Charles Chipiez

History of Art in Phrygia, Lydia, Caria and Lycia

Charles Chipiez

History of Art in Phrygia, Lydia, Caria and Lycia

ISBN/EAN: 9783744646086

Printed in Europe, USA, Canada, Australia, Japan

Cover: Foto ©Thomas Meinert / pixelio.de

More available books at **www.hansebooks.com**

HISTORY OF

Art in Phrygia, Lydia, Caria,

AND

Lycia.

FROM THE FRENCH

OF

GEORGES PERROT,

MEMBER OF THE INSTITUTE; PROFESSOR IN THE FACULTY OF LETTERS, PARIS,

AND

CHARLES CHIPIEZ.

ILLUSTRATED WITH TWO HUNDRED AND EIGHTY ENGRAVINGS

London: CHAPMAN AND HALL, LIMITED

New York: A. C. ARMSTRONG AND SON.

1892.

CONTENTS.

PHRYGIA, MYSIA, BITHYNIA, AND PAPHLAGONIA.

CHAPTER I.

CHAPTER II.

LYDIA AND CARIA.

CHAPTER I.

CHAPTER II.

CHAPTER III.

LYCIA

CHAPTER I.

CHAPTER II.

CHAPTER III.

CHAPTER IV.

LIST OF ILLUSTRATIONS.

TAIL-PIECES.

HISTORY OF ART IN ANTIQUITY.

PHRYGIA, MYSIA, BITHYNIA, AND PAPHLAGONIA.

CHAPTER I.

THE PHRYGIAN NATION.

HISTORY AND ORIGIN OF THE PHRYGIANS.

THE part the Phrygians played in the Oriental world is not so important as that played by the Hittites, but the modern historian knows next to nothing of the latter, whilst he is acquainted with the house, parentage, and family of speech of the former. The Phrygians appeared later on the scene of history; they lived in closer proximity with the Greeks, and left inscriptions, few and brief it is true, but written with characters the full values of which are determined. Herodotus and Xanthus of Lydia, who wrote about the fifth century B.C., are agreed in placing the cradle-land of the Phrygians, Mysians, and Bithynians in Thrace, whence they penetrated into Asia Minor across the straits.[1] Their testimony

[1] Herodotus, vii. 73; Xanthus, p. 5; *Fragm. Hist. Græc.*, C. MÜLLER's edit., tom. i. p. 37. Strabo (X. iii. 16) sums up the opinion of his predecessors, backed by the rich store of historical information which lay open to him, in the following words: "The Phrygians are a Thracian colony." So PLINY: "Sunt auctores transisse ex Europa Mysos et Brigas et Thynos, a quibus appellantur Mysi, Phryges, Bithyni" (*Hist. Natur.*, v. 41).

On the Thracian origin of the Bithynians, see also Thucydides, iv. 75; XENOPHON, *Anabasis*, VI. ii. 18; iv. 1, 2; *Hell.*, I. iii. 2; III. ii. 2; Herodotus, vii. 75, etc. The geographer clearly perceived that if Homer spoke of the Mysians and Thracians in the same line (*Iliad*, xiii. 3), this was meant to apply to those that had remained in Europe. The mistake of Herodotus (vii. 74), who writes of the Mysians and Lydians as one people, is easily accounted for from the fact that they fought under the same colours in the Persian army, and that long cohabitation on

was not wholly dependent upon the traditions the immigration might have left among the tribes established in the valleys of the Hermus and along the upper course of the Mæander; it rested also upon the fact that, many centuries after the separation, names of clans and localities were found east and west of the Hellespont, with scarcely any difference between them, beyond light shades of pronunciation. Nor is this all; the new country was sometimes called Asiatic Thracia, to distinguish it from Thracia proper. The like comparison was not possible between Phrygians and Armenians, albeit a close relationship was affirmed to exist between them. Herodotus, writing of the various nations which composed the army of Xerxes, says, "The Armenians are 'a Phrygian colony,'[1] equipped like the Phrygians, and when under arms obey a common chief." The little we know of their language would not belie the comparison thus instituted.[2] The terms, however, used by the historian imply an hypothesis unacceptable to our better informed judgment, since it is difficult to admit that the populations of Armenia were composed of tribes that had come from the west.[3]

the western coast of Asia had induced great similarity in their dialects and usages. Differences, no doubt, existed between them, but, though distinctly made out by natives, were not detected by strangers. Any one interested in the subject will find more texts in support of the Thracian origin of the people under discussion in F. LENORMANT, *Orig. de l'hist.*, tom. ii. pp. 366–371, and D'ARBOIS DE JUBAINVILLE, *Les Premiers habitants de l'Europe*, p. 168 and following.

[1] Φρυγῶν ἄποικοι, Herodotus, vii. 73. Cf. EUDOXUS, *Stephanus Byzantinus*, s.v. Ἀρμένιοι, and EUSTACE'S *Commentary*, 694. They went so far as to regard the appellatives Armenians and Phrygians as synonymous terms (CRAMER, *Anecdota Græca Oxoniensia*, iv. p. 257). JOSEPHUS (*Ant. Jud.*, i. 6) identifies the Phrygians with the descendants of the Togarmah of chapter x. of Genesis. Togarmah is generally taken to denote the Armenians.

[2] The relationship between the Phrygian and the Greek tongue was noticed by the ancients (PLATO, *Cratylus*, p. 410 A). Consult also LASSEN, *Zeitschrift der Deutschen*, etc., tom. x. p. 369 and following.

[3] FR. LENORMANT, *Les Origines de l'histoire*, tom. ii. pp. 373–379. Consideration of the earliest Armenian traditions has led him to the conclusion that the Armenians entered the country we now call Armenia from the west, and that when the Assyrians reached it for the first time, the people in possession were not Armenians, but Urartu, Urartû, Alarodians. On this hypothesis the Thracian emigrants who pushed furthest east would be Armenians. DUNCKER (*Geschichte der Alterthums*, tom. i. p. 383), whilst admitting the kinship between Phrygians and Armenians, holds the opposite view. He refuses to accept the testimony of numerous ancient texts, in which the migration of the Phrygians from Europe to Asia is stated, and holds it worthless. In his estimation it was just the reverse. If the same names are met with in Phrygia and Thracia, this, he holds, was because the parent tribes of both Phrygians and Thracians, coming from the east, left in Armenia a first colony; a

If affinity exists between Armenians and Phrygians, it may, perhaps, be otherwise explained. The two nations would have come of a parent stock, a main branch of the Aryan family—a branch which parted in far-off days, and formed two distinct ramifications. Of these, the one moved north of the Euxine and settled in the south-east of Europe, whence long afterwards they fell back upon Asia Minor; whilst the other entered the peninsula at the opposite end, through the passes of Caucasus, and the high levels binding it with the tableland of Iran. After centuries of separation, the two groups met again on the river Halys, which rises in Armenia, and whose lower course forms the line of delimitation between Cappadocia and Phrygia.

Further to discuss the question is outside our purpose. Neither the Thracians nor the Armenians ever had an individual art, so that in no part of this history will their name be recorded. If we have adduced traditions bearing upon the origin and ethnical affinities of the Phrygians, this was because they determine the question of race, and serve to establish their Aryan origin, further demonstrated by words of their language incised on stone hard by Seid al-Ghazi.[1] Their idiom might almost be considered a Greek

second group, Phrygians, Mysians, Bithynians, established themselves on the north-west of Asia Minor; then moving still further west, the bulk of the nation crossed the straits, and spread in the vast region that lies between the Ægean and the Danube. This is a theory opposed to almost all ancient texts, the universal belief of antiquity, and Duncker borrowed it from Otto Abel, who has not one good reason to show for it ("Phryges," *Real Encyclopëdie de Pauly et Makedonien*, p. 57). The few authorities he cites date from the Lower Empire, *e.g.* centuries after the events they purpose to relate.

[1] None of the scholars who have gone into the question have any doubt on the subject. See first Lassen's dissertation, already referred to (p. 2, note 2), entitled *Ueber die Lykischen Inschriften und die alten Sprachen Klein-Asiens.* In the second part (*Ueber die alten Kleinasiatischen Sprachen uperhaupt*) a large share is given to the study of the Phrygian language. The author, whilst giving the expositions of Jablonski, Adelung, Heeren, and De Lagarde, adds many observations of his own. The reader is referred to De Lagarde for a fuller account: *Einige Bemerkungen ueber êrânische Sprachen ausserhalb Erân's* (Gesamm. Abhand., 8vo, 1866, Leipzig). Chap. iii. pp. 283–291, deals with the glossary of Phrygian words preserved to us in ancient writers; but unlike Lassen, he makes no attempt to explain the inscriptions. Among the many correspondences these papers contain we will single out the following:—Hesychius (s.v.) formally states that Βαγαῖος was the Phrygian name of Zeus. Despite its Greek ending, due to lexicographers, it is not difficult to recognize the *bagha*, which in old Persian, and Zend as well, signifies deity. The word, with scarcely any modification, occurs in many other Indo-European languages. *Bog*, in Slavic idioms, has the meaning of deity.

dialect; "the Phrygians," it has been said, "are eastern Greeks," a term of comparison fully justified by the close relations which existed between the Thracians and the ancestors of the Hellenes in continental Greece. The witness borne by all antiquity was to the effect that the Greeks were indebted to Thracian tribes established in the valleys of Olympus and Pindus for the religious rites of Dionysus and the Muses. Orpheus was a Thracian bard.

We have still to consider the question of date. When did the migration take place which brought these Thracian tribes, so nearly allied to the Greeks, to the very heart of Asia Minor? To fix the year, or even the century, when the first of these clans crossed the straits is not once to be thought of. Thus stated, the problem would be insoluble; on the other hand, a highly probable solution may be reached by confining ourselves to determining the position that ought to be assigned to the Phrygians among the many peoples that succeeded each other in Asia Minor—at any rate, those who, thanks to the superiority of their culture, swayed their neighbours and played a leading part, each in turn. Of all the nations who figured on this scene, first in chronological order are the Hittites. The literary documents of Egypt exhibit them, in the days of Thothmes, Seti, and Ramses, as not only supreme masters of Northern Syria, but as wielding enough of authority over the peninsula to have induced innumerable hosts to cross the Taurus in order to fight for the kings of Carchemish and Kadesh against the Pharaohs in the valley of Orontes, and later, in the reign of Menephtah and Ramses III., to have threatened the Egyptian frontiers as well. Is it not likely that, had the Phrygians then inhabited the peninsula, they must, willingly or unwillingly, have been drawn into the general ferment impelling the native populations across the mountains on to Syria? Now, in the long list of nations banded together under the leadership of the Khetas, including the tribes called somewhat later, by the Theban scribes, "seafaring people," we look in vain for the name of the Phrygians. If contemporary texts containing the recital of these stirring events make no mention of the Phrygian group, was it not simply because the populations composing it had not yet abandoned their Thracian and Mysian cradle-land, nor crossed the straits, but still dwelt in Europe, where the bulk of the nation preserved their individual life and independence down to the Roman conquest? This hypothesis, the cumulative knowledge of Greece, the gleanings—for him who knows how to gather them—to be got out of the monuments in which the handiwork of the Phrygians has been recognized, everything in fact, tends to confirm. The caravan routes of the western coast, which led to Smyrna, Ephesus, and Miletus, served as connecting links from the earliest days, between the Ionians and the main group of the Phrygian nation—that which has left its name to the portion of the plateau comprised between the middle course of the Halys, the head springs of the Sangarius and the Mæander. We may assume that the traditions relating to Ionia reflected, though faintly, the memories the Phrygians themselves had preserved of their own past; now, these traditions show no proneness for carrying very far back the migration which brought the Phrygian tribes to the peninsula, since Xanthus of Lydia definitely places the event after the Trojan war.[1] As Strabo has already remarked, such an assertion is difficult to reconcile with the testimony of the Homeric poem, in which the Phrygians are represented as the neighbours and allies of the Trojans (XII. viii. 4, XIV. v. 29). The Greeks had no desire to be found to disagree with Homer; just as, for a long time, whoever handled ancient history was at pains to make his theories fit in with the Bible. Hence it was admitted that the Greeks who followed Agamemnon to Asia, found the Phrygians already at home there and in possession of a vast territory; nevertheless the migration of the Thraco-Bryges, even for

[1] Xanthus, p. 5. Herodotus does not give the date of the migration which brought the Thracians to the peninsula; if he asserts that the Phrygians had every right to consider themselves as the oldest people in the world, it was on the strength of the experiment made by Psammeticus, which he fully details (ii. 2), but which has no historical value. Its only point of interest resides in the fact that it testifies to that first awaking of a questioning intelligence, which in time was to expand into comparative philology and in our age to take rank among sciences. The two infants reared by Psammeticus in a secluded cottage, wherein no human voice was ever heard, in their first cry imitated the bleating of a goat, said to resemble "bec, bec," and one of the Asiatic Greeks in the king's body-guard forthwith identified the sound with the Phrygian word *becos*, bread. The anecdote simply proves the readiness of the Greek mind to find a solution, good or bad, to any problem presented to it. For the rest, the Phrygians might be "very ancient" in Herodotus' sense, and yet comparatively of recent date in Asia Minor. Arrian, in a passage preserved by Eustathes (*Denys Periegetes*, 322), says that the Phrygians passed from Thracia to Asia to escape the hardships consequent on the incursions of the Cimmerians. Inadmissible though this may be from a chronological standpoint, it is none the less important to show that authoritative writers were not disposed to carry back the migration under notice to remote antiquity.

writers who start from the above data, was not considered as an event which belongs to fabulous ages, and is lost in the twilight of time. Strabo, as we have seen, confines himself to saying that the tribes in question entered the peninsula before the Trojan war. At no time were the Phrygians, Mysians, and Bithynians, regarded by the ancients as the primitive inhabitants of Asia Minor, autocthones, to use the Greek expression.[1]

Strictly speaking, the witness borne by instances such as these might be questioned, but what enhances their weight is the fact that they coincide with the views suggested to the historian by monuments discovered within this century by Leake, Stewart, Téxier, and Ramsay, on this very soil of Phrygia.[2] Crowded in a narrow space, these memorials belong one and all to the region

[1] The saying Τὰ Ναννάκου, in the time of Nannakos, has been advanced in proof of the contrary hypothesis, as shadowing very far-off days; for old King Nannakos was represented as the Noah of Phrygia, and as having rescued his subjects from the Deluge. The coins of Apamœa Kibotos are witnesses to the popularity of similar legends in a portion of the peninsula during Roman domination; but earlier writers make no allusion whatever to the deluge in question. The oldest text in which it is mentioned is ascribed to Hermogenes, who wrote in the first, perhaps in the second century of our era (MÜLLER, *Frag. Hist. Græc.*, iii. p. 524). The dictum, "to weep over the days of Nannakos," is indeed found in a iambic poet, one Herodas, Heroudas (BERGK, *Poetæ lyrici Græci*, tom. ii. p. 796); but no one knows where he lived, nor is there aught to indicate the meaning he attached to the words Τὰ Ναννάκου. When Strabo (XII. viii. 13) tells us that *kibotos*, casket, coffer, was affixed to Apamœa of Phrygia, he does not in any way connect the surname with a deluge. It may be questioned whether the tradition of the Phrygian flood is in truth very old, and was not an importation of the Jews, who in very early days would have entered the country through Cilicia, and spread in the townships of the central plateau. The Acts of the Apostles show that Hebrew communities were established in Lycaonia in the opening years of our era. NÖLDEKE (*Untersuchungen zur Kritik des alten Testaments*, 8vo, 1886, pp. 154, 155) and FR. LENORMANT (*Les Origines*, 2nd edit., tom. i. pp. 440, 441) admit that traditions of a local deluge, akin to those which in Greece were connected with Deucalion, may have been current in Phrygia, but they acknowledge at the same time that such myths could not acquire any importance before the second century A.D., and were brought about by infiltration of Jewish and Christian ideas. This is proved in the name of ΝΩΕ, ΝΩ, engraved on native coins and clearly foreign to Phrygian myths.

[2] W. MARTIN LEAKE, *Journal of a Tour in Asia Minor*, 8vo, London, 1824. His journey was undertaken in 1800, in which year he visited the monument which bears the name of Midas written upon it. He was the first European who saw and made a drawing of the façade. An abridged account of his travels appeared in Walpole's Memoirs, under the title "Travels in Various Countries of the East."

JOHN ROBERT STEWART, *A Description of Some Ancient Monuments with Inscriptions*, etc., London, 1842. The letter-press is indifferent, and the plates, taken

where, by common consent, is placed the cradle of the Phrygian race—the scene, at least, upon which the nation unfolded and laid the foundation of a mighty kingdom. Here were many temples, and many votive objects put therein; the famous chariot, for example, upon which Alexander the Great rested his hand for a while,[1] and many sacred springs;[2] whilst the names of Gordios and Midas linger to this day in Gordion and Midaion, where once these kings were enthroned, but which are now reduced to mere hamlets.[3] These names, about which cluster so many fables, are prominent figures in the Phrygian mythic cycle; one might be inclined to regard them as purely legendary, but for the fact that they appear on the sculptured façades of the Phrygian sepulchres, written in letters not a whit more difficult to read than very old

from incorrect sketches, are far from satisfactory. The book is valuable on account of the inscriptions, copied, as a rule, with care.

TÉXIER, *Description de l'Asie Mineure*, tom. i. pp. 153–162, Plates VI.–LXI. The drawings are among the best brought home by Téxier; a few of them only require light corrections to make them quite exact.

G. PERROT, Ed. Guillaume et J. Delbet, *Explor. Arché. de la Galatie*, tom. i. pp. 135–186, 168–170, Plates VII., VIII. The little time the explorers had at their disposal obliged them to confine their observations to the so-called Tomb of Midas and the fortress known as Pishmish Kalessi, but they made very complete and careful tracings.

W. M. RAMSAY, *Studies in Asia Minor—1. The Rock Necropoles of Phrygia; 2. Sipylos and Cybele*, Plates XVII.–XXII. (*Journal of Hell. Studies*, tom. iii. pp. 1–68); *Some Phrygian Monuments*, Plates XXVI.–XXIX., pp. 156–262; *Sepulchral Customs in Ancient Phrygia*, Plate XLIV. (*Journal*, tom. v. pp. 241–262). No one knows more about this district, its history and antiquities, than Professor Ramsay. He has visited it no less than six times from 1881 to the present year; twice in 1881, and once in 1884, 1886, 1888, 1890. Unfortunately he cannot hold a pencil, and the sketches of M. Blunt, his companion in one of these expeditions, leave much to be desired, and, according to Professor Ramsay, are not always reliable. It is to be regretted that Professor Ramsay should not collect and publish in a separate volume the mass of useful matter he has gleaned.

[1] ARRIAN, *Anabasis*, ii. 3; PLUTARCH, *Alexander*, xviii.

[2] Midas *springs* were pointed out to the traveller in several cities of the Phrygian plateau; one was at Ancyra (Pausanius, I. iv. 5), a town whose foundation was ascribed to Midas, and another in the neighbourhood of Tymbrion and Tyraeon (XENOPHON, *Anab.*, I. ii. 13).

[3] Strabo, XII. v. 3: Πλησίον δὲ καὶ ὁ Σαγγάριος ποταμὸς ποιεῖται τὴν ῥύσιν· ἐπὶ δὲ τούτῳ τὰ παλαιὰ τῶν Φρυγῶν οἰκητήρια Μίδου, καὶ ἔτι πρότερον Γορδίου καὶ ἄλλων τινῶν, οὐδ' ἴχνη σώζοντα πόλεων, ἀλλὰ κῶμαι, μικρῷ μείζους τῶν ἄλλων, οἷόν ἐστι τὸ Γόρδιον καὶ Γορβεοῦς, τὸ τοῦ Κάστορος βασίλειον τοῦ Σαωκονδαρίου. On the probable position of Gordion, see PERROT, *Expl. Arché.*, tom. i. pp. 152–155. Midaion seems to have stood somewhat more to the south, on the old route which ran from Dorylaeum, now Aski Sheher, to Pessinus.

FIG. 1.—Inscription of the monument called "Tomb of Midas." RAMSAY, *On the Early Historical Relations*, Plate I., Fig. 1.

Greek inscriptions (Fig. 1).[1] Not only do we no longer find any trace of those Hittite hieroglyphs which still await decipherment, but the alphabet that may be restored from them (Fig. 2) is not derived, as was probably that of Cyprus, from an old system of writing, which seemingly obtained throughout Asia Minor before the introduction of Phœnician characters. What is more, it does not contain, as the Lycian, Pamphylian, and Carian syllabaries, letters of Punic origin, along with others borrowed from that Asianic alphabet which is found in outline in the literary documents of Cyprus. There is not one letter here which we may not expect to find in Greek inscriptions. The Phrygian alphabet was not derived directly from the Phœnician; for it does not contain all its letters, whilst it has a few not possessed by the latter; it was in all likelihood allied to it through one or other of the archaic Greek alphabets, either the Ionian, or rather that called

a	A A
b	B B
g	Γ
d	Δ Δ
e	E E E
v	F F
z	ʃ S S
i	I
k	K K
l	Λ
m	M M M
n	N
o	o O
p	Γ Γ
r	P P
s	ξ ξ ξ
t	T T
u	Y
ph	Φ

FIG. 2.—Phrygian alphabet. FR. LENORMANT, under the heading "Alphabet," in Daremberg and Saglio's Dictionary.

[1] Excellent copies of most Phrygian inscriptions will be found in the three plates subjoined to Professor Ramsay's interesting memoir, bearing the title, "On the Early Historical Relations between Phrygia and Cappadocia" (*Journal of the Asiatic Society of Great Britain and Ireland*, vol. xv. part i.). The third section of the memoir, "Archaic-Phrygian Inscriptions," is devoted to the Phrygian alphabet and its origin, together with a tentative decipherment and translation.

the "island syllabary."[1] The few short inscriptions of Thera (Santorin) are considered as the oldest in the Greek language, and in them the shapes of the letters still closely resemble Phœnician characters. Nobody has ever believed that these texts could be led back beyond the ninth century B.C.;[2] indeed, they are referred as a rule to the eighth, and sometimes as low down as the seventh.[3] We will stretch a point and accept the earliest date, though in all probability much too old; even so we shall be obliged to suppose an interval of many years, perhaps a whole century, between the Thera inscriptions and those of the Phrygian necropoles. A century at least was needed to effect the work of elaboration and adaptation, during which the sense of the writing underwent a change; the value of some of the characters preserved was modified, others were discarded, and not a few were created.[4] Finally the Greeks must be allowed time in which to transmit, some way or another, the use and practice of the alphabet to nations who, like the Phrygians, were not their immediate neighbours, but whom many natural obstacles separated from the Ionian and Doric cities of the seaboard. We are thus led back towards the end of the eighth century; and we reach the same conclusion through a correspondence that furnishes, so to speak, the proof of the operation, by collating and sifting the scanty data to be gleaned in history, intermingled with the brilliant tissue of fables, inseparable from Midas and Phrygia, as presented by the rich and capricious fancy of the Athenian dramatists. Thus Herodotus, in his narrative of the events which caused the throne of Lydia to pass from the Heraclidæ to the Mermnadæ, has the following:—"The founder of the new dynasty, Gyges, at first met with much resistance on the part of the friends of the old family; but the Delphic oracle having

[1] At first Professor Ramsay thought that the Phrygians had received their alphabet from the Greeks of Sinope (*Historical Relations of Phrygia and Cappadocia*, p. 27); and later, that they had derived it from the Phocæans and Cymæans, with whom intercourse was frequent and continuous (*Athenæum*, 1884, pp. 864, 865). There is this difficulty, that the Ionian syllabary would seem to have had no F, a letter largely used in all Phrygian inscriptions; hence Lenormant prefers to ally the Phrygian alphabet to that of the "islands," which would have entered the peninsula *viâ* Rhodes, where it was employed.

[2] LENORMANT, art. "Alphabet," p. 195.

[3] S. REINACH, *Traité d'Épigraphie grecque*, p. 181.

[4] AD. KIRCHHOFF, *Studien zur Geschichte des Griechischen Alphabets*, 3rd edit., 1887, p. 53.

declared in his favour, he was able to bear down all opposition and enmity. As an earnest of his gratitude, he laid before the shrine of the Delphian Apollo rich donations of gold and silver," described at some length, and, adds the historian, "To our knowledge Gyges was the first of the Barbarians who sent gifts to Delphi, the first at any rate since Midas, son of Gordios, king of Phrygia. Indeed, Midas had consecrated his throne, that upon which he sat to administer justice, a throne fully deserving to be seen, and this throne is exhibited on the exact spot where are the crateras of Gyges;"[1] that is to say, the Thesaurion of Corinth. If, as is generally held, Gyges reigned from 687–653, Midas should come, at the earliest, towards 700 B.C.[2] The influence of Greek culture had been unfelt before that date in the peninsula; and nothing was known of the sanctuary that played so important a part in the Hellenic world, before the unfolding of philosophy and scepticism—a part akin to that which the papacy filled in Europe during the Middle Ages. The greatest development, physical and spiritual, ever attained by Ionia was between the latter half of the eighth and the beginning of the seventh century B.C. She had already produced that marvel, the epic poem, and, with Archilochus, she created lyric poetry. In the domain of art she was beginning to chisel Parian marble; her architects were striving to bring out of the complex and undefined shapes of the Asiatic decoration they beheld around them, the elements of their column and entablature; they even sought proportions and lines, the felicitous selection of which was to make the fortune of that noble and attractive type with which her name will ever be linked. To this splendid display of inventive genius and activity corresponds a bold movement of expansion; the cities of Ionia turned betimes their vessels towards the main, and multiplied their counting-houses from the mouth of the Phasus and the Borysthenes to those of the Nile; when Miletus, along with Tyre, becomes the great emporium of the eastern basin of the Mediterranean. The Dorian cities of Caria, the Æolian townships of Mysia, though not with equal dash, join in

[1] Herodotus, i. 14.

[2] The dates 687–653 are those given by Gelzer, after Assyrian documents, and should be read in his admirable work bearing the title *Das Zeitalter des Gyges* (*Rheinisches Museum*, N. F., tom. xxx. pp. 231–268, and tom. xxxv. pp. 514–528). The first portion of the paper deals with the chronology and dynasty of the Mermnadæ. The work has lately appeared.

these manifold pursuits, and share the ebb and flow which attends on commercial enterprise. Built upon the shore, where its sinuous windings form natural havens, the vast majority of these centres owned but a narrow strip of land outside their walls; their population was not sufficiently large to render extension far inland advisable, for they would have run up against warlike tribes, the Carians and the Lydians, the Phrygians and the Mysians. The situation these populations held on the heights which dominate, whilst separating one from the other, the lower valleys of the Cayster, the Hermus, the Caicos, and the Mæander, gave them the control of the fertile plains washed by these streams in their lower course. The main outlet and general outflow of the inhabitants of these maritime cities was towards the sea; but most of the commodities for home consumption, as well as merchandise for exchange, were gotten from their inland borders, and further still. In order, therefore, to procure the necessaries of life and foster their trade, they were obliged to have friends, or, as we should now say, agents, in such districts as were closed to them, and where they could not settle with any chance of success. Thus commercial and personal intercourse led the way to relations of a friendly and social nature, between the chiefs of the great Achæan houses and those of the less barbarous tribes of the tableland; similar connections were sometimes drawn closer by matrimonial alliances.

During the seventh and the sixth centuries the kings of Lydia regularly chose their consorts from, or gave their daughters to, the patrician families of Ionia. In the preceding age, ere the Lydian empire had become supreme and interposed between the townships of the seaboard and the populations located on the central plateau, the Codridæ and the Neleidæ, those presiding families of the Greek colonies, had entered into similar relations with the sovereigns of the state that subsequently destroyed and absorbed Lydia. In the seventh century, a king of Phrygia espoused the daughter of Agamemnon, king of Cymæ, celebrated for her beauty and wisdom.[1] A certain Phrygios,[2] a prominent

[1] Heraclides of Pontus, περὶ πολιτειῶν (*Frag. Hist. Græc.*, MÜLLER, tom. ii. p. 216). Pollux (ix. p. 83) calls this same woman Demodike. She must have been the wife of the last king Midas, for to her was ascribed the introduction of coined money into Cymæ, Cumæ.

[2] PLUTARCH, *Fem. Virt.*, 16.

personage among the nobles of Miletus, who claimed descent from Neleus, is the hero of a story which Plutarch borrowed from some old historian; now, the name in itself is proof sufficient of the friendly intercourse which existed between the sovereigns of Phrygia and the Ionian princes, whose ancestors play so conspicuous a part in the Homeric poem.[1] If the names of Gordios and Midas do not appear in Homer, that may have been due to one of two causes: either he had no opportunity for introducing them, or, what is more likely, it was because those princes did not begin to reign until after the recension of the *Iliad* by the Rhapsodists; than which no better reason could be invoked in support of the comparatively recent culture of Phrygia. Had the epic singers been contemporaries of those monarchs, some passing allusion would be found in one or other of the poems to that fabulous wealth which the fervid imagination of the Greeks ascribed to the kings of Phrygia; Midas, that Midas who turned everything he touched into gold, would seem to have been for the Ionians, before Crœsus, the type of the monarch who could draw at will from inexhaustible treasures. The *Iliad*, it is true, makes repeated mention of the Phrygians as the allies of Priam; it places some of the tribes in Ascania, a region subsequently known as Hellespontic Phrygia;[2] it knows of others established in the interior of the continent on the banks of the Sangarius, who wage perpetual war with the Amazons, that is to say, with an enemy from beyond the Halys.[3] All are agriculturists, and

[1] It is Curtius' remark, *Hist. of Greece*, tom. i. p. 291.

[2] *Iliad*, ii. 860. The name of Ascania disappeared as a local designation; in the days of Strabo, however, the basin subsequently known as "Lake of Nicæa" still went by the name of Ascanian lake. One of Priam's numerous offspring, and the son of Æneas, are called Ascanius. Ascanius is a river of the Troad; the small group of islets fronting the latter are the Ascanian islands; the name is also found in a harbour situated on the Troadian and Lydian border. Ascania, according to Xanthus, was a European district, whence the Phrygians passed to Asia (Strabo, XIV. v. 29). Some hold that to have left so many traces in literary records, the name must have represented at one time the whole Phrygian people, or at least one of its tribes; an hypothesis confirmed by the fact that in the list of the sons of Gomer (Gen. x. 3), Ashkenaz, whom Lenormant would recognize as the father of the Phrygians, is placed side by side with Togarmah, the ancestor of the Armenians. The reader will find the reasons that invest the hypothesis with a great degree of probability in FR. LENORMANT, *Les Origines de l'histoire*, tom. ii. pp. 388–395.

[According to Lenormant and other authorities, Ascanios, Ascanius, is but the Greek rendering of Ashkenaz.—TRS.]

[3] *Iliad*, iii. 184–189; xvi. 718.

more renowned for the breed of their horses and skill in breaking them than for other earthly goods.[1] Moreover, in the *Iliad*, as also in a later poem, the *Hymn to Aphrodite*,[2] the chiefs who head the Phrygian forces are Phorcys and Ascanios, Asios and Hymas, Otræus and Mygdon—names to which there is no need to ascribe an historical value; in the "strongly walled cities of the Phrygians," Gordios and Midas reign not.[3] The vast majority of critics hold that the *Iliad*, as we possess it, has not materially changed since the ninth century B.C. Survey of the Epos and consideration of other intelligence bring us round to the conclusion reached a few pages back, namely, that if the Phrygians were already settled in the heart of the peninsula before the time of Homer, it was not until the year 800, or thereabouts, that they succeeded in laying the foundations of that state, which was to be the most influential in Western Asia down to the day when Lydia, under the leadership of Gyges and Ardys, entered upon the scene.[4]

Tradition told of Gordios, a tiller of the soil, as the founder of the dynasty; he was succeeded by his son Midas, and from that time the two names would seem to have alternated in the royal family; they were, perhaps, those of eponymous heroes of the Phrygian tribes, fabulous ancestors worshipped as gods.[5] Examination of the rare texts that bear upon this history permits us to make out, with more or less certainty, three Midases and four Gordioses.[6] The number of these princes is unimportant; the one

[1] *Iliad*, x. 431. [2] *Hymns*, iii. 111, 112. [3] *Ibid.*, 112.

[4] This result, to which several routes have led, is in perfect agreement with the chronology of Eusebius. He sets the beginning of Midas' reign in the fourth year of the tenth Olympiad, *e.g.* in 737 B.C. (ANGELO MAI, *Chron.*, p. 321). Eusebius had, it is true, put another Midas 552 years earlier, and made him coeval with Pelops (p. 291) and the foundation of Troy. All that can be urged is that the first data belong to the fabulous period of his tables, and have no historical value; whereas the second are comprised within the truly historical part of his work, when the materials he had to hand were of a very different character. The same observation applies to the date he assigns for the suicide of the last Midas (p. 324), which he places in the fifty-ninth Olympiad, clearly too late.

[5] The fact is proved for Midas, at least, who in the west of the peninsula was confounded with one of those gods whose worship prevailed down to the last days of paganism (Hesychius, s.v. Μίδας θεός). The representations of Midas on a certain number of painted vases are only to be explained by a similar confusion of the two names. See PANOFKA, *Midas auf Bildwerken* (*Archa. Zeitung*, iii. p. 92, 1845).

[6] See article entitled "Midas," *Real-Encyclop. Pauly.*

thing to be borne in mind, however, is that the Phrygian empire, after a prosperous existence of a hundred and fifty years, was ravaged (*circa* 660 B.C.), along with that of Lydia, by Cimmerian hordes. The king Midas of that day, unable to endure defeat, put an end to his existence by drinking the blood of a bull.[1] It was but a momentary calamity, which disappeared with the withdrawal of the Cimmerians; for Herodotus tells us that in the reign of Crœsus, the Phrygian king of that day styled himself son of Gordios and grandson of Midas.[2] The effect of the late invasion, however, had been to weaken and break up the country; so that its inhabitants offered little resistance to the Lydians when these, a few years afterwards, under the command of Alyattes and Crœsus, entered their territory, which they occupied as far as the banks of the Halys.[3]

Consequently, a space of two hundred or two hundred and fifty years may confidently be allowed as the duration of that Phrygian empire, which we credit with the monuments still extant around the springs that feed the western branch of the Sangarius. Strictly speaking, that state has no history, for its span of life was passed too far away from the coast. Until the day when the Greeks entered into intercourse or conflict with Lydia, nothing was known on the coast of the events that were taking place on the plateau. The scanty data we possess as to this empire relate to events which may be dated with certainty within a few years; landmarks, such as the reign of Gyges, the Cimmerian incursions, the wars of Alyattes and Croesus. Gordios, Midas, together with the monuments situate on the western rim of the great plateau bearing their names, belong, then, to what may be termed the historical period. We are better off in regard to another kingdom, which likewise left recollections of its power and wealth in the mind of the Greeks; we allude to a state skirting the Ægean, whose capital, fastnesses, and sanctuaries rose on the flanks and within the gorges of Sipylus, between the valley of the Hermus

[1] Strabo, I. iii. 21. Allusion to this suicide will be found in PLUTARCH, *Flaminius*, 20.

[2] Herodotus, i. 35, 45.

[3] Herodotus (i. 28) ascribes to Crœsus the subjugation of the peninsula to the banks of the Halys; but Alyattes must have commenced it, since a little further (i. 74) he shows him carrying on a war of six years' duration against Cyaxares. The valley of the Halys and the central plateau were doubtless the scene of this struggle; there is nothing to indicate that the Medes of that date went near the Mediterranean.

and the Smyrnian Gulf. As time rolled on, these heights were abandoned for the level plain below; populous cities, as Magnesia, were built in the plain, or on the shore, as Smyrna. But Sipylus, even when deserted, did not lose its hold on the regard of the natives; it continued to be venerated as the favourite abode of the great Asiatic goddess, Rhea or Cybele. The monuments, left by generations that had been the first to cast the seeds of civilization on a soil from which Greek genius was to reap such splendid fruit,[1] were visited with pious curiosity; but they elicited no questioning as to their chronological order, and whether due to one or several epochs.

The traditions relating to this commonwealth had assumed a mythic form; they led back to that fabulous age when gods descended upon earth and lived in intimacy with men; they clustered about two single names, those of Tantalus and Niobe, whose transcendent magnificence and insolent prosperity had roused the wrath of jealous deities, and caused their headlong fall. Then, too, had followed catastrophes as sudden as they were strange; earthquakes had shaken the mountain to its very base; yawning chasms had engulfed the royal city of Tantalis, with her prince and inhabitants, and amidst the crash of falling boulders streams had gushed forth from the abyss, and where once had been the proud city, stood now a lake, in whose waters at low tide the ruinous mass of palace and dwellings could be descried.[2] The legend of Niobe, daughter of Tantalus, whose numerous and happy offspring are all struck down, may be taken as foreshadowing the ruin of a brave and proud community, suddenly blotted out of the roll of nations by the wholesale massacre of its male adults.

Many are the variations of the myth of Tantalus and Niobe;[3]

[1] This is implied by Pausanias, who returns again and again to the curiosities of Sipylus, often in the following words: "As I myself saw on Sipylus."

[2] The *Odyssey* (xi. 582) puts Tantalus in Tartarus, but does not say to what misdemeanour he owed the famous punishment that goes by his name. PINDAR (*Olymp.*, i. 54–64) indicates as his crime the theft of nectar and ambrosia. On the destruction of Tantalis or Sipylus by an earthquake, see ARISTOTLE, *Meteorologica*, ii. 8; Strabo, I. iii. 17; XII. viii. 18; PLINY, *H. N.*, edn. Littré, ii. 93, v. 31. Pausanias writes that in his day the ruins of Tantalis were still to be seen in the depths of the waters (VII. xxiv. 13).

[3] These various traditions have been collected in book form, and discussed by K. B. STARK, *Niobe und die Niobiden in ihrer literarischen, kunstlerischen und mythologischer Bedeutung*, 464 pp. and 20 plates, 8vo, Leipzig, 1863.

the form given here is that which has found general popularity and acceptance. Among the various readings that have come down to us, one alone indicates, implicitly at least, the epoch to which the Greeks carried back the reign of Tantalus, and the dominion he exercised over the country that stretches from Sipylus to Ida; it represents Ilus, Ilos, Ilium, a prince of the Dardani, the founder of Ilium and grandfather of Priam, as having overthrown Tantalus and destroyed his empire.[1] To accept as sober fact the story according to which Ilus, to avenge his brother Ganymedes, had led a great force against Tantalus, is out of the question; but the tale suffices to prove that a far more remote antiquity was ascribed to Tantalus and his kingdom on Sipylus, than to the Phrygian empire of the Sangarius. For the chroniclers, to put an event generations before the Trojan war, was equivalent to relegating it away to that shadowy past, ere men had taken count of time.

If such traditions stood by themselves, they might be deemed of little moment; but it so happens that they are in perfect agreement with the monuments. Three of these rock-sculptures found in the Sipylus region have already been figured and described in the fourth volume of our history; namely, the two bas-reliefs at Karabel, and that colossal statue of Cybele, which for a long time was taken as a Niobe.[2] These works, it will be remembered, were assigned by us to the oldest civilization of Asia Minor, that which we designated as Hittite or Syro-Cappadocian; we based our assumption on similarity of type, style of workmanship, and graphic signs, which distinguish both these and the monuments of the basins of Orontes and the Halys.[3] On the other hand, nowhere in this district has the slightest trace been found of an alphabet derived from the Phœnician,—that which the Phrygians of the valleys of the Rhyndacus and the Sangarius borrowed from the Greeks when they wished to write their language; equally non-existent are those principles of ornament seen on the Midas monument, and the surrounding sepulchral façades. Had we no historical witness the mere sight of these monuments would enable any one of average intelligence to assign priority of date to the city and the culture of the population dominated by the rounded summits of Sipylus. To be noted

[1] Diodorus, iv. 74.

[2] *Hist. of Art*, tom. iv. Figs. 361, 363, 365.

[3] For the signs in question, see *Ibid.*, Figs. 364, 366.

also on these denuded slopes, will be other remains of a far-off past, consisting of bas-reliefs, structural and rock-cut buildings; which, though less striking and characteristic than the two pseudo-Sesostris and the Cybele, have, in our estimation, all the marks of high antiquity.

The difficulty is to find out to what branch of the human family belonged the race that has left so many marks of its existence and activity on the flanks of Sipylus. Is it necessary to attribute everything to those conquerors from the East, whose image we think we recognize graven on the rocky sides of the pass they carried with their arms? We trow not. The brave soldiers who measured their strength with Egypt, not always to the advantage of the latter, may, at the time when the superiority of their military tactics and armament ensured their undisputed supremacy in the western portion of the peninsula, have carried the point of one of their columns as far as here. But it is difficult to imagine that they remained long so far away from the Taurus, both slopes of which they occupied. Now, taken altogether, the monuments met with on Sipylus seem to testify to the long sojourn of a settled population. Near Magnesia, around the statue of Cybele, are altars and niches which in their turn testify to the homage paid to the gigantic idol from the day of its birth, and for centuries afterwards. On the lower hills, turned towards Smyrna, are stairways and galleries, redoubts, places of worship and tombs, all of which are partly built, partly hewn in the rock. One and all tell, as clearly as possible, that a people lived for many generations entrenched on these heights, but that when the Greek cities were founded on the adjacent shores, this same people had already lost whatever importance they had previously possessed; since epic and lyric poetry are alike silent about them, save their having once been mighty enough and rich enough to kindle the jealousy of the gods. The curiosity of the historian, which should not be so readily satisfied, but would seek to penetrate further, will have little more than a choice between two hypotheses. That of a Hittite colony established at some time on Sipylus is in itself very improbable; for no indication, however slight, can be produced in its favour either from history or legend. On the other hand, if already in the day of Herodotus the name of Phrygia Major, Great Phrygia, was confined to the elevated region stretching between the Halys and the Sangarius, the Rhyndacus and the

Mæander, a distinct impression was retained of a far-off age when the Phrygians had spread high up around the Mysian Olympus, the Idæan summits, and Sipylus. In the time of Strabo the name of Phrygia Parva, Small Phrygia, or Phrygia Epicteta, was still generally applied to the country ruled by these mountains.[1] It was an indefinite name, and answered to no existing division, yet is of great interest to us as a reminiscence of the old Phrygian empire, in that it serves to prove its extension to the Bay of Smyrna. We have a further proof of this in a passage of Strabo, where he expounds the difficulties that beset the historian who should try to fix the boundaries of the Phrygians and the Mysians. "This," he goes on to say, "is proved by the name of Phrygia, given by the ancients to the region of Sipylus itself. . . . They also called Phrygian Pelops, Tantalus, and Niobe."[2]

If, as universally held by the ancients, the Phrygians came from Europe across the straits to Asia Minor, it is natural to suppose that, once on the Asiatic side of the Bosphorus and the Hellespont, they tarried a while ere they ventured on to the thickly wooded heights of the interior; they would begin to spread along the comparatively clear coast, especially towards the south. In continental Greece, too, at the same time and in the same fashion, other Thracian tribes, following the chain of Pindus, reached Bœotia and Attica. The Phrygians would thus have pushed on to the rich plains which we know as Lydia, as far as, yet not further than, the Bay of Smyrna; since the southernmost territory specified by Strabo as within the Phrygia of the coast, which he distinguishes from Mediterranean Phrygia, is the district of Sipylus.[3] The more advanced post occupied this fort-like mass, which

[1] Strabo distinguishes (XII. viii. 1) "what is called Phrygia Major, the ancient kingdom of Midas, part of which has been occupied by the Galatians," from "Phrygia Parva, or, as it also is called to-day, Phrygia Epicteta, which extends along the Hellespont and Mount Olympus." The term ἐπίκτητος is of recent origin, and only dates from the kings of Pergamos; it designated the province these "acquired," in reality wrested, from the kings of Bithynia (Strabo, XII. iv. 3).

[2] *Ibid.*, viii. 2. So Athenæus, who, together with the whole antiquity from Homer, regarded Pelops as the son of Tantalus, states that within Peloponnesus are the tombs: τῶν μετὰ Πέλοπος Φρυγῶν (xiv. p. 626). Sophocles (*Antigone*, 825) calls Niobe: τὰν Φρυγίαν ξέναν Ταντάλου.

[3] Nevertheless, mention is made of Mydonians as inhabiting the neighbourhood of Miletus (ÆLIAN., *Hist. Var.*, viii. 5); of Bebryces, who, together with the Phocæans, would seem to have been engaged in holding in check the surrounding barbarous tribes (POLYÆNUS, *Strateg.*, viii. 37).

commanded at once the fertile valleys of the Hermus and the tranquil waters of a bay never stirred by the breeze. The advantages of such a situation as this ensured prosperity to the new kingdom, which was further increased by the winning of rich ores from rocks upheaved and fashioned by Plutonic agency. The wealth of Tantalus, rumour said, had been due to the mines of Sipylus.[1]

The art of mining and working metals was not learnt in Asia by the Phrygians; when they quitted Europe they were still a barbarous race. Those tribes that were left in the parent home of Thracia, around the Pangæus and Hæmus, were little better than savages at the time of the Roman conquest. If matters took a different turn with the children of that family who had settled in the Anatolian peninsula, it was because they were from the outset brought in contact with a more advanced people, one with the command, in part at least, of the processes that had long been the boast of the Egyptian and Chaldæan civilizations. These intermediate initiators and teachers were no other than the Hittites; those brave soldiers and ready inventors who had carried their arms and the use of their writing from the banks of the Euphrates and Orontes to those of the Ægean, from Carchemish and Hamath, even to the regions where later rose Smyrna and Sardis, Ephesus and Miletus. On many a point of the vast tract comprised within these boundaries, we have found unmistakable traces of the military power and creative energy of the Hittites; in Cappadocia and Lycaonia, for instance, are notable remains often of gigantic size, and in Phrygia and Lydia isolated figures carved on the native rock, with short inscriptions as yet undeciphered; everywhere, in short, east and west of the peninsula, we met with small objects, trinkets and seals, on which appear forms and types derived from Northern Syria. Instances such as these prove that Syro-Cappadocian culture, after having opened up the western highways with might and main, used these strategic routes for the purposes of trade, and guarded them by means of fortified posts, as we have seen at Ghiaour Kalessi.[2] One of these roads, taken by caravans, led to

[1] CALLISTHENES, *Fragm.*, 29 (*Scriptores rerum Alexandri*, collected by Ch. Müller, and placed at the end of Arrian's work, collect. Didot). Hence the Greek dictum, Ταντάλου τάλαντα (Thesaurus, s.v. ταντάλίζω).

[2] *Hist. of Art*, tom. iv. vol. ii. p. 714, Figs. 351, 352.

the Karabel Pass, where it divided: one running down to the furthest point of the bay, the other debouching into the marvellous plain of Hermus. If we have correctly made out the stages and guessed the terminus of this highway, would there not be ground for believing that, at the point where it reached the sea, a mart of exchange, both for merchandise and ideas, would almost immediately have sprung up; and should not this be the explanation of that precocious prosperity with which legend endowed the Tantalis of Sipylus, the proud city overthrown by Zeus, as elsewhere Sodom and Gomorrha were destroyed by Jahveh?

On this hypothesis Tantalus and his subjects would be Phrygians, as said tradition, but Phrygians formed in the school of those eastern conquerors whom we have tentatively called, to give them a name, Syro-Cappadocians or Hittites. Are commercial relations enough to explain borrowings and progress, or did the Hittites in their victorious march penetrate as far as these shores which unlocked the sea to them? Did they occupy for a time Sipylus, plant a colony there, a kind of outpost, whose population in due time intermingled with such of the Thracian immigrants as had been brought to these same slopes and ravines? Neither myth nor history will answer the question. The monuments of this district, however, exhibit features other than those seen on the examples of the upper valley of the Sangarius; they look older, and are directly derived from the art which created the sculptures of Pteria and Lycaonia. But for the enormous distance intervening between Sipylus and the Amanus and Laurus range, one would be tempted to attribute them to the Hittites. This we have done for the twin figures at Karabel and the Cybele near Magnesia; but when the reader, along with us, climbs the rugged sides of Sipylus, and discovers other very archaic works, will not the question arise as to whether all these, even to the Pseudo-Sesostris and the false Niobe, should not be assigned to the Phrygians of Sipylus rather than to transitory invaders? To these may belong figures whose outward signs and the place they occupy would lend themselves to such explanations; but there are difficulties not easily overcome in ascribing to hands other than those of the permanent inhabitants themselves, a work which, as the Cybele, Buyuk Souret, clearly shows long and patient labour. Our reason for including the Buyuk Souret with the Hittite series was (1) to make it as complete as possible, (2) because of the inscription accompanying it. It would have been wiser, perhaps, not to have detached it from the monuments that constitute the Sipylus unit, a group that would represent the effort and legacy of the first civilized state ever planted on the western coast of Asia Minor, within easy reach of the Archipelago, having the Hellenic peninsula right opposite. Of course, the Phrygians of Sipylus were not the first inhabitants of the line of coast that faces towards Europe. Before the influence of Eastern arts and industries had travelled thither, the physical and climatic conditions of this favoured land had attracted around the springs and mouths of rivers populations made up of pretty closely packed settlements. To inquire their name and origin would be vain, since history, nay, not even tradition itself, could travel so far back. The existence of these truly "prehistoric" populations, in the fullest sense the term implies, has been revealed to the world by the recent excavations of Dr. Schliemann in the Troad. From the bottom of the trenches opened in the sides of the hill at Hissarlik, was brought out a "stone civilization," if the expression may be allowed. Now, among the implements of every description that lay heaped together in the lower strata, dropped there by each generation in turn, no metal has been found; at least so rarely, that where its presence has been detected, we may reasonably set it down to accident—either some mistake in making up the journal from the notes, which may have got confused, or the falling in of a portion of an upper layer or crust, causing the regular order to be disturbed, so that articles that properly belonged to recent, or *at least much later* times, would be found in the lowest layers amongst the primitive ones. As to celestial types and ornamental forms of Egyptian and Chaldæan origin to be found almost everywhere, both on the coasts and the Mediterranean islands (whither they were carried by the Phœnicians), or distributed in the interior of Syria and Asia Minor by other intermediaries, they are non-existent at Hissarlik; at any rate, in pieces of genuine antiquity, such as unquestionably belong to the lowest strata. Here art and industry, though rude, betray independent effort; an effort akin to that which inspired the populations of the Ægean coast in their first struggles to emerge from barbarism, ere a double set of influences borne by land and sea put them in continuous touch with the civilized nations of Further Asia. A careful survey of the industrial products of the primitive art under notice, will form a natural introduction to the history of Hellenic art; we will call at Hissarlik on our way to Mycenæ and Tyrins.

In the race we promise to run, we are bound to complete our study of the productions of Oriental art ere making that turn of the road where lies Greece. That thousands of years divide the civilizations of Egypt and Chaldæa from those that unfolded later on the European side of the Mediterranean, is a fact we have tried to make clear; going back as far as possible to that mysterious past, whose far-reaching depths were unsuspected till yesterday. Thanks to recent researches and discoveries, the main results of which have appeared in our history, we are now able to measure the importance and originality of the work accomplished by the first civilized nations of the valleys of the Nile and of Europe. The course of our studies took us to the capitals where these nations had reared monuments both imposing and numerous; to Memphis and Thebes, Babylon and Nineveh, Tyre and Sidon. We saw by what means the methods invented by these active and influential centres were disseminated in an easterly direction. It remains to trace the effect of such teachings and example upon peoples who, although they never played a leading part in the world, contributed none the less, in a greater or less degree, to work up the materials which Asia transmitted to Europe. Hence the fitness of taking up each in turn, Phrygians, Lydians, and Lycians. These people lost their independence towards the beginning of the seventh century B.C., when they became subject to the Achæmenidæ. The result of this conquest was to bring democratic Greece into contact with the greatest Asiatic monarchy the world had yet seen, whose art, the youngest and the last derived from Oriental tradition, will form the larger portion of this volume. It is an art which, in the building and decoration of its monuments, could dispose of almost boundless resources; it will, therefore, detain us longer than those provincial and secondary arts, whose claim to our early attention lies in the fact that they stand first in chronological order.

In obedience to this principle we shall begin with the Phrygians, whose mythical cycle, often referred to by us, shows them as a compact political body in the days of Homer, to whom the name even of the Lydians is unknown. Our survey of Phrygian art will divide itself in two sections—one devoted to the monuments of Sipylus or Phrygia Parva, which, as a kingdom, had already ceased to exist when epic poetry had its birth; the other to those of that state of Phrygia Major, the last rulers of which belong to historical times. In this second group will be included a certain number of tombs recently discovered in Paphlagonia; here and there, north and south of the chain of Olympus, the arrangements in sepulchral architecture are precisely similar, at least in those tombs that are prior to the introduction of the Greek language and Greek arts into the centre and north of the peninsula. Were the Paphlagonians sprung, like the Phrygians, from a Thracian stock? We know not, save that the resemblance between the two sets of monuments seems to justify the comparison we have made.

CUSTOMS AND RELIGION OF THE PHRYGIANS.

The historian who desires to form a fair idea of the general culture, religious creed, and public worship of Phrygia is obliged in a great measure to rely upon authorities of comparatively recent date, unconnected, it would seem, with the period within which we wish to confine ourselves for the present. Such a course is justified by the oft-repeated statement, which will bear being mentioned afresh, namely, that Hellenic culture did not penetrate to, or take permanent hold on, the interior of the peninsula until the days of Alexander and his successors. And though its diffusion was universal and lasting, it proved ineffectual in stamping out the religion, legends, and usages, hallowed by a past so remote as to be counted by thousands of years. Hence it comes to pass that even the Greeks, in matters pertaining to religion and art, were actually influenced by the order of things they beheld around them. Under Roman rule, the temples of Pontus, Cappadocia, and Phrygia, of Bela, Comana, and Pessinus, to name only the best known, along with the lands attached to them, preserve a whole host of eunuch-priests and consecrated temple-slaves of either sex. The yearly festivals, which were wont on stated days to attract thousands of pilgrims to worship at the shrines, are as fully attended as of old. No need is there to rejuvenate or bring them up to date; their title of nobility and claim to the reverence of the multitude reside in their antiquity. Then, too, in many a sepulchre of old Phrygia, dating from the first and the second century of the

Christian era, imprecatory formulas continue to be incised, to scare away the impious who should presume to disturb the sacred repose of the dead.[1]

If the social conditions of the people in possession of the coast line of the Ægean were scarcely disturbed by the Macedonian and the Roman conquests, there is every reason to suppose that the old order of things was maintained during the Persian rule, which lasted two hundred and fifty years. Under the name of satraps, the heads of local dynasties preserved, almost everywhere, their hereditary power, and priests continued to preside over their theocratic principalities. Despite the apparent disappearance of ancient divisions, the various races who occupied the tableland were allowed to live their own life, subject to paying a small tribute and furnishing a certain number of soldiers in time of war. No government was ever found to govern less than that of the Achæmenidæ, nor was its policy ever directed to control the liberty of action of its subjects, who were left to work out their weal or woe unfettered. When we come to examine the monumental façades which are so plentiful in the cemeteries of Eastern Phrygia, we shall find that they continued almost unchanged during the space of about five hundred years, beginning from the eighth century B.C., down to, perhaps, the Seleucidæ. As time rolled on, Greek influence becomes perceptible in the proportion of columns, the shape of capitals, the character and make of entablatures, without prejudice, however, to the main dispositions or decorative themes, which are precisely the same as in the age of Gordios and Midas. It is a trite remark that religious conceptions, inasmuch as they are implanted in the inmost soul, offer a far greater persistency than artistic forms, no matter how beautiful or ancient, easily imitated, too, or borrowed. In Phrygia it took a very long time to bring about modification and change in existing forms, which were with difficulty replaced by fresh ones. If this

[1] The real significance of these formulas was first understood by Moritz Schmidt (*Neue Lykische Studien*, pp. 132-136). See also Professor Ramsay's recent dissertation, entitled "Phrygian Inscriptions of the Roman period" (*Zeitschrift für vergleichende Sprachforschung*, N.S., tom. viii. pp. 381–400). The formulas in question are more particularly found east and north of Phrygia; that is to say, far from the boundaries of Ionia and the district subsequently called the kingdom of Pergamus. These territories were, from the outset, marts of exchange, and, so to speak, the focus of the electric contact between Phrygians and Ionians; hence they became closely united together, nay, blended into one community, Greek in speech.

be so, how much more sedulously must observances relating to the public worship of deities have been watched over and preserved as relics bound up with the instincts and early awakening of these primitive societies? Contact with Greek polytheism did not materially affect the religions of Asia Minor or Syria, which kept their ground far more energetically, and were more successful in repelling alien influences, than those of the Italians and Gauls. This they owed to their intense spirituality; for, although they were acted upon by the new religion, they reacted and gave back in their turn quite as much, if not more, than they had received. Consequently, in trying to unravel the inner meaning and outward form of these cults, we may unhesitatingly draw from authorities acknowledged as such, Herodotus, Strabo, Diodorus, etc., as well as from later ones, who, when Greece ceased to create in the domain of art and poetry, set themselves to write the histories of the Hellenic race and of the various peoples who had preceded them in the country. In so doing they made use of the accumulated data which lay open to them at Pergamus and Alexandria.

The Phrygians were distinguished from their neighbours of Lydia, and the Greeks on the coast, in that they were essentially a nation of shepherds and husbandmen. From the earliest time they partially cleared out the forest-clad mountains, to feed numerous flocks and herds, which constituted one main source of the revenue of native princes, as it does to the present day. This was forcibly borne home to us as we sat at the door of our tents and watched the kine and yearlings roaming under majestic pines, or as we journeyed along the banks of the Sangarius, around its copious springs, which give the river from the outset a considerable volume of water, and render it unfordable save at rare intervals. If in summer herbage is scanty on the plateau an abundance of grass is always to be had on the first slopes of the hills. Homer extols the fiery steeds foremost in the chase led by the Phrygians (*Iliad*, ii. 862; iii. 185; x. 431; *Hymns*, iii. 138). Close at hand, Pan engaged Phœbus in unequal contest, when public opinion, as was to be expected, declared in favour of the greater god, and honest but imprudent Midas withdrew with ass's ears (OVID, *Metam.*, lib. xi., iv.[1]). However this may be, the same god

[1] The reference given is according to English arrangement, and not that which appears in the text.—TR.

reappears later under the name of Atys, the chief deity of the Phrygians, whom tradition depicted as a fair young shepherd of whom Cybele was enamoured.[1] Other instances might be added in proof of the rural bent of the Phrygians; their readiness in turning to account the natural fertility of the soil, which in many places is a soft tufaceous rock, easily disintegrated, and of marvellous productiveness. With them all that related to husbandry was deemed sacred: the husbandman, the ploughshare, and the patient oxen yoked thereto were under Divine protection. Death was the sentence passed upon the evildoer who misappropriated implements of husbandry or killed a plough ox.[2] The gold-plated chariot of their great ancestor, Gordios, had not been a war-chariot, but a lumbering cart which served him to garner his crops;[3] the plating had been of later days, so as to render it a fit offering to Olympus. Had not he commanded his winged messenger, the eagle, to alight on the yoke of Gordios's team, as an earnest of his future power? This was no other than the famous chariot placed in the Thesaurion at Corinth by his son Midas, and doubtless very similar to the clumsy *arábas* of the present day.[4] Then, too, the fabulous wealth of Midas had been foreshadowed in grains of wheat, carried by ants to his infant lips;[5] whilst his gigantic son, Lityerses, a king among reapers, gloried in the stoutness of his sinews, and overthrew everybody whom he challenged to single combat. His name it was which resounded in song in the lowlands at harvest time, or around the threshing-floor.[6] Others, again, were connected with the vintage, where Midas appears as filling the fountain, out of which Silenus is wont to quench his thirst, with the juice of the grape, so that the unsociable old man may be secured whilst overpowered by the unusual libation.[7]

Allusions to the potency of wine, its cheering effect on the hearts

[1] In a poem of Atys, partly reproduced by Origen (MILLER, *Philosophumena*, p. 119), he is called αἰπόλος, goat-herd; whilst Theocritus (xx. 40) calls him βουκόλος, ox-driver.

[2] Nicholas of Damascus (*Frag. Hist. Græc.*, tom. iii. p. 128, Müller's edition).

[3] ARRIAN, *Anabasis*, ii. 3; ÆLIAN, *De natura animalium*, xiii.; Q. Curtius, iii. 1.

[4] *Arába* is the Turkish name for a chariot drawn by oxen.

[5] CICERO, *De Divinatione*, I. xxxvi.

[6] Athenæus, x. p. 415, B; xiv. p. 419, A.; THEOCRITUS, *Idyls*, x. 41; Pollux, iv. 54.

[7] XENOPHON, *Anabasis*, I. ii. 13; Pausanias, I. iv. 5; Maximus of Tyre, XI. i.; PHILOSTRATES, *Life of Apollonius*, vi. 27. ARNOBIUS (*Adversus gentes*, v. 6) relates the same story of Agdistis, whom Dionysius overpowers with a generous vintage by the same means.

of God and man, abound in the Homeric poems, and prove the high esteem in which vine-culture was held; nor was there lack of flesh, which the Phrygians consumed in prodigious quantities, of milk and fruit, and of such rude comfort as is to be found in primitive communities (*Iliad*, iii. 401; xi. 184, etc.).

The Phrygians do not seem to have had a taste for warlike adventures or commercial transactions involving long voyages. They were content to sell their raw products, including, perhaps, metals, gold and silver, found on many a point of their territory; especially gold dust washed down by rivulets flowing down the rocky mountains. This it was which, as with their neighbours, the Lydians, gave "royal power to their kings;" and though they obeyed a military chief, they remained to the last a quiet, unoffending people. Thus it came to pass that, despite the strong position afforded by their hilly country, they fell an easy prey in turn to the Cimmerians and Lydians. Albeit accounted of slow understanding by their quick-witted neighbours, they could boast a mighty past, and were the first inland tribes that made use of an alphabet derived from Phœnician letters. They left no literature; but neither did their neighbours, the Lydians and Lycians, whose political existence was more brilliant, and extended over a longer series of years. Their writing, however, is known from the inscriptions already referred to. The substitution of the Greek for the Phrygian language was effected in the time of the Seleucidæ. The writers of that day, struck with much that was new and quaint in the narratives recounted to them, set about noting down the chief events and first struggles towards greater light—at least, as they appeared to them—of the beginnings of the people with whom they had become connected. In so doing much that it were interesting to know, myths, details connected with their religion and history, were rejected as rude and uncouth, altogether unworthy to figure in their pages; whilst many a fact was distorted or softened down to suit their prejudices. Nevertheless we are too severe in our strictures against the Greeks for the part they played in the reviving and editing of the folk-lore of these inland tribes, forgetting that without them the literary monuments in question would never have been heard of.

If the written records of the Phrygian nation consist of but a few obscure texts graven on stone, their tombs show them to have been possessed of genuine talent for plastic art. Were these non-existent, however, the nature of their legendary lore would be enough to prove their rare artistic gifts. They certainly were a vigorous, impassioned race, whose imagination, by turn graceful, tender, melancholy, and lively, is reflected in the myths which go by their name. They were great lovers of music, and, as the inventors of the flute, gave proof of real originality of mind. If not the first who had brought sounds out of the reed, as the Hellenes said, they had shown how much could be made of the simple instrument. On the margin of Lake Aulokrene, "the spring of the flute,"[1] it was further alleged, hard by Kelænæ, grew reeds of superior quality, emitting the most resonant sounds.

The close relationship between Armenians and Phrygians has been referred to; now, in the Armenian language *elegen* signifies reed, a word Greek lexicographers were unable to explain, albeit rendered familiar to them from about the seventh century B.C. by the *elegos* (whence elegy), poems of Callinus of Ephesus, and Archilochus of Paros,[2] which were heard throughout the cities of Ionia with due accompaniment of the flute. The Greeks passed readily from one mood to another, and took great delight in opposing the lyre to the flute; the deep dulcet tones of the former lulled the soul, whilst the shrill penetrating notes of the latter excited the nerves to quick resolve, often to deadly strife.[3]

[1] DUNCKER, *Geschichte des Alterthums*, tom. i. p. 384. BERNHARDY (*Grundriss der Griechischen Litteratur*, § 101, nn.) discusses at length the more or less absurd derivations put forth by Greek grammarians, in their vain attempts to prove the Greek origin of ἔλεγος. He is of opinion that it was an old Asiatic word, the real meaning of which was lost in its passage across Asia Minor and the Ægean. BOETTICHER (*Arica*, 34) derives ἔλεγος from *elegn*, reed, and *elegnery*, a flute made of reeds. On the other hand, HANS FLACH (*Geschichte des Griechischen Lyrik*, etc., 8°, 1883, tom. i. p. 158, note 2) connects ἔλεγος with a different group of Armenian words: *jegern* or *jelern*, misfortune; *jejerakan*, *jelarakan*, tragic, fatal, whence elegy, funeral song, to weep, to lament, etc. In our estimation Boetticher's theory, which would connect *elegos* with flute, is more likely to be right; for the word, at the outset, had not the exclusive meaning of plaintive poetry, and *elegn* comes nearer *elegos* than *jelern*, *jererakan*, and the like adduced by Flach. The hypothesis, too, is more consonant with what we know of elegiac poetry, in which Callinus (778 B.C.), Archilochus (685), Tyrtæus (684), Mimnermus, and Solon (558) excelled. Elegy was sometimes melancholy and mournful, sometimes amorous and martial; used, too, by moralists and politicians to air their ideas, or explain away their public action. The themes might be divergent, but the rhythm never varied, and as long as such pieces were sung, it was to music expressly composed for the flute.

[2] ARISTOTLE, *Politica*, VIII. vii. 8, 9.

[3] PLATO, *Republic*, iii. p. 399.

Each style of music had its partisans: Apollo led the choir of the lutists, and Pan and Marsyas were faithful to the native reed. Our duller northern sense is slow to grasp how impressions so wide apart, yet alike in their mastery, should have been aroused in the breasts of the ancient Greeks, albeit most of us can feel the difference of tone produced by wind or string instruments. Whether due to the complex and scientific character of modern music, certain it is that, except to southern nations who have retained much of the impressionable nature of primitive societies, it no longer is an all-engrossing force, a subjugation of the senses as irresistible and as much to be dreaded as inebriation.

The supreme sway music is apt to exercise over the impressionable mind of youth was fully acknowledged and taken into account by ancient philosophers in their educational plans. Plato banishes the flute from his ideal Republic;[1] and Aristotle[2] is of opinion that the young should not be exposed to music of necessity married to the captivating strains of elegiac verse which in his day still went by the name of Phrygian, as likely to lead to self-indulgence and debauchery of the worst kind. Nor were their apprehensions ill founded, for the melodies played on the flute bore strong and unmistakable signs of their origin; of having sprung up in the frenzied transports of public rituals to which the Greek gave the name of "orgies," and which were associated with the cults of Thrace, Syria, and Asia Minor.

The religious belief of Phrygia was but the worship of the powers of nature; its festivals were a sacred drama, the subject of which was the eternal struggle between life and death, light and darkness, youth and decay. Upon this theme a rich fancy rang the changes according to time and place. The waxing and waning of the moon, the revolution of the glittering spheres, the rising of the sun, its daily sinking below the horizon and its disappearance in the gloom of night, are phenomena well calculated to strike terror in the imagination of primitive man. Experience enables us to view with equanimity, if not with indifference, the varying phases of the complexes that sum up the universe. But it was not so in those early days, and we can imagine the anxiety with which men watched the rapid succession of the seasons in a region of climatic extremes. But yesterday the tableland lay under a

[1] PLATO, *Republic*, iii. p. 399.   [2] ARISTOTLE, *Politics*, VIII. vii. 8, 9.

white covering of snow, which the wind took up, tumbled about and cast from the heights, it being arrested by fretted rocks on whose surface the dust of summer still adheres. The moisture, helped by the sun, quickens even the bare stone, and covers it with soft green and a profusion of flowers which expand in the air their sweet perfume.

This is not the place for attempting to unravel the confused mass of the mythic cycle of Phrygia, which we only know in the garbled account of the Greeks, whom it moved to laughter, or the still more distorted version of Clement of Alexandria and Arnobius.[1] Yet all was not puerile, fanciful, and obscene in these myths as held by the fathers, for, despite multiplicity of names and whimsical variants applied to the same personage, we can go back to the time when the religion of these inland tribes was centred in a divine couple—a solar or god of heaven whom they worshipped as Papas,[2] father, whom the Greeks identified with Zeus, and a goddess, Ma, Amma, mother (Rhea, with the Romans), the personification of the earth.[3] Great reverence was paid to the female deity, in her character of goddess-mother, and the first place was assigned to her in all public festivities, contrary to the custom which prevails with people of different race. This was no other than Cybele, whose altar, accompanied by an inscription now

[1] In our account of the Phrygian religion we have followed M. A. MAURY, *Hist. des religions de la Grèce antique*, tom. iii. pp. 79–100; as well as DUNCKER, *Geschichte des Alterthums*, tom. i. pp. 338–390; ED. MAYER, *Geschichte des Alterthums*, tom. i. p. 253; and FRANÇOIS LENORMANT, *Sabasius* (*Revue Arché.*, N.S., tom. xxviii. pp. 300–389; tom. xxix. pp. 43–51).

[2] Arrian tells us that the Bithynians, who are nearly related to the Phrygians, call Zeus Papas: ἀνιόντες εἰς τὰ ἄκρα τῶν ὀρῶν Βιθυνοὶ ἐκάλουν Πάπαν τὸν Δία (*Bithyn.*, EUSTACHIUS, p. 565, 4). See also Diodorus Siculus, III. lviii. 4, who states that Atys was addressed as Papas in after times by the Phrygians.

Two names, supposed to have belonged to ancient towns whose site is unknown, are compounded with the form Manes; Manegordion, Manesion. Inscriptions and statues in honour of Men are plentiful during the Macedonian and Roman period throughout the peninsula. With regard to this god, his cult, and many appellations, consult GUIGNIAUT, *Religions de l'antiquité*, tom. ii. p. 962, and more especially WADDINGTON, *Voyage Arché. Le Bas*, v. Nos. 667, 668.

[3] *Etimologium magnum*, s.v. Amma; Stephanus Byzantinus, s.v. Mastaura, name of a Lydian town. Ἐκαλεῖτο δὲ καὶ ἡ Ῥέα Μᾶ καὶ [illegible] ἐθύετο παρὰ Λυδοῖς. Mā was likewise understood in the sense of mother by the Greeks. Μᾶ γᾶ, Μᾶ γᾶ (μήτηρ γῆ) is found in ÆSCHYLUS, *Suppl.*, 890–899. Μήτηρ ὄρεια, μήτηρ Ἰδαία (Strabo), *Phrygia mater* (Virgil), were exact transliterations from the various names borne by Cybele in her Phrygian home.

obliterated, has been discovered by Professor Ramsay. Fortunately for us, however, the two initial words, "Matar Kubile," written in sunk characters, can be easily made out (Fig. 3).[1]

Next in popularity and importance was the lunar god Men, whose cult spread throughout Asia Minor, and thence to Greece and Rome.[2] Statuary generally represents him as a man of youthful appearance.[3]

Greek and Latin writers, to whom we owe the little that is known of the Phrygian religion, mention, in relation with Cybele, a god whom they variously call Bagaios, Sabazius, Atys, and Agdistis.[4] That names so widely different should be applied to the same personage is rather puzzling at first; but philology will perhaps help us out of the difficulty. If, according to the best authorities, words said to belong to the Phrygian idiom admit of being explained by Indo-European roots, Bagaios was simply a generic term for god;[5] Sabazios, Sabazius, a eulogistic epithet signifying venerable, worthy of adoration.[6] The real and proper name of the god was Atys or Agdistis. Atys may be a dialectic variant, an abbreviation of the older and more complete form of Agdistis,

FIG. 3.—Phrygian inscription. RAMSAY, *On the Early Historical Relations*, Plate III.

[1] There is also the form Cybele, sometimes found in Greek lexicographers and in inscriptions of this goddess, which, like Fig. 3, seems to indicate a late modification of the name.

[2] Among the Thracians, who owned community of blood and religion with the Phrygians, Sabazius is a solar god (MACROBIUS, *Saturnalia*, I. 18). The great Phrygian deity was styled ποιμὴν λευκῶν ἄστρων (*Philosophumena*, Miller, p. 118), a periphrase clearly intended to designate the sun, and to be read in an ancient hymn cited by Origen, or whoever was the author of the book which bears his name. MACROBIUS (*Saturn.*, i. 22) identifies Atys with the sun: "*Solem Phryges sub nomine Attinis ornant et fistula et virga.*"

[3] In the psalms Men, lunar god, is described as the great "measurer."—TRS.

[4] It is possible that Agdistis may be a local name, as Dindymene, Sipylene, etc., applied to Cybele, according to the places in which she was worshipped. Pausanias (I. iv. 5) specifies a mountain, Ἄγδος, in Phrygia as the burial-place of Atys. Professor RAMSAY (*Sipylos*, p. 56) recognizes in ἄγδος the Phrygian word which signified mountain, and which he compares with the Greek ὄχθος, hill; whence Agdistis, "the son of the mountain." It may be asked whether "mountain" was not invented to explain a name which was no longer understood. In other forms of the myth, Agdistis has ceased to be a male god, and appears with all the attributes of Cybele.

[5] See p. 3, note, of this volume.

[6] Compare the Greek word σέβειν; Sanscrit, *sabhâdj*, honoured, revered.

which in process of time it wholly superseded.[1] Atys is the form usually used by poets and historians; we also find it as a proper name in Lydia.

The worshippers of Atys, as those of the Syrian Adonis, were in no sense of the word rapt and passive spectators of the rites enacted before them by the officiating priest. To them the oft-recurring drama was a thrilling reality, in which men and women all felt an interest and helped on the unfolding of the cosmic tragedy, during which were depicted the anomalies of terrestrial life, ever failing of its purpose, yet fulfilling it; arrested in its onward progress, yet bounding on with renewed energy. With a potency of which we can form no idea, the assembled multitude grieved for the orb which, pursued by the hurricane, grew wan and pale, and was presently engulfed with black clouds or the greater gloom of night; for the plants that wither under the hot breath of summer, whose foliage turns sere and whose sap ceases to run under the wintry blast. A few months later, the same multitude joyed in the return of light and warmth; it trembled with delight at the reawakening of the god, an event celebrated in a festival that was far away the more important of the two; it lasted six days, and consisted of two parts widely different in their import: a funereal pageant, followed by solemn rejoicings.[2] In both, the procession moved to the confused sound in turn of funereal chants, tambourines, cymbals, and flutes.[3] Branches of pine were carried on the shoulders of the worshippers as a symbol of undying life, a token that the dead they saw before them would rise again.[4] In this way they reached the grave previously prepared, into which the god was

[1] Greek manuscripts and inscriptions spell the name Ἄτυς, Ἄττυς, Ἄττης, indifferently. Scores of towns in Asia Minor, apparently compounded with the name of the god, have also the double consonant: Ἄτταια, Ἄττεα, Ἀττοῦδα, and the like. The first word of the inscription on the Midas rock (Fig. 1) shows the form ATEΣ.

[2] Pindar (Strabo, X. iii. 12) in a dithyrambic exclaims: "O mother of the gods, cymbals, tambourines, and bagpipes have struck up; young yellow pines are lighted in token that the festivity has begun." And in one of the so-called Homeric poems (xiii. 3, 4) Cybele is called "the goddess who loves the shrill-sounding crotala, the flute and loud tambourine." Propertius, xvii. 37; xvii.; MACROBIUS, *Saturnalia*, i. 18.

[3] LUCIAN, *Tragodopodagra*, 30–33.

[4] "*Quid pectoribus applaudentes palmas passis cum crinibus galli*" (ARNOBIUS, *Adversus gentes*, v. 10).

about to descend. As he was let down, the throng broke forth in wails and sobs, beating their breasts and tearing their hair.[1] In their religious frenzy, some lashed themselves with scourges furnished with bones that tore off great pieces of flesh, and fell a sacrifice to the deity;[2] others went further and offered their virility, dedicating the rest of their wretched existence to the god who had accepted their self-mutilation.[3] Thus each of these festivals swelled the number of eunuch-priests, who on public occasions were wont to lead the chorus of the devotees of Cybele. Under the name of Græco-Galli, they it was who during Persian, notably Roman rule, carried far and wide the rites and practices of the old Asiatic cults (Fig. 4).

FIG. 4.—Archi-Gallus. Capitoline Museum. DURUY, *Hist. des Romains*, tom. ii p. 528.[4]

[1] Μάστιξ ἀστραγαλωτή (PLUTARCH, *Contra Colotes*, xxxiii. 9). Consult also APULEIUS, *Metam.*, viii. 28.

[2] SUETONIUS (*Otho*, viii.) writes that as Otho moved against Vitellius, "*die quo cultores deum matris lamentari et plangere incipiunt.*"

[3] *Acuto silice* (Catul., xliii. 5); *rupta testa* (Juvenal, vi. 514). We find here, too, the sacredness of stone, in connection with the idea of sacrifice, as against metal (*Hist. of Art*, tom. iv. p. 373). It will be seen that the epithet *semi viri*, applied to the priests of Cybele by the Romans, was well deserved. With Italian brevity, the day of flagellations and self-mutilation was indicated in the calendar by a single but pithy word, "Sanguem." Julian's account of the "mysteries of the mother of the gods" (p. 168) coincides with the calendar, except that he omits to mention the two last days, *i.e.* Requies and Lavatio.

[4] The effeminate character of the eunuch-priest will be observed. From his ears depend heavy earrings; a diadem surrounds his brow, formed by three large coins that serve to keep in place the head-tire, which falls in rich folds behind his back. Long rows of pearls on either side of the face reach to his middle, where they rest in the horizontal folds of the shawl, and in a basket brimful of fruit, which he

The pageant attending the resurrection was in brilliant contrast with that which had preceded it. Branches of pine reappeared amidst the acclamations and the tumults of joy of the multitude, whose delight at the return of the god was translated by gambols and running about.[1] The music was in harmony with the new mood. It had been grave, sad, and slow before; now the clapping of hands, the dancing, capering, singing, and striking of brazen shields to mark the time, could scarcely keep pace with its phrenetic, bewildering movements.[2] In order to keep up or renew their flagging spirits, they had recourse to copious libations, until, overcome with fatigue and exhaustion, they one by one fell by the roadside, among the woodlands and vales whither they had wandered. The fifth day was given up to rest, so as to enable them to get over the effect of their violent emotions, and prepare them to return to the routine of daily life. The *lavatio*, or bath, occurred on the sixth and last day of the performance, when the puppet-god was carried to a clear running stream, stripped of its gay bridal apparel, and plunged into the water, even as a bride on the eve of her marriage.[3]

The favour enjoyed by Asiatic rituals away from their original

supports with his sinister hand; the dexter holding up an olive branch covered with berries. A thick golden chain goes twice round his neck, and from it hangs a golden shrine of Atys, whose image, crowned with the Phrygian tiara, is distinctly seen. Against the wall is a colonnette topped by a bearded bust, perhaps of the same Atys before his self-mutilation, or Zeus-Pater together with a scourge, flute, tambourine, and the mystic cystus.

[1] The solemnity of Cybele was opened with the Dendrophory, or carrying the pine to the temple—the *arbor intrat* of the calendar. With regard to the sacred tree, the fillets always surrounding it, as well as the place it occupied in these mysteries, see ARNOBIUS, *Adversus gentes*, v. 16; and ZOGA, *Bassi rilievi antichi di Roma*, tom. i. Plates XIII., XIV.

[2] LUCRETIUS, *De natura rerum*, ii. 621; APOLLONIUS, *Argonautica*, i. 1135–1139.

[3] The erection of the famous temple of Cybele and Atys at Pessinus was ascribed to Midas (Diodorus, iii. 58). In obedience to the injunctions of the Sibylline books, the Romans removed, by order of the Senate, the statue, *bætylus*, of the goddess to their city, where the rites connected with her mysteries seemed to have followed her. The Italians were particularly careful in washing every year, on the 6th of the calendar of April, her shrine in the waters of the Alno, a rivulet which falls into the Tiber close to Rome. This was in imitation of the ceremony which was yearly enacted at Pessinus, on the banks of the Gallus, a stream which flows through the town, where the *lavatio* could be performed, before it joins the Sangarius. It is evidently in allusion to this rite that Herodotus says, "The Phrygians used to celebrate the orgies of the river Gallus, a torrent which flows through the town of Pessinus" (*Hist.*, i. 35).

homes, the fascination they exercised over the civilized nations of the old world, are our justification for dwelling, in this place, upon the customs and the religion of a people which has left no images of its gods or heroes. Types which may be traced back to Phrygia and Lydia will be found in the sequel of these studies. Such would be Cybele, her head surmounted by a tall turreted crown, now enthroned, a lion at her side (Fig. 5), now driven in a chariot or riding the king of feræ (Fig. 6), along with a long list of gods and heroes—Menes, Atyses, Midases, and Marsyases, whose nationality is rendered unmistakable by the Phrygian cap and the trailing broidered robe. To these may be added the Amazons, whose noble type so often figures on ancient Greek vases, where they preserve the characteristics of their national costume. The orgies of Dionysius offered stupendous opportunities to the Greek artist for his portraiture of the human figure in all its varying outline. Under his touch it became a living, pulsating reality, the like of which had never been seen or attempted before; whether in the endless variety of fold of the disordered dress and dishevelled hair, caught up by the breeze, flying far behind, helping not a little the movement of the scene, or the audacious attitudes of the worshippers, men and women, whose conflicting passions, caused by wine and religious frenzy, struggled on to the surface, and were reflected in their whole being. If the name of the deity in whose honour festive bands moved on Mount Cithæron is different from that with which the sanctuaries of Asia Minor have made us familiar, the oldest examples of orgies are those of Cybele and Atys; during which nervous excitement trenched on those curious pathological phenomena designated in a general way as hysteria, and which in our day have received the careful attention of the medical profession. Our practical everyday life has nothing which resembles the tumult and rebellion of the senses, the periodical fits of madness, which seized the followers of Cybele during the performance of what may be termed their

FIG. 5.—Cybele seated on throne. Reverse of bronze coin. Cadi, Phrygia. DURUY, *Hist. des Romains*, tom. i. p. 534.

FIG. 6.—Cybele seated on a lion. Reverse of bronze medallion of the Empress Sabina, wife of Hadrian. DURUY, *Hist. des Romains*, tom. i. p. 524.

sacred carnival; deep gorges and forest gloom being the stage on which it was enacted.

We have taken advantage of the opportunity which offered itself here for giving some idea of these strange scenes, so as not to be obliged to refer to them again later on, when we meet on our path a whole series of works inspired by the Bacchanalia. The Greeks, it should be remembered, in the palmiest days of their political and artistic existence, never lost their taste for the gross pleasures afforded by the orgies, nor the tradition of their origin; for in their wildest transports they invoked, as occasion served, the Phrygian Cybele or the Thracian Dionysius. That which strictly belongs to Greek genius is to have been the first to feel, or at least to render, the beauty of the human form, as it revealed itself in the agitation and abandonment of the dance; its lines, as those of the drapery, changing with each step; the latter now clinging to the body, now filled with the breeze and carried over the shoulders of the dancers.

CHAPTER II.

PHRYGIAN ART.

SIPYLUS AND ITS MONUMENTS.

THE Sipylus forms a short range of mountains on the north of the Gulf of Smyrna, about ten leagues from east to west, by three or four broad. It naturally divides itself into three parts: the Iamanlar-Dagh, to the west, is but 976 m. high; the Manissa-Dagh, to the east, reaches 1500 m.; whilst the Sabanja-Dagh holds a middle course, and serves as intermediary between the other two[1] (Fig. 7). Each section has characteristic features of its own, engendered by difference of geological formation. Thus the western district, from the river Bournabat to Menemen, is a trachytic rock, with beautiful patches of red, black, and blue; but the eastern, which is far the most imposing, belongs to the secondary system, or the period intervening between eruptive and sedimentary formations. It rises high and formidable on the north and east sides, forming almost perpendicular walls, intersected by grottoes and gigantic faults, which seem to run right through the hill, with cones and hillocks towards the south of great beauty of form and colour, yellow, red, and brown. The

[1] Our description of the Sipylus and its monuments is derived from the following sources, to which we refer the reader who should wish to obtain ampler information:—TEXIER, *Description de l'Asie Mineure*, tom. ii. pp. 249–259; Plates CXXIX.—CXXXI. *bis*; HAMILTON, *Researches in Asia Minor*, tom. i. ch. iv.; A. CHERBULIEZ, *La ville de Smyrne et son orateur Aristide*, 4to, 1863 *et* 1865 (*Extrait des Mémoires de l'Institut national genevois*); CURTIUS, *Beiträge zur Geschichte und Topographien Kleinasiens* (*Abhandlungen* of the Berlin Academy, 1872, notably chapter headed "Alt Smyrna," with Plates IV. and VI.); WEBER, *Le Sipylos et ses monuments*, 8vo, 1880 (Paris, Ducher); KARL HEUMANN, *Ein Ausflug in den Sipylos* (WESTERMANN, *Illust. Deutschen Monatsheften*, Juli, 1885, Brunswick), 8vo; W. M. RAMSAY, *Newly discovered Sites near Smyrna* (*Journal of Hellenic Studies*, tom. i. pp. 63–74); *Studies in Asia Minor*, 2, *Sipylos and Cybele* (*Journ.*, tom. iii).

Iamanlar-Dagh lacks boldness of outline, afforded by precipitous cliffs and steep ravines; but from its long fretted line of crest, innumerable spurs run out towards the south, west, and east in curious fan-like fashion, seeming to invite the pedestrian to ascend their gentle declivity (Fig. 8). The summits may be stony and bare; but the slopes have enough vegetable soil, notably in the ravines, where the moisture drained from the mountains

FIG. 7.—Map of Sipylus. CURTIUS, *Beitrage*, Plate IV.

lasts for many a month, to enable the farmer to grow corn, vines, olive, and other fruit-bearing trees.

The western side, therefore, was marked out by nature to shelter from the earliest days a compact group, brought thither by proximity of a clement, unruffled sea, and a soil naturally productive. Consequently, here and here alone can we expect to find traces of a long settlement, with all that the term implies. The oldest structures must of necessity occur on the summit; but, as the conditions of life improved, they would gradually spread down the slopes on to the flat level around Bournabat, where the primitive tribe finally settled.

Its passage, however, has been obliterated by countless generations that have succeeded each other and contended for this rich, loamy piece of ground. Here, on the old road skirting the river Hermus, rose Magnesia, now Manissa, which, though much shrunk from its former size, has not ceased to be a bustling place, teeming with life and activity. On the other hand, the narrow ravines and precipitous sides of the Manissa-Dagh afford very insufficient space for figures, tombs, or temporary refuges, of course scooped out of the solid rock.

FIG 8.—The Iamanlar Dagh. Seen from the quay of Smyrna. WEBER, *Le Sipyle.*

Attention was forcibly drawn to this district in early days, both on account of the advantages it offered by land and sea, and the remains which connected it with a remarkable past. Pausanias, a native of this neighbourhood, writes of it as the seat of the Pelopidæ. "Our country," he says, "affords many proofs of the reign of Tantalus and Pelops, proofs that are extant to this day; to wit, the lake and the tomb of Tantalus, the throne of

Pelops on the summit of Sipylus,[1] above the Hieron of Mother Plastene" (v. 13). A little further on, he speaks of "the oldest known statue of the Mother of the Gods, to be seen in the district of Magnesia,[2] and of the rock that looked for all the world like

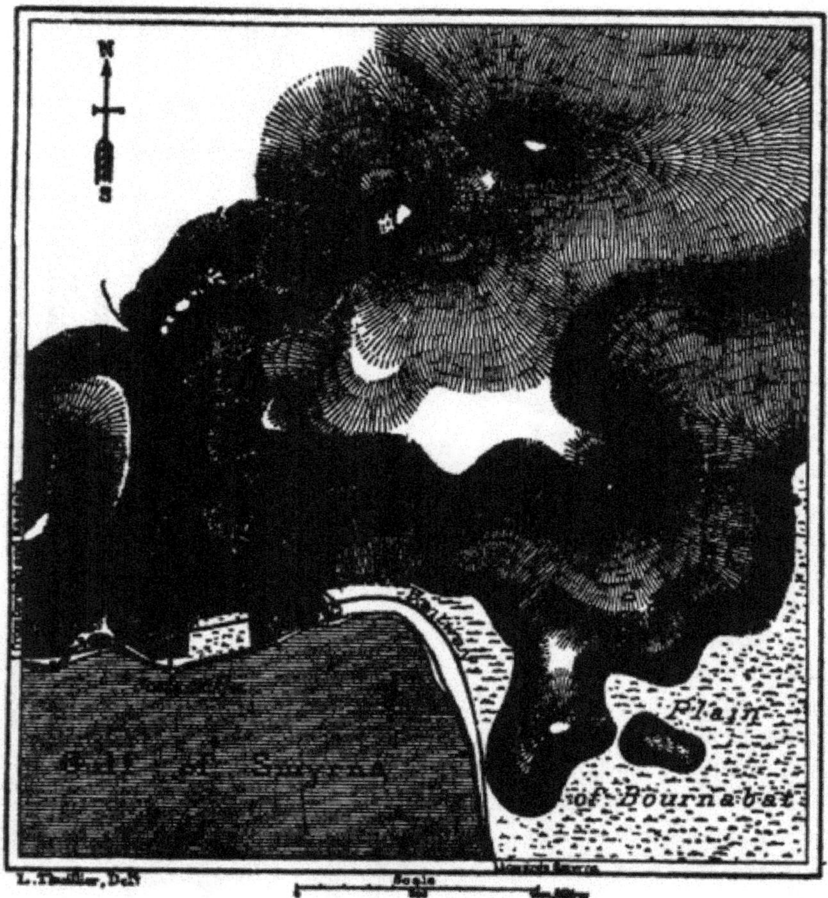

FIG. 9.—Topographical sketch of site north-west of Bournabat. CURTIUS, *Beiträge*, Plate IV.

a woman immersed in grief," which popular fancy identified with Niobe.[3]

[1] Weber translates Ταντάλου λίμνη by Tantaleis Harbour; but λίμνη is not synonymous with λιμήν, and, unless we suppose an error in the manuscripts, it must apply to one of the small lakes, the Kiz Gheul, or more probably still the Kara Gheul, actually found in the Iamanlar-Dagh (see Fig. 8).

[2] *Ibid.*, iii. 22.

[3] *Ibid.*, i. 21.

The monuments may be divided into two distinct groups, corresponding with the sharply defined regions east and west of Sipylus. Aided by the excellent map drawn for us by M. Hirschfeld (Fig. 9), we will begin with the remains on the Iamanlar-Dagh, specified by Pausanias, leaving for the last the statue of Cybele, on Mount Codine, and the curious rock which recalled the pathetic legend of Niobe, situate on the eastern side.

The site of the Iamanlar-Dagh group is fixed by the Tantaleis tomb. With this should be ranged other vestiges in the immediate

FIG. 10.—Post of observation on Sipylus. CURTIUS, *Beiträge*, Plate VI.

neighbourhood, bearing unquestionable marks of antiquity. The creek or primitive harbour, now covered by the alluvial plain around Bournabat, from which it takes its name, is found on the north of Smyrna. Facing the modern town of Haji Mūjor (Fig. 9) is an isolated hillock, which in former days was an island at the entrance of the harbour, and served to render its waters "as smooth as oil." If one ascends the undulating ground which, on the north, looks down upon the ancient haven, a necropolis, whose graves are all tumuli, is first met with, and a little higher up is the Acropolis, along with other structures cut in the solid rock, with general direction to west. These remains consist of terraces levelled out on the summit of a massive rock 15 m. long, but the use of which is not easy to make out.

Some think that thé site, commanding as it does the plain of Bournabat and the Bay of Smyrna, was used as a vedette (Fig. 10)—a supposition which would account for the steps leading to the esplanades, but would shed no light on the excavation, 2 m. long, cut in the centre of one of these open floors. Was this a grave or a trench, in which a man could lie unperceived as he scanned the surrounding country? Be this as it may, the fact that a fortress, numerous graves, stairways, platforms, and the like are crowded in a narrow space, leads to the conclusion that this was the site of the old city, by many centuries the senior of Greek Smyrna. Then, too, fragments of Cyclopæan walls, some running from north to south, intersected by others so as to form irregular enclosures, meet the eye along the whole side of the hill. Others, again, are barely visible above ground, and might be taken for walls built by the farmers to keep the earth in position, or pen their animals,[1] but for the distinct testimony of Téxier (who made a thorough study of the site and of all the monuments) to the effect that, although in places the stones are of varying size, they are so deftly fitted together as to produce a level surface, so that one is sorely tempted to make them coeval with the Acropolis and the neighbouring tombs. This elevated spot, with outlook towards the valleys of Smyrna and the Nif Chai, was the first to be inhabited; but the settlers do not seem to have been a seafaring or colonizing race, but to have chiefly relied on the natural productiveness of the soil and inland traffic.

The Acropolis, which forms the culminating point of these various remains, occupied a secondary summit 350 m. high—some 1250 m., as a bird flies, from the sea below. Half an hour's walk takes you to it, but the last part is a stiff bit of climbing. The south side is almost perpendicular, and its approach on the west is rendered difficult by quarries, whence was obtained the material for the erection of the rampart (Fig. 11). The hill, of which the summit forms an elongated plateau, measured lengthwise, is barely 45 m.

[1] TÉXIER (*Description*, tom. ii. pp. 255, 258) thinks that this was a long wall of enclosure, which served to connect the necropolis, together with public and private buildings, with the fortress. On the other hand, HAMILTON (*Researches*, p. 49) and G. HIRSCHFELD (*Alt Smyrna*) believe that all these walls are modern; whilst WEBER (*Le Sipylos*) would divide them into two sets, ancient and modern.

by 30 m. broad. It is divided in two parts: an outer court to the east, and an inner, fenced on the north, south, and west sides, C, D, by a double rampart, particularly noticeable on the north and east. Of wall G fragments alone exist, yet they suffice to show that it was parallel to C, D. The Acropolis was protected on the south by the natural escarp of the rock, to which additional strength was given by a wall wholly disappeared. Towards the east, where the hillock rises above the level of the plateau, are flat shelves with small oblong grooves, evidently made to receive the foundation stones of the outer wall. On the north side the gentle declivity of the hill made it necessary to resort to precautionary measures. These are found in a supporting wall which skirted the road, running along a narrow ridge up to a gateway about four feet wide, which it entered at right angles, and a square tower in front of it.

FIG. 11. –Acropolis of Iamanlar Dagh. Plan. WEBER, *Le Sipylos*, Plate I.

The approach to the Acropolis on the west was defended by ramparts scooped out of the projecting rock, which so narrowed the path as to allow only room for a man at a time (H). A huge excavation or ditch, hollowed in the rock on the left side of the path, whose wall below the escarp was almost perpendicular, is still seen (J). The ditch was covered by an outer wall on the left; a second (C, B, in plan), far the best constructed and the best preserved, crowned the talus (Fig. 12).

The constructive scheme of the area wall shows that it was the work of one architect, although it exhibits stones with vertical joints carefully squared at C, polygonal at B, with horizontal courses and oblique joints at O; thus yielding another instance of the danger of dating ancient structures from a small portion only. Builders in early days placed their materials exactly as they came from the quarry, without troubling themselves as to the effect they would ultimately produce. Blocks cut of the required shape, which should harmonize with a given style, were a late development.

It remains to notice two curious details. A ditch, approached by steps, enabled the defenders to take refuge in it when assaulted and obliged to withdraw into the fortress. The north-east angle of the external wall (B, Fig. 11), facing the ditch, was strengthened by a retaining semicircular wall, four courses of which still exist, and at a distance look like an unfinished tower. A quadrangular salience will be observed in the north face of the rampart which surrounds the eastern court (F, Fig. 11). This is divided into two equal sections by a partition of polygonal masonry, akin to the Acropolis properly

FIG. 12.—Northern wall of the Acropolis, seen from the outside. WEBER, Plate 1.

so called, save that the stones are smaller. The western court was a veritable redoubt, and numerous traces and fragments of walls bear witness to the effort of the builder to render it as strong as possible and capable of resisting sudden attacks from without. A hole towards the north-east corner, with rubbish lying in a circle, probably covers the site of an ancient cistern. The spade alone would reveal its true character, as also the real use of the walls at E, built of stones carefully dressed, forming a central square in the redoubt, measuring six or eight metres each way.

By no means the least interesting item of this Acropolis is the gateway (A, Fig. 11), with sides sloping upwards, giving it the appearance of a truncated arch (Fig. 13). It is closed at the top by two massive lintels of equal length, placed one behind the other. The exterior slab measures two metres by seventy-four centimetres, whilst the inner is ninety centimetres in height. It gave access to a slanting passage, at the end of which was probably a flight of steps leading to the esplanade, but now buried under stones that have fallen in. The roofing of the passage consisted of huge slabs.

We have already directed attention to the regularity of the material about the gateway, notably on the left side. It is self-evident that the unequal size of the blocks determined its having two courses on the dexter hand and three on the sinister. Here and there the lines are broken, even crooked; nevertheless there is a decided tendency towards horizontal courses. The subserviency of the builder to the stonecutter is marked throughout.

FIG. 13.—Gate to Acropolis WEBER, Plate I.

The principal eminence was selected as the site of the Acropolis, for the double purpose of making its defence an easy matter and allowing of efficient vigilance being exercised over the whole surrounding country. The necropolis was not exposed to the same risks, and could conveniently be placed on a lower grade, namely, the rocky slopes which descend towards the plain of Bournabat and overhang the ancient harbour (Fig. 9). The tumuli are about forty-five in number, and exhibit constructive skill enough. They are all stone-built and on the same pattern—a conical mass reposing on a circular substructure, itself in touch with the living rock.

Down to 1835, the more imposing, commonly called the Tantaleis tomb, could be descried from the quay; in that year it was explored by Téxier and a number of sailors placed at his disposal by the French admiral, Massieu de Clerval, stationed at Smyrna

(Fig. 14). The roof had already fallen in, but the sides were intact, and their present state is due to shafts sunk in the centre of the mass by Téxier. Before doing so, however, he had the tumulus carefully measured. The annexed woodcuts, as well as Téxier's verbal description, will enable the reader to grasp its inner arrangements.[1] Its diameter is 33 m. 60 c., or 105 m. 537 c. round. It forms a perfect circle, and is wholly built of small stones, laid out without mortar (Fig. 15). The centre is occupied by a rectangular chamber 3 m. 55 c. by 2 m. 17 c., and 2 m. 86 c. in

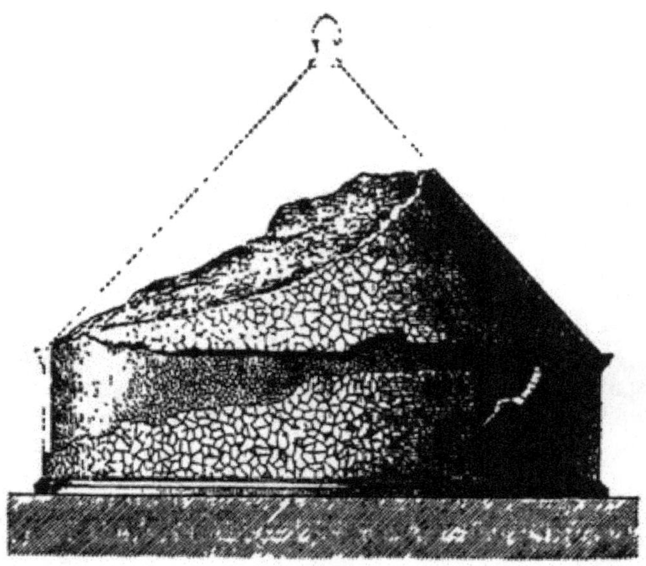

FIG. 14.—View of tomb of Tantalus before the excavations. TÉXIER, *Description*, Plate CXXX.

height under the centre of the arch (Fig. 16). The courses are horizontal throughout, and on average from 55 c. to 20 c. high. The vaulted appearance of the chamber is due to the corbel arrangement of the masonry; but there is no true arch, and, as a natural consequence, there is no key, the vacant space at the top being closed by a huge stone set on the last two courses (Fig. 17).[2] The mortuary chamber had no passage, and was

[1] TÉXIER, *Description de l'Asie Mineure*, tom. ii. pp. 253, 254. We have used WEBER'S *Sipylos*, pp. 19, 20, to check Téxier's narrative.

[2] Fig. 17 is after Weber, *loc. cit.*, Plate I. He was the first to notice that the curve formed by the ogee begins from the base of the chamber, and not, as stated

walled up after the body had been laid in it. The space around, measuring 3 m. 50 c., was tightly packed with stones of different

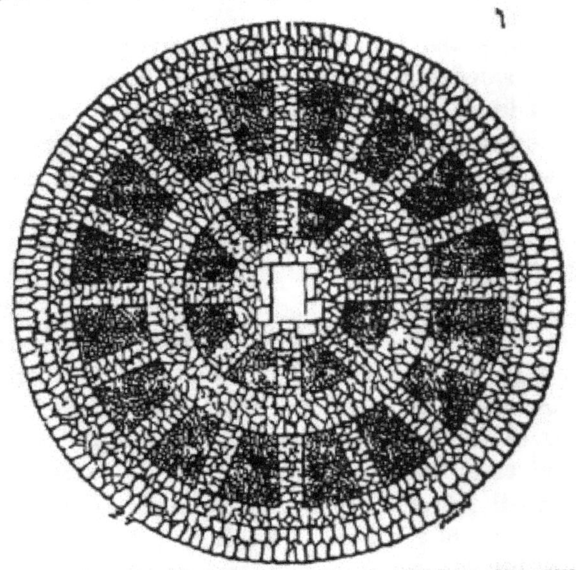

FIG 15.—Plan of tomb of Tantalus. TEXIER, *Description*, Plate CXXX.

sizes so as to fill up every interstice; eight partitions, 2 m. 70 c. long

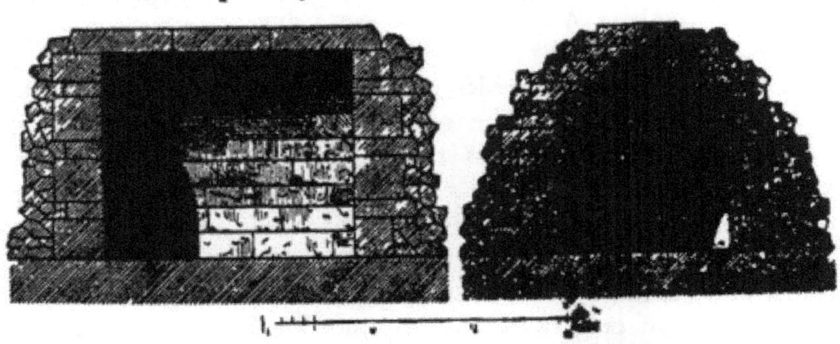

FIG. 16.—Chamber of tomb of Tantalus, Longitudinal section. TEXIER, *Description*, Plate CXXXI.

FIG. 17.—Chamber of tomb of Tantalus. Transverse section. WEBER, *Le Sipylos*, Plate I.

and three stones deep, ran from the central nucleus to a first

by Texier, from the third course. As to the hollows which appear towards the top and the middle of the wall, they are due to attempts doubtless made with a view to ascertain the existence of some secret passage to the grave-chamber ere it was closed up. Similar attempts proved vain, for nothing has been revealed save a stony mass.

circular wall, whence started other sixteen, which extended to the external wall, 3 m. 70 c. thick. The depth of this wall was not constant; thus the upper part was built of large stones and 2 m. 36 c. thick, whilst the lower was but 1 m. 50 c. To bring it to about the same strength, therefore, an internal and external casing was added. Outwardly, it was quite plain, the only attempt at decoration being a stylobate which rests on a rude plinth, the substructure of the tumulus, and a cornice of feeble salience.

It would be hard to conceive a better-devised construction, so as to enable it to withstand the action of the weather for many centuries. The intervening spaces between the partition walls are filled in with pebbles, closely packed and admirably put together, though without cement. Thanks to its solidity, the structure must have been preserved in good condition down to the last days of antiquity, protected as it was by the memories and traditions which attached to it. It was a striking object in the landscape—the first to greet the mariner on his return, the last to remind him of the home he left behind; bequeathed, too, said tradition, by revered ancestors, and one "that could not be buried out of sight"—*οὐκ ἀφάνης*, as Pausanias has it. Everything seems to indicate that the tumulus under notice is the Tantaleis tomb. When Téxier began his labours part of the roof was standing; given the diameter and the direction of the slope, the whole height, which he computes at 27 or 28 m., could be easily ascertained. The only data which present some uncertainty are the dimensions of the finial. This ornament has not been found, though it is not difficult to divine its nature. Around many other tumuli in the necropolis, whose decorative scheme and arrangement proclaim them coeval with the Tantaleis tomb, quite a large number of phalli of red trachyte have been discovered half embedded in the ground. In size they average from 40 c. to 1 m. 40 c. Primitive symbols of life and immortality, such phallic emblems, when introduced as finials, had exactly the same value as the rosette in Greek buildings. It is self-evident that the bases of all these phalli were intended to fit some cavity where they would not be seen, for they were left rough. Curiously

[1] It is curious that Téxier, who dug his way into the tumulus, should not have stated in what condition he found the grave-chamber. Did he pick up antique fragments? If so, he has kept the secret to himself.

enough, holes of corresponding size appear on the apex of the tumuli. The phallus is not uniform in shape—far from it—but evinces great variety. Among the more advanced forms are globular caps, with listel supported on stems (Fig. 18); elsewhere we find the usual conical ending (Fig. 19), and some few exemplars are mere cylinders with central swelling.[1]

The Tantaleis tomb, as the larger and more important of the group, rises at the top of a hill somewhat apart from the others by which it is surrounded, as a monarch by his subjects. These are closely packed together, connected sometimes by a wall, and one was found with two chambers. Being more lightly built than the larger tumulus, their state is even more ruinous, and treasure-seekers found less difficulty in bringing about their demolition. All have been opened from the roof or the sides, and in many instances nothing remains to mark the site but a heap of earth and rubbish. With the exception of these the plan can always be made out. Sometimes it is very similar to that of the Tantaleis sepulchre, doubtless built for a king, and as such must have been taken as pattern. The mortuary chamber has been walled up after the entombment, and a stone-work, set without mortar, made around it. It is intersected by partitions of channelled masonry, which, starting from the grave, extend to the exterior wall (Fig. 20). The

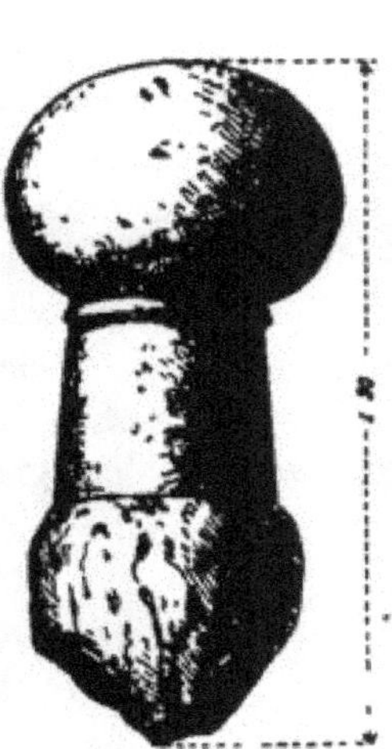

Fig. 18.—Terminal phallus. Weber, *Le Sipyle*, Plate II.

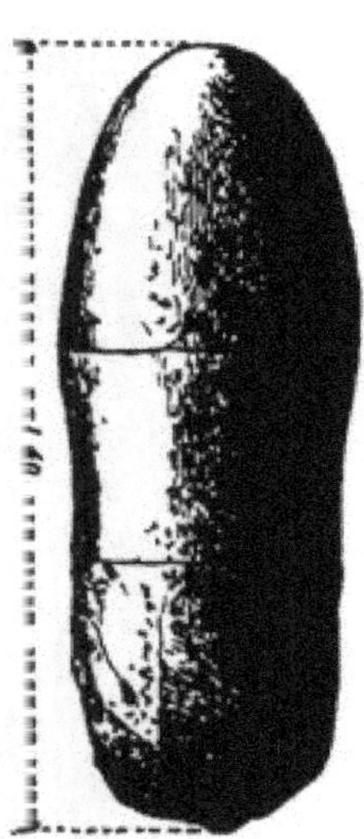

Fig. 19.—Terminal phallus. Weber, *Ibid.*, Plate II.

[1] About half a mile eastward of the colossal Cybele are tombs, and hard by Professor Sayce noticed between two triangular niches an immense phallus figured on the rocky wall (*Hell. Studies*, tom. i. p. 90).

The learned professor observes that the phallus in question is a stalagmitic formation.—Trs.

only difference is this: that as the tumulus is much smaller, multitudinous concentric circles were not required; hence from each angle of the central block, which is square, stone divisions of channelled masonry ran parallel one to the other, until they met the outside wall. There is yet a simpler type (Fig. 21), interesting from the fact that the flat arched chamber could be entered at all times by a broad passage covered with stone flags. It had no divisionary supports; a rude masonry of uncemented stones of average size extended from the central block to the circular wall. Large blocks were reserved for the substructure and the inner casing. Despite these drawbacks, it had enough solidity for its purpose. In the floor of some of these tombs, which is one with the living rock, a trough has been excavated for receiving the body. Around it may still be seen a shallow groove, which fitted the covering slab or stones. The orientation of the tombs is not constant, and, in each case, seems to have been determined by the hypsometric lines of the mountain. The Tantaleis memorial points north-east and south-east at an angle of sixty degrees.

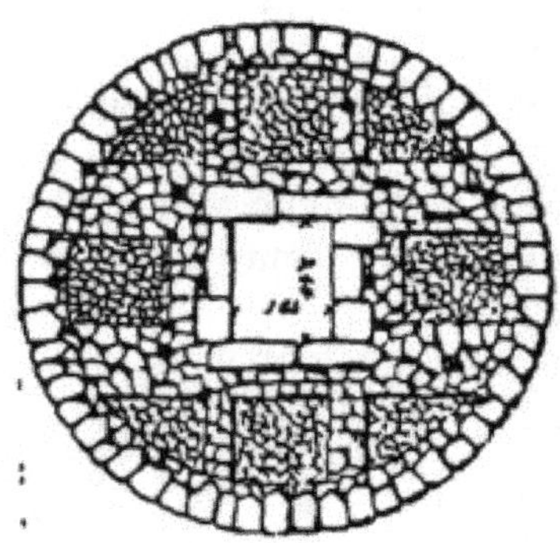

FIG. 20.—Tumulus of dry stones. TEXIER, *Description*, Plate CXXXI.

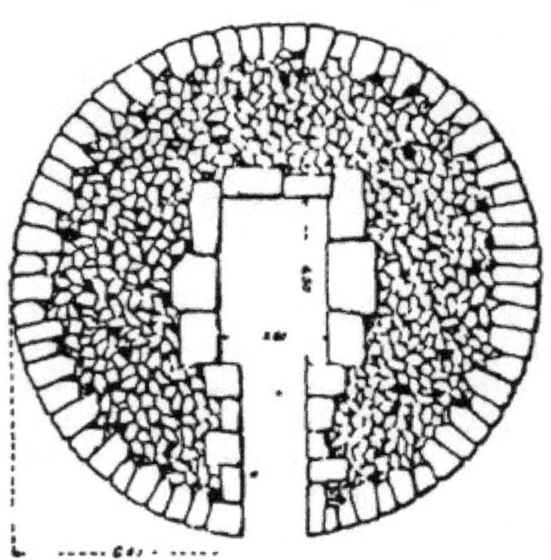

FIG. 21.—Tumulus of dry stones. TEXIER, *Description*, Plate CXXXI.

Remains of another important monument should be classed along with the Sipylus group, whose mode of execution, in part structural and in part rock-cut, they reproduce. We may consider the exemplar, therefore, as likewise the work of the people who placed their tombs betwixt the harbour and the fortress. The bold hillock which bears these ruins is further inland and on a lower plane than the Acropolis, on a line with the village of Petrota, towards the head of the valley washed by a stream, supposed to be the Acheleos. Its truncated summit, with vertical sides, forms a striking feature in the landscape which it commands; and to this circumstance it probably owes its modern name of Ada, "island."[1]

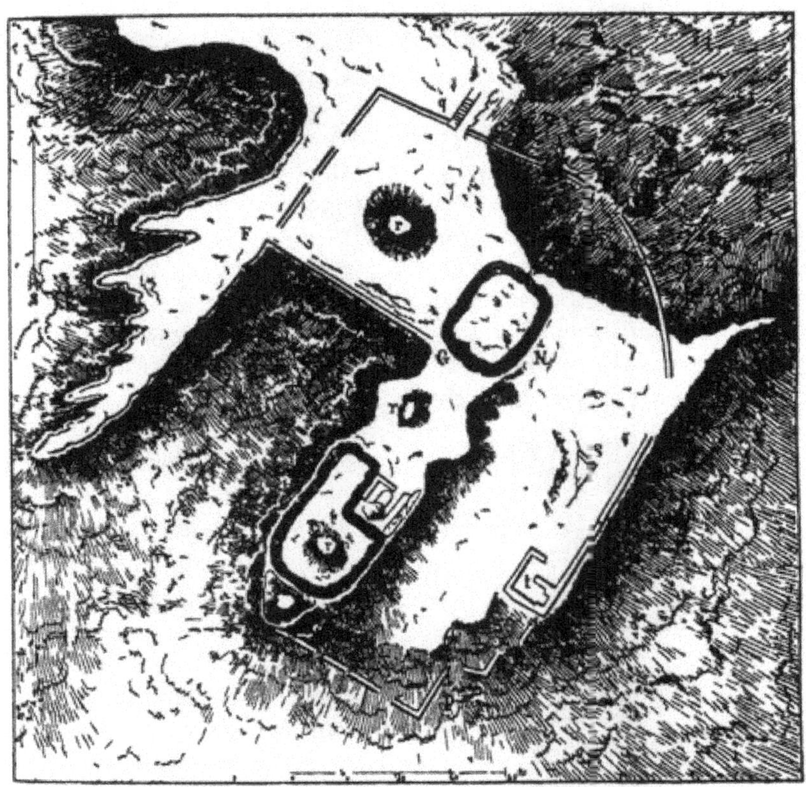

Fig. 22.—Plan of Sanctuary in the Iamanlar Dagh. Weber, *Le Sipylos*, Plate III.

It is a plateau more or less level, 70 m. by 20 m., which divides itself into three distinct parts (Fig. 22): a square, massive rock to the north, with precipitous sides 4 m. high (N in plan); an esplanade on a lower level with a circular hole in the middle, resembling the mouth of a cistern or well (R); and, by far the most remarkable feature, a gigantic rock, 22 m. by 13 m. broad which forms the southern extremity of the ridge (M). A deep chasm, 8 m. long

[1] Ramsay, *Newly discovered Sites*, p. 68.

by 4 m. wide and 4 m. deep, appears at the north-east angle (A in plan, Fig. 23). The bottom of this excavation is occupied by a kind of chamber open to the sky, 5 m. by 2 m. 20 c. (Fig. 24). The main walls are connected with one end of the grave-chamber by a thin circular wall; at the other they disappear under rubble and large blocks (*d*) which have rolled down into the excavation. The courses which form the walls of this chamber are very regular (Fig. 25); they are 36 c. high, and the length of the units varies between 39 and 72 c. Around it, distant 1 m., runs a polygonal wall which closed the entrance towards the north (Fig. 24, *c*, *b*), and protected the east side where the rock is not very high (H).

FIG. 23.—Sanctuary. Section through A B. WEBER, *Le Sipylos*, Plate III.

The esteem in which the monument was regarded may be gathered from the works of art surrounding it. As far as the configuration of the ground permits, which to the south and west breaks off and rapidly sinks, the ridge we have described is embraced, at a distance, by an external wall. It runs parallel to the two colossal rocks for 30 m. or thereabouts, towards the east, where a low ridge projects from the plateau. It follows the sinuosities of the cliff on the south-east, and forms salient and retreating angles of the utmost nicety (*p*), sweeping round the north-west side of the hill with a mighty curve (B, C, F, in plan). Here the cliff projects beyond the line of the wall into a kind of promontory, with precipitous sides; the rampart at first follows the ridge, then from F to C, where it terminated, it is carried in a straight line across the valley, and thus becomes a supporting wall to the plateau (Fig. 26). On the south face the rampart only extends as far as the rock M, where a ledge occurs, which it enters at right angles. Beyond it, the side of the hill being almost perpendicular, a wall became superfluous.

FIG. 24.—The Sanctuary. Plan of chamber. WEBER, *Ibid.*

The masonry of the rampart throughout, like the walls of the Acropolis, presents great variety. Thus, on the western and part of the eastern face (F, G, D, in plan), it is frankly polygonal; sometimes the courses are horizontal, but with oblique joints (E), whilst at C it very much resembles Hellenic work (Fig. 27). The principal entrance was approached by a flight of steps, which seems to have been on the northern face (*g*), where the wall breaks off suddenly, leaving a space 1 m. 50 c. wide. According to Weber (from

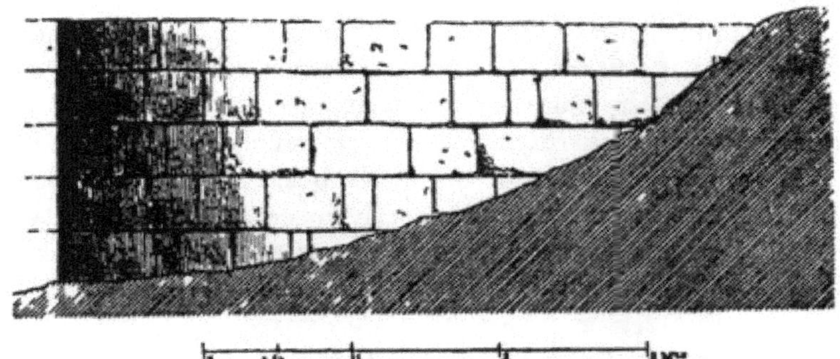

FIG. 25.—Sanctuary. Wall of chamber. WEBER, *Le Sipylos*, Plate III.

whom the foregoing description is taken), no traces of structures, to speak of, exist on the plateau, save the sinking in the northern court already referred to, and some few remains on the southern face (*s*, *t*). But these are so characterless as to throw no light on the nature of the original buildings.

FIG. 26.—Sanctuary. Section through F H. WEBER, *Ibid.*

For what purpose were the ramparts and the chamber erected, is a question to which no certain answer can be given. For although the first notion suggested by the presence of a rampart on an insulated plateau is that of a stronghold, there are features about it which seem to rebut such an hypothesis. In the first place, the fastness would have been very far removed from human habitation; in the

WEBER, *Ibid.*
FIG. 27.—Sanctuary. Surrounding wall on the north-west.

second place, the wall lacks the stoutness of that which crowns the ridge above the Tantaleis tomb, for nowhere is it more than 1 m. 20 c. thick; finally, there is no ditch, and it would have opposed a feeble barrier to the assailants. On the other hand, it harmonizes with our conception of a wall, the function of which was to enclose a given space adjoining a sanctuary; investing it with the character of a τεμενος, consecrated ground. How are we to explain, on the theory of a fortified place, the existence of the inner chamber scooped out of the solid rock with so much care? In what way could it have helped the defence? It is neither a silo nor a cistern. Neither is it a tomb; for both it and the chamber it contains are far beyond the usual dimensions—which hardly vary—of a mortuary oven, *i.e.* an oven-shaped tomb. Then, too, the walls bear no marks of having supported a roof; and we can scarcely conceive the possibility that the dead were left to themselves in the open.[1] Unaccountable as this would have been elsewhere, it would have been passing strange in this region, where hard by existed tombs with circular base; that is to say, the well-attested type of the tribe long settled here. Nor can we conceive that a primitive race would have laboriously excavated a spacious and well-enclosed area around a single tomb.

Setting aside similar explanations, the only possible conjecture left to us is that of a very ancient temple, with niche (the chamber) reserved for the symbol or the image of the deity worshipped in this "high place." By the light of what we know of the local cults, this deity can be no other than Cybele, enthroned among these hills. It is not to be supposed for a single moment that a statue was set up in this trench; but, as at Pessinus, it was doubtless a rude stone of peculiar shape. The arrangement of the sanctuary being considered, would point to an age when no statues were known, save colossal figures in high relief, cut in the rock, from which they were as yet unable to free themselves. In this hypothesis the general dispositions fall into place of their own accord, and become as clear as daylight. The area corresponded to those rude stone circles we have studied in Syria; within its enclosure the crowd of the faithful gathered themselves to celebrate

[1] M. Ramsay is inclined to see a fortress, which in the Greek period was already in a ruinous state, but continued to be visited for the sake of its sanctuary (*Newly discovered Sites*, p. 73).

their public rites.[1] The two rocky ledges at either end of the ridge overhanging the courts were as two gigantic altars on which sacrifices were offered in the light of day, *coram populo.* As to the *bœtylus*, the object of such homage, its rocky frame and double wall were sufficient protection against the weather, and, owing to the narrow entrance, the vast majority of the vulgar throng could be kept out, and none but the select few allowed to enter.

Was this the "Hieron of Mother Plastene," specified by Pausanias, and due to the early settlers on Sipylus, the same which the Greek colonists of Smyrna continued to surround with religious awe? In that case we must believe the report that the highest summit of the Iamanlar-Dagh, northward of it, was called the "throne of Pelops."[2] One of the faces of this particular peak towards the apex is broken off, and forms a ledge with a far-off resemblance to a gigantic seat. Its appellation was due to its peculiar shape, which was likely to strike the fancy of a primitive people; instances of which are to be found all over the world. Thus in many a French district are hills popularly nicknamed *Chaises de Gargantua.*[3]

Not to omit any item on this side of Sipylus, it remains to notice two fragments of fortified enclosures. One is found eastward of the necropolis which contains the Tantaleis tomb, on the lowest spur of the mountain, but close to it. It covers a much larger area than the citadel, and has its angles protected by round towers. To be brief, examination of the sites and of the walls leads to the conclusion that we are confronted by the Acropolis of the Smyrna of Homer.[4]

The second *enceinte* is found on the road which goes across the Belcaive Pass, along the valleys of the Nif Chaï and the Hermus, beyond the Sipylus barrier. It is the old road which from the remotest antiquity was followed by the inland trade of Smyrna, down to the opening of the railway (Fig. 7). North of the pass rises a conical hill, isolated from the mountain range on the south, and thus rendered a conspicuous object from every point of the Bournabat plain. On the summit are distinct traces of old

[1] With regard to the Syrian *bâmoth*, see *Hist. of Art*, tom. iv. ch. v. s. 2.

[2] Consult WEBER, *Le Sipylos*, pp. 30, 31. He remarks that the monuments referred to by Pausanias are all near the old road, which from Cordelio runs across the Iamanlar-Dagh to Menemen in the Hermus valley, and is still used by the natives when the country is flooded.

[3] Arthur's Seat, near Edinburgh, and many more will occur to the reader.—TRS.

[4] WEBER, *loc. cit.*, pp. 25, 26, Plate I.

walls, obviously remains of an ancient city and of its stronghold.[1] Some few yards below, eastward, is an extensive plateau, begirt by a wall. Then about midway up the hill, between two rocky ridges which descend towards the Turkish café (Belcaive), a wall 6 m. 50 c. thick, and here and there from 2 m. to 3 m. high, runs for about 50 m. with direction from north-west to south-west. Like the Acropolis of the Iamanlar-Dagh, its style of masonry exhibits great variety. Certain blocks left in the rough are very irregular; elsewhere the courses are nearly horizontal, set with dressed stones by no means of uniform calibre; nevertheless, the prevailing system is still polygonal. The rock was cut in places, and abutting on the wall is a circular ruin in which M. Weber recognizes a tumulus. "Fragments of pottery strew the ground; most are plain red without ornament, and not a few are of fine black ware, like ancient Greek vases, with here and there a bit of archaic make."[2]

From the day when the tribe settled here began to build the little town whose harbour is now covered by the Bournabat level, they must have been alive to the importance of closing the pass through which alone, by following the course of the Hermus, the enemy could descend upon them. Part of the population, therefore, occupied a post within easy reach of the plain and the slopes proper to cultivation, whence the defile could be easily guarded. A situation offering so many advantages must have tempted Greek colonists—who probably superseded the primitive settlers—to occupy the site and make use of the means of defence erected by former generations, whose name had passed out of men's memory.

The second group of the early monuments of Sipylus is found on its northern slope, in the Manissa-Dagh, eastward of the old site of Magnesia. Scholars had surmised that the race which, whilst cultivating the fertile plain of the Hermus, had its places of worship, its shelters, and tombs in the depths of the mountain, above or at the base of its formidable escarp, had probably left other traces of its activity in the neighbourhood of the colossal statue of their famous goddess Cybele. And this expectation recent researches have fully realized.

As you leave Manissa, coasting Sipylus up to the head of the valley, on some six hundred yards beyond the gigantic statue of Cybele, you suddenly come upon a narrow gorge, flanked by

[1] RAMSAY, *Newly discovered Sites*, etc., pp. 63–68; WEBER, *Le Sipylos*, pp. 114, 115.
[2] Ramsay, *loc. cit.*

vertical walls about 150 m. high (Fig. 28). About the middle of the gorge juts out a kind of spur with very precipitous rugged sides, called by the natives Iarik Kaïa (Twisted Stone), which, they tell you, bears on its summit the ruins of an old castle, Palæo Kastro. Of late years travellers have frequently succeeded in getting to the top of the bare cliff, a performance which requires elasticity of limb and a steady head; for, says Professor Sayce, you have to climb up, catching now at a projecting stone, now at some bush growing in the cleft of the rock. It appears that in olden times a path, wide enough for a mule, partly cut in the living rock, partly supported by artificial walls which were carried across

FIG. 28.—Topographic sketch of northern slope of Sipylus, east of Magnesia.

the chasm, led to the castle. Though it cannot now be used, it may still be traced in places "half hidden under a growth of myrtles and stones." A little further a grotto, 10 m. deep, is sighted, whose opening has been enlarged by human agency. Then comes a gateway, one of whose side posts was built and the other hewn in the rock—doubtless a sentry-box which served to guard and close the path. Presently, rising straight before you, is a rock which no sure-footed animal, let alone man, could possibly climb. But as you turn the corner there appears a split in the stone, which in Switzerland would be called a "chimney," and into this you disappear along with your guide. After feeling your way about for a few minutes you suddenly emerge on the upper ridge, now only accessible through this passage. A staircase, partly destroyed by a huge boulder which broke away from the cliff above, but of which steps may be seen hidden away under the brushwood, formerly led to the platform. It is an elongated plateau, 150 m. by 25 m., with a steep declivity; its highest point is 370 m. above sea-level, and its lowest 325 m., yielding a difference of 45 m. (Fig. 29). The site looks almost too forbidding for human habitation; nevertheless five or six cisterns, bottle-shaped, are met with, along with remains of houses in stages, on to the very brim of this thin, dizzy ridge. Thanks to the incline of the ground, the rocky mass was cut away in such a fashion that only the side and back walls, and sometimes the partitions between one apartment and another, were left adhering to the soil (Figs. 30, 31). The façade, now disappeared, was artificial, and must have been constructed with adobes and stone chips; for nowhere do we find blocks of a certain calibre, real prepared stones. On the other hand, burnt tiles are not rare; some are quite plain, others of a more complicated make served to cover the joints, thus implying that a certain degree of care was bestowed upon the roof. The number of these dwellings, connected one with the other by short flights of steps, is computed at twenty-five. To the rear of the uppermost a rectangular excavation, 1 m. 10 c. by 1 m. 55 c., by 1 m. 30 c. deep, has been cut in the living rock. Its faces are finely polished (Figs. 32, 33). M. Humann, who was the first to describe this tiny, quaint Acropolis, is inclined to recognize it as the throne of Pelops, which used to be shown on the summit of the hill above the Hieron of Mother Plastene.[1]

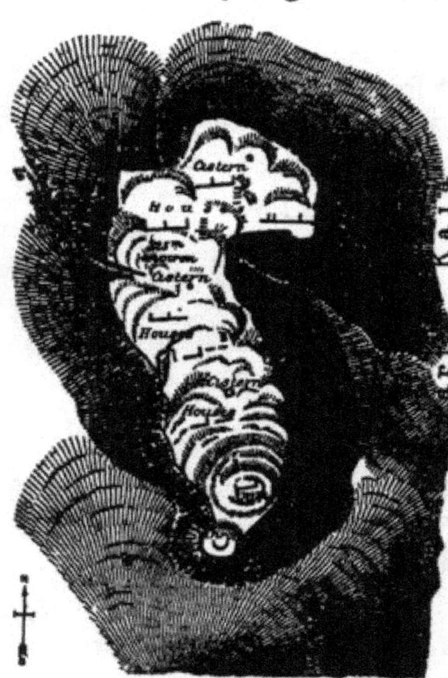

FIG. 29.—Topographic sketch. After Dr. Fabricius.

[1] Our description is abridged from M. HUMANN's *Ein Ausflug in den Sipylos*, p. 10, of which a new illustrated edition has just appeared, entitled *Die Tantalosburg mittheilungen*, 1888. To Dr. Fabricius of Berlin we are indebted for Figs. 28, 29, 30, 33, as well as a discursive letter upon Iarik Kala, which he visited in

What tends to give colouring to this hypothesis is the fact that on the edge of the plain, near the entrance to this narrow pass, recent excavations have brought to light the site of a temple of this goddess, where she was addressed by the name of Μήτηρ Πλαστηνή; that is to say, the very title given her by Pausanias.[1] Striking though this may be as a coincidence, it fails to carry weight with it. In the first place, the feeble salience of the rock which, according to him, was held as the seat of the great ancestor, was not visible from below. In the second place, even when the path was in its prime, the difficulty of ascent was too serious a drawback to have tempted many people making the experiment.

FIG. 30.—Plan of houses. After Dr. Fabricius.

Obviously the throne of Pelops was a conspicuous feature in the

1885. Consult also WEBER, *Le Sipylos*, pp. 118, 119, and Prof. RAMSAY, *Sipylos and Cybele*, pp. 35–37.

[1] The name of Πλαστηνή, under which this goddess was worshipped here, occurs in ancient manuscripts. But as neither inscriptions nor coins have it, Sichelis, Dindorf, and after him Schubert, took upon themselves to replace Πλαστηνή by Πλακιανή. It is now universally acknowledged that the manuscripts were correct, an example which should warn editors to pause ere they tamper with ancient texts; notably in relation to proper names and local epithets which, though unknown to fame, were none the less current in the districts where they are found. Πλακιανή was a surname of Cybele which obtained in the Troad. The temple in question is said to be about an hour eastward of Magnesia, *e.g.* hard by the statue of the goddess. On its site several bas-reliefs of a votive character have been discovered, representing a woman accompanied by lions, in which it is not difficult to recognize Cybele. On one of the sculptures appears the following inscription, published in the *Bulletin de Correspondence hellénique*, 1887, p. 300:—

ΜΗΤΡΟΔΩΡΑ ΑΠΟΛΛΑ	Μητροδώρα 'Απολλᾶ
ΜΗΤΡΙ ΠΛΑΣΤΗΝΗΙ	μητρὶ Πλαστηνῇ
ΕΥΧΗΝ.	εὐχήν.

Another inscription, in very good preservation, mentions the temple in which the votive monuments in question were deposited, along with one Apollonius Skitalas, son of Alexander, who is said to have built or rather repaired it. What is wanted here is a squeeze, so as to learn whether the restoration dates from the Seleucidæ or the Roman empire.

view, with some kind of resemblance to a seat, upon which popular

FIG. 31.—Rock-cut dwellings. From Ch. Humann.

FIG. 32.—Niche hollowed in the rock. From a photograph of Charles Humann.

fancy had fastened, as it had for the rock which recalled to those in the humour for it the sitting form of a woman "grieving because her children were not." We rather incline to believe, with Dr. Fabricius, that this was a vedette, whence the watch, comfortably sheltered behind the cliff, had a full view of the path from its first winding up the steep side of the hill.[1]

We have not seen the ruins specified by Humann. Bearing in mind, however, the straits to which the Mussulman conquest reduced the populations of Asia Minor, we should be tempted to think that a village, almost as inaccessible as an eyrie, might, after all, date from the Byzantine rule, but for the fact that M. Humann seems to have no misgivings as to the high antiquity of these remains. Needless to add that the avowed opinion of so experienced an explorer of the Asiatic peninsula is entitled to serious consideration.[2] In its favour are those cisterns and domestic dwellings excavated in the living rock, together with the kind of parapet, 1 m. high, obtained in the rocky mass by the same process, which is visible on many a point along the edge of the precipice.[3] Similar structures, reserved for the most part in the cliff upholding them, have struck all travellers who have seen them with the strong resemblance they bear to those on the Pnix at Athens.

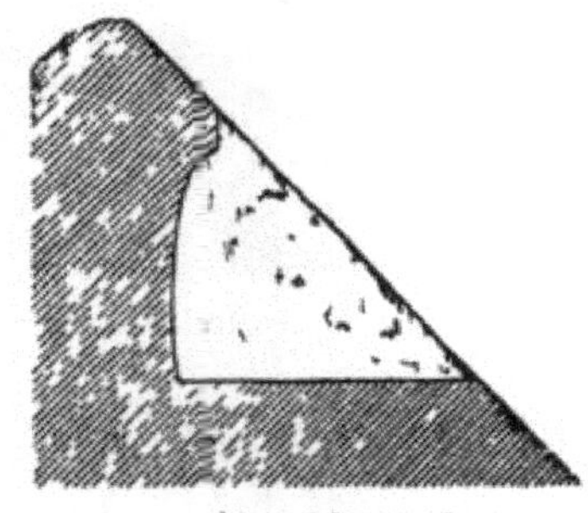

FIG. 33.—Niche hollowed in the rock. Longitudinal section. After Dr. Fabricius.

Such constructions (we have adduced and shall yet adduce numerous instances) were of long standing, and lasted many centuries with the older inhabitants of these provinces, until a more advanced culture caused them to adopt a more convenient style.[4] Our leanings are all for considering this elevated site as the Phrygian Acropolis, where the population of the town below could find temporary shelter whenever a sudden panic overtook

[1] M. Fabricius admits the possibility that the term "throne of Pelops," under which the vedette is popularly known, may be due to a late period.

[2] MM. Ramsay and Fabricius are equally positive on the subject.

[3] The detail is due to M. Ramsay, *loc. cit.*, p. 36.

[4] M. RAMSAY (*Sipylos and Cybele*) states that, besides multitudinous pieces of plain red ware, he picked up a fragment of black pottery recalling Greek vases. No conclusion, however, can be reached from a single piece of this kind. In the early stage of Hellenic civilization the village may have been inhabited by woodmen or other colonists who supported themselves from the land produce.

them. The town in question may have been Tantalis, which, according to Pliny, preceded Magnesia, and was destroyed in one

FIG 34.—Tomb hollowed in the rock, near Magnesia Perspective view HUMANN, *Ausflug*, Fig 1.

of those seismic convulsions of frequent occurrence along the coast.[1] The appalling earthquake of 1880 is vividly remembered by the Smyrnians, when broad masses of the mountain, being loosened, rolled down into the plain, with trees and crops adhering. In like manner Tantalis was buried in Lake Salæ (now a pond at the entrance of the pass leading to

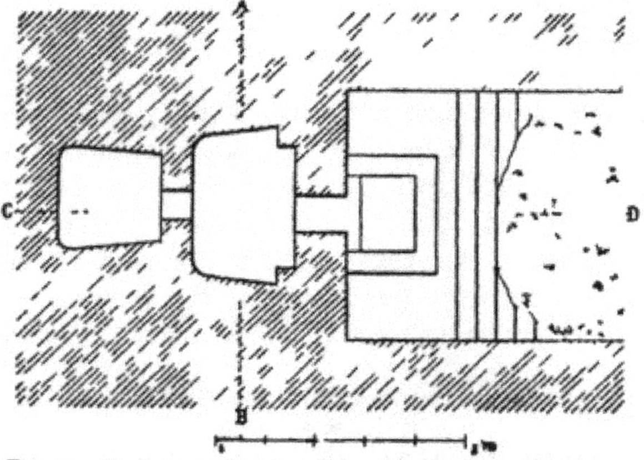

FIG 35.—Tomb near Magnesia. Plan HUMANN, *Ausflug*, Fig. 3.

[1] M. HUMANN (*Ausflug*, etc., p 7) does not seem to be aware that the tomb under notice was published before him by STEWART, *Ancient Monuments*, Plate II. The drawing of the latter, however, is so imperfect as to be worthless for the purposes of science. Weber's sketches (*Trois tombeaux archaiques de Phocée*, pp

the fortress), whose waters reflected the ruinous walls of the antique city.

To the people who preceded the first Greek colonists on Hermus (founders of Magnesia) should likewise be attributed a funereal monument, met with about four hundred yards east of the ravine (Fig. 34). It is known in the country as the tomb of St. Charalambe, and is entirely scooped out of the living rock, in a talus which dips to the south-west at an angle of forty-five degrees. In this ledge of rocks was first sunk a broad staircase open to the sky, whose lower steps are hidden under accumulated earth. It led to a platform, in the centre of which a two-stepped landing has been reserved. The topmost step is level with a passage which gives access to a first chamber, followed by another corridor and a smaller chamber (Figs. 35, 36).

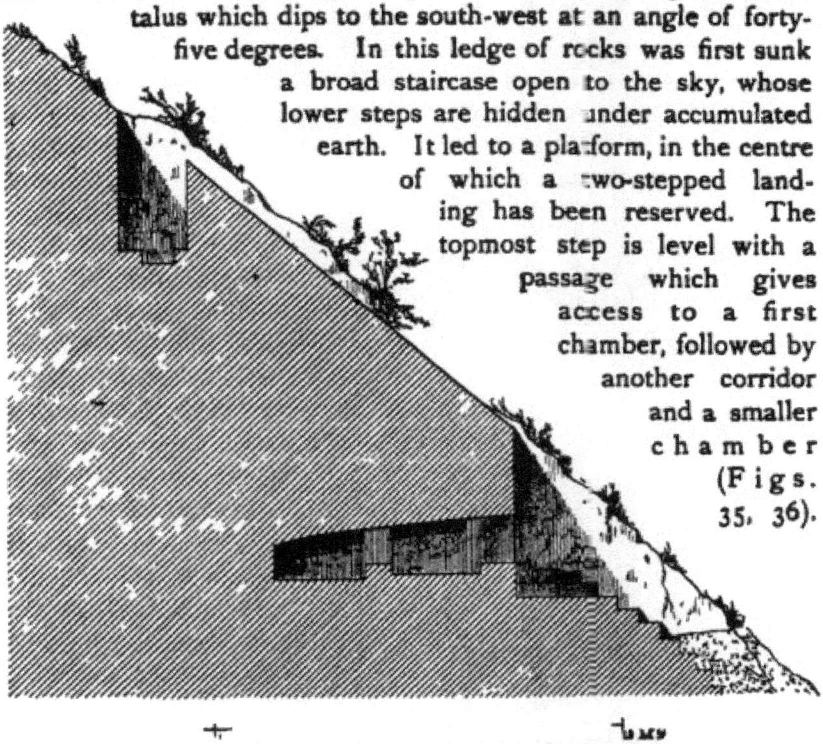

FIG. 36.—Tomb near Magnesia. Longitudinal section. HUMANN, *Ausflug*, Fig. 2.

The ceiling of both apartments is slightly arched, its height diminishing from front to back, and the result is a somewhat oven-like aspect (Fig. 37). The two doorways are not on the same axis; that of the inner is a little to the west as regards the exterior opening. There are no signs of troughs or stone couches, but along the western wall, a little above the ground, runs a double ledge, upon which rested the heads of the corpses laid out on the

136–138, Figs. 11–15) agree in all essentials with M. Humann's illustrations. See also RAMSAY, *Sipylos and Cybele*, p. 37.

floor of the mortuary chamber. The ledge is non-existent on the opposite wall.

About the exterior doorway no trace of hinges or frame was found. The passage must have been closed by a heavy slab rolled up against the opening, which may have been broken in early days by treasure-seekers. The inner work is rudimentary enough. The stone-cutters reserved all their thought and care to smoothing and polishing the outer faces; this they did so well and thoroughly as to leave no mark of the chisel. Above, the hypogee table, 9 m. 50 c. by 5 m. 60 c., was levelled out, with a deep groove which separates it from the stony mass by which it is enframed (Fig. 38). The advantages of a similar arrangement are twofold: despite its simplicity it invests the whole with a monumental aspect, whilst it serves to isolate the tomb, and to guard it as well. The rain water that falls on the surface of the rock is thus collected in a double gutter and discharged on either side some distance in front. Thanks to this precautionary measure, the façade is unimpaired, and looks almost as fresh as if carved but yesterday. Nevertheless not one among the explorers who have studied this hypogee hesitates in assigning to it a remote antiquity. There is no inscription, nor the slightest sign of mouldings which might indicate a

FIG. 37.—Tomb near Magnesia. Transverse section. WEBER, *Trois tombeaux*, Fig. 13.

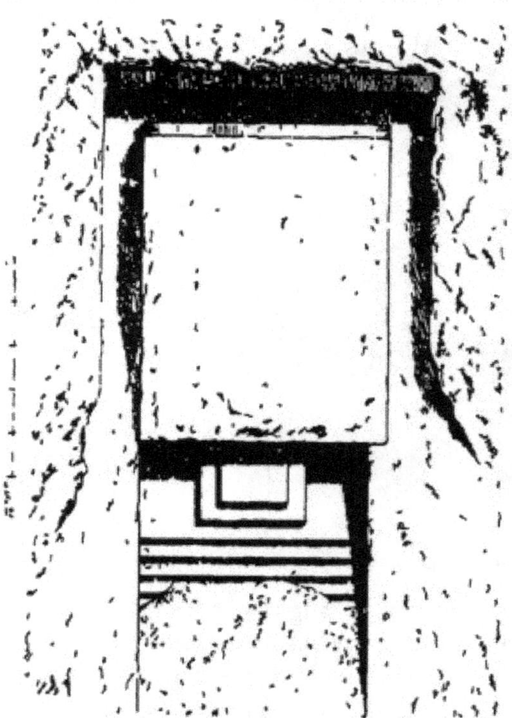

FIG. 38.—Tomb near Magnesia. Horizontal projection of upper part. HUMANN, *Ausflug*, Fig. 5.

Greek origin; the processes resorted to for its erection are identical with those met with in the Phrygian tombs of the Rhyndacus and the Sangarius valleys. Here, too, the effort to isolate the grave-chambers and provide a hollow space, more or less complete, between it and the mass of stone in which it has been hollowed, is occasionally seen. For the rest, the guiding principle and the data are exactly similar; although the frontispiece has been given a fixed and sharply defined shape, it none the less preserves a solid and severe rusticity, in perfect accord with the grand plans of the mountain, and the broken lines of the native rock which covers and enframes it. Two other tombs, lately discovered, should be added

FIG 39.—Tomb near Phocæa WEBER, *Trois tombeaux*, Fig 6

to complete the number of monuments found in the region of Hermus. They are said to be old, due, perhaps, to the age which preceded the birth of the Greek cities.[1] One, called by the Turks Sheitan Haman (the Devil's Bath), is hard by Phocæa; and the other, which bears the Greek name of I Pelekiti, is about two hours' walk eastward of the ancient ruins of the same city, near the road which leads to Menenem. There is nothing remarkable about the first. Like the Charalambe tomb, it consists of two chambers, but in the floor of the inner apartment was hollowed a grave in the form of a trough.[2] The other is somewhat curious.[3] The im-

[1] WEBER, *Trois tombeaux*, etc., pp. 129–136.

[2] See Weber's plan, sections and elevations.

[3] M. Solomon Reinach informs me that the above tomb was published as far back as 1831, in 1 vol. 18mo, now very rare, entitled *Fragments d'un Voyage en Italie, en Grèce, et en Asie*, 1829–1830, par Gautier d'Arc, Consul de France.

pression it produces is that of a small country church with a square tower (Fig. 39). Thus, upon a parallelopiped base, 8 m. 80 c. by 6 m. 25 c. by 2 m. 40 c. high, have been cut four grades which were ascended on the eastern side; and on these, again was left a cubical block, 1 m. 90 c. in height, surmounted by two low steps. The monument did not end here, for on the top appear marks as of some object torn off. This our illustration, although on a reduced scale, shows very distinctly. Was the crowning member ornamental, a "stepped" pyramid, rosette, or symbolic device, like the phallus of the tombs around Bournabat? To this question no answer can be given, for the breaking off has been too cleanly done to admit even of conjecture. But if the terminal form is sadly to seek, the internal dispositions

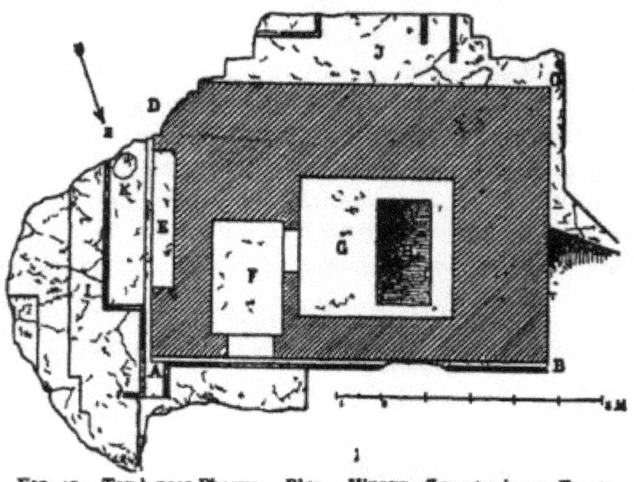

FIG. 40.—Tomb near Phocæa. Plan. WEBER, *Trois tombeaux*, Fig. 7.

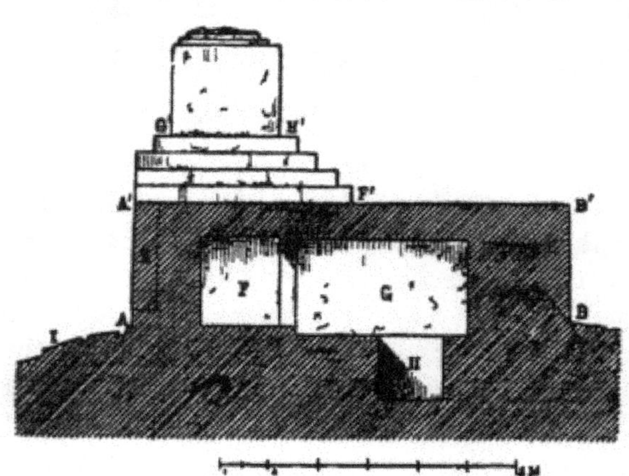

FIG. 41.—Tomb near Phocæa. Longitudinal section. WEBER, *Trois tombeaux*, Fig. 8.

The author was a member of the Société Royale des Antiquaires, a fact which he does not seem to have remembered save in this single instance, his short narrative being wholly taken up with picturesque and sprightly anecdotes of a more or less personal character.

are very well preserved (Figs. 40, 41). A door leading to a kind of small ante-room opens in the northern wall, F, whence the chambered grave, properly so called, is entered. The ceilings are flat, and the grave is a trough cut in the floor, H. As at Charalambe here also, the skill of the artist was chiefly directed towards the exterior; be it in polishing the rock surface around the base, cutting grooves on the north and south sides, I, J, for the outflow of the water, or piercing the small circular tank, K, in one of the corners. The north, south, and west faces are quite plain. On the other hand, the eastern face is profusely decorated: first, by an elongated window-shaped niche, divided into four compartments; then a cornice with ornamental ancone slightly salient beyond the rocky wall. On this side the pyramidal base of the cubical block has no steps. Despite these irregularities, in its pristine state, the tomb from its very quaint appearance was not wanting in attractiveness.

When we drew up our list of the older monuments of Sipylus, or at least of the most noteworthy, nothing was said about sculpture: not because the art for that period was unrepresented, since even at the present hour are works of the highest interest, such as the bas-reliefs of Sesostris, described by Herodotus, and the Cybele of Mount Codine, seen by Pausanias; but because the inscriptions about these images prove that they were executed in the period preceding the introduction of letters derived from the Phœnician alphabet, when characters akin to the Hamathite obtained throughout Asia Minor. Hence we were obliged to class the figures under notice with the series of monuments which, for want of a better name, we have termed Hittite. To these sculptures we have nothing to add, except a bust discovered by M. Spiegelthal near the village of Bouja, situated in a mountain eastward of Smyrna, called Tashtali.[1] His description, which we borrow, was written before the mutilation of the monument by the fanatic natives. M. Dennis, her Majesty's Consul at Smyrna, had it removed by night so as to save it from further dilapidation, and secretly despatched to the British Museum in 1869.

To quote from the German explorer: as you ascend the path leading to the alpine village of Bouja you pass a sinking of some 8 to 10 m. deep, and 100 m. long, surrounded by a wall composed

[1] A. MARTIN, *Trois Monuments des environs de Smyrne, lettre à M. G. Perrot* (*Revue Archl.*, Nouvelle Série, tom. xxxi. pp. 321–330).

of stone blocks piled one upon the other without cement. At one end of the depression, pierced in the solid rock, is a kind of arcade which opens into a grotto extending far into the depths of the mountain, but which is choked up by the falling away of the calcareous stone. On either side of the grotto are stone seats, finely polished. Externally, right and left of the doorway, runs a gallery one metre wide, which seems to have been made to facilitate the duty of the watch set to guard the cavern. The grotto was

FIG. 42.—Rock-cut bust. Drawn by A. Martin.

originally entered by a staircase, the lower steps of which are now buried under rubbish, which has gathered to a considerable height in the hollow. It is possible that a clean sweep of the detritus would result in curious finds. Every detail about the grotto indicates that it was formerly a fane. The wall planted in a hollow is assuredly not a defensive wall; whilst the rock-cut benches inside the grotto, and in especial the bust which only a few years ago (1868)[1] stood over the doorway (Fig. 42), are as unlike what we should expect to find around a fortified enclosure as can well be

[1] WEBER (*Le Sipylos*, p. 113) says, "Une grotte se trouvait *au dessus* de la tête."—TRS.

imagined. The sculpture, 1 m. 50 c. by 60 c., appeared upon a bold salience of the rock. The head looks full face, with flat nose, low retreating forehead, rounded chin, elongated eyes raised at the outer extremities. The hands meet in front; a necklace of large beads is around the neck. The face is quite smooth, and without a trace of beard. Horns appear on either side of the cheeks where ears should have been, recalling the horns of Ammon. The position of the figure over the doorway of a sacred place is conclusive evidence of its being the image of a deity. By what name are we to address him? Were the locality on the mainland of Greece, we could confidently say that a subterranęous fane was dedicated to no other than Pan or the Nymphs. Here, however, we are in the realm of that Cybele who maintained her sway over Sipylus and the hilly tract which it overshadows with its mighty crown to the latest times. It may be urged that a smooth face is no sure sign of sex, since it may with equal propriety belong to a youth as to a woman; whilst horns, as a rule, are associated with gods. Ammon, Hercules, personified rivers. But may not horns, as symbols of strength, have been now and again attributed to a goddess, the embodiment of endless creative force, the tamer of wild beasts whom she obliged to draw her chariot? And does not the figure whose body is lost in the depth of the cliff admirably lend itself to represent the Divine Being so intimately allied with the mountain he inhabited as to be called ἡ μήτηρ ὄρεια, the mother of the mountain?

This is not the place for attempting even a conjecture as to the date of the monuments we have passed in review. The time, if it should ever come, will be after we have duly studied Phrygia properly so called, where the Phrygian race had, if not its capital—it never owned a place deserving of the title—at least its political and religious centre, its principal sanctuaries and royal necropoles. On the upper course of the Sangarius, monuments are far more numerous; they have, if we may so speak, a first beginning of civil life written upon them, for they bear inscriptions which, despite obscurities, permit us to name with absolute certainty the people who made them, and to fix a proximate date to them. On our home journey from our exploring quest, we shall feel qualified to add to the weight of the hypothesis suggested to us by historical and mythical data; basing it upon resemblances in style, mode of workmanship, and general dispositions. We shall bound over the vast tracts which as yet have yielded no monuments of ancient date, on to the uplands where the various races which first peopled Asia Minor maintained their customs, traditions, and cults against the encroaching genius of Hellas.

ARCHITECTURAL CHARACTERISTICS OF PHRYGIA PROPER.

It is doubtful whether Asia Minor, rich throughout in beautiful sites and grand scenery, can offer a corner which in picturesqueness will compare with that which may be seen on the western side of the Sangarius, in the neighbourhood of Pessinus, where Strabo informs us (XII. v. 3) that in his day the inhabitants still preserved the memory of their kings. The region in which the relics connected with these old chiefs are found lies about two days' journey to the south-east of Koutahia, a place generally chosen as the starting-point of their journey by travellers. Leaving the town, the way leads across a white dusty plain, but sundown brings you to the low hills, with clustering pines, in advance of the mountains. Here a valley is entered, and a gentle though continuous ascent brings you to the village of Kumbet, the second station after Koutahia, situated 150 m. above the latter.[1] The tedium of the journey is tempered by the beauty of the landscape, which improves with every hour; the country is finely undulated, the hill-tops well timbered, and pines, the great tree of this district, are so artistically grouped along the slopes—where, despite a general dearth of water, great herds find an abundance of grass down to June—as to suggest English scenery. The Iuruk tribe, amidst which we found nightly shelter, owned no fewer than a thousand heads of horned cattle. In summer these semi-nomadic shepherds camp out in egg-shaped tents made of felt, or in shanties built of unsquared timber. The framing is put together without clamps or pins; the beams for the walls are laid side by side as close as possible, and made to project and overlap each other at the four corners. To keep them in place the under beams are mortised to about half their thickness. The roof consists likewise of a rude frame of unsquared beams, horizontally placed at some distance from each

[1] M. E. Guillaume, who was my travelling companion on the occasion, gives the following barometric measurement: Koutahia, 920 m. above sea level; Kumbet, 1060 m.

other and built up so as to form a curvilinear skeleton; upon this are laid square posts as compactly as they can be laid (Figs. 43, 44).[1]

The configuration of the soil is very peculiar; for it is neither of the nature of the lowlands, nor can it be called alpine. The whole region from Kumbet to Seid el-Ghazi, Khosrev Pasha Khan, and Eski Kara Hissar, is a succession of valleys with flat flooring, from 100 to 1000 m. wide, dipping with slight variations from north to south. The valleys are separated one from the other by thick formations of rocky masses, 40 to 50 m. in height; now sloping upwards to a narrow ridge, now terminating in tablelands of some extent (Fig. 45). By reason of the crumbling away of the rock above, their base is a chaotic wilderness of boulders heaped up in confusion to a considerable height. The ground is undulating throughout, and the rocks rise up into low hills, connected with, albeit they do not belong to, the snow-capped mountains extending far away. Trees of fine growth spring out of the clefts of the rocks. Here

Fig. 43.—Wooden house near Kumbet. After M. E. Guillaume.

Fig. 44.—Wooden hut near Kumbet. After M. E. Guillaume.

[1] Vitruvius, in his chapter entitled "Origin of Domestic Architecture," describes this mode of building of general acceptance in Asia Minor, notably at Colchis, in the following words:—"Four sets of trees, two in each set, of the length required for the width of the house, are laid parallel to each other on the ground. They are met contrariwise at the extremities by other trees, whose length is equal to the space between the horizontal trunks, so as to form a kind of rough frame. This is then placed upon the perpendicular beams, which form the corners of the house and serve as supporting pillars. Planks are laid across as near to each other as they can be laid," etc. (II. i. 4). In reality the system has always been in vogue wherever a plentiful supply of timber is to be had; for example, in Lycia and towards the Euxine.

and there are volcanic cones broken up into a thousand fantastic forms, in strong contrast with the plain whence they shoot up. The formation is a coarse conglomerate, yellowish in colour, nowhere very hard, yet varying considerably in firmness and density.[1] The salt lakes, and generally the geological formation of the soil, clearly indicate that the central plateau emerged from an inland sea. The waters, raised by successive volcanic efforts, were hemmed in on all sides by a double and triple belt of massive lofty ridges, which they had slowly to undermine and pierce, ere they found an outlet into the oceans sur-

FIG. 45.—General view of Kumbet.[2]

rounding the peninsula. At first the waters that escaped from the rocky walls were nothing but rivulets; but ere long they gathered themselves into impetuous streams, as they descended the broad grades of the elevated tableland towards the Euxine and the Mediterranean. During their course they often helped to fill lakes that had suddenly emerged and as suddenly disappeared, in one of those upheavals which helped to build up the plateau,

[1] A small fragment of the Midas rock has been handed to me by Professor Ramsay. I had it analyzed by M. Munier-Chalmas, who returned it with the following note :—"The stone I examined is the result of volcanic agency in the Miocene or Pliocene period. It is a rhyolithic tufa, with fragments of pumice and obsidian. The microscope reveals the presence of broken crystals of quartz, orthose, oligoclase, and amphibole, sprinkled in the shapeless mass; along with a fragment of an older rock or micaceous schist with blue crystals."

[2] The above sketch is by M. Tomakieviez, from a photograph of M. Gustave Fougères, of the French School at Athens. It faces the tomb we study and represent a little further on.

and caused that part of Phrygia which is wholly formed of irruptive rocks, to be called Phrygia Combusta. During these periods, which may be counted by thousands of years, the many streams which descend from these heights carved a tortuous bed around the more friable rocks, the eddy acting as battering-ram in shaping them into every possible contortion of lofty pinnacle and narrow promontories, rending their flanks into dark caves, deep crevices, and fissures, or polishing the hard-grained stone into vertical walls.[1] Strolling about the neighbourhood of Seid el-Ghazi (ancient Nacoleia) I was forcibly reminded of the Forest of Fontainebleau, whose configuration science explains as likewise due to fluvial energy.

Before the primitive inhabitants were provided, as they are at the present day, with forged iron, they could not resist the temptation of excavating their houses into the friable rock they had everywhere at hand. Moreover, even when they had tools with which they could rapidly fell and cut up pines of the required length and size, they continued to take shelter, at least in the winter months, in stone habitations hollowed in the depth of the hill, or those isolated rocks which shoot up on many a point of the valley. The winters are cold here; for, though Kumbet is but 150 metres above the level of the surrounding plain, it is more than 1000 metres above the sea. At such an altitude the nights are fresh, nay, cold throughout the year. Thus, at 6 a.m. on the 12th of June, the thermometer marked six degrees above zero; and albeit the time was summer, we were often kept awake in our wooden huts, by the sharp frosty air, and had to take in turn feeding the fire through the night. Dwellings like these are of a certainty picturesque, but they are positively no protection against the wind, and very little against the rain, which latter penetrates through chinks and fissures large enough for the hand to get through. Nor was it much better when we tried to stop the gaps with straw and clay, for these were presently turned into mud and washed down inside by the driving rain, whilst the chaff, left to itself, was taken up by the wind and tossed about our faces. As for the wraps and blankets we put up before the apertures, they

[1] There was some uncertainty about the name of the site occupied by Seid el-Ghazi. Prymnessus, whose coins during the Roman domination bear the effigy of Midas, was proposed. The researches of Professor Ramsay in 188[illegible] have definitely settled the question. "Prymnessus," he writes, "was at Seulun, three miles south-east of Afium Kara Hissar," on the postal road which runs from this city to Konieh.

only made matters worse, in that they swelled like so many bladders and blew out into the middle of the room, discharging a veritable hurricane about us.

In conditions such as these, it is no wonder that, whilst living in forests, habits which seem to suit regions where timber fails should have persisted for centuries. Writing of the usages in vogue among the Phrygians, Vitruvius employs terms which clearly indicate that the district he has in view is Phrygia Combusta, which joins on Lycaonia, where trees are only seen in gardens.[1] And, indeed, on this side, in the territory of Urgub, Kumbet, and Utch Hissar, the faces of the tufaceous rocks are entirely honeycombed with artificial grottoes.[2] That some were tombs is rendered indubitable by the inscriptions which accompany them; and it seems no less certain that a vast majority were appropriated to domestic and religious uses, even as they are at the present day. Troglodyte dwellings, it should be remembered, are too deeply rooted in the habits of the people ever to have been out of fashion. Thus, towards the northern extremity of the rock upon which the village is perched, are remains of a spacious mansion, of which a plan was made by Professor Ramsay (Fig. 46). The foundation walls, mostly reserved in the thickness of the mass, are still two and three metres in height. But where the rock failed, in front, recourse was had to masonry set in courses of squared units. Professor Ramsay recognizes the women's quarter in a block of buildings entered by a long winding passage, H, and separated from the rest of the habitation. He finds a bedroom, C, dressing-room, E, and bath-room, F. The floor of the latter is paved with a different stone, and shows a small duct cut through the rocky wall to carry off used water, G.[3] The mansion served as

[1] II. i. 5: "Phryges vero, qui campestribus locis sunt habitantes, propter inopiam silvarum egentes materia eligunt tumulos naturales, eosque medios fossura distinentes et itinera perfodientes dilatant spatia quantum natura loci patitur."

[2] With regard to these Troglodyte hamlets, see *Hist. of Art*, tom. iv. Fig. 389; and MORDTMANN, *Die Troglodyten von Cappadocien* (*Mem. zum Akademien Munchen*, 1859). Strabo reports that in his time native tribes in the Taurus range still lived in caves and grottoes (XII. vi. 5). We observed similar caves at Beibazar and Istamos in the Sangarius basin. The hewing of these chambers is rendered easy by the loose texture of the stone. Thus at Martkhane, near Urgub, Barth slept in an apartment 25 feet long by 13 broad, and 10 high, which his host informed him had been cut in the space of thirty days by one single workman.

[3] RAMSAY (*Hell. Studies*, x. p. 177) writes: "We enter the harem through the winding passage, H, and reach first the large women's sitting-room (A in his plan,

domestic dwelling until quite recently. During the Byzantine rule, the apartment D was apparently turned into a Christian chapel. The whole pile seems to have been inhabited by a Turkish agha, who rebuilt part of the walls with small stones and covered the

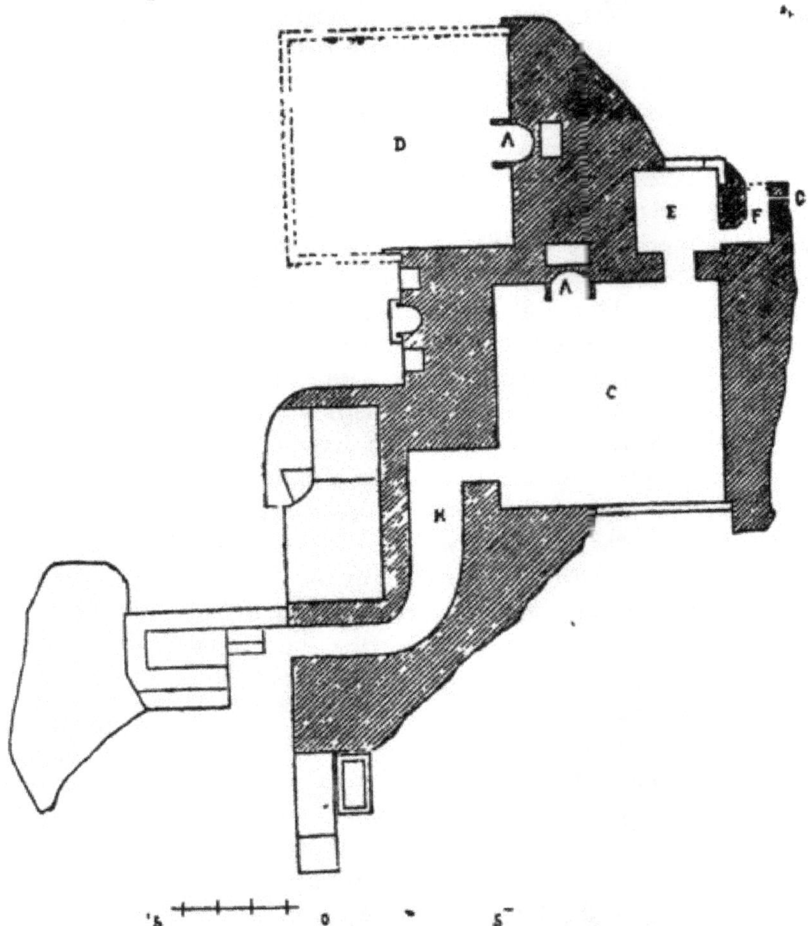

FIG. 46.—Plan of rock-cut dwelling, Kumbet. From Professor Ramsay.

whole with a coat of plaster. To him also should be ascribed the decoration over the mantelpieces, which Barth wrongly deemed

C in Fig. 46), then the little bedroom, B (E in Fig. 46), and finally the bath-room, D" (F in the above figure). M. Perrot also makes the larger northern room, D, of the ἀνδρωνῖτις a Christian chapel; it is the smaller middle chamber below (marked E in Ramsay's plan) that has been used for that purpose.—TRS.

to be antique,[1] but the fireplaces cut in the living rock must be old Phrygian work, A.

It certainly is an interesting and somewhat rare phenomenon to find the mingling of the two styles of architecture thus employed simultaneously, the principle of which is so widely different; the one using none but combustible materials, the other taking advantage of every salience in the earth's crust to excavate abodes for the dead and the living as well. The subterraneous house, as a rule, is only resorted to in localities where timber fails altogether, as in Egypt, but in especial in that Lycia whose sylvan scenes we shall ere long have occasion to visit,[2] where, too, the co-existence of the two modes led to curious results. In order to invest the façades of the hypogeia with monumental aspect, pieces of carpentry, mouldings akin to those cut in a wooden post, have been copied in stone. Shapes, therefore, which in the wooden house were organic members, and formed an integral part of the construction, have been endowed with a purely decorative value. Nor are these the only items which have thus been turned from their natural use; yet other instances of similar transpositions and adaptations are met with in this rock-cut architecture. From work done in the loom or with the needle, the Phrygian ornamentist likewise borrowed the designs which served to fill the field of his frontispieces so as to ensure variety of aspect.

The district in which occur the monuments whose main characteristics we have broadly sketched occupies but a narrow strip in Kiepert's excellent map. Eastward it follows the edge of a wooded tract, with Koutahia on the west, Seid el-Ghazi on the north, and Eski Hissar on the south. It corresponds to the ancient territory of two Phrygian towns of a certain importance, Nacoleia and Prymnessus, and is quite close to the first. We do not hear of Meros (which will be found near Kumbet on the map) until the time of the Eastern empire; in the reign of Justinian it was a large borough with a bishopric. When we wrote our *History of Art*, no map of the canton had been published; hence it was no easy matter to get a clear notion of the relative situation of the monuments from the verbal description of travellers. Professor Ramsay was good enough to place at my service drawings

[1] The miserable ornament and modern woodwork about the chimney was accepted as old by the German traveller BARTH (*Reise von Trapezunt*, etc., p. 95).

[2] *Hist. of Art*, tom. i. pp. 507–516; tom. v. book ix.

and observations taken on the spot, and afterwards to revise the topographical sketch made from them by M. Thuillier. Each tomb has been carefully numbered so as to enable the reader to determine approximately, at least, the place each occupies in the map (Fig. 47).

A first glance at the sketch reveals the fact that if the tumuli under notice are scattered all over the place, they nevertheless form two principal groups: one towards the north-east around the

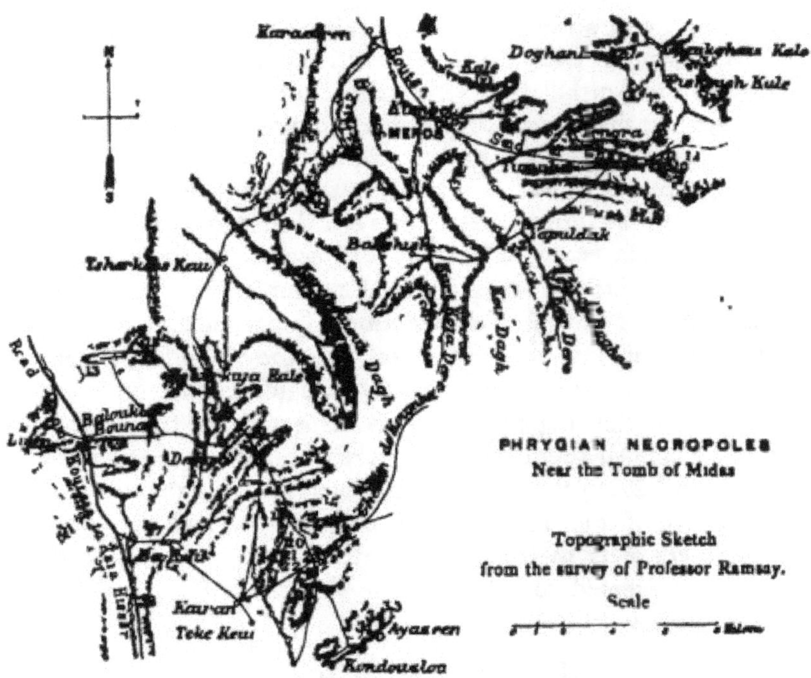

FIG. 47.—Phrygian necropoles. Topographic sketch.

Midas monument (9 in plan), and the other twenty miles to the south-west, near the village of Ayazeen. For convenience' sake, therefore, we shall follow Professor Ramsay and call them respectively the Midas necropolis and Ayazeen necropolis. The above appellation has no pretension to accuracy, and has no other merit than that of facilitating the finding of a particular tomb in either cemetery. The northern or Midas necropolis has been known since 1820, when it was visited by Leake, and subsequently by Téxier, Stewart, Barth, Mordtmann, and finally by me. That of

Ayazeen was discovered by Professor Ramsay, from whom we have borrowed all we have to say about the tombs it contains. If the tract rendered famous by monuments which reveal an art remarkable for originality has no geographical frontiers by which it can be easily traced on the map, the characteristics it offers are sufficiently marked and distinct to enable the observer to single it out from the adjacent country. It consists throughout of volcanic formations, more or less friable, which favour and seem to invite excavations. The works suggested by the nature of the rock, far from being everywhere uniform, exhibit wonderful variety, whence we may surmise that many generations had a hand in these hypogeia. Nevertheless resemblances between those considered old, as against the comparatively modern, are sufficiently strong to warrant the conclusion that they were the outcome of one art—a national, or rather a local art—which in these secluded sylvan scenes was faithful to the forms and subjects it had started with. To these it clung with characteristic tenacity for generations, defending them against the seductive style and the nobler taste of the sons of Hellas. Nor is this all; the exceptional importance which attaches to these monuments lies in the fact that they manifest numerous instances of the use of an alphabet and idiom that have left no traces outside this region. As was suspected by travellers who first came across these lovely picturesque valleys, there is every reason for believing that such inscriptions represent the writing and the language of the Phrygians, a people who, had they not put their seal wherever their chisel was allowed to play on these rocks, would have seemed to belong to the domain of fable rather than of sober history.

FUNEREAL ARCHITECTURE.

"The Phrygians," wrote Nicholas of Damascus, "do not bury their priests, but set them up upon stones ten cubits high."[1] No instance has been found in Phrygia in support of this assertion. Arguing from analogy, and assuming, as we are inclined to do, identity of blood between the tribes that founded the commonwealths on Sipylus and the banks of the Sangarius, what we should expect to find here would be burial-places in the form of tumuli. The type, as a matter of fact, cannot be said to be unrepresented in Mediterranean Phrygia, where numerous remains of artificial

[1] *Frag. Hist. Græc.*, Muller's edit., tom. iii.

mounds have been traced.[1] Professor Ramsay, in a letter to the *Athenæum*, dated December 27, 1884, thus describes the one specimen he was able to examine with some care: "The tumulus is bounded by a circle of square blocks, half imbedded in the ground, which have fallen from the top and sides of the mound. I was informed by a native that one of the stones had graven characters upon it, and with the help of four villagers, a pickaxe, and wooden poles to serve as levers, we succeeded in setting up the block, when it turned out that the signs were akin to the hieroglyphs of Cappadocia."[2] The tumulus in question is south of the village of Bey Keui, in the pass marked 28 in the map.

The finding of Hittite characters in the bowels of a tumulus might be taken as conclusive evidence that cognate monuments met with in Phrygia are anterior to the time when its inhabitants elaborated an alphabet which they derived from the Phœnician. However remarkable the discovery may be, it would be rash to advance an opinion from one solitary instance, and it is well to wait until the remaining mounds shall have been examined. We may regret that the explorations were allowed to stop here, and that no attempt was made to find out whether such mounds contain chambered graves. However that may be, the fact remains that, speaking generally, tumuli in Phrygia form the exception, not the rule. If the first owners of the soil, the Syro-Cappadocians, or, after them, the early bands of Phrygo immigrants who occupied the district, made use of this mode of sepulture, the habit did not last. All Phrygian tombs are hypogeia.

Of all the monuments in this district, the most famous is certainly that which since 1824 is known by archæologists under the name of the Midas tomb[3] (Fig. 48, 9 in map). Its size,

[1] *Hell. Studies*, 1882, p. 18.

[2] RAMSAY, *Athenæum*, p. 884. It seems strange that the author should never have published the inscription.

[3] Leake brought the monument to the knowledge of the world in 1800.—TRS.

See Professor Ramsay's observations in respect to our cuts, Figs. 48, 49. Whilst acknowledging that our general view of the Midas rock is far away the best that has been published, he still finds it inexact in some respects. The explanations he puts forward as to the character of the meander displayed on the Phrygian tombs are too long for reproduction, and we refer the reader to *Hell. Studies*, x. pp. 149–156. Here more than ever the need is felt of having the image as understood by Professor Ramsay placed side by side with that which he criticises. Knowing the sureness of hand and the pains taken by M. Guillaume when at work, we are loth to believe his drawing faulty, as affirmed by Professor Ramsay.

the singularity of its ornamentation, the mythical name of "Midas" written on the façade, its situation at the head of the valley amidst picturesque rocks fringed with gloomy firs, have all helped to bring it out from among the rank and file surrounding it, which are either lost in the depths of plantations or buried out of sight in the clefts of the rock, a small aperture on the apex and an insignificant rude front being alone visible. The royal monument, on the other hand, has no trees to take from the proportions of its fine frontage (which starts from the ground, giving it an amplitude not to be seen anywhere else) and stupendous base of rock, 7 or 8 m. high; nothing, in fact, diverts the eye of the beholder from Iasili Kaïa (the Great Written Stone), as the native woodmen style it. Like a magnet, it has attracted and attracts every traveller who has visited or visits these parts; it is the first he wishes to see, and when he leaves it for a while, it is only that he may return to it. He makes it his head-quarters, the better to examine it.

Our visit was in 1861. Solicitous as we were to push on to Ancyra, where a long and important work awaited us, we made all the same arrangements to spend the night in a neighbouring tomb, so as to devote another day to the monuments of the Midas necropolis. But Fate willed it otherwise; this time in the guise of a heavy storm of rain and wind, which broke out during the night and did so much damage to our photographing apparatus, that it was rendered useless for the time. As the Midas plateau was not down in our programme, we did not feel justified in wasting the time requisite to take measurements, and make hand-sketches and photographs with a light camera of the tombs it contains. Reluctantly, therefore, and with heavy hearts, we set our faces towards our real goal, followed by the regret of not being able to tarry here for one week at least, so as to take exact measurements of the principal tombs, which even now have not yet been acquired to archæology. Five and twenty years have gone by, and the sequel of the *History of Art* takes me back to these very woodlands and picturesque rocks, that I may properly characterize and define the style and processes of Phrygian art from the remains it has left behind. Once again in my essayal approximately to date and classify the tombs met with in this region, the Midas rock, better than any other, will serve as starting-point and term of comparison for tombs, the oldest of which may perhaps go

Fig. 48.—Monument of Midas.

back to the eighth century B.C., whilst the more recent may be coeval with Alexander and his immediate successors.

The monument deserving of this high place of honour may be described as a sculptured frontispiece cut in the face of a vertical wall of tufa 20 m. high, bounded on one side by an immense chasm where the road passes, and on the other by rocky masses which close the ravine called Doghanlou Deresi (Hawk Valley). It is a rectangular table, 11 m. 74 c. by 12 m. 50 c., separated from the rough portions of the rock by a shallow groove, the crowning member being a very low triangular pediment. A device composed of a double volute, the centre of which has disappeared, appears above the tympanum. The remaining parts, including the ornament and the inscriptions, are in a marvellous state of preservation. The lettering on the left describes an oblique line on the virgin rock, almost parallel to the slope of the frontal; that to the right runs from top to bottom in a vertical line on the outer edge of the upright. Finally, pierced in the face of the slab, is a false door or niche, framed by triple jambs with a slight inward slope, and in retreat one from the other, the effect of which is to deepen and narrow the opening towards the top—a contrivance taken up again by the builders of the Romanesque and Gothic style of architecture. The second lintel or architrave rests upon rectangular saliences or bracket-like shapes (Fig. 49).[1]

If from the main and more striking lines we pass on to details, we shall find that the façade is wholly covered with geometrical forms, either graven or in relief, be it on the flat pilasters, the horizontal fascia, under the coping of the roof, and even the field of the tympanum. A star-like pattern, composed of four lozenges whose centre is marked by a smaller lozenge, surrounds the frontispiece. Under the gable are, first a row of squares of larger calibre, then other two rows of smaller ones, placed edge-wise so

[1] We have intentionally had the false door drawn on a larger scale than the rest of the monument, because it was inadequately figured in Téxier's book, and from him reproduced in many works. The plate in question, however, is on the whole better than the vast majority to be found in his volume, and has but two inexactitudes: one is his having placed the vertical inscription on the virgin rock, when it should be on the outer edge of the jamb; whilst his shadows are all too strong, giving a depth to the niche which it does not possess in reality. Again, there never was here a funereal bed, as shown in his sketch; whilst the meander pattern right and left of the door widely differs from that traced by his pencil.

as to form what is technically called the key device. The greater intricacy of the main design is more apparent than real, in that its elements are wholly rectilinear. It is a continuous meander, forming and limiting spaces of varying size and shape, which are occupied by rows of crosses and small elongated dots. The form, meanders and crosses have a relief of 13 c., and occupy the inner slab, which, as already stated, is 11 m. 74 c. in height, by 12 m. 55 c. in width.[1] We do not vouch for the absolute accuracy of

FIG. 49.—Monument of Midas. False door. Drawn by E. Guillaume. *Exploration archéologique*, Plate VI.

measurements we had no time to verify; but they cannot be far removed from reality.

To the left of the façade, on the level, appears a small grotto roughly cut, 1 m. 60 c. wide, 75 c. deep, one side of which is 1 m. 35 c. and the other 1 m. 82 c. high. Over it is incised an inscription in large Phrygian letters, 30 c. high and 1 c. deep,

[1] Our figures are taken from TEXIER, *Description*, tom. i. p. 154. A sketch of Sir C. Wilson, kindly forwarded to me by Professor Ramsay, gives the following measurements:—Width of sculptured slab, including pilasters, 16 m. 62 c.; width of surface occupied by meander, 12 m. 39 c.; height of the same, 12 m. 16 c. (the figure is obviously too high, for Sir Charles's sketch shows a greater difference between breadth and height than appears from his measurements); mean width of pilasters (they are not quite alike), 2 m. 13 c.; height of the whole, 21 m.

and, like those on the frontispiece, should be read from left to right. This is not the place for attempting to unravel the meaning of these texts; nevertheless, regard should be had to the uppermost and longer inscription graven on the native rock (Fig. 1), as likely to be helpful in determining the nature of the monument itself. The prominent place it occupies, its length of line (13 m.), the size and clearness of the characters, each separated by a dot, so as to make confusion impossible; finally, the issues involved in these alphabetical signs;—everything combines to attract the eye and draw attention to it. Transliterated in Roman figures, it reads thus: "*Ates arkaie Fais akenanola Fos midai la Faltei Fanaktei edaes.*"

It is self-evident that the first word is the nominative singular of the radical *atu, attu,* the great Phrygian god, the Atys, whom classical writers represent as the inseparable companion of Cybele. The name seems to have enjoyed popular favour, for Herodotus (i. 34) tells us that a son of Crœsus and an old king of Lydia (i. 71) were so called; and Strabo writes that it was the official title of the high priest of Cybele at Pessinus.[1] Discarding the next two words of doubtful reading, we come to the dative form of the familiar name of Midas; those which follow *la Faltei* and *Fanaktei*, being in the same case, are supposed to be his honorific or patronymic appellations. Curiously enough, if we drop the initial letter F of the second word—instances of which may be observed in cognate languages—we have the Greek dative ἄνακτι, ἄνακτει, from ἄναξ, prince. *Edaes*, on the other hand, is the third person of a verb, which in Phrygian probably represented an Indo-European root, signifying to establish—in Sanscrit *da-dha-mi*, to establish; Greek, τί-θε-μι; German, *stellen, stabilire, établir, poser.*[2] Hence the words known at present yield the following formula: "Atys . . . dedicated . . . to king Midas" (Ἄτης . . . Μίδᾳ . . . ἄνακτι . . . ἔθηκεν).[3]

[1] *Hist. of Art*, tom. iv. p. 659, n.

[2] G. CURTIUS, *Grundzuge der Griechischen*, etc., 3rd edit., 1869, p. 238, No. 309.

[3] For more details respecting the conjectures that may be adduced about the words still undeciphered, and the reasons for considering *edaes* as a third person of an aorist, see RAMSAY, *Hist. Relat. of Phrygia and Cappadocia*, pp. 29, 30. Professor Ramsay persists in considering the Midas monument as a funereal memorial, whilst we would rather attribute to it a commemorative and religious character (*Journal*, x. pp. 149–156). No grave-chamber has been found at Iasili Kaia, nor in one or two cognate façades, and until a discovery which would settle the question is made,

Philologists who have studied the Phrygian texts, and every traveller who since Leake has visited the district, are agreed in accepting the testimony borne by the inscription, to the effect that this important work was executed in honour of king Midas. On the other hand, opinions are divided as to whether we are confronted by a real tomb, in which were formerly deposited the mortal remains of the prince, or a mere cenotaph, a commemorative monument, the use of which was to keep green the memory of a mythic ancestor, an eponym hero, the founder of the monarchy worshipped as a god.

The idea that rises uppermost from the contemplation of the monument is naturally that of a sepulture, whilst the rank of the illustrious dead buried in it would account for the abnormal size and decoration of the façade; but if a tomb, where is the funereal chamber? Texier, one of the early explorers of the Phrygian necropolis, was at first inclined to see in the cavity formed by the false door, a niche in which the body was deposited, and formerly closed by a covering slab (Fig. 49). On maturer reflection, however, he seems to have abandoned the notion, closer inspection having shown him that a recess 84 c. in capacity would ill accommodate the corpse.[1] We may add that if the body was placed, or rather squeezed, in the niche under discussion, a slab, of necessity very thin, with joints manifest to all, would have been the only safeguard against violation, and would have invited rather than repelled the vulgar curiosity and rapaciousness of subsequent generations. Lastly, had there been a stone to disguise the hollow, the surrounding rock would show the marks left by the covering slab; but nothing of the kind occurs, nor is there the slightest indication of any mode of sealing having been here. And against any lurking doubts, we may adduce a false door in

we feel justified in upholding our hypothesis whilst fully conscious of the difficulties which beset it. Then, too, I very much doubt if the small niche to the left-hand side of the monument, even enlarged as Professor Ramsay has it in Fig. 16, could ever have been a royal tomb, inasmuch as it is level with the ground and would have been too easily entered. Professor Ramsay (p. 186) states that in one inscription of the Midas rock there occurs a Phrygian word which may signify *grave-chamber*. The decision as to whether *sikeneman* presents the degree of probability which he attributes to it must be left to philologists.

[1] Texier, after describing the Midas monument and other two near it, goes on to say, "Could it be possible to regard the central niche of the former as having served as chambered grave, nothing of the sort can be deduced from the latter." (*Description*, tom. i, pp. 154–158).

Fig. 50.—Delikli Tach. Perspective view. Drawn by E. Guillaume. *Exploration archéologique*, Plate V.

which precisely the same arrangement is reproduced; it is found in a façade, which certainly belongs to the art and the people who created the Midas monument. It is the most westward specimen of Phrygian activity. As an advanced post, it rises alone of its kind on the slopes of Mysian Olympus, close to Harmanjik, in the middle valley of the Rhyndacus, and is called by the natives Delikli Tach (Holed Stone) (Fig. 50). On the information yielded by a passage of one of our predecessors we repaired thither, that we might observe it with the care it deserves.[1] We will describe it in this place, as helpful to understand in what light one is tempted to view the Midas monument, when obliged to abandon the notion of the niche being a funereal chamber.

FIG. 51.—Delikli Tach. Detail of doorway. Drawn by F. Guillaume. *Explor. arch.*, Plate VI.

Delikli Tach stands towards the extremity of a rocky ridge twisted into the most fantastic shapes. The thick mass advances like a promontory into a narrow gorge, at the bottom of which flows one of the many small affluents of the Rhyndacus. Its position over the path (probably an old road) which runs from Harmanjik to Mohimûl, and the almost white colour of the cliff in which it is excavated, cause it to be seen at some distance. The broad massive rock has been rent into three unequal parts, with jagged outline of varying depth. The two

[1] *Researches*, tom. i. p. 97. In Hamilton's book the Phrygian tomb is described in ten lines, and represented by one simple sketch.

masses on the right and left have not been touched by the chisel, and preserve their uneven and natural saliences. But the central fragment was cut in such a way until a façade-like aspect was obtained, terminating in a very pointed pediment. A false door, preceded by three steps, enframed in wide double posts, appears in the middle of the façade, at about one-third of the whole height of the rock (Fig. 51). The effect of the whole is satisfactory. The marriage of simple architectural shapes with the virgin portions of the rock is exceedingly happy; we find here united the picturesque rugged outlines of nature, with the human interest supplied by a work of art, and the latter, as an index of the mind that created it, never fails to excite our curiosity and call forth our sympathies.

The circular opening seen in the pseudo-door is certainly a late, perhaps a modern degradation, made by treasure-seekers to enable them to penetrate into the inner chamber, which they supposed to exist behind. The irregular cutting of the narrow aperture is enough to prove that it did not form part of the original plan, but was hastily pierced to the size of a dormer-window to allow a child to get in, when, being disappointed in their object, they suspended their operations. But for this, however, the real and only entrance, near the summit of the rock, would not have been suspected. Now, anybody by putting his head through the aperture can see the well into which the body was lowered, as it was conveyed to its last abode. The grave where the body was laid was no more than the bottom of the well or chimney, 4 m. 30 c. high, opening towards the middle of the vertical façade. Reference to our perspective section, through transverse axis (Fig. 52), shows that, as soon as the dead was placed in his stony bed, the mouth of the well was sealed down with care by two stout slabs, the marks of which—60 c. apart—may still be seen. Their arrangement and the salience of the upper stone over the one below are indicated by dotted lines in plan (Fig. 53). As the walls of the well would not be seen, little care was bestowed on their appearance and effect, so that they were left almost in the rough; the builders being content to invest the sepulchre with the utmost solidity, so as to guard it against unwelcome visitors and profanation. As at Iasili Kaia, here also the false door is furnished with a double case; the second or inner being set back from the first. The general arrangement is identical, and the differences are

FIG. 52.—Delikli Tach. Perspective section through transverse axis. Drawn by C. Chipiez

reducible to two. Thus, at Delikli Tach, upon the second

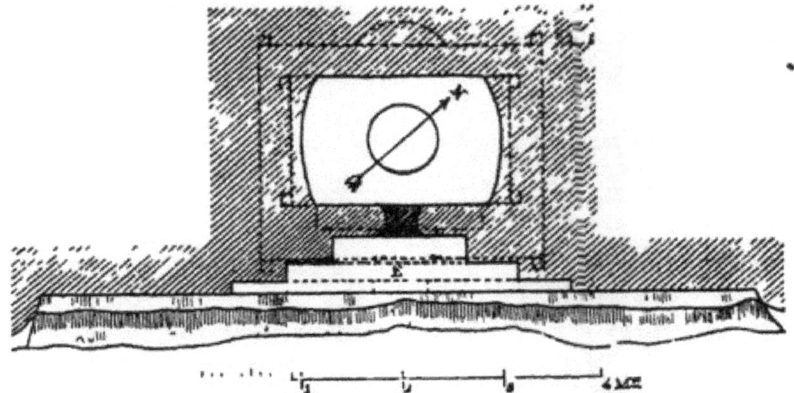

FIG. 53.—Delikli Tach. Plan of tomb. Drawn by E. Guillaume.

lintel, which projects far out beyond the jambs and forms a kind of ancone (Figs. 54, 55), are three large intermitted tores.[1] The adjustment at Iasili Kaia was simpler, and exhibits neither tores nor ancones. Then, too, no trace of painted ornament has been found about the Midas monument, nor in the tombs around it. At Delikli Tach, on the other hand, many portions of the rock still exhibit stuccoed patches, white, black, and red. The latter colour in especial abounds on the vertical face of lintel, F, and soffit, E (Fig. 54). Lintel and soffit—and, owing to its sheltered position, notably the latter—still preserve remnants of a scroll painted white on black—at least, so it looked to us—with red in the middle, which occupied the whole length (Fig. 56)

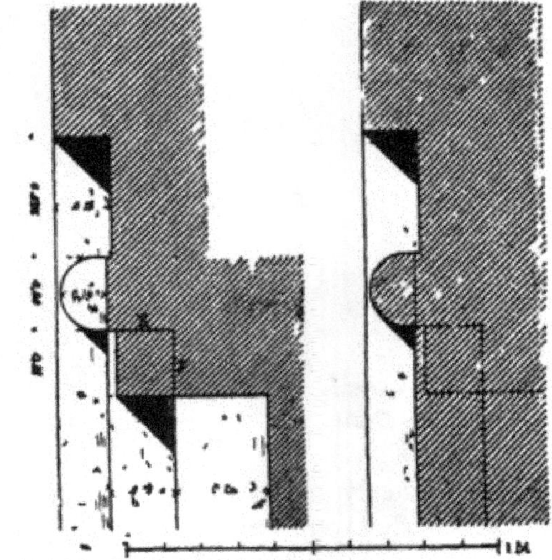

FIG. 54.—Delikli Tach. Profile of lintel on inner jamb. By E. Guillaume. *Explor. archt.*, Plate VI.

55.—Profile of lintel on external jamb. By E. Guillaume. *Explor. archt.*, Plate VI.

[1] In Fig. 51 the left tore has disappeared, but has been restored in our illustration.

of the stone. Applied ornament seems also to have been resorted to in the decoration of this façade; for between the small circular niche which appears above the mouth of the well and the commencement of the frontal are holes which are far too regular not to be artificial. They suggest the notion of having served to fix metal plates.

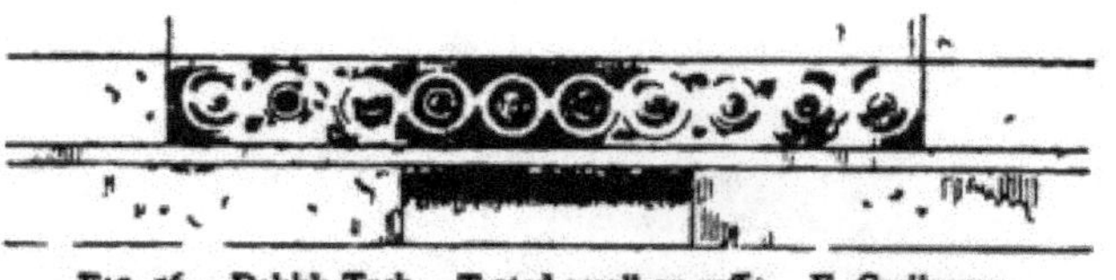

FIG 56 —Delikli Tach. Tinted scroll on soffit E Guillaume. *Explor archéol.*, Plate VI

A good many niche-like hollows, seemingly artificial, look out of the rocks surrounding Delikli Tach They are so ruinous, however, that plans and measurements are out of the question, nor is it possible to advance an opinion as to their original purpose Here and there may also be traced remains of other cuttings. Thus, for instance, our general view (Fig. 50) exhibits steps which formerly led to the top of the rocky mass, in the depth of which the tomb was hollowed. We found no vestige whatever in the neighbourhood to mark the existence of a town which had here its necropolis Nothing was gained by our study of the ground at this particular spot, and very little is to be hoped from two single letters—all that remains of an inscription, apparently very short, incised on the inner jamb of the false door on the left-hand side. Bits of colour still adhere in the hollow of the letters, which are reproduced, one-fifth of their actual size, in our illustration from an impression taken from the stone (Fig. 57).

FIG 57 —Delikli Tach Characters incised on jamb of door *Explor archéol.*, Plate VI

Fig. 58 — Rock cut façade

If *per se* these two letters have no meaning whatever, they are valuable and of great interest in that they permit us to formulate a probable conjecture in regard to the relative age of the two monuments we have juxtaposed. They are not found in the alphabet which the Phrygians borrowed from Greece, instances of which are given in our cut representing inscriptions met with on the rocks around Nacoleia (Fig. 2). On the other hand, they have been identified in a somewhat more complicated form—one on a fusaiole from Hissarlik; and the other, composed of two sets of parallel lines, both on fusaioles, a clay patera brought out of a tomb at Thymbra within the Troad, and in Cypriote inscriptions.[1]

The deduction to be drawn from the coincidence is the following. The two characters under discussion belonged to one of the many varieties of the alphabet we called Asianic, which, by way of reduction and simplification, was derived like the syllabary of Cyprus, where the older form persisted longer, from Hittite hieroglyphs, which obtained throughout Asia Minor before the introduction of Phœnician letters. Agreeably with this hypothesis the Delikli Tach tomb would have been excavated before the Phrygians received from the Ionian Greeks the alphabet they made use of at Iasili Kaia and the sepulchres surrounding it, and, as a natural consequence, it is older than the tombs in the neighbourhood of Nacoleia.

Our supposition is in accord with the character of the monument and its close resemblance with the Midas rock. In both there is great contrast between the rude massive rocks enframing the façade and the frontal surmounting it, whilst their shapes and architectural members exhibit intelligent proportion and symmetry. The only difference is that at Delikli Tach all was regulated on simple lines; little or no effort was made to heighten the effect of the pediment and inner slab by ornament, which, like rich drapery, covers the whole façade at Iasili Kaia. We may be permitted, therefore, to consider Delikli Tach as the first exemplar of a type invented by the Phrygians, a type they improved and perfected in the upper valley of the Sangarius, where they had their political and religious centre for a period of two or three centuries.

[1] PERROT, *Explor. Arch.*, p. 107. Sayce, appendix written for Dr. Schliemann's English edition of *Ilios*. We have shown in another place that the letter on the right is not a double one, the repetition of the lines being purely ornamental; the ligatures belong to the decadence of a system of writing, and not to its initial period.

During our expedition in Asia Minor, we went straight from Delikli Tach to Iasili Kaïa, where the striking family likeness observable between the two monuments was brought home to my companion, M. Guillaume, and myself, with perhaps greater force than if a longer interval had interposed between one journey and another. Arguing from exterior analogies, we judged that they might extend to the interior. But we did not for a moment deem it possible that the sinking or false door could ever have been a grave. We were inclined to think that there was behind it a real mortuary chamber, entered by a shaft as at Delikli Tach. The next thing was to find the entrance, which we were disposed to seek at the summit of the rock, behind the broken finial crowning the pediment.[1] One of our party, M. Delbet, volunteered to climb up the rock, so as to test the truth of our hypothesis; but his attempts were unsuccessful, and as we could not spare the time it would have taken to procure ladders, ropes, and so forth for the purpose, we were fain to abandon the undertaking.[2] Professor Ramsay, with true British tenacity of purpose and British elasticity of limb, succeeded in scaling the rocky wall, "whose top is so narrow that he could sit on the edge as on the back of a horse, pushing himself along with his hands." But he found no sign of an orifice to the well he was in quest of. He had, however, ample opportunity for observing that "as the stone is a soft conglomerate, a deep chimney of this kind would split it like a wedge."

If the notion that the Midas rock is a tomb be persisted in, there is no other alternative but to seek the grave towards the foot of the rock; or, rather, our only chance of discovering the entrance to the mortuary chamber is to clear away the silt and potsherds that have gathered in front of the façade to the height of three or four metres. The spade alone can clinch the question. On the other hand, no instance of such an arrangement can be adduced in the whole Phrygian necropolis. Hence the question we have asked before may be asked again, as to whether we are confronted by a real sepulchre, or a simple commemorative monument, whose imposing dimensions, elaborate and skilful workmanship, are witnesses to the homage rendered by the princes of the eighth or seventh century B.C. to the eponym hero, the legendary ancestor,

[1] *Explor. Arché.*, pp. 105, 106.

[2] RAMSAY, *The Rock Necropolis of Phrygia* (*Journal*, 1882, pp. 16, 17).

Fig. 59.—Rock-cut façade.

whose name they adopted and to whom they paid divine honours.[1] Viewed in this light, the niche to the left was a shrine in which lamps and offerings were deposited as tokens of regard to the ancestral god.[2]

What tends to confirm our conjecture is the fact that in the same neighbourhood are other two sculptured frontispieces, whose tops, covered by a fine growth of pines, can be easily reached; but where, despite diligent search, no well, nor the semblance of a pseudo-door, have been detected.

The most important, because of its inscription—the longest known in Phrygia—is Fig. 58 (4 in plan). It consists of no less than five lines, three of which follow the slope of the roof below and above it on the native rock. Then a horizontal line appears on the frontal in the place usually occupied by the frieze in a Greek entablature, ending on the dexter hand on the rough stone; whilst

[1] We plead guilty to having misquoted Hesychius. The error arose from our having, contrary to our invariable custom, taken the lines from a book which happened to be close at hand, where the misprint occurred, and not from the original as we should have done. They should be read as follows:—Οἱ ὑπὸ Μίδα βασιλευθέντες ἐσέβοντο, καὶ ὤμνυον τὸν Μίδα θεόν, ἣν τίνες μητερα αὐτοῦ ἐστι τίμεσα λεγουσεν. As may be observed, "Mida" is in the genitive case, whilst θεόν is in the accusative, and agrees with the feminine article την; hence the construction is, "The goddess of Midas," doubtless Cybele, who was said to be the mother of the great ancestor of the Phrygians. Even in this form the passage may be adduced in favour of the opinion I put forth: Midas, whose name so largely figures in national legends as the son of a goddess, came to be considered in the light of a heroic or semi-divine character.

[2] Of the inexactitudes complained of by M. Ramsay, I find but one of any relevancy (*Hell. Studies*, x. pp. 161–163). It occurs on the left side, which should have been left incomplete, whilst we have left out a few squares which occur on the right side. (See *Ibid.*, ix. Fig. 13.) The fact is that the ornament of the façade was never finished; we forgot to warn our draughtsman, and when the mistake was discovered it was too late to be remedied. M. Ramsay makes a great deal of our having distributed six nails on each of the double doors of the pediment, when one panel should have but four. In truth, a venial error. We might with far better reason reproach him with having produced, in 1888, a picture which shows no trace of the characteristic sinking which surrounds the façade, and imparts thereto a niche-like aspect; upon which he vehemently insists in 1889. This our illustration, albeit containing two wee nails in excess, brings out very distinctly.

The slight discrepancy between the text and the translation in regard to the tombs of the Ayazeen necropolis and the Midas city is due to the fact that I have written this part with the help of the additions and corrections at the end, so as to save the reader trouble and put him at once in possession of the whole evidence.—TRS.

the last forms a vertical line outside the right-hand upright. If, on the one hand, the text, out of which the words "Materee" and "Materan" are alone understood, occupies a larger space, on the other hand the decorative scheme is conceived on simpler lines than at Iasili Kaia. The frame, made up of square posts surrounding a field carefully smoothed over, but quite plain, is the only portion which has been carved. Towards the top of the inner slab, a tiny square niche has been pierced, which seems to belong to the

FIG. 60.—Tomb in the Ayazeen necropolis. *Journal*, Plate XXI

primitive plan. Other niches, circular in plan and elevation, are seen above and to the left of the pediment.

The presence of the long inscription well agrees with the character we are inclined to ascribe to this façade. We own to feeling some degree of hesitancy in respect to Fig. 59 (5 in plan), which exhibits no inscription on its front, no chambered grave in its rear. In general plan, however, it is identical with Fig. 58; whilst on the rock which serves as foundation to the inwrought façade appear small niches and stone benches which seem to imply

Fig. 61.—Rock-cut façade. Perspective view.

that the site was much frequented.[1] All the same, it does not help us to explain how a people in possession of a system of writing should have laboriously cut out of the solid rock a commemorative monument, which was to perpetuate the memory of a god or royal personage, without taking the trouble to record his name. Here more than ever are explorations needed around, above, and at the base of the rock, one of whose faces bears as elegant and well adjusted a decoration as was ever executed by the Phrygian chisel. Had this been a tomb, the absence of a Phrygian text should cause no surprise; since, with one notable exception, instances abound with chambered graves, troughs or stone beds, that leave no doubt as to their sepulchral character, which yet are innocent of any literary document.

FIG. 62.—Plan of tomb at Bakshish. After Wilson.

The number of monuments respecting which it is impossible to pronounce a decided opinion is reducible to three or four. Real tombs, on the other hand, may be counted by hundreds; but as they are pretty much alike, a sequent description would involve wearisome iteration, and would only result in loss of time. We propose, therefore, to single out such exemplars as will serve as types for the many. The grave of a certain number of these is entered, as at Delikli Tach, by a

FIG. 63.—Tomb showing mouth of well. After Ramsay.

[1] TÉXIER, *Description*, tom. i. p. 157, Plate LVIII.; Stewart, Plates IX., X.; BARTH, *Reise von Trapezunt*, p. 92. We have corrected Téxier's drawing with the aid of sketches handed to us by Professor Ramsay; hence it has been possible to represent more exactly the rosettes and the central acroterion.

perpendicular shaft; in most, however, the opening is in the centre of the façade.

For obvious reasons we are unable to dwell at length upon the tombs around Nacoleia, because the information to hand is far from being as minute and complete as that derived from our notes in regard to Delikli Tach. Professor Ramsay has made no plans of them, and confines himself to the general statement that the tombs in the great necropolis of Ayazeen offer a close analogy to the Midas monument.[1] The only one he describes is Fig. 60 (24 in plan), whose sculptured front is akin to the royal memorial, save that it has no false door. It is locally known as Maltash, the stone of the treasure. About 45 c. behind the frontispiece an oblong shaft, 4 or 5 m. deep, was cut down into the rock, in the floor of which appears a rectangular grave, now exposed and distinctly seen from above. The covering slab was probably removed by treasure-seekers when they broke the top of the pediment; the shallow groove, however, into which the stone fitted, is visible to the present day in the sides of the rock.

We are a little better off respecting a beautiful tomb south of Bakshish[2] (1 in plan). From the data furnished by the various travellers who have visited it, we have been able to evolve the general view[3] (Fig. 61), plan (Fig. 62) and sketch (Fig. 63). The latter shows the groove for the covering slab on the apex of the monument and the situation of the chimney.

The most remarkable specimens of memorials of this class, from a decorative standpoint, are found about three miles northward of Ayazeen, with entrance to the grave in the centre of the façade, as that of a house. The lion, which in Pteria is figured about the city and palace portals, or as support to the throne, watches here over the last abode of prince and grandee. The device seems to have found great favour in funereal architecture. The tomb in which

[1] *Studies*, p. 17.

[2] The rock bears a Phrygian inscription, but so much worn as to have been undetected on Professor Ramsay's first visit, when the sketches we reproduce were made.

[3] Stewart, Plate VII. The general view was drawn, under the supervision of M. Chipiez, from original sketches made on the spot by MM. Wilson and Ramsay, including a photograph taken by the latter during a recent visit. The lower part of the façade is much worn, and the geometrical forms hopelessly obliterated by the influence of the weather. At the extreme eastern point of the Midas plateau is another tomb of the same general type as that at Bakshish. It is cut free from the rock, except the back, which is engaged. The roof slopes on either side (*Journal*, x. p. 166, Fig. 19).

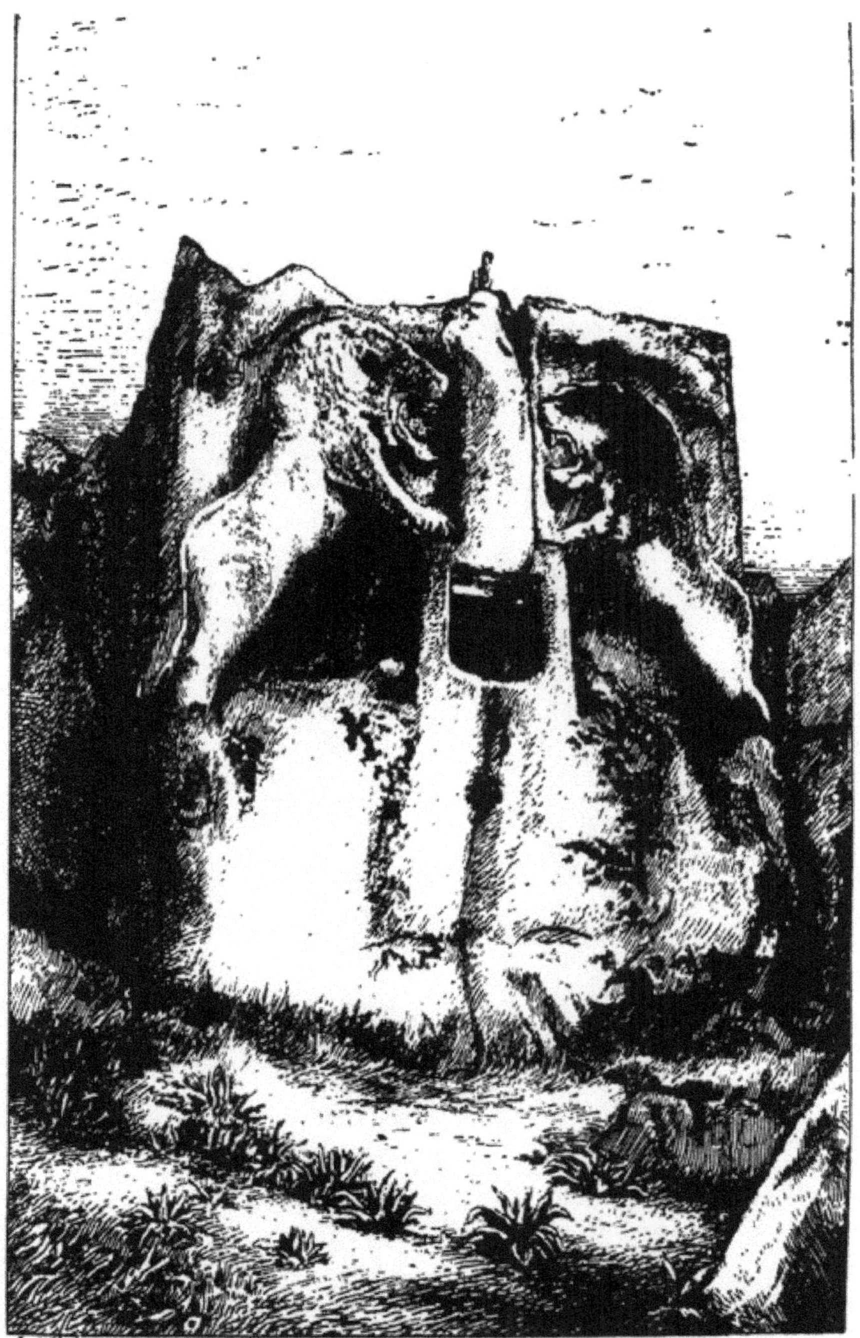

Fig. 64.—Tomb in the Ayazeen necropolis.

it is seen to the best advantage belongs to the group under notice, where the rocks, without being hard, are firmer than about Ayazeen. Hence in the perpendicular faces of the cliffs, which hem in the plateau on all sides, have been pierced chambered graves with gaping mouths, so high up as to require ladders and other contrivances to reach them. An immense rock, jutting from the plateau above, has been rudely fashioned into a parallelopiped block, wholly void of mouldings; a plain small doorway appears in the usual position, 6 m. above the ground (Fig. 64, 21 in plan). Over the lintel of this door is carved a slightly conical obelisk, topped by a capital, the outline of which brings to mind that of the echinus in the Doric capital. It is flanked by rampant lions, one on each side, their fore paws resting on the door-posts in threatening attitude and mouth wide open, as though to warn off the sacrilegious from the tomb. Beneath each of the lions is a little cub, kept in deep shadow by the larger figures, in more senses than one; the heads of the latter are almost level with the top of the slab, and monopolize the whole attention.[1] The chamber is small, archaic, and of no interest.

Professor Ramsay states that there are eight other tombs at least in this necropolis, whose façades are enriched by the lion device; some of them, however, belong to a very late period.

Had it been preserved, the finest and perhaps the oldest specimen of sepulchral decoration yielded by the lion device would be found in a hypogee, some 90 m. beyond that which we have just examined (22 in map). But, unfortunately, water and Plutonic agency have broken it to pieces. The site it once occupied is covered with immense blocks six and eight metres long, and of proportionate thickness. Huge fragments are scattered or piled up on the ground in picturesque confusion (Fig. 65).

The fragments in question excited the curiosity of Professor Ramsay, who since then returned to the spot in 1884 and 1887, bent upon unravelling the history these stones had to tell. He went

[1] M. Blunt's photograph, from which St. Elme Gautier drew Fig. 64, was taken late in the day, when the whole monument was in deep shadow; hence he failed to bring out the cubs. They were given more prominence in Plate XVII., *Journal of Hell. Studies*. The shape of our pilaster does not agree in every respect with the verbal description of Professor Ramsay, written in consequence of a second visit to the monument (*Athenæum*, December 27, 1884, p. 864). The fact that the adult animals are without mane, coupled with the presence of two cubs, leads to the conclusion that the sculptor intended to represent lionesses (*Journal*, ix. pp. 368, 369).

to work lever in hand, "turning about the less heavy blocks, slipping in between those that could not be moved, sinking trenches around others, so as to examine the lower face of fragments touching the ground." The result of his investigations is as follows :—

Like the tomb decorated with a pair of lions, this, too, was

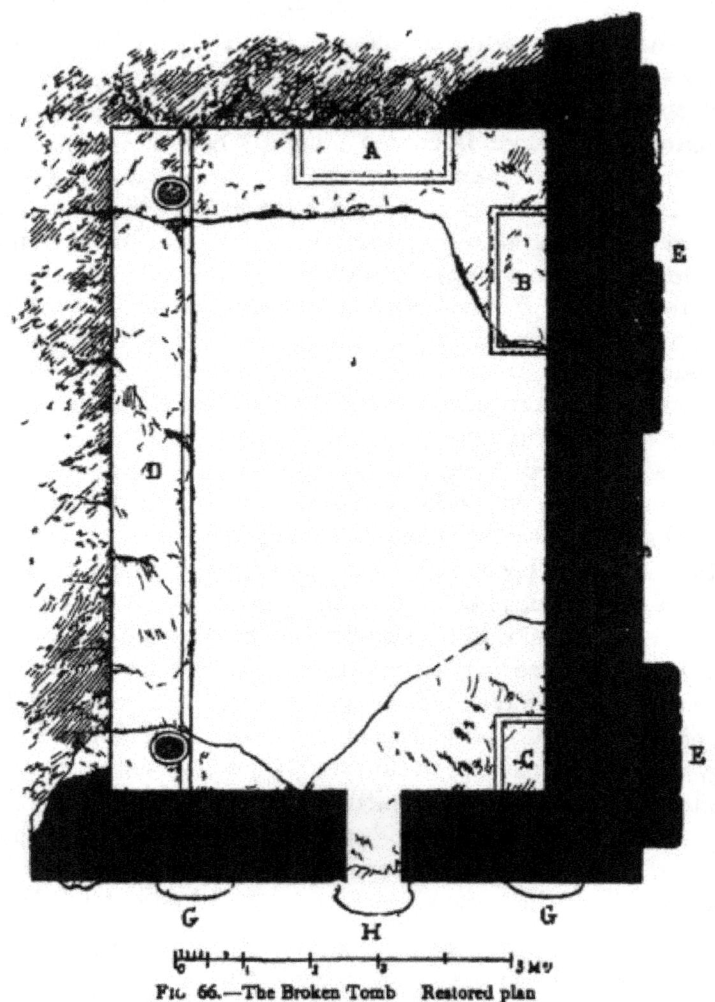

FIG. 66.—The Broken Tomb Restored plan

hollowed in the face of a projecting cliff, along with grave-chambers of less importance, of which two sides at least, west and north, were disengaged. The door was in the north side (Fig. 66). The south wall of the hypogee, which formed the end or back

FIG. 65.—The Broken Tomb   Drawn by St. Elme Gautier from Blunt's photograph.

wall of the chamber, is almost unimpaired, for it was cut in the solid mass of the hill. Thus the width of the apartment, 6 m. 29 c. by 3 m. in height, is obtained, as well as the shape of the roof, which had a double slope, a king-post as support to the side-rafters like carpentry work. The same arrangement was repeated in the north face, save that the door appears in the position occupied on the opposite side by the bed (Fig. 67). A funereal couch is hollowed in the back wall of the grave-chamber (Fig. 68). In the north-west side of this appears a seat, whilst a second mortuary bed occupies its west face (Fig. 69). Between it and the settee there occurs a gap. A passage, 1 m. 6 c. by 1 m. 21 c., ran along the eastern side; two columns at least, one at either end, supported its roof; that in the back wall is still in position, whilst the fragment, now lying on the ground, which formed the north-east angle, shows the marks left by the upper part of the second pillar (Fig. 70). The base of these supports is a large torus; above the shaft, a palm of elegant design expands on the inner side of the column, facing the interior of the chamber, of which a perspective view is given (Fig. 71). The two funereal beds, the settee, portico, and sculptured faces, are witnesses that a more complicated arrangement

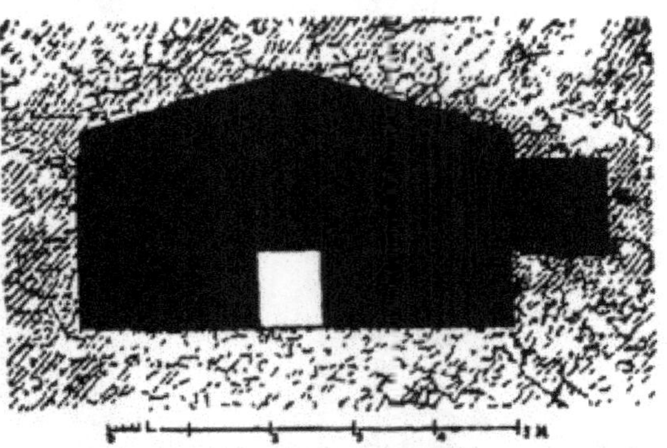

FIG. 67.—The Broken Tomb. Restored transverse section through the north face.

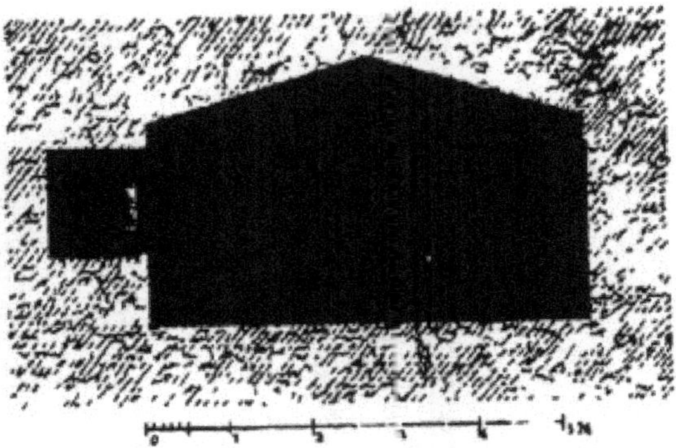

FIG. 68.—The Broken Tomb. Transverse section through end wall of vault.

and monumental aspect were aimed at in this tomb, the like of which has not yet been met with in the Phrygian necropolis. The exterior decoration was equally ambitious.[1]

Both sides freed from the mass were carved. No less than three lions, cut in very high relief, adorned the western face; two

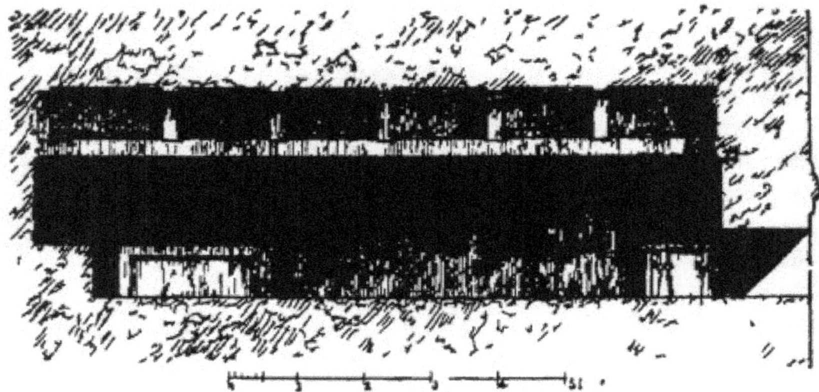

FIG 69.—The Broken Tomb. Restored longitudinal section through west face.

stood rampant, with their raised fore-paws pressed against each other (Fig. 66, E, Fig. 122). The action of the animals has been made out from their fore-paws, which were discovered still

FIG 70.—The Broken Tomb. Restored longitudinal section through east face.

[1] We are happy to say that our restoration of the broken tomb is in perfect agreement with Professor Ramsay's (*Journal*, ix. pp. 354–364, Figs. 1–9). His "inner restoration" corresponds in every respect with the perspective view offered by M. Chipiez (Fig. 71), and reference to his inner sections (Figs. 4 and 7) will tell the reader the position occupied by the pictures in the building. This is carefully indicated by dotted lines.

adhering to the external portion of the fragment;[1] the other, or inner side, had a mortuary bed (Fig. 65, right-hand block). Of the third lion on this side, the head and shoulder are extant (Fig. 65, on the left). It was near the north-west corner (Fig. 66, F), and faced north (Fig. 121), his back turned against the pair. Taken from the tip of the nose to the back of the neck, it measures 1 m. 28 c. The pose of the animal must have been very similar to that of the two lions seen at the entrance of tomb (Fig. 64).[2]

Finally a bas-relief, composed of three figures, took up the whole of the northern side (Figs. 117, 118). It represented two warriors (Fig. 66, G G) in the act of spearing a Gorgon-like monster, whose head appears over the door (Fig. 66, H). This side is now broken into two huge blocks. The larger fragment answers to the north-west angle of the tomb; it still preserves the settee (Fig. 66, C), the head and shoulder of the lion (Fig. 65), and the best half of the northern façade. Our woodcut shows its present situation. The block bearing the right-hand warrior, the door, and the Gorgon has its external side turned against the ground; as also the second fragment with the left-hand warrior, but this has suffered far more from the fall and the weather, and looks as if excoriated, the helmeted head of the hero being the only part visible. Nor are these the only lacunes; the block to the dexter hand betrays no trace of the lower part of the figures. Did the artist content himself with busts, or did he sculpture full-length figures? The latter hypothesis is the more likely. The chances are against the door having been on the level, but they are many for its having been high up in the façade, so as to afford ample space below it for figures of normal size. It is to be deplored that the tomb we are considering should have met with so untoward a disaster.

[1] This is the fragment very imperfectly figured in the first instance in *Hellenic Studies*, 1882, p. 222, Fig. 6, and of which a better drawing was published in the same *Journal*, vol. ix.

[2] It is a matter for surprise that M. Ramsay's labours with regard to this tomb should have resulted in the discovery of but the two fore-paws of the lions facing each other. Hence he raises the question, which he answers in the negative, as to whether the body of the animals ever existed. Two single isolated paws standing out from the wall without rhyme or reason would, in truth, have been an odd device. He thinks it not improbable that the bodies of the animals may have been utterly destroyed when the chamber fell in, part of whose walls was crumbled to dust. Whilst having our doubts on the subject, and not having seen the tomb, we cannot but accept (though under reserve) the restitution offered by one who has explored the site with untiring perseverance and curiosity.

Had it been preserved, no finer or more important specimen of Phrygian art could have been held up for our admiration; inner arrangement and monumental sculptures, all combine to render it a fit companion to the Midas façade.

In the pillar supporting the sloping roof, we recognized a wooden post imitated in stone; but we are unable to pronounce in regard to the obelisk-like shape seen over the doorway (Fig. 64). It has suffered too much from the weather, its contours are too indistinct to permit of a conjecture one way or another. On the other hand, it is pretty certain that the object which appears in the same position in one tomb of this necropolis is a phallus.[1] Of the idea and feelings which led to this symbol being set up on the top of a funereal mound, above the entrance to a grave-chamber, where it sometimes forms the sole decoration, we have spoken in another place. This is well exemplified in the tomb called Pishmish Ḳalessi (Fig. 100, D), from the fortress which rises on the summit of the crag in whose flank the grave-chamber was hollowed. Its arrangement will be easily grasped by reference to plan (Fig. 72), elevation (Fig. 73), and transverse section through the vestibule (Fig. 74) made by M. Guillaume in 1861, the date of our visit when we brought this interesting specimen to the knowledge of the world.

FIG. 72.—Plan.

FIG. 73.—Façade.

FIG. 74.—Section through A, B.

Figs. 72–74.—Tomb near Pishmish Kalessi. PERROT and GUILLAUME, *Explor. Arché.*, tom. i. p. 146.

The tomb consists of a vestibule and a chamber, the latter having two funereal beds. The entrance of each apartment bears traces of pivot-holes for the door or covering slabs. A runlet was cut in the exterior grave so as to drain percolating water. In the centre of the pediment was a stave or pole, with a triangular cap, and streaked by three vertical striæ. The notion that this sturdy upright was copied from a piece of carpentry need not be entertained, for a wooden post would have been inadequate to uphold

[1] The explorers familiar with the tombs of Phrygia are almost unanimous in viewing the object in question as a linga (BARTH, *Reise von Trapezunt*, p. 94; PERROT and GUILLAUME, *Explor. Arché.*, p. 146).

the heavy frame of the roof. Some have thought that this was a stick with a Phrygian cap;[1] but nothing proves that the cap in question, which only crops up on very late monuments, was at that time the national head-dress of this district of Asia Minor; and, what is more, will any one explain its meaning on the top of a pole, and its business about a tomb? On the other hand, we can easily account for the part played here by the phallus, as well as the significance that may have been attached thereto. Did we not observe it in Cappadocia, as centre-piece of an ædiculum, a place usually reserved to the deity?[2] Was it not put on the summit of tumuli in the neighbouring necropolis of Smyrna?[3]

As to the conventional form it has assumed here, it may be explained on utilitarian principles, in that the artisan could fashion in no time, and at small expenditure of labour, those cippi in stone or wood that were so important a feature of the naturalistic religion of Syria. The frequent parallelism Hebrew writers establish between Asherahs, sacred poles, and Ashtoreths or Astartes, goddesses of love and life-giving, led us to suspect that cippi—found in such abundance in Phœnicia and in her dependencies—had a phallic meaning.[4] The sample we reproduced from Kition[5] is precisely similar to that which served as model to the Phrygian sculptor; a symbol he again figured in the Yapuldak tomb, which likewise belongs to this necropolis, and which, from an artistic standpoint, is in advance of the Pishmish Kalessi example (Fig. 75).[6] In each case plinth, quadrangular cube, and pyramidion are identical; making up a type which from Southern Syria must have passed to the Hittites—worshippers of Ashtoreth, and spread from the valley of the Orontes and Cilicia to Cappadocia and throughout Asia Minor. Hence it came to be regarded as an indispensable adjunct in the public worship of the various nations, whose religion was based on the great concept of an eternal and never-ceasing creative force, and a deep sense of the homage it should receive. This is the type we are inclined to recognize

[1] This was the opinion of the late Mordtmann, the companion of Barth (*Reise von Trapezunt nach Scutari*, p. 93).

[2] *Hist. of Art*, tom. iv., pp. 646, 653, Fig. 321.

[3] *Ibid.*, tom. v. p. 51, Figs. 18, 19.

[4] *Ibid.*, tom. iii. p. 385.

[5] *Ibid.*, tom. iv. Fig. 203.

[6] Stewart, Plate XV.; BARTH, *Reise*, p. 93; RAMSAY, *Journal of Hellenic Studies*, tom. iii. pp. 256, 257, Plate XXVIII. n. 4.

in the Hittite character (Fig. 76), which in Cypriote writing appears in a more cursive form.

The tomb whose façade we reproduce (Fig. 75, 2 in map) is

FIG 75 —Tomb at Yapuldak Elevation of façade and section through axis of the same *Journal*, Plate XXVIII

found at Yapuldak. It consists of three chambers in a row extending right through the hill, and may be likened unto a tunnel with opening at either end, or east and west. The hypogee opens on to a spacious platform facing eastward, with parapet cut in the stony mass, down it the rock has not been touched, and has been left in its native state. On this side, too, was certainly the path taken by the funereal procession and the friends of the deceased, as they wound up the gentle acclivity of the hill, conveying the dead to these artificial grottoes The efforts of the decorator were concentrated on the posterior façade, which faces northward and dominates the valley; whence, about half-way up, the wrought front may be

FIG 76 —Hittite character WRIGHT, *The Empire of the Hittites*, 2nd ed, Plate X, 1, 4[1]

[1] The sign is likewise figured by PROF. SAYCE, *Monuments of the Hittites*, p. 28, n. 3—TR.

descried standing out from the almost perpendicular ledge of rocks. A man must needs have sureness of foot and a head not given to dizziness to scramble up these, catching at every projecting stone until the base of the monument is reached. Here he may sit down on the cornice, about 50 c. broad, which forms a kind of parapet along the front, and examine it at his leisure; conscious, however, that the slightest movement backwards will send him spinning some 40 m. below.

The bay is 25 c. above the soil and cir. 50 c. above the floor of the first chamber; so that it looks like a rent in the rock rather than a door properly so called. Its width is somewhat less towards the top than the bottom. This gentle, almost imperceptible salience of the lines one upon another, extends to the fascias surrounding the door, which form as so many frames around it. In the tympan, right and left of the rude obelisk just described, are two walking animals face to face. Stewart saw in them two horses; Barth and Ramsay are both of opinion that the one on the right, which still preserves some sort of outline, has a faint resemblance to an ox, and is as far removed from a horse as can well be. The worn state of the other does not permit to give formal expression as to the species to which it belongs.[1]

The three chambers are small, and the roof-shaped ceiling has a double slope. Over the inner door, which communicates with the second chamber (assuming the main entrance to have been on the west side), is carved a pillar with volute capital. It is the sole ornament of the interior; no couches, no troughs for receiving the bodies. In face of the bare aspect and exiguous dimensions of the chambers, it is not easy to conceive how they could have been subterraneous dependencies of a domestic dwelling, which formerly stood on the platform, the inner side of which leans against the cliff.

But what even more tells in favour of its being a tomb is the characteristic symbol carved on the posterior façade, a symbol we have observed about the doorway of an hypogæe whose funereal purpose cannot be questioned.

As far as we have gone, the monuments we have described betray no arrangement, no element which may be taken to denote acquaintance with and imitation of alien models. This does not apply to a large number of tombs in this very district, and more

[1] M. Ramsay is rather inclined to think that it is a horse.

particularly those of the Ayazeen necropolis. Here multitudinous indications enable us to grasp that the artisans were beginning to feel the influence of Grecian art, albeit in the main they still adhered to the traditional processes of a former age. A certain class of subjects—animals in pairs, for example, whether passant or rampant—had taken too firm a foothold on Phrygian soil not to have

FIG. 77.—Tomb near Ayazeen Façade *Journal*, 1882, Plate XXVI.

been maintained for many centuries. Two or three specimens will suffice to give the reader some notion of this intermediary and composite style.

MM. Ramsay and Blunt were the first to make known an hypogee which, to judge from the number of its troughs, must have been an important family vault. It was decorated by a porch, but the whole of the richly ornamented façade is much defaced (Fig. 77, 32 in map). It is entirely rock-cut; of the two columns which upheld the entablature, one has disappeared without leaving a trace, and of the other the upper part alone remains in position, hanging from the architrave. Right and left of the twin pillars appear two salient members which terminated in small frontals. Were they supported by colonnettes, so as to render them proportional to their surroundings? Had the chisel carved an ornamental device or inscription upon it? In the worn state of the stone surface, nothing can be affirmed either way. The entablature is formed by an architraved cornice, the profiles of

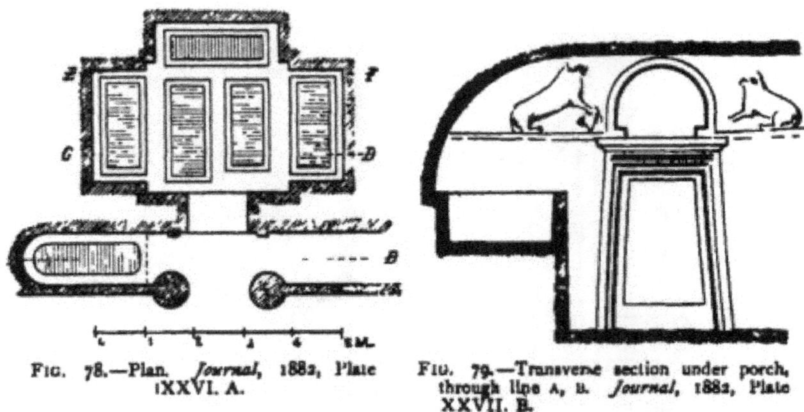

FIG. 78.—Plan. *Journal*, 1882, Plate XXVI. A.

FIG. 79.—Transverse section under porch, through line A, B. *Journal*, 1882, Plate XXVII. B.

which are repeated on the sloping sides of the very pointed pediment crowning the whole. The details about frontal and entablature should be noticed. In the middle of the tympan appears an indistinct object.[1] Was it a Gorgon's head, or rather a simple wreath? It is difficult to say. Behind the porch is the entrance to the tomb, a bay with sloping jambs (Fig. 78). Within the porch, flanking the arch which appears over the lintel, are two semi-rampant lions face to face (Fig. 79); a device repeated on the end wall of the chamber opposite the entrance (Fig. 80). The decorative scheme had variety. Thus, on the inner side of the wall in which the door is pierced, were two oblong panels which, to judge from their shape, contained human forms, but so hopelessly obliterated that no explorer has cared to

[1] *Some Phrygian Monuments*, p. 262, Plates XXVI., XXVII.

commit himself as to their sex (Fig. 81). Over the door, equally ill-determined and obscure, is repeated the subject, which externally occupies the centre of the frontal. The whole apartment was set out for the accommodation of the dead; the end and side walls had each a niche, arched at the top, and troughs were hollowed in the floor of the chamber. No room was found for a late arrival, so that a couch had to be cut within the porch on the left-hand side.

A similar mingling of architectural and ornamental forms may be observed in other hypogeia around this tomb and the flank of the hill, in which the lions reappear.[1] Of the many tombs Professor Ramsay has published, we will content ourselves with

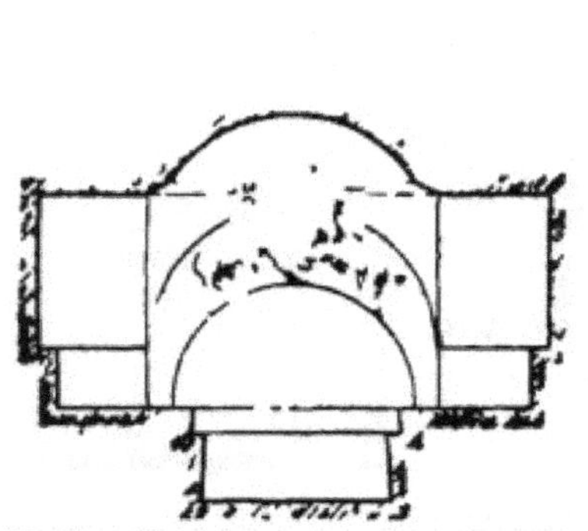

FIG. 80.—Transverse section through line A B. *Journal*, Plate XXVII

FIG. 81.—Transverse section through line G D. *Journal*, Plate XXVII C.

singling out the example whose façade is adorned by two Ionic columns (Fig. 82, 31 in map).

Nor is this the only necropolis wherein works of an art slowly undergoing transformation are met with; instances likewise occur in the northern district, in the neighbourhood of Nacoleia. The most curious specimen of this class is the fine tomb, still in very good preservation, cut at the base of the rocky ridge upon which the village of Kumbet is planted (Fig. 83). It has a great advantage over the tombs of this canton in that it has been studied by an architect,[2] whilst the good condition in which it is found

[1] *Hell. Studies*, Plates XXVII–XXIX.

[2] G. PERROT and GUILLAUME, *Explor. Arché.*, pp. 138, 342, 368. The following figures (Figs. 84–88) are reproduced from drawings made by Guillaume. Sketches of this tomb had been previously published by Stewart, pp. 6, 16, by LABORDE,

Fig 83.—The Kumbet Tomb. General view. From a photograph of J Delbet

renders it an admirable subject for comparison. Then, too, we enjoyed a liberty of action unknown to our predecessors, whose operations had been impeded by the situation of the Agha's kiosk, built right over the monument. His public room stood over the tomb proper, whilst the grave-chamber was turned into a store-room. This particular Agha, said the old men of the place, was

FIG. 82.—Tomb at Ayazeen. *Journal*, Plate XXIX.

one of the last representatives of old-fashioned Derey-Beys, or independent native princes, and noted for his atrocities; suspicious, too, of any European lurking about, pencil in hand, as boding no good to the konak. By stealth only, and whilst this terrible ogre was enjoying his siesta, did De Laborde at last succeed in

Voyage d'Asie Mineure, pp. 78, 79, Plates XXIX., LXIV., LXV., *Barth, Reise*, p. 90. But as these travellers gave no plan or measurement of the memorial, no good or exact idea could be formed of its style.

making a drawing of the tomb. As for its occupant, he was put to death by order of Sultan Mahmoud; and the upper story he had added to it has been empty ever since, and is rapidly falling into decay. Our illustration of this picturesque konak is from a photograph taken at the time of our visit (Fig. 83). Nothing would have been easier than to clear its base of the silt that has gathered around it, but for the fact that we found the village

FIG. 84.—Façade of the Kumbet tomb. Drawn by E. Guillaume. *Explor. Archl.*, Plate VII.

deserted of its inhabitants, who had betaken themselves to their tents during the summer heat, and were camping in the woodlands some two or three leagues away.

Like the Midas rock and the Delikli Tach, the Kumbet tomb is no more than a sepulchral front cut in a rocky mass, the stone surrounding it being left in the rough (Fig. 84). Steps appear on the left side, but whether coeval with the tomb or comparatively recent, it would be difficult to say. Their purpose, whatever it was, could certainly not be to reach the chimney, obtained, as at Delikli Tach, in the vertical plan of the tomb above the grave-chamber. There never existed here an opening of this kind, as everybody may see for himself if he will take the trouble of entering the double grave, pierced right through the rocky mass in which the tomb occurs (Fig. 85). The false bay of the older rock-cut façades has been replaced by a real door, surrounded by double mouldings, which opens in the centre of the frontispiece. Curious discoveries might be ours, had attempts been made to ascertain the possible existence of a substructure, and study the old soil hidden under accumulated earth, which can scarcely be more than fifty centimetres below the present level, proved by longitudinal section (Fig. 86). Right and left of the door, between the jambs and the outer edge of the façade, appears a sculptured figure. On the dexter hand it is the front part of a bull, with a hump on his back, like the bison of America and the Indian zebu; the variety no longer exists in Anterior Asia, but we find it figured on the autonomous coins of this province, on those of Ancyra,[1] Eumenia,[2] Kibyra,[3] as well as in the bas-

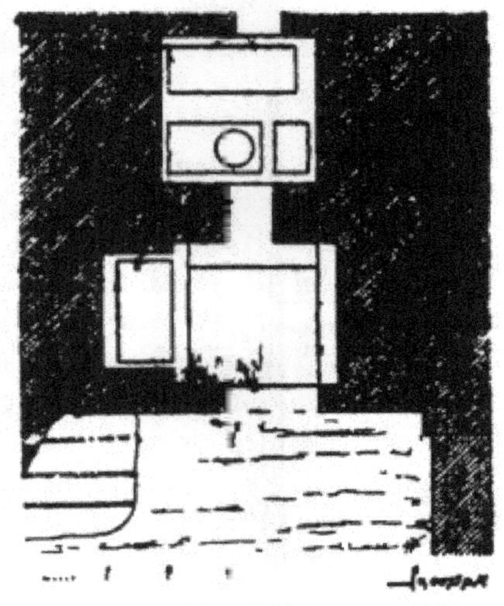

FIG. 85.—Kumbet tomb. Plan. *Explor.*, Plate VII.

FIG. 86.—Kumbet tomb. Longitudinal section. *Explor.*, Plate VII.

[1] MIONNET, *Médailles grecques et romaines*, tom. IV. p. 219.
[2] *Ibid.*, p. 293.
[3] *Ibid.*, p. 28, *Supplément*, tom. VIII. p. 533

reliefs of the theatre of Aizani.[1] On the other side, owing to the depth of the silt, we could descry nothing. The drawings of our predecessors, however, show a Gorgon's head.[2] Over the doorway ran a cornice, now almost obliterated, and over it again was a bas-relief flanked by semi-balusters. The middle of the field is occupied by a double-handled vase of simple, elegant design. Numbers may be seen in our museums, labelled "Italo-Græco," whose contour is precisely similar. A lion and a lioness are seen on either side of the vase; they look at each other, and advance as if to drink out of it. The bas-relief is separated from the frontal by a narrow cornice, upheld by large modules or modillions which reappear under the side beams of the roof; but between each module come out small heads finely carved (Fig. 87). Below them are dentals. The corona of this pediment is allied to the native rock by an elegant foliate scroll, terminating at the angles and at the top in graceful rich palmettes and acanthus-shaped leaves (Fig. 88). Such is the external aspect of the monument. If we pass the rectangular door and enter the chamber, we shall find a single vaulted grave scooped in the left wall. A passage narrower than the entrance gives access to the second chamber, which is somewhat lower than the first, with semi-circular arch. Its arrangement is different: three sarcophagi of unequal size are pierced in the floor, and at the bottom of one opens a circular hole which sinks into the rock. It was filled with earth. To our thinking the work about the walls and troughs is less good than that of the first chamber, and betrays hurry and a modern hand, as if this had been a later addition pieced on to the original

FIG. 87.—Kumbet tomb. Sculptured head in cornice. *Explor.*, Plate VII.

FIG. 88.—Kumbet tomb. Palmette at angle of cornice. *Explor.*, Plate VII.

[1] PHILIPPE LE BAS, *Voyage Arch.*, fol., Plate XIV.

[2] In Stewart's Plate the head is shown with luxuriant hair; two concentric circles are all Bartle has given.

plan. What tends to confirm our hypothesis is the inscription, in large letters, engraved over the doorway by which the second chamber is entered (Fig. 89). It reads as follows :—

ΕΟΛΩΝ ΚΕ ΕΝΘΑ Σόλων κε[ῖ](ται) ἔνθα.[1]

The shape of the characters, as well as the contractions, prove their late origin, and may be dated from the Roman dominion, in the third or second century of our era. Its interest resides in the fact that it testifies to a habit with which numerous instances have made us familiar.

FIG 89.—Kumbet tomb. Inscription *Explor.*, Plate VII.

In the last centuries of antiquity, it often happened that, to save themselves the trouble of hollowing a fresh tomb in the depth of the rock, they took possession of those the men of old had prepared for themselves, when, no doubt, the first to be usurped were the most ancient. The more recent were guarded either by the surviving members of the families who had consecrated them, or, at least, by the stringency of the laws which the Treasury, interested in the matter, had enacted for the purpose. No such obstacles were to be apprehended in the earlier monuments, in which were buried the nameless sons of a forgotten race, whose pinch of ashes had been scattered to the four winds of heaven, and which, moreover, had long since been desecrated and rifled. Thus, under the golden rule of the Antonines, one Solon, a native magnate, found it convenient to appropriate to himself a tomb of a certain repute. Then it was that the second chamber was added, with the inscription giving the name of the owner. As to the opening in the farthest wall of this chamber, we found it choked up by potsherds and stones; so that we failed to make out whether it was coeval with the monument, or whether it had been pierced through the thin rocky wall by the Agha, to enable his servants to enter the vault, used as lumber-room, through the courtyard.

Externally we found no trace of stucco; but in the hollows, notably about the palmettes at the sides, are still patches of vivid red. Internally, a rude gorge, ornamented by vertical stripes of

[1] With regard to the restitution of the above text, see PERROT, *Explor. Arché.*, p. 140.

the same colour (Fig. 89), appears as part of the cornice above the second doorway (Fig. 86, N); a mode of enrichment likewise found in cavettos of similar aspect, both on the monuments of Egypt and the capitals of antæ in the Propylæa at Athens.

As last example of the transition period we will cite another

FIG. 90.—Tomb at Yapuldak. Drawn by Blunt.

tomb at Yapuldak (Fig. 90, 2 in map[1]), the complex decoration of which attracted the attention of MM. Barth and Ramsay. Although ruder in manipulation, this façade resembles the Kumbet example in too many points not to come very near it in date.

[1] Ramsay, whilst sending us his sketch of the Yapuldak tomb (Fig. 90), which we reproduce, warns us against that made by Barth, as quite incorrect. The reader will find a plan, elevation, and sections of this same tomb in *Journal*, x. Figs. 28–33, pp. 182–184. Internally, the head of the Gorgon is repeated in fantastic varieties over the doorway and the three graves or arcosolia. The monument seems to be one of the youngest in the necropolis.

Thus rectangular door, shape and size of pediment, modillions, and dentels in the cornice which form the coping, proneness to adorn the top and angles of the frontal by means of devices which, if less elegant, have none the less the same value, are identical in both, even to the shield in the middle of the tympan. Differences are shown in the two columns, in touch with the wall, on either side of the doorway which uphold the entablature; the pilasters at the outer edge of the façade, and the rudimentary capitals upon which are put dissimilar objects. Of these, that to the right seems to be a vase, or funereal urn, instances of which are plentiful in these hypogeia. Bandelets and necklaces intervene between column and pilaster, whilst a foliate scroll above the lintel graces the doorway. The ornament throughout is very much injured, and the general aspect is further marred by rectangular niches pierced in the façade, but for what purpose it would be hard to guess. With the advent of Christianity the tomb must have served as chapel or domestic dwelling.

As years rolled by, Hellenic art crept in and became dominant in Phrygia and the peninsula generally, and replaced all that had gone before. About the centre of the [illegible] necropolis which surrounds the Midas monument, a tomb is descried, which, like one of the exemplars in Pteria, goes by the name of Gherdek Kaiasi (the Rock of Marriage) (Fig. 91, 3 in map).[1] The architecture of the façade is clearly Hellenic Doric, with all the elements characteristic of the order. If the columns are smooth, it is because the fluting, which is easily obtained when the shaft is made up of several pieces, cut and prepared in the stone-yard, would have offered real difficulties; and required a whole system of scaffolding, with a support of great size taken from the actual mass of the rock. Hence, reverse curves, or

[1] *Hist. of Art*, tom. iv. Fig. 345. The monument is a double chamber, which the peasantry imagine contains husband and wife, whence its name "Gherdek Kaiasi" (the Rock of Marriage). It has been published by Stewart, Plate XII., and by TEXIER, *Description*, Plates L[illegible] LXI. But the elevation of the latter, he informs us in the text, is a restoration (tom. i. pp. 158–162). Part of one column alone remains in position hanging from the architrave. M. Ramsay writes that the Doric façade, our Fig. 91, after Texier, is inexact. I suspected as much. On the other hand, it is to be regretted that he has not thought fit to supply a better one himself. As far as he can recollect, he says, the monument has a more massive character, the pillars are stouter than Texier represents them. I must demur against the words put in my mouth, that "in style it was Roman Doric;" what I did say was that "it recalled the attenuated proportions of Roman Doric."

flutings, are, as a rule, non-existent in the rock-cut façades.[1] With this exception, the frontispiece of this tomb is that of a Greek temple; but it is neither the temples of Pæstum, the

FIG. 91.—Gherdek Kaiasi. Restored façade. TEXIER, *Description*, Plate LX.

Parthenon, nor the Propylæa of the Athenian acropolis, which are thus recalled, but rather the slender proportions, the wide

[1] For the Doric order, this is exemplified in the tombs at Paphos (*Hist. of Art*, tom. III. Fig. 161), and in the Jewish tomb which goes by the name of St. James, at Jerusalem (*Ibid.*, tom. iv. Figs. 143, 144); for the Ionic order, in the so-called tomb of Absalom (*Ibid.*, Figs. 141, 142). We can do no more in this place beyond referring the reader to the monuments, illustrative of the two orders, which have been published in our former volumes.

intercolumnation of Roman Doric, well exemplified in the temple of Heracles at Cori. The monument cannot be carried back beyond the Seleucidæ; it may even date from the days when Phrygia formed part of the kingdom of Pergamos, or of the Roman empire.

We find greater difficulty in fixing the dates of those monuments in which the true arch is seen side by side with the triangular pediment; inasmuch as there are elements about them which persisted down to the opening years of our era in well-known tombs of Caria and Syria. Nevertheless, sundry indications lead to the inference that our Phrygian tombs belong to an older epoch, and are the outcome of a local art which, though in a certain degree open to Greek influence, was by no means slavish, and still clung to the methods of former ages. Of these signs we will single out the most noteworthy.

In many of these monuments, chevrons form the ornament of the archivault which appears over the doorway, a device never used by the Greeks in that situation. Such would be a tomb in the Ayazeen necropolis (30 in map), whose façade displays, moreover, a pair of lions carved over the entrance, and a shield in the tympan (Fig. 92).[1] This chevron device brings to mind, though in an abridged form, the crenellations the Assyrian artist distributed about his fortresses.[2] It likewise occurs in Cappadocia, as robe-ornament of the deity who occupies the centre of an ædiculum carved in the Pterian sanctuary.[3] Then, too, as a rule in our monuments, frontals are taller and more pointed than in Greek buildings. Their mode of attachment is clumsy; for they are not the prolongation nor the development of the entablature, upon which they rest as a hat would, without being an integral part of it. The profiles of the moulding are very simple, and resemble archaic Greek make rather than the soft, undulating outlines of Græco-Roman structures, found in plenty throughout the southern districts of the peninsula. Thus in the tomb which, beyond all others of this series, has been most minutely described, we find as terminal moulding at the sides of the frontal, a deeply inclined but rude form, with none of the characteristics of a Greek

[1] M. Ramsay has handed to me a drawing of another rock-cut façade, in which chevrons likewise encircle the arch.

[2] PLACE, *Ninive et l'Assyrie*, Plate XL.; *Hist. of Art*, tom. ii. Figs. 76, 155, 156, 190.

[3] *Hist. of Art*, tom. iv. Fig. 314.

cyma; whilst the entablature of all these frontispieces sins against canonical proportions.

But we find its counterpart, or nearly so, at Persepolis, where, as

FIG 92.—Tomb at Ayazeen. *Journal Hell. Studies*, 1882, Plate XXVIII.

in Phrygia, the architraved cornice is never seen without a row of dentels under the corona of the frontal. The same remark applies to the rock-cut columns, every one of which has points in common with one or other of the types which constitute classical architecture, but so divergent in many respects as to preclude being classed in a distinct order. In one of these tombs (Fig. 92) the capital

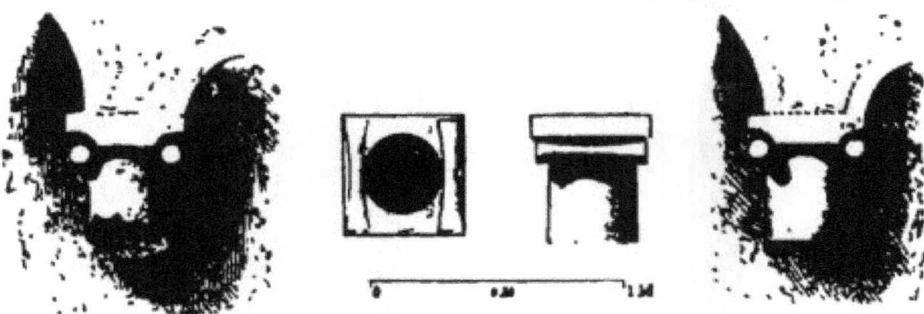

FIG. 93.—Ionic capital. Present state. Perspective view. *Journal*, 1882, Plate XXIX.

FIG. 94.—Ionic capital. Plan. *Journal*, Plate XXIX.

FIG. 95.—Ionic capital. Lateral elevation. *Journal*, Plate XXIX.

FIG. 96.—Ionic capital. Elevation. *Journal*, Plate XXIX.

is composed of two members, which play the part of the echinus and abacus in the Doric capital. The result of this is that it somewhat resembles the latter; the contour, however, is different, and the somewhat slender column rests upon a base. In another tomb (Fig. 82), the capital is formed of two thin rolls, with so deep an inward curve as to be separated from the abacus found at the springing of the arch (Fig. 93). The interest which attaches to this capital, both in plan (Fig. 94), side view (Fig. 95), and elevation (Fig. 96) is our reason for reproducing it. In principle the motive is the same as in the Ionic capital; but how wide the difference between the dryness of these cushions and the elegance and amplitude of the volute! Again, we are reminded of the Corinthian capital (Fig. 97) in the calathiform of Fig. 77,[1] with its ring of leaves under the lower part; save that

FIG. 97.—Calathiform capital and profile of shaft and entablature. *Journal*, Plate XXIX.

[1] Some kind of likeness exists between this Phrygian capital and that of a tomb near Mylassa, in Caria, which Téxier was inclined to date from the Roman dominion (*Asie Mineure*, 8vo, p. 648, Plate XXVII.). There is no doubt about the forms enfolding the Carian capital being acanthus leaves, whilst the influence they betray

the latter are sketchy, without salience, and barely outlined. They are more developed and their characteristics are better brought out in the pilaster of the Broken Tomb, in which a colossal lion appears (Figs. 98, 99). Here also the base of the column is not unlike the Ionic, whilst the terminal palmette is akin to that which expands above the volute of certain stelas figured on Greek vases.[1]

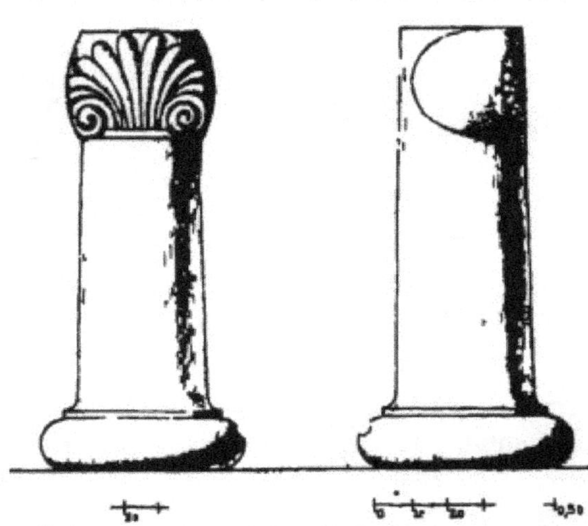

FIG. 98.—Elevation and profile of pilaster in Broken Tomb Drawn by Ramsay.

On the other hand, the palmette in question bears just as much analogy to that which crowns a stela discovered in Assyria, at Khorsabad, by M. Place.[2]

How great the embarrassment of the scholar who enters upon the study of Phrygian architecture, will be easily understood. Thus, many a detail looks as the dawn and harbinger of Greece; many another is only to be explained by the light and traditions of Asianic culture, and one pauses before not a few to which either origin might be assigned at will. The characteristic touch which more

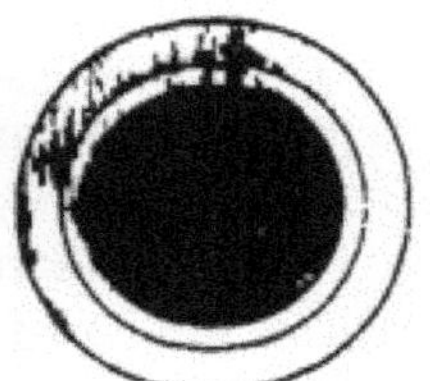

FIG 99.—Pilaster of Broken Tomb Plan above base. Plan at the commencement of capital. Drawn by Ramsay.

to Greek models is no less certain. The blocking out, however, before the ornament was proceeded with, must have offered a mass very similar to that of the Phrygian capital. The basket-shape was in full swing during the rock-cut stage of architecture, and no doubt continued in the habits of the native artisan, even when he had learnt how to dress stone and fashion the capitals and shafts of his columns out of the same material.

[1] CHARLES CHIPIEZ, *Hist. critique des origines de la formation des ordres grecs*, p. 273, Fig. 130.

[2] *Hist. of Art*, tom. ii. p. 270, Fig. 110

than any other betrays the relationship these monuments bear to those of Cappadocia, and through these to the art of Assyria and Chaldæa, is the feeble salience of the sculptures seen on these façades. The geometrical, vegetable, animal, and human shapes which adorn the doorways, tympans, and frontals of these frontispieces, with rare exceptions, are chiselled in flat relief and all the living forms drawn in profile. The processes by which they were obtained are precisely similar to those of the figured decorations encountered beyond the Halys, the Taurus range, and the valley of the Amanus, works which we ranged under the denomination of Hittite monuments.

Among all these façades, that in which the highest and boldest relief was attained by the Phrygian sculptor is the Kumbet tomb (Fig. 84). The heads of the lions and the vase stand out from the field with a relief of thirteen centimetres and seven centimetres respectively. This furnishes us with a first token that the monument is younger than many others in these necropoles; its outward appearance, however, is not as thoroughly Greek as Gherdek Kaiasi, for instance; it still belongs to the transition period, and must be ascribed to native art. The themes treated by the sculptor are those selected in preference by the Syro-Cappadocian ornamentist. Such would be eagles and lions figured in pairs face to face, a phallus, a tree, vase, or candelabrum interposing between them, and likewise encountered on many a point of Phrygia. This same subject (animals in pairs) appears on the cylinders and sculptures of Mesopotamia, as also in Cappadocia; whilst Phrygian tombs are witnesses to the special favour it enjoyed with the indigenous artificers, whether on the threshold or above the entrance to their hypogees. But if the data are very primitive and archaic, the technique denotes a more advanced stage and a later date. Compare the Kumbet lions with the Kalaba example[1]—also due perhaps to Phrygian activity—and those of Figs. 64, 65, met with in the necropolis under consideration, and you will perceive at a glance the wide-reaching distance which divides them.

When the artist set about chiselling the Kumbet animals in the rocky mass, he had freed himself from the conventionalism resorted to by his predecessors for indicating the hair, the muscles of the fore-leg and the shoulders. This is very visible in the model-

[1] *Hist. of Art*, tom. IV. p. 713, Fig. 350.

ling, at once bolder, rounder, and smoother; but its commonplace facility does not compensate for the loss the work has sustained in dignity and vigour. As was observed a few pages back, the shape of the double-handled vase, which occupies the centre of the field, is both simple and elegant, and its contour may be seen in countless Italo-Greek specimens deposited in our museums. Hellenic influence is, perhaps, even more apparent in the architectural domain. False openings, as at Delikli Tach, with cumbrous jambs in retreat one upon the other, and no less massive lintels, have disappeared; in their stead are real doors, with frames less refined, but which none the less recall those of Hellenic portals. True, this likewise occurs in the Ayazeen necropolis; but the bay of these façades (Figs. 64–67) tends to narrow above and widen below, and by inference this is at least a sign, a presumption, of relative antiquity. The fact that the jambs at Kumbet are straight leads one to believe that the models from which Phrygian art drew its inspirations had stepped beyond the archaic period. The same impression is left by observation of the entablature. Not only is it quite distinct from that of the oldest façades—those bearing Phrygian inscriptions—it is also more complex, and shows greater skill and technique in its elaboration, than in those tombs wherein trapezoidal doors obtain. Over the entablature in question was a real cornice, the deep salience of which is cause of its almost complete destruction, making it a matter of conjecture as to the nature of the profile and the moulding composing it. Had it been preserved we should, in all likelihood, find in it all the essentials of a Greek cornice, with something of the light and shade which are never absent from Hellenic compositions. What confirms our conjecture is the arrangement of the sides of the pediment. They consist of members largely introduced in classical architecture, and appear in the same situation, the same order, and almost the same proportions. Thus dentels and modillions are figured under and above the corona respectively. Over it again stands out a cyma, and terminal palmettes, corresponding to the antefixes of Greek frontals, unfold at the angles and the apex of the pediment. In Greek taste, too, averse to monotony, are those small heads between modillions, sculptured on the soffits, which appear to have yielded great variety of types.

Despite these and other resemblances, the Kumbet tomb is not yet a thorough-going Hellenic work; the proportions of its façade are not those which would have commended themselves to an Ionian architect called in from Phocæa or Ephesus. The modillions have a breadth, shape, and relief unknown to Greek modules, and the angle of the pediment is more acute than in classic buildings. There are no columns; the very peculiar cornice belongs to no distinct order, and in some respects it still recalls a primitive wooden construction.

The inference to be deduced from analysis and comparison alike is that the monuments we have just passed in review form a continuous series, without break or discrepancy. We are led by almost imperceptible stages from those of unquestionable hoary antiquity on to exemplars which testify to the inroads Grecian art was making in the inland districts of the peninsula, foreshadowing its final and complete victory. Hence, it behoves us to guard against a conjecture, apt to arise in the mind of the archæologist by superficial and hasty inspection of the façades under consideration. Many a tomb of Caria, Pamphylia, and Lycia displays forms which at first startle the student by their seeming strangeness, but when dissected and examined in detail, they turn out to be nothing more than Greek shapes, the poor or clumsy style of which is due to imperfect technique, local habits, or corrupted taste. Thus, about this and that structure one had been inclined to think very old there crops up a characteristic feature, a dated inscription which discloses the fact of its being the work of the decadence, of the second or third century A.D.

In like manner, there is danger of antedating, doubts are felt, in regard to a number of monuments of the Ayazeen necropolis. Similar doubts we think we have forestalled. Here, in this district where the old Phrygian kingdom had its political and religious centre, all the monuments explorers have disinterred or reported are certainly the fruit of a primitive national art. The difference between them resides in the fact that some travel back to the age when this art created types and adopted processes of its own, whilst others belong to the period when, unwillingly and whilst disputing the ground step by step, it began to yield to the greater charms continental Greece was offering to her neighbours. The monuments embraced within the period which has the Midas rock at one end and the Kumbet tomb at the other, the older as the more recent, are all prior to the triumph of Hellenic genius—a triumph which, prepared by the conquests of

Alexander, took a long time in gaining a foothold in the more distant provinces of Asia Minor, and was finally completed by the proconsols, prætors, and procurators of Rome, when the whole country, swampy steppes and hilly range, was intersected by military routes. In taking up, then, monuments so very much later than the fall and consequent loss of independence of the Phrygian kingdom, we have not outstepped the limits within which must be confined this part of our History of Art. Study of the little that remains of their fortresses and sanctuaries will bring out with even greater force and vividness the truly archaic and original character of the civilization under notice.

RELIGIOUS ARCHITECTURE.

Neither in Phrygia nor Cappadocia are found traces of temples constructed with a view of placing in them the image of the deity. But as in Pterium, here also, sanctuaries and fortresses, steps leading to them, sacrificial altars, along with the divine simulacrum, to which was addressed the homage of the multitude, seem to have been wholly rock-cut.

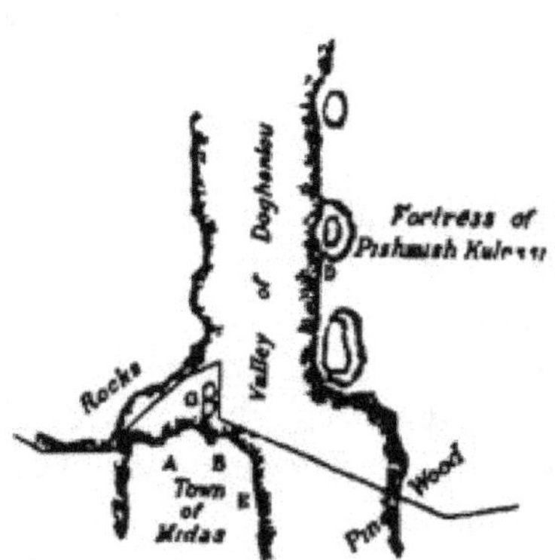

FIG. 100.—Valley of Doghanlou and town of Midas. *Explor. Arch.*, "Itinéraires," Feuille C.[1]

The more important of these sanctuaries are open to the sky: but it seems not improbable that temples, or, to be accurate, subterraneous chapels, also obtained.

There is reason, we think, to recognize as places of worship a certain class of monuments which at the outset were supposed to be tombs, but in which dispositions appear ill in accord with the hypothesis of a sepulchral function.

Thus southward of the ravine locally called Doghanlou Deresi (the Hawk Valley) shoot up broad masses of rock bounded by a perpendicular cliff, in the depth of which monumental façades, akin to that bearing the name of Midas, have been cut (Fig. 100).

[1] Legend of map: A, tomb figured by Texier, Plate LVIII.; B, Midas monument; C, masses of rock honeycombed with graves; D, tomb (Fig. 72); L, other tombs (Fig. 123).

The stony mass terminates in an oblong plateau dipping southward, where may be traced surfaces levelled out with care, stairways, altars, a variety of symbols, inscriptions, rock-cut walls, perhaps the back walls of houses leaning against the cliff.[1] The esplanade was formerly surrounded by a built wall, the blocks of which have almost all disappeared; but the marks left in the tufa by the lower units may still be traced. This fortified level is what M. Ramsay has called the "Midas town." It was reached by a path, like-

FIG 101 —Rock cut altar and bas-relief. *Journal*, Plate XXI

wise rock-cut, which took its start about two hundred metres south of the Midas rock, and ascended in a gentle curve from the valley, having on the right a vertical wall of rock, on which a series of eight figures in flat relief have been carved, as if to represent a procession descending from the heights towards the valley

[1] I and M. Guillaume did not visit this plateau, hence our map (Fig. 100) contains but a general outline of the northern portion of the cliff The account which follows is borrowed from M. Ramsay, to whom redounds the honour of having discovered this group of monuments (*Hellenic Studies*, vol. III pp. 6–17, and 41–44, under the title: "Studies in Asia Minor"). But he made no plan of the unit, and did not attempt to give a methodical and complete description of it. His information respecting it has to be gleaned and sought out in various papers.

below. Each and all are very much worn, and the drawings by which they are known are not sufficiently minute or exact to allow us to define their style.[1] Until further details are to hand, therefore, they cannot be considered as works executed by the subjects of the Gordioses and Midases. Some thirty yards beyond, just before reaching the summit, the road widens, and there appears straight before you a sculpture representing a personage clad in a short tunic, and grasping a kind of sceptre in his left hand, and hard by a huge two-stepped altar cut in the living rock (Fig. 101, 10 in map). The high antiquity of the figure is unquestionable; in front of it we recognized signs of the Hittite writing; and this obliged us, so to speak, to class the bas-relief in the series of monuments of Syro-Cappadocian art.[2] In so doing there was no intention on our part to detach it from the group to which it by rights belongs; our aim was simply to make the sequence of figures associated with ideographic characters as complete as possible. This system of ideographs preceded in Asia Minor the introduction of alphabets derived from the Phœnician syllabary. Both altar and bas-relief were fashioned by the same hand. The latter represented one of the tutelary gods, under whose protection the small Phrygian city was placed. Close at hand was a stone table or shelf, upon which offerings were laid. The place constituted what may be termed the temple-gate,

FIG 101.—Rock-cut altar.

[1] RAMSAY, *Hell Studies*, "Studies in Asia Minor," Figs. 1, 2.

[2] *Hist of Art*, tom. IV. pp. 721, 722, Fig. 363.

where preliminary devotions were performed ere the precincts were entered.[1]

Traces of high places, sanctuaries open to the sky, abound on the plateau and several points of this district; of which half a dozen or so, borrowed from M. Ramsay, are reproduced here. A ledge and a niche occur above the altar of the first of these (Fig. 102), the latter was meant, perhaps, to receive a lamp or a statuette, and might be taken for the altar of a Roman Catholic chapel. *Per contra*, the terminal form of the altars (Figs. 103[2]–105) is

FIG 103.—Rock cut altar

FIG 104.—Rock cut altar.

[1] M. Ramsay at first mistook the sinking which may be seen behind the altar for a mortuary bed. But on a subsequent visit he discovered that what he had taken for a funereal trough was in reality a grave made to receive the stones of the lower course (*Hell. Studies*, p. 12).

[2] The bœtulus and the lower steps of this altar are broken away

a kind of milestone rounded at the top, seemingly of the nature of a bœtulus, sacred stone. That which justifies us in attributing a holy character to the stone in question is the fact that it reappears in another monument situated in the centre of this plateau (Fig. 106, 11 in map), whose rude ornamentation allows us to guess its true import; this appears in the shape of two concentric circles or discs carved side by side on the

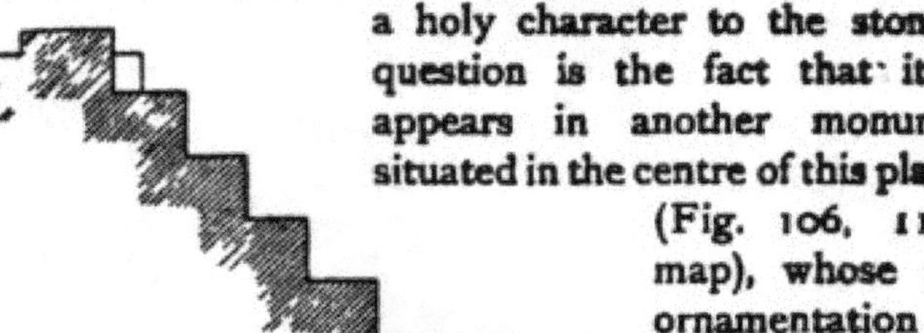

FIG. 105.—Rock-cut altar. Section through altar.

FIG. 106.—Rock cut altar. From drawing and photograph of Ramsay.

stela. The curved lines enframing them, which terminate on each side in a curl, bring to mind the head-dress of the Egyptian Hathor,[1] an arrangement we observed in Asia Minor in the

[1] *Hist. of Art*, tom. i. Figs. 40, 342, 343.

monuments of Hittite art, both about the sphinxes at Eyuk,[1] and the colossal figures of the façade at Eflatoun.[2] Curve and ringlet, turned outwardly at the end, are identical in all.

Finally, to complete the series, we will cite a last monument, a shrine found on the rim of the plateau, right over the path which leads to it. The surface of the stela is dressed with care, but void of ornament. On the other hand, close by, on another part of the rock, is a figure which, despite its diminutive size and roughness of make, at once reminded M. Ramsay of the

FIG. 107.—Figure of Cybele. *Journal*, 1882, Plate XLII.

colossal Cybele on Sipylus (Fig. 107, 11 in map). Seen full face, the pose is that of a sitting figure, for the knees stand out 10 c. from the body. The right hand has disappeared, but in the left is carried a shallow bowl (*phiale*), the one attribute most sedulously preserved in Grecian art to the Asiatic goddess. That this picture was intended as a representation of Cybele is confirmed by the inscription MATAP KTBIAE, to be read over a pedestal of the same nature in the necropolis of Ayazeen (18 in map). In this figure, which we recognize as Cybele, the features, as on the stela just described, are not indicated, and the head is a mere round ball. This same conventional treatment of the divine

[1] *Hist. of Art*, tom. iv. Figs. 323, 327.

[2] *Ibid.*, tom. iv. p. 737.

simulacrum was repeated on the sacred stone, where, the better to emphasize the meaning, the hair was added.

The Phœnicians now and again made use of this very same abridged process for those stelas which Carthage manufactured in prodigious numbers; where Tanith is figured, now standing, now reduced to a mere bust, whilst at other times the divine representation is reduced to a head wreathed in plaits of hair arranged as those of our Cybele.[1] The whole difference consists in this, that whilst the superior skill of the Phœnician sculptor enabled him to chalk in with a few strokes nose, eyes, chin, etc., his Phrygian colleague suppressed every detail and carried simplification to its utmost limits.

Are the two heads (Fig. 106) figured on the stela emblematic of the worship rendered here to twin paredre deities, or is the repetition intended to convey the notion of the power of one and the same divine personage? The answer to this query might perchance be had, could the Phrygian inscription of two lines incised on the wall dominating the sacred stone be read.[2] No translation of the text, however, has yet been made, and, moreover, it seems pretty certain that we possess but the half, and that other two lines were protracted on the right-hand side of the stela. But all this part of the monument has been detached by an earthquake or the action of the weather. One side being intact, it would be an easy matter to restore the other. In its original state the monument, though simple, was not void of a certain degree of dignity.

In some respects these hypæthral shrines recall the high places of Syria and Palestine;[3] they differ from them in that neither stone altar nor bœtulus were left in the rough, but have been fashioned by metal implements. The Phrygians do not seem to have been imbued with the notion that contact with forged iron would pollute the stone and rob it of its sacred character. Hence they freely used pick and chisel to excavate small temples, akin to the Egyptian speos, close by these open places of worship. It is a sanctuary

[1] *Hist. of Art*, tom. iii. Fig. 16.

[2] Consult RAMSAY, *On the Early Historical Relations*, Plate I. n. 6, p. 33.

[3] *Hist. of Art*, tom. iv. pp. 371, 372, 375–385.

We are all familiar with the following passages:—"So Moses commanded the children of Israel to build an altar of whole stones, over which no man hath lifted up an iron." Again: "Thou shalt not lift up any iron tool upon them," *e.g.* stones to build an altar.—TRS.

Fig. 108.—Arslan Kaia. General view. *Journal of Hellenic Studies*, 1884, Plate XLIV.

of this kind that we propose to recognize in a monument which, at first sight, the traveller who discovered it placed among funereal hypogeia.

This monument—unfortunately much injured—is hard by the village of Liyen (Fig. 108, 13 in map) and goes by the name of Arslan Kaia (the Lion Rock). The physical formation here is a stratified tufa of varying degrees of hardness; some layers are quite soft, and the sculpture is not protected against the weather by overhanging rocks. Arslan Kaia is cut in the face of a tall isolated rock, of sugar-loaf shape, which rises to the height of some twenty metres on a steep grassy slope.[1]

The rocky mass has been chiselled on three sides, so as to present three vertical faces, looking respectively east, south, and west. The southern side is the most important. It forms a rectangular surface, in the lower part of which the door is pierced, topped by a pediment crowned by a curvilinear device, analogous to that of the Midas monument. Here, however, it seems to terminate in two serpents' heads. The inner slab was formerly covered with geometric shapes, of the nature of those so well preserved at Iasili Kaia—meanders and crosses, but so defaced that an occasional fragment is all that can be made out; so that no attempt has been made to indicate them in the annexed woodcut (Fig. 109). There is also a Phrygian inscription along the horizontal fascia that divides the triangular pediment from the rectangle or inner slab, but so hopelessly obliterated that it could not be transcribed with any hope of success, even when brought close to it by a ladder.[2] The decoration of the frontal, thanks to the salience of its sloping beams, is in a better state of preservation. It is composed of two winged sphinxes, passant and face to face, but separated by the supporting column. They are seen in profile, their heads turned towards the spectator, the ears large and prominent, but the features are worn quite flat. A long curl hangs down over the shoulder of each. A band of meander pattern runs along the two sloping sides of the pediment. The whole is carved in very low relief.

[1] Our views of the monument have been obtained from M. Ramsay's sketches, which, he observes, "were confined to the wrought part of the stone, and that the draughtsman made them too high, causing the rock to look taller than reality" (*Journal*, Plate XLIV.; *ibid.*, 1884, p. 241).

[2] *Ibid.*, p. 243, n. 2.

The eastern face of the monument is entirely taken up by a huge rampant lion. He stands on his hind legs, and his fore paws rest on the angle of the pediment; the head, almost disappeared, towered high above it. The lower part of the figure is in better condition. It would be natural to find his pendant on the other side, and no little surprise is felt in meeting in his stead a diminutive figure of different type and movement. It is a passant griffin, much injured, whose head faces eastward, and probably

FIG 109.—Arslan Kaia Western side *Journal*, Plate XLIV

ended in an eagle's beak like those of Assyria, which may have served as models (Fig. 109). Griffins and sphinxes alike have the tips of their wings outwardly curved in the form of a round knot.

Our journey round the monument has brought us back to the main face in which the door is pierced; the disposition of this recalls the simulated openings at Delikli Tach and Iasilį Kaia. In the present case, however, we are confronted by a real bay; one, too, intended to be always open. The two wings of the door are figured in relief against the sides of the little chamber into which the door gives admittance. On each valve of the door, near the top, is a row of nails which served to fix a bronze lining. On the right wing is a defaced ornament, which may be a lock, or possibly a knocker. The door gives access to a little rectangular chamber, whose end wall is taken up by a very curious sculpture (Fig. 110). It represents two lionesses who stand on their hind legs, face to face, and rest their fore-paws against the head of a central figure, in which, despite its dilapidated state, we recognize a woman wrapped in long drapery, with a tall ovoid tiara upon her head. This woman can only be a goddess, and that goddess Cybele, the great local deity, whom lionesses she has tamed surround in playful attitude, and in whose company she travelled round the ancient world. The image was carved in relief fully a foot high, but the soft volcanic tufa was unsuited for a relief standing out so boldly, and the front part has fallen off, leaving only an uneven surface with the outline of the figure. The movement of the arms, however, can be made out from the difference of the angles at the elbows. The right hand, it would seem, was placed over the bosom, and the left hand over the middle—an attitude rendered familiar to us from scores of simulacra of Asiatic goddesses.[1]

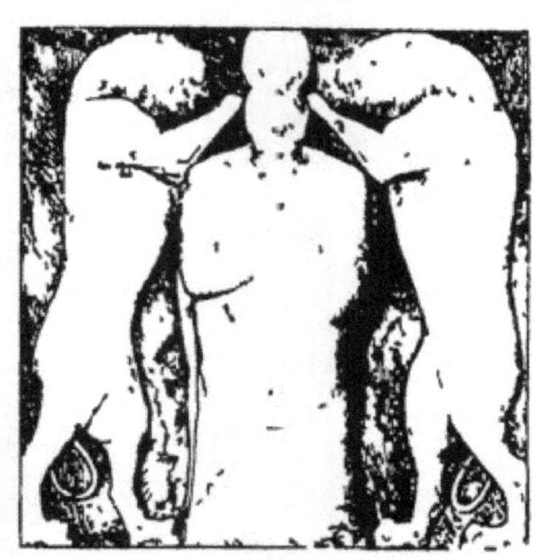

FIG. 110.—Arslan Kaia. Sculpture on the end wall of chamber. *Journal*, 1884, p. 285.

Had the stone in this district been more compact, we should, doubtless, find many another instance of this type. Thus, near the fine tomb already described (Fig. 64) a similar idol, albeit even more defaced, ruder and smaller than this, stands in a little niche three metres high (Fig. 111).[2]

It will be understood, therefore, that if we left out from among the number of tombs the hypogeum of Arslan Kaia, it was because nothing about it betrays a funereal purpose. Every sepulture, in

[1] *Hist. of Art*, tom. iii. Figs. 381, 382.
[2] RAMSAY, *Hellenic Studies*, vol. v. p. 245

view of the function it is called upon to fulfil, must be closed. We have seen what precautions were taken in the oldest Phrygian sepultures to ensure the repose of the dead. The grave-chamber was made inaccessible save by a shaft, which, being on the summit of a lofty rocky mass, could be easily concealed under a clod of earth or brushwood. In all those instances where the tomb was entered by a real door, we mostly find the grooves in which fitted the covering slab. Here, however, not only is there not the slightest trace of closing, but the wings of the door are actually figured thrown back against the wall: a disposition which, if ill suited to a sepulchre, is quite appropriate to a sanctuary. If we pass through the bay, which seems to have been invitingly left open, so as to attract the wayfarer to penetrate into the chamber, we shall find in it neither troughs, niches, nor couches scooped in the floor or let into the walls; but facing us is an image whose religious character is unquestionable. Will it be urged that the goddess whom we see carved on the wall appears here as patroness of the dead and guardian of his eternal repose? But naught like it is met with in those chambers that leave no doubt as to their funereal purpose. Moreover, there are no data, figured or literary, to induce the belief that Cybele ever filled the office of sovereign of the nether world, custodian of the departed.

FIG 111.—Niche, with figure of Cybele After Ramsay

From all appearance, therefore, the Arslan Kaia chamber is akin to those subterraneous sanctuaries we have studied in Egypt,[1] Phœnicia,[2] and Arabia,[3] as well as those we shall find in

[1] *Hist. of Art*, tom. i. pp. 408, 409–427, Figs. 234–249.
[2] *Ibid*, tom. iii. pp. 258-261, Fig. 197.
[3] *Ibid.*, tom. iv. p. 389, Fig. 204.

Greece, where, as a rule, they were dedicated to Pan and the nymphs. We should also be inclined to consider the smaller artificial grotto contiguous to the Midas tomb (Fig. 48) in the light of a chapel, or shrine, in which traditional rites were performed in honour of the ancestral god, to whose memory was consecrated the imposing façade bearing his name and titles. Indeed, the whole district we have just gone through is brimful of similar rock-cuttings, which like dark patches dot the face of the rock along the roadside. Here offerings were deposited, according to the locality, either to ancestral gods, manes, or national deities. The Phrygian workman was not content with chiselling the image of his gods in the solid rock, cutting altars, excavating sanctuaries and grave-chambers in which the bodies were laid; he likewise provided places of refuge for the rural population who, along with their live stock, lived in straggling homesteads in the clear portions of the forest. Fastnesses were needed, and everywhere the relief of the soil offered capital defensive positions. The more gentle slopes were turned into perpendicular walls, and rendered inaccessible by engineering; stairways, parapets, fortified posts, everything was obtained from the stony mass, which, with the stone-cutter, became as soft as clay in the potter's hand.

MILITARY ARCHITECTURE.

There are numerous hillocks in this district to which the natives give the name of Kaleh (fortress). In fact, on the sites thus denominated rise Gheugheuz Kaleh, Doghanlou Kaleh (in map), Tshukurja Kaleh (14 in map), Aktshe Kaleh, and many more; each and all exhibiting traces of the hand of man, and of his having been stationed here.[1] Of these (the castle of Pishmish Kaleh, Burnt Fortress) may be taken as type of the class (Fig. 100).[2] It occupies the summit of a rectangular mass, terminating in a kind of table upheld by almost perpendicular rocks (Fig. 112). The lower belt of the hill is covered with vegetation, but above it the sides are so rugged and precipitous as to require a long détour to reach the top. At first, the rock, with its grades almost up to the summit,

[1] Aktshe Kaleh (Silver Fortress) is not marked on Ramsay's map. From my notes, it should be to the northward of Pishmish Kaleh, a little way beyond it.

[2] PERROT and GUILLAUME, *Explor.*, pp. 145, 169, 170.

looks like a Byzantine castle;[1] and as you ascend the winding path there appears a chasm in the hillside, bridged over with characterless materials—baked bricks, squared stones, chips of all sizes and shapes, fixed in beds of mortar. But the aspect of man's work completely changes as you reach the other side, more particularly the plateau. This had been levelled out, save towards the centre, where the rugosity of the tufa is so slight as to render it unnecessary. On this short and narrow plateau chambers and cisterns were hollowed, loop-holes pierced in the living rock (Fig. 113). When they set about levelling out the area, upon which

FIG 112 Pishmish Kaleh View of hill Drawn by E GUILLAUME, *Explor Arché*, Plate VIII

they intended to place a garrison, the rock was cut in such a way as to leave along the outer edge a kind of wall or parapet, which, measured from the area, averages from 1 m. 25 c. to 7 and 8 m. on the south and north faces respectively. In the latter was the main entrance, if the name may be given to a gap left in the wall between two huge blocks, broken away at the base, but joining at the top (Fig. 114).[1] Towards the north-east angle rises a wall built of large units put together without cement. The rampart was thick enough to be used by soldiers on their round. Flights of steps, still in good condition on many a point, and seen in our illustration, led to the platform, whence the garrison could roll down stones and pour missiles on the enemy, whether they tried to get

[1] The view is taken from point H.

over the glacis, or force their way in through the gate from the winding path. The gateway faced north, and was covered by an outer work on a lower level, a few yards in front. It formed a round tower (1 in plan), having in its rear a sentry-box, likewise

FIG. 113 — Pishmish Kaleh. Plan. *Explor. Arch.*, Plate VIII.

rock-hewn, in which soldiers on guard were posted. Built walls only occur where the rock was not thick or salient enough to allow of a rampart being reserved in the mass, as for instance at the south-east angle. Here the lower courses of the artificial wall consist of large blocks almost everywhere regularly fixed, but with irregular joints—a style of masonry which recalls that of the

Acropolis on the southern declivity of Sipylus, near Smyrna (Figs. 12, 13).

Besides the principal gateway, G, there was another entrance, or rather another means of egress, towards the north-east angle of the plateau. Here a flight of twenty-four steps, cut in the depth of the cliff, extend down to the base of rocks bearing the fortress. Two-thirds of the stairway are open to the sky; the rest is hidden under the vaulted roof and the stones which have fallen from above (A in plan). At the point where the steps break off[1] (M in plan), there appears a sort of housing, with a groove on either side, six centimetres wide; which, to judge from a small hole in the roof and the upper floor, must have served to work pulleys, by means of which a portcullis could be let down or hoisted up at will. The underground passage, which from the bottom of the stairway led outside, has the appearance of a natural cavity; its existence may have suggested the idea of scooping out the steps. It brings to mind the grotto of Aglaurus, at the foot of the Athenian Acropolis, due to a similar slit in the rock, through which the citadel could be entered.[2] As is well known, its discovery by a soldier of Xerxes led to its surrender.

To return: the defenders, when sorely pressed, could escape unperceived in the gloom of night by this secret passage, or suddenly fall upon the besiegers. In doing so, however, they ran the risk of the enemy taking possession of the entrance, either by force or through a traitor, and thus have their retreat cut off. Within the citadel they had only to lower the bridge to be safe against surprise.[3]

The stairway in the northern face (G in plan) is neither so well preserved, nor does it disappear in the bowels of the earth; its purpose was simply to bring the threshold of the gateway up to the level of the platform. On the opposite side, towards the south-east angle (L in plan), two internal spurs have been reserved in the stony mass. They are cleanly cut, each with a pair of vertical

[1] Width of stairway above, 1 m. 55 c.; width below, 1 m. 30 c.; height from the lowermost step to the fortress level, 7 m. 20 c. This leaves a mean altitude of 30 c. for each step.

[2] E. BEULÉ, *L'Acropole d'Athènes*, tom. i. pp. 27, 157.

[3] With regard to secret passages, we may remind the reader of that which in Pterium ran under the wall, with outlet into the ditch (*Hist. of Art*, tom. iv. p. 620, Figs. 304, 308).

FIG 114.—Pishmish Kaleh Rock-cut rampart Inner view Drawn by GUILLAUME, *Explor Archl.*, Plate VIII

grooves down the inner face. A rectangular excavation, 10 c. deep, occurs between the two saliences, with a corresponding one in the parapet. Spurs, grooves, and artificial hollows seem to indicate that an apparatus had been prepared on this spot, either to serve as war engine or derrick, which by means of pulleys would haul up heavy loads.

It is not likely that a garrison was stationed here all the year round; the green sward of the woodlands hard by had greater attraction than the plateau, now swept by the wind, now heated like a furnace; but every measure was taken to ensure the prompt victualling of the stronghold and place it on a defensive footing. The district around is well timbered; so that nothing was easier than to run up wooden huts, akin to those which the natives build at the present day. These, however, offered but a poor shelter against wintry blasts, hence weather-proof dwellings were pierced in the solid rock. Three such chambers, 3 m. high, exist in the western face of the *enceinte* (C C), the thickness of whose walls reaches 85 centimetres. The top of the monolithic mass was levelled out, and was approached by stepped-like cuttings.

This esplanade shows numerous traces of the work of man—ditches of varying shape and size, B B′ B″. Of these a few may have been graves; but others are too large to have been put to such usage. Thus, between pointed saliences which towards the centre of the platform rise above the level, there occurs a rectangular excavation 4 m. 74 c. long by 1 m. 70 c. wide, and 2 m. deep. Still visible about the ruins are holes that served to fix the slabs or beams closing the vault. This can only have been the store-room. A little beyond we find a circular hollow, B‴, which looks like the mouth of a cistern or silo, now obstructed and nearly filled up. Another hollow, completely choked up with earth, appears at point K; the deep incline of the soil seems to denote that this was the entrance to a subterraneous passage, hollowed under the platform. Nor should a good-sized shelf, about 40 c. high, pierced in the east wall, E, be left unnoticed. This seems to have been a fireplace, for on one side is a rounded hole clearly intended to receive a cauldron. On the exterior wall of chamber D may be read, incised in letters nine centimetres high, the following inscription :—ЄIC ΘЄOC; Εἷς θεός, "There is but one God."

It is universally known that this formula—examples of which

abound in Syria, the Sinaitic peninsula, and Egypt—was much in vogue during the first centuries which witnessed the triumph of Christianity.[1] Will it be inferred that in these two words we have the signature of the nameless workman who cut, as with a knife, this citadel in the living rock? It is too late in the day to be required to give proofs that work of this kind was in the habits of the older inhabitants of the peninsula, the people who started its civilization. Later on, in certain parts of this same region, subterraneous chambers, which men of old had hollowed by thousands in the flank of the mountains, continued to be utilized as tombs, sometimes as domestic and religious abodes; such processes resulting from the inexperience of the constructer were discarded, but little was added to the legacy of the past. They knew how to build with stone and brick, with or without cement. When an elevated site was to be fortified, it was found easier to plant a wall on the rock, and raise covers behind it, than laboriously to cut rampart and subordinate defensive works in the mass of the cliff.

It was certainly not the Byzantines, in perpetual dread of fresh invasions from without, who could have attempted so laborious a mode of construction. The one thing required was the greatest amount of labour in the shortest possible time. Hence the architects of Justinian made a lavish use of mortar when they repaired or rebuilt fortresses, the long list of which is pompously set forth by Procopius. We are inclined to see here a hasty restoration, dating from the first incursions of the barbarians, when above the large blocks with which the lower portion of the walls at the north-west angle are built, there followed a chain of bricks and smaller stones ill put together. The beams in this section of the wall are in good preservation, and are enough to prove their comparatively modern date. In those troublous times, when the emperors of Constantinople fought for the possession of Asia Minor against Arab captains and Turkish emirs by turn, the citadel must have been repeatedly attacked and repaired. Barth thought to recognize, in places, the masonry of the Seljoukides.[2]

The inscription, at any rate, is contemporaneous with the first restoration of the fortress, which had been abandoned and suffered

[1] G. PERROT, *Explor. Arch.*, p. 145, n. 1.
[2] BARTH, *Reise von Trapezunt*, p. 91.

to fall into decay in those centuries of peace which marked the rule of the Roman emperors, but which was now set on a proper footing of defence. It is incised with too much care, the letters are too large to be explained as the passing whim of a casual tenant. Quite a different conjecture is suggested. Shut up in this stronghold, which he was to defend against the enemies of the empire and of his faith, the commanding officer of those days may have been a fervent Christian, who wished to affirm his creed in the face of barbarians. When he impressed on stone the holy formula, it may have been from a desire to consecrate to and place under the protection of the new god a peculiar structure due to pagan generations.

Our detailed account in respect to Pishmish Kalessi will dispense us dwelling at any length upon kindred monuments. All we know of the neighbouring heights, seemingly appropriated to the same uses, is that the rocky mass furnished the material out of which were obtained walls, ramparts, fortified posts, levelled spaces, cisterns, stores, stairways, and so forth. At the foot of the hill which bears the village of Yapuldak is a subterraneous passage, now blocked up, which led towards the plain and a stream. Travellers who have visited the site have no doubt as to its having been inhabited;[1] they incline to think that on one of these artificial platforms there stood a princely mansion. A plan of this Acropolis and its wall of enclosure, made by M. Ramsay, will be found in *Hellenic Studies*. He likewise succeeded in taking the plan of a house at Kumbet, where the old city is covered by the modern village (Fig. 46). Works similar to these are also reported from the Ayazeen necropolis, in the rear of the Broken Tomb, where, on the plateau upheld by escarps, hypogeia are seen in vast numbers.[2] If on the summit of several rocky masses are met vestiges of the work of man, the site where they are most marked is undoubtedly the plateau, on one side of which the Midas monument is sculptured. It brings to mind the "violet hills" of Athens, notably the Pnyx and the Museum, where the bare rock covered under clustering asphodels testifies to the laborious activity of the race whose narrow houses, closely packed together, rose in

[1] BARTH, *Reise*, etc., p. 93.

[2] With regard to the remains of fortifications which occur on the little Acropolis some three miles north of Ayazeen, see *Journal*, vol. ix. pp. 352, 353. For plan of the Yapuldak Acropolis, see *Journal*, vol. x. p. 180, Fig. 26.

stages on those heights.[1] The Midas level is on too small a scale to have been the site of a city properly so called; but the tribal chiefs may very well have had a temporary abode here, which they inhabited for a few weeks two or three times a year, when the ceremonies connected with these sanctuaries took place amidst the assembled multitudes gathered around them. It is not to be supposed that the place was left to itself; there always was a nucleus of stationary people—care-takers entrusted with the treasures of the chieftains, priests who watched over royal and private tombs, or sacred rocks bearing the names of ancestral deities, altars and speos in honour of Cybele.

Future explorers cannot well devote too much attention to this tiny spot, which seems to have been the official centre, the chief place of a canton where the Phrygian race has left in greater abundance than anywhere else the monuments of its cults, language, and individual culture. They should bring back with them exact tracings of all the curious dispositions the rock has preserved to this day. Such documents, if they ever come to hand, will be of inestimable value to the historian.

SCULPTURE.

We have now gone over all the monuments of any importance in this district, and the reader cannot have failed to notice the insignificant space given to sculpture. This is everywhere in flat relief; nor is there aught to be compared to the extensive figured processions which cover the rocks of Pterium.[2] With the exception of a ram above life size, there is not a single statue, great or small. This particular ram was discovered lying on its side, half embedded in the earth, among Turkish graves near the village of Kumbet.[3] With the help of some villagers, MM. Wilson and Ramsay succeeded in setting him "on his tail," for the nature of the ground and the thickly interspersed gravestones, says the latter, precluded his being set on his feet. It is a rectangular block of stone, 1 m. 44 c. long by 76 c. high, and 35 c. thick. Except the head, which comes out beyond the block, the relief of the general outline and the legs is indicated by a shallow groove on the side of the slab, after the manner of Pterian sculptures at Boghaz Keui and Eyuk, for

[1] RAMSAY, *Hellenic Studies*, tom. iii. p. 6.

[2] *Hist. of Art*, tom. iv. § vi. ch. iii. 4; ch. iv. § 2.

[3] RAMSAY, *Studies*, pp. 25, 26.

example, where we studied the curious mingling of parts in low relief opposed to others worked in the round.[1] The head is much

FIG 115—Stone ram Left side *Journal*, 1882, Plate XX

injured; the horns and the tail—the flat broad tail of the sheep of the country—are the only distinct features that serve to identify

FIG 116—Ram carved on stone Right side RAMSAY, *Journal*, 1882

the kind of animal to which they belonged. Thus, we find here the same conventionalism, the same compromise, the same want of power in setting free the living figure from the mass of stone where it lies imprisoned, which characterize Cappadocian art (Figs. 115, 116).

[1] *Hist. of Art*, tom. iv. pp. 548, 611, 581.

A curious thing about this image is that the artisan grafted on it a second which has no relation to the first; thus he put a bas-relief, bounded by a double strip, on each face of the stone. On the one flank are three objects with long horns apparently belonging to wild goats, and on the other flank two horsemen, and above them two birds on the wing. A hunting scene was clearly intended here. The manipulation is inexpressibly barbarous; but the situation of the birds is precisely similar to that of numerous instances seen in the bas-reliefs of Assyria and the metal bowls of Phœnicia.[1] It would be difficult to imagine aught more strange than these data, workmanship ruder or clumsier, particularly the horses and their riders.

As to the function of the ram, it is easily guessed. He had a pendant, and the pair decorated the threshold; they were regardant, *e.g.* with heads turned away, and played the part of the huge winged bulls of Assyria, the lions of Comagena (of which several were found in place), and the sphinxes and lions at Eyuk.[2] Thus may be explained the awkward overcrowding, which sins against the canons of good taste. The primitive artist, in his endeavour to enhance the importance and power of his patron, bethought him of no better contrivance than to figure him at his favourite pastime, the pursuit and capture of big game. Both at Nineveh and in Upper Syria, in that Hittite palace, of which the ruins are seen at Sinjerli, the basalt and alabaster casing of the lower part of the walls is covered with scenes descriptive of the main episodes of royal existence.[3] In this instance, the house of the tribal chief was, perhaps, no more than a wooden konak, like that of the Dere Bey at Kumbet (Fig. 83). Two huge stone blocks set up at the gateway were all the Phrygian artist had to hand; and in his anxiety to do the best he could with them, finding, moreover, no other available space, he carved the hunting scene on the flanks of the ram.[4]

[1] *Hist. of Art*, tom. iii. pp. 767, 793.

[2] *Ibid.*, tom. iv. pp. 533, 534, Fig. 269.

[3] *Ibid.*, pp. 530, 535, 559, 680.

[4] Milchhofer sees in this ram a funereal symbol, which he compares with those seen in the bas-reliefs of Caucasus and the tombs of Armenia (*Wilderdenkmäler aus Phrygien und Armenien, Archæ. Zeitung*, 1883, p. 263); but Armenian presentations of the animal, such as these, are after the Christian era, one bearing the date of A.D. 1578. To try to establish a link between monuments separated by so wide a space in time seems very risky. Our explanation has this in its favour, that it does

The Phrygian sculptor then, even in works apparently of remotest date, now and again tried his hand at reproducing the human form. Of this we have proof in the image which stands near a sanctuary of the Midas plateau (Fig. 101). This image is decidedly in advance of the two horsemen we have just described, yet it betrays so unskilful a hand as to have no style, it being mere child work. As to the figures sculptured along the roadside which leads to the plateau,[1] there are data about them which raise the question as to whether they do not belong to a very late period—the first or second century of our era, when the monuments, in far better condition than they are now, were visited as a curiosity. At that time the inhabitants of this region were fully conscious of the glorified interest attaching to these Phrygian myths. The poetry and art of Greece had done much towards their development; nevertheless, here in their primitive home they preserved much of their primary character, nor was their hold upon the native populations much less than of old. That the latter were justly proud of the traditions relating to their past is shown by the coins of this period, which bear on one side the name and effigy of Midas (see tail-piece, end of chapter).

It is quite possible, then, that some local worthy, in the day of Augustus or the Antonines, had these pictures carved on the rocky wall as a reminiscence of the chief episodes which the old legends current in the district had to tell. Does not M. Ramsay identify one figure with Marsyas, hung up to be flayed?[1] If the modelling of the image is mediocre in the extreme, the arrangement of the theme belongs to Greek statuary. Now, as proved by the whole array of Syro-Cappadocian sculptures, the archaic art of the peninsula had nothing to say to undressed models, and never figured them but amply draped. Finally, we are told that "the two pictures heading the procession are exceedingly thin in proportion to their height." And slender proportions are neither in the habits of Asiatic sculpture, nor, in a general way, in those of archaic art, which prefers thick-set dumpy forms. M. Ramsay

not outstrip the domain of archaic art, and is referable to a disposition which exemplars furnished by Babylon and Nineveh brought into repute throughout Anterior Asia.

[1] RAMSAY, *Studies*, Figs. 1, 2.

[2] *Ibid.*, p. 6.

goes on to say that the distinguishing feature in some of these figures "is a certain ease and grace in their outline, especially in the line of the back."[1] All these details put together, as well as variety of pose, would appear to preclude the notion of remote antiquity. We should be inclined to think that the one picture really old is that near the altar (Fig. 101); all the rest would be Græco-Roman sculpture, but due to provincial or, if preferred, rural art. The habit of carving bas-reliefs in the flank of rocks persisted very late in Asia Minor, as in Syria and Persia. Any one interested in the subject will find numerous specimens by turning over the leaves of our *Exploration Archéologique*, Plate XII., as well as in works of our predecessors, Téxier, Le Bas, Stewart, and others who have worked in the same field.

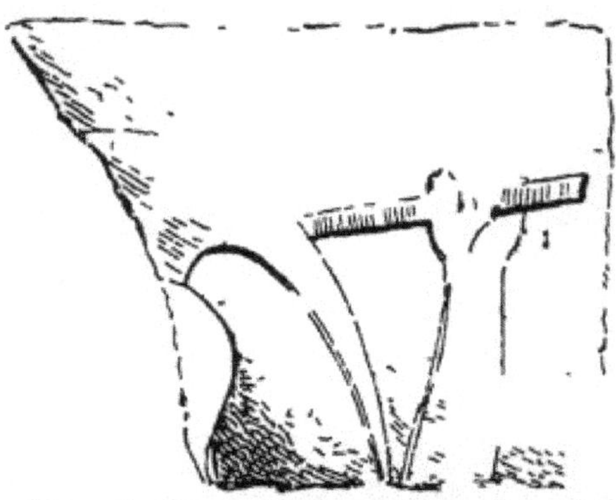

FIG. 118.—Bas-relief of Broken Tomb. Drawn by St. Elme Gautier after Ramsay.

On the other hand, we must recognize as a production of indigenous, of true Phrygian art, the sculpture which decorates the northern front of the hypogee we have called the Broken Tomb (Fig. 65). It represents two warriors, one on each side of the slab, in conflict with a monster (Figs. 117, 118). Each carries a heavy circular shield on the left arm; the other is raised, and holds a spear which runs into the head of the enemy. Our knowledge of Phrygian mythology is too scant to

[1] RAMSAY, *Studies*, p. 7. M. Ramsay does not share our doubts as to the great age of the processional figures (*Journal*, x. p. 167). The question is not one to be solved away from the monuments or photographs of the same, as in my case. Hard by the figures under consideration is one with two characters in front that would appear to be Hittite. This figure, apparently very different from the others, I engraved in *History of Art*, tom. iv. Fig. 355, from a sketch placed at my disposal by M. Ramsay; to-day he produces another drawing, which he declares is more correct than the first, and is intended to show the great similarity of profile common to all these figures (*Mittheilungen Athens*, xiv. Fig. 4). Granting the absolute accuracy of his last image, when placed side by side with Fig. 5, it will, perhaps, be found that his hypothesis is weaker than our own. At all events, the worn state of these monuments makes it very difficult to assert one way or another with any degree of confidence.

FIG. 117.—Bas relief of Broken Tomb. Drawn by St. Elme Gautier after Ramsay.

enable us to give a name to the twin knights, but the meaning of the symbol they embody is easily grasped. The part the warriors enact is analogous to that which the gods and heroes of Assyria and Persia are made to play, whether on cylinders or sculptures adorning the portals of Chaldæan palaces, where they are seen strangling a lion, or plunging their sword in the griffin's throat. Here their function is sharply defined by the situation they occupy, which is that of protecting genii of the grave; they guard the dead against the demon. Of the monster, nothing remains but an immense head, drawn full face; the outline, it would seem, of the Medusa of Greek statuary. That the rudimentary, rough style of the image was intentional—the eyes are not even indicated—is proved by the surrounding parts of the sculpture, which declare a far more advanced stage of art.

The horseman on the dexter hand of the doorway[1] alone remains in position (Fig. 117).[2] The other half of the stone is broken, save the chip bearing the arm which holds the spear, and which we reproduce from the joint efforts of MM. Ramsay and Blunt in Fig. 118. Despite the smallness of the size of the fragment, a certain restoration is rendered possible by the position of the spear, the end of which protrudes beyond the bay.[3] The perfect resemblance of limb and feature between the two actors in the scene extended to their attitude, which was the exact counterpart one of the other. The bare arm is well drawn, the movement natural and satisfactory; it stretches out well. The lower part of the figures is wanting; one was cut across the chest by the fall of the stone which formed the north-west corner, and the other is banked up to a little above the knee. The lower edge of our illustration breaks off somewhat above this place, the reason of which will be found in footnote. Hence we cannot say whether the legs were encased in gaiters; but the other items of his armour are those which the epos and ancient Greek pottery

[1] The position of the remaining horseman has been corrected from the errata.—TRS.

[2] M. Ramsay admits that our illustration (Fig. 117) gives a better idea of the relief than his engraving (Fig. 9, *Journal*, ix. p. 363). He observes that the ringlets of the Gorgon are *on the side*, and *not* on the edge of the relief, for the simple reason that details so disposed would not be seen in a figure drawn full face.

[3] M. Ramsay, during his visit in 1881, took a sketch and measurement of the fragment, from which the skilful pencil of M. Blunt produced the original of Fig. 118. It should be observed that the worn part of the stone is left out.

ascribe to the heroes of Homer. These consist of a breast-plate, or thorax; a circular shield; a sword stuck in the belt, with short slender hilt protruding from a large sheath; a heavily crested helmet with neck, nose, and cheek pieces, which latter could be raised or lowered at will.[1] The crest was a very striking item, formed of two parts: a bird's head and a ridge or narrow band of metal, crescent-shaped, the φαλος of the poets. I know of no Hellenic monument better calculated than this to help one to grasp the meaning of the lines describing the phalanx led by Patroclus against the Trojan Sarpedon: "Men against men, shield against shield, helmet against helmet, with shining crest, over which waved wisps of hair. The men in the second row, as they lowered their heads, touched the helmets *falling on the shoulders* of the men in front, so close against one another were the combatants."[2] The crest depicted here has a deeper projection on the brow and on the nape of the neck than is to be found on Greek vases, on which the figures are black (Fig. 119). Then, too, in paintings the topmost part is fixed throughout to the metal ridge, whereas here the only mode of attachment between crest and helmet-cap is a hook-like projection, which cannot have offered the same solidity (Fig. 117).

FIG. 119.—Helmet, from Greek vase with black figures. HELBIG, *Das Homerische Epos*, p. 298.

There are points in the treatment of the face which should not pass unnoticed. Thus, no doubt to save trouble, the eyeball is not indicated; nose and lips approach the negro type.[3] There is no moustache; the upper lip is shaved, but a small pointed

[1] HELBIG, *Das Homerische Epos*, etc., 1887, pp. 298–300.

With regard to "Homeric armour," consult Leaf, *Hell. Studies*, iv. pp. 281–304; Dennis, iv. pp. 11, 12.—TRS.

[2] *Iliad*, xvi. pp. 215–218.

The above lines would appear to be a paraphrase, inasmuch as they contain more than I could find in the text.—TRS.

[3] If these characteristics are non-apparent in the illustration, writes M. Ramsay (*Journal*, ix. p. 366), that is because neither his travelling companion nor himself was able to reproduce faithfully what he saw. He straightened the nose, thinned the lips, and refined the contour beyond reality.

beard falls below the chin. This mode of dressing the beard was in vogue among the nations of Syria and Asia Minor from the eighteenth Egyptian dynasty; whence it passed to Greece, where it persisted down to the classic age.[1] Long-pointed beards, akin to those of our sculpture, appear in the golden masks of Mycenæ.[1]

The surface upon which the figures are carved is 5 m. 78 c. long by 2 m. 20 c. high. If we suppose the pictures when complete to have been whole figures, they would average from 2 m. 40 c. to 2 m. 50 c.; that is to say, far above life size. Despite conventional treatment and too precise a symmetry, effect and nobility were assured to the sculpture by sheer size, truth, and breadth of movement. It conveys in full the idea it was intended to express. There is a felicitous contrast between the huge grimacing head of the Gorgon and the proud bearing of the two victors. The former is a whole head taller than her adversaries; the legs are bent at the knee and wide apart, so as to allow the feet of the three actors to rest on the same plane: an arrangement which leads one to imagine a pose for these figures akin to that exhibited in archaic Greek sculpture, to express the idea of swift running.

The bas-relief under notice, unknown but yesterday, occupies a place quite by itself in the art productions of Phrygia. In effect, when the native artist wished to endow his great goddess Cybele with a body, all he was able to do was a gigantic puppet, in which no attempt was made to indicate the features of the face, the nature and arrangement of fold in the drapery. We feel that when occasion offered to attack the human form, he was utterly unable to grapple with it. Thus, in one of the sanctuaries of the plateau, where the latter would seem to have its place marked out, did not he shirk the difficulty and replace the divine simulacrum by an emblem suggesting it (Fig. 106)? On the other hand, in common with all primitive artists, he is far more at home in his presentation of animal forms; and in this domain he gives proof of genuine talent and natural gifts. Thus, in the group in which Cybele is represented between two lionesses (Fig. 110), whilst the effigy of the goddess is no more than a kind of head-stone or pillar, the general outline of the animals is drawn with precision, and the movement is exactly what it should be. The same impression is felt in presence of the colossal lion,

[1] HELBIG, *Das Homerische Epos*, 2nd edit., pp 147–256.

who has given the name of Arslan Kaia to a monument met with in the neighbourhood of Liyen (Fig. 108). Neither modelling

FIG 120.—Lion of Broken Tomb Drawn by St Elme Gautier from a photograph.

nor details were indicated within the image; but the contour has enough of frankness to enable one to appreciate the justness of feeling which regulated the proportions of this huge sketch, which the sculptor, with rare boldness, flung high up on the rocky wall.[1] In point of interest, perhaps no manifestation of the plastic art of Phrygia can compete with the lion (Fig. 120), now reduced to a mere fragment, and which belongs to the tomb on whose exterior the two warriors are carved (Fig. 65).

Measured from the nose to the back of the neck, this lion was 2 m. 30 c.; that is to say, far beyond the Arslan Kaia exemplar, whose relief it also surpassed. The latter, about 15 c., was obtained by cutting round the outline parallel lines at right angles to the ground of the stone. High relief, however, was not used by the artist for modelling the flesh, the planes of the shoulder being alone marked; the latter is more salient than the neck, to which it is not allied by a curve as in nature, but by clean cutting at the edge. The other details—hair and folds of skin on the forehead, muscles of the shoulders—are marked by sharp, rigid strokes, which recall the processes of engraving rather than those of sculpture. The mane, which contributes so much to invest the lion with his peculiar physiognomy, was well brought out by the artist in a series of tightly curled ringlets, carved in the plane of the bas-relief, very similar to those that surround the faces of archaic Greek statues. The work is continued in a different form on the vertical edge surrounding the slab. Here tufts of hair are indicated by oblique parallel lines incised on the slight ridge. But this very rudimentary mode was not confined to a portion of the work, where it must almost have been lost to view; the same herring-bone pattern is found on the more apparent sections of the sculpture, from the ear along the cheek, where it perhaps marks the mane fringe, thence under the chin, the breast, the shoulder, where it corresponds to the wrinkle seen above the joint, the back of the quadruped, and finally on the fragment bearing the two paws, which, we think, belong to other two lions (Fig. 122). The slab was broken off just at the point where the fore-parts are joined on to the body; but the head, the most carefully wrought portion of the animal, remains.

Exception must be made for the ear, which is nothing but a triangular surface with a deep salience on the plane of the face.

[1] Our illustration is from a sketch taken from below and too near the object. The result has been, M. Ramsay informs us, somewhat to alter the proportions of the lion, and make him look more lank than he is in reality.

It is small in comparison with the size of the head, as a lion's ear should be. The eye is deeply cut, and the eyelid frankly projects, with a clean vertical edge, from the eyeball. The muscles about the cheek, the wrinkles of the nose, are rendered with truth and decision as if from direct observation of the living animal; other details, however, would seem to belie such a conclusion. If there are no teeth in the upper jaw, that is because they were broken when the block fell in, but the marks left by them are still distinct. Those in the lower jaw are well preserved, and curious to behold in a lion's mouth. Instead of the nail-shaped, sharply pointed teeth proper to animals of prey, it is the broad, flat molars of herbivorous animals which make their appearance here. Yet it seems probable that when these sculptures were executed the lion still haunted the hilly range of the peninsula; he fills too important a place in the Homeric poems, his habits and physiognomy are painted in too lifelike, vivid colours, to induce the belief that the dwellers of the Ægean coast only knew him from the accounts of travellers and the more or less conventionalized portraitures of Oriental art.

Despite these inexactitudes and the very arbitrary mode in which certain details are handled by the artist, the figure had its modicum of beauty and dignified aspect. What was its attitude? In all likelihood the lion was rampant, as in several monuments of this neighbourhood (Figs. 64, 79, 92). Our illustration (Fig. 121) shows how M. Ramsay thinks the animal can be restored. Of the other two lions carved, he thinks, on the same face of the tomb (F in plan, Fig. 66) nothing is left but two paws, opposed one to the other—a movement suggestive of two animals set up against each other in true Oriental taste and fashion (Fig. 122).[1]

The decoration of the broken tomb is perhaps the masterpiece of Phrygian sculpture. Next comes the exemplar with two lions standing on their hind legs, and separated by a pillar. The work, though in better condition, betrays a more rudimentary style, and the relief of the two great figures is not so accentuated; in both, however, the joints, muscles, and folds of skin are indicated by the same process. The main front faces north, and is for the most part covered with greenish moss. As the figures are considerably above the ground, details are not easily made out, but the eyes,

[1] The two restitutions (Figs. 121, 122) are made from sketches by M. Ramsay; the parts restored are merely outlined.

ears, wide-gaping mouth, protruding tongue, and the teeth in the lower jaw are easily discernible. The sculptor made the head and shoulders larger than life. The exaggeration was perhaps intentional so as to add to the effect, and intensify the appearance of strength and power of the two colossal animals. The pose is very frank and the meaning of the group easily grasped. Despite

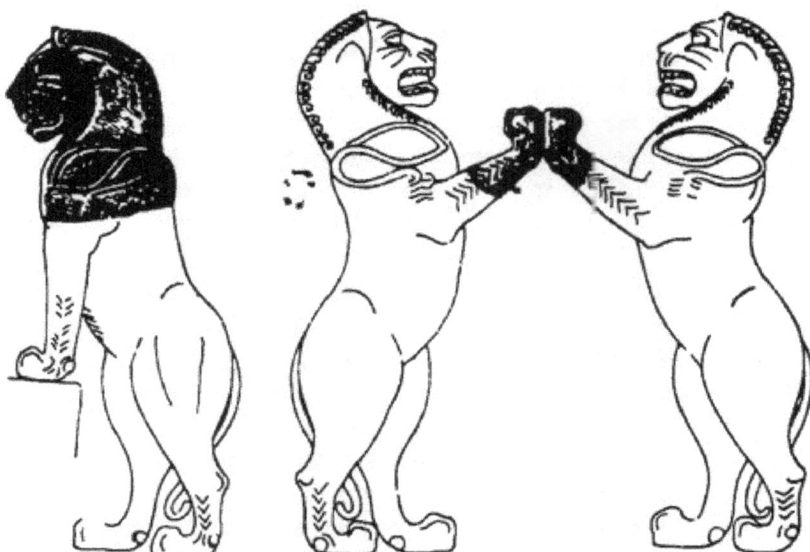

FIG. 121.—Broken Tomb. Restoration of rampant lion.

FIG. 122.—Broken Tomb. Restoration of the two lions face to face.

the rudimentary character of the execution, the two figures, boldly flung athwart the living rock, have a fine air enough.

However simple, then, Phrygian art is not without merits. That in which it is most deficient is variety. At no stage of its development does it seem to have known how to model in the round boss; it never rose above flat relief, and even then the process is only applied to a very limited number of themes. It is possible, however, that some of the types it created or borrowed have not come down to us; many a picture chiselled in the rock may have been destroyed by the fall of the tufaceous mass, one of whose faces it ornamented. Excavations, such as would be likely to bring to light bronzes and terra-cottas, have not been attempted hitherto in Phrygia; yet there is no reason to suppose that the Phrygians were ignorant of the method of casting in bronze or fashioning clay. The ancients mention a female statue of bronze; which would seem to have been put over the tomb of one of the Midases; probably the king who married the Greek Demodikè of Cymæ.[1] A line of one of the Rhapsodists, referring to the figure, is extant, and in the true spirit of the age the statue is made to speak—

"I am a bronze maiden, on Midas'-tomb I lie."[2]

Where was the tomb? We are not told, and do not propose recognizing it in the monument we have described, albeit we can imagine a bronze statue to have stood on the ridge of the rock, over the double volute crowning the pedestal (Fig. 48). At all events, it is difficult to admit that the line in question is a pure invention; the meaning of the epigram would be pointless, unless we suppose it to have been applied to a well-known work. Even supposing the object in question to have been executed in Ionia for a foreign prince who was popular and well thought of there, the fact remains that it had to be despatched to Phrygia, where it served as model and diffused at the same time a taste and practice in the art of working metals.

Up to the present hour, Phrygia has yielded no intaglios or small figures, whether in clay or bronze. Nevertheless, those princes who knew how to write, who sent objects of art as presents to Delphi, could not but have signets of their own; this is rendered the more probable that the usage of the seal was firmly established among the neighbouring nations. Of late, the attention of archæologists has been called to cylinders and cones whose *provenance* and peculiar make stamp them as the work of a local art proper to Asia Minor.[3] But what is still undiscovered are seals wherein the image would be associated with alphabetical characters, akin to those manifested on the inscriptions of the Nacoleia district. When intaglios shall appear with real Phrygian lettering, such as we see on the Midas monument, a new and curious chapter on glyptic art will have to be opened.

[1] Diogenes Laertius, i. 89; PSEUDO-HERODOTUS, *Life of Homer*, ii.; C. F. BERGK, *Geschichte Griechische Litteratur*, tom. i. p. 779.

[2] Χαλκέη παρθένος εἰμὶ Μιδέω δ' ἐπὶ σήματι κεῖμαι. The verse was ascribed now to Cleobulus, one of the seven wise men, now to Homer.

[3] *Hist. of Art*, tom. iv. pp. 665–774; HEUZEY, *De quelques cylindres et cachets de l'Asie Mineure* (*Gazette Archh.*, 1887, pp. 55–63).

Ornament and Industrial Arts.

A country where, as in Phrygia, sculpture has had but a mediocre development is not likely to yield rich and varied stores in architectural ornament. Of its artistic productions only the merest wrecks have been preserved, so that the study of decorative composition is confined to sepulchral façades. The framework and inner shapes of these are borrowed—the first from timber constructions; the latter, by a long way the most advanced in style, from patterns worked in the loom or with the needle.

The number of stone buildings would seem to be very small in the valley of the Sangarius. This is to be accounted for by the soft loose texture of the rock, a poor material to work upon at best, and the abundance of timber. As soon as the subterraneous abode ceased to satisfy the growing needs of the population, when something more spacious, airy, light, and gay was required, oaks and pines furnished the elements out of which the house was made. The result of this is that here stone has not the forms belonging to it, as in Egypt for example, whether in the façades or the doorways of mastabas, the sarcophagi and stelas of the older empire,[1] where the shapes are unmistakable imitations of carpentry work. It is a wholesale imitation, flagrant and servile; not only traceable in the leading lines, but in the minutest details as well. The Phrygian façade, without one exception, may be described as a rectangular space, comprised within a frankly accentuated frame, surmounted by a triangular pediment (Figs. 58, 59), in which all the essential parts of the front of a wooden house are reproduced. Thus, the false pilasters bounding the frontispiece right and left are copies of wooden posts, found at the angles of the square as main-stays to the building. The plain band upheld by the pilasters is the tie-beam of unsquared timber, deeply mortised at the sides to let in the pilasters and keep them in position. The elongated triangle crowning the frontispiece is the gable and framing which support the roof, of which every detail of the timber structure is literally rendered in the stone-work; back-rafters and trusses meeting in the centre, where they form a double volute. The latter could easily be obtained from wood, either in the main end of the beam, when a deep salience of contour and corresponding channel were

[1] *Hist. of Art*, tom. i. pp. 508–516.

desired, or carved almost flat on applied pieces. In countries, as Switzerland, where timber architecture has never been out of fashion, the top of many a gable will be found ornamented by the volute device.

The subordination of stone to lignite types, and the effort to

FIG. 123.—Tomb near Iasili Kaia. Elevation. Téxier, Plate LVII.

imitate them, are not confined to the exterior of these façades. We find them also as projecting beams of a flat ceiling in a chambered grave of this necropolis, and, again, in the first apartment of a tomb westward of Iasili Ḳaia, whose ceiling reproduces the disposition of a pointed roof, along with its purlins, cross-beams, and covering. The tomb was noticed by Téxier, of whom we borrow elevation (Fig. 123), plan (Fig. 124), and section (Fig. 125).[1] His tracing, however, shows no sign of the detail in question, which we were the first to point out, of which a fair idea may be gained from M. Guillaume's sketch (Fig. 126).[2]

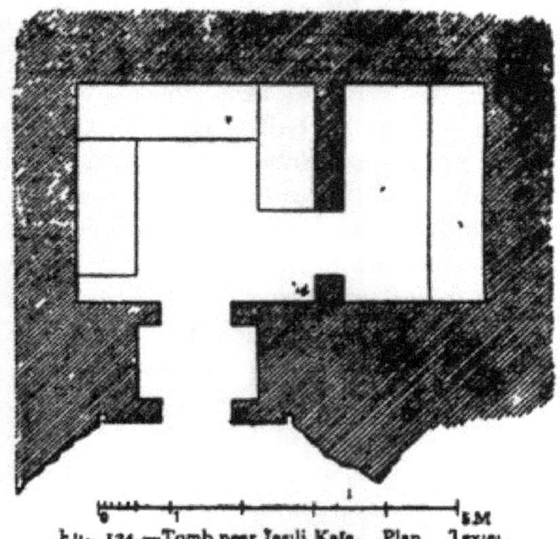

FIG. 124.—Tomb near Iauli Kala. Plan. Texier, Plate LVII.

Imitation of wooden forms extends from the exterior to the interior of the building, where it may be traced in pieces of furniture. Thus, within the tomb figured above were funereal beds for the bodies, cut in the solid rock (Fig. 125).[3] They are much too plain to be considered, like those M. Heuzey brought out from the depths of a tumulus at Pidna, as copies of costly furniture, luxurious couches, metal-plated, upon which the wealthy reclined at banquets. These are modelled on the ordinary instances to be found in every house, of which the hypogeia are faithful representations.

FIG. 125.—Tomb near Iauli Kala. Transverse section. Texier, Plate LVII.

Among other ornamental details to be mentioned as imitated from timber structures, are those raised roundels about the pediment, which bring to mind the salient knobs seen on the door-valve (Fig. 58). It would even seem that a door-handle was

[1] TEXIER, *Description*, tom. i. p. 156.

[2] PERROT and GUILLAUME, *Explor. Arché.*, tom. i. pp. 146, 147.

[3] HEUZEY and DAUMET, *Mission archéo. de Macédoine*, Plates XX., XXI.

identified in the middle of the panel, whilst the lozenges carved about a number of these frontals are supposed to be reminiscences of joists (Figs. 48, 58, 59). When similar squares appear under the side beams of the pediment, as in the Midas rock, such a value may be given to them; as to those in the inner slab, however, set out in sets of five, so as to form crosses, it is more natural, perhaps, to consider them as belonging to the category of designs imitated from carpets or embroidered stuffs. Lozenges, squares, crosses, meanders, all the forms that ornament these sculptured fronts, are of the kind the looms and the broideries of Asia Minor easily produce at the present day; be it on those justly prized carpets made in the province which answers to the Lydia and Phrygia of olden times, or the bodices and aprons the native women embroider for themselves, even to the rosettes seen now and again on these frontispieces (Fig. 59).[1]

The way to read these rock-cut monumental fronts is this. The tomb here, as elsewhere, is but a copy of the house. But the house which had served as model was wholly enclosed in masses of timber, pinned to supporting beams at the angles, which yielded no space to speak of whereon to trace furniture or ornament so as to introduce variety into the scene. Consequently the ornamentist was compelled to seek in other fields forms which it was not in the nature of a lignite architecture to furnish. These he found in profusion in the sumptuous webs, for which the country has been noted from the earliest age; where they served as floor and wall covering, drapery to divans—of which an instance is found in these tombs

[1] Stewart was the first to notice the striking analogy which exists between sepulchral and textile ornament (*Description*, p. 9); whilst M. Ramsay (*Studies*, iii. p. 27) lays particular stress on the resemblance these sculptured fronts bear to hanging carpets.

This theory, which he strenuously advocated in 1882, he now abandons in favour of terra-cotta and metal inlays; and he holds that the style of ornamentation which appears on these fronts "is but the imitation in stone of some kind of tile-work, *e.g.* the covering of a flat surface, floor, wall, and so forth, with a pattern of tiles or of square plaques of bronze" (*Journal*, x. p. 153). To this view we will oppose the following remarks:—It is not easy to conceive how wooden structures, the forerunners of the rock-cut façades, could be ornamented by a terra-cotta or a bronze lining, because, as a rule, coloured inlays are applied to stone and brick. Moreover, the forms we find here are those invented by the mat and basket maker or the weaver, which he elaborated by opposing strips and threads of various colours to one another. The principle of the Phrygian decorative scheme is the chess-board pattern, met with among people and nationalities the most diverse in the early manifestations of their industries.

(Fig. 126)—or curtains to doorways, to exclude sun and dust and allow free access within as well. Native imagination supposed the decoration of these frontispieces, whether funereal or commemorative, to be one of those richly tinted veils hung up in front of the door—an hypothesis which provided the ornamentist with a theme which he could easily work out as fancy prompted him. It is even possible that the imitation of tapestry was carried further than might be surmised from the present state of the monuments; and that, to bring out the geometric shapes composing the decoration, recourse was had to tinted grounds, red and blue. Vestiges of polychrome ornamentation have not, it is true, been observed about these vast surfaces, but this may be due to the flat relief of the forms, which offered but little protection against the weather. The observations of myself and M. Guillaume respecting Delikli Tach and Kumbet, the only tombs that have been traced by an architect, would tend to confirm the above conjecture.

FIG. 126.—Tomb near Iasili Kaia Perspective view of main chamber HEUZEY, "Recherches sur les lits antiques considerés particulièrement comme forme de la sépulture" (*Gazette des Beaux Arts*, 1873)

At Delikli Tach (Fig. 56)[1] the whole front was covered with a coat of stucco, where, in the most sheltered parts, painting was still visible. At Kumbet there were no remains of plaster; nevertheless distinct traces of red are distinguishable in certain hollows, especially about the palmettes at the angles. Within the vault, over the second doorway, there appears a kind of Egyptian gorge, ornamented with red vertical stripes, as part of the cornice (Fig. 89).[2] Again, in other tombs of the same village (7 in map), we noticed stripes of the same tint which served to divide the wall of the chamber into compartments or panels. The Phrygian ornamentist knew, then, how to use the brush in order to complete or supplement work done by the chisel, and heighten the effect of certain mouldings or paint them on a flat surface. This being granted, is it not at least probable that the stone-cutter, in order to impart more cha-

[1] *Hist. of Art*, tom. v. p. 97. [2] PERROT et GUILLAUME, *Explor Archl.*, p. 168.

racter and effect to these units, the relief of whose form is so slight, had recourse to the same expedient? A few well-chosen pigments were all that was needed to obtain a brilliant decoration, in tones that could be seen from afar, and in imitation of a resplendent veil which the piety of a later generation had hung athwart the rock, in the depths of which reposed the venerated dead.

Some thirty centuries have elapsed since then, in the course of which all that goes to make up the habits, manners and customs, the language and religion of a race, even to the inhabitants themselves, everything has apparently changed many a time in Asia Minor. Nevertheless, the traveller is startled by resemblances as unforeseen as they are curious and frequent between the present he observes, and that past whose image he tries to reconstitute. Should his wandering steps take him northward of the Midas rock, to the little town, now the capital of the canton, in which rises the tomb where are deposited the remains of Seid el-Ghazi, the victorious lord, a saintly hero of Islam, he will find it hung with Turkish or Persian carpets and costly shawls, soft in texture and of brilliant colours. Precisely the same thing is seen about the vault of the mosque at Hebron, where the patriarchs Abraham, Isaac, and Jacob are supposed to rest, but which may have been erected by the Maccabees; and, again, about the turbehs at Broussa and Constantinople, the burial-places of the Osmanlis.

The inference to be drawn from this general employment of drapery is that the Phrygians also veiled those vats or troughs and mortuary couches, found in multitudinous tombs, whose patterns were identical with those carved with so much care on the façades of the monuments. Plates of metal may also have been applied to these frontispieces. We thought to recognize the marks left by them about the sealing-holes of the Delikli façade, towards the top.[1] Should our visual observation be confirmed, it would strengthen the conjecture suggested by a text which does not seem to have been noticed before;[2] and the question may be asked as to whether bronze figures, analogous to the one referred to above as having stood over the Midas tomb, did not adorn the summit of some of these monuments. But as with the question of the part colour played in the ornamentation, that of metal also, can only be settled by minute and thorough exploration. Should

[1] PERROT and GUILLAUME, *Explor. Arch.*, p. 112.
[2] *Hist. of Art*, tom. v. p. 182, 183.

this be undertaken by one possessed of the requisite patience, we doubt not but that interesting discoveries would crown his efforts, without prejudice to past labours in the same field. The innate love for colour of nations rejoicing in perpetual sunshine is well known; the data to hand, though scanty, make it probable that the Phrygians formed no exception to the general rule, and that, externally and internally, the sculpture and sombre sheen of metal were relieved by strongly coloured backgrounds. The fancy can picture these multi-coloured surfaces standing out in bold relief from the clear azure sky, the low tones of the rock, and the rich varying greens of the surrounding leafage. Yet all may be illusion and a snare, and until the sculptured fronts have been narrowly examined, bringing ladders or scaffolding in touch with the topmost parts, supplementing vision by "touch," so as to lay hold of the slightest signs of the primitive intentions and dispositions, it would be rash to advance a decided opinion.

That which characterizes the monuments we have just reviewed, or at least those of them the true type of which is to be found in the Midas rock, is the union, in the same unit, of two distinct sets of devices; the one suggested by wooden shapes, and the other by patterns familiar to the weaver and the embroiderer. Nowhere have we met, outside Egypt, nor shall we meet on our path so intimate a blending of two categories of forms, and if there is a Phrygian ornamentation properly so called, it should be approached and defined from this its individual standpoint. Side by side with elements sprung from local habits and indigenous industries are others that may be viewed in the light of importations, as having been transmitted to the Phrygians through the medium of their neighbours of Cappadocia. It was Oriental art which gave them the idea of setting up animal figures at the portals of their palaces, of which the shapeless, unwieldy Kumbet ram is the sole representative (Figs. 115, 116); from it, too, were borrowed lions in pairs, rampant or passant, separated by a pillar, a vase, or other object. We have seen Assyria and Chaldæa lavish these symmetric groups both about the walls of their royal buildings and the woven fabrics they exported wherever a market was open to them. Thence also came feathered sphinxes, whose wings curled in front, and which bring to mind the sphinxes of Anterior Asia, rather than those of the Nile Valley (Fig. 109).

Particularly interesting would be a detailed study of the architectural forms manifested in these monuments; but in order to do this properly and judge of the nature of the ornamental scheme, drawings on a much larger scale than those to hand would be requisite. Then, too, following up the points in touch which a certain class of capitals seem to have with Ionic, Doric, and Corinthian capitals—albeit not copied on any canonic types of Greek architecture—would give rise to curious remarks. Are the analogies in question previous to the age when Hellenic architecture differentiated and fixed its types, or mere distortions more or less barbarous? We incline to the first hypothesis. The profiles of the mouldings in all these façades are those of an archaic style rather than one of decay (Fig. 127). Another sign of remote antiquity is the very marked sloping of the jambs about the doorways (Figs. 75, 79, 92). If a certain degree of hesitation may be felt in regard to the calathiform capital, found in very late monuments (Fig. 97), including the exceedingly simple exemplar with a far-off resemblance to the Doric, this does not apply to those capitals whose forms approach those proper to the Ionic order. The latter are found in tombs, which, like the Yapuldak (Fig. 75), belong to the oldest group of hypogeia contained in these necropoles. Here, over the door leading from the second to the third chamber, is a small column with double volute—a detail which was not lost upon the traveller who saw it; but he neither described it with precision, nor was his visual appreciation carried into his sketch, where it is barely outlined.[1] As to the capitals encountered in the Ayazeen necropolis (Figs. 93-96), it is not easy to see in them borrowings from classical models; one is rather inclined to range them in the category of those forms we have called Proto-Ionic, the outlines of which were first observed in Chaldæa and Assyria, and which would naturally come next after the series of those figured in the ædicula of Iasili Kaïa, in Pterium.[2] Thus each

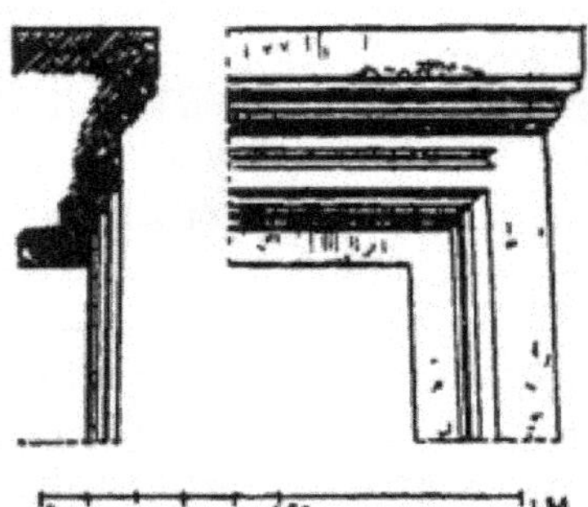

FIG. 127.—Tomb of the Ayazeen necropolis, showing door-frame and profile of its mouldings.

[1] BARTH, *Reise von Trapezunt*, pp. 93, 94.
[2] *Hist. of Art*, tom. iv. pp. 694, 695, Figs. 314 321.

day adds to the evidence we already possessed, and tends to confirm the hypothesis formulated by antiquarians, to the effect that the Ionian Greeks found the device in full swing among the dwellers of the tableland and the upper valley of the peninsula. This type they refined and perfected into the beautiful architectural member they were so fond of introducing in most of their edifices; and though they did not actually invent it, they certainly gave it its graceful, charming curves, and deserve to have their name inseparably attached thereto.

If in the course of our analytical retrospect we have not once made mention of vegetable ornament, that is because the Phrygian

FIG. 128.—Scroll on sepulchral façade. After Blunt.

craftsman rarely derived his decorative forms from the inexhaustible store furnished by the leafage, fruit, vegetables, and flowers of the woodlands amidst which he lived. In this department all we can mention are characterless leaves surrounding the basket-shaped capital (Fig. 97), the mediocre and rudely carved chaplets in the façade of the tomb (Fig. 93), and finally the scroll, executed in good style, which forms a kind of frieze below the frontal in one of the principal monuments of the northern necropolis (Fig. 128). Its arrangement is precisely similar to that of the scrolls formed by the lotus bud and flower, which Assyria seems to have borrowed from Egypt.[1] If the Assyrian artist improved upon his Egyptian model, in that the elements of the group, buds, flowers, and curved lines are better allied one to the other, so did the Phrygian outstrip him. Thus the leaf-stem is replaced

[1] *Hist. of Art*, tom. ii. p. 319, Fig. 134, 136.

by a double volute, which imparts greater amplitude to the ornament. It has already something of the character of those spiral devices so largely introduced on vase-painting by the Greek artist. Was the form we reproduce in the annexed illustration (Fig. 128) derived from an Oriental model? Perhaps so, up to a certain point, and having regard to the very peculiar way narrow shapes are opposed to large ones, as well as to the mode of attachment; but the resemblance to Asiatic art is more intelligible on the hypothesis of imitation than of native ingenuity. Moreover, the rosette, thrice repeated within the field and above the tympanum (Fig. 59), belongs to the "properties" of the Mesopotamian artist. A piece of stuff of Chaldæan manufacture, doubtless, suggested the notion of putting there scroll and rosette. But that which would seem to belong to the Phrygian artisan is his having discarded the flower of the tepid waters of the Nile for the fruit and leafage of the oak and pine, of abundant growth in his native valleys, and a familiar object to his countrymen. As to the spirals curling round the base of the leaf, it may have been induced by direct observation of nature, the tendrils of creepers, which in many a northern district of Asia Minor climb the boles and branches of trees. Such a locality, on the middle course of the Sangarius, is present to me now, which I visited in early spring, when my olfactory nerves were gratified by the delicate sweet perfume which the bloom of the wild vine spread abroad.

To sum up: the chief characteristics of Phrygian decoration would seem to reside in the development of the device under notice, the substitution of the oak for the lotus, as well as the blending of wooden types and tapestry patterns; so that it may justly put forth claims to its share of invention and originality. These merits would certainly be more patent, had any remains of Phrygian industry come down to us—armour, furniture, jewellery, and woven fabrics. Unfortunately the sculpture of the Phrygian race was not sufficiently advanced to trace, as in Egypt and Assyria, the faithful and lasting image of tools, utensils, ornaments, and so forth that served them in their daily life.

The only local industry of which, by the aid of the form seen on the stone façades of the necropolis, some notion may be gained is that of tapestry. But if we are to accept the decoration of the Midas rock as a copy of carpets worked at that time in the villages of Phrygia, we are bound to admit that they were much simpler than the webs of Egypt and Assyria. The tapestries issued from the workshops of Babylon and Anterior Asia were figured; the borders often taken up by flowers and leaves and long rows of animals, real or fantastic, of whom Orientals have always been enamoured. Here, on the contrary, the patterns are entirely made up of geometrical combinations. Tomb Fig. 89 forms the only

FIG. 129.—Turkish woman at her loom. BENNDORF, *Reisen*, tom. i. p. 18, Fig. 12.

deviation to the general rule; hence we may assume that vegetable ornament took up but a narrow space. Nowadays, whether under the roof of the stay-at-home Turcoman or the black tent of the nomad, the goodwives are the sole makers of those carpets for which demands have so steadily increased during the last twenty years or thereabouts. In this and other particulars, matters are probably as they were in olden times; nor is the loom, of which two varieties exist, much changed.

The more elementary (?), technically called "high warp," is used for webs of a plain description (Fig. 129[1]). It consists of two movable cylinders, supported by uprights which enter the ground, held together by cross-beams. Round the upper cylinder, mortised at the sides, is rolled the warp, and round the other, fitted into holes at the end, the web as this is completed. The

FIG. 130—Comb of carpet-makers. *Reisen*, tom. i. Fig. 13.

warp is stretched upon the frame and divided by the weaver into two leaves, which are kept apart by a thread passed alternately between the threads of the warp, and by small sticks. The warp consists of balls of coloured wool, some on the ground, others suspended to a cord, stretched across the frame, at the height of the weaver's hand. These worsted threads she dexterously twists and knots, two at a time, into the lengths of the warp. When a series of courses is completed, she strikes the warp from top to bottom with a heavy-handled comb (Fig. 130). The result is a twisted, rather than a woven tissue. The fact is hard to realize that this rude frame is on exactly the same principle as the complicated modern loom, with its array of cylinders, glass tubes,

[1] Our illustration is taken from *Reisen in Lykien und Karien beschrieben*, by Otto Benndorf and Georg Niemann, folio, Wien, 1884; a work from which we shall freely borrow in this part of our volume. The loom figured on p. 189 was photographed by the explorers from one belonging to a Turkish household settled hard by Cnidus. Plate VIII. (*Reisen*) shows a frame akin to this set up in the open near a Iürük encampment. Our verbal description is mainly due to Professor Karabaceck, whose knowledge of Oriental tapestry is well known (*Reisen*, p. 19). We have also consulted Muntz' excellent manual, *La Tapisserie*, 12mo, Quantin (*Bibl. de l'enseignement des Beaux-Arts*).

and tracings on the warp,[1] in which the Gobelin tapestry is manufactured at the present day, with seven or eight skilled artisans at work on the same piece. Nevertheless, guided by racial instinct, the poor Turkish woman, with her imperfect tottering frame, will turn out so marvellous a picture of the native wilderness of flowers as will justly rank, in the eyes of a true *connoisseur*, far above the costliest products of Paris or Manchester.

None but high-warp frames have been traced on ancient monuments, an instance of which appears in a painting at Beni Hassan,[2] whilst Greece furnishes a vase from Chiusi, in which Penelope is figured sitting at her loom with a vertical frame.[3] It is probable, however, that the low-warp or flat frame was known in antiquity; in which, as the name implies, the cylinders are horizontal or parallel to the ground, and the crossing of the warp is done by a downward movement of the treadle, which is moved with the foot.[4] Work made on the horizontal frame is analogous to our calicoes. This frame is used at the present day in those towns of Asia Minor where carpet manufacture has acquired a certain importance.[5]

Phrygian women, writes Pliny,[6] were the inventors of work done with the needle or embroidery, in which they excelled. Even now, whether along the coasts or in the interior of the peninsula, women adorn their bodices, aprons, and head-coverings, the towels presented to the guests before and after meals, coverlets, etc., with geometric shapes, clustering flowers and leaves,

[1] This is done by means of a transparent paper, on which a sketch of the picture to be copied is countertraced in sections as the work advances.—TRS.

[2] *Hist. of Art*, tom. i. Fig. 25.

[3] The vase in question has been published by CONZE, *Monumenti dell' Istituto Arche.*, tom. ix. Plate XLII. Fig. 1; reproduced by MUNTZ, *La Tapisserie*, p. 31.

[4] In both looms the weaver is obliged to work on the back of the piece; but as the face is downward in the flat frame, it is much more difficult to detect and mend a fault; for in the vertical loom he can step in front and correct, as he advances, the smallest mistake. With regard to tapestry, woven stuffs, and so forth, the reader will find valuable information in the South Kensington Handbooks—*The Industrial Art of India*, by G. C. M. Birdwood; *Textile Fabrics*, by the Rev. D. Rockford. Consult also HAMILTON, *Researches*, vol. ii. p. 111.—TRS.

[5] Plate VII. (*Reisen*) has a photograph of one of these primitive frames. It is certainly helpful in giving a general idea of the apparatus, but it would perhaps be difficult to make a satisfactory drawing from it.

[6] *H. N.*, viii. 74: "Pictas vestes apud Homerum fuisse (accipio), unde triumphales natæ. Acu facere id Phryges invenerant, ideoque Phrygioniæ appellatæ sunt . . ."

sometimes threads of gold and silver, formed into picturesque designs, exquisite in tone and workmanship. It is work that will bear being looked into, where nature is reproduced with truth and great freedom of interpretation at the same time; that is to say, the very qualities which tapestry and embroidery should possess.

TOMBS IN PAPHLAGONIA.

In the district whose antiquities we have described in the foregoing pages are monuments proper to it and encountered nowhere else; they cluster around the frontispiece upon which the name of Midas is to be read, and consist of those façades where forms borrowed from timber enframe ornament with forms seemingly imitated from tapestry designs. Such façades are further characterized by inscriptions, the lettering of which belongs to the syllabary we have called Phrygian. If nothing of the kind has been seen hitherto outside Phrygia, *per contra*, in the adjacent province of Paphlagonia, a recent explorer, M. G. Hirschfeld, reports the existence of several tombs exhibiting singular analogies with such exemplars of the Ayazeen necropolis as are adorned by a porch.[1]

The name of Paphlagonia was given in antiquity to that portion of the peninsula whose boundary line was formed on the north by the Euxine, the Halys on the east, the Parthenius on the west (beyond which lived the Myrandynians and Bithynians), and Mount Olgassys on the south.[2] The latter belongs to the Olympus range, whose summits rise between the central plateau and the low valleys watered by streams discharging their waters in the Black Sea. It is emphatically a hilly, well-timbered region, albeit here and there the hills open out into plains of no great extent, but of marvellous fertility, due in part to the abundant

[1] G. HIRSCHFELD, *Paphlagonische Felsengraeber*, etc., with seven plates (*Abhandlungen der Kaiserliche Akademie der Wissenschaften, Berlin*, 1885, 4to).

[2] Xenophon extends further east the boundaries of Paphlagonia, beyond the Halys and the mouth of the Thermôdôn; perhaps on the testimony of Hecatonymus, the Sinopian envoy at that moment in the Greek camp. Among the many difficulties the Greeks, according to his account, would have to face, he seems to suppose that before they attempted to cross the Thermôdôn, they would have had to fight the whole force of the Paphlagonians (*Anabasis*, V. vi. 9). In another passage (*Ibid.*, VI. i. 1) Xenophon tells of a collision between Greek marauders and Paphlagonians, as having taken place in the neighbourhood of Cotyora.

supply of water, in that the lower range of mountains run parallel to the coast line and oblige the streams to wind round their base ere they reach the sea or lose themselves in the Halys. On the coast, Sinope, a Milesian colony, had been a flourishing centre from the eighth century B.C., and in its turn had given rise to Amastris, Sesamos, Kytoros, Ionopolos, or Abonoutikos. Thus she multiplied havens along the line of coast, in which her merchantmen could take shelter, whence a brisk trade could be carried on with inland tribes.

Lost amidst woodlands, these tribes are little known; nevertheless, it would appear that they were closely related to the Cappadocians, and spoke like these an Aramaic idiom, a fact which permits us to class them with the family of Semitic nations.[1] However that may be, we learn from Xenophon, the first man of note who visited this district before Alexander the Great, that they were less rude and savage than their neighbours, the Tibarenians and the Mosynœci. The Ten Thousand did not traverse Paphlagonia, but took ship and skirted its coast as far as Cotyora, where they encamped. Here their general received the delegates sent by the Paphlagonian chief, Corylas, whose barbarous magnificence and fine steeds drew forth admiring expressions from the Greeks.[2] The power of Corylas must have been considerable, to judge from the high estimation in which he was held by a city like Sinope, her foremost citizens styling themselves royal guests, pensioners.[3] The Sinopian envoys, for private reasons of their own, did their utmost to prevent amicable relations being entered into between the Greek captains and Corylas; hence to dissuade the former from crossing the Paphlagonian territory, they may have exaggerated the military force of the barbarians,

[1] Herodotus, in writing of circumcision and the nations among whom it is practised, goes on to say, "The Syrians, who occupy the banks of the Thermôdôn and the Parthenius . . .;" thus confounding under one denomination the Cappadocians and Paphlagonians. Strabo (XII. iii. 25), whilst stating that many local appellatives are common to Paphlagonia and Cappadocia, bears witness to the resemblance existing between the dialects current on either side of the Halys. PLUTARCH (*Lucullus*, 23) speaks of Sinope as situated in Syrian territory. Finally, Denys Periegetes (v. 970–972) specifies two Syrias—one in Lebanon, the other stretching far away to Sinope washed by the flood, inhabited by Cappadocians.

[2] XENOPHON, *Anabasis*, VI. i. 2.

[3] *Ibid.*, V. vii. 11.

when they affirmed that they could move 120,000 men into the field, including a well-mounted cavalry.[1]

The meaning covered by these words is that the powerful maritime centre had every interest to secure the amity of native chiefs, who could at any moment oblige her inhabitants to keep within her walls, and close up the routes followed by her trade with Phrygia, Cappadocia, the distant provinces of the Taurus, and the basin of the Halys. The bulk of her transport, as well as her import traffic, was right through Paphlagonia. Her caravans, laden with all manner of manufactured goods, collected in the workshops of Ionian cities, moved slowly along the circuitous mountain path, distributing them everywhere. They brought back in return not merely hides, but corn and wool; not only mineral substances, such as minium or vermilion, but textiles, bronzes, ivories, enamelled terra-cottas, jewellery—in fact, the whole luxury of the East. Thus was created a flux and reflux which led through the land of the Paphlagonians; so that these could not wholly escape being influenced by two sets of cultures, the Greek and the Asiatic, between which they acted the part of middlemen. The transactions in which they took part brought them in touch with polished nations; similar relations, and the models created by skilled labour thus brought to them, could not but awake in their breasts a taste and feeling for the refinements of life. The fact, therefore, that monuments within the territory of Paphlagonia bear upon them the impress of noble and considerable effort, should cause no surprise.

Towards the centre of Paphlagonia, in a valley which we may well imagine to have been thickly populated from the earliest age, hard by the little town of Kastamouni, Kastamboul, there appears a whole series of tombs hollowed in the depth of a low cliff of a certain length.[2] Some notion of the general arrangement of the whole may be formed from the annexed plan (Fig. 131). The principal hypogæum (1) is preceded by a portico composed of two square pillars, about 4 m. high, and corresponding antæ. These pillars are without base; above is a rude capital with cavetto and abacus. Over this again an architrave and pediment, which

[1] XENOPHON, *Anabasis*, V. vi. 9.

[2] The name of Kastamouni does not appear in history until the thirteenth century of our era, but the presence of ancient remains about the place leads to the inference that a settled population had long been established here.

latter has suffered much from the weather (Fig. 132). Within the tympanum, right and left, are winged quadrupeds, whose four paws rest on the ground. The figure separating them appears to be that of a female clad in a long robe. Pierced behind the columns, a door, not quite in the middle of the wall, leads to a rectangular chamber, whose sides are smoothed over with care. The curves of the ceiling, in imitation of a tent covering, should be noticed (Fig. 133). The chisel has reproduced on stone even the rollers which in the light construction uphold the frame.

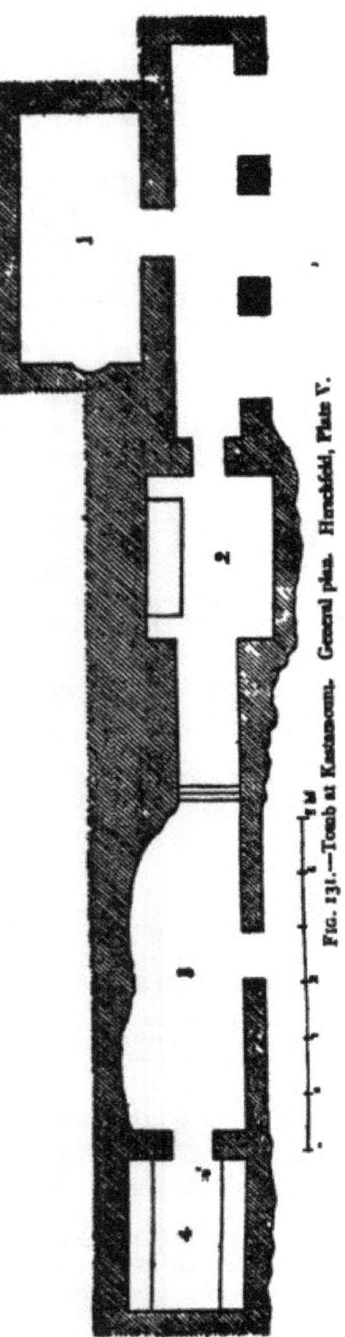
FIG. 131.—Tomb at Kastamouni. General plan. Hirschfeld, Plate V.

At the southern extremity of the porch, a small door opens into a second and smaller chamber, whose roof and main beam recall a lignite structure (Fig. 134). The funereal bed is found in a niche, the external face of which is akin to that of a wood panel. Nor does the hypogeum end here; beyond are two steps by which the apartments 3 and 4 are reached (Fig. 135), the last one alone containing graves hewn in the floor. Taken together, these chambers measure 22 m. 7 c. from north to south. All the tombs we have met with in Asia Minor up to the present time had but one, or at most two sepulchral chambers. This is the first instance of a family vault, with its row of graves, like those found in such abundance in Phœnicia and Judæa.

Although imperfectly described,

the hypogeum was pointed out by MM. Shanykof and Mordtmann, some time before M. Hirschfeld visited it. But he was the first to light upon the tomb called Hambar Kaia (Barn Rock), situated in a deep valley of the Halys, marked "Terra incognita" in Keipert's map.[1] The vault is hollowed in the northern face of a mass which juts out from the body of the hill, along the right bank of the river, into a kind of promontory (Fig. 136). The frontispiece, to the height of 13 m. 70 c., is inwrought with a gentle upward slope, but the lines of the porch by which the chamber is entered have all been maintained in a vertical plane.[2] The result has been to leave along the whole front, between the talus and the base of the columns, a ledge or step 7 m. long and 74 c. wide (Fig. 137). Above it, by way of balustrade, the rock was cut into three lions couchant, seen in profile.

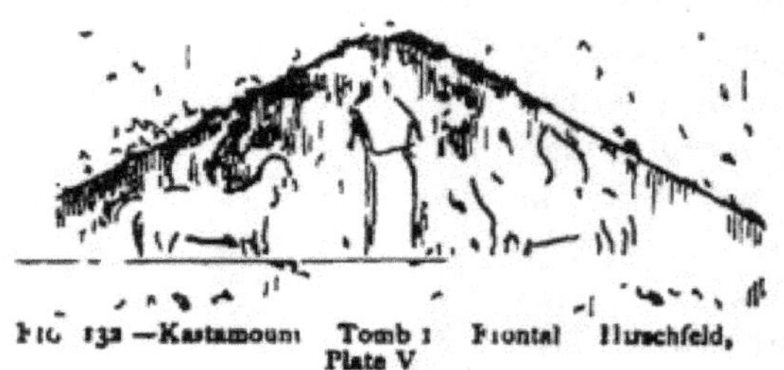

FIG. 132.—Kastamouni. Tomb 1. Frontal. Hirschfeld, Plate V.

FIG. 133.—Kastamouni. Tomb 1. Ceiling of chamber. *Ibid.*

FIG. 134.—Kastamouni. Tomb 2. Transverse section of chamber. *Ibid.*

FIG. 135.—Tomb 4. Transverse section of chamber. *Ibid.*

Their sides are left in the rough, and adhere to the cliff, whose slope they continue. Except for the back, head, and paws, it would be hard to make out the kind of animal to which they belong. They have suffered very much from the weather; their pose, however, would seem to be pretty near the same as that of those bronze lions which in Assyria served as weights.[3] The porch, whose floor is

[1] For a detailed account of the monument and of its geographical position, consult M. HIRSCHFELD, *Memoir*, pp. 9, 11.

[2] M. Hirschfeld estimates the angle made by the talus with the vertical line at 12°.

[3] *Hist. of Art*, tom. iii. pp. 566, 567, Plate XI.

Fig. 136.—Hambar Kala. Hirschfeld, Plate I.

on a slightly higher level, is enframed by a double fascia; the height of its three columns, including base and capital, measures 3 m. 13 c. (Fig. 138). Their short massive appearance is due to the marked diminution of the shafts towards the top.[1] The base is a very large torus and narrow listel; the capital, which is quadrangular, consists of three platbands put one upon the other; their salience beyond the shaft, even the topmost, is very feeble. A mere outline served to distinguish the pediment which stood over the portico from the surrounding rock; there is no cornice to define and shelter its field, so that wind and rain have played havoc with the figures carved on the inclined surface. Distinguishable with the first morning light, however, are a bird at the left angle of the frontal, and a quadruped, seemingly a lion, in front of it. The decoration was in all likelihood symmetrical—an hypothesis borne out by the fact that remains of outline are visible on the other side, where we may suppose that bird and lion were repeated (Fig. 139). The door is neither central with the porch, nor with the apartment to which it gave access. The sepulchral chamber is quite plain, with a roof-like sloping ceiling, and a recess or mortuary shelf pierced in the further wall, 55 c. above the soil, and 95 c. wide. The monument stands well. The architect entrusted with the building was singularly happy in the selection of the site, high up in the cliff, overhanging the flat stretch below. The rude proportions of the columns harmonize

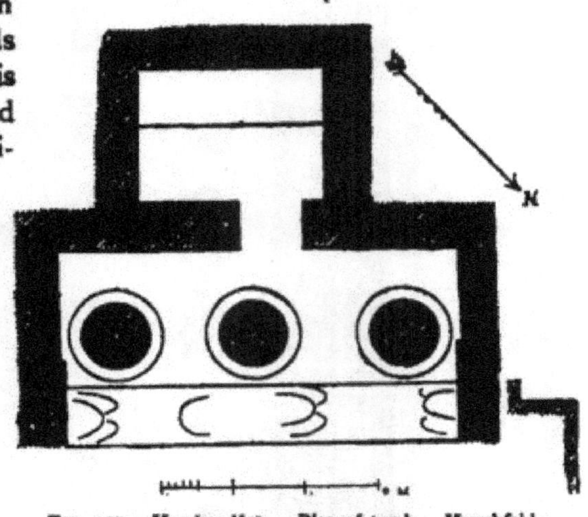

FIG 137.—Hambar Kala. Plan of tomb. Hirschfeld, Plate V.

FIG 138.—Hambar Kala. Column. *Ibid.*

[1] The upper diameter is 19 c. less than the lower, a considerable difference in a height of 2 m. 19 c. measured by the shaft.

with the amplitude of the rock in which they are carved. The eye is forcibly drawn to their light colour, and when there, it lingers to note the skilful contrast between the polished fasciæ and the sombre rugosity of the virgin rock, between the incline of the talus and the perpendicular lines of the architectonic whole. No

FIG. 139.—Hambar Kala. Façade of tomb. Hirschfeld, Plate II.

less remarkable is the shape of the monument itself, terminating as it does in a triangular pediment, which, despite irregularity of outline, recalls the classic frontal.

The Iskelib group, the last of the series, is farther away from the sea, on the edge of the central plateau. It is called after the town of the same name, situate southward of Kutch Dagh, a little way beyond the left bank of the Halys. The tombs are excavated in the depth of a huge rock, towards the base, bearing on its

FIG. 140.—Iskelib. General view. Hirschfeld, Plate III.

summit walls, which M. Hirschfeld identifies with Tavium, the capital of the ancient Trocmes, or Eastern Galatians.[1] As for ourselves, we find no reason to change the opinion formulated in another place, to the effect that the site of Tavium must be sought on the right bank of the Halys, close by Nefez Keui.[2] Whichever view may be taken, the fact remains that the Iskelib tombs are anterior to the occupation of the district by the Galatians.

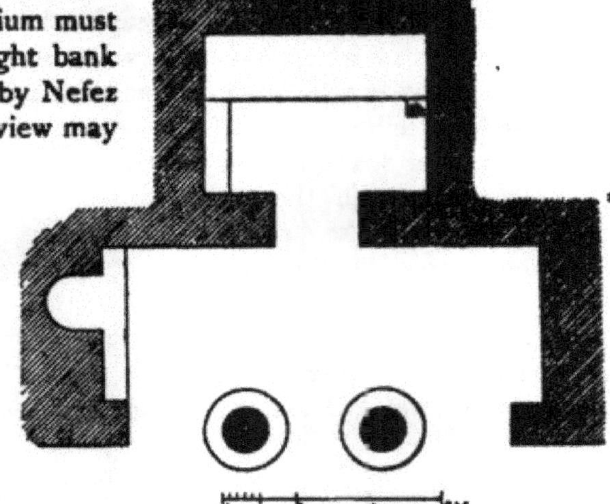

FIG. 141.—Iskelib. Tomb I Plan. Hirschfeld, Plate VI.

There are four sepulchral chambers, one on the ground-floor and the other three on the second tier; the more important one being in the centre (Fig. 140). It is preceded by a porch composed of two stout columns and corresponding antæ (Fig. 141). The whole height of the pillars is almost 3 m. (2 m. 98 c.), of which 57 c. go to the base and 29 c. to the capital. The base, though a trifle more complicated than the Hambar Kaia exemplar, is likewise bell-shaped (Fig. 142), and rests upon a thin plinth, 93 c. at the side, a narrow listel uniting

FIG 142.—Iskelib Tomb I Elevation of portico *Ibid*

[1] *Monatsberichte Akademien Berlin*, 1884, p. 1254. Ainsworth is almost the only modern traveller, besides Hirschfeld, who visited Iskelib. But he does not seem to have had an inkling of the importance of these monuments; at any rate, no trace of it appears in his narrative.

[2] PERROT et GUILLAUME, *Exploration archéologique*, tom. i. pp. 289-292

it with the shaft. The resemblance extends to the capital, likewise on a rectangular plane, made up of a slightly salient cavetto and abacus. The architrave is a smooth flat band; above it appears the pediment, which is wrought with care and slightly sunk. An indistinct object, figure or pillar, occupies the middle of the frontal, the upper part of which has been wantonly destroyed; hence no decided opinion can be advanced as to the nature of the symbol from the least telling portion (Fig. 140).

The vault is spacious, and nearly half of it is taken up by a grave in touch with the end wall. Its vault-like ceiling and the profile of the mortuary couch should be noticed (Fig. 143). A diminutive shelf is pierced on a lower plane along the left wall. The situation of the tiny grave at the entrance of the porch on the right-hand side is doubtless the reason of its present poor condition (No. 2). In the lower tomb (No. 3) the one pillar of the vestibule has disappeared; traces of it, however, are visible about the floor and the lower face of the architrave (Fig. 144). The support was removed to facilitate access to the adjoining room and the esplanade, when the tomb was turned into a domestic abode. The mutilation is all the more to be regretted that the work, to judge from the listel framing the end wall, shows careful manipulation (Fig. 145). Base and capital might have yielded interesting details. A door opens into the first chamber,

FIG. 143.—Iakelib. Tomb I. Transverse section through end of chamber, and profile of mortuary couch. Hirschfeld, Plate VI.

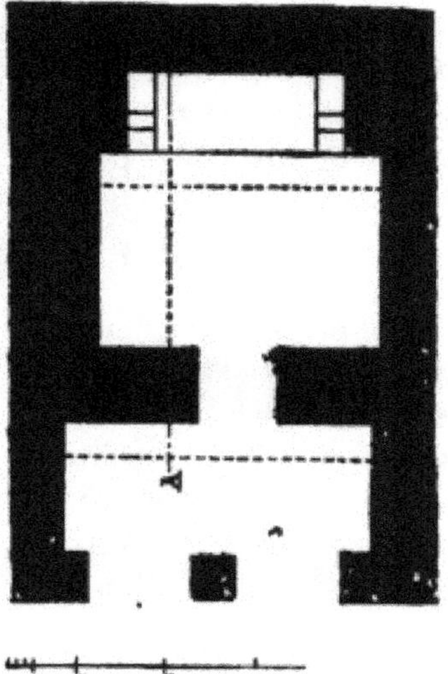

FIG. 144.—Iakelib. Tomb III. Plan. *Ibid.*

lighted by a narrow window; the diminutive apartment seen behind it is the grave properly so called. Both have roofs with sloping sides; but the slightly projecting band, which in the main chamber serves as point of junction between the vertical walls

FIG. 145.—Iskelib. Tomb III. Transverse section under porch through C D. Hirschfeld, Plate VI.

FIG. 146.—Iskelib. Tomb III. Longitudinal section through A B. *Ibid.*

and the superincumbent ceiling, is not repeated in the smaller tomb (Fig. 146).

As in many Phrygian tombs, we find here also a pillar in the middle of the tympan, which is an exact copy of the wooden post of a loft. Like it, it is composed of a thin plinth or

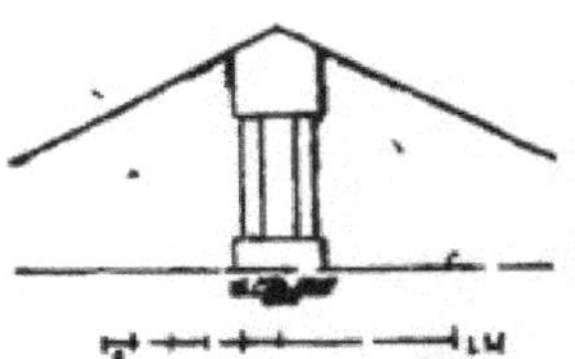

FIG. 147.—Iskelib. Imitation of a wooden loft. *Ibid.*

FIG. 148.—Iskelib. Tomb III. Section through E F. External face of mortuary couch. *Ibid.*

shoe, three square posts, and the whole is topped by a capping upon which rest the cross-beams (Fig. 147). Again, the ceiling of the further room forms a canopy over the anterior face of the grave, divided into four panels like a wood partition, and as unlike stone forms as can well be imagined (Fig. 148). This applies to the shelf, 60 c. wide, upon which the body was laid; its outer rim is rounded off, whilst the two semi-rolls at the back stand out from the rocky wall. All these details show care and finish.

The fourth tomb, whose base is about three metres above the

ground, stands somewhat apart to the westward of the group we have just described. Its general arrangement is precisely similar to that of the other tombs; but its state of preservation is not so good, nor does it favourably compare with any of them in point of workmanship. The interest which attaches to the monument

FIG. 149.—Iskelib. Tomb IV. View of façade. Hirschfeld, Plate IV.

resides in curious details, of which more anon, not encountered hitherto in Phrygia nor Paphlagonia.

The portico is enshrined, as at Hambar Kaïa, in a double fascia (Fig. 149). The rude columns, 2 m. 80 c. high, resemble the stems of coniferous trees, and, like these, taper towards the top. The upper diameter of the shaft is one-third less than the lower (95 c.): to this fact the supports owe their squat and massive appearance. The bases are much injured. There is no sign of plinth or listel; nothing but a very salient torus *cir.* 1 m. 40 c. in diameter. The most striking detail appears in the rectangular capitals, 50 c. high, 95 c. at the side, and 73 c. on the face. Upon this are carved the head and paws of an animal, which M. Hirschfeld thinks were intended to represent a lion. The whole is much worn.

FIG. 150.—Iskelib. Tomb IV. Plan. Hirschfeld, Plate IV

The bases and corresponding antæ—the latter absolutely void of moulding—fill up the whole depth of the porch, so that no passage exists between them and the wall behind (Fig. 150). A niche, irregularly shaped, occurs at the end of the gallery on the right-hand side. A doorway, 80 c. in height, leads to a narrow grave-chamber, whose altitude, measured from the central point of the vaulted ceiling, is barely 1 m. 80 c. (Fig. 151). A stone bench runs along the left and the back wall; and near the entrance was pierced a mullioned window in the shape of a cross.

It remains to notice some curious points about the pediment. Like the Hambar Kaia exemplar, it is quite plain, without a cornice, a mere isocele, 1 m. 25 c. high; a light *resault* alone separating it from the rough surface of the rock (Fig. 149). One is surprised to see here two winged *putti*, carved in flat relief within the tympan, and turned towards each other. In the hand of one is carried a label, a fruit or vase in that of the other. Owing to the indistinctness of the details, it is impossible to say which. The pose of the figures, seeming to fly across the solid pediment as in mid air, is incongruous, and ill agrees with the simple and sober taste of remote antiquity. This is one reason for suspecting that the decoration is younger than the tomb. The impression thus created is strengthened by the character of the subject, in which no one can fail to recognize a Greek Ἔρως;

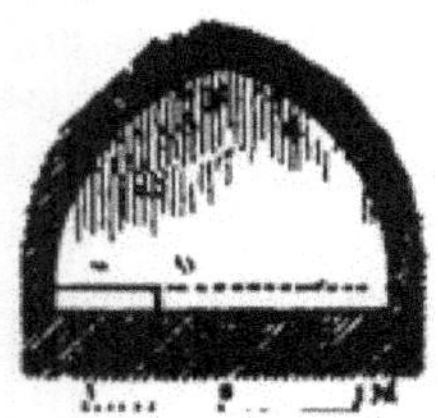

FIG. 151.—Iskelib. Tomb IV. Transverse section through back of vault. *Ibid.*, Plate VII.

a commonplace device the ornamentist of the Lower Empire introduced wherever he found a bare corner.[1] Indeed, the bas-relief betrays the ease and freedom, the nerveless make of the Roman period. This detail apart, the Iskelib tomb is precisely similar to the monuments with which it has been compared; like them it bears the stamp of an age when the influence of Greek culture had not yet made its way into the interior of the peninsula. The conclusion which forces itself upon the mind is that the cupids are an addition of the second or third century of our era, when the long-abandoned tomb received a new tenant. The so-called vault of Solon in Phrygia (Fig. 89) is a conspicuous and certain example of one of those tardy misappropriations. Thanks to this procedure, a man could give himself the luxury of a rich place of burial at little or no cost. All he had to do was to excavate a second chamber, restore the façade, write an inscription over the doorway, and the thing was done.[2]

The artist found here, as at Kastamouni, a pediment altogether devoid of ornament, and his horror *vaccui* prompted him to fill in the space with figures, that would rejuvenate the monument and clothe it in the fashion of the day.

Along with these should be ranged first a tomb found at Tokat in Pontus, with a small and irregular chamber, and porch upheld by a single pillar;[3] besides two other monuments, which seemingly belong to the same series. They are encountered in Paphlagonia: one near Tach Keuprü, ancient Pompeiopolis, the other close to Tshangri, formerly Gangra.[4] All these monuments belong to a region which is pretty fairly delimitated by history and geography; albeit these are not their only claims to be classed under one head. If, in some respects, they recall exemplars already met with either in Cappadocia or Phrygia, their resemblance to one another is so great, that had they not been found closely packed together, one would have been led to put the same label over them. A primary feature they have in common is that in Paphlagonia we see no traces of precautions

[1] M. Hirschfeld (BENNDORF, *Reisen in Lykien und Carien*, tom. i. p. 80) observes in regard to a large sarcophagus, scarcely as old as the Antonines and found at Sidyma in Lycia, that nude winged figures form the acroteria of the frontal depicted upon it.

[2] *Hist. of Art*, tom. v. pp. 135, 136.

[3] HIRSCHFELD, *Paphlagonische Felsengræber*, p. 24, Plate VII. 3.

[4] *Ibid.*, p. 25.

taken to conceal or render access to the mortuary chamber difficult, as is the case in the older Phrygian tombs; graves with wells are non-existent. Then, too, throughout Paphlagonia, porches are the due accompaniment of tombs of some importance, and are generally associated with a rudimentary, unadorned pediment; a characterless outline alone interposing between it and the uneven surface of the rock. But in Phrygia the pediment only occurs in tombs upon which the word "recent" might be written, and are always enframed in a cornice more or less salient, which continues that of the entablature. And again, in the Paphlagonian façades, pillars sufficiently resemble one another to permit of their being classed in one distinct order; whilst if we except Fig. 149, in which a lion's head forms the capital, base and crown are nearly alike. In the Ayazeen necropolis, however, where scores of tombs are adorned by porches, the shape of supports is exceedingly varied. Nor is this all; mortuary couches are by no means the rule in Phrygia, whilst in the basin of the Halys scarcely a tomb is without them. Here, too, doors are all on the same pattern—a small opening devoid of ornament, nearly always rectangular, and *cir.* 1 m. above the ground (Fig. 152). In Phrygia portals are much taller, trapeziform, on a plane with the portico, and wreathed in a frame made up of several mouldings.

FIG. 152.—Iskelib. Tomb I. Section under porch. Hirschfeld, Plate VI.

It follows, therefore, that the craftsmen who fashioned the tombs at Hambar Kaia and Iskelib had no hand in building the monuments met with in the upper valley of the Sangarius on the Phrygian plateau; their habits are not precisely similar, and preference is given to other arrangements. Externally, the Paphlagonian ornamentist does not make use of certain themes, such as patterns derived from tapestries, which are so popular with his Phrygian colleague. What most resembles the hypogeia of the Paphlagonian group is the tomb of Alajah, situate on the right bank of the Halys, in Western Cappadocia.[1] Its size and general disposition, everything, brings to mind that which we have just described; if no frontal appears above the architrave, a decorative form occurs over the window of the side chamber, whose value is precisely similar. Instances observed here are reproduced in the small tomb at Tokat; their significance is sufficiently great to constitute a special type, which we propose to call the northern type of the Asiatic tomb.

The type has an individuality *sui generis*, albeit in many respects closely allied to that which we have studied in Phrygia. Nowhere is this more conspicuous than in the position and general aspect. Here as there, a happy instinct presided over the choice of the rocky masses, in whose flanks tombs were to be hollowed; it warned the architect to put his façade neither too far nor too near the spectator; it taught him the height at which it would dominate the plain and produce the utmost effect.

A distant likeness is apparent between tombs of widely different arrangement; Hambar Kaia and Delikli Tach, for example (Fig. 50). The upper contour of the stone is wrought in the former, and left in its native ruggedness in the latter. In both a rude frontal follows in a general way the movement of the architectural composition, and serves to separate shapes created by art from shapes traced by nature itself. Both testify to a far more ephemeral style of architecture than could be derived from stone buildings, be it in the outline of frontals, the mouldings of entablatures, the form of ceilings, the arrangement of capitals, the division into panels of vertical surfaces, the extent of which will require ornament. The same symbols obtain in the north and the centre of the peninsula. Thus the lion, which in Phrygia is placed high up on either side of the tomb to guard the entrance, crouches here before the portals (Fig. 136). Elsewhere he has taken his stand on the top of pillars, the better to watch the approaches to the abode of the dead (Fig. 149). At other places animals in pairs appear face to face in the field of the pediment; now a lion and a bird are brought together, now griffins separated by a female figure, who is no other than the great goddess, the tamer of feræ (Fig. 132). One and all of these motives passed under our eyes when we visited the Phrygian necropoles. Within certain limitations, then, the funereal monuments of Phrygia and Paphlagonia may be

[1] *Hist. of Art*, tom. iv. vol. ii. Figs. 344–347.

rightly considered as constituting, to use the language of naturalists, a genus, which comprises not a few species. Many a conjecture on the origin of this local art and the probable date of its chief works, many a remark as to style and peculiar characteristics of workmanship, are equally applicable to the two series we have been led to form and place side by side.

GENERAL CHARACTERISTICS OF PHRYGIAN CIVILIZATION AND ITS INFLUENCE UPON HELLENIC CULTURE.

Some surprise may be felt that so large a space should be apportioned to the Phrygians in this study. Our line of conduct was prompted by the historical part this nation, viewed in the light of recent discoveries, has suddenly acquired in the estimation of antiquarians. For some time past science has busied itself in drawing up the inventory of the benefits the Asiatic Greeks, from the earliest days, derived by contact with their continental neighbours, the numerous tribes they found established on the soil of the peninsula. The task was rendered exceedingly difficult because the peoples which at one time divided Asia Minor among themselves have not sown and left everywhere, as did the Phœnicians, the instances of a brisk and thriving industry. If in the days afar off armour, jewellery, domestic furniture, etc., were deposited in their tombs, these have long been empty. Hence it comes to pass that, in order to divine the inner meaning of their creeds, manners, and customs, we are fain to turn to the rocks they fashioned, the chambers they hollowed in their depths, the sculptures they chiselled, *e.g.* where these have not been obliterated by the weather. Tombs in Lycia may certainly be counted by hundreds, or rather thousands; but nearly all belong to what we have called the second period, and betray the influence of Grecian arts. Of the activity of the Pamphylians and Carians, nothing remains but a few tombs imperfectly traced, and short inscriptions that still await decipherment. The once rich and populous Lydia is represented by a single group of tumuli and her coins. The kingdom of Gordios and Midas did not play so grand a figure in the old world as that of Alyattes and Crœsus, but yet it can boast of rock-cut monuments so plentiful and varied as to enable the student to arrive at a pretty fair notion of the peculiar genius of its people and the help they gave in handing on plastic types and indispensable industries.

The first thing to be determined is the nature and importance of the borrowings the Phrygians made from the culture of Syro-Cappadocia, whence they seem to have derived the main elements of their beliefs and those rites which Greece long afterwards acknowledged as having received from Phrygia. The Asiatic Greeks who lived in daily intercourse with the Phrygians were content to adopt the sacred orgies they found in full swing among this people, without troubling themselves as to their cradle-land. Our curiosity is more exacting; it aims at tracing back their origin, and the evidence it finds on its path leads irresistibly to Cappadocia. If we have understood them aright, the great figured decorations carved upon the rocks of Pterium reveal concepts and represent ceremonies the main lines of which are precisely those that are supposed to characterize the religion of Phrygia. If we are unable to give a name to one of the two deities, that with the turreted head-dress, long robe, and supporting lion may unhesitatingly be regarded as the prototype of the Cybele of Sipylus and Dindymus.[1] Dances analogous to those of the Græci-Galli are depicted in the procession; some of the actors in the pomp bear a strong family likeness to those eunuch-priests who held the first rank in the sacerdotal order of Cybele. Be that as it may, self-mutilation did not originate with the Greeks, or with any Aryan people whose usages are known to us. It is a rite proper to Syrian cults, and was practised by the Semites, the White Syrians of Herodotus, established beyond the Halys, from whom it passed to the Phrygians. As much may be said of the phallus, put over Phrygian and Lydian tombs alike; were proof required of its importance we could point to the situation it occupies in an ædiculum carved upon the walls of the Cappadocian sanctuary.[2]

If the Thracian tribes in spreading eastwards compelled the Syro-Cappadocians to recede before them, only slowly and by degrees did they succeed in displacing them on this side of the Halys, in the course of which they became imbued with the social

[1] *Hist. of Art*, tom. iv. vol. ii. Fig. 320. The question may be asked as to whether we should not recognize a Cybele, under a different form, in the very curious figure at Iasili Kaia, in which the arms and legs of the deity are made up of lions' muzzles and bodies respectively.

[2] *Ibid.*, Fig. 331, pp. 385, 646, 653.

and religious ideas of the conquered. It is even possible that certain groups of the old population kept their ground in the neighbourhood of the sanctuaries they had consecrated, and that with revolving years they mixed and were so intimately fused with the new-comers, as to be undistinguishable from them. As we have just said, they transmitted to the younger nation their idea of the divine principle, the practices with which the gods were honoured and the symbols that served to translate their notions of them. The legacy handed down by an alien race was the basis upon which Phrygian genius worked, but which it seems to have enriched and unfolded in such a manner as to deserve to have its name linked with that religion and cultus of Cybele and Atys, to which the Græco-Roman world reserved so long and brilliant a career.

Types and emblems such as these were probably not the only means of expression the Phrygians received from the primitive owners of the land. When they wished to fix their ideas, the only possible system of signs offered to their use were Hittite hieroglyphs, whose finest specimens occur in the inscriptions found in the valley of the Orontes. If writing was known to the subjects of Tantalus, these were the characters they employed. Was theirs the hand, or that of the preceding generations, that engraved in the flank of Sipylus the hieroglyphs still to be seen near the Pseudo-Sesostris and the so-called Niobe? We incline to the latter hypothesis, and ascribe to the Hittites the few cognate signs met with in the very heart of Phrygia, close by long inscriptions in Greek letters.[1] What cannot be attributed to a people whose writing was little more than a string of images are those characters we discovered upon a tomb which, like the Delikli Tach example, unquestionably belongs to the Phrygian series of monuments (Fig. 57). The letters in question belonged to one of those Asianic alphabets, derived, as the Cypriote, from Hittite hieroglyphs through a method analogous to that which gave birth to the Phœnician syllabary.[2] Consequently there was first a Phrygian alphabet before that represented by the inscription of the Midas monument and others of the same type, in common use at the time when the Phrygians had no teachers outside their eastern neighbours, the Cappadocians.[3]

[1] *Hist. of Art*, tom. iv. Fig. 553. [2] *Ibid.*, p. 519.

[3] We are at one with M. Hirschfeld in considering Cappadocia in the light of

Thought has means other than writing to express itself; so that the Phrygians learnt yet another lesson at the Hittite school, and derived from it the first rudiments of art. Their princes, however, even in the heyday of their power and prosperity, do not seem to have been moved by the lofty ambition which had fired the tribal chiefs beyond the Halys. But these, in their encounters on the battle-field and their transactions of a more peaceful character, had been brought in touch, albeit transiently, with the wonders of Egyptian and Mesopotamian culture.

To sum up: Phrygian art stands as near as possible to Hittite art, as this does to that of Chaldæa and Assyria. It is the attenuated reflex of a far-off focus of light, whose rays have of necessity lost much of their splendour during their transit across the mighty Taurus range. Take for example the palace, the masterpiece of Assyrian architecture, represented in Cappadocia by edifices such as those at Boghaz Keui and Eyuk; these, though plainer and on a reduced scale, reproduce the plan and special details of the Ninevite buildings. On the other hand, no such data have been traced in the ruinous structures of Phrygia, so that the question arises as to whether its tribal chiefs were not content to put up with a wooden dwelling. The Kumbet ram (Figs. 115, 116) is the one solitary instance which seems to indicate that an attempt was made here to reproduce a disposition to which Eastern builders were most faithful. But even so, it is not proved that the said ram was one of those janitors we have met everywhere at the threshold of royal mansions, from Persia to Cappadocia.

The same impression is produced when we oppose Oriental to native sculpture. Whatever its purpose, the Kumbet ram looks shapeless as against not only the noble winged bulls at

an important centre of culture (see *Die Felsenreliefs in Kleinasien und das Volk der Hittiker*, p. 70). We deeply regret that his memoir, aptly entitled *Zweite Beitrag zur Geschichte Kleinasien*, should have appeared after the publication of our fourth volume. His observations and deep insight are of the kind that cannot be passed over lightly, and could not but have been of service to us; whilst we should have been at pains to explain more fully the reasons which lead us to differ from him. We might perhaps have been brought to agree on many a point respecting which disagreement is more apparent than real. The only serious point of dispute between us is that Cappadocia and Syria are more intimately connected than M. Hirschfeld is willing to admit.

Khorsabad and Nimroud, but the Boghaz Keui lions, and the Eyuk bull as well.[1] Besides, this fragment is isolated, for no other has been found in Phrygia; all the other instances of its statuary consisting of figures that are one with the mass in which they are carved, and all are modelled on those images in high, moderate, or flat relief, which the primitive owners of the soil chiselled in the flank of the hill. Again, is there aught that in any way resembles the remarkable bas-reliefs of Pterium, whether in magnitude, the number of the figures, or quality of workmanship? The only attempt in that direction is the inexpressibly poor and barbarous hunting scene depicted on the flanks of the Kumbet ram (Figs. 115, 116). The two idols of Cybele (Figs. 107, 110) are of the nature of highly conventionalized symbols, rather than portraitures of the living form. Of the original aspect the colossal Cybele at Magnesia[2] may have offered, it is now impossible to judge, save that such gigantic proportions as these testify to rare boldness of chisel.

In Phrygia, on the contrary, both in sanctuaries open to the sky and subterraneous chapels, the simulacra we have found are but clumsy, timid pieces, devoid of the one quality of size. As to the bas-reliefs of the Broken Tomb (Fig. 117), and more particularly the images decorating the walls of another sepulchre of the same group, they cannot be discussed here, since they already betray the influence of Greece.

Viewed as disciples of Cappadocian culture, the Phrygians are much inferior to their masters. The fact, however, that they were humble imitators and pupils is undeniable. Method and habit in attacking the solid rock in order to bring out the image, and, above all, identity of types, everything, proves it. The seated Cybele holding a patera (Fig. 107) is a replica of the Sipylus example;[3] as to the lions the goddess caresses (Figs. 64, 84, 110),[4] the notion of making them her companions did not originate with the Phrygians. Another point still more significant and equally foreign to the soil is the oft-recurring device about Phrygian frontispieces made up of two animals, one on each side of some object. This object may be a phallus (Fig. 75), a pillar (Fig. 109), a vase (Fig. 84); the animals, winged sphinxes (Fig. 109), bulls (Fig. 75), and oftener lions (Figs. 64, 84). The artist is allowed

[1] *Hist. of Art*, tom. iv. Figs. 298, 339, 340.
[2] *Ibid.*, Fig. 365. [3] *Ibid.*, tom. iv. Fig. 365. [4] *Ibid.*, pp. 650, 651.

a certain latitude as to the posturing and elements of his group, subject to one condition, that it shall be without prejudice to its general character. The lion device stands out amongst all others as that most dear and familiar to the Assyrian ornamentist.[1] It is the one he lavished wherever he found a space, both as decoration of his palaces, furniture, textiles, and jewellery. Caravans carried the latter to the nations of the West, so that the device became fashionable throughout Asia Minor. From Cappadocia it passed to Phrygia; thence, step by step, it reached Greece, where it obtained civic rights.

Of the animals thus brought in relation and opposed to one another in this theme, some, the sheep, the ox, and the horse, were indigenous, and could be copied from life. Pure creations of the fancy, however, were certainly borrowed from their inventors. Such would be the winged sphinx which occupies the middle of the frontal in the façade of a chapel (Fig. 109); such the griffin (Fig. 108) in the flank of this same rocky mass. The wings of the sphinx are designed like those of Assyria, and more particularly Phœnicia; their tips are curled in front towards the head of the animal.[2] As to the lion, he would seem to be a borrowed type.

To judge from certain details, notably the treatment of the mouth, it is clear that the sculptor had never beheld the animal, or, at least, had never looked him narrowly in the face with the intention of making his portrait. Silhouette and general outline were taken from Cappadocian artists; these in their turn had been inspired from the models furnished by Assyria. Assyria, with her vast jungles swarming with ferine, her royal hunts at which they were brought down by dozens, alone lived, if we may so speak, in intimacy with the lion, and could thus hit off his physiognomy. The type she had created was offered to the gaze of the Syrians in countless structures that rose in the broad strip of land separating the Euphrates from the Orontes valley and the oasis of Damascus, a kind of border line, the object of frequent and long disputes between Syrians and the kings of Calach and Nineveh. Nor was its circulation confined within these landmarks; seals, carpets, small pieces of furniture of every description,

[1] *Hist. of Art*, tom. ii. Figs. 95, 124, 138, 139, 265, 280, 331, 348, 399, 409, 430, 443.

[2] *Ibid.*, Fig. 249; tom. iii. Figs. 73, 76, 547, 552, 593.

served to diffuse it among all the peoples in touch with the markets of Mesopotamia. Imitations sprang up everywhere, and everywhere it retained something of the interpretation the plastic art of Chaldæo-Assyria had imparted to the noble forms of the king of feræ.

Along with characteristics common to all are differences due to personal temperament and the greater or less degree of skilfulness of the imitators. The workshops of Phœnicia issued countless proofs from this one type; in their hands, however, it assumed a redundancy of outline not found in the original. Their commonplace facility attenuated the accents put there by the firm, vigorous chisel of the Assyrian sculptor. These accents the Hittite artist did his best to preserve; but his lack of training caused him to exaggerate them. Tradition of this somewhat vulgar make is very apparent in the Phrygian lions. In order to bring out this resemblance, it will be enough to call attention to one characteristic detail, namely, the expedient resorted to by the stone-cutter to mark the shoulder-joint and the salience of the muscles. Here and there they are indicated on the limb by a raised line, oval shaped, instanced in a stela at Merash,[1] the Kalaba lion near Ancyra,[2] and the colossal lion which formed the external decoration of one of the finest tombs of the Ayazeen necropolis (Fig. 120). Observe, also, the strokes, forming a herring-bone pattern, which in the latter work serve to show where the mane ought to be, but scarcely aim at representing it; do not they remind us of the process employed by the Eyuk sculptor to render the deep folds of skin about the face?[3] Conventional treatment, dryness, and hardness of make are inherent to both, and place these works far behind Assyrian models; nevertheless, the Kalaba lion,[4] and even the Eyuk bull, are superior to the art productions of Phrygia of the same class—they are instinct with more truth and movement than any animal figures the Phrygian necropolis has to show.

Relations in matters of taste and workmanship, resemblances of types and methods, are likewise traceable in the scanty architectural forms revealed in the frontispieces of the Phrygian tombs. One of them is distinguished by a column, whose capital, though simpler and more primitive, in some respects

[1] *Hist. of Art*, tom. iv. Fig. 282.
[2] *Ibid.*, Fig. 340.
[3] *Ibid.*, Fig. 350.
[4] *Ibid.*, Fig. 339.

approaches the Doric (Fig. 92). It should be compared with the pillars at Gherdek Kaiasi, in Pterium, which also belong to the category of supports sometimes called proto-Doric.[1] We have laid particular stress on the basket-shaped capital, made up of leaves, which recalls many an Egyptian capital. Are we to view it as a unique survival of a really primitive type imported to Syria and Cappadocia from distant Egypt? The conjecture is fascinating; yet the tomb is certainly not among the oldest, and more than one monument of the Roman period could be named in Asia Minor, with capital richer and more complicated, it is true, but not without analogy with the one we are considering. If the particular order is still *sub judice*, the fact remains that we find introduced here, in a variety of ways, a decorative form of special interest to us, because of the large and brilliant use Greek genius was to make of it. We allude to the Ionic volute, whose beginnings have been made the subject of such hot disputes. The volute device may, perhaps, have been applied to surfaces other than that of columns; in which case it might be recognized in the inverted curve which appears as acroterion in the vast majority of pediments (Figs. 58, 59). But elsewhere we find it again in its real function, as crowning member to columns and pilasters; an instance of which occurs in one of the best executed façades (Fig. 61), where it is lavished, and furnishes at the sides and summit of the pilasters the elements of a somewhat elaborate design. Finally, as columnar capping in a pair of tombs of later date (Fig. 90), where it is chalked in with a careless hand, the narrow tight rolls of Figs. 93 and 96, if somewhat meagre and rigid, constitute all the same a capital not devoid of elegance. We think we have made it clear, then, that the Phrygians largely utilized the volute in their decorative schemes; a motive we tracked from Mesopotamia to Syria, on to Phœnicia and Cappadocia. Its presence in Phrygia forms one more link between her art and that of the people of Anterior Asia. It may be that we also should turn to Phrygia for the secret of resemblances which it would be hard to explain, had her monuments, like those of Lydia, perished without leaving a trace. When the temples of Miletus and Ephesus were built, the Ionians had not yet penetrated into Cappadocia; they had not beheld, figured on the Pterian rocks, the columns in which we think to recognize the rude outline of

[1] *Hist. of Art*, tom. iv. Fig. 344.

the noble architectural type with which they have had the honour to link their name;[1] but their intercourse with the well-to-do peaceful agriculturists, whose kine and corn they purchased, whose cults they adopted, and to whom in return they gave their alphabet, was frequent and intimate. In Phrygia, then, carved on wood and stone, they everywhere saw the graceful involúcrum, now serving to lessen the thrust put upon the supports, now as pleasing ornament to pieces of jewellery, artistic furniture, and ivories brought by overland and sea routes.[2] Which, among the widely different and numberless objects challenging their attention, struck their fancy most, made them intellectually richer? We know not; save that, so far as we can guess from what has been preserved in the rock-cut monuments, Phrygian architecture must have furnished more than a useful suggestion to those receptive and curious minds.

The Greeks found something more among the Phrygians than the time-honoured volute, which had long been acknowledged as among the properties of Oriental art. Phrygian architecture was neither derived from Chaldæa, where stone is unknown, nor from untimbered Cappadocia proved by the tombal façades which are modelled upon edifices inhabited by the living. It has little to say to lignite constructions, and the exclusive use of timber gave a form to the building which is markedly different from that obtained elsewhere from stone and brick. In countries where rain and snow are not rare, the framework of the wooden house ends necessarily in a sharp ridge; a roof whose double slope describes on either side of the building a gable, of which the angle may be acute or the reverse as climatic requirements or the taste of the builder shall direct. Who does not know the importance given to the pediment in Grecian temples, where slanting lines form as happy a corona to cella and porticoes as can well be imagined; yielding, moreover, ample space upon which the ingenuity of the sculptor can be exercised? Now, the pediment is no more than a sharply defined gable, bounded at the beginning of the angle by a horizontal bar, the salience of the cornice. This form we have met once only in the course of studies in which is reflected all that remains of Oriental art. Reference has already been made to the curious architectonic shape which occurs in a

[1] *Hist. of Art*, tom. iv. pp. 694, 695, Figs. 314, 321.
[2] *Ibid.*, tom. ii. Figs. 71, 76–80; tom. iii. Figs. 51–53.

bas-relief, representing the temple of a town in Armenia about to fall into the hands of the Assyrians.[1] It is probable that the temple in question, situate within a cold, forest-clad region, was likewise wholly built of wood; if the Ninevite artist took pains to make a faithful copy of it, this was because he had been struck by its singular aspect, altogether different from the buildings he was wont to put in his pictures. It was a whim of no consequence, one that titillated the imagination, as a remembrance of distant campaigns, but which the Assyrians had no intention of imitating; their architecture, humble and submissive throughout its career, followed implicitly the prescriptive rules and methods of Chaldæan art.

Matters were different with the populations of the west; for on the one hand they shook off the thraldom of tradition, whilst on the other hand, whenever they looked abroad in Phrygia and Lydia, they beheld types which had originated in wood, but were imitated on stone, in the face of rocks in which Phrygians and Lydians alike hollowed their tombs. If they found there forms and arrangements to their liking, adapted to their taste and needs, there was nothing to prevent their appropriating and making use of them. Hence it comes to pass that the wooden house, as it is built and lined in certain parts of Asia Minor at the present day, may have furnished some of the elements seen in the first essayals of the Greek builder. The particular notion suggested to him in this way was to put a triangular pediment over the rectangular slab of the façade—an arrangement whose principle and model he was not likely to discover anywhere among the peoples he frequented.

There is less need to insist upon a disposition met with in several tombs of the necropolis and the oldest Greek buildings. We mean to say the slope at the sides which renders the top of the bay narrower than the base (Figs. 75, 79, 92). The arrangement is not sufficiently bound up with the processes and exigences of a timber architecture to warrant its being considered as a distinct feature of Phrygian buildings, or explain its presence in other localities, as borrowed from wooden types. The same thing may be said of the meander, which plays so important a part in Phrygian ornament, and which the Greek decorator has so often introduced into his work (Figs. 48, 49, 60). The woollen textiles

[1] *Hist. of Art*, tom. ii. Fig. 190.

and embroideries manufactured by inland tribes, and which they despatched to the markets of the coast, helped, doubtless, to accustom the eye with the pattern; yet the theme is so naturally suggested by the weaver and the mat-maker, as to be found among peoples that have never had any intercourse one with the other. It is as frequent on Peruvian and Mexican vases as on those of Greece; so that the Ionians may have discovered it for themselves, as they plaited bulrushes and handled the shuttle ere Phrygionic tissues served to furnish their dwellings.

Differences bearing exclusively on details admit, then, of being explained without calling in the hypothesis of imitation or borrowings. In the same rank with the frontal shape, which we noticed for the first time when we began to visit Phrygia, should be placed a type of burial also found there, or at least in a territory occupied for a while by the Phrygians. We were careful to make tracings of the few exemplars then known. It is a type we shall meet again, both in the Lydian kingdom, where it seems to have persisted almost down to the fall of the last national dynasty, and on the other side of the Ægean, in Greece proper, where it is represented by monuments certainly older than the tomb of Alyattes. This type is the stone tumulus, sometimes protected by a casing of well-dressed units. The internal arrangement consists of a chamber of sufficient strength to shelter the corpse, and, as a rule, of a passage leading to a doorway. But the difficulty is this: these tumuli are empty and mute, and so can tell us nothing of their history, whilst the monuments in the district of Nacoleia are signed, so to speak, and approximately dated by the people who reared them. Nevertheless the Greeks, even when supreme masters of the lower valley of the Hermus, never regarded their forefathers as the creators of the tumuli which it contains; those on Sipylus they ascribed to the quasi-fabulous Tantalidæ, and they could tell the names of the kings who had reared the Lydian monuments The sum of evidence tends to prove that the tombs with circular base are a legacy of the civilization which in this district preceded that of Hellas. The fact, moreover, that we have observed nothing like them in Egypt or Mesopotamia, Syria or Cappadocia, is another point in favour of the argument which would consider the very particular type seen in the neighbourhood of the Smyrnian bay as neither of Oriental origin nor an importation thence; but as having been introduced by Thracian tribes, which spread under various names and occupied the whole of the north-west corner of the peninsula. Of all these nations, the Phrygian would appear to have been the first to reach a state of cohesion and a certain politico-religious importance. Hence, in the absence of positive data respecting the primitive history of these populations, it seems natural to connect the people who first set the example of so burying their dead in Asia Minor, who furnished the model of monuments such as the famous tombs at Mycenæ, with a Phrygian stock.

It may be objected that the funereal architecture of the Phrygians of the Sangarius (who, in virtue of the witness borne by history and that of the inscription, alone deserve the name) is imbued with characteristics other than those that appear on the southern slopes of Sipylus in the Tantaleis necropolis, where rock-hewn vaults are the rule and tumuli the exception. The objection was disposed of when we defined the nature of the rock, which everywhere around Nacoleia is even with the surface; but wherever it could be readily worked, it was simpler to excavate tombs than to undertake the long arduous process of building a somewhat complicated vault. Do not we find hypogeia in those parts of Sipylus where soft calcareous formations rather than hard trachytic rocks obtain? The nature of the soil and a settled condition of life may have brought about rapid changes in the habits of the people under consideration.

In a minute study such as this, it was impossible to avoid taking up conjectures one by one as they presented themselves. Towards the twelfth century B.C., perhaps even earlier, Thracian clans began to appear in Asia Minor, where they would seem to have taken advantage of the clear space left by the great migratory movement, which we find recorded in Egyptian documents; when, like bees, part of the native population swarmed and dispersed themselves along the coasts of the Mediterranean. Ere long the Phrygians, one of these tribes, founded, within the region comprised between the Hermus gulf and the mouth of the river of the same name, a state that owed much of its prosperity to the strong position it had secured for itself, along with the rudiments of civil life its inhabitants had learnt in their intercourse with the cultured people of the central plateau. These still continued to send their merchandise to those seaports they had formerly visited as conquerors. On a coast where natural harbours alternate with promontories, which clustering islands prolong far out into the sea, they owned perhaps the largest and safest. In conditions such as these, a race of hardy mariners soon sprang up, who spread in the Archipelago, perhaps even on the coasts of continental Greece, along with the home produce of the rich Hermus valley, the raw material brought by caravans from Cappadocia and from farther still, to the markets of the seaboard. It is but an hypothesis that we offer, but an hypothesis apparently confirmed, and on the one hand by traditions connecting the Tantalidæ with Peloponnesus, on the other by truly curious analogies observable between certain very antique monuments found within the Argolid and those of Phrygia.

When or what the causes that wrought the downfall of the state on Sipylus, it is impossible to say. Its pristine importance, due at the outset to its situation as a natural bulwark, was already lost during historical times; and it became little more than a store-room for the memory, a holy mount. Following on the foundation of the Greek colonies, all movement and bustle had migrated to the lowlands and the narrow strips girding the sea. But the new-comers, the Æolians of Magnesia and of Smyrna, as they settled, some to the north, and others to the south of Sipylus, learnt of their predecessors traditions which told of the wealth and power of the ancient rulers; their glowing fancy, exercising itself on this theme, drew forth the myths of Tantalus, Pelops, and Niobe. In the same frame of mind, they adopted the cults they had found established in the country, and became fervent worshippers of the Phrygian Cybele; and whilst they raised her new temples, they continued to surround with pious reverence her old simulacra and the sanctuaries that were one with the holy mount. Thus the old state of Phrygia outlived itself in the impress it left in the soil and the religion it bequeathed to its heirs. But towards the tenth or ninth centuries B.C. the Phrygians of the Lower Hermus ceased to exist as a nation; for the tribes that go by that name in the epos are grouped around the head-springs of the Sangarius; they still try to extend eastward, and this brings them into conflict with the Amazons, that is to say, the warlike populations of Cappadocia. The various stages in the onward march of the Phrygians, starting from the shores of the Ægean and Propontis on to the Halys, may be guessed from the monuments themselves. Thus the tomb at Delikli Tach, situate in the Rhyndacus basin, looks older than any of the sepulchral monuments in the necropoles around Nacoleia. The decorative scheme is simpler; and, a still surer criterion, the signs by which it is accompanied are older than any alphabetical writing. The Greek epos does not know the Gordioses and the Midases; when it was composed the names of the founders of the Phrygian power had not yet re-echoed in the Ionian and Æolian cities; hence we think we may assume that the Phrygians did not constitute themselves into a political body, under that dynasty, before the eighth century B.C. To organize themselves into a well-ordered state may well have taken in a hundred years, during which they developed the resources of the country, opened up continuous relations with their eastern neighbours, the Cappadocians, on the one side, and the Greek-speaking populations of the western coast on the other. Besides, if we are not mistaken in refusing to seek a tomb behind the façade upon which the name of Midas may be read, it will give us one more reason for putting a pretty late date upon this considerable work, which was not undertaken the day after the death of the personage. The notion must have come much later, when the memory of the ancestor was productive of successes and benefits to his descendants, when the first Midas, magnified by the legend that already attached to his name, was nothing more for the new generations than the founder of the monarchy, the glorious father of a whole race of kings, an eponymous hero, to whom divine honours were rendered.

Consequently, it is towards the end of the eighth or the beginning of the seventh century B.C. that we would place the Midas monument and the more important tombs surrounding it, characterised by forms imitated from carpentry work, designs borrowed from tapestry, and, above all, the use of an alphabet derived from the Phœnician syllabary. We feel greater embarrassment in trying to assign a date to another group of monuments, those frontispieces of the Ayazeen necropolis, in which are seen true bas-reliefs, figures of men and lions.

Are these façades older or more recent than such exemplars as exhibit a wholly geometrical decoration? M. Ramsay is inclined to think them more ancient. He finds in them types taken from Cappadocia, and resemblances of detail to which we referred a little way back. In his estimation, real Phrygian art started into being later, when the ornamentist, shaking off the yoke in which alien traditions had held him a prisoner so long a time, set himself to reproduce on stone all the shapes that made up the wooden house in which he lived, together with the patterns the women around him worked in the loom. If his decorative scheme is neither rich nor varied, it has yet the merit of being a faithful portraiture of the homely scenes in which it arose, and of having been kept within the limits imposed upon it by the material at hand. If it cannot be denied that the period covered by the frontispieces of the Midas necropolis is, in some respects, much the most interesting for the historian, it does not help us to understand how so simple, one might almost say so poor an ornamentation, can have succeeded one in which the living form and its potential diversity held so large a place. Art, like poetry, is progressive, and does not move from the complex to the simple, but follows an inverse course. It is possible that the clumsy pictures on the flanks of the colossal Kumbet ram, those modelled about the Yapuldak tomb by so unskilful a hand as to render it almost impossible to guess the kind of animal they stand for, as well as the rough-drawn images of Cybele seen near the tombs and sanctuaries of the plateau, preceded what may be termed the classic age of Phrygian art; but the whole group of the Ayazeen necropolis bespeaks a later epoch. The architecture is more complicated and of quite a different nature. Nothing in it betrays imitation of a timber construction; neither the columns with their varied capitals, nor the membering of mouldings with their elaborate profiles and wealth of subjects, nor the general arrangement in which the curved forms of the portico mingle with combinations of straight lines, which elsewhere cover the whole field. At the same time sculpture properly so called, has assumed an importance it had not in the other series of monuments. Griffins and winged sphinxes abound; gigantic lions are set to watch at the threshold of sanctuaries and tombs, whilst others, of smaller calibre, are seen in pairs within the tympans of frontals. Nor is this all; the human face looks out of at least two of the better class of tombs, and furnishes the theme of a large bas-relief belonging to that fine hypogeum, the destruction of which is so much to be regretted. Mr Ramsay's patient labour among these fragments, in the course of which he succeeded in turning about and discovering nearly all those that originally decorated the main wall, has caused him to abandon the hypothesis he had at first taken up. There is nothing in it to recall Capadocian art, either in the theme, workmanship, or accessories; in order to find some analogy thereto we must address ourselves to the archaic work of Greece, and especially ancient vase-painting. The figures have no longer the highly conventional posture which the bas-reliefs of Pterium, and those of other localities allied to the same school, have familiarized us with; the arms are detached from the body.

Accessories show quite as notable a change. Thus the shield is circular, the breast-plate composed of metal pieces, and the helmet has little resemblance to the Hittite cap, but is a real covering and protection for the head; as to the huge crest crowning it, its explanation and appellative are to be sought in Homer. We have observed nothing like it either in Assyria or in the long series of rock-cut sculptures of Asia Minor, those representing the primal civilisation of her inhabitants. The panoply of the two warriors who run their spears in the Gorgon's head, on the façade of a Phrygian vault, is that of the Greek hoplite, those Carian and Ionian mercenaries whose "scaly" armour terrified the populations of Syria and Egypt, when, towards the middle of the seventh century B.C., they appeared on their borders and took part in their quarrels.

The bas-relief of the Broken Tomb does not even go so far back. It plainly shows that the sculptor who modelled it had been, in some way or other, under the influence of Hellenic art. Now, to find, in Greece, figures on marble or the body of vases drawn, as these, with so remarkable a sureness of hand, we must fain descend to the latter half of the sixth century B.C. We should, therefore, incline to date the execution of both vault and sculpture somewhere about that time—a date that will, perhaps, be questioned by drawing attention to the make of the lion. The latter is much more archaic than the two heroic lance-bearers,[1] and originates, as the other colossal figures encountered in this canton, from a type created by the sculptors of Mesopotamia; this type, when transplanted in Syria and Cappadocia, assumed a very peculiar and heavy aspect, due to sheer massiveness. If the attitude is different, the general appearance of the figure is pretty near the same as in Pterium, and the rendering of certain details is identical. Is this to be taken as a proof that the inner and external decora-

[1] With regard to the apparent anomaly, due to imperfect technique, between the workmanship of the lion and the human figures, *vide* p. 172 and note [2].

tion was undertaken at two different times—say, at an interval of a hundred years? There is no need for such an hypothesis. The monument, with its more complicated arrangement than any other exemplar of the Phrygian necropolis, is the outcome of a single effort, and the apparent anomaly is readily explained. As the lions were mere decorative figures, the work of carving them was left to craftsmen who repeated a traditional type, numerous instances of which already existed in the necropolis. This does not apply to the bas-relief in the cemetery, which is unique of its kind. The man for whom it was carved, a petty local prince under the jurisdiction of the Persian satrap of Daskylion, wished to have something out of the common, when he ordered the image of genii, guardians of the tomb, to be set at the entrance of the burial place which was to receive his mortal remains. To this end he called in a sculptor whose training had brought him in touch with the Greek world of the Ionian coast, where art was even then making such prodigious strides towards perfection.

The Broken Tomb, then, belongs to the opening of the second period of the development of Phrygian art. General arrangement and selection of forms, the whole architectural scheme, still bears the stamp of early habits and local taste, whilst the ornament is entirely borrowed from that old repertory of devices and symbols which had satisfied older generations. But in the frontispiece of the funereal chamber we have a sculptured page dictated by a new spirit, written by a different hand.

The same analytical test, applied to the neighbouring hypogeia, would result in the same remarks; we should see that the primitive forms and national subjects have undergone gradual modification by contact with Hellenic art; and, as in the Kumbet tomb (Fig. 84), the theme is still thoroughly Asiatic, thoroughly Phrygian if preferred, whilst the manipulation of bas-reliefs and mouldings testifies to a more refined and elegant taste.

The Kumbet exemplar, therefore, cannot be carried back beyond the end of the fifth century, and may, after all, date from the fourth century B.C.[1] Ancient traditions, whether of general

[1] HIRSCHFELD (*Paphlagonische Felsengräber*, p. 41) does not consider the tomb older than the fourth century. He compares it with the Lycian tomb at Myra (published by TEXIER, *Description*, tom. iii. Plate CCXXV.), in which the subject—the deadly conflict between two animals (a lion and a bull)—is strictly Oriental, whilst the architectural types belong to the Ionic order, of universal usage in the peninsula during the two last centuries of the pagan era.

adjustment or details, were discarded in the tomb of Gherdek Kaïasi; it is no more than a Greek monument of the decadence, one we might as readily expect to see elsewhere as in Phrygia (Fig. 91), and in all likelihood is coeval with the Seleucidæ, mayhap the Roman proconsuls of Asia. On looking at it, we feel that when the artist designed it all meaning and tradition of rock-cut architecture were already forgotten; the slender supports of the façade, the wide intercolumnation which separates them, ill agree with the massiveness of the native rock in which the sepulchre was hollowed. Taken as a whole, it falls short of the air of strength and solidity which a rock-cut structure ought to possess.

The fact of Oriental types having died exceedingly hard about the tombs in the vicinity of Nacoleia is to be explained by the memories and associations which attached to the canton. Packed away in a hilly well-timbered region, untraversed by the military or commercial highways, it was in the nature of things that it should have lain forgotten by Greek and Latin writers—by those, at least, who have come down to us. Mention of it may have been made in the pages of those monograms entitled Φρυγιακὰ (*Histories and Descriptions of Phrygia*), but such works are lost. Fortunately for us, the silence of texts is supplemented by monuments both varied and numerous; they permit us to guess that the situation of this district did much to mould the character of the real Phrygian people, those of the Gordioses and Midases, as well as the light in which they were held by their Hellenized descendants, who for centuries were wont to engrave on their coins the effigy of their ancestor Midas (see tailpiece, end of chapter), and who, in the age of the Antonines, would not have readily believed in the efficacy of the formulas incised on their funereal stelas, had not letters of their ancient and, doubtless, obsolete language been interpolated with them. The tribes that fought the battles around the head-springs of the Sangarius, the echo of which reached Homer, tribes that secured to their descendants possession of part of the plateau of Asia Minor, had here their first religious and political centre. Under the protecting shadow of rock-hewn strongholds, they gathered themselves around sanctuaries, consecrated, mayhap, by the former owners of the soil, whose religion was adopted and continued by the new-comers. As the spring came round, these sylvan scenes would resound with the voice of young life; lambs, kine and colts that frolicked under the vault of undying pines in sheer wantonness of youthful spirits. Here twice a year were celebrated the mysteries of Cybele and Atys, the king and the heads of the various clans taking part in the ceremonies. Tents and temporary booths were set up on the greensward, whilst prince and nobles, during the festivities, occupied roomy wooden houses planted on artificial esplanades, of which we found traces on many a point; "konaks," they would be called at the present day, very like the kiosk of the old Dere Bey of Kumbet (Fig. 83). There never was here a town, as we understand the term—as Apamæ and Celenæ, Pessinus and Ancyra, for example. Real Phrygian cities, of which many are still important centres, were built on better chosen sites, lending themselves more readily to supply the wants of an agglomerated population all the year round. In this district water fails during the hot summer months, but with the autumnal rains of October silvery rills reappear, when along their banks cattle find an abundance of coarse tall grass to the end of June.[1] Picturesque rural retreats such as these seemed marked out for those *al fresco* festivities, *panegyria*, which have never been out of fashion with Eastern races, Greeks, Syrians, and Turks. With the return of each season, woods and meadows, even as the valley of the Alphæus during the Olympian games, would fill with the hum, the stir and merriment of thousands of human voices, married to the confused sound of flutes and tambourines; the multitude passing, with scarcely any transition, from frenzied joy to black despair. The cares and routine of daily life were for the time suspended or forgotten; every sense was employed in celebrating the public rites of the national gods. On such occasions visits were paid and sacrifices and libations made to the manes of ancestors who had wished their tombs to be placed under the special tutelary wing of Cybele, whose style and image appeared on these same rocks.

[1] To find a perennial spring, says Barth, one must needs go as far as the neighbourhood of Doghanlou Deresi (8 in map) and Gherdek Kaiasi (3 in map), some two hours north of the Midas monument. This is one reason which prevents us seeking there the "town of Gordios" (Γορδίου πόλις), also named Gordion, supposed to have been "the hearth (cradle) of ancient Midas," writes Plutarch (*Alexander*, xviii.); a conjecture overthrown by Arrian, who says of Gordion, "It is found on the river Sangarius" (*Ana.*, i. 29), a situation which does not by any means fit the site we have called "Midas city." Arrian's testimony, especially upon matters relating to Asia Minor, is generally correct.

The main cause why the monuments under notice were saved from destruction is to be accounted for in the fact that there never was here a great urban population. The contempt and discredit that fell upon the old beliefs when the antique world fell to pieces caused sites, formerly the objects of frequent pilgrimages, to be neglected and forgotten by all save tillers and woodmen. Thus it came to pass that until the beginning of the present century, when these monuments were discovered by travellers, there had been nothing to disturb the dust gathered around what may be called the museum of Phrygian art. Had these works perished, like others of the same kind and style that doubtless once peopled the necropolis and cities of Phrygia, there would have been one more lacuna, hard to fill in the history of civilization and of the plastic arts. We should have been unable to form a correct estimate of the influence exercised upon the Greeks by certain nations of Asia Minor, both as middlemen and creators of not a few architectonic and ornamental forms. Nor is this the only title the relics of Phrygian art offer to the lively interest of the observer; what adds to their importance is the fact that here, perhaps, are to be found the oldest traces of the influence Greece (from having at first received on all sides) began to exercise over nations who had been her first instructors. This she did with characteristic vigour and power.

The first symptoms of this singular phenomenon, this returning wave, are manifested on the monuments of Phrygia. The Greeks, in the opening years of the seventh century B.C., gave their alphabet to an independent community settled far enough from the shores of the Ægean. This was ere long followed by Grecian architecture and Grecian sculpture. At this school, Phrygian artists learnt the secret of imparting just proportions and freedom of movement to the human form; they accustomed themselves to enclose within mouldings of greater variety and refinement symbols dear to their ancestors, when internally and externally a gradual change spread over their façades.

Thus, on the soil of this vast mountainous peninsula, where the sons of Hellas owned but a narrow strip fringing the sea, new forms, new ideas stole in on every hand, which traffic and example helped further to disseminate long before any Greek captain had scaled, with his army, the terraced hills in advance of the inland plateaux. The battles of the Granicus, Issus, and Arbela were no doubt of great service in opening more widely existing routes, breaking down the last barriers; but military action alone would have been powerless to effect a radical and lasting change in the condition of the world, had not a long period of tranquillity prepared the way, during which a propaganda, pacific and fruitful, was carried on, which contributed not a little in bringing about the final result, the definitive triumph of Hellenic genius, and the subjugation of the whole East to the commanding superiority of Greek civilization.

LYDIA AND CARIA.

CHAPTER I.

THE LYDIANS, THEIR COUNTRY, HISTORY, AND RELIGION.

THE Lydia of Greek historians and geographers was comprised within the small basin of the Caÿster, the lower and middle valley of the Hermus, and extended as far as the right bank of the Mæander, which served as line of delimitation between it and Caria. "Homer," says Strabo, "was unacquainted with the Lydians."[1] The country subsequently so named is styled by him "pleasant Mæonia."[2] Should the two names be taken to designate two different peoples who succeeded each in the country, or were they applied to twin groups of the same race, the last one of which finally obtained the upper hand? There is a greater degree of probability for the latter hypothesis; since the Lydian nation, as is well known, was made up of several tribes. The appellative Lydian would seem to have been borne by the tribe settled around the middle Hermus, and to have gradually extended to the whole people. This was mainly due to the foundation of Sardes, whose commanding situation would of itself secure to its owners a marked ascendency over the other clans. The ancients were fully conscious of the comparatively recent period of that city and its fortress. This they expressed after their own fashion, when they said that Sardes had risen after the Trojan war.[3]

From the Greek lyric poets of the seventh and sixth centuries, we get the first glimpse of Lydia and the Lydians. As to the little that is known of their history, we are mostly indebted for it

[1] Strabo, XII. viii. 3; XIII. iv. 5.

[2] HOMER, *Iliad*, iii. 401; xviii. 291. The name of Mæonia was not wholly wiped out; under Roman domination it was still applied to a city and district north of Philadelphia, between it and Mount Tmolus.

[3] Strabo, XII. iv. 5.

to Herodotus and Xanthus of Lydia.[1] The latter was an Hellenicized Lydian, who wrote in the early part of the fifth century. His book is unfortunately lost; and it may be questioned whether the fragments that have been preserved by Strabo, notably Nicholas of Damascus, really belong to the old logographer, and not rather to a far less reliable writer, one Dionysius Skythobrachion, who seems to have compiled a history of Lydia during the Alexandrian age, which he published under the venerable name of Xanthus.[2] Such a suspicion, in a certain measure, throws discredit on the testimony of Xanthus, who on many points is at variance with Herodotus; nevertheless there is a tendency to believe that, though the Alexandrian rhetorician may have embellished and added many stories of his own to the work of his predecessor,[3] whose great name he pirated, he yet, on the whole, closely followed him. From the citations we infer that he was a man given to the observation of nature, one, too, who had lived in the country; for he is circumstantial and precise in his remarks respecting the natural phenomena to which Lydia owes its peculiar configuration; nor is he less well informed as to its antiquities. Such things would have had no interest for the pedantic bookworms of Pergamus and Alexandria. It is possible that had the work of Xanthus been preserved in its entirety and in the language in which it was originally written, its testimony, in matters pertaining to Lydia, would be found of even greater weight than that of Herodotus himself. He was familiar with the native language, which had not yet fallen into desuetude through the diffusion of the Greek tongue; he was thus able to consult the archives of the country, which were of no small importance for the work in hand.[4] The main thread of Herodotus's narrative is made

[1] BERGK, *Poetæ lyrici Græci*, 3rd ed.; Sappho, Frag. 85; Anacreon, Frag. 18; Hipponax, Frag. 15; Xenophanes, Fr. 3, etc.

[2] See notice upon Xanthus and the fragments preserved in tom. i., *Fragmenta historicorum græcorum*, Ch. and Th. Muller.

[3] Nicholas of Damascus, a famous rhetorician of the Augustan age, probably borrowed the substance of the fourth and sixth book of his *Universal History*, dealing with Lydia, from Dionysius Skythobrachion's work, rewritten and arranged to suit the taste of the day. Lengthy fragments exist of these two books, notably the second (*Fr. Hist. Græc.*, tom. iii.); if mixed up with much that is purely romantic and fantastical, there are yet curious data which would seem to belong to Xanthus himself.

[4] Nicholas of Damascus (Frag. 49, 21) says of a certain Spermios, who would seem to have occupied the throne for the space of two years: ἐν τοῖς βασιλείοις οὐκ ἀναγράφεται. As to the time when Xanthus lived, see Letronne's notice (*Œuvres choisies*, tom. i. pp. 203–206, 8vo, 1883, Leroux).

up of gossiping stories current in the Greek cities of the seaboard; more particularly hearsay evidence he had picked up at Delphi, where the stupendous gifts the shrine had received from the last kings of Lydia had served to keep green the memory of their names. It may be easily guessed that in such an atmosphere facts would necessarily undergo notable change and disfigurement, so as to enhance the importance of the oracle and prove its infallibility.

This is not the place for endeavouring to reconcile the conflicting evidence found in Herodotus with that ascribed to Xanthus, or to enter into the very obscure question as to the chronological order of the Lydian kings. Of the history under notice we require no more than what will help to understand the monuments. Herodotus reckoned three dynasties as having succeeded each other in Lydia: the Atyadæ, Heraclidæ, and Mermnadæ.[1] The first is purely fabulous; born of the vanity of the Lydians, and of their desire to possess a past no less remote than their eastern neighbours. We feel on scarcely more solid ground with the Heraclidæ, to whom Herodotus assigns five hundred years duration and twenty-two princes, since it is self-evident that a mere string of names, wholly bare of facts, could only have been obtained by artificial means; exception may, perhaps, be made for the two or three last reigns. With the Mermnadæ history may be said to begin.

The exact date of the advent of Gyges, the founder of this dynasty, is not fixed with any degree of certainty. What seems pretty sure is that Greek chronographers put it too far back; on the basis of Assyrian documents it is now moved on to the seventh century B.C.[1] On the other hand, the date of the overthrow of Crœsus and the taking of Sardes, his capital, by the Persians in 546 B.C. may be relied upon. It enables us to compute the reign of the Mermnadæ at a little over a hundred and fifty years, during which they raised the Lydians, who up to that time had been of no account in the world, to the first rank in the peninsula, and masters of more than half of it. If Lydia ever produced original works, we may affirm beforehand that they belonged to this period,

[1] Herodotus, i. 7.

[2] Gelzer, who has studied with care the early period of Lydian history, gives the following dates as the result of his calculations. According to him, Gyges reigned from 687 to 653; his son Ardys from 652 to 616.

the only one when her people were united enough, powerful and rich enough, to have a culture and an art of their own.

The monuments in question are unfortunately very few, and in the number there is not a single inscription, or a text, or even half a dozen letters, which would give us the clue to the Lydian language, or, at any rate, its alphabet.[1] Consequently we have not, as in Phrygia, the resource of turning to the language in order to extract therefrom some little light upon the origin and the ethnical affinities of the people. All we can do is to take down the testimony of the ancients, without the possibility of checking it.

Herodotus represents the Mysians as a branch of the Lydian stock, from which it had separated at some time or other[2]—an assertion confirmed by Xanthus, since he gives formal expression to the effect that the spoken dialect of the Mysians held a middle course between that of the Lydians and the Phrygians.[3] Linguistic research has established in full the opinion of the two historians. Thus of the few Lydian words which lexicographers have rescued from oblivion in their glossary, most are susceptible of being explained by roots common to Sanscrit and cognate Indo-European languages.[4] Some of these words are found both in the Lydian and Carian, others in the Lydian and Phrygian idioms.

Still further proofs may be adduced, on the authority of Herodotus, in support of the near kinship between Mysians, Lydians, and Carians, since he affirms that they looked upon themselves as of one family, and that, in virtue of this consanguinity, the temple

[1] Unknown characters have been discovered, which, had they been submitted to a competent authority, might have turned out to be Lydian inscriptions; for M. G. Hirschfeld thus wrote in 1870, "Whilst the works for the construction of the railway were proceeding, huge blocks of stone were dug up at Sardes, on which appeared unknown characters, resembling, it is said, cuneiform characters. Further information is to follow" (*Bulletin de l'Institut de correspondance archéologique*, 1873, p. 225). The promise thus made was never fulfilled. One is also tempted to see a Lydian text in the monument uncovered by Fontrier at Ak Hissar, ancient Thyatira (S. REINACH, "Chron. d'Orient," *Revue arché.*, 3ᵉ série, 1886, tom. vii. p. 165). An impression of it was shown to Professor Sayce, but he confined himself to the statement "that, whatever the characters might be, they were not Hittite." During Professor Sayce's excursion in Lydia, he was informed of the existence of a rock-cut inscription in cuneiform characters (?) to be seen in a secluded corner of Mount Tmolus (*Journal Hell. Studies*, 1880, p. 88).

[2] Herodotus, vii. 74; *οὗτοι* (the Mysians) *δέ εἰσι Λυδῶν ἄποικοι.*

[3] Xanthus, Fr. 8. Another native writer, Menecrates, furnishes a like intelligence (Strabo, VII. ii. 3).

[4] PAUL DE LAGARDE, *Gesammelte Abhandlungen*, pp. 270–276.

of Carian Zeus, at Mylasa, which no stranger was allowed to enter, stood open to Lydians and Mysians.[1] If, setting aside local cults, which are very imperfectly known, we consider solely the broader features of the creeds which obtained in the west of the peninsula, we shall be able to say that the religion of the Phrygians and Lydians was identical. The most important temples of Lydia were consecrated, as in Phrygia, to the great goddess who personified the creative power of Nature—she whom the Asiatic Greeks (heirs and pupils of the nations they had found settled on the soil) worshipped, now under the name of Cybele, as at Smyrna, and now under that of Artemis, as at Ephesus. Atys, the inseparable companion of Cybele and the lunar god, Men, were honoured as much in Lydia as in Phrygia. Lydian and Phrygian myths represented the hero Mânes as the founder of their respective national dynasty.[2] Then, too, the basis of religious belief and the character of public worship of either country are very similar, save that myths in Lydia have assumed a very peculiar form and complexion. Such would be that out of which the Greeks spun the tale of Heracles and Omphales.

Let it be demonstrated, then, that whether the Lydians originally came from Thracia, or entered Asia by another route, they none the less belonged, as all their neighbours, to the Aryan family. If this was for a long time a moot question, if the Lydians were considered as Semites, it was on the strength of a verse in Genesis;[3] but this curious chapter (tenth) has no longer the authoritative weight it once had, even in the eyes of orthodox commentators.[4] Besides, it is now generally acknowledged that the ethnographic, or rather ethnogenitic, classification which the author of the genealogies strove to establish corresponds, at least in its general outlines, with the geographical table of the distribution of the human families over the earth's surface. Thus, to the north and south are people descended from Japhet; the sons of Ham hold Southern Syria

[1] Herodotus, i. 171.

[2] PLUTARCH, *Isis and Osiris*, 24; Herodotus, i. 94, iv. 45; DENYS OF HALICARNASSUS, *Roman Antiquities*, i. 27. Mânes has been compared with the Indian Manû and the Teutonic Mannus. It would be more risky, perhaps, trying to do the same for the Cretan Minos.

[3] Gen. x. 22: "The children of Shem; Elam, Asshur, Arphaxad, Lud, and Aram."

[4] LENORMANT, *Les Origines de l'histoire d'après la Bible et les traditions des peuples orientaux*, tom. ii. p. 324.

and Africa, and between the two stands the family of Shem, to which the sacred writer belonged. The nations of each group, represented by these various names, are ranged as near as possible as they would be on the map. One of two things may have happened: either the scribe of these tables put the Lydians between Chaldæa (Arphaxad) and Syria (Aram), or the appellative may denote a tribe of Mesopotamia unknown to us under that name; or it may have been altered through a copyist's error.[1]

Whichever conjecture be adopted, the reasons that tell in favour of the Lydians being nearly related to the nations who inhabited the west of the peninsula, between the Halys and the Ægean, are far too weighty to be upset by an isolated doubtful and obscure passage. On the other hand, it is not to be denied that Semitic culture would seem to have had a deeper and more lasting hold on them, than on any of the tribes settled within the northern edge of the central plateau between the Halys and the Euxine; in other words, on Phrygians, Bithynians, and Mysians. Traditions, language, and public ceremonies all testify to the relationship and interaction existing between these various populations.

The national legends allied Ninus, the head of the second Lydian dynasty, to Chaldæa and Assyria, when they made him the son of Belus.[2] All reminiscence of Eastern conquerors had been blotted out by the later splendour and magnificence of the victories and the power of the Sargonides and of Nebuchadnezzar. Nineveh and Babylon had caused Carchemish to be forgotten; nevertheless, some faint trace, it would seem, had lingered in the memory of the Lydians, as to the relations which had once existed between their ancestors, not with the great military states of Mesopotamia, but with the masters of Syria. Lydian princes, it was said—Mopsos, Ascalos—had carried their arms as far as Ascalon.[3] Similar tales, if they contain a residuum of truth, can but allude to a share taken long ago in the wars the Khetas had waged against Egypt. However closely allied the Lydians may have been with the Mysians and Phrygians does not preclude the possibility that they were the first to reach the peninsula, early enough to join in the ambitious

[1] This last notion is the one adopted by M. JULES HALÉVY (*Recherches Bibliques*, p. 165). It is for Hebrew scholars to criticise the correction proposed by him.

[2] Herodotus, i. 7.

[3] Xanthus, Fr. ii. 23.

designs and lust after plunder of the "league of the seafaring nations," which had caused Pharaoh to tremble on his throne.[1]

These distant expeditions and advanced posts to the southward were, after all, but incidents of little moment in the life of these populations; the two sets of influences brought about by conquest and commerce were far more reaching in their consequences. It will not have been forgotten that the Syro-Cappadocians at one time extended their dominion as far as the Lower Hermus, and here, in the vicinity of Smyrna and Magnesia, are found signs of their peculiar writing and types created by their art. Consequently the origin of the Heraclidæ should be sought, not in the valley of the Euphrates, but among the primitive owners of the peninsula, as likely to furnish the explanation to the names of Belus, Bel, and Ninus, which latter headed the list of that dynasty. If we know nothing of that remote age, more than one indication permits us to guess the effect of the continuous relations the Lydians entertained with that Syrian nation who, holding both sides of the Taurus, ended by gaining a firm foothold on the middle Halys, in the very heart of Cappadocia. It is possible that the Phrygian and Lydian Atys may have originated with Atar, Ates, who appears as a local deity in Northern Syria.[2] The divine name Ate is compounded with several names of the sovereigns of Lydia—Sandyattes, Alyattes; and its place as a suffix is in accordance with the formation of theophore names in the idioms of the western Semites.[3]

A conspicuous figure in the Lydian legends is that of Iardanos, the father of Omphalos, a name which vividly recalls the principal stream of Palestine, Jordan, *the* river.[4] Instances such as these deserved to be noticed, inasmuch as they suggest conclusions confirmed in full by all we know of Lydian religions. Purely

[1] M. Maspero, however, thinks that Chabas erred when he recognized the Mæonians in the list of the "sea-people;" in his opinion the group of hieroglyphs, the object of the discussion, yield "Iliouna," not Maouna. On the other hand, he is inclined to see, in the oft-cited name of Shardana, the ethnic encountered among the Greeks (who had no *she*) in the name of Sardes city.

[2] Upon the god Ate and the texts in which he figures as one of the elements of a made-up name, see ED. MEYER, *Ueber einige semitische Goetter*. iii. (*Zeitschrift der Deutschen Morgenlaendischen Gesellschaft*, xxxi. pp. 731, 732).

[3] Similar names would be formed like Hebrew proper names ending in *el*—Joel, Abimael; or an abridged form of Jahveh—Adonijah, Elijah.

[4] The correspondence is due to ED. MEYER, *Geschichte des Alterthums*, tom. i. § 257.

Semitic were those sacred prostitutions which Herodotus notices with astonishment as existing among the Lydians,[1] as well as in Cyprus, whither they had been imported from the same source.[2] The stamp of Syrian cults is even more distinct in the myth of Atys, slain by a wild boar raised against him by Zeus, wroth at the divine honours paid to the former;[3] in which we at once recognise the great Byblos myth, that of Adonis-Tamuz. Again, in the story told by Herodotus of Atys, the eldest son of Crœsus, who is killed by Adrates during a boar's hunt, one is tempted to see a later and somewhat modified form of the same myth.[4] The theme is invariably that of a fair youth, tenderly beloved, who falls a victim to an impure, loathsome monster; stirred by the catastrophe which had engulfed the powerful family of the Mermnadæ, popular fancy demanded of fable the elements it spun around the tragic event, so as to deepen the interest attaching to a great empire overthrown, together with the royal family which had created it.

When did the warlike people whose power was supreme in Cappadocia cease to overrun as conquerors the basins of rivers that descend towards the Ægean, or, at any rate, maintain their ascendency, based upon superiority of arms and civilization? When did the Lydians constitute themselves into a well-ordered independent state? These are questions which it is hard to answer. The Assyrian horizon, down to the reign of Asur-nat-sirpal, was bounded in this direction by the Amanus and the Taurus range. As to the Greeks of the coast, they at the outset lived with their eyes fixed upon the sea by which they communicated with their brethren; not until ambitious princes arose, who began to threaten and molest them in their rear, did they turn their faces in that direction. From that hour, self-defence compelled them to interest themselves in the events that were taking place in Lydia, the rebound of which would ere long be felt on the littoral. It caused them to acquaint themselves with the names, deeds, and character of the kings of Sardes. Henceforward, Western Asia has a history of its own; and albeit, down to the Persian conquest, it is still mixed up with many fables, it contains, none the less, a

[1] Herodotus, i. 93, 94. [2] *Ibid.*, 199.

[3] This was the rendering of the myth as presented by the poet Hermesianax, a native of Colophon, familiar, therefore, with the legends of Lydia.

[4] *Ibid.*, 36–46.

certain number of well-established facts and dates, which latter, within a few years, may be fixed with certainty.

The glimpses we catch in the preceding period are to the effect that when the Phrygians, towards the tenth century B.C., established themselves on the central plateau, the Syrian tribes were obliged to fall back and fortify themselves beyond the Halys; the newcomers then formed around the head-springs of the Sangarius and the Mæander a thick curtain of sedentary populations, behind which the Lydians were able to constitute themselves into a nation. When the mist that had shrouded them for a long time began to disperse, they appear as a feudal state, in the reign of the last Heraclides; their principal districts are presided over by those subordinate dynasties, whose bloody quarrels and rebellions greatly curtail the power vested in the nominal sovereigns enthroned at Sardes. The title of "king's companion"[1] made of the nobleman possessing it a kind of grand vizier, the keeper of the double-edged axe, symbolic of supreme authority, and therefore the real head of the state. Two families—both allied to the reigning family—the Tylonidæ and, above all, the Mermadæ, contended for so exalted a situation. Now, it happened that the mayor of the palace of the last Heraclid was a Mermnad of the name of Gyges, who, to possess himself of the throne, murdered the king, variously called Sandyattes and Candaul by Xanthus and Herodotus. A long civil war followed, and in the end the usurper saw his authority universally acknowledged.[2] This revolution, the first well-known event in the history of Lydia, was big with meaning for the Asiatic Greeks, and would seem to have made a profound impression upon them. Hence it is that the name and individuality of Gyges speedily passed into the domain of fiction. Herodotus and Plato make him the hero of an extravagant tale, in which foolish king Candaul, the owner of a magic ring which renders its possessor invisible, is brought to an untimely end by his indiscreet vanity.[3] Though no less strange and fabulous, Xanthus's version lacks the piquancy and happy turn of phrase, the

[1] This may be gathered from a passage where Plutarch (*Greek Questions*, 45) alludes to the king's companion and axe-bearer as symbolic of supreme power. Cf. Nicholas, Fr. 49, i. 30.

[2] The data to be found in Nicholas of Damascus, Fr. 49, relating to the change of dynasty, has enabled Gelzer to reconstitute with a great degree of probability their sequence up to the enthronement of Gyges.

[3] Herodotus, i. 8–13; PLATO, *Republic*, ii. 3.

cunning art, of the above writers.[1] The astonishment and awe aroused in the Ionian cities were deep and profound at the sight of a people concentrating themselves under the command of an energetic and gallant captain, for the avowed purpose of attacking their neighbours and moving back their frontiers in every direction; who, whilst their hands were full in quelling internal disturbances, had allowed the Greeks to spread along the coast, ascend the course of the rivers up to a certain distance, and occupy the fertile stretches around Magnesia. As soon as they became conscious of their strength, they regretted having given up to another people so many fertile deltas, so many fine harbours hollowed beneath high promontories, when the desire to have an outlook towards the sea became too strong to be resisted. Lydia is one of the most favoured, the most fertile regions of the peninsula. The winter is milder and the summer less dry than on the central plateau, and its situation near the sea also causes more rainfall. The vine, olive, and fig tree prosper on the lower hills; the slopes of Tmolus and other mountains are, and above all were, covered with forests of pine, oak, and beech. These slopes now are brown and bare, and have never recovered from the wanton neglect, and worse, brought about by ages of wretchedness and misery which followed on the fall of the Roman Empire. In the plains, many of which are extensive, the soil consists of a fat ooze, left by the overflowing of streams after they have rid themselves of the pebbly mass wrenched from the flanks of the mountains, when their course becomes sluggish and peaceful, and lends itself to the purposes of irrigation, so that the land can be turned to pasture or ploughed fields at will. The best-mounted horsemen of Asia Minor were Lydians, because they had an abundance of grass.

The clemency of the heavens, the variety and plentifulness of rude creature-comforts, which an inexhaustible soil provided for man and beast, all conspired to ensure the well-being of the inhabitants; and when a lucky chance raised in their midst intelligent and energetic chieftains, what more natural than that a remarkable development, political and military, should have been the result? That which also contributed to the rapid growth and prosperity of the commonwealth was the happy choice of the site upon which was built their capital—a site easily identified, whether from indications

[1] NICHOLAS OF DAMASCUS, *Frag. Hist. Græc.*, tom. iii. pp. 384, 385.

scattered up and down in history, or the magnitude of the ruins still to be seen, or the name of Sart, which, handed down by tradition, is applied to a few huts, the sole representatives of the once great centre. The most frequented route of all those that descend from the Phrygian uplands, the "royal highway" of Herodotus,[1] as it emerges from the ravines of the Hermus, towards the flat level, is met, nearly opposite, by Mount Tmolus, whose highest ridge faces south and bounds the plain; whilst in the direction of the north-west it throws out a long narrow counter-fort, whose abrupt and almost vertical slopes are about five or six kilometres from the river.[3] A low hill connects this spur with the mountain mass;

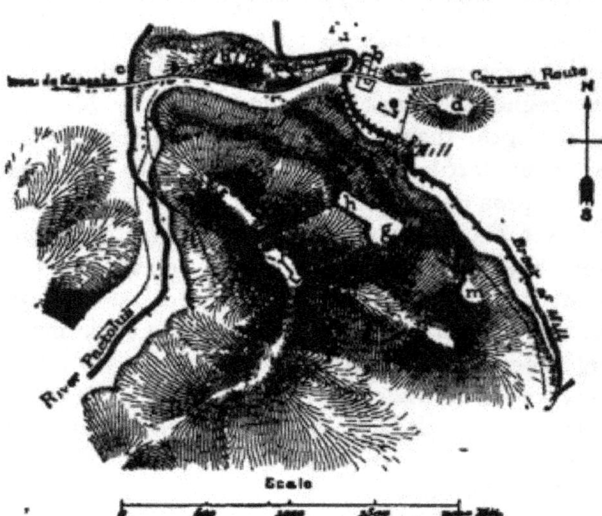

FIG. 153.—Site and ruins of Sardes Topographical sketch. CURTIUS, *Beiträge zur Geschichte und Topographie Kleinasiens*, Plate V.[2]

[1] Herodotus, v. 52.

[2] Legend of map: *a*, hut, *b*, coffee-house and grocer's shop; *c*, piers of ancient bridge; *d*, rubbish heaps; *e*, church (ancient gymnasium); *f*, church; *g*, theatre; *h*, stage (*stadium*); *i*, vaulted double door; *k*, ruin, Lower Empire; *l*, substructures; *m*, odeum (?); *n*, gibbet facing the Acropolis: *o*, upper citadel; *p*, advanced works of citadel; *q*, substructures of temple; *r*, supporting walls; *s*, remains of city wall; *t*, temple said to be of Cybele; *w*, bearings of tomb of Alyattes.

[3] Our description is chiefly borrowed from E. CURTIUS, *Beiträge zur Geschichte und Topographie Kleinasiens: Sardes*, pp. 84–88 (*Abhandlungen* of the Berlin Academy, 1872). See also TEXIER, *Asie Mineure*, 8vo, pp. 252, 253; STARK, *Nach dem Griechischen Orient*, *Reise-Studien*, 8vo, 1874; SAYCE, *Notes from Journeys in the Troad and Lydia*, pp. 86, 87 (*Hell. Studies*, 1880); J. SCHMIDT, *Aus Constantinople und Kleinasien*, pp. 150–153 (*Mittheilungen d. d. archæ. Inst. Athens*, 1881. A plan of Sardes, forming part of an unfinished and undated work, despite jerky and indifferent execution, has likewise furnished some curious documents (TRÉMAUX, *Explor. archl. en Asie Mineure*, Hachette). Useful information was also had from Gregorovius's account of a visit paid in 1882 to the ruins of Sardes, containing a brilliant sketch of the history of Lydia, and a graphic description of its physical

then the ground shoots up into a sharp ridge, the culminating point of which is two hundred metres in height (Fig. 153).[1] A deep sinking, or ravine, occurs east and west of the ridge; in the one which is all but dry in summer flows the Pactolus after rainfall, whilst the other, fed by a copious perennial spring, has enough of water to turn a mill. These waters, it would seem, were utilized in olden days by draining them into a ditch that covered the town to the northward, whence they ran to join the Pactolus, to fall together into the Hermus. The principal quarter of the city, now occupied by the bazaar, and the rendezvous of caravans, was on this side, and faced the point where the two streams met. From the bed of the torrent to the foot of the hill are spacious platforms which support the houses and structures of the town; it was an open city both in the day of the Lydian kings and the Achæmenidæ; the whole effort of the defence was directed to the citadel.[2] Little need was there to aid the work of nature; even now the steep rugged paths leading to the summit, once girded by a wall, are climbed with great difficulty (Fig. 154).

Rising on the site where the mountain more nearly approaches the river, the fortress commanded and watched over the adjacent country far and wide. Under its protecting shadow, each year since the advent of Gyges, as the spring came round, the Lydian cavalry assembled in the grass meadows around, and formed themselves into those squadrons that were wont to be away the whole summer on warlike expeditions. At the outset, aided by the Ionians, Gyges had seized the whole of Mysia, from the Gulf of Adramyttion to the farther bank of the Rhyndacus.[3] Had not the new king, in order to strengthen his as yet tottering throne, asked for the moral support of the Delphic oracle at the beginning of his reign, and repaid it with a liberal hand?[4] Had not he helped the

aspect ("Sardes," *Kleine Schriften zur Geschichte und Cultur*, tom. i. pp. 1–47, 18mo. Leipzig: Brockhaus, 1887).

[1] The market of Sardes extended along the two banks of Pactolus. See Herodotus, v. 101.

[2] This may be inferred both from Herodotus's account of the siege of Sardes by Cyrus (i. 80–84), and the attack directed against it, fifty years later, by the Athenians and Ionians (v. 100, 101). In both instances the defenders of the place gave up to the enemy the lower city, and withdrew themselves into the citadel.

[3] Strabo, XIII. i. 22.

[4] Herodotus, i. 14; Nicholas of Damascus, Fr. 49.

Milesians to found the colony of Abydos, on the Hellespont?[1] Were not soldiers of fortune, whether Carians or Ionians, bent on adventure and plunder, sure to get both while serving under his banner?[2] The good understanding was of short duration. Intercourse with the Greeks, mayhap friendly visits to their flourishing cities, roused in the breast of a prince already master of a vast territory, and the head of a brave and well-equipped

FIG 154.—View of Acropolis at Sardes, taken from the left bank of the Pactolus, opposite the temple of Cybele. CURTIUS, *Beiträge*, Plate VI

nation, the ambitious design of subjecting these inventive minds and energetic characters, of confiscating for his own benefit so brisk an industry and maritime commerce, along with multitudinous workshops and harbours, all their power and riches. He first attacked, but failed to carry, the fortified cities of Smyrna and Miletus; he was more successful before Colophon,[3] and possession of the place gave him the control of the Cayster and cut up Ionia into two halves. Gyges was indeed defeated and slain by the Cimmerians

[1] Strabo, *loc cit.*

[2] Mention is made by Herodotus (i. 77) of the mercenaries the Mermnadæ kept in their pay.

[3] Herodotus, i. 15, 22, 26.

in 650 B.C.; but neither his death nor his defeat were fraught with grave consequences. The invaders, after having ravaged the peninsula, retired as suddenly as they had come; and, once the storm was over, the Lydian monarchy resumed the work—momentarily interrupted—at the point where it had been left. Ionia had suffered quite as much as Lydia; but the latter, with Ardys and his three successors, Sadyattes, Alyattes, and Crœsus, was not only able to reconstitute her military power, but to harass the Greek maritime cities with repeated and frequent attacks for the space of a hundred years. Jealousy of one another prevented these small communities banding together for the purpose of opposing a stout resistance against the common foe; singly they could not levy a sufficient number of troops to oppose with any hope of success the cavalry squadrons which the Lydian princes, at all times, were able to pour into their territory. Miletus, despite the gallantry and excellence of her infantry, was compelled to renounce keeping the field; for at each fresh attack her soldiers had to withdraw behind the walls, whence they beheld the burning of their homesteads and their crops, the falling of their olive trees under the axe. No courage is proof against a long-enforced inactivity. The fall of Smyrna was followed by that of Ephesus, and, if we except Miletus, there was scarcely a town that did not pay tribute towards the end of Crœsus's reign. On the other hand, the Lydian empire had by degrees spread as far as the Taurus range and the Halys, and the latter would thenceforth form its boundary line towards the Median empire. The treaty of 585 B.C., between Cyaxares and Alyattes, after years of warfare, provided a family alliance between the two dynasties, and fixed the great river as frontier of the two empires.[1] Thus Lydia belonged to Asia, be it from the despotic character of her monarchy supported by a large army, or the relations she had opened in the day of Gyges with Asur-nat-Sirpal, or those she subsequently entered into with the Medes, inheritors of the Assyrians, along with the Babylonian successors of Nebuchad-

[1] Herodotus (i. 73, 74) specifies all the peoples subject to Crœsus as if they had been subdued by him; Crœsus, however, did but complete the work commenced by his predecessors. Nicholas of Damascus (Fr. 65) speaks of the war Alyattes waged against the Carians; but the long struggle he likewise carried on with the Medes must have taken place near the Halys, perhaps on the eastern bank.

nezzar,[1] and the Saït rulers of Egypt.[2] On the other hand, the conquest of Ionia, in opening the Ægean to Lydia, awoke in her sovereigns a new train of thought: that of fitting out a fleet for the conquest of the Cyclades.[3]

The wildest ambition seemed to be within the grasp of these fortunate conquerors, when their power suddenly collapsed; induced not by internal turmoils and rebellion, but because of a revolution in the south of Iran, which caused supremacy to pass from the Medes to the Persians. In an evil hour Crœsus conducted an expedition across the Halys against the new masters of Anterior Asia; an indecisive battle was fought in Cappadocia, in which Cyrus would seem to have had the advantage, for he soon reappeared in Lydia, and completely routed an army hastily collected together, which was sent to impede his progress and prevent his advance on Sardes. All in vain. At the end of a fortnight's siege the Persians took by surprise a citadel deemed impregnable, in which, together with his family and his treasures, Crœsus had shut himself up.[4] Sardes became the seat of a Persian satrap, and the Lydians from that day disappear as an independent nation. Though brief, the part they played as a political force was not without its effect on the unfolding of antique civilization.

Not the least curious feature of this history, covering the period between the enthronement of Gyges and the taking of Sardes, is the nature and character of the relations the Lydians entertained with the Greeks; since it would seem that hostilities and mutual acts of kindness went hand in hand together. Each day served to bring the two people nearer and unite them more intimately. Thus in the time of the Heraclidæ, Ardys, expelled from Lydia by a usurper, finds refuge in the Æolian city of Cymæ.[5] Somewhat later, with the reign of the following dynasty, Lydian princes espouse Greek women, and give their daughters in marriage to Ionian nobles.[6] A merchant of Ephesus supplies the sinews of war, and enables Crœsus to undertake a warlike expedition.[7] Finally, when Cyrus, ready to march against Sardes, invited the Ionians to raise the standard of rebellion against masters they

[1] Herodotus, i. 74, 77. [2] *Ibid.*, 77. [3] *Ibid.*, 27.
[4] Herodotus, i. 75-84. [5] Nicholas of Damascus, Frag. 47.
[6] Herodotus, i. 92; Nicholas of Damascus, Frag. 63; ÆLIAN, *Hist. Var.* iii. 26.
[7] Nicholas of Damascus, Frag. 65.

had so often resisted, every town was loyal to a man.[1] If such was the state of affairs, it was because, despite the many evils the Mermnadæ had inflicted upon Ionia, they could rightly have assumed the style of "Philhellenic kings," as many Oriental princes did a few centuries afterwards.

If no means were spared to incorporate the maritime centres with their empire, this arose from the regard and admiration they had for the Greeks, and the consciousness of the superiority of their genius. Not only had Gyges and his successors sent rich offerings to the shrines of Asiatic and continental Greece,[2] but they also kept their artists employed,[3] welcomed their philosophers to their court,[4] and kept up relations of the most amicable nature with Miltiades, tyrant of Thracian Chersonesus, and the Athenian Alcmæonidæ.[5] If temples, during their campaigns in Ionia, suffered from the ravages of war, they were rebuilt, at their expense, on a grander and nobler style than before.[6] Thus, it was Crœsus who supplied the money for the building of the temple of Artemis at Ephesus.[7] And the Lydians, when menaced by Persia, turned for help to Sparta and Athens.[8] What further proves the great popularity Crœsus enjoyed in the Grecian world, is the fact that his misfortunes did not rob him of the halo which had been his. Pindar, long after the fall of Sardes, cites him as an instance of the persistency with which fame preserves the memory of princes whose liberality has won them the esteem and admiration of their contemporaries: "The benevolent virtue of Crœsus," he says to Hieron, "dies not."[9]

That which helped not a little to reconcile the Ionians to the dominion of Lydia was the wealth of the latter. The Greeks were a shrewd, keen-witted people; they could behave heroically in an open fight, but when luck was against them, they readily

[1] Herodotus, i. 141.

[2] *Ibid.*, i. 14, 25, 50–52, 92; Theopompus, Frag. 184; MÜLLER, *Frag. Hist. Græc.*, tom. i.

[3] Herodotus, i. 25, 51.

[4] *Ibid.*, 27, 29. If chronology tells against Solon having been the guest of Crœsus at Sardes, there is a great degree of probability that Bias of Priene and Pittacos of Mitylene visited the place. No one would have dreamt of taking Solon to the Lydian court, had not other sages been right royally entertained there.

[5] Herodotus, vi. 37, 125.

[6] *Ibid.*, i. 19–22.

[7] *Ibid.*, 92.

[8] *Ibid.*, 56, 69, 70, 83.

[9] PINDAR, *Pyth.*, i. 184: οὐ φθίνει Κροίσου φιλόφρων ἀρετά.

adapted themselves to the masters with whom more was to be gained than by staying away. The economy of the ancients was of the simplest; in their estimation the prosperity of the Lydians and the vaunted opulence of their princes were sufficiently accounted for by gold extracted from the depths of their mountains or picked up in the torrents of Tmolus.[1] But though it is pretty certain that veins of the precious metal were then won from auriferous rocks of quartz for the benefit of Lydia and Mysia,[2] nothing proves its having been obtained in quantities that would compare with the amount the kings of Macedonia quarried in after years from the flanks of Pangæus. As to the Pactolus, its reputation was doubtless due to the inflated language of poets; for the gold-finders who washed and sifted its sands, of a certainty, created but a small fraction, perhaps a very small fraction indeed, of the wealth Alyattes and Crœsus would seem to have possessed. Other agencies contributed a much larger share in the formation of treasures which were the wonder of the Greeks. In the first place should be named those soldiers who, after plundering half the peninsula in the interest of their chiefs, compelled the population to pay tribute; then came agriculturists, who utilized this vast and fertile territory, either as pasturage or arable land and vine-culture; craftsmen of either sex who, in the urban as in the rural workshop, practised those high-class industries already in vogue in the days of Homer;[3] merchants who served as middlemen between the Greek ports and the productive centres, as well as the markets of the whole of Anterior Asia. Herodotus says that "the Lydians were the first retailers."[4]

[1] Herodotus, who has often been reproached with undue credulity, says nothing of the kind (i. 93, v. 101); he confines himself to the statement that the deciduous torrents of the Lydian mountains carry along with them gold particles. It is by much later writers that the Pactolus is described as the main source of Crœsus's wealth (Strabo, XIII. iv. 5). Upon the gold of Pactolus, consult TCHLATCHEF, *Le Bosphore et Constantinople*, 8vo, 1864, pp. 232–242. This traveller supposes that towards the seventh century B.C. the stream came upon a rich gold ore, which it disintegrated and worked out after a number of years, and as a matter of course ceased to produce gold in any quantity. The geological formation of Tmolus, as is well known, does not belie the above hypothesis; it accounts, too, for the exaggerated language of later times, as a reminiscence of what had once been a substantial fact.

[2] Strabo, XIV. v. 28; Pseudo-Aristotle, *περὶ θαυμασίων ἀκουσμάτων*, 52.

[3] HOMER, *Iliad*, iv. 141–145.

[4] *Πρῶτοι δὲ καὶ κάπηλοι ἐγένοντο* (Herodotus, i. 94).

So stated the assertion is incorrect, since Egypt and Phœnicia had small vendors long before Lydia. What Herodotus means, and says after his own fashion, is that the Lydians had a natural turn and genius for trade, which in their hands acquired a singular activity. At any rate, it was not retail, carried on in the shops of some street in the bazaar, but wholesale trade that gave the Lydian Pythius his enormous wealth, which he placed at the disposal of Xerxes when the latter marched against Greece.[1] Even if we only reckon the actual worth of the precious metals, the capital Pythius is said to have possessed would amount to the considerable sum of more than £3,200,000.[2] Pythius was a citizen of Celænæ, situate by the head-springs of the Mæander, on the road which, a little beyond Colossoi, branched off in several directions, down the valleys leading to Miletus, Ephesus, Sardes, Magnesia, and Smyrna. I picture him as not unlike one of those Greek or Armenian merchants I have known in Asia Minor and Syria, for whom caravans travel between Smyrna, Messina, Alexandretta or Beyrout, and Angora, Konieh, Cæsarea, Aleppo, or Damascus.

Transport of raw products and manufactured objects served to swell the royal coffers; for it is probable that all imports and exports were heavily taxed, and that there existed fixed rates for everything sold, which were collected on the spot. Hence the gold and silver that filled the royal treasury chambers in the citadel of Sardes were derived from deductions made by the sovereign upon capital continually created and renewed by universal labour. No wonder Greek imagination found some difficulty in realizing this enormous accumulation of the precious metals.[3] In the Hellenic world, capital was divided between a number of cities, and again subdivided between the well-to-do citizens of each town, so that it could not be condensed and amassed in one receptacle, as in Lydia, where the prodigality of the prince, however great it might be, could never exhaust it, since it always received more specie than it gave back to circulation. It is possible, nay probable, that what was in truth very considerable may have been exaggerated, notably by later writers, when their fancy

[1] Herodotus, vii. 27–29.

[2] *Ibid.*, *loc. cit.*

[3] Archilochus found no more appropriate expression to denote the largest conceivable fortune than the following: Οὔ *μοι τὰ Γύγεω τοῦ πολυχρύσου μέλει* ("The wealth of Gyves, he who is possessed of so much gold").

ran away with them.* Nevertheless, when Herodotus enumerates the presents Crœsus consecrated to the Delphic shrine on the eve of his disaster, he doubtless reproduces the figures furnished him by local archives.[1] We know now from the inscriptions at Delos, those of the Parthenon and of many more sanctuaries, with what order and precision the great temples of Greece kept their accounts. It has been computed that Crœsus's offerings of massive gold, the weight of which, says the historian, was 117 bricks and 1 lion, are equivalent to 6448 kilogrammes, or, at the present value of gold, to nearly twenty millions of francs (£800,000). If to this be added all the other objects of unweighed gold and silver mentioned by Herodotus, and we reckon these at only one-half of the above sum, we shall find that the splendid liberality of the Lydian king amounted to nearly one million two hundred pounds sterling.[2] There was, then, an abundance of the precious metals in Lydia, the royal treasury was full to overflowing, and considerable quantities were distributed among private individuals. On the other hand, the great commerce of the country was one of traffic; it exported products derived from the soil or created by national industry; it not only imported foreign goods from the old cities of the East, but others manufactured nearer home, upon which Greek genius was beginning to put the stamp of its taste. Similar transactions added daily to the common wealth of the nation, and were facilitated by a metallic reserve far in excess of that of their neighbours, a fact which doubtless suggested to them a notion that had not occurred to their predecessors, the industrial peoples of remote antiquity, the Egyptians, Chaldæans, and the Phœnicians themselves.

The first step in commerce had everywhere been the barter of one species of goods or produce for another. Thus a monument at Memphis, in Egypt (Fig. 155), shows housewives going to market and purchasing shoes, vegetables, and liquids, which are paid for with fans, glass-beads, and other small objects. Inscriptions incised beside the personages render ambiguity as to the meaning of the picture impossible. Exact equivalents cannot be obtained by a similar process, nor is it an easy matter to balance differences when they exist. As soon as commercial transactions expanded, however, as soon as they were carried on not only

[1] Herodotus, i. 50, 51.

[2] P. DE TCHLATCHEF, *Le Bosphore*, etc., 8vo, pp. 237, 238.

between the inhabitants of one village, or of one town, but between men of different tribes and different nations, the need of a medium of exchange was felt, which should facilitate despatch of business, and which, by common consent, should always and everywhere be accepted in discharge of all and any purchase, without obliging the vendor, by way of compensation, to accept goods he did not require. This medium, at once commodious and easily transported, possessed, too, of intrinsic value which was recog-

FIG. 155.—An Egyptian market, from a tomb painting of the fifth dynasty. *Gazette Archl.*, 1880, Plate XVI.

nized by all, was supplied by the precious metals, gold and silver, and, to a certain extent, bronze also. At the outset their use was restricted to dust and irregular pieces; by degrees, however, they were replaced by crenated bars, ingots, rings, and plates, or flat pieces, with notches so graduated as to correspond with the scale of weights, down to the feeblest. Ingots of this kind are often figured on the monuments of the civilized nations of Egypt and of Anterior Asia, in the very act of having their weight tested. This is shown in our woodcut (Fig. 156), as well as in scores of inscriptions. Ingots were a primary form of specie, which, though showing a decided advance, still left much to be desired.[1]

[1] Upon the coinage of the early nations, see FR. LENORMANT, *La Monnaie dans l'Antiquité*, tom. i. pp. 93–124.

One could never be sure as to the genuineness of their composition; hence assays became indispensable for ascertaining weight, fineness, and portion of alloy.

The most important innovation, the true innovation of genius, which transmuted the still imperfect ingot into money, was the adoption of a constant mark which, affixed to that of the sovereign, should by its bare presence remove all suspicions. By this official stamp the State vouched for the standard and weight of its metallic coinage, which it had issued "as signs of value," and

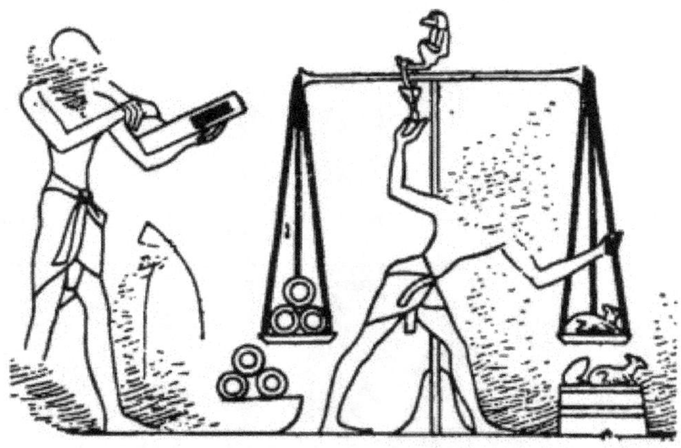

FIG. 156.—Weighing gold ingots in Egypt. After a painting at Thebes. WILKINSON, *The Customs and Manners of Ancient Egyptians*, 2nd edit., vol. i. Fig. 7.

"the world was saved from perpetual weighing;"[1] whilst public authority was rewarded for interposing in the interest of the community, by having its money accepted without question. By this one act the specie acquired a current value which had not belonged to the ingots of the preceding epoch. At the same time the service rendered to commercial transactions put the government in a position to circulate its coinage in every country subject to its jurisdiction. Strictly speaking, the right assumed by authority is only legitimate as far as the money is genuine and what it purports to be; should it fail of these conditions, no enactment of the law, however stringent and severe, will make it effective, or prevent the depreciation of a coinage whose nominal worth is much below its intrinsic value.[2]

No coined money—as is now proved—was struck before the

[1] ARISTOTLE, *Polit.*, I. vi.

[2] LENORMANT, *loc. cit.*, pp. 93, 94.

opening years of the seventh century B.C., and the honour of the invention rests between the Greeks and the Lydians; that is to say, between two nations almost sisters in blood, and both occupying the basin of the Ægean Sea. Two traditions obtained in the ancient world in regard to it, both supported by authorities of the greatest weight. The lexicographer Pollux, a judicious and well-informed man, in face of the conflicting evidence found in various authors, hesitates "to settle the question as to whether the Argian Pheidon or the Lydians first struck coins."[1] The question is precisely where classic antiquity left it.[2] For some—Ephorus, followed by Strabo,[3] Ælian,[4] and a goodly number of later writers,[5] as well as continental Greece generally—the first coins were those bearing a tortoise on the obverse, which Pheidon, king of Argos, caused to be struck in the island of Ægina, which formed part of his dominions. On the other hand, Herodotus says, "To our knowledge the first men who struck money of gold and silver were the Lydians."[6] The same testimony is borne by an older writer, Xenophanes of Colophon, who made the ancient history of Lydia his special study.[7] The gold of Gyges, the staters of Crœsus, were likewise adduced as having passed as currency.[8] The evidence we now possess enables us to assert that the two traditions rest on a real base, and coincide with two distinct facts; namely, that the first gold coins were issued by the kings of Lydia, and the first silver money by Pheidon in Ægina. This last fact is connected with the institution of the oldest system of weights and measures known in Peloponnesus, and is universally attributed to that prince—whose authority seems to have extended over a large portion of that province—by historians who have handled the subject.[9] But which of the two monetary issues is entitled to

[1] Pollux, ix. 83.

[2] We do little more than give a summary of Lenormant's very precise and lucid exposition (*La Monnaie*, I. iii. 2).

[3] Strabo, viii. vi. 16.

[4] ÆOLIAN, *Hist. Var.*, xii. 10.

[5] The *Paros Chronicles* (i. 45, 46) record certainly the fact that silver coins were struck at Ægina by Pheidon, but nothing is said as to having been the first issued.

[6] Herodotus, i. 94.

[7] Pollux, ix. 83. Xenophon was born towards the end of the seventh century; he is the author of a poem entitled Κτίσις Κολοφῶνος.

[8] Pollux, iii. 87. Γυγάδας χρύσος, Κροίσειοι στατῆρες.

[9] Herodotus, vi. 127; PLINY, *Hist. Natur.*, VII. lvii. 7 (ed. Littré); Pollux, x. 179, from whom we learn that Aristotle, under the heading "The Constitution of the

priority? To whom should the honour of the invention be attributed with a greater degree of probability?

The witnesses in favour of the kings of Lydia seem more worthy of belief than those upholding the pretensions of the Æginetans; they are older and nearer the facts they purpose to relate. Xenophanes was a contemporary of Alyattes and Crœsus, and had seen the use of coinage gradually spread from the Lydian empire to the Ionian cities. If Herodotus lived after the fall of the Mermnadæ, he yet was the senior by a hundred years or thereabouts of Ephorus; more than this, he was born and his youth was spent in a region where, in his day, considerable quantities of specie, formerly issued by the Lydian monarchs, were doubtless still in circulation, and he was more curious and better informed than the rhetor-historians of the Isocrates school. The fact that the self-conceit of the Greeks would not permit them readily to acknowledge the superior claim of the Lydians is another reason why we should believe the testimony of Xenophanes and Herodotus; for nothing short of titles of unquestionable authority would have compelled the former to yield the palm of honour to others.

Historical chronology cannot be depended upon to solve the question, since no date is more controverted than that assigned to the reign of Pheidon. If certain instances would seem to mark the eighth or even the ninth century B.C. as a possible date, there are others which oblige us to go down to the middle of the seventh century, in order to find, in Peloponnesus, a range of circumstances in accord with the great and special part attributed to Pheidon. Hence it is that the eminent historian of Greece, Ernest Curtius, has embraced the latter hypothesis.[1] In his estimation Pheidon was a contemporary of Gyges, but somewhat his junior, and still a youth when the Mermnad bore down all opposition and firmly seated himself on the throne of Lydia.

The best way for settling the point at issue is to address oneself to the monuments, for superficial inspection will suffice to bring out clearly the importance of the witnesses we have adduced. No extant series of coins bear so primitive and old an aspect as the silver pieces of Ægina, and certain "electrum" examples

Argians," subjoined to his great collection, devoted part of a chapter to the weights and measures instituted by Pheidon; the *Paros Chronicles*, i. 45, 46.

[1] E. CURTIUS, *Hist. of Greece*, tom. i. p. 299, n. 3.

which are generally attributed to the kings of Lydia. The latter, as struck by the Lydians, will alone engage our attention in this part of our history. Our reason for assigning a Lydian origin to them rests upon the following data:—The vast majority of similar pieces (found in our museums) were collected in the environs of Sardes.[1] The type seen on them is in harmony with the hypothesis we uphold; it is a lion, whose image Crœsus sent to Delphi,[2] which, carried round the ramparts of Sardes,[3] made them impregnable, and, last not least, it is the animal sacred to Cybele, the great goddess of Asia Minor. In other specimens the head of the lion is opposed to that of the bull, and numerous examples have already shown us how dear was the device to Asiatic art; the juxtaposition of the two animals would seem to have had a symbolic value.[4] Moreover, many of these pieces are in electrum, that is to say, the metal *par excellence* of Lydia.[5] The Greeks gave the name of *electrum*, pale gold, to a natural alloy of gold and silver in varying quantities. The electrum obtained from the auriferous sands of Tmolus and minted by the Lydians contains seventy-three parts of silver to twenty-seven of gold.[6]

The use of a coinage, of which the alloy was not constant, is in itself a strong presumption of remote antiquity; since Herodotus tells us that later, in the reign of Crœsus, moneyers took to refining gold destined for coinage, so as to bring it nearer to standard. The form and aspect of the pieces in Lydia, which are little more than ingots ovoid shaped, betray the gropings of a nascent art far more effectually than imperfection of the metal employed. Then, too, on these kind of huge lozenges flattened at the rim, appear hollows or striæ on one side, and three deeply incused stilettos or puncheons symmetrically arranged on the other.

[1] RAWLINSON, *Herodotus*, i. p. 713. [2] Herodotus, i. 50. [3] *Ibid.*, 48.

[4] *Hist. of Art*, tom. ii. Fig. 443; tom. iii. p. 652, Figs. 475, 476, 544, 624. One of these stilettos is in the shape of a fox's head, symbolic of Dionysios, who in Lydia was called *Bassareus*, fox. *Bassara* was the name of the fox among certain barbarous people (*Thesaurus*, *s.v.*).

[5] SOPHOCLES, *Antigone*, 1037–1039:

Κερδαίνετ' ἐμπολᾶτε τὸν πρὸς Σάρδεων
ἤλεκτρον, εἰ βούλεσθε, καί τὸν Ἰνδικὸν
χρύσον.

[6] BARCLAY V. HEAD, *Hist. Numorum*, Introduction, Plate XXXIV.; FR. LENORMANT, *La Monnaie dans l'antiquité*, tom. i. pp. 190–194. The periphrase "white gold," λευκὸς χρυσός, was sometimes used instead of ἤλεκτρον by the Greeks (Herodotus, i. 70).

The oldest coins of Ægina have a far-off resemblance with the metallic bars of former days, which served as medium of exchange; the ingots are still oblong instead of approaching a more or less circular shape;[1] so that their primitive rough appearance might at first sight be taken to denote priority of date as against those of Lydia. But if the puncheons seen on the coins we attribute to Gyges show better workmanship than those issued at Ægina with a tortoise impressed on the obverse, the difference admits of easy explanation. In the seventh century B.C., Asia Minor was greatly in advance of Greece; her art and the crafts allied thereto testified to a development and surety of hand which training and experience alone can give. The fact which apparently decided the question of priority of date is that the oldest coins of Lydia, as compared with those heading the Ægina series, do not, as these, entirely fulfil the conditions which, in antiquity, constituted and defined coinage. The pieces clearly belong to an early epoch of transition; they are still ingots, of the kind once circulated in Egypt and throughout Asia, but the stamp of public authority has conferred upon them all the essentials requisite in a coinage, as a medium of traffic and public convenience. On the other hand, a gigantic step onward was made with the advent of the coiner's block, when impressions in relief could be obtained; and this enormous progress is non-existent in the earliest gold staters of the Lydians. Consequently pieces, no matter how rude in make, but on which types in relief appear, have no claim to be considered as the oldest, since they carry the mark of a new and progressive stage in the coiner's art; and to this stage belong the oldest silver coins of Ægina.[2]

Herodotus would seem, then, to be right when he awards the honour of the invention of coined money to the Lydians; save that it is inaccurate, as regards the Lydia of that time, to speak of

[1] In the famous temple of Hera, at Argos, were shown bars (ὀβελίσκοι) said to have been consecrated by Pheidon, as a standing witness of an old usage his inventions had caused to be set aside (*Etymol. Magnum*, *vide* ὀβελίσκος).

[2] For a comprehensive survey of the Lydian coinage, besides Lenormant, see BARCLAY V. HEAD, *The Coinage of Lydia and Persia*, which appeared in the *International numismata Orientalia* from 1874–1877 (Trübner and Co.). In it (p. 19) the author discusses in full the reform attributed to Crœsus. Each number is accompanied by excellent plates in photogravure, which form a separate work. The same questions are more briefly treated in *Hist. Numorum*, pp. 545, 546, by the same author. M. C. SOUTZO, *Systèmes monétaires primitifs de l'Asie Mineure et de la Grèce* (*Revue Roumaine d'Archl., d'histoire, et de philologie*, tom. ii., 1883).

gold and silver as having been issued conjointly. The latter should have been omitted. The oldest silver coins that can be assigned to Lydia, with any degree of probability, are of a much less archaic type than the electrum examples; and numismatists agree in not carrying them back beyond the age of Crœsus. This prince is generally credited with the introduction of a double standard, pure gold and pure silver, which took the place of electrum, the standard of which was not rigorously defined. This wise and happy reform, it is said, largely contributed to the increase of commercial enterprise and the wealth of his kingdom. Be that as it may, the silver coins under consideration, whether they were struck in Lydia or in the Greek cities of Asia Minor, are markedly younger than the first tortoise examples of Ægina. As these, their type is in relief, and of good workmanship. It is highly probable that the mint at Ægina issued the first silver coins.

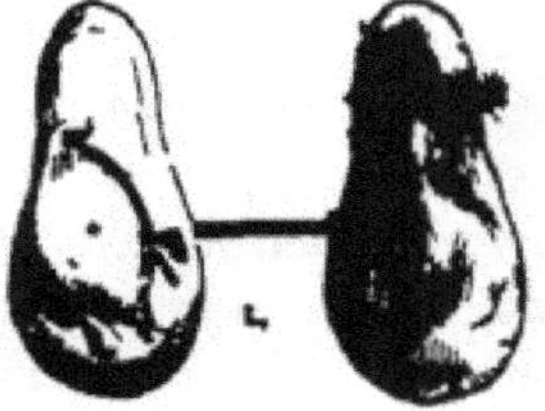

CHAPTER II.

ART IN LYDIA.

ARCHITECTURE.

WHEN we described the necropolis and the tumuli in the neighbourhood of Smyrna, it was with a certain degree of hesitancy that we connected the above monuments with the quasi-fabulous monarchy of the Tantalidæ.[1] We feel no such embarrassment when we try to fix the origin and approximate date of the cognate tombs of the necropolis near Sardes, called *Bin Tepe* (the Thousand Mounds).

The kings of Sardes had their sepulchres on the farther side of the Hermus, to the northward of the town and close to it (Fig. 157). The monuments were still pointed out to travellers in the day of Herodotus and Strabo. The descriptions of the site, form, and dimensions of these tombs by ancient writers, are sufficiently near reality to have enabled modern explorers to identify them. In a remarkable passage that will bear repetition, Herodotus has the following :—[2]

"In Lydia is seen a work much superior to those we admire elsewhere (I would, nevertheless, except the monuments of the Egyptians and the Babylonians); it is the tomb of Alyattes, the father of Crœsus. The wall around it consists of large stones, and the rest is of earth heaped up. It was erected at the expense of merchants who retail on the market-place, of craftsmen and courtesans. Five termini, put on the top of the monument, were extant in my time, and inscriptions indicated the share which each of the three classes had had in the building. Measurements show that the portion of the courtesans was far the largest, because every one of the girls in the country of the Lydians practises prostitution;

[1] See pp. 48–53.

[2] Herodotus, i. 93.

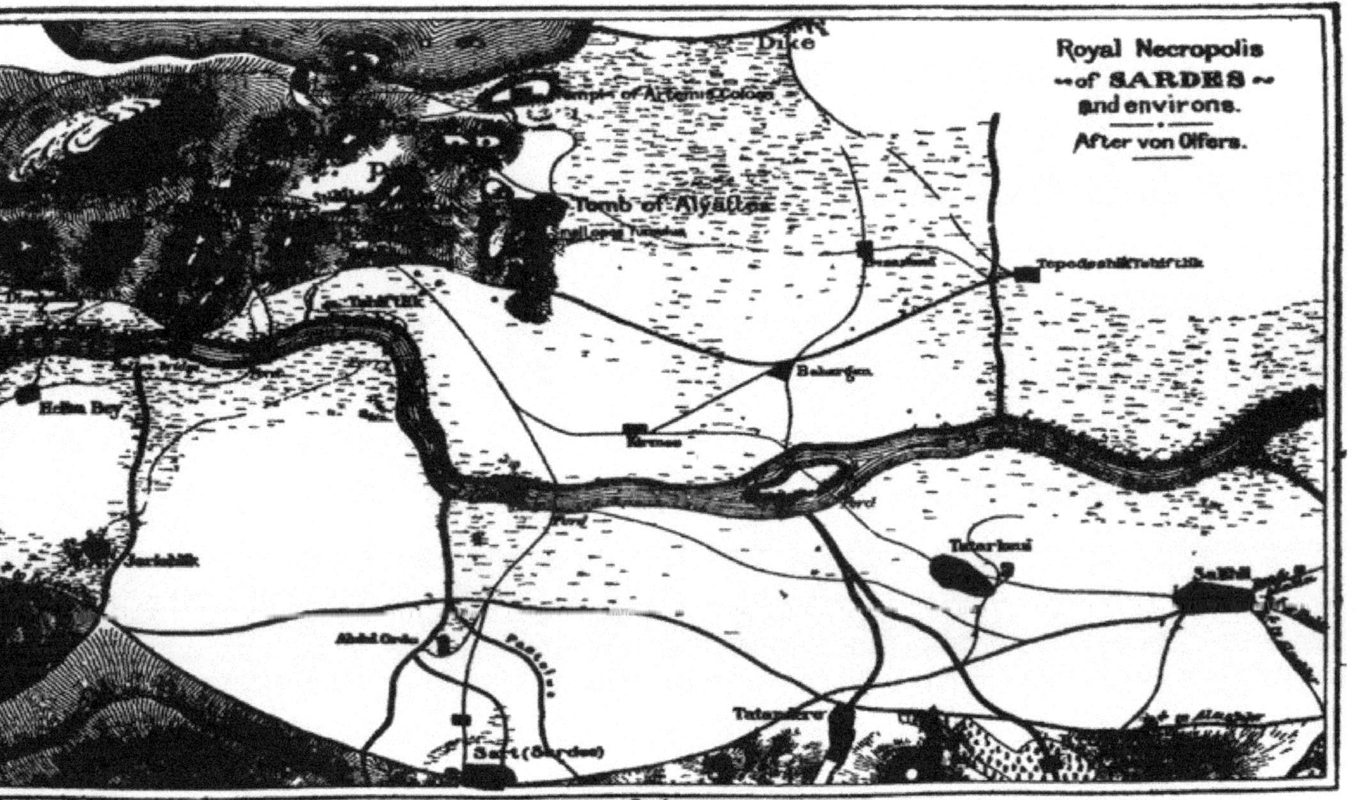

Fig. 157.—Royal necropolis of Sardes and its environs. After Von Olfers' map in *Abhandlungen* of the Berlin Academy, 1858.

they earn their dowry by it, and continue the trade until they marry; they have the right to choose their husbands. This monument is 6 stadia 2 plethra (1171 m. 65 c.) in circumference, and 13 plethra (400 m. 75 c) wide. Close by is a large lake, which, say the Lydians, never dries up. It is called the Lake of Gyges. All is exactly as I have said."

To this graphic account may be added the bearings given by Strabo of these respective sites, the only portion of his narrative which adds to our knowledge: "Forty stadia (7400 m.) from Sardes is a lake called by Homer Lake of Gyges, but which sub-

FIG. 158.—View of tomb of Alyattes, from the south. Von Olfers, Plate IV.

sequently changed its name into that of Coloæ. . . . The tombs of the kings are sprinkled around the Lake Coloæ; that of Alyattes (Fig. 158) looks towards Sardes; it is an immense embankment of earth, kept in place by a tall base of stone." After alluding to the statement of Herodotus as to the share girls of bad repute had in the building of the tomb, he adds: "This explains why the royal mausoleum was formerly called the Courtesans' Monument. Certain historians assure us that the Lake Coloæ was excavated by the hand of man to receive the surplus waters of the rivers" (XIII. iv. 5, 7).

It would be impossible to have clearer or more exact indications;

nevertheless Strabo errs in placing Coloæ so close to Sardes.[1] The only lake near the town is the Mermereh Gheul; the artificial knolls, called Bin Tepe, some of colossal size, are situate on the southern bank of the stream. Seen at a distance, from Sardes for example, they might be taken for low hills closely packed together; when near them, however, they appear in regular rows which follow the undulations of the ground until they are lost to sight. Their symmetrical arrangement is so conspicuous as to have struck every traveller who has visited them, so that no doubt is left in their mind that they were artificially made.[2] From the fact that there is little or no difficulty in exploring them, it might have been expected that they would have been searched long ago. From some unexplained cause, however, these masses were left untouched until the consul-general of Germany, Spiegelthal, had the happy idea of sounding their depths. His first attempts were made around the smaller tumuli, but he presently gave up the undertaking and attacked the mound, which for all the world looks like a low hill, and whose exceptional dimensions singled it out as the tomb of Alyattes.[3]

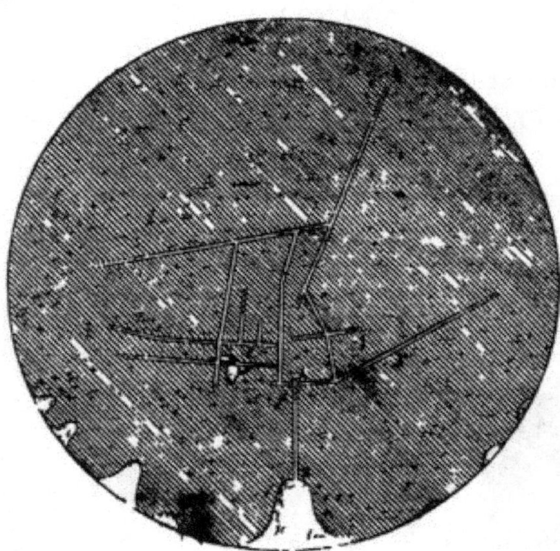

FIG. 159.—Plan of tomb of Alyattes. Von Olfers, Plate III

[1] The real distance is but some twelve kilometres; the discrepancy is probably due to some confusion in the figures which crept into the text. It should be remarked that the suburb of Sardes, in the time of Strabo, may have stretched far away to the northward, across the plain.

[2] CHANDLER, *Travels*, p. 263; HAMILTON, *Researches*, tom. i. pp. 145, 146; TEXIER, *Asie Mineure*, 8vo, pp. 258, 259; PROKESCH VON OSTEN, *Erinnerungen*, iii. p. 162.

[3] *Monatsblatt der k. P. Akademie der Wissenschaften zu Berlin*, 1854, pp.

In its present state this tomb is still sixty-nine metres above the level of the plain. The turf covering the mound was cut to some depth around its base, when the stone construction which formed the shell of the vault was disclosed; more cuttings were made across the mass to the centre, occupied by the funereal chamber, in which, doubtless, had been deposited the royal body, but which the explorers found empty.

During his borings, Spiegelthal found traces of other galleries that, in all likelihood, had been made in antiquity by treasure-

FIG. 160.—Perspective view of the interior of tomb.

seekers (see plan, Fig. 159, A, B). He followed their direction and thus attained his goal.[1]

700–702; and in *Abhandlungen* of the same learned society, 1858, pp. 539–556, appeared a memoir, by Von Olfers, entitled "Ueber die Lydischen Koenigsgraeber bei Sardes und der Grabhuegel des Alyattes nach den Bericht des Kaiserlichen Generalconsuls Spiegelthal zu Smyrna," with lithographed plates.

[1] The trench A, B in map (Fig. 159) was opened by Von Olfers, when he came upon galleries that had been excavated by treasure-seekers. By clearing and following them, he reached the mortuary chamber.

The situation of the vault is fifty metres south-west from the centre. The walls are built of large blocks of grey marble, smoothed over and finely cut, and held together by leaden dovetails (Fig. 160). But right at the top, beneath the ceiling, runs a band, forming a kind of frieze, which was left in the rough. After the deposition of the body, the door was closed with marble slabs, smoothed away at the edges, whilst the rest is rough-cut (Fig. 161). In front of the door is a passage, which was entered

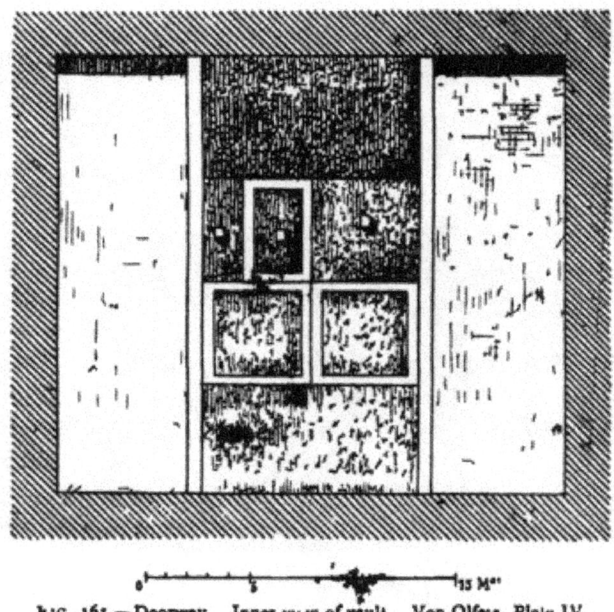

FIG. 161.—Doorway. Inner view of vault. Von Olfers, Plate IV.

from the south, looking towards Sardes (Fig. 162). Its walls are of square blocks of the same marble; they appear channelled, and contrast with the plain faces and framing, scarcely touched by the chisel. As soon as the vault was closed, huge stones were rolled and heaped against it, the better to block the passage. The roof is arched, but the vault, though mediocre, has not moved. The covering of the mortuary chamber consisted of horizontal slabs, some of which have been displaced by earthquakes. No trace of the sarcophagus was found; it doubtless was of wood, and destroyed by the first treasure-finders. On the other hand, numerous fragments of vases of Oriental alabaster and of clay were picked up. Above the ceiling of the mortuary chamber, charcoal was discovered heaped up to about two metres —the remains apparently of the temple-store which served to consume funereal sacrifices.

The royal mound consists of two conical masses put one upon the other, each with a truncated summit, the topmost being some-

FIG. 162 Passage Von Olfers, Plate IV

what more depressed than the one below (Fig. 163). The lower part of the cone, to the height of eight metres, is native rock; then comes a circular wall of large units, fixed without mortar, which serves to keep in place the earthwork within the circle. The whole may be likened to a pie, of which the wall is the crust.[1] Here and there, the rock shoots up above the surrounding level, and projects internally beyond the wall line into the void, which it helps to fill (see plan, Fig. 159). Between these peaks, the artificial mass was disposed in regular layers, one of clay, one of

[1] The total height of the tumulus is sixty-one metres, and the artificial mound from the top of the built wall, forty-three metres.

yellow mud, and a third of lime mixed up with sand. Measured from the level of the plain, the circular base is twenty-six metres; it supported the mound properly so called, which had a facing of bricks at least towards the apex (Fig. 164), and ended in a platform, where the excavators found one of the boundary stones named by Herodotus, lying on one side, but still *in situ*. Its diameter at the base is 2 m, 85 c. (Fig. 165). In it we recognize a phallus akin to those encountered in the Tantaleis necropolis. Another, one-fourth the size of this, was discovered at the foot of the mound. To judge from the respective bulk of the two stones, as well as the situation in which they are found, we may conclude that the larger was that which once stood in the centre of the platform, whilst the other was one out of the four distributed around it, and which, being close to the edge, rolled over the talus.

FIG. 163.—Section of tumulus through south-north line. Present state. Von Olfers, Plate II.

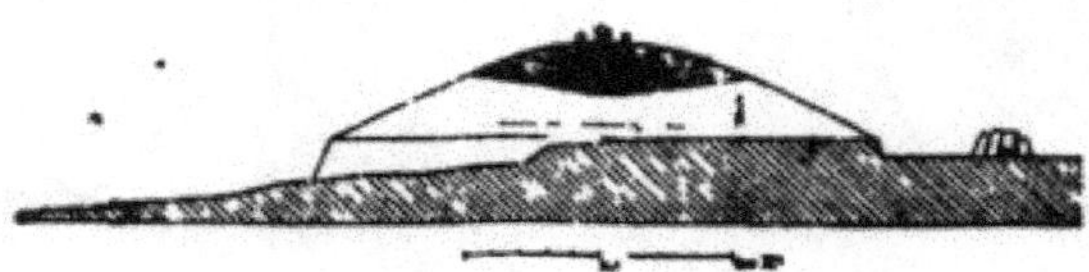

FIG. 164.—Section of restored tumulus. *Ibid.*, Plate IV.

FIG. 165.—One of the stone termini. *Ibid.*, Plate III.

The remaining three cannot be far off, and are, doubtless, buried under accumulated *débris*. There is no trace of an inscription anywhere about the stones. Herodotus did not actually climb the sepulchral mound of Alyattes; he was content to see it from Sardes. His mention, therefore, of a stela that should have been somewhere on the outside of the monument may be due to one of two causes. Either he was the dupe of his guide, as every traveller ignorant of the language of the country he happens to visit knows to his own cost, or his memory may have played him false, and made him confuse the said stelæ with the milestones of the upper platform.

On the other hand, the measurements given by the historian coincide very nearly with those taken on the spot, and must of a necessity relate to the same monument. The one error in his computation is clearly due to his having mistaken the diameter for the circle, since a circle of 1172 m. would yield a diameter of 373 m., and not 403 m. If we take the 373 m., which are the real figures of Herodotus, and compare them with the 355 m. obtained by Spiegelthal for the diameter measured at the foot of the wall, we shall only find a divergence of 18 m. between the two sets of measurements. Accepting Spiegelthal's figures as final, the monument was 1115 m. round.

If these dimensions be set against those of the Cheops Pyramid, they will make one realize how the Lydian monument should have reminded the historian of what he had seen in Egypt and Chaldæa. The Great Pyramid is certainly taller than the tomb of Alyattes, but its circumference is much less, being no more than 935 m 96 c. Then, too, in its pristine state the Lydian sepulchre must have looked far more imposing than it does now, with its wall buried under rubbish, and its sides deformed by deep furrows or sinkings. The deepest of these looks towards the old capital (Fig. 157). Traces of a carriage-road have been found in the direction of the Hermus and Sardes, with which it communicated either by a bridge or a ford. It led to the necropolis, and thence to a temple of Artemis Coloæ not far distant.

The monument, then, considered as a whole, was not devoid of grandeur, and testified, if nothing else, to a great effort. The tomb of the warlike monarch, who had moved the frontiers of Lydia on to the banks of the Halys, was the principal ornament of a necropolis embracing sepulchres other than royal mausoleums; since no less than a hundred distinct mounds have been made out,[1] whilst in a district where tumuli obtained, we may take it that many more have been destroyed, either by the action of water or the ploughshare.

As stated above, Spiegelthal began by exploring some of the

[1] The figure is that given by Spiegelthal; Hamilton and M. Choisy say about sixty mounds.

smaller tumuli, but the public has not been given the result of his researches. Hence our information in regard to them is derived from a work lately published by M. Choisy, a French traveller, who visited the Lydian necropolis in 1875. When he reached the spot he discovered that several tombs had recently been opened and cleared—by whom no one seemed able or willing to tell—so that he had ample opportunity to study the secondary tumuli, and analyze the character of their architecture.[1]

Despite slight differences which it is unnecessary to point out, these tombs may be reduced to one single type (Fig. 166). Thus the mortuary chamber beneath the conical mass is a low and tiny apartment flush with the soil, whose dimensions are appreciably uniform, no matter the importance of the covering mound. In round numbers these dimensions are 3 m. 50 c. for the principal face, 2 m. for the opposite side, and 2 m. in height. The direction of the main sides is east and west. The walls are of hewn blocks, with counter-walls of small uncut stones or rubble at the back. Large flags formed the ceiling of the chamber. A door pierced in the southern face was closed by a stone plug that exactly fitted the door-frame. It communicated with a passage that ran for some distance, and was presently lost in the mass itself. The wall-facings of the apartment were left, as a rule, in an incomplete state, whilst the passage is subdivided into sections, added on at different times, whose execution gets ruder in ratio to its distance from the mortuary-chamber. All the details betray evident precipitation.[2]

FIG 166.—Lydian tomb Plan CHOISY, *Note*, Fig 1

M. Choisy completes these general indications with a double set of drawings. The main dimensions of the first tomb (Fig. 164) are the following: length of chamber, 2 m. 94 c.; width, 2 m. 1 c.; height, 2 m. 2 c.

Passage: width, 1 m. 51 c.; height, 1 m. 98 c.

[1] AUGUSTE CHOISY, *Note sur les tombeaux Lydiens de Sardes avec planches et plusieurs figures dans le texte* (*Revue Archéologique*, N.S., tom. xxxii. pp. 73–81).

[2] *Ibid.*, p. 74.

Fig. 167 gives a perspective view of the slab that served to close the cell, of which a good view is given in plan. Transverse section (Fig. 168) shows the door open. In Fig. 169 we have two sections of the passage, built of well-prepared units; the sections are pieced on, but not united one with the other; the remaining portion of the gallery is of small stones, and the whole surrounded by the earthwork.

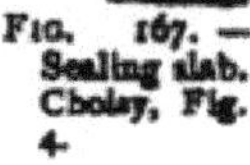
FIG. 167.—Sealing slab. Choisy, Fig. 4.

The next tomb (Figs. 170–173) is a variant of the preceding one. The piers have an inward salience, whose incline is about 20 c. per metre. Dimensions of chamber: length, 2 m. 83 c.; width on the ground plane, 1 m. 94 c.; width flush with the ceiling, 1 m. 52 c.; height, 2 m. Width of passage: 1 m. 29 c.; height, 1 m. 72 c.

The last monument (Figs. 174, 175) is a simple chamber without any vestige of a passage, 2 m. 60 c. by 1 m. 65 c., and barely 1 m. 19 c. in height. In Fig. 176 are figured the two sides of the unfinished casing, much enlarged; they are supposed to be raised from the ground and seen from below. Fig. 177 indicates the place usually occupied by the chamber, and the gallery by which it is approached. The earthwork has been obtained by conical layers regularly arranged around the axis of the mound. The lower zones have a steep incline, which grows less with each successive band.

FIG. 168.—Transverse section. *Ibid.*, Fig 3

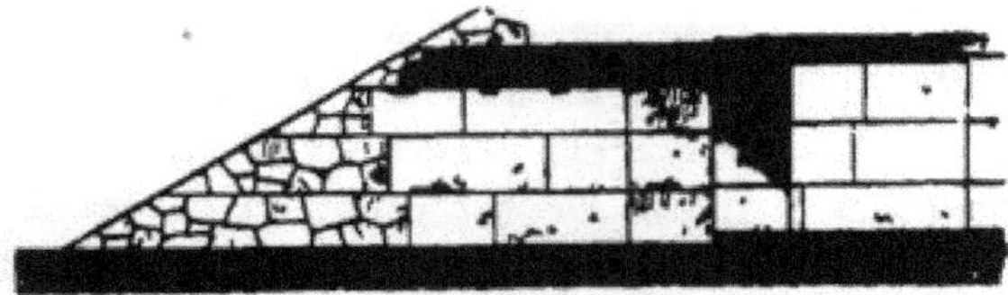
FIG. 169.—Longitudinal section *Ibid.*, Fig. 2.

FIG. 170.—Lydian tomb. Plan. *Ibid.*, Fig. 5.

"Indications such as these permit us to understand how the work was carried on. Two gangs were employed at it; one composed of journeymen to raise the earthwork, and the other of masons to build the vault. For the greater convenience of the two parties, whom close contact would have seriously hindered, the tomb-chamber was built away from the centre, so as to leave here an open space for depositing the material which was to form

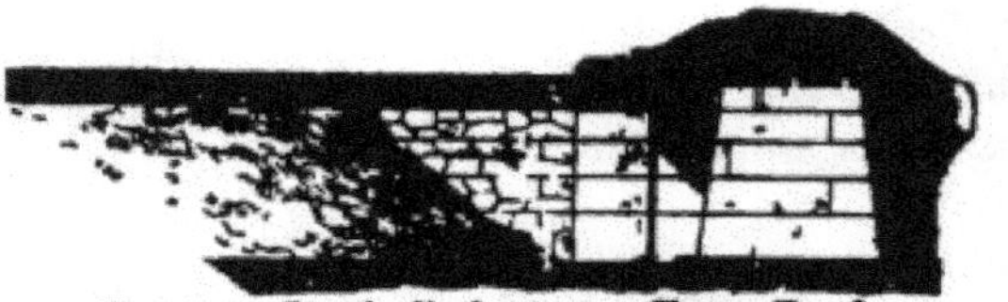

FIG. 171.—Longitudinal section. Choisy, Fig. 6.

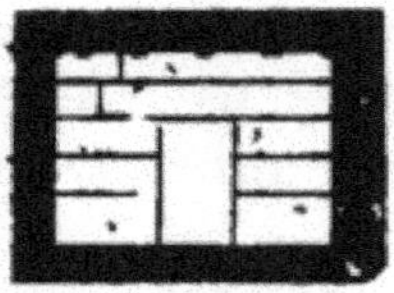

FIG. 172.—Transverse section. *Ibid.*, Fig. 7.

the mound-core. The earthwork went on adding to its size by degrees until it reached the cell which it encompassed, all but a narrow space reserved for the passage branching off on the south face. As the filling progressed and grew larger, the gallery, whose function was to keep the entrance free, was lengthened out; hence the fragments of masonry everywhere observable about these passages. Here and there even, to save time, dressed stones were abandoned for small units in their native rudeness (Figs. 169, 171). When complete, the body was deposited in the tomb, the door was sealed, and the cell left to itself amidst its earth surroundings; but its smallness, coupled with careful construction, saved it from being crushed under the enormous pressure.

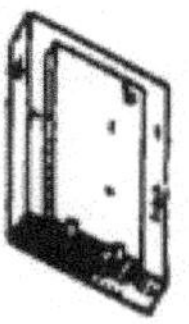

FIG. 173.—Sealing slab. *Ibid.*, Fig 8.

"The galleries by which it was approached, being less firmly constructed, were more liable to give way under superimposing weights; and to prevent so untoward a catastrophe they were entirely filled inside with earth, proved by the state of absolute obstruction in which they are found, and the absence of an opening of any kind at their extremity.

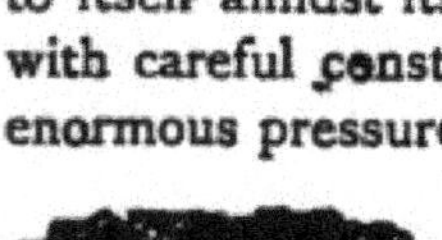

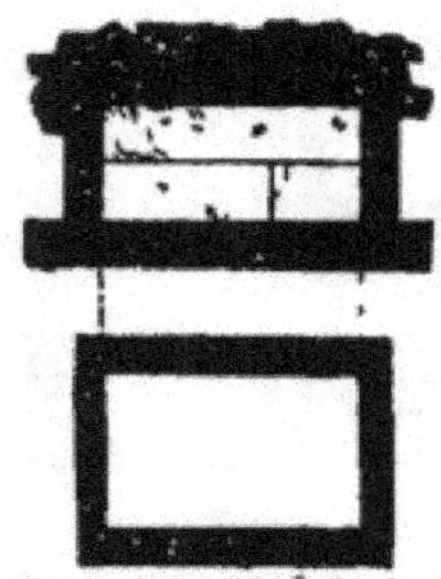

FIGS. 174, 175.—Lydian tomb. Plan and longitudinal section. *Ibid.*, Figs. 9, 10.

"Thus the progress of the labour explains itself. If now we look into the processes with which the stones were made ready for use, we shall trace analogies between the methods of the Lydians and those of the Greeks, which cannot assuredly be considered as fortuitous. The blocks are prepared exactly as those of Hellenic monuments of the best epoch. When time failed for dressing beforehand those intended to line the walls, we find grooves around the unfinished units to guide the stone-cutter in the completion of his work (Fig. 176)—a mode of execution likewise followed in the Propylæa at Athens. But when the blocks were put in place ready cut, near the salient angles and along the edges, seams in relief have been reserved to prevent the effect of violent contact (Figs. 168, 169, 172). Very similar precautions were resorted to at Segesta, in Sicily, in placing the architrave. As with the Greeks, here also, the covering slabs of the chambers are horizontally placed; and the result is a ceiling instead of a vault. When the builder feared to see the slab of his ceilings break under downward weight, he reduced the span by approaching the two supporting walls (Fig. 171). "In this way the Greeks perpetually ensured solidity to their platbands; the lintels of their doorways are laid upon piers whose intervening space is less towards the top than at the base."[1]

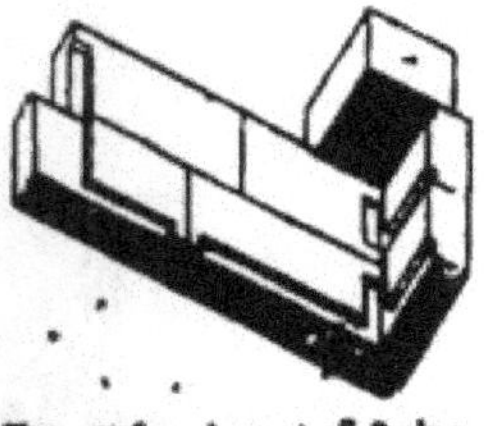

FIG. 176.—Aspect of facing. Choisy, Fig. 11.

A curious detail will be observed: wherever the masonry in the galleries is of small units, we find them neither cemented nor set up dry, but imbedded in soft mud; the mark left by the trowel for smoothing it down is still to be seen. No example has been quoted of so primitive a mode in the monumental constructions of antiquity.

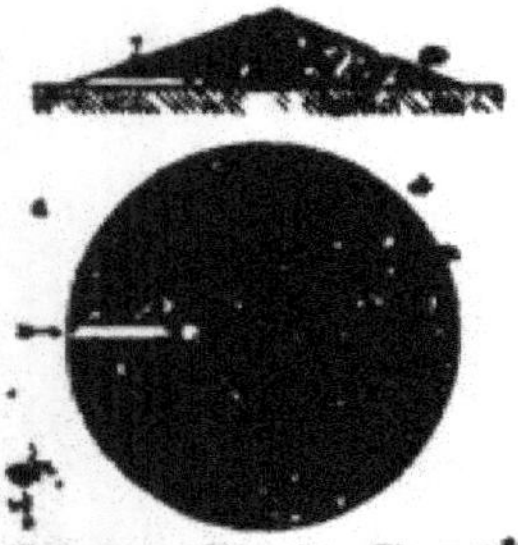

FIG. 177.—Tumulus. Plan and section. *Ibid.*, Fig. 12.

All the precious objects deposited in these tombs have disappeared. M. Choisy collected on the site chips of resinous wood, probably remains of ancient coffins, along with iron clamps that served to hold them together; fragments of pottery, bits of a fine alabaster vase with an elongated profile, and finally stone beds upon which the Lydians laid their dead. All these couches were cast out of the vaults when the excavations took place; but from the pieces that were then collected, it has been possible to restore a whole bed (Fig. 178). The funereal couch was upheld by two supports of unsquared stone, the upper face of which was slightly sunk, in

[1] CHOISY, *Note*, pp. 76, 77.

imitation of the depression made by the body upon a mattress, and at either end the corner bulged out with a hollow in the middle, as would a pillow upon which the head has rested. In the front face of the stone bed is an ornament in the shape of a patera; to judge from the thinness, as well as from the palmette design decorating them, the feet carved on the anterior face of the supporting slabs would appear to be copied from a bronze couch. In many of these beds, when there was not time enough to chisel the stone, the painter's brush was used in the decoration. Vestiges of colour, red and green, are distinguishable on another couch, a transverse section of which is given in Fig. 179. Thus the Greek key along the edge of the pillow was merely painted; so were the stars decorating the lateral face

Fig. 178.—Funer bed.

of the mattress, the "rays" of which are partly green and partly red. The drawing of these stars is inaccurate and bad, and indications of hurry, we might say precipitation, are patent everywhere. But all the same, the design and ornament of this piece of furniture bespeak the frank and firm treatment of a late period. On the other hand, no tombs with Greek inscriptions have been discovered in this plain. The Hellenicized Sardes of the Achæmenidæ, of the Seleucidæ, and of the kings of Pergamus, had her cemeteries closer at hand. In Bin Tepe we have the ancient Lydian necropolis, that in which the heads of the great families had wished to repose beside their kings; but there are no data to warrant the supposition that, as time went on, people continued to be buried there. Consequently we may regard these tombs as anterior to the defeat of Crœsus; the more recent would date from the first half of the sixth century B.C. This hypothesis is not belied by the style of the mouldings, or the aspect of the many fragments picked up during the excavations in this field of the dead.

FIG. 179.—Funereal bed, with painted ornaments. Choisy, Plate XIII. A.

The tumuli situate near Lake Coloæ were not the sole instances to be found in this district. A fragmentary text of Hipponax, unfortunately very much corrupted, describes a number of similar monuments, which the traveller met with on the road to Smyrna leading across the Lydian territory.[1] If we suppose the above highway to be that which ran from Ephesus to Smyrna (Hipponax was a native of the former city), we might recognize as one of the tumuli specified by the poet that to which a great expert in matters relating to this region has drawn the attention of the learned world.[2] It stands about two miles northward of Ephesus, in the

[1] Hipponax, Frag. 15 (BERGK, *Poetæ lyrici Græci*, tom. iii).

[2] G. WEBER, *Tumulus et hiéron de Bélevi, sur l'ancienne route d'Éphèse à Sardes,*

valley of the Caÿster, near a rocky hillock in which was excavated a primitive sanctuary; apparently replaced under the Roman dominion by an Ionic temple, the remains of which strew the ground. Some hundred and twenty yards from these ruins, in a westward direction, rises a hill whose top was transformed into a tumulus, which rules the valley. The result was obtained at little expenditure of time and labour; all that was needed was to build a retaining wall at the foot of the hill, which effectually prevented the slipping of loose soil over the talus and preserved the integrity of the mound. The masonry of this wall is more regular than that of the tombs around Sardes. It is made up of alternating courses of varying height, which bring to mind what is called Hellenic stone-work. The blocks, set out without mortar, are "bossed" and show careful execution. An ingenious contrivance was resorted to in order to guard against the sliding of stones consequent upon a lateral thrust (Fig. 180). At twenty-five centimetres from the external border of the unit,

FIG. 180.—Tumulus at Belevi. Notch in rock. Weber, Plate I. Fig. 2.

FIG. 181.—General view of tumulus. Weber, Plate I. Fig. 2.

was cut a groove or notch eleven centimetres deep, which exactly fitted a seam in relief cut in the upper stone; so that it was able to oppose the utmost resistance to pressure acting from the apex of the tumulus towards the circumference. The best view of the whole tumulus and of the substructure is obtained from the south side (Fig. 181), where stood the entrance (Fig. 182, O). This, to

8vo, 16 pages and two plates. The village is marked in Kiepert's map under the slightly changed name of Beledi.

judge from the arrangement of the wall, was not likely to be distinguished by any architectural devices. At the top of the mound, which is slightly rounded, a few blocks of limestone are sprinkled about; remains, it may be, of a crowning respecting which no opinion can be advanced.

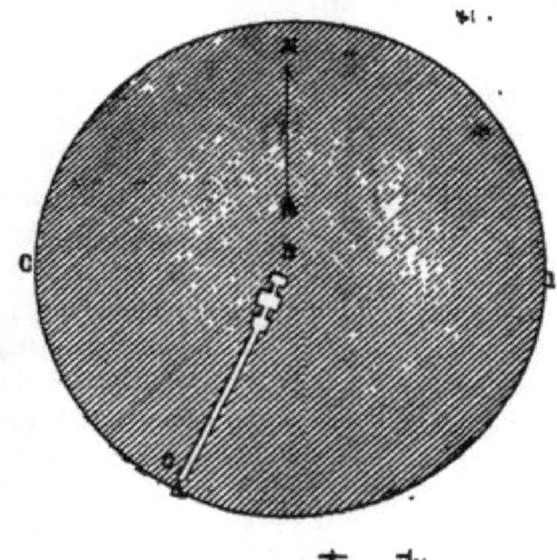
FIG. 182.—Plan of tumulus. Weber, Plate I. Fig. 3.

The action of rain water has nearly blocked up the opening of the passage, which can only be entered by crawling on all fours (Fig. 183). It is roofed over with large slabs of limestone, and is very low to about eight metres from the threshold, when it suddenly slopes upwards to a height of close upon two metres, to sink very gradually again. The gallery leads to a series of chambers, whose level is sunk one metre (see plan, Fig. 184). The first is little more than a widening of the passage. Its walls, as those of the other two apartments,

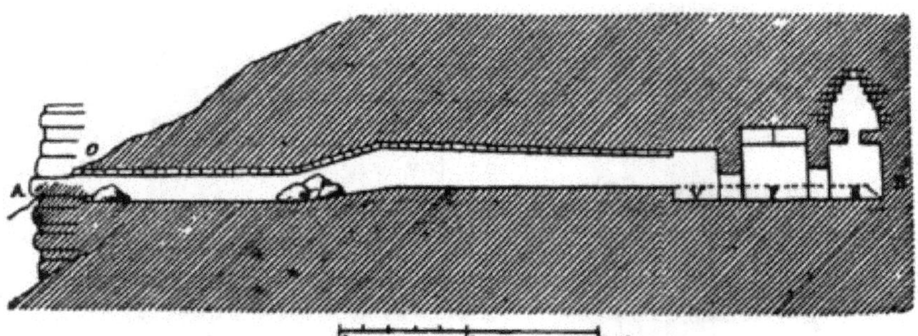
FIG. 183.—Longitudinal section. Weber, Plate I. Fig. 3.

are made of stones of large calibre, smoothed over with care. The next room is 2 m. 50 c. by 2 m. 70 c. wide. Here the builder found the space to be covered much too large for the materials at hand; to get over the difficulty he put triangular blocks at the four corners of the chambers, thus making a rectangle within a rectangle and reducing the opening. The only attempt to decorate the bare surface of the walls is found in a tiny cornice, a simple quarter round, which surrounds the roof of the vault (Fig. 185).

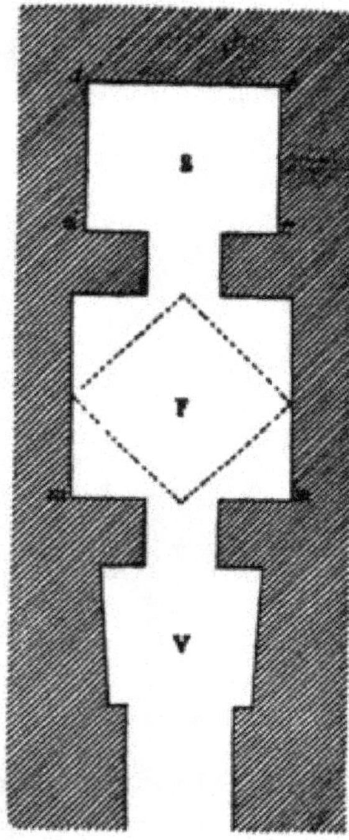

FIG. 184.—Plan of chambers. Weber, Plate I. Fig. 7.

The eastern and western walls are straight, as in the Tantaleis tomb of Smyrna (Fig. 186). Springing from the other walls, at a height of 1 m. 55 c., is a corbel arch, made of two courses of four blocks, two on each side (Fig. 187). Fearing that the system would yield under the weight of accumulated earth, the builder placed a discharging chamber above the roof, which is entered by an opening pierced in the vault. The material employed in the building of this loft was not prepared with the same care as in the other sections of the structure; nevertheless the end aimed at was obtained by setting the courses slightly in advance one of the other, thus narrowing by degrees a space of more than two metres in height.

The fact that the tomb has been opened for centuries, explains the absence of a funereal bed and of any fragment by which it might be approximately dated. The explorer who has described it insists on the regularity of the material employed, and is led to infer from it that the tomb was erected under Greek influence, at an age when the taste was felt for a better and more perfect art than could have been known to the contemporaries of Alyattes and Crœsus. The drawings he has furnished are inadequate, however, and on too small a scale to permit us properly to judge of the difference between the two sets of monuments.

FIG. 185.—Perspective view of second chamber, F. *Ibid.*, Fig. 5.

But we may remark that regular courses are the rule about the walls of the tumuli at Bin Tepe; whilst tall and low courses, which are pointed out as characteristic of Hellenic masonry, are seen in the Tantaleis tomb (Figs. 16, 17). The method is identical in both; and if in this solitary instance the execution is better, the fact may be due to its having been erected at greater leisure. It is just possible, therefore, that the tomb under discussion may be anterior to the Persian rule; as it is quite as likely to have been constructed at a later age, for a wealthy Lydian, a tyrant of Ephesus, in imitation of the old royal tombs. This type of burial is very similar to that of the tumuli of the Troad, within which Achilles and Ajax were supposed to rest; it brought to mind the heroes of the *Iliad*, along with the kings of the old local dynasties, Gyges and Crœsus, whose names stirred and filled the imagination of men with legends no less remarkable than those connected with the epos. The effect of these reminiscences and the ideas they brought in their train was seen in the funereal architecture, which here and there harked back to ancestral models, as late as the third century of our era,[1] in the full swing of Alexandrian culture. About the Belevi monument, however, are data that make it unnecessary, nay forbid, our travelling so far down; instanced in the awkward expedients resorted to for covering the two main chambers, which betray the gropings of inexperience and unskilfulness. What seems most probable is that the tomb is not much later than those around Sardes, and that, like them, it was allied to the traditions still current in the country at the time of its erection. Hence we shall not greatly err in ascribing it to the latter half of the sixth century B.C. This it is that has led us to put it to the account of Lydian art.

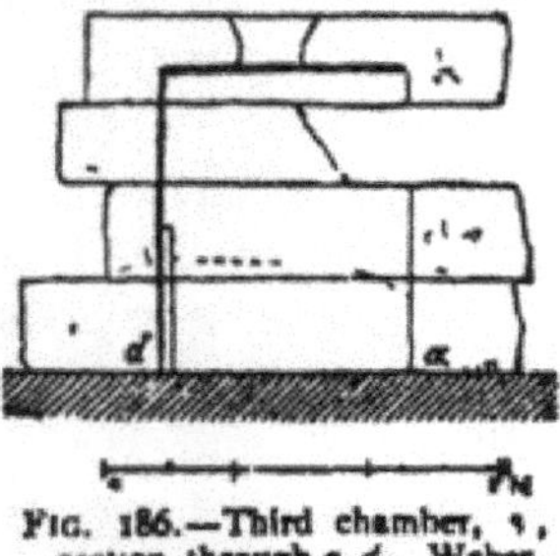

FIG. 186.—Third chamber, , section through a, d. Weber, Plate I. Fig. 6.

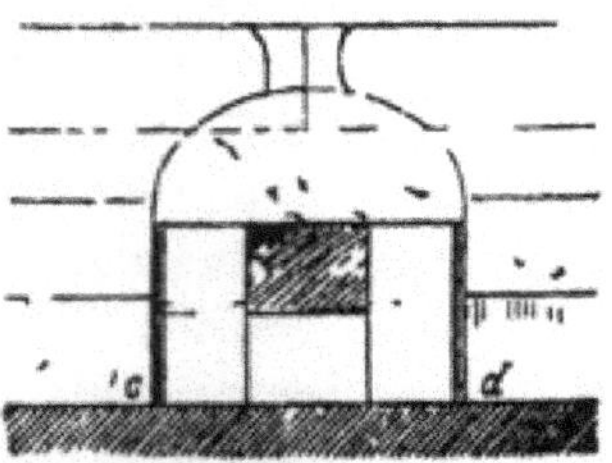

FIG. 187.—Third chamber, ; section through c, d.

[1] See *Beitraege zur Geschichte und Topographie Kleinasiens*, Curtius, p. 53, note by Adler; *Klassische Baudenkmaeler zu Pergamon*, pp. 55, 56, with drawings from Plate III.

Considered as a whole, the dispositions of the tombs we have just surveyed belong to the type encountered everywhere in the Smyrna necropolis. Nevertheless, when placed side by side and looked into critically, slight differences become apparent. Thus the internal arrangement of the Tantaleis tumulus is a dry stone-work of small units (Figs. 14, 15). Around Sardes the pebbles are replaced by a system of radiating and concentric walls, and superimposed layers of earth and concrete rammed in as tight as possible. In Lydia the base of the tumulus is a truncated cone; it is barrel-shaped at Smyrna. Here, too, the sepulchral chambers are found in the centre of the mound; but at Belevi, in the royal necropolis of the Mermnadæ, they never occupy that situation. The resemblances between the two groups of funereal edifices are sufficiently marked to justify the conclusion that they are the work of one race, a race which, on the slopes of Sipylus, as at the foot of Tmolus, were faithful to habits taken up, perhaps, in their cradle-land, and brought with them from Europe to Asia. But different hands worked at the two sets of buildings. On the other hand, differences are striking enough in the arrangement of the plan as well as the processes of execution, to induce the belief that they were due to two people and two different ages. This hypothesis is in harmony with our knowledge of the history of the Lydians and the Phrygians, their original affinities, and the difference of their ultimate fate.

Funereal architecture is the only branch of that noble art which has left traces on the Lydian soil. On many a point of Lydia were sanctuaries, whose foundation and repute led back to the far-off days of national independence. Such would be the temple of Cybele at Sardes, and that of Artemis Gygæa, hard by the lake from which she was called. It is highly probable that here, as at Ephesus, the name of Artemis covers that other name of Anahith, so soon forgotten, or one or other of those goddesses who, in the eyes of Asiatics, personified the creative power of nature—the power that calls forth beings into existence, to destroy them when their hour is come to make way for new generations. The site of both edifices is thought to have been identified; what remains, however, or rather all that is found above ground, belongs to very late reconstructions. The two Ionic columns still standing on the right bank of the Pactolus, and fragments of an entablature lying on the ground beside them, were part of an edifice certainly not older than the Seleucidæ,[1] perhaps even later (Fig. 154).

Of the temple of Artemis Gygæa, or Colonæ, only three Doric columns are left, along with remains of a frieze on which appears a lion's head, and an archer with a pointed cap. Details are wanting; but the very fact that forms belonging to one of the canonic orders have been employed suffices to show that here also we have a building Hellenic in character.[2] Examinations made at this point might yield interesting results; for the temple in the day of Strabo was one of the most honoured in Asia, and we know that the veneration which attaches to sacred places is in direct proportion to the antiquity ascribed thereto.[3] Marble was used in rebuilding these temples, but we have proofs that bricks, in the reigns of the Lydian kings, were likewise employed in edifices of great size. Under the action of air and water, formations such as gneiss, the main constituent of the Tmolus mass, crumble away and furnish an excellent clay. The fact that Lydia in old days gave her name to a special type of bricks suggests the notion that they were manufactured on a large scale for exportation. Thus in Italy clay units one foot and a half by one in width were called "Lydian bricks."[4] Nor have bricks ever gone out of fashion in Lydia; their usage is universal at the present day for house covering. The excellent quality of the native clay led Lydian builders to apply it to ornamental purposes, in the same way as the Chaldæan masons had done before them; but it never entered into the scheme of the Greek architect. A German traveller[5] mentions having seen, on the right bank of the Pactoclus at Sardes, colossal drums in terra-cotta lying on the ground amidst accumulated rubbish. In the days of Augustus there was here an old brick building called *the Palace of Crœsus*,

[1] CURTIUS, *Beitræge*, pp. 87, 88, Adler. STARK (*Nach dem griechischen Orient*, p. 394) shows very forcibly that it by no means follows that the two Ionic columns represent the temple of Cybele, a temple which, according to Herodotus, disappeared in the general conflagration of Sardes. We have no information as to the site of this temple, and a city of the importance and magnitude of Sardes must have had other sanctuaries, notably in the Græco-Roman period.

[2] The only data we possess in regard to these ruins were borrowed by E. Curtius from the notes of Spiegelthal (*Artemis Gygæia, und die Lydischen Fuerstengraeber*, *Archæ. Zeitung*, 1853, pp. 148–161, more particularly p. 152).

[3] Strabo, XIII. iv. 5.

[4] PLINY, *Hist. Natur.*, xxxv. 49.

[5] GREGOROVIUS, *Kleine Schriften*, tom. i. p. 15.

within which the elders withdrew themselves on market days, to avoid the turmoil and bustle going on around them. To have fulfilled the condition of a place of rest, the house must have stood in the lower city; for requiring old men to climb up the high and steep hill upon which the citadel was perched, would have been anything but a relief to their shaky aged limbs. The foundations at least of this important edifice must still exist, and would in all likelihood be found on one of the platforms staged between the flat level and the precipices terminating the Acropolis on the north.

The fact that the palace lasted more than five centuries, is strong evidence that it was built of bricks baked in the kiln. Raw bricks were largely employed in the building of private houses; these, if we are to believe Herodotus, 500 B.C., were nothing more than huts thatched with reeds; and even in those instances when the walls were made of brick, the roof was invariably thatched;[1] hence it was that one of these ephemeral huts having been set on fire, the flames soon spread to the whole town and brought about its destruction. Until the Persian conquest (divided from the Ionian rebellion by a little over forty years), buildings of great importance, as the tomb of Alyattes and the palace, were only erected by the kings and grandees of Lydia; so that the town, which was open, had the appearance of a huge village.

SCULPTURE AND NUMISMATICS

If not a single sculptured work remains which may be attributed to the Lydians with any reasonableness, this is to be accounted for in their marked preference for built tombs, those in which the vault is hidden away in the depths of the tumulus. Had they, like the Phrygians and the Paphlagonians, hollowed the sepulchres of their kings in the living rock, bas-reliefs would have been preserved about Tmolus and the neighbouring hills, akin to those we have met on the central plateau. But rock-sculptures are rare within the Lydian territory, and, to judge from their execution, they clearly belong to the time of the Roman dominion.[2]

[1] VITRUVIUS, *De Architectura*, ii. 10; PLINY, *loc. cit.*, XXXV. 49.

[2] In *Voyage Archéologique* of Le Bas, Plate LV., "Itinéraire," are reproduced three bas-reliefs, the originals of which are found at Ammam, in the Upper Hermus,

If under the circumstances we could not expect to see figures flung athwart the face of the stony cliff, we had hopes that the tombs of Lydia would yield small objects, such as bronzes and terra-cottas; those that have been opened, however, have revealed nothing of the kind, whilst the small figures sold by dealers of curios at Constantinople and Smyrna are almost always of uncertain origin. Reference was made a little while ago to a quadrangular stone covered with writing on three of its faces,[1] which was discovered at Ak-Hissar (ancient Thyatira). On the fourth face was incised a man's figure, whose head and bust are completely obliterated; the legs, which are inwardly bent and wide apart, are alone preserved,[2] so that little is to be made out of the monument.

Coins are the only instances left to us from which to obtain some notion of the way the Lydians understood and rendered the human form. The pieces in electrum, divided into two different systems, are the oldest creations of the coiner's art in Lydia; both of which had their origin in Mesopotamia. In the one which is generally called Babylonian, the unit of weight is a mine of 505 grammes, divisible into 60 parts of 8 grammes 415 c. each; in the other, known as Græco-Asiatic or Phœnician, the mine is equal to 1010 grammes, and its sixtieth part is 16 grammes 13 c. The lighter mine would seem to have been introduced in the interior of Asia Minor, by the Syro-Cappadocians and the Phrygians; whilst the heavier mine was carried to the coasts and the islands of the Ægean, and thence to continental Greece, by the Phœnicians. We do not propose entering into details as to the expedients which followed the invention of coinage, and which were taken up by the Lydians and Ionians in order to fix the relation between the three precious metals employed in succession in the issue of money. Any one interested in the subject should consult a standard work in which are duly set forth the different cuts that were adopted for each of the metals, and the simultaneous introduction of the sexagesimal

north-east of Kulah, on the Ghediasû; that is to say, in the district formerly called Mæonia. The sculptures are descriptive of religious scenes connected with the cultus of Atys. In the one he is seen under a pine, a tree sacred to him; in the next he is surrounded by a pack of hounds; whilst in the third, he is borne in the arms of his worshippers, who are about to lay him in the tomb.

[1] *History of Art*, tom. v. p. 242, note 1.

[2] A squeeze due to M. S. Reinach has been deposited in the Bibliothèque de l'Institut.

and decimal division, by means of which the end aimed at was more easily reached.[1] The important thing to be remembered is the fact that the lighter pieces were struck at Sardes to facilitate the caravan traffic carried on between the Euphrates valley and Lydia; whilst the larger, heavier mine would seem to have been more particularly employed in the commercial transactions of the Mermnadæ with the Greeks of the seaboard. The interest these pieces have in our estimation does not reside in their specific weight, but in their form and the image impressed thereon; we study them as monuments of the arts of design. The moneys attributed to the age of Gyges and Ardys are all in electrum. On one side are markings or striæ, but no impression made with the die; on the reverse, three deep indentations, oblong in the middle, square on either side. In these hollows are symbols in relief, sometimes very indistinct. The most curious is seen in Fig. 188, exhibiting a running fox within the narrow slit cut right across the piece. Here and there, despite the smallness of the image, the animal is distinguishable and easily recognized;[2] in the majority of cases, however, it is guesswork rather than vision. On the smaller ingots, as the half and other fractions of the stater, the markings of the punches are more or less rude and irregular.

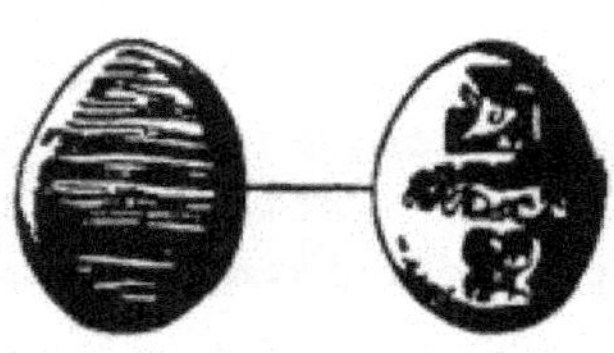

FIG. 188.—Lydian coin. Electrum. British Museum.

The Greeks of Miletus, Ephesus, Cymæ, and Phocæa, who had in very early days adopted the electrum, then the gold coinage of Lydia, showed no less alacrity in making their own the new invention, the advantages of which were patent to all. But they soon improved upon the medals they had borrowed from the Lydians, and made a great step onward when they took the image out of the bed in which it lay in shadow, and set it up in the light of day, on one of the faces. To this progressive stage already belongs a specimen attributed with a great degree of probability to

[1] See FR. LENORMANT, *Monnaies royales de la Lydie*, pp. 184–196; BARCLAY V. HEAD, *Coinage of Lydia and Persia*, pp. 1–7; *Hist. Num.*, "Introduction," pp. xxviii.–xxxvi.

[2] Some have denied the existence of the fox in the situation referred to in the text; but it is plain enough in Fig. 188, which was drawn by M. St. Elme Gautier, from an impression kindly forwarded to us by Mr. Barclay V. Head of the British Museum.

Sandyattes or Alyattes (Fig. 189). On one side are seen the foreparts of a lion and a bull, back to back, or rather neck to neck;[1] on the other, a square hollow produced by the relief of some hard substance, upon which was placed the blank piece of metal to be struck by the hammer. At the first blows the pattern on the die enters the metal and prevents it moving out of place. We propose to assign the same origin and date to another stater, bearing the head of a lion turned to the left, with open mouth and protruding tongue (Fig. 190). The reverse of certain pieces, with a lion couchant on the obverse, and head turned away to the left, is like that of the earliest coins ever issued, proving that old puncheons were used over again (Fig. 191).[2]

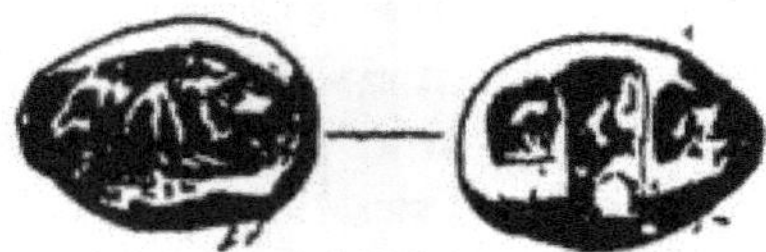

FIG. 189.—Lydian coin. Electrum. Cabinet des Médailles.

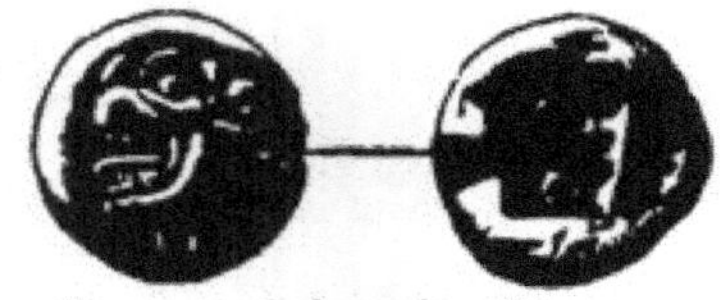

FIG. 190.—Lydian coin. Electrum. British Museum.

As stated, Crœsus appears in history as a monetary reformer. Now, the Greek cities of Miletus, Ephesus, and Phocæa began to issue staters and fractions of the same, in pure gold, as early as the reigns of Alyattes and Sandyattes, the father and grandfather of Crœsus. In the lifetime of Alyattes, Crœsus was made governor of Mysia, and was thus for years a near neighbour of Phocæa, a circumstance calculated to bring home to him the many advantages of the new coinage, whose standard was more closely defined than that of the electrum pieces struck by his predecessors. On his ascending the throne, therefore, he ceased to coin electrum, and put in circulation new pieces of gold and silver. He is fathered with two gold staters, of varying weight,

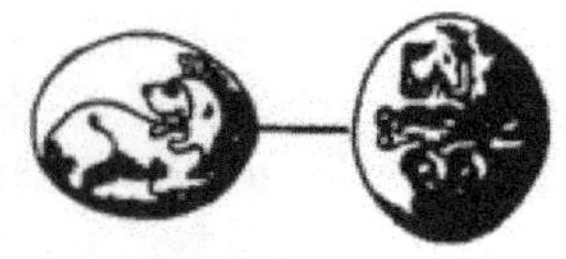

FIG. 191.—Lydian coin. Electrum. British Museum.

[1] The images are so blurred as to challenge the question whether we should not rather see in them bulls; but arguing from the pieces ascribed to Crœsus, in which the lion and the bull are quite distinguishable, has led to the conclusion that in this instance also the coiner meant to depict the two inimical animals.

[2] It is uncertain whether the coins in question should be ascribed to Sardes or Miletus (BARCLAY V. HEAD, *Hist. Numorum*, p. 545). The balance is in favour of Sardes from the fact that the fox appears on them, an image not seen on the later pieces of Miletus.

corresponding with the two systems current in Lydia proper and the neighbouring provinces. As to the silver stater issued by this prince, it was the tenth part of his gold stater. Thanks to these wise measures, Lydian pieces were readily accepted, not only throughout the empire, from the Halys to the Ægean, but outside the frontiers as well; whilst in every market of the seaboard they more than held their own against the coinage struck by the Ionian cities.

No matter the metal of which the coins were made, whether large or small, all that came out of the royal mint at Sardes have one uniform type: the foreparts of a lion and a bull face to face, the former with open mouth, the latter with protruding horn (Fig. 192); on the reverse, two hollow squares, made by two dies with rude irregular surface.

FIG. 192.—Gold Lydian coin. Cabinet des Médailles.

Of the types that appear on these coins, the lion and the group made up of the lion and the bull, alone belong to the "common properties" of Oriental art. The lion seems to have held in the national myths of Lydia as large a place as in Cappadocia and Phrygia.[1] As to the manipulation of all these pieces, it is in perfect harmony with the origin and the date we ascribe to them; the forms of the animal have the somewhat rigid precision which we found everywhere to be the characteristics of analogous works, from the palaces of Assyria to the Phrygian necropoles. It is not to be denied that the Lydian staters, with types on relief, have little to differentiate them from those that were struck nearly at the same time by the cities of the seaboard; a resemblance, than which no more likely hypothesis can be adduced than that Ionian engravers were called to Sardes by Alyattes and Crœsus. In the sixth century B.C., Ephesus and Miletus would not have condescended to take their types from people they called *Barbarians;* the art of Ionia was too far advanced; it moved from progress to progress with too bold and independent a mien, to have permitted her to look beyond her frontiers for such borrowings as these. On the other hand, at that time Greek sculpture, in its representation of the animal form, notably the lion, was still archaic and a slavish imitator of Oriental models; it needed no effort nor shifting of its lines to enable it to turn out images for the Mermnadæ in perfect

[1] See *Hist. of Art*, tom. v. p. 262.

accord with those with which the country was familiar. One would be tempted, however, to exclude from coins of this kind that with a lion's head (Fig. 190), where details are imbued with a certain degree of heaviness and exaggeration, that remind one of the workmanship of the Phrygian necropolis (Figs. 64, 130).

INDUSTRIAL ARTS.

The capital potter's clay that made the fortune of the Lydian bricks was equally fitted to taking any form the potter at his wheel chose to impress upon it. Ceramic industry, to take the word in its widest sense, seems to have been very flourishing in Lydia. Certain types of drinking-cups were said to be of Lydian invention.[1] The fragments of vases collected by Spiegelthal in the mortuary chamber of Alyattes, including remains of flasks in Oriental alabaster, do not belong to the high-class objects above mentioned, but to the common everyday earthenware (Fig. 193). Nevertheless, not one of these pieces, even the plainest without a trace of ornament (Figs. 194, 195), but testifies to advanced technique. The paste, when broken, is light red and of very fine texture; it has been well potted, and so nicely turned on the wheel as to have yielded a contour of the utmost regularity.[2]

FIG. 193. — Alabastron. Third of actual size. Von Olfers, Plate V. Fig. 10.

Parallel bands running round the body are the sole decoration of the most carefully fashioned vases (Fig. 196). On another fragment, dots arranged in circles appear between the bands (Fig. 198); whilst concentric circles are exhibited inside the bowls (Fig. 199). A drinking cup, of which only a tantalizing small piece remains, was furnished with a handle whose design and attachment were not void of elegance (Fig. 197). Variety, whether of tone or designs, is sadly to seek. The ornamentist used little more than whites or yellow ochres or both combined, of varying depth, which he opposed to dull browns. Precisely similar in character are a

[1] Critias, cited by Athenæus, x. p. 432, D. It is regrettable that the passage should have been tampered with.

[2] VON OLFERS, *Ueber die Lydischen Kœnigsgraeber bei Sardes*, pp. 549, 550.

few tiny bits picked up in another tumulus of this same necropolis (Figs. 200–202).[1] The largest of these (Fig. 200) has beautiful black lines on a field of reddish yellow. If, as far as we can judge from these much too rare and minute fragments, the ceramists of the age of Alyattes were thoroughly masters

FIG 194.—Vase found in tomb of Alyattes Third of actual size Von Olfers, Plate V Fig 7

FIG 195.—Vase found in tomb of Alyattes Third of actual size *Ibid*

of the secrets of their art, it must be confessed that they were deficient in imagination. It was not at their school that the Greek potters of the maritime cities could learn to paint figures on their vases. No terra-cotta statuettes or small bronze figures have been found in Lydia up to the moment we write; the soil

FIGS 196–199.—Fragments of vases found in tomb of Alyattes Third of actual size Von Olfers, Plate V. Figs 2, 3, 6.

of Sardes still awaits to be stirred from its very depths. Professor Sayce, who explored its ruins, "satisfied himself that the remains of the old Lydian city in the valley of the Pactolus lie at a depth of more than forty feet, both below and above the temple of

[1] In regard to the vase-fragments figured in next page, the result of Dennis's excavations, see the critical account from the pen of Cecil Smith (*Classical Review*, 1887, tom. i. p. 82).

Cybele."[1] It is matter for surprise that excavations offering no difficulty should not yet have been made.

In that Lydia whose wealth was the admiration of her neighbours, the art of working metals cannot but have kept pace with

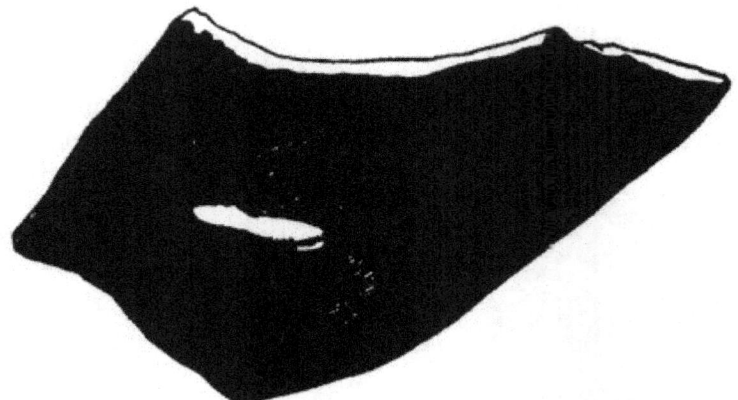

FIG. 200.—Fragment of vase from Bin Tepe Third of actual size. British Museum.

ceramic industry. Within a region where gold and silver were found in abundance, trinkets of the precious metals must have been made and worn. As samples of Lydian jewellery should be

FIGS. 201, 202.—Fragments of vases from Bin Tepe. Actual size.

mentioned the remarkably fine personal ornaments in pure gold, now in the Louvre (Figs. 203–208). They were found in the vicinity of Aidin (ancient Tralles), *e.g.* on the boundary line between Lydia and Caria.[2] Professor Ramsay, in one of his many visits to the

[1] SAYCE, *Notes from Journeys in the Troad and Lydia*, p. 85 (*Hell. Studies*, 1880).

[2] A. DUMONT, "Note sur des bijoux trouvés en Lydie" (*Bulletin de correspondance hellénique*, 1879, pp. 129, 130). The trinkets in question are fully described in the

country, was told that the trinkets in question had been taken out of a tumulus—a not improbable statement; for if nothing of the kind has been discovered in the tomb of Alyattes, the fact is due to its having been rifled in antiquity; whilst the score or so of tumuli that have been recently opened in Southern Caria have yielded a variety of gold objects, jewels, tubes, pieces that were sewn on dresses, spirals, rings, fibulæ.[1]

"The main piece is a thick gold slab or plaque, shaped into a semicircle; a horizontal tube, held in place by four rings, divides the field into two unequal sections; above is a narrow band whose space is entirely taken up by a row of discs, ornamented, like the rings, with a beaded edge (Fig. 203). A double twist surrounds the sides and the top of the oblong panel. Diminutive bulls' heads stamped on gold leaf appear in the two central discs; a navel is the only decoration of Nos. 2 and 5, whilst the remaining ones at either end exhibit two huge rams' heads. Below the cylinder, towards the top of the semicircle, are three heads of different animals; a bull in the centre, flanked by hawks of considerable size. Each of these discs has a central hole into which is let the neck of the animal. The way it was secured at the back was not by soldering, but by turning down the end piece (see Fig. 204). Below, in the middle of the slab, is a small female figure in slight relief, whose hieratic pose, dress, and hair arranged

FIG. 203.—Lydian plaque. Height, 68 c.; length, 77 c. Louvre. Drawn by St. Elme Gautier.

Catalogue des objets d'art antiques, terres cuites, bijoux, verrerie, made by M. Froehner for the sale of the Hoffman collection (May 26, 27, 1886). The letterpress is accompanied by a capital coloured plate, 4to, 1886, Plate XX. Its only drawback is that the objects appear too fresh and new.

[1] PATON, *Excavations in Caria*, pp. 68, 69 (*Journal of Hell. Studies*, 1887).

in true Egyptian fashion seem to indicate a goddess. The arms, which are bare, hang close to her sides; she is nude down to the waist; from it the body is wrapped in drapery entirely covered with a beaded pattern, of great fineness and

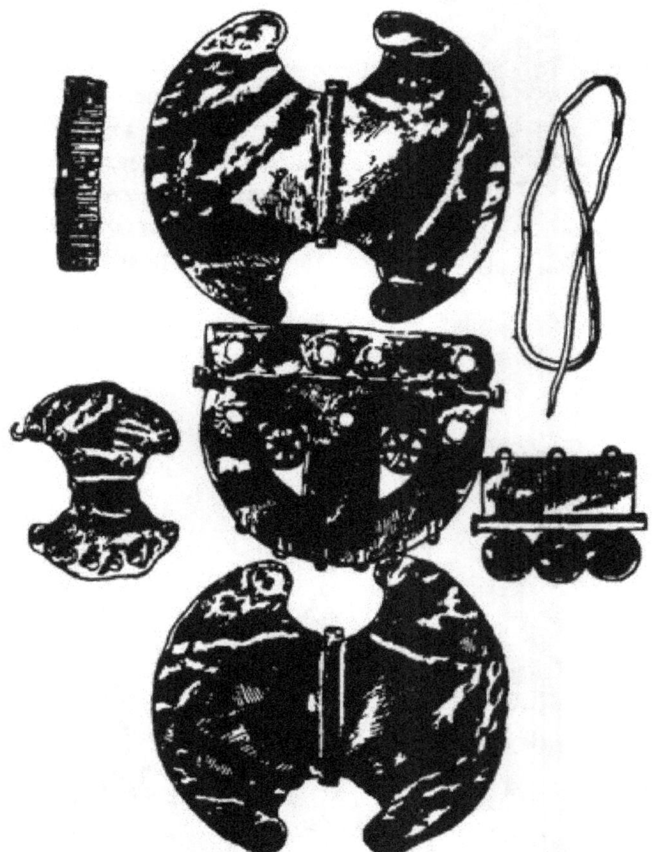

FIG. 204.—Back view of Lydian trinkets. *Bulletin de correspondance hellénique*, 1882, Plate V.

delicacy, made up of lozenges and triangles. A double row of beaded chevrons, and a pearl border running round the edge of the semicircle, complete this rich ornamentation. Nor should the six loops fixed at the back, below the lower rim, destined to receive pendants, go unnoticed."[1]

The next is an oblong slab, likewise topped by a tube, with

[1] FROEHNER, *Catalogue*, pp. 49, 50.

two masks, very similar in style to the goddess, separated by a rosette encircled within a narrow band (Fig. 205); above the tube, are three discs with central navel; and granulated work. Many of these ornaments of double gold leaf have a vertical tube; they are simpler in plan and execution than the preceding, and are cut in the shape of a double-edged axe (Fig. 206). The largest specimens have a pearl border, and the crescents terminate in a fluted knob or button, one on each side. More pearls are arranged cross-wise in the field. In another plaque, precisely similar but smaller, the pearls are replaced by filigree work. Other two discs are juxtaposed and surmounted

FIG. 205.—Lydian trinket. Height, 35 c; length, 89 c. Louvre. Drawn by St. Elme Gautier.

FIG. 206.—Lydian trinket. Height, 99 c.; length, 89 c. Louvre. Drawn by St. Elme Gautier.

by a tube, adorned by three sets of rings and a granulated edge (Fig. 207). They are followed by two more discs of exactly the same type, but without tube, and sixteen ornaments semi-cylin-

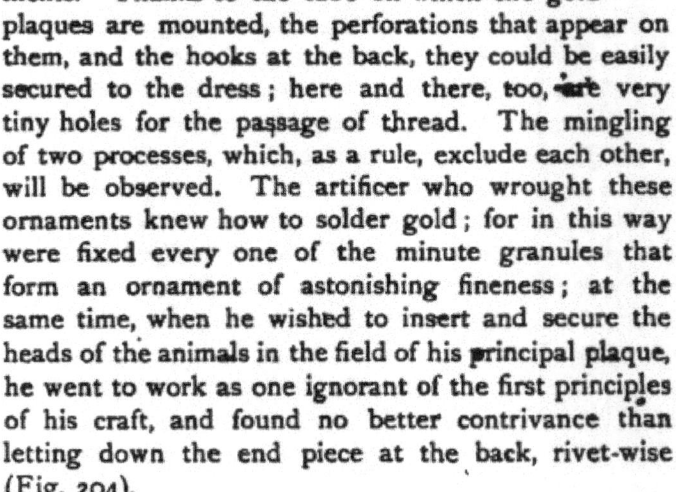

drical in shape, or annulated, with staples at the back for attachment (Fig. 208). The last object is a simple twist of gold thread of considerable size; with an oblong hole at one end. The twenty-five pieces which made up the treasure, have all the appearance of having come out of one workshop, and of being the work of one hand. We have here the remains of one or two sets of ornaments. Thanks to the tube on which the gold plaques are mounted, the perforations that appear on them, and the hooks at the back, they could be easily secured to the dress; here and there, too, are very tiny holes for the passage of thread. The mingling of two processes, which, as a rule, exclude each other, will be observed. The artificer who wrought these ornaments knew how to solder gold; for in this way were fixed every one of the minute granules that form an ornament of astonishing fineness; at the same time, when he wished to insert and secure the heads of the animals in the field of his principal plaque, he went to work as one ignorant of the first principles of his craft, and found no better contrivance than letting down the end piece at the back, rivet-wise (Fig. 204).

FIG. 207. — Lydian trinket. Height, 16 c.; length, 36 c. Louvre. Drawn by St. Elme Gautier.

That these jewels are the outcome of an advanced art is proved, both by the plaques of metal beaten out into great thinness with the mallet, and the *repoussé* work done with the graver; it testifies to an art that makes light of difficulties, and knows how to turn out forms and ornament pleasing to an educated eye. If these trinkets are from the hand of a Lydian, they must have been wrought in the time of Gyges or one of his successors. The heads of the animals adorning them recall those on Lydian coins of the same period, characterized by firm vigorous make. On the other hand, if we find here elements borrowed from Egypt, their presence is to be accounted for in the relations entered into between the Lydian empire and Egypt from the advent of the Mermnadæ, the latter furnishing Egypt with those Carian mercenaries, whose profession took them backwards and forwards

FIG. 208. — Lydian trinket. Length of either cylinder, 48 c. Louvre. Drawn by St. Elme Gautier.

between the two countries. In the preceding period, Lydia had been unacquainted with the Delta, and her art had no other repertory to draw from than that of Syro-Cappadocia. Another hypothesis which has nothing improbable about it may still be adduced; namely, that the jewellery we are considering might, after all, be of Punic fabrication. The points of resemblance it presents with those admirable pieces that came out of a tomb at Camiros are both striking and numerous.[1] There is the same mingling of human and animal forms, of heads wreathed in the *klaft;* whilst the situation given to the female image on one of the pieces from Camiros and another from Aidin, is precisely similar to that of our goddess, save that there it is full face, quite nude, and half dressed here. The image is supposed to be the Asiatic goddess Qadesh, who appears on Egyptian monuments with so peculiar a physiognomy.[2]

Whether these ornaments were fashioned in the kingdom of Crœsus, or brought by an adventurer from Syria or Egypt, matters little, and does not preclude the fact that their exquisitely fine workmanship could not but render them objects as rare as they were costly. Long before Lydian craftsmen were capable of executing pieces as complicated as these, jewellery whose chief value resided in the material of which it was made, must have been turned out by much simpler and more expeditious methods. By means of a mould of some hard stone, personal ornaments, pieces to be sewn on to garments, small figures or amulets, could be cast in vast numbers. The mould of serpentine figured on next page was used for making pieces of this kind (Fig. 209). It was found a few years ago near Thyatira, and placed in the Louvre collection.[3]

That the slab, 15 centimetres thick, is a jeweller's mould, is proved from the fact of the gutters that appear upon it, and which can only have been used to receive or drain the liquid metal. Similar moulds have been found in Assyria; but the interest that attaches to this particular one is the size and character of the

[1] The gold objects in question are due to the excavations of M Salzmann. They form part of the Louvre collection, and an account of them will be found in *Revue archl.*, 2e Série, tom. viii. pp. 1–6, Plate X.

[2] PIERRET, *Le Panthéon égyptien*, p. 46.

[3] A circumstantial account of the mould in question, discovered by M. S. Reinach, may be read in his paper, "Deux moules asiatiques en serpentine" (*Revue arché.*, 3e Série, 1885, tom. v. pp. 54–61). The memoir has been republished in a separate volume, under the title *Esquisses archéologiques* (8vo, Leroux, 1888), pp. 44–51.

figures that make up the pattern. One is a nude woman; the hands point to her breast, and the abdomen and the pelvis are rendered with gross realism. Examples of this clumsy insistance have already been figured in this history, in reference to the terra-cottas of Susiana and the ivories of Assyria.[1] Left of this personage is another somewhat smaller, robed in the long tunic of a Chaldæan priest, with six flounces of crimped work. The

FIG 209.—Mould of serpentine Actual size Louvre Drawn by Wallet

characteristic gesture of the female figure, the absence of any drapery, proclaim the goddess-mother, Istar or Anahith, of the religions of Anterior Asia.[2] From the fact that the dressed personage has no special attribute, we find greater difficulty in giving him a name; one is tempted to recognize in him a god rather than a priest, since the images produced by the mould would be meaningless, unless they were portable puppet-gods or Lares.

The other subjects incised on the slab of serpentine are less

[1] *Hist. of Art*, tom. ii. Figs. 16, 231, 232.

[2] *Ibid.*, pp. 82, 505, 507, 606; tom. iii. pp. 419, 450, 455, 610, 783, tom. iv. pp. 532, 808.

important. The lion on the right, with a ring on his back, recalls those that were discovered at Nineveh,[1] and which served as weights. We may take it as a sure sign that the pattern was most in favour and widely diffused. The singular part about it is the stick he holds between his paws. Next to Anahith, on the left, appears an altar, or four-storied tabernacle; the two uprights at the sides spread palm-wise into six points or fingers, whilst between them protrudes a semi-circular form. Very similar tabernacles are depicted on a certain class of Mesopotamian monuments.[2] The globular shape brings to mind the round stela which crowns the stone-cut sanctuaries in Midas city (Figs. 103, 104, 106). As to the diminutive circular shield and the rectangle that take up the rest of the field, all that can be made of them is that they are large-headed buttons, whose function was to put the finishing touch to dress or furniture. The left disc, in the lower corner, looks like a six-rayed star.[3]

The divine types and subsidiary devices which accompany them so closely resemble those of Chaldæan tradition, as to challenge the query whether the mould may not, after all, have been brought from Mesopotamia to Asia Minor, by one of those strolling jewellers one often meets in the East in the present day, at long distances from their native place.[4] On the other hand, the work is so exceedingly coarse and rude, the design hard and conventional, that it would reflect the greatest discredit on the technique of Chaldæan artists to father it upon them. On the contrary, if we suppose a people inferior to the Chaldæans from a cultured standpoint, whose mediocre engravers copied mechanically foreign models, coarse, heavy manipulation will no longer surprise us, but will appear quite natural. No matter what the rights of the case may be, it is none the less hard to believe that uncouth works such as these were fabricated in the age of the Mermnadæ, under whose rule Lydia was in direct relationship with Egypt and Assyria on the one side, whilst on the other she was beginning to feel the influence of Ionian art, which at that time was fast progressing towards perfection. As far as workmanship will enable us to judge, the slab would seem to be many

[1] *Hist. of Art*, tom. ii. Plate XI.

[2] *Ibid.*, Figs. 68, 79, 233, 301.

[3] Compare the sidereal shapes figured on Chaldæan stelas, *Ibid.*, Fig. 10.

[4] *Ibid.*, tom. iii. p. 448.

centuries older, perhaps, than the reign of Gyges; and would, therefore, lead back to the period when the only intercourse Lydia had with the great civilized nations of Anterior Asia was through the intermediary of the Syro-Cappadocians, when Greece was not. What the images engraved upon it specially recall are the most barbarous works of what we have called Hittite art; for example, the bas-reliefs of the Eyuk palace.[1]

The cabinet of antiquities of the Bibliothèque Nationale has another mould of serpentine, the origin of which is unknown (Fig. 210). It represents a man and a woman standing side by side. His dress is a short tunic falling short much above the knee, and a mantle thrown over one shoulder, leaving apparently the other arm and the legs exposed. He wears a long thick beard, and his head is covered with a kind of pointed helmet. The arms are bent and rest upon the chest, a movement repeated by his companion, whose fingers point to, but do not close upon her breasts. Her arms and bust are frankly nude, but the skirt, her only item of dress, reaches to her ankles. Upon her crescent-shaped head-dress are traced geometric characters. Her luxuriant hair falls in thick ringlets on either side of her face. The two bars rising obliquely on each side of her, may perhaps be explained as remains of the apparatus required for casting the figure.

FIG. 210.—Mould of serpentine. Actual size. Cabinet des Antiques.

When the mould under notice was discovered some twenty years ago, and attention drawn to it, it was attributed to the twelfth century A.D. and described as an image of *Baphomet*, to which the Templars, said their enemies, were wont to offer idolatrous homage.[2] At that time, however, the ancient art of Asia was so imperfectly known as to render the mistake excusable. Our better informed judgment cannot hesitate to recognize in it a monument precisely

[1] *Hist. of Art*, tom. iv. Figs. 328–338.

[2] CHABOUILLET, *Catalogue général et raisonné des camées et pierres gravées de la Bibliothèque impériale*, 8vo, 1858, No. 2255.

similar to those that have been collected in Assyria and Asia Minor. It is made of the same material as these, and certain details are amazingly alike. If the execution betrays a lighter hand than appears in the Louvre specimen, there is no doubt as to the treatment of the dress having been copied on the same models, instanced in the horizontal bands which make up the flounced skirt, and the markings of the same in imitation of crimped work. Broadly speaking, the details that distinguish the female figure under consideration from that of the Lydian mould are but trifling; if she is partly dressed, if her gesture is somewhat modified, the divine type and characteristic attitude are exactly alike. As to the male figure, his head-covering is the pointed cap so often seen on the rock-cut bas-reliefs of Asia Minor, and the seals of her primitive inhabitants.[1] The two horn-like appendages flanking the helmet resemble the uræus-shaped ornament about the cap of the chief personage in the bas-relief at Ghiaour-Kalessi.[2] Finally, at the sides, on a line with the brow, there seems to be a holed (two ?) salience, akin to that which appears in the same situation about a bronze figurine from Central Anatolia.[3]

The instances that have been adduced render it highly probable that both the smaller and the larger slab are from Asia Minor. In the former exemplar, the figures are less removed from reality; there is more precision and sureness of hand than can be claimed for the Louvre mould, but it exhibits a certain degree of dryness, which, it has been justly observed, seems to indicate that its fabricator was accustomed to metal engraving. Taken altogether, it looks less ancient than the Thyatira intaglio, but this notable difference may be due to another cause; it is just possible that the monument originated from a more important centre, whose craftsmen had better patterns to work from and better training.

If there are reasonable grounds for believing that the use of high-class jewellery was in great favour in that Lydia so rich in precious metals, it is likely that the demand for luxurious art furniture and fine apparel, soft tissues for furnishing the palaces of princes and the houses of people of distinction, was fully as great. Thus the stone-beds of the Lydian tombs are more ornate than those of the Phrygian necropoles. Observe how much simpler in composition is the specimen we descried in one of the vaults at

[1] *Hist. of Art*, tom. iv. pp. 546, 562, 692, 722, 744, 760. [2] *Ibid.*, Fig. 352.
[3] *Ibid.*, Fig. 367.

Doghanlou Deresi (Fig. 211),[1] as compared with the fragments that came out of the tumuli at Bin Tepe (Figs. 178, 179). Fine clothes were part of the "soft vanities" which the wise Greek philosopher, Xenophanes of Colophon, rebuked his countrymen as having learnt of the Lydians.[2] From their neighbours of Sardes, says the poet, "the Ionians had borrowed those robes of purple in which they were wont to appear in the agora, those gold ornaments that glittered in their profusely scented hair.[3] Data such as these suggest the idea of an existence at once luxurious and brilliant, well calculated to dazzle and charm the Greeks of the coast. It was at Sardes more particularly that they beheld and admired those many-coloured robes, whose elegant and varied designs the vase-painters of a later period were to introduce in their pictures of Oriental and mythical personages, Priam and Paris, Atys and Midas, the Amazons and Omphales. Textiles were among the early industrial products that found favour and flourished in Lydia, and, despite the many vicissitudes and political changes that have swept over the country, they have ever continued to be made with taste and success. Sardes was justly proud of her short-nap carpets, for which high prices were paid.[4] At the present day the so-called Smyrna carpets are manufactured at Gherdiz (ancient Gordis) and Ushak, on the Upper Hermus; that is to say, within the limits of ancient Lydia.

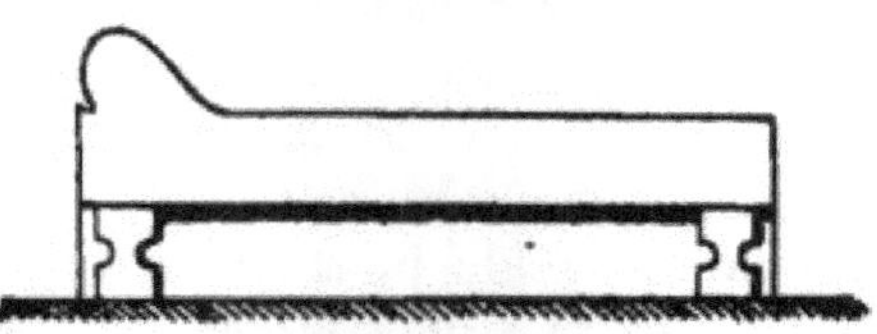

FIG. 211.—Funereal Phrygian couch. Drawn by G. Guillaume.

Fine beautiful work done by Lydian women was not confined to weaving and embroidery. There were other handicrafts they carried on with equal skill and patient labour. Of these one is incidentally mentioned in the *Iliad*, where Homer sees the white skin of one of his heroes suddenly stained with blood, and turning

[1] The bed in question is found in the tomb described, pp. 121, 122, Figs. 72–74. See Heuzey.

[2] Xenophanes, Fr. 3: Ἀβροσύνας δὲ μαθόντες ἀνωφελέας παρὰ Λυδῶν (BERGK, *Fragm. Lyr. Græc.*, tom. ii.).

[3] Προῄεσαν διησκημένοι τὰς κόμας χρυσῷ κόσμῳ, says Athenæus (xii. p. 526, A). His reading (doubtless after Phylarchus, whose witness he invokes) of Xenophanes's line is thus rendered in our text: αἰχαλέοι χαίτῃσιν ἀγαλλόμενοι εὐπρεπέεσσιν.

[4] They were designated as ψιλόταπις or ψιλόδαπις (Athenæus, vi. p. 255, E).

red around the wound inflicted by the sword. He compares it with ivory dyed with purple by the hand of a Lydian or Carian woman, as she sits at her work and decorates the bridle destined for the war-horse of the king, a bridle that all the other warriors will covet.[1] The harness of the famous Lydian cavalry was doubtless ornamented with inlay, a mode of enrichment that has never been out of fashion in the East, abundantly proved by the specimens exposed for sale in the bazaars of Bagdad and Cairo.

GENERAL CHARACTERISTICS OF LYDIAN CIVILIZATION.

The task we have taken upon ourselves involves the collecting of the minutest remains in which the hand of the Lydians may be traced, together with the most casual literary mention having reference to their art and industry. Nevertheless, if our attention had no other criterion outside the monuments that exist above ground to guide it, there is no doubt but that Phrygia would appear worthy of a larger place than Lydia in this history of civilization. But, though specious, the conclusion would be unsound, and in danger of being upset in favour of the Lydians, whenever explorations among the ruins of Sardes—which cannot be long delayed—shall furnish proofs of the constructive and industrial superiority of Lydian craftsmen. Besides, even now, before the discoveries are made, traditions that have come down to us testify to a country whose political and international action was far in advance of anything Phrygia can show. The Phrygians were above all tillers of the ground; they raised cereals, reared cattle and sheep. Agriculture was equally in favour with the Lydians; their meadow land nourished kine as numerous, and a breed of horses which for the space of a hundred years and more made their cavalry the best in the Oriental world. Their practical turn of mind and trading propensities, however, found uses for their horses other than those of war. Long processions were to be seen slowly trending their way along the paths that follow the course of the Hermus, the Caÿster, and the Mæander, laden with fruit from field and orchard; merchandise obtained from their Asiatic or Greek neighbours, as well as the manifold productions of their workshops; woven fabrics and carpets, tiles and vases of home manufacture; gold won from the depths of Tmolus, which the

[1] HOMER, *Iliad*, iv. 141–145.

crucible had converted into portable bars. The productive activity of the colonist, the artisan, and merchant had more to do with creating the wealth of Lydia, than all the washings of her auriferous sands, the contemplation of which gave the Greeks their first insight into the power of capital.

In a restricted sense, a phenomenon of a similar nature had already taken place in Phrygia. The Greeks nowhere extracted the noble metals from their soil; they only obtained them by way of exchange. This it was which caused their lively imagination to exaggerate the importance of the gold fields the Phrygians were supposed to possess in the flanks of their mountains, and the beds of their torrents; they invented tales which, sprung from childish credulity and wonderment, a later age endowed with moral and philosophical import. The untold wealth of Midas had been no good to him; it disappeared along with that of the country, both during the Cimmerian invasion and the wars that had to be carried on against the Medes and the Lydians. The affairs of Lydia took a different turn, and she retained her autonomy for another hundred years. In the meanwhile, her military preponderance caused a large proportion of the capital, that had accumulated for centuries in the most thriving parts of the peninsula, to flow in the royal treasury. Thanks to her commerce and industry, the difference of exchange was always to her benefit, so that whatever gold came out of the soil circulated within the territory, either for the use of her princes and merchants or that of the country generally. The superabundance and plethora of the noble metal suggested the first idea of an invention which will ever shed lustre on the Lydian name.

The glory of Phœnicia is to have made the civilized world richer with an alphabetical writing; that of Lydia to have given it a monetary system. This she did when she put a stamp upon her ingots, thereby endowing them with a fixed official value, that made them acceptable and things to be desired throughout the vast empire, which had Sardes for its capital.

In the sequel of this history, we shall show what splendid use the art of Greece and Rome made of the double field yielded by the two faces of the coin, and how medal-engraving became one of the most flourishing branches of sculpture, one that was productive of the richest and most exquisite harvest. No effort of plastic genius conveys, in the same degree, the impression of stupendous difficulties overcome, as a certain class of pieces that wring our admiration at the way the engraver managed to introduce in so limited a space an image which, however reduced, is endowed with a breadth only to be found in the noblest statue. We marvel how, with so feeble a relief, he was able to put every feature in its plan, and faithfully render the modelling of the face, the roundness of the living form. If of a truth we are right—and we think we are—in believing that to the practical and ingenious mind of the Lydians we are indebted for an invention that was forthwith taken up by the Greeks, in whose hands types created by statuary were multiplied and sown broadcast, this is sufficient reason why history should be interested in the Lydian people, and should feel in duty bound carefully to seek and describe the scanty remains of their civilization.

Nor is this the only thing which entitles Lydia to be considered as worthy of solicitous regard. The phenomena we have observed in Phrygia are likewise manifested here, but with much greater intensity. We allude to the ascendency which, towards the end of the seventh century B.C., the genius of Hellas began to exercise over that Asia of which she had at first and for centuries been the client and disciple, when, with a sudden reversing of the parts, she not only carried her interference on the eastern coasts of the Mediterranean, but some way inland as well, and penetrated with each succeeding age further into the interior of a continent her hosts were to conquer under the leadership of Alexander.

If the action of Hellenic civilization was felt with even greater energy within the boundaries of Lydia than in those of Phrygia, it was because Sardes is closer to the sea than Pessinus and Ancyra, because contact between Lydians and Ionians was direct and uninterrupted, and mutual intercourse more rapid and intimate. Whilst monarchical Lydia, by sheer superiority of arms, reduced the Ionians to a state of vassalage, these turned the tables upon their masters and morally subdued the kingdom. When Crœsus fell, he was on the point of declaring himself a Greek prince; he was already in the enjoyment of the rights belonging to a Delphian citizen,[1] and had he lived, he would, doubtless, have obtained the privilege of sending his horses to run the races at the great public games of Greece, and Pindar would have celebrated the victories of one of his successors, as he did those of Gelon, Hiero, and

[1] Herodotus, i. 54.

Arcesilas. In time the Mermnadæ would have acquired on the east of the Ægean Sea a situation analogous to that which the Philips and the Alexanders won for themselves on the north of this same sea. All that would have been required of a Mermnad prince, to be accepted on equal terms into the body of the Hellenic nation, would have been to trump up a pedigree connecting him with the mythic lover of Omphales, or some equally famous hero. Had history taken that turn, the world would have been given the spectacle of an Asiatic Macedon, in which the great natural gifts of the Hellenic race, her energy and intelligence, her love of liberty, which had been fostered by municipal franchise of long standing, all would have been placed at the service of a great military power. Greek culture would have spread to the Halys, and perhaps beyond the Taurus range, two hundred years earlier than it actually did.

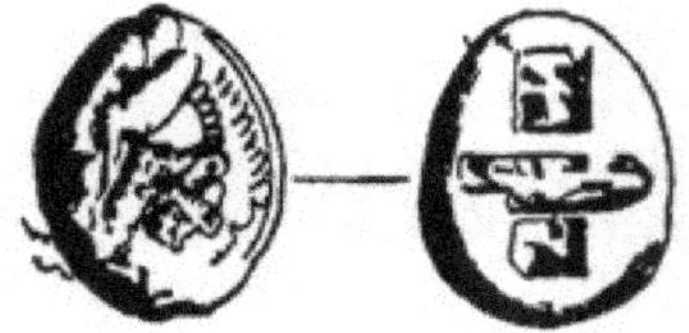

CHAPTER III.

CARIA.

HISTORY OF THE CARIANS.

THE name of Caria was applied in antiquity to a hilly district, southward of Asia Minor, which stretches between the mouth of the Mæander and the impetuous stream called the Indos (Doloman Tshai). The latter descends from Cibyratides and falls into the sea opposite Rhodes. It is a country bounded by the mountain chains of the Messogis, the Cadmos, and the Salbacos, which serve to separate it from Lydia on the north, and Southern Phrygia on the east; whilst the lofty mountains of Lycia oppose a formidable barrier on the south-east.[1] Caria belongs almost entirely to the Mæander basin; its shores are broken up throughout into very salient peninsulas and deep gulfs; but whilst the maritime frontage of Lydia and Mysia fell into the hands of the Ionian and Mysian Greeks, the Carian population managed to retain most of their coast line. The province counted little more than three important Greek centres, of which two rose at the extremity of long promontories in touch with the continent by a narrow tongue. These, to take them in their order from north to south, were potent Miletus, the acknowledged queen of Ionia until the day when her well-sheltered roadstead, which served her as harbour, was silted up by the deposits of the Mæander; next came Halicarnassus and Dorian Cnidus. Veritable ships riding at anchor, these cities derived their main resources from maritime enterprise; hence they were content with suburbs of no great extent, and, except in their immediate neighbourhood, all the rest, dominated by the crested heights of Latmos, was occupied as of

[1] Strabo, XIV. ii. 1.

yore by the Carians. It was a coast whose every winding formed a safe anchorage, whilst behind each jutting cape or slit in the mountain, were narrow creeks in which the mariner could find shelter, and when all was snug the crew could drop on the fine sanded beach.

Caria was conquered by the Mermnadæ, and became a mere dependency of Lydia; before the fortune of war, however, had brought about the reunion of the twin nations, the kinship existing between them had been fully recognized. Thus, when the Carians were asked as to their origin, they told Herodotus that their ancestors, as those of the Lydians and Mysians, were brothers of the respective names of Car, Lydos, and Myses. It was owing to this primitive affinity, they said, that the Lydians were permitted to pay homage to their national deity on the same footing as themselves.[1] The god in question, whom the Greeks identified with Zeus, was worshipped under the name of Labrayndos, Labraundeus, Labradenos, near Mylasa, where he had a temple. The qualificative was not a local proper name, but derived from λάβρυς, the Lydian word for "axe," which he carried in his hand (see tail-piece, end of chapter).[2]

Proper Carian appellatives, whether of individuals or places, have naught that is Semitic about them;[3] nor are the few common nouns preserved in the glossaries of lexicographers to be explained

[1] Herodotus, i. 171; Strabo, XIV. ii. 23.

[2] Λυδοὶ λάβρυν τὸν πέλεκυν ὀνομάζουσι (PLUTARCH, *Gr. Questions*, 45). Many other words are put forward as common to Lydian and Carian, or at least sufficiently near one to another as to yield, when submitted to analysis, identical roots (see glosses bearing upon γλοῦς, thief; Μάσαρις, or Μάρσαρις, a surname of Dionysios among the Carians, which appears to be a dialectical variant of the Lydian Βασσαρεύς; Κανήβιον, "dog-city," a Carian centre, with the initial καν is likewise found with the same signification, in the Lydian name Κανδαύλης. The double-edged axe often appears engraved, as a kind of coat of arms, above the Greek inscription of Caria (*Bull. de corr. hell.*, xi. p. 310).

[3] See the list drawn up by Haussullier (*Bull. de corr. hell.*, 1880, iv. pp. 315–320) and Sayce ("The Karian Language and Inscriptions," *Trans. Bibl. and Archæ. Soc.*, vol. ix. part i., 1887). The only local Carian name that looks Semitic is that applied to Mount Cadmos, rising to the eastward of the Mæander valley. In the first syllable may be easily recognized *kadem*, east. We can well understand how the Phœnicians, as they ran along the coast of the Ægean, on the tract of their counting-houses and mines, should so have designated a conspicuous landmark bounding their horizon in the east. The fact that the appellation has survived them may have been due to the natives having caught it up of the Phœnicians, with whom they were in perpetual intercourse.

by Semitic methods, whilst a certain proportion are easily traceable to Aryan roots.[1] In the seventh century B.C. the Lydian language was written with an alphabet of from thirty-three to thirty-five letters.[2] Of these the vast majority was derived, through the intermediary of the Doric syllabary, from Phœnician characters, whilst the remaining signs had their origin in one or other of those older systems we have called Asianic alphabets, and which, by way of reduction and abbreviation, came out of Hittite hieroglyphs, so as to express sounds proper to Carian.[3] Caria, up to the present hour, has yielded but one inscription written with the syllabary under notice, so that our knowledge of it is chiefly derived from Egyptian *graffiti* (Fig. 212).[4] The texts are all very short, and, as a rule, consist almost entirely of proper names; nevertheless there are a few nominal and verbal forms which seem susceptible of being inflected and conjugated as the nouns and verbs of the Indo-Germanic languages.

FIG. 212.—Carian inscription. Zagazig, Egypt. Sayce, Plate I., No. 111.

We know next to nothing of the religion of the Carians; at least, what we know is taken from documents relating to an age when the Carians used Greek as their speaking language. It is generally acknowledged that the Carian religion admitted of orgiac and bloody rites, of the nature of those enacted in honour of Cybele and Atys;[5] that, as in Lydia and Phrygia, the plaintive, soul-moving melodies of the flute likewise obtained here.[6] From such indications as these we surmise a people addicted to the worship of the great goddess of nature, whom the Greeks of Asia Minor designated in places as Cybele, whilst elsewhere they confounded her with Artemis;[7] but the cult which more than any other left traces

[1] DE LAGARDE, *Gesammelte Abhandlungen*, pp. 267–270; SAYCE, *The Karian Language*, pp. 5–9.

[2] See Plate I. Sayce's memoir, in which all the characters, with their certain or probable values, are duly set forth.

[3] *Hist. of Art*, tom. iv. p. 95; tom. v. p. 218.

[4] Professor Sayce's memoir, dated 1887, has a complete collection of all the inscriptions which may reasonably be regarded as Carian, and three plates containing fac-simile reproductions and transcriptions, including explanatory notes of the texts.

[5] Herodotus, ii. 61.

[6] Eustathius, commentary to verse 791 of Denys Periegetes.

[7] The Hecates of Lagina, near Stratonice, where she had a temple, was perhaps no more than a Greek form of the Asiatic deity (TACITUS, *Annals*, iii. 62). In regard to the public rites of which she was the object, consult the inscriptions

and authentic monuments of its existence is that of the supreme god, honoured not only within the territory of Mylasa, but on many a point of Caria, where sanctuaries, each the centre of a local confederation, were in high repute as late as Roman times.[1] Of the different names used by epigraphic texts to designate this deity, who seems to have been endowed everywhere with pretty much the same character, two are specially deserving our attention, namely, Ὀσογώς, an epithet applied to the Carian Zeus, and which certainly covers a word of the ancient native idiom;[2] and the title of Ζηνοποσειδῶν, which again and again occurs in the inscriptions of Mylasa.[3] The term seems to indicate that the great deity of the Carians was both god of heaven and of the sea. Thus, at certain seasons, the paving-stones of the temple at Mylasa were supposed to be washed by sea waves, although a distance of eighty stadia (twelve kilometres) separated it from its seaport.[4] Nothing of the kind has been discovered in Lydia; nevertheless, in the time of the Mermnadæ, she had annexed to her dominions the whole of the western coast. These conquests, however, had come too late to effect any permanent influence on her religious and social condition. Her gods, as those of Phrygia, dwelt on lofty summits and in gloomy forests; they were indifferent to storms, which they did nothing to raise or quell, and the worshippers that frequented their shrines were ploughmen, horsemen, artisans, and caravan-traders.

collected by Sir C. Newton (*A History of Discoveries at Cnidus, Halicarnassus, and Branchidæ*, ch. 24, and Appendix, tom. ii. pp. 780–803), as also those published by the syndicate of the French School at Athens, brought back from a recent visit to Caria (*Bull. de corr. hell.*, tom. v. pp. 185–191; tom. xi. pp. 3–30, 145–162). The Hecates under notice had her "mysteries," a fact which suggests ceremonies akin to those that distinguished the Phrygian cult. We should like to hear something more about the "key pageant" (κλειδὸς πομπή, or ἀγωγή), which, from the sacred precincts, repaired to the neighbouring town of Idrias, subsequently called Stratonice, amidst an immense concourse of people (*Bull.*, xi. p. 47).

[1] Within the territory of Mylasa alone were three temples in honour of Zeus, *i.e.* one to Zeus Carios, common to Carians, Lydians, and Mysians; another to Zeus Osogos, and the third to Zeus Stratios, also called Labrandeus, from the name of the mountain crest, where it rose about midway between Mylasa and Alabanda (Strabo, XIV. ii. 23). With regard to Zeus Panamaros, the tutelar deity of Idrias, see Deschamps and Cousin, *Bulletin*, xi. pp. 373–391; xii. pp. 82–104.

[2] Osogos is sometimes met with in an undeclined form, as Ὀσογῶα, and at other times we find it inflected. Consult Waddington's Commentary, No. 361, Part v.; *Voy. Archl.* of Le Bas; and *Bulletin*, xii. pp. 13–14.

[3] Bœckh, *C. i. gr.*, No. 2700; Le Bas, *Voy. Archl.*, Part i. No. 361.

[4] Pausanias, VIII. x. 4.

Wholly different was the temper of the Carians; when they appear on the historical scene, set up by Greek genius, they could already boast a long past spent in maritime adventure; and though details escape us, reminiscences of their former deeds lingered for centuries in the eastern basin of the Mediterranean. They themselves preserved the traditions of a time when they had overrun the Ægean as their special property on their voyages round their settlements, in and out of the isles speckling her vast bosom, as well as certain points of the Greek mainland, where they founded Hermione, Epidaurus, and others of minor fame.[1] In that remote period they had been accompanied in their daring enterprises by the mysterious Leleges, whose love of adventure or booty was in unison with theirs. It would appear that whilst the Leleges established themselves in Laconia, Bœotia, and Megarides, the Carians, true to their maritime instincts, occupied Argolid,[2] and spread along the coast line which later was called Ionia and Æolia, where they selected the sites and built the first dwellings of those cities which, under the name of Ephesus and Miletus, were to attain so brilliant a destiny.[3] To what stock belonged the Leleges, and what language did they speak, are questions it is impossible to answer; since when Greek historians first began to write, they were already forgotten, and had disappeared without leaving a trace. Nevertheless, popular tradition persistently allied their name with the antique tombs and fortresses with which Caria was interspersed;[4] it further stated that in order to people his newly built capital, Mausolus, the famous Carian dynast, had forcibly carried off the inhabitants of six villages of the Halicarnassian peninsula.[5] If the ancients were unable to solve the problem as to the nature of the link which had formerly bound Carian and Lelege, it is not likely to be settled by modern research. The view of Herodotus, or rather Pherecydes, and many other writers, to the effect that the name of Leleges was one of the many designations by which the Carians were known,

[1] Herodotus, i. 171; Thucydides, i. 8; Aristotle, cited by Strabo, VIII. vi. 15; Strabo, XIV. ii. 2.

[2] Aristotle, cited by Strabo, VII. vii. 2; Pausanias, III. i. 1; IV. i. 2.

[3] Strabo, VII. vii. 2; XIII. i. 59; XIV. i. 21.

[4] *Ibid.*, VII. vii. 2; XIII. i. 59.

[5] *Ibid.*, XIII. i. 59. PLINY (*Hist. Nat.*, v. 29) ascribes, doubtless from lack of memory, this same measure to Alexander the Great.

the distinctive of a tribe belonging to the Carian group, is, on the whole, that which seems most probable.[1]

Be that as it may, under one name or another, the Leleges certainly played an important part in those far-off days, which merge and disappear in the cloudland preceding the Homeric horizon. Along with the Carians, they would seem to have been the first who boldly turned their light skiffs towards the Sporades and the Cyclades, over the space stretching from Asia Minor to Crete and the more distant coast of the Hellenic peninsula;[2] the first, in fact, who opened up relations between these many lands, which once set on foot were to go on to the end of time. Traders and pirates as occasion served, they sailed, as the Phœnicians had done before them, from Asia to Europe, and from Europe to Asia. Their cargoes consisted of the products of the soil, of fabricated goods, and slaves; women they had surprised at the public fountain, labourers snatched from their field occupations. The bands would land at night, conceal themselves in the neighbouring thicket or a rocky cave, and emerge from their ambush with the first morning light, when, falling upon whatever they found within reach, they carried all on board ere time was given for sounding the alarm. It was a violent procedure, yet, strange as it may seem, productive of the happiest results, in that it brought together people who, but for these compulsive displacements, would ever have remained estranged one from another. Interchange, whether of ideas or beliefs, or of outward symbols consequent on the latter, would have been impossible; nor would instruction of a more practical nature, crafts, and industrial secrets peculiar to each have been learnt.

The date when the Carians first began to lose ground may be put at the first appearance of the Punic galleys in the Ægean; for, as pupils of Egypt and Chaldæa, and intermediaries between these and the countries bordering on the Mediterranean, the

[1] Herodotus, i. 171.

[2] Strabo, XII. i. 59; XIV. i. 3; Pausanias, VII. ii. 8. Homer (*Iliad*, x. 428), in his enumeration of the Trojan allies, distinguishes Carians from Lelegians, the fact in itself does not in any way invalidate the conclusion that the twin groups had originally sprung from the same family. A native historian of Caria, Phillippos of Syangela, states that the Leleges occupied towards the Carians a position akin to that of the Helots towards the Lacedemonians, and the Penestes to the Thessalians (*Athenæus*, vi. 271, B.). A passage in Plutarch (*Quæst. Græc.*, 46) would seem to bear out the assertion.

Phœnicians represented a culture superior to that of Caria. Then came by turn Greeks, Ionians, and Dorians, who in their progressive stages gradually drove the Carians out of the island, or became fused with such of them as had not been expulsed or annihilated. Hence it came to pass that in or about the eighth century B.C. the Carians ceased to exist as a compact and distinct group, save in that province of Asia Minor which has preserved their name. But although they had long been playing a losing game, and had been obliged to withdraw more and more before the invader, they had lost none of their roving proclivities, and their name as soldiers stood as high as ever. Herodotus credits the Carians with three inventions that were afterwards adopted by the Greeks;[1] namely, the fashion of putting plumes about their helmets, and ornamental figures on their shields, which they shifted and kept in place by means of a leather strap slung over the neck and left shoulder, and also fitted with a handle; for until then, every one who made use of a shield carried it without a handle."[2]

We must turn to Caria, therefore, for the prototype of the Greek hoplite; as also for the example she gave to the sons of Hellas, of selling their services to Asiatic and Egyptian monarchs.[3] Both Carians and Ionians penetrated into Egypt as early as the reign of Psammeticus I., and henceforward the flow never ceased.[4] Better armed and of a more bellicose disposition than the natives of the Delta, thoroughly versed, too, in their profession, they formed, under commanders selected from their own ranks, the main force of the armies the Saït Pharaohs moved in the field. These had established them in what were called "The Camps," on the Pelusiac branch of the Nile; whilst the Ionians occupied the other side of the river. Somewhat later, in the reign of Amasis, quarters were also given them at Memphis.[5] Of these mercenaries, whom age or wounds had unfitted for active service,

[1] Critias, a poet of the fifth century B.C., referring to the inventions due to different nations and different cities, expresses himself as follows:

Θήβη δ' ἁρματόεντα δίφρον συνεπήξατο πρώτη,
φορτηγοὺς δ' ἀκάτους Κᾶρες ἁλὸς ταμίαι.

[2] Herodotus, i. 171.

[3] To talk of a Carian, in the seventh century B.C., was synonymous with soldier of fortune. Thus Archilochus (BERGK, *Poetæ lyrici græci*, Frag. 24): Καὶ δὴ 'πίκουρος ὥστε Κὰρ κεκλήσομαι.

[4] Herodotus, ii. 152.

[5] *Ibid.*, 154.

all did not return home; many found it so snug that they permanently settled in Egypt, where they became dragomans, like the Greeks and Maltese at the present day.[1] The bronze statuette of Apis, in the Boulak Museum,[2] with a bilingual inscription on its base (in Egyptian hieroglyphs and Carian letters), is not the only instance which testifies to the part the Carians played in Egypt; even without the great authority of Herodotus, the notes they have left behind them would have led us to guess as much. Thus, from Ipsamboul to Memphis, their names are incised on the rocks of the Nile valley and the walls of temples, side by side with those of Greek or Syrian adventurers and Punic traders. Professor Sayce has collected and transcribed fifty Carian *graffiti*, and fresh researches cannot but add to the number. Of these, forty or thereabouts were discovered at Abydos.

If the language and writing of the Carians have left most traces in the Nile valley, monuments, architectural and artistic, which may be ascribed to this people, have not been found outside Caria. Do all such monuments lead back to the period of the independence of Caria? Did they witness the rise and fall of the Mermnadæ, the conquest of the Persians? We do not care to commit ourselves to a decided opinion; besides, it matters little. The inscriptions seen about the principal sanctuaries tell us plainly how faithful were the Carians to their gods and local cults, even in the full swing of Roman dominion; hence we cannot admit that change of masters induced them easily to change their methods, whether in their constructions, mode of burial, vase types, jewellery, and so forth, with which they had long been familiar. All the monuments, therefore, encountered on native soil, wherein Grecian style and Grecian taste are non-apparent, may be considered as Carian.

FUNEREAL ARCHITECTURE.

Those tombs which in the time of Strabo were pointed out as being due to the Leleges, have seemingly been identified by modern travellers on different points of the Carian coast. A few, simple in construction, belong to the neighbourhood of Iasus. They are chambers built of schistose blocks set up exactly as they

[1] Herodotus, ii. 154.

[2] The Egyptian text reads thus: "To the life-giving Apis, Prâm interpreter" (SAYCE, *The Karian Language*, pp. 15, 35).

came from the quarry (Fig. 213), the larger units having been reserved for the ceiling. These chambers are, as a rule, half embedded in the ground, and vary in size according as they were to receive one or several bodies.[1]

Towards the extreme end of the peninsula of Halicarnassus,

FIG. 213.—Tomb near Iasus. Texier, tom. III. Plate CXLVI., Fig 8.

bearing to the southward, rises the Acropolis now called Assarlik; and whether it corresponds to Syangela or Termera, there is no doubt as to its marking the site of one of those Carian or Lelegian cities whose importance, towards the fourth century B.C., gave way before Halicarnassus, one of the most flourishing centres of

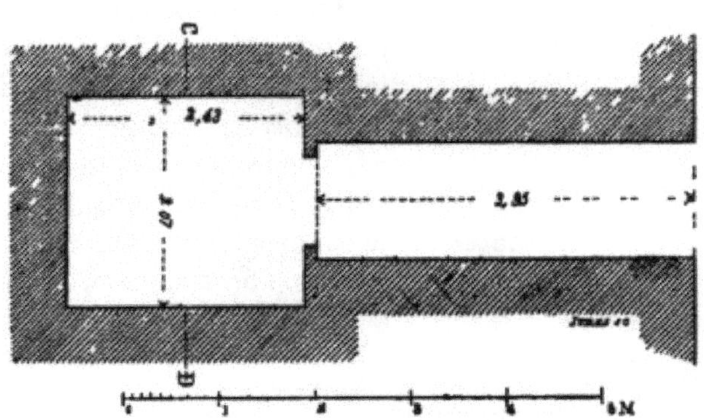

FIG. 214.—Tumulus at Assarlik. Plan. PATON, *Excavations*, p. 67.

Asia Minor, during the reign of Hekatomnos and his successors. Near the citadel is a necropolis of considerable size, which attracted the attention of Sir Charles Newton some thirty years ago,[2] and which has been more recently studied by M. Paton,

[1] TEXIER, *Description*, fol., tom. iii. p. 141; explanatory of Plates, 146.

[2] NEWTON, *A Hist of Discoveries at Halicarnassus, Cnidus, and Branchidæ*, p. 583.

who made excavations among the tumuli;[1] his drawings for the most part, however, are so imperfect as not to deserve reproduction.

Some of these tombs, commanding as a rule an elevated

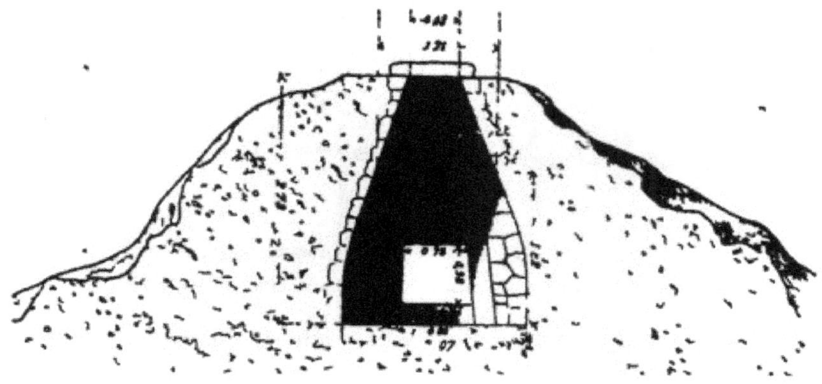

FIG 215.—Tumulus at Assarlik Transverse section PATON, *Excavations*, p. 67.

position, belong to the tumulus-type, examples of which are so plentiful throughout Lydia. Thus, Fig. 214 shows a vault entered by a covered passage, roofed by large slabs; both it and the chamber are hidden under a mound made up of earth and

FIG. 216.—Tumulus at Gheresi. *Ibid.*, p. 80.

small stones. Above the grave-apartment the end stones of each course are corbelled out beyond one another, thus producing the effect of an arch (Fig. 215). In another of these tombs, which has had more care bestowed upon it, the hollow at the top was closed by an enormous stone, at least 4 m. 35 c. long (Fig. 216). A plan

[1] W. R. PATON, *Excavations in Caria* (*Hell. Studies*, tom. VIII pp. 64–82).

of the tumulus will be found in Fig. 217. But the circular wall that surrounds the mound at a distance, and forms a kind of sacred

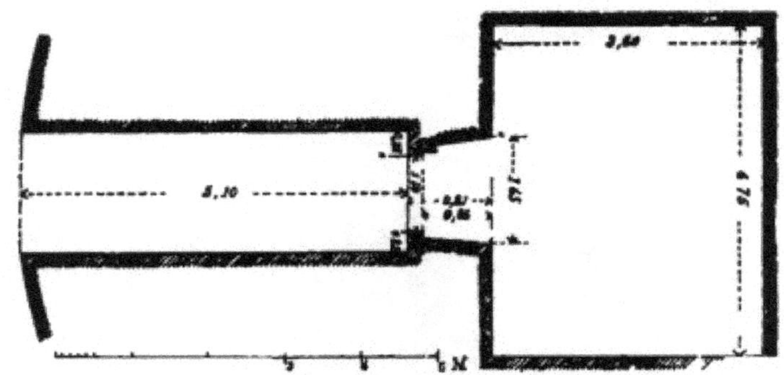

FIG. 217.—Tumulus at Gheresi. Plan. PATON, *Excavations*, p. 80.

area, is peculiar to these monuments and is never met with in Lydia (Fig. 218).

Of the vast majority of the tombs that certainly existed here, nothing remains but a low, ill-constructed wall of two or three irregular courses, which bounded the tumulus and upheld the mass. Lack of a casing to protect and support these walls is cause that the rains have penetrated the tumulus and carried down stones and earth, heaping them upon the ground.

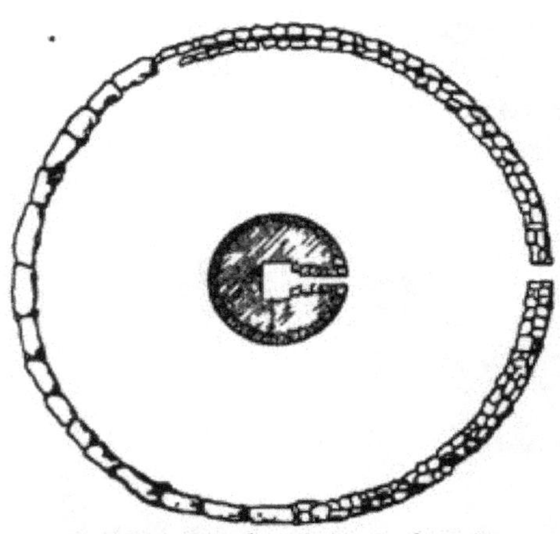

FIG. 218.—Tumulus with its circular wall. Plan. *Ibid.*

The fact that no funereal beds have been found here, akin to those of Phrygia and Lydia, is pretty convincing proof that the Carians practised incineration. The tombs in this necropolis were not all of the same size and on the same pattern, for, side by side with those of a certain importance, we come upon quite a large number of small, unpretending graves, mostly put within rectangular recesses which are fenced by a low wall. The tower-like structure

(Fig. 219) belongs to a necropolis some three miles southward of Halicarnassus. Its discovery is due to MM. Winter and Judeich. It is obvious that we are confronted here by a sepulchral *enceinte*, respecting which unusual precautions were taken to protect the dead against the living; instanced in several ditches surrounding it, as well as huge blocks set up around the graves, the larger stone being placed lintel-wise over the entrance. A doorway lower than this appears at the further side; the wall out of which it opens is built of stones of the smallest pattern. It may be modern, and have been used to pen cattle.[1] The

FIG 219.—Funereal enceinte Caria *Mittheilungen*, xii p 225

tombs found within *enceintes* of this description were mere hollows, and recall those at Iasus; they are fenced round now by huge tiles, one for each side, now by the same number of stones. A larger unit, rounded and flattened towards the edges, serves as lid. Such contrivances are no more than boxes, some 30 c. wide by 45 c. Bodies could not lie at length in them. They were meant to receive the ashes of the dead, which have been found either on the bare earth, more often in a terra-cotta vase, a large pithos with pointed base. Nor were urns the only pieces of furniture about these tombs; smaller vases of more varied shape, arms, and personal ornaments are often met with, both within the vaults of tumuli and the receptacles sunk in the surface of the soil.

[1] WINTER, *Vasen aus Karien*, pp. 224, 225; in *Mittheilungen des K. d. Instituts, Athenische Abtheilung*, tom. xii. pp. 223, 224.

RELIGIOUS AND MILITARY ARCHITECTURE.

The temples of Caria, as those of Lydia, were all rebuilt after the fourth century B.C., on the actual sites of the primitive ones. The public ritual which had marked the old religion was continued without a break in the new buildings; so that they retained, for example at Lagina, a very distinct physiognomy. At the present day, however, all that remains are Corinthian and Ionian capitals of mediocre workmanship, fragments of friezes carved by second-rate Greek artists; in which dry, finicky make are the distinguishing features, as indeed in all buildings erected by the successors of Alexander and the Roman proconsuls.[1] These unlovely *débris*, which commonplace ornament does nothing to redeem, may perhaps conceal remains of primal structures which excavations, that should go deep enough, would bring to light; when, who knows but that we might come upon ex-votos that Carian soldiers had offered to their "god of hosts," or their Zeus Stratios, on their return home after the many adventures and hardships they had experienced with Psammeticus, in his distant campaigns up the Nile as far as Nubia, of the expeditions Alyattes and Crœsus had carried across the Halys against Medes and Persians? *Per contra*, on the crested heights where the primitive inhabitants built their first cities, more than one wall fragment is seen with no resemblance to Hellenic work.

If there is a monument more likely than another to tempt one to seek in it a very old specimen, such as popular fancy, in the day of Strabo, connected with the early owners of the soil, it assuredly is the singular rampart discovered by Téxier near Iasus, and which he calls "Leleges' Wall." Its length is several kilometres; and its trace on the mainland is within a certain distance of the shore, and contiguous to the islet bearing the Greek city; it runs over a broken uncultivated tract, without trace of habitation. The fact that the defences, towers, and resaults of the wall under notice are turned towards the sea, forbids seeking in it advanced works of the Iasians to protect their suburbs against invasions from the interior. The notion that it was intended to cover the territory of a city on the main-

[1] As regards the remains of the temple of Lagina, see NEWTON, *A Hist. of Discoveries*, Atlas, Plate LXXVII.

land, to prevent a landing, which city may have been Miletus, whose southern limit joined on that of Iasus, would seem to be the more likely, but for the other fact that this formidable rampart could be attacked on another point of the gulf, and taken from the rear. Consequently we are left to wonder why so great an effort should have been made for so small and uncertain a result. Moreover, the dispositions exhibited in the trace of the wall are very dissimilar from those of Greek fortifications (Fig. 220); nor does the masonry, in which stones of enormous calibre and

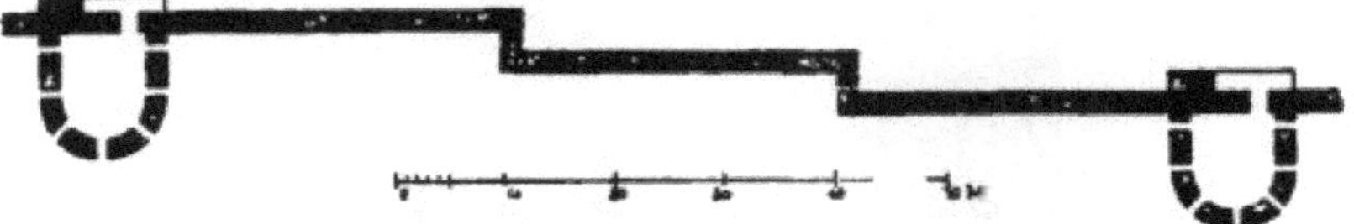

FIG. 220.—Plan of the Leleges' Wall. TÉXIER, *Description*, tom. iii Plate CXLVII.

irregular courses obtain, in any way resemble that of structures of the Argian colony at Iasus, for example, the continuous rampart set up around their islet. The latter, along with its square towers, is built of great blocks of white marble, "bossed," 70 c. in height;[1] whilst the outer face of the wall on the mainland is barely touched by the chisel (Fig. 221). Téxier was the first to draw attention to the Leleges' Wall, to call it by the name he gave it, which well deserves to be studied with more care than it has as yet received; and it is matter for surprise that, of the many travellers who have visited Caria since the French explorer, not one should have responded to the appeal he directed to his successors.[2] It is just

[1] TÉXIER, *Description*, tom. iii. p. 137. In respect to the Greek city of Iasus, see E. L. HICKS, *Iasus* (*Hell. Studies*, viii. pp. 83–118).

[2] The architect Huyot, and after him Alexandre and Léon de Laborde, had visited Iasus before Téxier; the result of Huyot's researches were not given to the world. Made aware by a passage of Laborde (*Voy. de l'Asie Mineure*, fol., p. 93) of the interest of Huyot's notes and drawings deposited in the Manuscripts Cabinet of the Bibliothèque Nationale, I lost no time in consulting them. They are headed: "*Notes d'un voyage de Paris à Smyrne*, 1817–1821, autographe, Fonds français, nouvelles acquisitions, 664; 2 vols. in-fol., de planches 5080, 5081." No sketch of the wall on *terra firma*; but the problem propounded by the gigantic construction seems to have excited Huyot's curiosity, as will appear from his own words, p. 236: "On the mainland, on the other side of the small harbour skirting the seashore, runs a low mountain chain. A long wall, with towers flanking it on the land side, descends, ascends, and runs out to a considerable distance. Main entrance in the valley. Facing the gate, a platform upon which may have been a temple. This wall is a stupendous structure which embraces nothing but bare rocks, and no trace

possible that, were a complete tracing of the rampart made, some sort of guess might be hazarded as to the intentions of the forgotten authors of a work which, though rude, they endowed with a certain degree of grandeur by sheer massiveness and extent. The towers, distributed over the length of the rampart at about

FIG 221.—Gateway in the Leleges' Wall TEXIER, *Description*, Plate CXLVII

100 m. one from the other, form a semi-circular salience over the curtain (Fig. 222); their thickness, at the height of the window, is 4 m.; that of the wall, 3 m.; and the height of the courses averages 1 m. (Fig. 223).

of other buildings, nor would it have been possible to erect any save within a few narrow corners. Nevertheless there must have been here a large population. The construction of the wall is good. At stated intervals are round towers, furnished with small doorways. Between the towers, resaults and the same kind of openings. Both gates and resaults seem to have been provided for the double purpose of facilitating sorties and preventing the enemy approaching the wall. Here and there, pierced towards the top of the wall, are openings level with the ground on the city side, but at a considerable height towards the plain."

The wall of another Carian city, Alinda, whose ruins cover a considerable area, should be noticed. "The towers which flanked the rampart of both Acropolis and city are almost entire. They

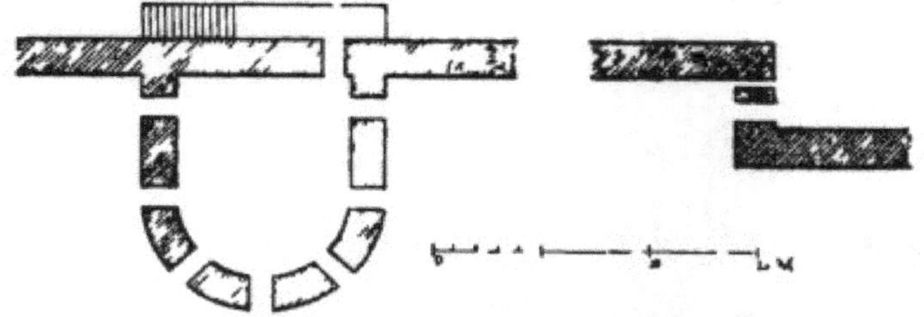

FIG. 222.—Leleges' Wall. Plan of tower and adjacent rampart. TEXIER, *Description*, Plate CXLVII.

were provided with banquettes and loopholes for the defence. Above them, on a peaked rock that dominated the town and even the Acropolis, rose a fortified tower, whose function was to guard

FIG. 223.—Leleges' Wall. View of tower. *Ibid.*, Plate CXLIX.

so important a point."[1] Fig. 224, after M. Trémaux' plan, shows the direction of the wall and the towers distributed about it. It will be observed that its most oblique course is from the first to

[1] TRÉMAUX, *Exploration archl. en Asie Mineure*, fol.

the second tower, planted on the culminating point of the Acropolis.[1] Farther on, in front, appears a detached tower, a phrourion (guarded post) (Fig. 224).

The city wall at Assarlik, of which Sir C. Newton made a drawing, offers pretty much the same aspect as that near Iasus;[2] there is great tendency to regular courses and vertical joints. It is probable that we have here the most perfect style of masonry achieved by the primitive inhabitants, ere they put themselves under Greek tuition; whilst their first constructive attempts may be sought in a wall of this same district. It runs along the rock that forms the crest of

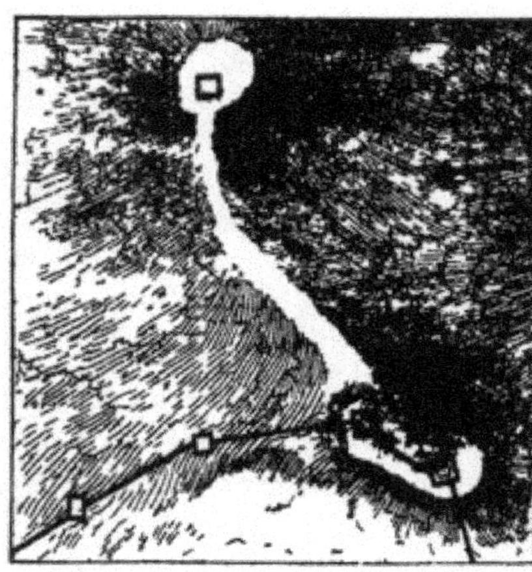

FIG. 224.—Portion of plan of Alinda.

FIG 225.—Wall near Myndus. PATON, *Excavations*, p 66.

the peninsula, west of Myndus harbour, and descends to the sea edge (Fig. 225).

[1] Cf. PHILON, *Traité de fortification*, viii. 6 and 13, in the translation of M. de Rochas d'Aiglun, *Principes de la fortification antique*, 8vo, Duchar, 1881.

[2] NEWTON, *A Hist. of Discoveries*, pp. 503–586.

It would be vain to multiply examples of this kind; those we have cited suffice to show that if the Carians and Leleges were not solicitous, as only the Greeks have been, to impress upon whatever work came from their hands, even to a simple wall, a mark of beauty and grace, they nevertheless knew how to use materials of such size and solidity, as to have withstood the neglect of thousands of years.

INDUSTRIAL ARTS.

The physical formation of Caria is very similar to that of Lydia, and potter's clay of equally excellent quality is plentiful; hence, one of its towns, Tralles, was famous for its pottery, which it largely exported.[1] Pliny wrote that in his time the brick palaces of Attalus and Mausolus were still standing; the former in this same city of Tralles, the latter at Halicarnassus.[2] Recent excavations have confirmed the testimony of the Roman writer; they have proved that baked clay was applied in this district to many and diverse uses—that they were not content to fashion vases of every size and shape for domestic purposes, but had their coffins made out of it as well. Thus, within recently explored necropoles, we sometimes find ashes in large clay jars ending almost in a point below, and at other times in chests or sarcophagi of the same substance.[3] But whether these vases were put within jars and sarcophagi, or set in the tumulus-chamber or the grave against the coffin, a sufficient number has been found to enable us to gain some idea as to the habits and taste of the Carian potters.

As in Lydia, the clay is a rich reddish yellow, fine in texture and well prepared. The lightness of the handles and the variety of types show that the artisan was already proficient in his craft. The vast majority of vases were decorated, and the form is obviously meant in those whose surface is covered with a coating of a dark brown pigment; such would be a kind of bowl which, along with other vases, came out of a necropolis hard by Tshangli, near, it is supposed, the ancient site of Panionion (Fig. 226). Most of the pieces have ornamental designs, composed of ring-

[1] PLINY, *Hist. Nat.*, xxxv. 46. [2] *Ibid.*, 49.

[3] W. R. PATON, *Excavations in Caria*, pp. 70, 73, 75–79; F. WINTER, *Vasen aus Karien*, pp. 226, 227.

like bands turning round the body (Fig. 227); the lines sometimes intersect concentric circles that are parallel to the main axis of the vase (Fig. 228); sometimes, in the blank spaces about the

FIG. 226.—Carian pottery. Winter, p 229.

FIG. 227—Carian pottery. Ibid.

FIG 228.—Carian pottery Paton, p 74

middle, we find triangles whose apex is turned towards the neck (Fig. 229); whilst the spiral device, that distinguishing feature

FIG. 229.—Carian pottery. Winter, p. 229.

FIG. 230—Carian pottery. Ibid, 230.

of Mycenian ornament, appears upon a vase now at Smyrna, and which is said to have come from Mylasa (Fig. 230).

The decoration of these and other pieces of the same nature is purely geometrical; nevertheless we have indications that the

Carian artist sometimes aspired to a higher standard, in at least two vases of the same fabrication, wherein are introduced shapes borrowed from the living world.[1] They came out of a tomb near Idrias, where they had lain along with human ashes in a huge funerary jar, resembling at all points the examples of the Assarlik necropolis. To name them in their ascending scale, the less important is a two-handled bowl (Fig. 231). The band below the rim stands out in light against the dark ground, and between the vertical bars, dividing it into a number of panels, the brush has traced roughly suggested birds. These, though imperfectly seen in our illustration, thanks to the bits of colour that still adhere to the piece, are quite distinct in the original. The second vase is

Fig. 231.—Vase from Idrias. Winter, p. 226.

Fig. 232.—Vase from Idrias. *Ibid.*

exceedingly curious. It has a very protuberant contour, but its long narrow neck and handle are broken (Fig. 232). The markings of the latter are plainly seen on the body.

The decoration consisted in part of bands, turning round the body at irregular intervals; but a more complicated arrangement than any from the same workshop is found in the lines that appear in the centre (Fig. 233). The meanders and oblique lines cross each other at acute angles, and form triangles, the surface of which is now sprinkled with dots, now taken up with fine trellis-work, now with the checker-pattern, which we observed in Cyprus, and which likewise occurs on countless Greek vases of the archaic period. The special interest which attaches to this piece is the figure introduced at the side of the

[1] WINTER, *Vasen aus Karien*, pp. 226, 227, 232–234.

ewer, opposite the handle. Though roughly outlined, the double row of pointed teeth is distinct enough to suggest a carnivorous and ferocious animal; as to the genus to which it belongs, it would be hard to say. The lion is out of the running; his physiognomy was too familiar to make it possible for any Oriental artist to have so disfigured it. Stress is laid by some on the hump which appears on the back, and which is proper to one kind of bull as well as the bear; the teeth of the former, however, are not nail-shaped, but large and flat. At first sight, there would seem to be a greater degree of probability in recognizing here a Bruin, an animal found in the Taurus range at the present day, and which formerly may have haunted the then well-timbered ravines of Tmolus and Latmos. There is nothing to forbid the conjecture; yet certain details, the disposition of the teeth, length of tail, and elongated body, ill agree with the bear hypothesis; but if we suppose that the unskilful artist intended to portray a hyena, all difficulties would seem to vanish. Thus, when moving, the hyena arches her back as in our illustration; nevertheless, it is hard to explain that if a hyena was indeed meant, the artist should have omitted to indicate the characteristic and abnormal length of the fore-legs of the animal, that make it look when at rest as if standing on its hind legs.

FIG. 234.—Carian pottery. Paton, p. 74.

The pigments used in the decoration of these vases are of that dull opaque colour encountered on very antique Greek vases. Here black and white bands stand out on a light-yellow ground; there the form is painted in with a brownish-red colour. In the largest specimen (Fig. 233), the form is in three tones; the lines are dark violet, the animal and the bands round the body brick-red, whilst the dots scattered over the field of the triangles are light green. Colours of this kind were not fast, and are easily rubbed off; so that great care has to be exercised in cleaning the pieces. The shapes are generally very simple, and not devoid of elegance; that of the three-footed specimen, with a single

FIG. 233.—Vase from Idrias. Showing detail of ornament. Actual size. Winter, Plate VI.

handle at the side and spout in front, recalling the aspect of a lamp, is somewhat more complicated (Fig. 234). Medium-size or small vases were hand-painted; whilst the large jars and the slabs, out of which sarcophagi were made, had the ornament stamped in, impressed on the wheel whilst the clay was wet and soft. Spirals (Fig. 235) that remind one of the stelas at Mycenæ, chevrons, and a rudely chalked-in ovolo device are the due accompaniment of pithoi (Fig. 236). As to the slabs of terra-cotta that formed the walls of the sarcophagi, besides the usual meander, we find rosette devices very similar to those seen on Mycenian pieces of jewellery (Fig. 237). Of these, the simplest is a star composed of eight rays or bars (Fig. 238). Elsewhere it has but six points, but the intervening space is filled in with the tooth device (Fig. 239). A decided step in advance is observable in the ornament of the two remaining

FIG. 235.—Fragment of pithos. After Paton, p. 71.

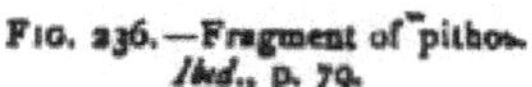

FIG. 236.—Fragment of pithos. *Ibid.*, p. 79.

FIG. 237.—Slab from sarcophagus. One-fourth of its actual size. *Ibid.*, p. 75.

slabs. In the one two zones of chevrons, frankly separated by concentric rings, surround the central star (Fig. 240). No star appears in the other, the space being wholly taken up by the willow pattern, which is made to radiate around a central ring, and is intersected by five presiding lines, dividing the circle into six equal segments (Fig. 241). The arrangement of the rosettes is felicitous. As we observed before, it proves that the artist was no mere tyro, but one who could skilfully handle the elements of design to decorate his surfaces.

The remark holds good in respect to the industrial objects that have been found in the Assarlik necropolis. They are fragments of gold twist, of which one was a light ring; and plaques of the same precious metal, with very simple ornament made up of lines beaten out. A specimen shows a hole at both ends, large enough for the passage of a very slender nail or thread; hence it could be applied or sewn on to a

FIG. 238.—Slab from sarcophagus. One-fourth of actual size. After Paton, p 76.

FIG. 239 —Slab from sarcophagus. One-fourth of actual size. *Ibid.*, Paton, p. 75.

FIG. 240.—Slab from sarcophagus. One-fourth of actual size. *Ibid* , p. 75.

FIG. 241 —Slab from sarcophagus. One-fourth of actual size. *Ibid.*, p. 77.

garment.[1] Bracelets, spirals, and bronze fibulæ are not rare. The only specimen which is intact will be found at Fig. 242.

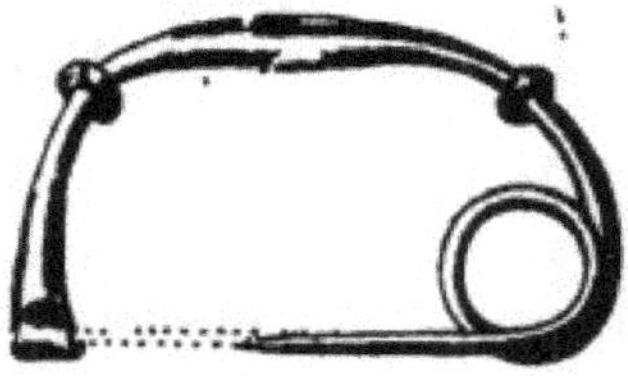

Fig. 242.—Bronze fibula. Actual size. After Paton, p. 74.

On the other hand, defensive arms, spear-heads, knife-blades, with point often twisted, are all of iron.

General Characteristics of Carian Civilization.

We have endeavoured to give as complete an inventory as possible of Carian culture, but the results we have reached are far from satisfying our curiosity. Nevertheless we will point out the most salient features, such as are likely to linger in the memory.

The constructive methods of the Carians had nothing to distinguish them from those of the other nations of the peninsula. Like these, the materials they employ are varied, and are the natural outcome of the progress of time and advance in manual arts. To walls built of roughly squared blocks there succeeded others in which units were still put one upon another without mortar, with courses more or less regular, precisely as in Cappadocia, Phrygia, and Lydia. On the other hand the arrangement observable in the sepulchral architecture of Caria is also met with in Lydia, but nowhere else. Both south of the Mæander and in the valley of the Hermus, the shape to which preference is given in tombs of some importance is the tumulus type, along with a covered passage and internal chambered grave. There is another correspondence: owing to the superior quality of their clay, Carians and Lydians alike largely built in brick, and were noted for their skill as potters. The resemblance between fragments of vases collected in the royal necropolis at Sardes with those that came out of Carian sepulchres is truly remarkable. Forms and colours are identical, and the principle applied to the

[1] Paton, *Excavations*, pp. 68 and 70, Figs. 7, 11–13.

ornament is the same in both. True, a couple of vases have been picked up in Caria which testify to the effort the artist made in order to step beyond a simple combination of lines, and draw his inspirations from living nature, whilst Lydian ceramic industry affords no example of so ambitious an aim. This, we maintain, is purely accidental: a lucky hit which attended on the Carian excavations. In fact, it would be preposterous to assume that what was achieved at Idrias and Mylasa was impossible in a capital such as Sardes; the more so that the same taste and the same methods obtained throughout the south-western part of this region. The remark applies in full to jewellery. Thus golden plaques, hammer beaten, have been found as plentifully in Caria as in Lydia, proving, moreover, that here as there the precious metal was put to the same uses. The human and animal form appear only on a brace of vases that were dug up with others at Tralles; all the specimens from the environs of Halicarnassus have no other than geometric forms. The only sensible conclusion to be drawn therefrom is that certain pieces were more elaborately wrought than others, and that forms of a higher order were selected for the decoration. On the other hand, it should be borne in mind that Tralles stands on the border between Lydia and Caria; hence the personal ornaments that have been brought to light there may be carried to the account of either indifferently. If we have assigned them to Lydia, it was because their elegance and richness awoke in our mind the remembrance of the proverbial opulence tradition ascribed to the subjects of Crœsus.

No traces of sculpture have been discovered in Caria or Lydia. Some authorities hold that the lacuna could be easily filled up. Not a few of the archæologists who have busied themselves with the origins of Grecian art are inclined to attribute to the Carians those tiny, shapeless statuettes that are found in vast numbers in and out of the Cyclades (Fig. 243).[1] According to them, such pieces are the work of the Leleges and the Carians, and date from those far-off days when these people sailed over the Ægean in every direction, and peopled its islands and the coasts of Peloponnesus as well. We will confine ourselves for the present to the following prejudicial remark:—Cappadocia, Paphlagonia,

[1] Tiesch was the first to broach the notion ("Ueber Paros und Parische Inschriften" in *Abhandlungen der Muenchener-Akademie*, 1834, p. 585, P. A.). Cf. L. Ross, *Archæ. Aufsaetse*, tom. i p. 855; *Vorgriechisches Graber*, pp. 52, 53.

Phrygia, and the region of Sipylus offer countless rock-sculptures to the gaze of the traveller, but not one instance has been reported from Caria. The excavations that have been made in the Carian necropoles have yielded naught beyond vases and jewels; small figures, whether of stone, bronze, or terra-cotta, that might in any way remind us of the primitive statuettes of the Archipelago are non-existent. To admit that the Carians fabricated the figures in question, we must suppose that they did so before they migrated to Asia Minor, since as soon as they were in possession of the province that goes by their name, contact with the Phrygians on the one hand, and the Lydians on the other, was a daily occurrence. The art of these was sufficiently advanced to serve as model to the Carians, who then ceased to reproduce types puerile and barbarous in the extreme, when the same order of ideas prompted them to adopt the tumulus-type as mode of entombment—a type absent in the Archipelago, but of which multitudinous specimens exist in Lydia. The hypothesis is a fascinating one, and has the merit to remove many difficulties; its greater or less degree of probability, however, is dependent on ulterior discoveries which should reveal monuments in Asia Minor akin to the oldest tombs of the Cyclades. Then, and only then, we should be in a position to follow the track of this restless wandering people, even as we followed that of the Phœnicians, from their native coast of Palestine on to those of Spain; then only would it be legitimate to recognize in the incipient fabricators of these coarse idols the primeval inhabitants of the Greek islands on the one hand, and on the other the ancestors of those Hellenes who, in the day of Homer and afterwards, occupied the region south of the Mæander. Until this comes to pass the question under notice must at least remain doubtful.

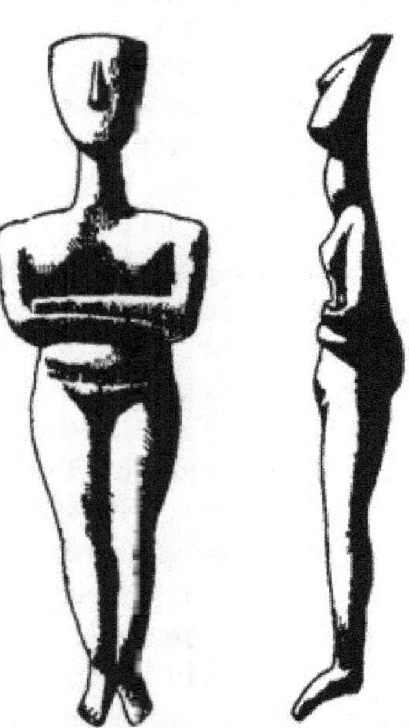
FIG. 243.—Stone statuettes. Actual size. LE BAS, *Voyage Arch.*, "Monuments figurés," Plate CXXXIII.

On the other hand, if we maintain a prudent reserve, and give up attempting to reach the cloudland where the insular Carians are lost to our gaze, if we forbear crediting them with works which tell us nothing as to their authors, it will simplify matters not a little, in that it will leave nothing more than a stay-at-home people, with a language and religion closely allied to those of the Lydians, from whom they are henceforth (the sixth century B.C.) inseparable. Nevertheless, the situation of many of their centres within deep bays, or at the extremity of jutting headlands, as well as their worship of a sea-god, whom the Lydians knew not, distinguished them from the latter. Then, too, even after the loss of their autonomy they still retained something of their wandering habits, which they satisfied by enrolling themselves as mercenaries and dragomans; in which capacities they visited Syria, and especially Egypt, where many remained in respectable positions. Such expeditions imply voyages from the Nile valley to that of the Mæander; and during one of these, perhaps, the Carians may have carried to Lydia the pieces of jewellery found at Tralles. The fact that their love of adventure and turbulent disposition lived with them even when they inhabited cities they had raised, along with temples in close proximity to the necropoles in which their dead reposed, is confirmatory of the legend that told of the part played by the Carians in pre-historic times, and of their maritime sway.

The historian is thus brought round to an hypothesis from which at first his prudence recoiled, and which he now refrains examining in detail until the day when he shall be in a situation to compare on the one side the monuments collected in the Cyclades with those dug up at Hissarlik and Thera, and on the other hand the instances representing the culture of Mycenæ.

LYCIA.

CHAPTER I.

THE LYCIANS—THEIR COUNTRY, HISTORY, AND RELIGION.

THE COUNTRY.

LYCIA is a country of Asia Minor, bounded on the south by the Mediterranean, Caria, and the deep gulf now called Macri on the west, Pamphylia and the open roadstead of Adalia on the east. Its line of coast towards the south is nearly as marked as that of Cilicia, Tracheia or the rough, and is constituted by the powerful spurs which Taurus throws out in this direction. Their broad base covers the whole surface of the province, and in antiquity each mount had a particular name. From west to east was, first, Anticragos, which rose high above Telmessus (Macri); and Cragos, a mere prolongation of the first, stretching close up to the sea, where it terminated in formidable escarps. Then came Massikytos, some of whose numerous peaks rose far above those of the mountains along the coast, being more than three thousand metres in height, that is to say, the region of everlasting snow.[1] It is now called Ak-Dagh (Mont Blanc), and, like this, is the central knot of the somewhat complicated system of the mountains in which it stands. It is connected with Mount Solyma by the Susuz-Dagh; but Takalu-Dagh, to the south-westward of the province, in the rear of the ancient site of trading Phaselis, reaches an altitude of two thousand four hundred metres; further north, the long ridge of *Klimax* (the "Ladder") leaves no more than

[1] The snow disappears on the southern slopes during the months of July and August, but it remains throughout the year on those looking north.

a footpath between its precipitous sides and the sea, which disappears under the flood as often as a sea wind prevails. In Mount Solyma is seen the subterraneous fire which gave rise to the fable of the Chimæra;[1] the shepherds round about utilize the flames that leap out of a slit in the rock to cook their dinner.

Lycia can boast of but one valley really deserving the name, open enough and spacious enough to have been split up into several divisions, each with an important centre embosomed amidst gardens and well-watered fields, which covered the gentle slopes of the last counter-forts of the mountain towards the plain, and supported houses, public edifices, and acropoles. The valley is known as Sibros or Xanthus (Eshen-Tshai) (Fig. 244); its length from the sea where it abuts to the rocky gully out of which the river escapes is about fourteen leagues; its mean width is from three to five kilometres, whilst its direction, in a straight line from north to south, affords the shortest and most convenient route to those making their way inland. The other valleys of Lycia, —Myros (Dembre-Tshai), Arycandos (Bashkoz-Tshai), Limyros (Alaghir-Tshai)—are little more than gaps hollowed out in the rock by water agency. Flat level is seldom found except at the mouth of streams, where a narrow strip exists between the sea and the heights, due to the deposit of ages. Then, too, higher up the mountains, dominating numerous havens formed by the indentations of this jagged, rugged coast, appear here and there levelled spaces, just broad enough to afford a foothold to man between the escarps of the cliff and the gentler slopes, which he covered with vineyards and fine plantations of olive. As time went on lack of room induced him to utilize the tiniest eyelets, lost in the depths of the mountain—such as Phellus, for example. Beyond the snowy peaks eastward of Xanthus, which the traveller descries from the sea, the aspect changes, for here vast plateaux with a

[1] In regard to the orography of Lycia, and the correspondence to be established between ancient and modern denominations, we have relied on Kiepert's map, in *Reisen in Sud-westlichen Kleinasien*, fol., Vienna, tom. i.; *Reisen in Lykien und Karien*, described by Otto Benndorf and Georg Niemann, 1884, with forty-nine plates in photogravure and eighty-nine figures in the text, tom. ii.; *Reisen in Lykien, Milyas, und Kibyratis*, published by Eugen Petersen and Felix Luschan, 1888, forty plates in photogravure and eighty-six figures. A much reduced copy of this same map will be found in *Geschichte der Lykier*, by Oscar Treuber (12mo, 1887, Stuttgart). The work is a brief but exact summary of the best-known writings bearing upon the geography and history of Lycia.

mean elevation of a thousand to twelve hundred metres[1] (Fig. 245) stretch away to enormous distances. Properly speaking, however, these uplands no longer belong to Lycia.

The waters drained by these plateaux, after many a long winding,

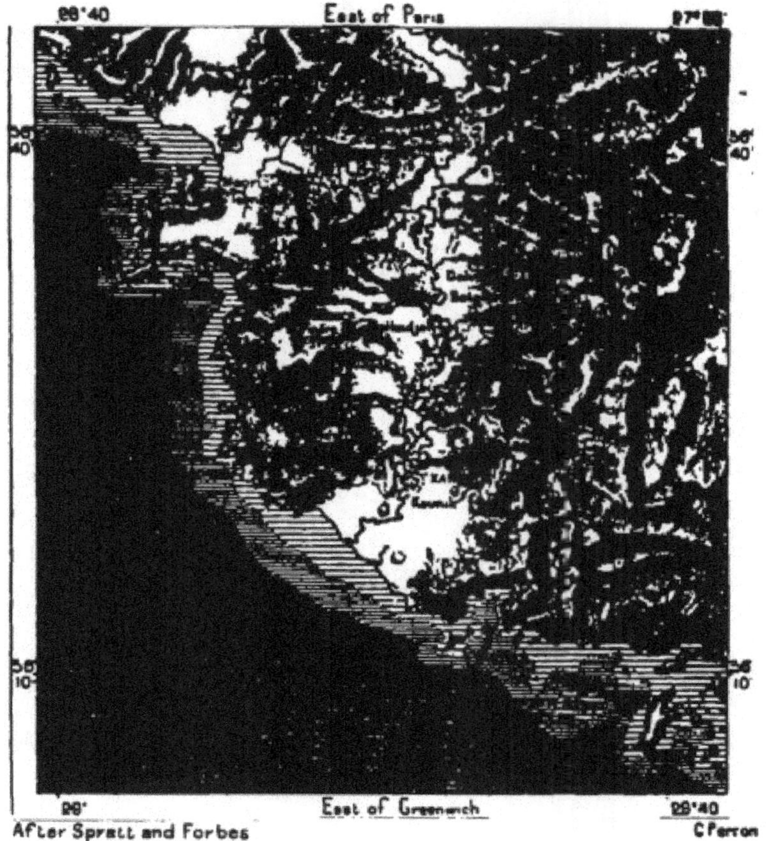

FIG. 244.—Valley of Xanthus.[2] From the *Nouvelle Géographie*, by Elisée Reclus.

fall into the Mediterranean or spread themselves into inland lakes, whose overplus escapes through subterraneous abysses; but the

[1] The name geographers give to the plateau under notice is Elmalu, from a bustling modern town, the largest and most important in Lycia.

[2] The names of ancient towns in this and the next chart (Fig. 245) are more lightly marked so as to distinguish them from modern centres.

high plains themselves are allied to those of Cabalia, of Cibyratides, and of Southern Pisidia, which they continue with hardly any change of level, whilst on the Mediterranean side they are reached by long steep ascents and passes closed during the winter months. Lycia, on the contrary, is well timbered throughout, so that it offers little opportunity for the raising of corn. The lower slopes are covered with green patches of maple and fine oaks (*Quercus ægilops*), and towards the bottom of the valley torrents disappear

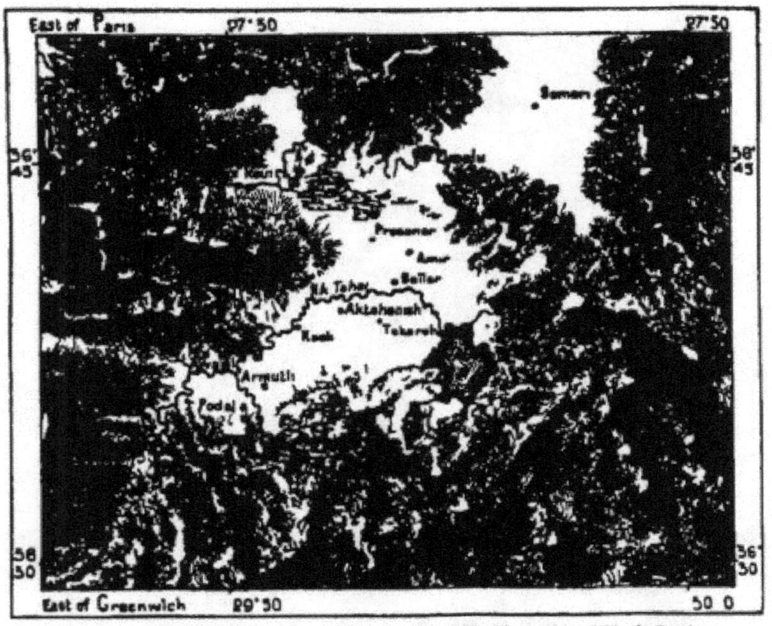

FIG 245.—Plateau of Elmalu. After the *Nouvelle Géographie* of Elisée Reclus.

under the wide-spreading branches of planes which form a perfect arcade over them, and, as you follow the trend of the coast, high up in the flank of precipitous cliffs, out of every fissure in the rock are pines, which look as if suspended in mid air. Farther inland they appear in great clustering groups. And higher up still, in the vicinity of snow are met trees of a different kind, such as delight in cold—dark zones of firs and the yet gloomier cedar. Thus it will be seen that forests, which in many other parts of Asia have been utterly destroyed, here have battled with success against the neglect and waste of centuries.

One of the distinguishing features of Lycia, is the marked contrast of climate and the variety of vegetation which meet the traveller as he goes up the valleys abutting to the sea. Along the shore he sees none but lemon and orange groves, the monotony of whose line is broken by pyramid-like cypresses and tall feathery palms. A few hours' walk brings him to a colder zone, where the walnut, cherry, pear, and apple—in fact, all the trees of Europe—grow in abundance. A day of this continuous ascent amidst hill and dale, his ear caressed the while by the refreshing sound of the waterfall below, lands him in Alpine scenery, which vividly recalls Switzerland and Tyrol.[1] In such conditions as these, all that is needed to escape the extreme of heat or cold is a simple shifting of abode. The seasons, which here may be expected with the regularity of clockwork, give the signal for the start. Twice a year, spring and autumn, the whole population is on foot. Every lowland village owns, somewhere in the highlands, its *ayala*, or summer encampment, generally situated in the clearing of a forest or on its outskirts. Towards the end of May, all the roads are covered with the migratory population, driving before them their flocks and herds, when the stranger who happens to be travelling on these roads must needs stand aside many times in the day, to let them file past. All are eager to escape from the pestilential, burning shore, where every green leaf has withered under the scorching rays of the sun, to go and live three or four months in the cool atmosphere of the hills, near living springs, under the grateful shade of trees, where, too, their animals will find an abundance of grass. Even the most frequented ports are ere long abandoned by all except half a dozen or so of poor wretches, custom officers and shopkeepers, compelled by their professional duties or interests to remain; the former have to keep an eye over the sailors belonging to the ships stationed on the coast, whilst the latter are busy administering to their creature comforts. The example is catching, and more than one mountaineer forsakes his alpine hut for the plain, so that many villages in the higher uplands are deprived of part of their population during the winter months. A few possess on the seaboard a plantation of olives whose berries are ready to be gathered, or a plot of ground that needs sowing, whilst others will go on the farms as shepherds and journeymen.

[1] The distance, as a bird flies, between the spot where the Xanthus breaks through the rocky wall of the Cibyratides plateau, and where it reaches its lower valley, is but some ten kilometres; the difference of level, however, is eight hundred metres.

When the country was sprinkled with flourishing cities teeming with population, the Lycians must have been less prone to move from place to place than their descendants. Within the towns were buildings with very thick walls, roomy houses of great solidity, standing in shady gardens kept green by irrigation; nor was the air along the shore rendered deadly by pestilential miasmas, rising from the harbours (as at Patara, for example), which now are turned into so many swamps. Hence, whether along the sea edge or in the towns of the lower valleys, a large proportion of the inhabitants were stationary. Nevertheless, habits such as these so naturally find their explanation in climatic exigencies as to make it difficult to imagine that they do not travel back, at least within certain limits, to antiquity itself.[1] The hills are everywhere so near the plain, the slopes so steep and rugged, that one and all of these tiny communities doubtless found within their own territory the needful summer station.

If climate and vegetation are not constant in Lycia, its physical formation, on the other hand, is pretty much the same everywhere. The breccia and facilite found in the lowlands were detached from the mountains above, and precipitated down there. Formations of schist and serpentine occur to the south-eastward, in the mountain chain that skirts the Bay of Adalia; the rest of the thick mass is a calcareous stone, which shoots up into perpendicular walls above ravine and valley. Its degree of compactness varies in places, yet it lends itself everywhere to be cut with ease; whilst its texture is fine enough and hard enough to have kept the shapes and inscriptions traced upon it by the chisel, infinitely better than the vast majority of the tufaceous rocks of Phrygia. Its colour is generally milky-white, like marble; hence it is that travellers have often been deceived by its aspect, unmindful of the fact that no marble exists in Lycia. The rare monuments of that material encountered in the country are of foreign origin.[2]

[1] What makes one suspect that at that time social and religious existence was momentarily suspended, at least in the maritime cities, is a passage of Herodotus in reference to the oracle of Apollo at Patara, to the effect that he was silent during the summer months (i. 182; SERVIUS, *ad Æneida*, iv. 143). Again we read (Herodotus, i. 176) that when Xanthus fell to the hand of the Persians, eighty families were out of town (ἔτυχον τηνικαῦτα ἐκδημέουσαι)—a circumstance which suggests the idea that the households in question had left the city for their summer station before it was surrounded by the enemy.

[2] BENNDORF, *Reisen*, tom. i. p. 39.

The soil of Lycia is frequently agitated by earthquakes,[1] as the ruinous mass of more than one town amply testifies.[2] But for these seismic convulsions tombs and buildings would be intact; at least, in the vicinity of poor homesteads, whose inmates have no desire of re-using the materials of ancient structures. The thriving little town of Macri is a case in point; before many years are past the fine remains of ancient Telmessus will have completely disappeared in building new houses for the accommodation of the citizens of the modern centre.[3]

HISTORY.

There are good reasons for identifying the Lycians (Λυκοί) of classic tradition with the "Louka" of the Egyptian texts, where their name first appears in history, side by side with the Iliouna, the Shardhana, and the Shakalosh, those seafaring people whose repeated onslaughts carried terror into the heart of the Pharaohs of the nineteenth and twentieth dynasties.[4] That which gives a high degree of probability to the above assumption is not dependent upon mere similarity of names, but rests on the fact that the tribes with which the Louka were associated in their campaigns against Egypt would seem to have likewise originally come from Asia Minor, where they have left traces of their transitory passage or long sojourn. There is but one difficulty in the way; to wit, the witness of Herodotus to the effect that the name the Lycians brought with them to the peninsula, that by which they were still known by their neighbours when he wrote, was not "Lycian," but "Termilæ" (Τερμίλαι).[5] As a native of Carian Halicarnassus, whose bargemen certainly frequented the near ports of Lycia, Herodotus could not fail to be well informed. Nor is this a solitary assertion; other historical

[1] PLINY, *Hist. Nat.*, ii. 98.

[2] BENNDORF, *Reisen*, tom. i. p. 50.

[3] Reference has already been made (*Hist. of Art*, tom. v. p. 323, n. 1) as to the monuments now disappeared, but which were standing when Huyot visited the ruins near Macri. Those interested in the subject will find the monuments under notice reproduced in a series of drawings covering eighteen sheets in his vol. i. of plates, which he never published.

[4] DE ROUGÉ, "Extrait d'un mémoire sur les attaques dirigées contre l'Égypte par les peuples de la mer," in *Revue Archt.*, N.S. 1867, tom. xvi. pp. 39, 96, 97.

[5] Herodotus, i. 173; vii. 92.

texts,[1] and the Lycian inscriptions themselves, bear the same testimony. These, though they do not lend themselves to being deciphered, have alphabetical signs whose value is known. Now, the word ΤΡΧΜΕΛΑ has been found in them scores of times.[2]

Herodotus, then, did not err: yet it is just possible that the name Termilæ, Tramelæ, was no more than the particular appellation of a Lycian tribe which, by extension, was applied to the whole Lycian people by imperfectly informed neighbours. Examples of appellations used in a double and triple sense might be cited *ad infinitum*, *e.g.* as applied to nations of any importance in the world's history; such would be the Jews, Greeks, Germans, and many more. In this particular instance, we have every reason to believe that the more general and oldest appellation was certainly that which persisted down to the last days of antiquity, the one by which the inhabitants of this province designated themselves on the coins bearing the legend: *κοινον Λυκίων*, "Lycian confederation." Homer furnishes a further proof of this. He stands about midway between Ramses III. and Herodotus, and he knows as little of the Tremilæ as the Egyptian scribes; whilst the Lycians play a conspicuous part[3] in all the battles of the *Iliad*, in which they bear themselves bravely and far outnumber the other allies of Troy.[3] Then, too, the description the poet gives of the country whence Sarpedon and Glaucus led out their forces in aid of the Trojans in their straits, coincides with Lycia. "It is very far removed from the Troad;"[4] "brawling Xanthus flows in its midst;"[5] and if this were not enough, he adds: "The Solymi are the constant enemies of the Lycians."[6] No uncertainty exists as to the exact position of the country held by the Solymi; it was the tract ruled by Mount Solyma, and the latter, according to geographers, is represented at the present day by Taktalu-Dagh.

[1] Stephanus Byzantinus, s.v. Τρεμίλη; Menecrates of Xanthus; MÜLLER, *Fragm. Hist. Græc.*, tom. ii. p. 343, Fragm. 2.

[2] The name "Tramela" may be read in the great inscription of the obelisk discovered at Xanthus, and in the Lycian texts found at Antiphellus, Myra, Limyra, etc.

[3] This is implied in the oft-repeated phrase, "Trojans and Lycians," used by the bard to designate the assembled forces opposed to the Greeks (*Iliad*, iv. 197; vi. 78, etc.).

[4] . . . *μάλα τηλόθεν ἥκω*, says Sarpadon. *Τηλοῦ γὰρ Λυκίη* (*Iliad*, v. 478, 479).

[5] *Ξάνθου ἄπο δινήεντος* (*Ibid.*, ii. 877).

[6] *Ibid.*, vi. 184, 185, 204.

Why did the poet seek a people so far removed from the scene of action as were the Lycians, when he could so easily have found others better fitted, one would think, to fill their place—the Paphlagonians, Phrygians, and Mæonians, for instance, whose situation was comparatively near the Troad? Inspection of the materials out of which the *Iliad* was composed, now irretrievably lost, would doubtless give us the clue to the secret cause which prompted Homer in his selection. But even as it is, we think we can understand that if he acted in that way, it was because he was vaguely reminiscent of the relationship that once had existed between the ancestors of Hector and those of Sarpedon. Are not Tros and Tlos, one the name of the Trojans, the other that of a Lycian city, doublets, twin forms of the same word made slightly different by pronunciation? Troad has a river called Xanthus, but so has Lycia. Again, is there not some degree of probability that not only did the Lycians inhabit a canton of Mysia, the valley of Æsepus, but that they had spread along the coast, where later rose the Ionian centres? This, we think, may be inferred both from certain lines in Homer, as well as numerous traditions found in later writers.[1] In this supposition, the northern Louka would be a rear-guard of the bands which had at one time overrun Asia Minor and Lycia; when, along with the Iliouna, they sallied forth and broke through the Egyptian frontiers. Swept away from their homes by the wave of the barbarous invasions which, in the seventh century B.C., laid waste the peninsula, they were, in time, fused with the adjacent populations amongst which they had found shelter; whilst those of their brethren who settled south of Taurus prospered, and

[1] Pandarus is represented in the *Iliad*, both as a native of Lycia (v. 105, 173), and the chief of the Trojans "who dwell at the foot of Ida and drink the black water of Æsepus (ii. 824, 825). The historian of Alexander, Callisthenus, basing his narrative upon the testimony of the elegiac poet Callinus, wrote that Sardes was twice captured; first by the Cimmerians, then by the joint efforts of the Treræ and the Lycians (Strabo, VIII. iv. 8). The former seem to have been a Thracian clan which met the Lycians in their southward progress, when they marched together against rich Lydia. Of course, the southern Lycians were outside their line of march. When the Ionians, driven from continental Greece, settled in Asia Minor, not a few of their bands, says Herodotus (i. 147), chose their leaders from among the descendants of Lycian Glaucus. On the other hand, Pausanias numbers Lycians among the component parts of the primitive population of Erythræ, prior to the arrival of the Ionians there (VIII. iii. 7). In regard to the question under notice, consult TREUBER, *Geschichte*, pp. 14–18, 50, 51.

were left alone behind the insuperable bulwarks of their mountains, so that they could retain their name, the originality of their language, and their customs.

If we thus look upon the southern Lycians as the last representatives of a tribal group whose chequered existence was shared by the forefathers of the Trojans, we shall more easily understand how they came to occupy the situation, which the legendary lore collected by Homer assigns to them. It enables us, at the same time, to dismiss, as baseless, the explicit statements of Herodotus, to the effect that the Lycians had originally come from Crete, and that their name was due to the Athenian Lycon, son of Pandion.[1] In all likelihood, when Herodotus wrote his narrative, the last assertion had been recently coined, trumped up at Athens, whose policy it was to establish an historical link between Attica and Lycia, so as to induce the latter to enter the maritime federation set on foot by the Cimons and Pericles, with the object of compelling the cities on the coast to pay tribute.

Only for the sake of the thing shall we record the attempts that have been made to put a meaning upon the word "Lycian." The derivations that have been proposed are all taken from the Greek language. The Greeks of Rhodes and of Caria, it has been urged, as they steered towards the Asiatic coast, leaving the great island in their rear, saw the sun emerge from behind Cragos; in their ignorance they imagined that the god of light had his dwelling somewhere among those dazzling heights they had never scaled; hence they came to call the people who inhabited them Leukoi,[2] the "Luminous" ones, *i.e.* Orientals. The conjecture is ingenious; the fact, however, that if the Lycians are one with the Louka of the Theban inscriptions, they were so named long before the existence of Greeks in Caria or Rhodes, makes it unnecessary to argue the point.

Nor are these the sole tokens by which we may recognize in the Lycians, a people that had constituted themselves into a compact political body, centuries before the migratory movement of the Greeks in the eastern basin of the Mediterranean took place. The Lycian language is known from numerous texts,

[1] Herodotus, i. 173.

[2] From the root *luc*, signifying light both in Greek and Latin (G. CURTIUS, *Grundzuge der Griechischen Etymologie*, 5th ed., 1879, p. 160). Upon the various derivations of Leukoi, see TREUBER, *Geschichte*, pp. 28, 29.

some of which are of considerable extent; that of the Xanthus obelisk having no less than two hundred and fifty lines. The words of these texts are separated by dots, so that it is easy to make out the different parts of speech, which bilingual inscriptions, Lycian and Greek, help further to elucidate, and if the vocabulary is all but undeciphered, some notion of the nominal and verbal inflections has been gained. These enable us to guess at an exceedingly peculiar idiom, which most philologists class in the Aryan family of speech. But what place should be assigned to it in the family unit, and to which of its groups it should be allied, is a question regarding which prudent critics do not care to commit themselves.[1] As will be remembered, no such difficulty exists for Phrygia, whose language closely resembles Greek.

The marked originality of the Lycian idiom is in itself a strong presumption of remote antiquity. If the Lycians are indeed allied to the Indo-European stock, they must have separated from their congeners long before the Italiote, Greek, and Thracian tribes left their primeval home, in that their respective tongues offer among themselves striking analogies on the one hand, whilst on the other they have distinct correspondences with Sanscrit and ancient Persian.

Study of the Lycian alphabet leads to the same conclusion (Fig. 246). Like that of Phrygia and Caria, it was derived from the Phœnician syllabary, through the channel of a Greek alphabet which has been recognized as that current in the islands, and which was also in vogue in a district near Rhodes. To judge from the lettering in the vast majority of cases, as found in such inscriptions, as would seem to date somewhere in the interval of two hundred years separating the Persian from the Macedonian conquest, the aspect of the characters is even less archaic than that of Phrygian letters; their tracing is more regular, and the

[1] LASSEN, "Ueber die Lykischen Inschriften und die alten sprachen Kleinasiens," in *Zeitung der deutschen morgenlaendischen Gesellschaft*, tom. x. pp. 325–388; MORITZ SCHMIDT, *The Lycian Inscriptions after the Accurate Copies of the late Augustus Schönborn*, 1868; *Neue Lykische Studien*, 1869; SAVELSBERG, *Beitraege zur Entzifferung der Lykischen Sprachdenkmaeler*, Bonn, 1878; *Beitraege zur Erklarung der Lykischen Sprache*, Bonn, 1878. Carl Pauli, in his dissertation, *Eine vorgriechische Inschrift in Lemnos* (Leipzig, 1886), touches upon the question of Lycian characters (p. 590 and following). He inclines to connect Lycians and Etruscans with the Pelasgians, whom he considers as neither Semites nor Aryans, and consequently distinct from the Thracians.

à	A P
ā	X
ē	↑
è	E
ī	I
ì	Ŧ
v	B b
ō	B B
ū f	+
v	Ж ⋇ ⋇
ŏ	Ж Ж
u	Ѱ Ѱ Ѱ Ѱ
u	Ѱ Ѱ Ψ Ѱ Ψ
γ	O
g	V
c [2]	< >
d	Δ
z	I
k	K
l	Λ
m	M Ⲙ M
n	N N N
p	Γ Γ Γ
r	P
s	ϟ ϟ S
t	T
ʒ	F
"	Ж

FIG. 246.—Lycian alphabet.

downward strokes have a nearer approach to the vertical;[1] but whilst the characters which appear in the monuments of Midas (city?) are wholly borrowed from the Greeks, those of Lycia, in the mode of writing, betray traces of an older stage, of a period when her people employed the system of signs which the primitive inhabitants of the peninsula had derived from Hittite hieroglyphs. Thus, out of the twenty-eight letters of which the Lycian alphabet is composed, four are common to the Cypriote syllabary,[2] whilst two or three cannot be traced either to Phœnicia or Cyprus, and may likewise have originated from the older source. There is, then, reason to believe that when the Lycians adopted the Greek alphabet, not finding in it all the signs that were required to express certain sounds in their language, they retained a few of those they had hitherto employed, which they transferred to one or other of those Asianic alphabets, whose complicated arrangement caused them to be discarded everywhere, except in the island of Cyprus.

We feel the same impression when we try to collate the scanty data that historians have handed down to us relating to the institutions of Lycia. "This people," says Herodotus, "have a peculiar custom not met with among

[1] F. LENORMANT, "Alphabet," p. 209, in *Dict. des antiquités de Saglio.*

[2] SAYCE, "Inscriptions found at Hissarlik," p. 910, in SCHLIEMANN, *Ilios, City and Country of the Trojans.* London: Bell and Co.

any other nation; the Lycians, in order to define their name, add thereto their mother's, and not their father's. If you inquire of any of them to what family he belongs, he will give you the name of his mother and the ascendants on his mother's side. If a freeborn woman cohabits with a slave, her children have the right of citizenship; but if a freeborn man, no matter how exalted his rank, has children by an alien or a concubine, they remain outside of the city,"[1] *e.g.* they can have no civic rights. A much later writer, Nicholas of Damascus, but who had access to documentary sources now lost, corroborates the formal assertion of Herodotus, adding that family substance descended in the male and not the female line.[2]

It must be admitted that inscriptions show but very faint traces of the superior condition women are supposed to have enjoyed in Lycia;[3] the texts in question, however, are comparatively recent; whilst we may assume that the action of Hellenic culture in its onward progress could not but efface local habits, rendered all the more easy that it did not clash with written laws, for the simple reason that the Lycians, we are assured, knew of no other except custom and usage.[4]

We have no reasons for discrediting the data bearing upon the earliest relations between the two people. If the habit under consideration had not been current among the Lycians, it is not in the least likely that the Greeks would have conceived the notion of attributing it to them. On the other hand, we can well realize their surprise when brought face to face with such a reversion of parts; one too diametrically opposed to their customs, and therefore all the more calculated to attract their attention. The system which was still in force in the time of Herodotus, is what modern lawyers call *matriarchate*, of which vestiges have been traced among people and nationalities the most diverse, and which is generally considered a survival of a very primitive state of society, leading back to a period when the family had not yet constituted itself by marriage, when the relations of the sexes

[1] Herodotus, i. 173.
[2] *Fragmenta Hist. Græc.*, tom. iii. p. 461.
[3] In regard to this subject read Treuber's observations, *Geschichte*, pp. 121–124.
[4] Heraclides Ponticus, Fr. 15 (MÜLLER, *Fragm. Hist. Græc.*, tom. ii. p. 217). This same writer also alludes to the Lycian "gynecocracy," as he styles the ruling station of women in Lycia.

were solely guided by the whim of the moment or chance meetings.[1]

Whatever path we take, then, we shall reach the same result; the Lycians of the classic age were the remnant of a people that figured in that primitive Asia Minor which, from the Amanus to the Ægean, was under the ascendency of the Hittites, of their arms and culture. It is possible that many of their tribes were swept away, amidst the stir of populations and the bloody strifes consequent upon it; but some, we cannot say when, found shelter in the narrow strip of land that goes by their name, amidst the depths of lofty mountains where they could be easily isolated, and where they peacefully dwelt for centuries; whilst it is not unlikely that in the present occupiers of the soil we have their descendants. Most travellers who have visited the country think they recognize the sons of the ancient owners of the soil in the inhabitants of the upper valleys of Lycia, and that they are Turks only in name.[2] They base their opinion upon the nobility of types of the population, their dress, and the persistency of certain usages which bear the stamp of remote antiquity. They were converted to Islamism towards the end of the Middle Ages, so as to retain possession of their homesteads, precisely as many Greeks have done, whether in Pontus, Crete, Bosnia, or Albania. But none the less, the blood that flows in their veins, according to these same authorities, is not different from that which pulsated in those of the companions of Glaucus and Sarpedon. Invaders, as a rule, show no great predilection to establish themselves among the hills; for, besides being already occupied, they have very few attractions to newcomers, who would not feel safe among them, and would, moreover, find life exceedingly hard. Hence it is that the populations of mountain regions neither change nor are renewed with the same facility as on the tableland and the plains.

When the first Lycian tribes crossed Taurus, following the beds of the torrents that descend from its heights on their way southward, it was on the banks of the Xanthus that they settled. For

[1] CURTIUS, *Hist. Græc.*, tom. i. p. 96, n. 1.

[2] This is the view of Dr. von Luschan, Benndorf's companion during a journey to Lycia, a succinct exposition of which will be found in a paper under the heading, "Anthropologische Studien," in *Reisen*, tom. ii. chap. iii. In it are found curious details respecting the very peculiar manners of the Taktadshi group, "plank-makers;" a people whose sole avocation, as their name implies, consists in the preparation of timber.

Homer, Lycia and the valley of the Xanthus are one and the same thing. When he speaks of "broad Lycia,"[1] it is the valley of the Xanthus which is mirrored in his mind's eye, the only one to which the epithet could be rightly applied (Fig. 247). But this privileged canton had not been wrested without strife from the Solymi and the Milyes,[2] who were in possession. It was a long

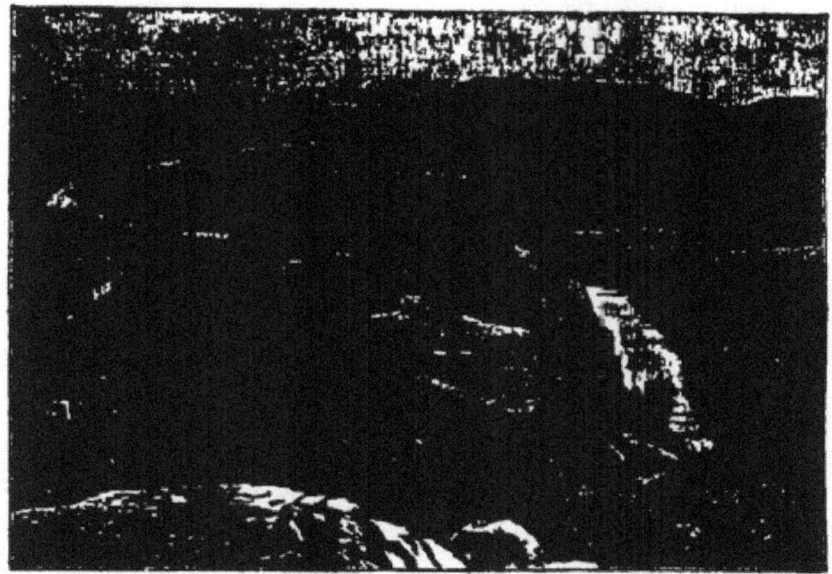

FIG. 247.—The Xanthus Valley. DURUY, *Hist. des Grecs*, tom. iii. p. 253.[3]

guerilla warfare, during which the Lycians gradually but steadily gained ground, and in the end drove the natives on to the coast

[1] Λυκίη εὐρείη (*Iliad*, vi. 173, 188, 210, etc.).

[2] Strabo (XII. viii. 5; XIV. iii. 10) is aware that the primitive inhabitants of the district under consideration went by the name of Milyans and Solymi, and that the term Lycian was of later date; but he seems to think that the various names were applied in succession to one and the same people, an hypothesis not very probable in itself, and distinctly opposed besides to the formal testimony of the *Iliad* (vi. 184, 204), where the Lycians are described in conflict with the Solymi from generation to generation. Then, too, he contradicts himself, and confutes his own statement, when he speaks of the language current in Cibyratides, not as "that of the Lycians," but that which was spoken by the Solymi.

[3] The above view is borrowed from Plate XIII. vol. i. of the *Reisen*. It is taken from a height north of Xanthus, facing south. Above the river rises the rocky eminence upon which stood the citadel; to the west of the rugged mass are still a few buildings of the city, half hidden amidst bushes. The sea is seen in the distance.

turned towards Pamphylia, and the elevated plateau in touch with Pisidia. Were the Milyes and Solymi of Semitic blood, as has been supposed? There are no data to prove or disprove the hypothesis.[1] The only thing we do know for certain is that no Lycian inscriptions have been encountered east of Massikytos.

Homer makes no mention of Lycian cities whose picturesque remains, set in a grand frame of mountains, are the admiration of every traveller. This, however, may have been due to the fact that when he wrote the city, with all the term implies, had no existence in Lycia, and that it started into being by contact with the Greeks of Rhodes, of Phaselis, and of the Carian coast. That the Lycians were stimulated by what they beheld in these intelligent centres, is proved by their adoption of an alphabet the chief elements of which are borrowed from one of the systems of Greek writing. Under Hellenic influence and the increase of wealth, the heights upon which the early immigrants had set up their hamlets gradually became veritable cities, with due accompaniment of citadels, public buildings, and necropoles. This change was accomplished somewhere about the sixth century B.C., when Harpagus, a lieutenant of Cyrus, marched against Lycia after having subdued the Ionians and Carians. Xanthus sent a force to check his advance; but it was routed in a battle fought outside the city, when the disordered troops retreated behind the walls of their citadel, set fire to the place, killed their wives, children, and slaves, and met their own death as they madly rushed into the ranks of the enemy.[2] Lycia had kept aloof from the Lydian empire,[3] but had she felt herself menaced by her ambitious and turbulent neighbour; and many of her other towns (there is no reason to suppose that Xanthus stood alone) must have followed the example of the latter, and have surrounded themselves with ramparts behind which they could defend their territory. If we but hear of Xanthus, it is because her tragic end was so

[1] The testimony of Chœrilos (cited by JOSEPHUS, *Against Apion*, i. 22) has been adduced in regard to this subject, to the effect that he numbers among the soldiers who followed Xerxes in his expedition against the Greeks, "a Phœnician-speaking nation who occupy the Solymian mountains;" but Josephus identifies them with the Jews, and he would seem to be correct, since the poet, the better to define the situation of this people, adds, "close by a vast lake." No such thing exists in Lycia; if, on the contrary, we turn to Palestine we shall find the great Asphaltic Sea.

[2] Herodotus, i. 176.

[3] *Ibid.*, 28.

memorable an episode in that campaign as to have been bruited afar. Frightened into submission by so great a catastrophe, the other towns opened their gates to the Persian conqueror, and engaged to pay tribute. This is the reason why the historian does not name them in his succinct narrative; but whilst Xanthus was the chief centre of the lower valley of the same name, Pinara and Tlos were undisputed mistresses of the middle valley. The

FIG. 248.—View of Tlos. FELLOWS, *Lycia, Caria*, Plate VI.[1]

former rose at the head of a gorge on the right bank of an affluent which descends from Anticragos; whilst on the left bank Tlos, from its lofty and impregnable Acropolis, planted on one of the last counterforts of Massikytos, watched over the plain which it ruled (Fig. 248). Then came Pidnaia and Patara, seated likewise

[1] The view is borrowed from Plate XXIII. tom. i. in *Reisen*, and is taken from an eminence to the north of the river. Above it is seen the rock that supported the Acropolis; whilst to the left of the rugged precipitous mass are still descried a few structures, representing the western portion of the city, amidst a tangle of bushes, with the sea in the distance.

opposite one to the other, like two sentinels, guarding a bay, with good anchorage at the entrance of the Xanthus valley, the latter being flanked on either side by mountain chains.

Patara, to judge from the extent of its ruins, was far the more important of the twin cities. Here Apollo had an oracle which was already famous in the day of Herodotus.[1] The gulf, like all the harbours through which passed the traffic of the valley, is turned into a marshy delta, and made impassable by brakes of reed-cane and tamarisks, so that the student finds it difficult to explore this and similar sites.

The Xanthus basin, with its numerous walled towns turned towards the sea and crowded in a narrow space, not only proves that it was the seat of a dense population, but the very heart of Lycia. Pre-eminent among them all was Xanthus, the "metropolis of the Lycian nation,"[2] as she proudly styles herself in the inscriptions of the Roman period. Nor was this a vain boast, since the sacred building of "Letoon," in which the delegates of the confederation were wont to assemble, lies at no less than four kilometres to the south-east of the town.[3] Again, ancient geographers, notably epigraphic texts, tell of the situation of cities in Lycia in and about the sixth century B.C. Such was Telmessus (Macri), the principal port of the Cragos region, which better than any other could communicate with the island of Rhodes. She already possessed, in the reign of Crœsus, a school of soothsayers, famed throughout the peninsula.[4] Much narrower than the

[1] Herodotus, i. 182.

[2] BENNDORF, *Reisen*, tom. i. No. 92.

[3] With regard to the ruins that are visible about the place, read *Ibid.*, chap. xi.

[4] Herodotus, i. 78. It has been argued that Telmessus did not become a Lycian city until the fourth century of the old era (TREUBER, *Geschichte*, p. 103). From the fact that it figures separately in the list of the tributaries of Athens (*C. I. Attic*, pp. 19, 22, No. 37, and pp. 104, 118, No. 234), as well as the statement of Theopompus to the effect that it had fallen to the hand of the Lycian king Pericles (Theopompus, Fr. 111 in MÜLLER, *Fragm. Hist. Græc.*, tom. i.). But it would seem probable that the Telemessus (*sic*) of the Athenian list, referred to an inland town of Caria, north of Halicarnassus, and consequently had nothing to do with Lycian Telmessus (SIX, *Monnaies lyciennes*, p. 93). As to the passage in Theopompus just mentioned, all we can say is that Telmessus, being separated from the Xanthus valley by the lofty chain of Cragos, carried on its existence for ages independently of the rest of the nation. Nothing indicates that it was either a Greek colony or a Carian centre. All the monuments found there bear an unmistakable Lycian physiognomy. The simplest thing is to consider it as having been peopled in very early days by Lycians. The same remarks apply to Kadyanda, a

Xanthus valley, that of Dembre-Tshaï, or Myros, was not as thickly populated. It has many windings; and is squeezed in between rocky walls which, in places, are perpendicularly cut; with the melting of the snow the waters devastate the land, and leave little that will repay cultivation. Nevertheless, the site of not a few small towns has been traced, whose inhabitants lived on the produce of meadow land and the fine forests stretching away on the neighbouring hills; these were Arniai, Kandyba, and Phellus, the latter being already mentioned by Hecatæus.[1] Nor should Myra, the most important centre of this district, be left out; its site is fixed with no less certainty, whilst the ground covered by its necropolis, as well as the shape of the tombs, impart thereto a very primitive aspect. At the entrance of this same valley, between the thick mass and the sea, rose Antiphellus, and Aperlæ, and Sura, ever ready to enter upon commercial or piratical emprise as occasion served. Finally, bearing to the eastward, Limyra looked down upon the fertile plain watered by the torrents which fall from the Elmalu plateau and the eastern slopes of Mount Solyma. In this brief enumeration we have omitted more than one town whose name is recorded either by ancient writers or inscriptions, and have confined ourselves to such as contain literary documents, along with monuments whose features are sufficiently distinct to permit us to see in them the representatives of cities travelling back to the days of Lycian independence. Their list will doubtless grow longer, inasmuch as travellers report many other sites where the ruins betray this same stamp of antiquity. For the present the difficulty is to identify them with one or other of the many names of Lycian cities preserved by ancient geographers, notably Stephanus Byzantinus.

The internal affairs of Lycia are very imperfectly known, down to the opening years of our era. From that day forward, Greek and Latin documents are plentiful, and furnish us with many a curious detail in regard to the social and political condition of the province. In the preceding epoch Greek inscriptions are

little way to the north. The Indus valley, wild and unpopulated, formed a sharply defined frontier between Lydia and Caria.

[1] Stephanus Byzantinus, *s.v.* Φελλος. If Hecatæus placed Phellus in Pamphylia, it was because, in his time, the boundaries of the different provinces of the peninsula were as yet undefined. For Hecatæus as for Homer, Lycia, strictly speaking, was the basin of the Xanthus.

short and rare, and, besides, few are older than the successors of Alexander. As already observed, Lycian inscriptions still await decipherment, with the exception of half a dozen formulas or so, that add nothing to our knowledge. As to historians, they take little heed of this small people, who, hidden behind a belt of mountains, like a tortoise in its calipash, had no part in the quarrels of the great powers of the world.

That which in a large measure enables us to supplement the insufficiency of literary data, is the study of the configuration of the soil, along with the ruins that are sprinkled on its surface. The Persian empire was not one where the central government was strong enough, its policy systematic enough, to make it possible to frame laws that should be binding on every subject, irrespective of race and language; laws, in fact, whose constant and lasting action would attenuate differences bearing on local customs, and sometimes succeed in effacing them altogether. The Lycians were subject to the Achæmenidæ in name rather than in fact; Darius comprised them in the satrapy of Iaouna, the chief of his divisions, and they were supposed to contribute four hundred talents[1] as their share of the tribute levied upon the province; yet in 300 B.C. Isocrates wrote, "No Persian king was ever lord of Lycia."[2]

Mountains in Lycia entirely cover the soil with their ramifications, and subdivide it in so many distinct sections as to have made it impossible for any one captain or city to unite the territory into one state. The pre-eminence of Xanthus was purely honorary. Lycia, that Eastern Switzerland, was carved out by nature for cantonal existence, and was bound sooner or later to drift into a federal system. People of one family and language, inhabiting valleys which mountains keep apart, ere long feel the need of breaking through their isolated position, of meeting at festivals common to both, and frequenting market-places open to all. Lycian federacy, as described by Strabo,[3] would appear to have constituted itself late enough after Alexander the Great; conscious that union of all the clans is the surest means of being respected abroad; but its organization had certainly been prepared by more than one essayal, more than one compact concluded at the end of perhaps years of warfare between adjoining townships, those

[1] Herodotus, iii. 90.

[2] ISOCRATES, *Panegyric*, 161.

[3] Strabo, XIV. iii. 3.

of the Xanthus valley for instance. We can read by the light of many signs that temporary groups, partial leagues had been formed, before the great association (*temp.* Augusto), in which figured twenty-three towns, each with a number of votes proportional to its size. Thus, both in official documents—such as the list of tributes paid to Athens by the allies—and histories, the natives of this province are often designated as "the Lycians," an expression which seems to imply that they were considered as one body of people.[1]

Again, all the Lycian coins struck under the so-called rule of Persia belong to a uniform monetary system; whilst the same symbol appears on the reverse of the vast majority, leading to the inference that they were destined to circulate throughout the territory of Lycia.[2]

And again, the monuments, architectural or sculptured, tell the same tale, presenting as they do uniformity of aspect from one end of Lycia to the other. This we should find hard to explain, unless we admit that, despite the splitting up of their territory into numerous fractions due to natural causes, the Lycian people, in very early days, possessed federal institutions, rude and imperfect no doubt, but which served none the less to keep alive the memory of primitive union among all their children. We know not how these cantons were constituted and what form of government they obeyed. It would seem that each had an hereditary nobility, out of whose ranks were selected princes who sometimes succeeded in bringing under their authority several neighbouring towns. One curious feature to be noticed is the importance the city acquired in Lycia, an importance that may be gauged from the passionate devotion of her citizens. In time of peace her inhabitants vie with one another to endow her with fine buildings, and raise monuments in her midst that shall perpetuate the memory of their exploits and munificence; when pressed sore, rather than surrender her to the foe, they elect to bury themselves under her ruins. Nor is this an imaginary picture. Twice in the course of her existence is Xanthus said to

[1] In regard to the subject under notice, see TREUBER, *Geschichte*, p. 112; Herodotus, i. 90, vii. 92; ISOCRATES, *Panegyric*, Λύκιοι καὶ Ισωντελεῖς; *C. I. Attica*, 161; Diodorus, XV. xc. 3.

[2] SIX, *Monnaies lyciennes*, 8vo, 109 pages and two plates (*Extrait de la Revue numismatique*, 1886, 1887).

have offered such an example to the world;[1] once at the time of the Persian invasion, and long after, when she was besieged by Brutus, Cæsar's murderer.[2] We find no parallel instance, either in the north or the centre of the peninsula. Hence the idea suggests itself that if a people made up of ploughmen and woodmen, rose to a notion of the city and devotion consequent upon it, long before the tribes of Cappadocia, Phrygia, and Paphlagonia, it is probable that they had learnt it by contact with the Greeks of Phaselis and Rhodes; the more so that they built their towns in imitation of Hellenic centres, and provided each canton with a capital whose Acropolis commanded the country around. Those who first copied Greek models could not but have found it a convenient scheme. Quarrels, in regard to a piece of woodland or pasturage lying close to the border, must often have occurred between these small communities. During similar affrays the immense advantage of placing man and beast in safety behind fortified walls must have been felt on all hands.

Lycia is washed on three sides by the sea, which advances in between the saliences of lofty promontories and forms bays, closed against the wind blowing from the main by a barrier of clustering islands; it lies peaceably at the foot of mountains that yield an abundance of timber of excellent quality. Consequently, as soon as the Lycians turned their eyes towards the sea, they could have as many ships as they needed, which they not infrequently ran, as privateers, against the Rhodians.[3] There is no doubt that a certain amount of maritime traffic was always carried on in and out amongst these coasts, unbroken, like those of Caria and Ionia, into fjord-like bays which advance far inland and continue the great fluvial valleys, hollowed by nature for the very

[1] As the formal statement of the text is rebutted in the footnote, I thought it better to make the sense dubious, so as to prepare the reader for what is to follow.—TRS.

[2] APPIAN, *Civil Wars*, iv. 76–80; Dion. xlvii. 34. There seems to be no foundation in the story according to which the Xanthians once again met their death rather than surrender to Alexander, during his progress through Lycia (APPIAN, *loc. cit.*, iv. 80). Arrian, who is so exact, has naught about it, and represents Lycia as having submitted without striking a blow (*Anabasis*, i. 24). As to Diodorus, if he mentions so tragic an event, it is that he may credit the Pisidian town of Marmara with it (xvii. 28). The second catastrophe was an invention of the rhetors, in whose eyes the Xanthians were bound to go through the same tragedy every time an enemy knocked at their gates.

[3] Heraclid. Ponticus (MÜLLER, *Fragm. Hist. Græc.*, tom. ii. p. 21).

purposes of trade, which it has always followed and will continue to follow to the end of time. Lycian valleys, not excepting those of the Xanthus basin, appear short and narrow, as against those of the Mæander, the Caÿster, the Hermus, and the Sangarius. Their precipitous sides and gullies become so many brawling torrents in the rainy seasons, rendering them impassable during many months in the year; so that they can never serve as ways of communication between the seaboard and the central plateau of Asia Minor. The country is thus reduced to its own resources, but these are sufficiently great to provide the elements of a brisk trade. As we have seen, only a small portion of the soil is under cultivation; but even when every foot of ground was made productive, it can barely have yielded grain enough for home consumption. The rearing of cattle and the timber of the forests must at all times have been the sole industrial means of the country. Its exports at the present day are still sheep and oxen, which are shipped off to Rhodes; and wood, whether for combustible or building purposes, which finds its way to Smyrna, Beyrouth, notably Alexandria. In such narrow conditions as these, it was yet possible for the native population to live a happy, though frugal and humble life. The fact of their having been squeezed in between their elevated narrow valleys cannot but have fostered a conservative turn of mind; hence it is that we find them retaining longer than any of their neighbours on the Asiatic coast, the use of an alphabet and a language peculiar to them, along with institutions such as the "matriarchate," which elsewhere disappeared much sooner. Then too, even when conversant with all the arts of Greece, they for centuries went on repeating in their necropoles forms suggested by the only style of architecture they had known at the outset—that which, in building the house, used none but squared and unsquared pieces of timber.

CHAPTER II.

ARCHITECTURE.

FUNERARY ARCHITECTURE.

THE Lycians, to consider them only during the period of their independence, have left but few monuments outside of their tombs; but they are of so marked a character as to have struck travellers such as Leake, Fellows, Téxier, Spratt, and many more, who, in the beginning of this century, revealed them to Europe along with the country in which they occur. In the number of these tombs (of which plans and drawings were made), very few travel back to the period within which we wish to confine ourselves in this history of art. The vast majority of the exemplars we shall cite are later than the Persian conquest, and not a few, accompanied by Greek inscriptions, date from the Macedonian era. Nevertheless, we shall find that the original aspect of these monuments was not suggested by Grecian art, since the forms that are proper to the latter, have naught comparable to the bulk of those that appear in the Lycian necropoles.

To account for the fact that types so peculiar as these should have persisted ages after their creation, we must suppose that they were truly indigenous, with all the term implies; and had originated from practices, imposed by the nature of the materials employed, intimately bound up with the life of the Lycian people, who persistently clung to them even when their statuary had made itself thoroughly Greek in style, and borrowed most of its themes from Hellenic myths, to decorate these very tombs. Consequently, whatever be the date, real or supposed, these strange monuments carry about them, and which Lycia alone possesses, we are entitled to figure them here as survivals and witnesses of a remote past, as true representatives of national architecture.[1] Sepulchral mounds are unknown in Lycia, and are proper to flat countries. If we have met the type on the borders of the Smyrnian bay, in the Hermus valley, and the coasts of Caria, it is just possible that we ought to look upon it as the survival of an old habit contracted in far-off days, when Mysian and Phrygian tribes still occupied the plains of Thracia; a type they had brought with them when they invaded Asia Minor, and which long practice caused them to retain for a while at least. The neighbouring tribes of Lydia and Caria borrowed it from them. The populations that inhabited the western part of the peninsula were all closely related; the languages they spoke resembled each other, and some of their cults were common to all; hence amalgamation between many of these clans had been easy, and so complete that they could not be distinguished one from the other. Not so with the Lycian people. Wherever they came from we find them entrenched behind Taurus apart from the rest. Their territory was a network of narrow valleys, and the rock was everywhere to hand, but of sufficient softness to lend itself to be attacked without much effort, and of sufficient firmness to retain almost entire shapes traced by the chisel. Hence it is that from the outset, tombs were excavated in the depth of the stone. Rectangular niches are recognized on all hands as the most ancient type; these are generally met with in the neighbourhood of towns, their dark apertures looming out of the face of tall walls perpendicularly cut.[2] They are cut to a depth of about two metres, and quite plain; the rock in places is perfectly honeycombed with them, so that a little way off—below the Acropolis at Pinara, for example—the stone surface looks as if covered with gigantic wasps' nests. Such niches are open, and seem always to have been open; nor is there much probability that thieves, even the most reckless and daring, would have cared to risk breaking their necks in order to rifle them. They are almost all inaccessible, so that to excavate even the lowermost scaffolding had to be set up close to the calcareous rock, and

[1] Our account of Lycian tombs is no more than a summary of Benndorf's exposition in *Reisen*, pp. 95–113, tom. i. chap. ix. By far the greater proportion of the woodcuts found in the book are reduced copies of Niemann's skilful and accurate pencil drawings. Others are taken from the photograph plates of von Luschan, which serve to illustrate Benndorf's work.

[2] BENNDORF, *Reisen*, tom. i. pp. 48 and 96, Plates XVIII. and XL.

a whole apparatus of pulleys fixed to the apex of the cliff for the upper specimens. Similar recesses may have received human ashes, but there is no reason why corpses enclosed within coffins should not have been safe in them, since nothing short of a pair of wings would enable one to get so high up. Then, too, it is probable that these niches are not all of one date, or very ancient; since we know that they continued to be pierced in the flank of the hill for the accommodation of the poor, even when funerary architecture, bent upon gratifying the conceit

FIG 249.—Wooden house in Lycia. Restoration of primitive type. BENNDORF, *Reisen*, tom. i. Fig 53.

of the wealthy, had learned to fashion more complicated stone shapes.

The most original tomb of Lycia is also the most ancient, and the reproduction on stone of a wooden construction. It admits of many variations, but they are all reducible to one type, the characteristics of which are clearly brought out in the annexed diagram (Fig. 249), due to M. Niemann, the architect who accompanied M. Benndorf to Lycia. Upon a plinth which represents the ground, or rather the low wall which was to prevent the planks from coming in contact with the damp earth, rest the lower cross-beams, A, B. It will be observed that the mode of connecting these and the various timbers that make up the frame is by scarfing, well seen in the side-posts, C. At the angle where the pieces meet, we sometimes find the broad head of a pin, driven in to secure the work. D is a double girder, which not only prevents the uprights from spreading, but supports the principal rafters that form the under portion of the roof, and ties them in at their feet as well. Then comes the real covering, which is horizontal, and consists first of small beams closely put together,[1] the extremities projecting well beyond the façade, upon which were laid beds of earth beaten down. Above it is the cornice, composed of three beams set lightly in advance one of the others, and made to cross at the four corners. It thus constitutes in plan a salient and stout capping, well calculated to keep in place the clay underneath. Our illustration (Fig. 250), which represents one of these sepulchral façades, will enable the reader to grasp the disposition of this class of roofs.

FIG. 250.—Tomb at Keuibashi. BENNDORF, *Reisen*, tom. i. Fig. 80.

The spaces between the main beams of the principal façades are filled in with a wood framing of square pieces, which divide the surface into recessed panels, like those of a ceiling, the number of which is regulated by the size and height of the fabric. The back and side walls are quite plain and closed with flat boards, which the sculptor often utilized by covering the rock-cut tomb with bas-reliefs (Fig. 251). The wall-plates or horizontal beams, N, I, K, that divide the surface into compartments, correspond with the stories of the wooden hut, and, together with the uprights, support the joists of the floor, or ceilings, M. A side view

[1] In a tomb at Pinara the round beams of the roof are replaced by square joists, but this is the exception, not the rule (BENNDORF, *Reisen*).

of our model leaves the impression that the timber hut has two stories above the ground floor: in the tomb, however, in order to enhance the effect of the frontispiece and the importance of the funereal chamber, the horizontal beam of the first story has been left out, so that door and panels are two stories high. If the door in our illustration is not indicated, it is because vaults were sealed with a slab fitting a grove—a mode of closing improper to wooden constructions. The size of the pieces that make up the false timber-framing is proportionate to the scale of the tomb in which they occur. In a general way the uprights have a mean square of thirty centimetres, whilst the diameter of the small round beams is about ten centimetres.

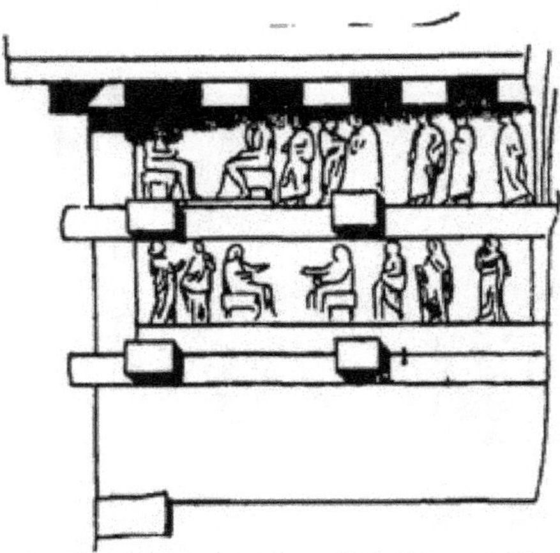

FIG 251.—Tomb at Hoiran. Lateral eastern side. BENNDORF, *Reisen*, tom. ii. Fig. 16.

Here and there, particularities of a purely decorative nature are observable in the type we have just reconstituted, which cannot be explained by the exigencies of the materials, and must be ascribed to the individual taste or whim of a nation. Such would be the crocket-like ending of the cross-beams, B C (Fig. 249). In order to find aught resembling it, we must needs travel to the far East, to Japan, the doorways (*tôri*) of whose temples exhibit, placed lintel-wise upon wooden shafts, beams turned up at the extremities exactly like these.[1] Then, too, the light salience of the entablature is quite as remarkable; for its straight profiles, unbroken by curves of any kind, were not calculated to throw off rain water.

It would be vain to deny that more than one detail about the structure under consideration is exceedingly singular; yet its main lines are decidedly those of an ordinary timber structure, which any chance artisan could reproduce at will. When we see with what constancy the dispositions we have described reappear in every tomb, we are loth to believe that the type to which they

[1] BENNDORF, *Reisen*, tom. i. p. 95, Fig. 52.

gave rise was the work of a single day, invented for the sole purpose of entombment, and the conviction forces itself upon the mind that it is no more than a petrified wooden house, the copy of a style of domestic dwelling which at one time obtained throughout the country. On the ground floor were the stables, the household occupied the rooms of the first story, over which was the loft or store-room. For the rest, the building was of the simplest description—no oblique joining of the timbers, no gable roof; and as its component parts were apt to shrink and give way, it always failed in the one essential of solidity. Finally, as every man who has travelled in Syria has learnt to his cost, horizontal roofs are doubtless capital screens against the heat, but their very flatness unfits them for throwing off the rains that fall in great abundance for days together during the winter months. A system with serious drawbacks such as these would never have been retained unless coeval with Lycian civilization itself, long habit having made its creators insensible to its defects. A parallel case may be observed in Japan, where for thousands of years the natives have been faithful to a style of house, of which the timber framing is still more elementary than that which we surmise behind the veil of the rock-cut sepulchre.

Some have advanced the opinion that tombs of this kind are an exact representation of a funereal pyre.[1] The notion is so strange that we find some difficulty in understanding how it ever was allowed at all. Is it conceivable that the Lycians would have endowed their pyres with so complicated a shape, and have been at the trouble of squaring and connecting timbers about to be destroyed? The conjecture is all the more risky that the internal dispositions of these sepulchres presuppose that bodies rather than human ashes were deposited in them. The remains of stone houses, said to exist on the site of Lycian cities, are adduced in support of the above theory; but similar remains are seldom found except in districts where wood is scarce. Moreover, wherever irrefragable evidences have permitted to fix the date of such fragments—at Istlada, for instance—it is found that they do not lead back to high antiquity.[2] From the day when Lycians adopted Greek models, the chief citizens, those with Ionian sculptors in their employ, must have directed them not only to decorate their tombs, but to construct them stone

[1] SEMPER, *Der Stil*, i. pp. 230, 315, 318, 430, and following.
[2] BENNDORF, *Reisen*, tom. i. pp. 30, 99.

houses as well, so as to be distinguished from the rank and file. Around the stately edifice, however, the lower classes lived in houses that were but a development of the wooden hut—a conjecture which the study of the ruins combined, with the evidence of historians, to bear out in full. Of all the places within Lycia, not one perhaps has kept the vestiges of the past in better preservation than the elevated plateau of Cragos, where once rose the little town of Sidyma, whose every stone structure, no matter how small, is not only standing, but almost entire. The fact that no traces of houses are met with leads one to suppose that they were wholly built of wood;[1] and, if so, their destruction must have occurred at a comparatively recent period, since the town is not heard of as of any importance until the Roman dominion. There is nothing improbable as to a tiny centre lost upon the silent plateau having disappeared. Do not we find a parallel instance in Xanthus, the chief city of Lycia, twice consumed by fire; and if a few hours sufficed to bring this about, is it not because, as Constantinople and Broussa until within a few years, they were built of combustible materials? Houses in Lycia, it is needless to say, were not lighted with petroleum; had they been of stone, therefore, they could not have been so easily burnt down.

The vestibule of far the most important tomb in the necropolis at Pinara displays curious bas-reliefs representing, it is supposed, views of the Lycian cities that were subject to the prince who was buried there. They are bare outlines of the walls, gates, and main buildings of four cities, with tombs crowning the summit of mounds or ridges of some extent (Figs. 252, 253).[2] Two out of the views would seem to be copies of timber structures. Thus the second row of edifices situated in the upper city, seemingly consists of two blocks of masonry three stories high, entered by a portal raised on several steps. Rudely outlined as it is, the building recalls none the less those vast seraglios of Asia Minor, where in more than one town I have seen the governor of the province giving audience.

To return: the structures to the left exhibit a very marked salience

[1] BENNDORF, *Reisen*, tom. i. pp. 60, 99.

[2] *Ibid.*, pp. 52-54. The above views were published by Fellows; but his imperfect drawing led to conclusions wide of the mark. Thus, for instance, a sarcophagus seen from its short side (Fig. 252, lower panel) was mistaken for a building with cupola. Our woodcuts are from copies made for Benndorf at the British Museum, and consequently far more reliable.

between the second and third story. Was not this intended for the extremity of the cross-beam which projects beyond the angle of junction? Could a more graphic allusion be devised to the mode of connecting timbers together, to which we have repeatedly drawn attention? Be that as it may, no ambiguity exists as

FIG. 252.—Views of cities, Pinara. Benndorf, tom. i. Fig. 36.

to the nature of the construction which in the next bas-relief (Fig. 253) occupies the upper part of the lower picture on the right. Here the façade, over which appear the ends of the joists and wall-plates, is divided into panels, very similar to carpentry work. There is but one point which is doubtful: namely, whether the building in question is a real house made up of beams and planks or one of those tombs hollowed in the rock, in the fashioning of which the stone-cutter tried his best to imitate wood methods.

Stone as well as timber buildings, according to localities, are

FIG. 253.—Views of cities, Pinara. Benndorf, tom. I. Fig. 37.

encountered in Lycia at the present day; yet even where the walls of the house are of unsquared blocks of stone, united with moist clay, wood always plays an important part in the construction. The modern house is no longer a mere timber-framing, like that displayed or guessed at in the antique rock-cut tomb. The walls are made of dry stones held together with a little mud; the flat roof, however, is still covered with beds of clay, and upheld by posts engaged in the wall, but outwardly free, so as to provide

FIG. 254.—House at Ghendova. BENNDORF, *Reisen*, tom. i. Fig. 49.

a double gallery to the rustic house of two stories (Fig. 254). Where the dwelling has but one story, an open verandah or porch is built, sustained by a number of pillars, for the convenience of the inmates, where they can sit or move about as well. The more general type is seen in Fig. 255.[1]

FIG. 255.—House at Ghleuben. BENNDORF, *Reisen*, tom. i. Fig. 26.

It is not the domestic abode, then, which has preserved the primitive type as revealed in the Lycian tomb; but curiously enough it crops up in those stone rooms found in the vast majority of Lycian villages. They differ, however, in one particular from the model that forms the object of our study, in that the roof has been raised so as to slope

[1] BENNDORF, *Reisen*, tom. i. p. 100.

its sides for the throwing off of rain water, which would damage the stores put in them. Sometimes, as in Fig. 256, the king-post is tied in at its head by the principals, where they cross at the angles; sometimes the struts are visible in both gables (Fig. 257), so that, with the exception of the roof, the resemblance is startling between these granaries and the hut we have restored after the sepulchral façades. Here again, both girders or wall-plates and joists, all the pieces of the timber frame up to the first story (M, M), are united together by scarfing, and the ends left very salient. The larger beams are found at the angles and serve as posts. Pierced above man's

FIG. 256.—Lycian store-room. FELLOWS, *An Account*, etc., p. 129, Fig. 32.

FIG. 257.—Lycian granary. BENNDORF, *Reisen*, tom. i. Fig. 56.

height in the middle of the façade, is a door barred and locked, but so low that to pass within anybody but an infant must crawl.

The fabric does not rest on the humid ground which would soon damage its sides, but is raised on large stones.

Perhaps the most curious method for connecting timber is that which appears in Fig. 258, where the planks that form the walls of the structure are made to cross at the sides within a foot of their heads, and the result is a very quaint aspect. This mode of piecing wood together is not in the habits of the Turk or Greek joiner, whether of the towns or plains; and we find no trace of it in their carpentry work.[1] It is proper to Lycia, or, to speak correctly, to mountain regions where wood is plentiful; and is a contrivance which makes iron bolts and nails superfluous. We noticed it in the hilly tract of Olympus,

FIG. 258.—Hut at Kurje Keui. PETERSEN, *Reisen*, tom. i. Fig. 58.

FIG. 259.—Granary at Villards de Thônes. Drawn by Marie Perrot.

in Bithynia.[2] It is still used in the construction of domestic dwellings and barns, whether in Lycia or the upper valleys of Savoy. Look at the sketch on p. 365, made by M. Niemann (Fig. 258), representing a guard-room which stands at the crossing

[1] BENNDORF, *Reisen*, tom. i. p. 100.
[2] *Hist. of Art*, tom. v. p. 73.

of a road somewhere in Lycia; could anything be found more closely resembling the granaries that meet the eye of the tourist in Savoy, as he makes his way up the slopes of Aravis (Fig. 259)? Social conditions must undergo profound transformation, in order to effect definite change in rural districts, where the tendency is to remain what the surroundings and natural resources of the soil have made them at the outset. Take the Swiss village—not, of course, one kept up by visitors, like Interlacken, which is no more

FIG. 260.—Tomb at Holran. BENNDORF, *Reisen*, tom. i. Fig. 24.

than a number of hotels, but the real typical village, lost among the hills—and you will find that houses there are identical with those that obtained in the day of Ariovist.

If this be true as regards Europe, it must surely apply with greater force to Lycia, where villages have, in all likelihood, not much changed in aspect since the fabulous age of Glaucus and Sarpedon; with this notable difference, that when all the country was flourishing and more densely populated, the houses of the peasantry were doubtless more spacious, and built with greater care. As a rule, rock-cut tombs reproduce but a front view of the house which served them as model. Sometimes imitation of reality is carried further. This happens when a lateral wall is added to the façade, so that we obtain a side view of the primitive Lycian house as well. Fig. 260 shews the street corner of a necropolis hard by the village of Hoiran, whose ancient name is as yet unknown, in which the two modes of representation may be observed. Now and again the effort of the copyist has outstepped beyond this, and prompted him to disengage the long sides of the building, so as to leave only the back adhering to the cliff (Fig. 261). Though more seldom, he even went so far as to completely isolate the tomb, and set free its four sides (Fig. 262). The false construction is, then, a faithful image of the house, or store, which, created by domestic architecture in far-off days, was taken up by funerary architecture, and repeated without a break for centuries.

FIG. 261.—Tomb at Pinara. BENNDORF, *Reisen*, tom. i. Fig. 37.

It is easy to grasp the ideas and feelings that led the Lycians to endow their tombs, on the outside, with the aspect of the house. To them, as to other nations of antiquity, life beyond the grave was but the continuation of that which man had led in the light of day. It was natural, therefore, to put him in a building which should recall that in which he had spent the days he had been allotted on earth. A curious point to be noted here is that the interior of the tomb has no correspondence with its exterior.[1] To obtain out of the living rock the members of carpentry displayed on the outside, great expenditure of time and labour were required; and all we find behind the façades so curiously wrought is a chamber without trace of moulding, and so low that a man could not stand upright in it. The mortuary chamber often contains three couches; one pierced in the farthest wall, and the remaining two

[1] BENNDORF, *Reisen*, tom. i. p. 96.

on each side of the vault. It is but very seldom, too, that double rows of rock-cut niches, like those of the Phœnician vaults,

Fig. 262. Bi Renn, XXX

occur here; whilst vestibules preceding the chamber form the exception, not the rule. Such would be the Pinara exemplar connected with a sepulchral chamber (Fig. 263), of which a perspective view is given in Fig. 261. It was an open vestibule, divided into two sections by a pilaster, wherein we recognize a copy of the beam which in the wooden house upheld the roof of the pent-house. The entrance to the hypogeum was closed with a slab, and stood behind this kind of porch; but it was neither on the axis of the vestibule nor of the chamber—an irregularity that may have been due to the shape of the rock in which the sepulchre was excavated. As to the doorway, if in defiance of the laws of symmetry it faces a side opening in the porch, it was to facilitate the passage of the bodies.

FIG. 263.—Plan of tomb Pinara BENNDORF, *Reisen*, tom. i Fig 34

Nowhere in this region do we find rows of chambers, such as obtained in the centre of the peninsula; whilst no attempt at architectonic effect is perceptible in the specimens whose approaches testify to more ambitious aims. Hence it is that Lycian tombs, even the most ornate, always remind us of what they originally were—mere holes, just large enough to receive a corpse.

No transition is observable between the primitive tomb and that which simulates the front of a wooden house covered with a flat roof; so that we are led to conclude that, from the day when they adopted this mode of construction, imitation of carpentry work was everywhere faithful and complete There is but one notable deviation from this universal rule. In addition to the terrace-roof sustained by small beams (roundels), we find a second covering, a roof with double slope, which, seen front-ways, yields a curvilinear gable, ogee-shaped (Fig. 264).[1] Some have supposed that this was in imitation of those light constructions set up, in warm countries, on the terraces terminating the houses, so as to screen the inmates against the sun or evening dew, and which become the living apartment during great part

[1] Instances of an arched gable roof, though less frequent, are also met with Such would be the covering of a tomb at Hoiran (BENNDORF, *Reisen*, tom. i. p. 33, Fig. 25).

of the day, and, in summer, during the nights as well. Such appliances, however, are no more than tents sustained by stakes;[1] but the ogee-shaped attic of the Lycian tomb, like the rest of the façade, is very similar to carpentry work made up of large pieces of wood (Fig. 264), such as joists, the heads of which project beyond the main rafters, with two false tie-beams and a strut

FIG. 264.—Tomb at Myra. TEXIER, *Description*, tom. iii. Plate CCXXVII. Fig. 3.

properly so called, both being maintained in place by struts, exactly as in Phrygian tombs (Figs. 58, 59). Then, too, the angles and the apex of the gables are often ornamented by appendices which, both here and in Phrygia, play the part of what the Greeks

[1] BENNDORF, *loc. cit.*, p. 105. In the Biblical passages collated by Benndorf in proof of his theory, the word in the texts, to designate the construction under notice, is rendered by σκηνή, tent, by the Greek translators.

call acroteria. These, in Fig. 264, from a tomb at Myra, are represented by rude balls; whilst a façade at Pinara displays, in the same situation, the horns and ears of a bull (Fig. 265). Was this ornament designed to bring to mind the sacrifice offered to the dead at the time of his entombment, or does it testify to a custom dear to the Lycians, in common with many country people at the present hour, of setting over the doorways of their houses or enclosures the head of a bull, of a horse, or other animal? Be that as it may, it was practised in Greece, where it was allied to a religious idea;[1] and from it may have been derived the device known as "bucrane" or bucranium.

FIG 265.—Tomb at Pinara Benndorf, tom. i. Fig 33

The feet of the side pieces of the curvilinear roof are comprised between the beams, which not only kept down the beds of clay, the real covering of the house, but prevented the main rafters from spreading. Here, again, every detail lends itself to the conjecture that we are confronted by a faithful copy of a model once familiar to every eye; moreover, we have reasons for supposing that a certain number of these Lycian châlets had a pointed loft just large enough for a top room or store, in which wood, forage, etc., could be stowed away, very similar to the triangular attics of the Swiss châlets. This last class of loft

[1] With regard to the above question, read what Benndorf has to say about it in *Rasen*, tom. i. p. 52, n. 3

likewise appears in the funereal façades of Lycia; but, as a rule, the tombs in which it occurs (Fig. 266) look younger than those with gable roofs. In countries where winters are severe, the

FIG. 266.—Tomb at Antiphellus. TEXIER, *Description*, Plate CCI.

ogee-shaped attic was a better covering than a flat or even a triangular roof, in that the snow could more easily slip down its sides, and must therefore have been widely employed in those regions. What proves that the curvilinear roof obtained in certain cantons is the fact that from it was derived the form of the Lycian sarcophagus (Fig. 267). Some two thousand of these sarcophagi, of which the short side reproduces the front of a house, have been encountered in Lycia, and in Lycia only. They consist of a very ponderous movable lid, furnished with saliences which served as handles, and a vat into which were put the bodies of the family one after another; whilst underneath is often found a kind of vault or *hyposorion*, in which the servitors found their last rest. These funerary monuments are sometimes built; sometimes both vat and base supporting it are cut in some rocky mass.

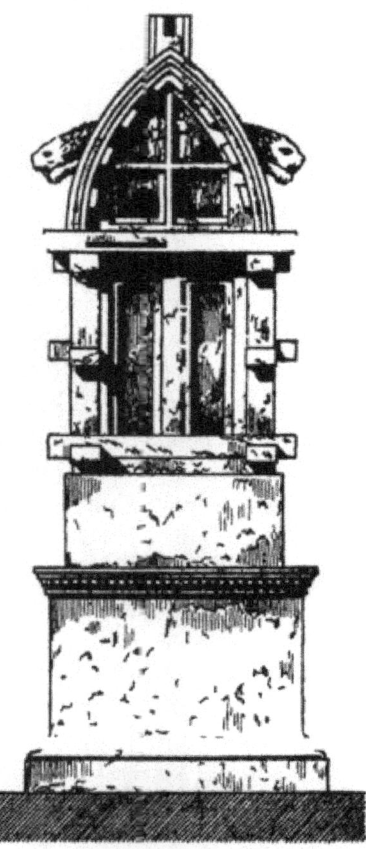

FIG 267.—Sarcophagus at Antiphellus. TEXIER, *Description*, Plate CCXXVII.

This is not the place to describe the varieties offered by sarcophagi of this kind. The example we have adduced suffices to show that the creations of Lycian architecture, one and all, even those in which one would least expect it, were influenced by and derived from timber constructions. So far we have given a summary of the architectural shapes distinctly peculiar to Lycia; it remains to note a monument which does not seem to come under that denomination, and which is known as the Tomb of the Harpies, from the figured bas-reliefs that decorated it, now in the British Museum. The removal of the sculptured slabs that formed the sides of the chambers is the cause of its present disfigured and mutilated aspect. It is a type made up of a square mass, tower-shaped, in which the mortuary chamber is perched under a flat and very salient roof, which expands into a dais-like shape. To give the reader a good idea of this kind of tower, we will reproduce a specimen from the Xanthus Acropolis, which has not been ravaged (Fig. 268).

The rocky mass was cut in such a way as to leave a "stepped" plinth and rectangular tower, with a recess or vault above, formed of four slabs of marble,[1] and a couple of tombs of the usual type below. The doors to the chamber in this and other sepulchres at Xanthus were all small, whilst a vault at Ghieul Bashi is but eighty-five centimetres by nine; making it self-evident that similar tombs could only be used by practising incineration.

The height of these sepulchral monuments averages from three to six metres; their number is small, and does not amount to more than about fifteen throughout the extent of Lycia;[2] they would seem to be the oldest tombs as yet discovered in this region. Such would be Figs. 273–275. Considered as a whole, the group leaves the impression of a type that never became popular, but was restricted to a few great families, and abandoned in very early days. The more recent tower-sepulchres would date from the fourth century B.C. In our estimation, the explanation offered as to the origin and character of the monuments under notice, has completely failed of its purpose. They have been compared to the funerary towers of Persia, and the question has been asked whether we are not faced here by tombs built for Persian satraps; but one of these exemplars at least, that at Ghieul Bashi, does not lend itself to the above hypothesis, in that it may very likely be older than the conquest of Lycia by Harpagus, and that the hold of the Achæmenidæ over the province was purely nominal. Again, the Tomb of the Harpies, which, with its bas-relief, is far the most carefully wrought of the series, does not reveal a single point that could in any way remind us of Persian creeds. Admitting for the moment that a vague resemblance is perceptible between the Lycian towers and those of Meshed-i-Mūrghāb and Naksh-i-Rustem, the differences are distinct enough to nullify the hypothesis of direct imitation, and relegate the likeness, real or supposed, to the domain of coincidence. It is just possible that the notion of the tower-shaped tombs was suggested by those watch-towers of frequent occurrence in regions whose territory is divided between hostile clans, and that the guard-room perched on the top of the slender edifice became the mortuary chamber. Timber towers may have obtained at an early age, but the combustible materials of which they were

[1] BENNDORF, *Reisen*, tom. i. p. 87.

[2] A list of the sepulchres in question will be found in *Ibid.*, pp. 107, 108.

FIG. 268.—Funerary tomb at Xanthus. BENNDORF, *Reisen*, tom. i. Plate XXV.

made exposed them to be easily burnt down; so that the advantage of using stone in their construction must ere long have been recognized. The idea of having a lofty and stout burial-place may first have occurred to a local magnate, who would thus continue to look down upon the familiar streets and squares of his native city, in which he had played a conspicuous part.

We will not pursue farther the history of funereal architecture, inasmuch as it forms no part of our scope to study monuments which, whilst preserving features borrowed from primitive and local types, are thoroughly permeated with the spirit of Greece. To sum up, the tomb is by a long way the most characteristic monument of Lycia. Nowhere else do we find so large a number of sepulchres executed with greater care; and, in especial, nowhere else do we find such minute precautions taken, as are here revealed, to place the mortal remains under the tutelary wing of the gods, and—the better to secure them against profanation—under that of the future generations inhabiting the city. Care is taken to interest them in the repose of the human ashes, by settling upon them the pecuniary fines to which desecrators rendered themselves liable. Laws enacted against the disturbers of the dead appear sooner in Lycia than in any other place, whence the practice spread to the rest of Asiatic Greece. Such, at least, is the conclusion that may be deduced from the comparative study of funerary inscriptions.[1] It is, then, probable that from the earliest time the cult of the dead had a considerable importance in Lycia; and, perhaps, when we are able to read fluently Lycian texts, they will tell us the particular form the religion of the tomb, common to all the other peoples of antiquity, had assumed with this nation.

TOWNS AND THEIR DEFENCES.

Every traveller who has visited Xanthus has noticed that the principal tombs, instead of being put outside the city walls like those of Greece, stand amidst the ruins of the upper town, a practice that seems to be peculiar to Lycia. Such would be the monument of the Harpies (Fig. 268) and other funereal towers, along with huge sarcophagi figured above. The habit, though remarkable, might have been surmised by a single glance

[1] HIRSCHFELD, "Ueber die griechischen Grabschriften welche Geldstrafen anordnen," in *Koenigsberger Studien*, 1887, 8vo.

at the views of towns depicted on certain Lycian bas-reliefs; notably in one of the pictures from Pinara, where funerary monuments of different types are mixed up with edifices comprised within the ramparts (Figs. 252, 253); as well as a representation of

FIG 269 — View of a Lycian city *Monumenti dell' Instituto*, tom x Plate XVI

the same nature at Xanthus (Figs. 269, 270),[1] which forms part of the sculptures displayed on the building known as the monument of the Nereids. The latter represented the military exploits

FIG. 270 — View of a Lycian tomb *Ibid*

of a prince or satrap of the fourth century B.C., and the places he was supposed to have besieged or taken. Over the crenelated wall of one of them appears the upper part of a monument, with a

[1] MICHAELIS, "Il monumento delle Nereidi," p. 117, in *Annali dell' Istituto di corrispondenza archeologica*, 1875.

sphinx as crowning member, in which we recognize a quadrangular stela, akin to the large Xanthus exemplar surmounted by a sphinx between two lions.[1] The latter bears a bilingual inscription in honour of a descendant of a local magnate, by name Harpagus.

What must have contributed to imbue Lycian centres with a pre-eminently singular physiognomy, were those wooden buildings we think to recognize in the sculptured views (Figs. 252, 253).

The towns were built upon heights difficult of access. But where the escarps of the rock did not forbid an attempt at an escalade, built walls were resorted to, of which the oldest portions display polygonal masonry. The vast majority of these places, however, must have undergone so many sieges, requiring the defences to be so often repaired, as to make it doubtful whether

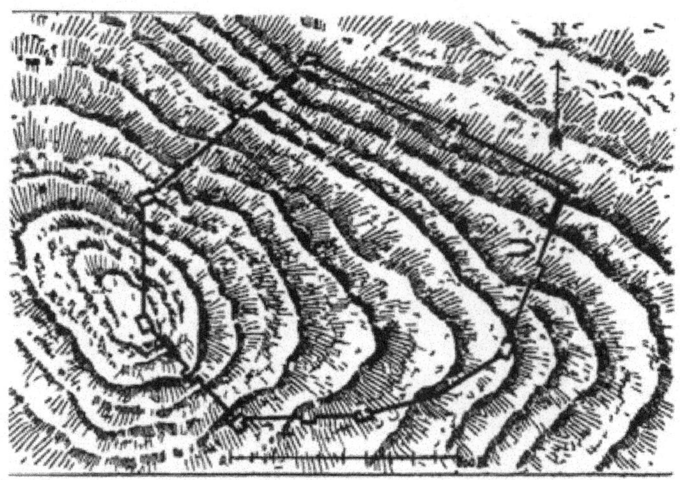

FIG. 271.—Plan of fortress, Pidnai. BENNDORF, *Reisen*, tom. i. Fig. 75.

any portion of the primitive work can be traced below the reconstructions. Xanthus affords an instance of this; so that to find a unit homogeneous in all its parts, we must fain turn to the ruins of simple fortresses, that have never been touched since the day when they were abandoned. Such would be the *enceinte* found in a remarkably good condition close to the mouth of the Xanthus river, bearing to the west. It was a fortified castle called Pidnai,

[1] Prachow has published by far the best reproduction of the monument under notice, in *Antiquissima monumenta Xanthiaca*, Plate II. Fig. 1 (fol., St. Petersburg, 1871, two pages of written text and six plates of lithographs).

which covered the territory of the Xanthians against the incursions of mountaineers inhabiting the Cragos region.[1] The wall in question stands on the summit of a low hill, and the space it embraces forms an irregular polygon (Fig. 271). It is constructed with stones of medium size, very well dressed and fixed, in almost always regular courses, without a sign of mortar (Fig. 272). The citadel had but two openings—one on the north and the other on the east side. The rampart is broken at unequal distances by

FIG. 272.—Wall of enclosure, Pidnai. BENNDORF, *Reisen*, tom. 1. Fig 71.

eleven rectangular towers, standing out boldly from the curtain, and at some points still rising to a height of ten metres. The thickness of the wall is about one metre; the top, which is covered with large slabs, ends in a crenelated edge, made up of unsquared blocks set in mortar, perhaps a later addition. The towers were pierced with loopholes, windows, and doorways, and the latter were made to open into the area. The top of the rampart was reached by very steep flights of low steps, which led from the upper or second story of the towers. On the walls are still the ledges whereon rested the joists of floor and ceiling.

[1] BENNDORF, *Reisen*, tom. i. p. 124.

Without aiming at elegance, the structure throughout evinces that the masons who constructed it were familiar with fortification works.

Very similar square towers are likewise figured in the bas-reliefs (Figs. 252, 253, 269, 270). In these, however, the wall runs along the base of the hill upon which the town was built, and both soar upwards towards the Acropolis. Lycian centres did not emerge from their plate of armour to descend and expand in the low level, until the peace brought about by Roman dominion. In the preceding age, wars between rival and neighbouring cities had been frequent; so that the Lycians were not content to surround their dwellings with a belt of ramparts to guard them against their enemies, but readily engaged in works of greater extent. Thus, about a league to the north of their town, the Xanthians barred their valley with a wall which leans against a counter-fort of Massikytos, and runs for a distance of some four kilometres close up to the river, where it abuts on a kind of redoubt, or exercising ground crowning the hillock. The materials of which the wall is made, consist of blocks of great size irregularly cut, leaving interstices which are filled by small units. Here, doubtless, was fought the battle specified by Herodotus between Persians and Lycians, when the latter were obliged to fall back and take shelter behind the walls of their chief town.

No monuments exist in Lycia from which to obtain an idea of its temples, such as they appeared before they were rebuilt in Greek fashion, *e.g.* like the edifices whose remains are still visible at Patara and other points of the country. But for the nature of timber structures, which dooms them to prompt destruction, we might perhaps have lighted upon the outline of what has been sometimes called *hut temples.* If we except Macri and Elmalu, at the present day, throughout Lycia, mosques, at first sight, are not distinguishable from the houses of the peasantry by which they are surrounded; so that we should not grasp the purpose for which they were erected, had not the builder taken the precaution to write *Mirhab* on one of their walls.

CHAPTER III.

SCULPTURE.

THE tomb, the principal varieties of which we have passed in review, whether rock-hewn or built of well-dressed units, was decorated by reliefs as soon as the circumstances of its owner permitted him to indulge in the outlay. Thus the fine series of sculptures in the British Museum are the spoils of a few tombs in Xanthus; whilst the liberality of half a dozen or so of *dilettanti*, coupled with the energetic action of MM. Benndorf and Niemann, have added to the wealth of the Vienna Museum, a collection of reliefs which decorated the Heroon at Ghieul Bashi.[1] We do not propose to describe or figure similar works, or those of the like nature that are still *in situ*. Originality of a high order they certainly possess, be it in the details of costume and more particularly in the themes handled by statuary;[2] their execution, however, is thoroughly Greek, betraying in every line the hand of Ionian artists or their pupils; so that they belong to Hellenic art, where we shall find them when we come to treat of the latter. For the present it suffices to show that if from the latter half of the sixth century B.C., Lycia, violently drawn out of her isolated situation by the Persian conquest and included in the satrapy of Ionia, employed Milesian and Ephesian craftsmen to decorate the tombs of her princes and chief citizens, she had not waited until that day to carve upon the façade of her sepulchres the human and animal form.

[1] BENNDORF and NIEMANN, *Das Heroon von Gjölbaschi Trysa*, Vienna, 1888. This elaborate work brings to our notice the reliefs and details of the Heroon. The plates, thirty-four in number, are executed in line engraving, a process rendered perhaps advisable by the dilapidated state of most of the bas-reliefs.

[2] In regard to the peculiar nature of the themes referred to, consult PETERSEN, *Reisen*, tom. ii. pp. 193–196.

Benndorf inclines to consider the bas-reliefs (unfortunately much injured) which he discovered at Trysa, near Ghieul Bashi, as the most antique instances of the plastic art of Lycia (Figs. 273–275).[1] They decorated the external sides of a funereal square tower now fallen on the ground and lying on one of its faces, so that only three sides are visible. It is very similar, although not so lofty as the Xanthus specimen (Fig. 268). The top part of the plaques is broken away, and the figures seen on the remaining surface are below natural size. This, coupled with their very flat appearance and indistinct outline, may likewise have been brought about by the weather. They most probably formed part of one of those funerary processions exhibited around the body of those antique vases called *dipylon*.[2] The least damaged slab (Fig. 273) shows the lower extremities of five men walking one after another, their faces set to the left. On the arms are carried round shields. On the next appear the busts and legs of an equal number of figures;

FIG. 273.—Bas-relief on tomb, Trysa. BENNDORF, *Reisen*, tom. ii. Fig. 9.

FIG. 274.—Bas-relief on tomb, Trysa. *Ibid.*

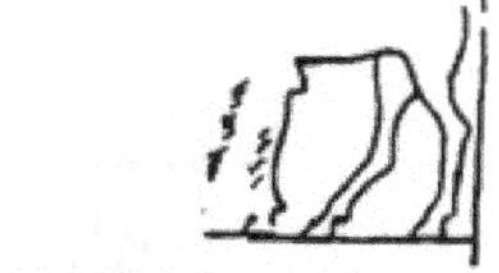

FIG. 275.—Bas-relief on tomb, Trysa. *Ibid.*

their hands stretched in front as if they held something, perhaps an object about to be offered (Fig. 274). Of the relief on the third slab nothing is left but the hind part of a horse and the heel of a rider (Fig. 275). These files recall many a figured decoration, Oriental and archaic in style; for example, the processions seen about Cypriote sarcophagi;[3] those on the engraved bowls of Phœnicia,[4] and the profusely ornamented ostrich eggs

[1] PETERSEN, *Reisen*, tom. ii. p. 13.
[2] RAYET and COLLIGNON, *Hist. de la céram. grecque*, pp 23–30, Fig. 19, Plate I.
[3] *Hist. of Art*, tom. iii. Figs. 415, 416.
[4] *Ibid.*, Figs. 548, 549.

which Etruscan tombs have disclosed;[1] and, lastly, those instances to which reference has already been made as occurring on golden pieces of jewellery found at Corinth.[2] The theme is one among the most in favour with nascent plastic art, and was suggested by the spectacle of those martial pomps, composed of the associates in arms and retainers of the chief whom they mourned

FIG 276.—Tomb at Xanthus British Museum Small side Length 1 m 13 c Drawn by St Elme Gautier.

as they moved around his funereal pile, the pathetic details of which are recorded in the *Iliad*.[3]

To the same class of monuments belong other reliefs, properly put next to the above in the British Museum, and which would seem to rank among the oldest specimens that have come to us from Xanthus (Figs. 276–280).[4] Unfortunately the stone or stela which served as background has been destroyed, hence no

[1] *Hist. of Art*, tom. III. Figs. 626, 627.

[2] FURTHWAENGLER, "Archaischer Goldschmuck" (*Archæ. Zeitung*, 1884, pp. 99–114).

[3] *Iliad*, xxiii. 134.

[4] A certain number of lions are left in Xanthus, which look fully as archaic as those in the British Museum (BENNDORF, *Reisen*, tom. I. Plate XXVIII.).

opinion can be put forth as to its original height. This does not apply to its shape, which was oblong and not square in plan; proved by the unequal length of its faces, two being long and two short. The latter are occupied each by a lion couchant. The head of the animal in Fig. 276 is much injured; but his action, which is that of a fond parent licking his cub, upon which he caressingly rests his paws, is easily read. A corner and side view of the next slab is obtained in Figs. 277, 278, representing the

FIG 277.—Tomb, Xanthus. British Museum. View of corner.

conflict of a lion with a bull. The latter has fallen; his head, from which life has departed, is thrown so far back that the horns touch the ground, to which he is held by his victor. As to the long sides, they are partly broken. On the one are carved three figures—a horseman, seemingly nude, who moves towards the right (Fig. 279); he is followed by a man on foot, probably a slave, unarmed, and clothed in a short tunic; the warrior who comes next walks in a contrary direction from the other two. The interest which attaches to the last figure resides in the shape of his helmet, furnished with a top-piece of metal, crescent shaped, which extends from nape to forehead—a detail, it will be remembered, exhibited in a bas-relief of Phrygia (Fig. 117); whilst the circular shield is not only akin to the examples seen on the earliest vase-painting of Mycænæ, but to all the monuments of widely different origin in this part of the world, including the Trysa bas-relief, to which we refer the reader (Fig. 274). It is difficult to hazard a guess at the significance of the disc carved in front of and level with the head of the warrior, which a shallow groove, sunk in the stone, separates from his helmet. Is the object hung high up against the wall a shield? Of the other long slab nothing remains

FIG. 278.—Tomb, Xanthus. British Museum. Long side. Height, 93 c.

but a group occupying about one-third of the surface, and enframed within a border in relief (Fig. 278). It probably had a pendant at the other end, whilst between the two pictures stood the doorway. This sculpture produces one of the themes dear to Oriental art, *e.g.* the struggle between a man or god and a lion.[1] The two foes stand upright, face to face; with his left hand the hero clutches the mane of the beast, whilst with his right hand he buries a huge sword in his flank, unconscious the while that the claws of the brute are tearing his shoulders and side. The pose is wholly

[1] *Hist. of Art*, tom. ii. Figs. 322, 337; tom. iii. Figs. 471, 472; tom. iv. Fig. 266.

conventional; if, in order to be more realistic, the artist had aimed at varying the traditional treatment, if he had so handled

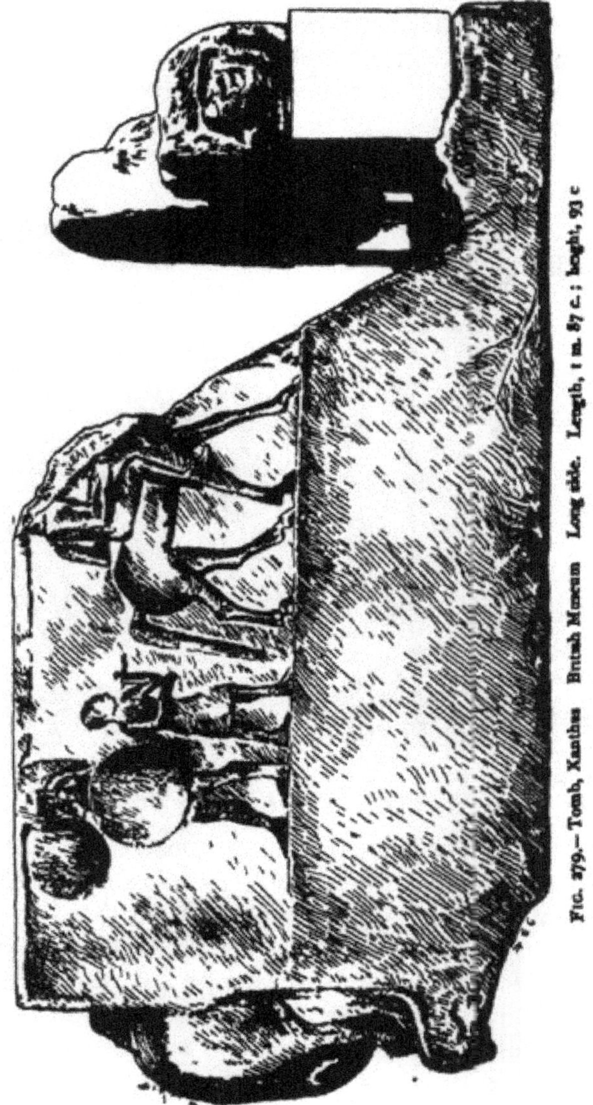

FIG. 279.—Tomb, Xanthus British Museum Long side. Length, 1 m. 87 c.; height, 93 c.

the subject as to raise doubt in the mind of the spectators respecting the issue of the conflict, the symbol would have ceased to be understood. The idea it awoke was that of a victory obtained by a powerful and beneficent being over the powers of evil. To have the notion grasped, it sufficed to posture the figures exactly as the public was accustomed to see them, without changing an iota as to aspect and position. The presence of this traditional element serves to explain the inequalities observable here and there in the workmanship. Could aught, for instance, be conceived more rigid in treatment than the group of the lion and

FIG. 280.—Tomb, Xanthus. British Museum. Small side. Length, 1 m. 20 c.; height, 93 c. Drawn by St. Elme Gautier.

his victor? A bolder handling is already perceptible in the figures carved on the other long side; the horseman stands well.

But a greater step in advance was made in the pair of lions at either extremity. If there is still a certain degree of clumsiness in some of the details, if the cub and the head of the lifeless bull are not exempt from awkwardness, we nevertheless feel that we have here a really superb work, and that the attitude of the lion lying on his victim is felicitous and expressive, notably when seen sideways, as in Fig. 280. It conveys to the utmost the idea of force when at rest; the manipulation is broad, rich, subtle, and pre-eminently characteristic. We guess at the powerful muscles beneath the skin; but they do not detach themselves and project beyond the flesh with the somewhat hard firmness which is in the habits of the Assyrian sculptor, neither do we find the dryness of execution and conventionalism which we had occasion to observe in Phrygia.[1] Here, on the contrary, nothing could be more faithful than the rendering of the rich masses of floating hair falling low over his forehead. Travellers tell us that the lion still has his lair in the Lycian Taurus; so that the artist could go to nature for his portrait.

Of the two monuments we have studied, that of Trysa may, perhaps, travel back to the seventh century B.C.; as for the other, it evinces a far more skilful chisel, and would therefore date from the sixth.[2] However that may be, the pair have all the appearance of being the outcome of an art as yet uninfluenced by that of Ionia, in that their themes belong to the properties of Asiatic culture. Phrygia, too, set up lions as guardians of the tomb (Figs. 64, 65); and the hero near the doorway (Fig. 280), who has just slain the king of the forest, brings to mind the group of two warriors running their spears into the Gorgon's head (Fig. 117). The situation they occupy about the entrance to one of the most important tombs of the Sangarius necropolis is akin to that of the Lycian figure. The difference is one of style. Ample and naturalistic in Lycia, it is dry and frigid in Phrygia. The inhabitants of the former country would seem to have had quite a natural talent for plastic arts—a fact that inclines one to believe that they did not give up practising them, even when they sought examples and teaching among their neighbours of the Mæander and the Hermus valleys. Consequently, in the vast array of bas-reliefs ornamenting the tombs of the Lycians, a goodly number were doubtless executed by native artists, trained at the school of Ionian masters. But whilst to a certain extent they modified their style, in other respects they remained faithful to old local traditions. Hence it is that they continued to multiply figures of lions, and went to the repertory of Oriental arts for their forms. Such would be the conflict between the lion and the bull; the group where the stag is slain by the king of the beasts; lions and sphinxes set up in pairs face to face.[3] Very similar subjects were largely reproduced on

[1] *Hist. of Art*, tom. v. pp. 178, 179.

[2] M. Benndorf inclines to think that the sculptures in question are anterior to the Persian conquest (*Reisen*, tom. i. p. 88).

[3] FELLOWS, *An Account of Discoveries in Lycia*, 1841, plates opposite pp. 174, 187, 197; TEXIER, *Description*, tom. iii. Plate CCXXV.; PRACHOW, *Antiquissima monumenta Xanthiaca*, Plates IV.–VI.

coins (see tailpiece, end of chapter). One thing to be noted is that the Chimæra, so often met with in Cyprus, is conspicuously absent in Lycia, where we might expect it would crop up in bas-reliefs and monetary types. On the other hand, the man-headed bull of Assyria and Persia is not rare.[1]

A habit that should be very ancient in Lycia, since it has never been out of fashion, is the use of colour to give point to the decoration. Vestiges of pigments have certainly been discovered about mortuary towers, acknowledged on all hands as among the archaic types of Lycian tombs. Thus the panels of one of them were tinted, whilst elsewhere we find them ornamented by carving unrelieved by colour.[2] Again, the ground, in more than one bas-relief of subsequent ages, was painted blue or red, and the dress yellow or violet.[3] It was the same with architecture, where, over numerous rock-graven inscriptions, the brush of the painter has been drawn, and the lettering picked out in red or blue.[4] And so it happens that in the pure light which recalls that of Attica, man took pleasure in adding here a little and there a little to the wealth and variety of brilliant harmonies that charm the eye; the light yet vivid tints he applied to sculptures and edifices, stood out from the dull white of the limestone, their point and sparkle being enhanced by the sombre green of pines, the azure of sky and sea, and the dazzling splendour of snowy peaks on distant Taurus, glorified by the rays of the sun.

[1] SIX, *Monnaies lyciennes*, Nos. 90, 93, 95, 143, 144.

[2] BENNDORF, *Reisen*, tom. i. p. 87.

[3] FELLOWS, *An Account*, etc., plate opposite p. 199; TEXIER, *Description*, tom. iii. pp. 208, 239, 240.

[4] DE GOBINEAU, in his "Catalogue d'une collection d'intailles asiatiques" (*Revue archéologique*, N.S., 1874, p. 239), assigns to Lycia an intaglio picked up in Mesopotamia; in so doing he is entirely guided by the device figured upon it, in which he thinks he recognizes Pegasus and Bellerophon. But inasmuch as the inscription is in the Aramaic language, we incline to ascribe the stone to Lycia. Ménant has included among Persian intaglios a cylinder in Le Clercq's collection, which represents the offering of a dove to a seated goddess, by a personage whom he identifies with an Achæmenid prince, because of his head attire and dress (*Recherches sur la glyptique orientale*, tom. ii. Plate IX. Fig. 2, pp. 174, 175). Yet the male figure is wanting in some of the attributes that would define it with absolute certainty, such as spear and bow; whilst the pose of dove and goddess, and, indeed, the execution throughout, recall the bas-reliefs on the Tomb of the Harpies at Xanthus. One is tempted to ask, with M. Heuzey, whether we are not confronted here by a Lycian monument, in which case the male figure would naturally be a dynast of Lycia. An inscription in Lycian characters could alone confirm the conjecture, but that is sadly to seek.

The glyptic art of Lycia, like that of Phrygia, is as yet an unknown quantity. To my knowledge no cylinders, cones, or intaglios of any kind have been published with inscriptions in Lycian characters incised upon them. They alone could give us the clue by which to distinguish gems engraved for and by the Lycian people. We cannot suppose for a moment that they were without seals; these instances of their activity, however, are confounded in our collections with Oriental and Greek intaglios.

Lycian numismatics do not enter into our scheme, at least in this history, because recent investigations tend to prove that the oldest coins of Lycia, those struck in Xanthus with a hollow square and a wild boar (see tailpiece, chapter i.), are not older than the seventh century B.C.[1]—a period when the administrative and commercial relations established by Persia between the subjects of her vast empire began to penetrate Lycia, whose borders, whether towards the sea or land, had hitherto been closed against alien influences. The specie she issued about this time was of Lydian weight, but as she found it; that is, much reduced from its weight standard by long circulation. Lydian coiners had certainly drawn their inspirations from the staters of the great Ionian cities, but they also created distinct and useful types of their own; contrary to Lycia, whose coins are destitute of originality as to size, workmanship, or the types figured upon them. The device of many of her coins is the "triskelis," or so-called "triquetra,"[2] a name derived from three serpents' heads which usually figure in the field, much after the fashion of those supporting the famous tripod at Delphi, consecrated by the Greeks to Apollo after the battle of Platæa. The number of heads is not constant; some coins having as many as four—"tetraskelis," whilst others have but two—"diskelis." The Greeks connected the symbol with the cult of Apollo, which they represented as very popular, and of hoary antiquity in Lycia.

[1] SIX, *Monnaies lyciennes*, p. 6.

[2] Literally, three-cornered, triangular, triceps. The number of heads may have been regulated by the different size of the coins in question, probably answering to different values.—TRS.

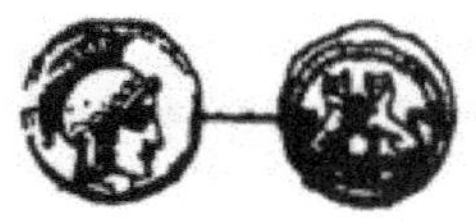

CHAPTER IV.

GENERAL CHARACTERISTICS OF LYCIAN CIVILIZATION.

IT would be natural that some surprise should have been felt at the place we have assigned to Lycia, inasmuch as the plan pursued in this history does not extend to that class of Lycian monuments which have most occupied the attention of archæologists. In so doing we were actuated by the fact that Lycia, in virtue of her origin, alphabet, language, and certain sides of her plastic art, belongs to that very old world of Anterior Asia whose development preceded, as it prepared, the unfolding of Hellenic culture. Nowhere is her primæval social state more evident, than in the curious rock-inscriptions seen on the façades of tombs built in imitation of wood structures.

Timbers are connected at right angles in the valley of the Nile. This habit of the Egyptian builder arose out of his predilection for perpendicular and horizontal lines, which led him carefully to banish from the walls and roofs of his edifices oblique pieces. The fact that the woods within reach of his hand were mediocre in the extreme, that stately beams could not be obtained, nor square pieces of any length, and far less curvilinear ones, may have had something to do with, but was not the sole reason for a choice which endows his wooden house with its look of firmness and chest-like aspect, since he carried these same elements into constructions scarcely needing them, in those light open structures, which we attempted to restore from paintings where they often figure. In both classes of buildings he had recourse to almost smooth faces and flat attics. With him square vertical beams play an all-important part; they are put close to each other over the whole surface, the only voids being those required for the piercing of doorways and windows, whilst their width is so feeble as only to allow of narrow divisions or panelling.

On the other hand, the balance between uprights and cross-beams hangs pretty even in the carpentry work of Lycia. Here the wall-plates of the wooden frame stand out boldly at either side, whilst the roof often presents oblique and even curved pieces, which cannot be obtained except in timbers of excellent quality, handled, too, by skilful craftsmen. Again, whether the house covering is flat or a roof with double slope, instead of the small boards, slender fillets, and tenuous rods employed by the Egyptian carpenter, we invariably find large divisions such as stately oaks, many centuries old, and pines of enormous bulk alone could furnish.

Difference in the quality of the materials to hand is the chief cause why methods proceeded on different lines in the two countries. If the woodwork of Lycia is distinguished by ampler and firmer shapes than that of Egypt, this, as already stated, was because it was cut in timbers of superior quality, which enabled the artisan to resolutely divide his surfaces into great divisions, whilst the frank salience of his timbers provided more accentuated effects of light and shade over the façades. The art of the carpenter is more advanced, the types he created are nobler, because they are less minute, and the eye can more readily take in the presiding lines of the construction, the skeleton frame of the structure.

Our reason for having insisted on these peculiar monuments is that they naturally lead up to the manifestations of Greece in this domain, where we shall have much to say as to the way her architects constructed their timber frames. Unlike the Lycians, the idea never seems to have dawned upon them of compelling stone to reproduce wooden forms; and yet they were placed in surroundings that recall those of their Lycian colleagues, since they had, though less plentifully perhaps, the same kinds of woods at their disposal. Consequently, when the time comes for us to reconstruct Hellenic timber-work, we shall turn to that of Lycia for more than a useful hint; in the mean while it will aid us in reconstituting the wood-piles which upheld the esplanades of Persia.

ADDITIONS AND CORRECTIONS.

Page 7, note. To the list that Professor Ramsay has published upon the antiquities of Phrygia, should be added the memoir entitled, "A Study of Phrygian Art" (in *Hell. Studies*, vol. ix. pp. 350–380; vol. x. pp. 147–189). This essay is not yet the realization of the wish expressed by us, to the effect that Professor Ramsay should undertake a complete description of that district; for we find in it no more than remarks upon matters of detail, thrown out as they suggested themselves to the mind of the author. The first part is taken up with a disquisition upon the ethnic affinities of the Phrygians, their entrance into Asia Minor, the history of the state they founded, and the origins of their art. Professor Ramsay's ideas coincide, in the main, with those I have expressed. He then supplements the account contained in former papers with regard to several monuments, such as the Broken Tomb, the Lions' Tomb, Midas city, and he touches upon the relations between Phrygian and Mycenian art, a question of vital interest for archæology. The second part is little more than a critical review, a kind of errata, of that portion of our history dealing with the monuments referred to above. According to Professor Ramsay, it would appear that we have not always grasped the drift of the documents he forwarded to us. Whilst acknowledging once more his liberality, we must remind him of the state of the drawings he placed at our disposal, incomplete as they were, fragmentary and often contradicting one another. Besides photographs and drawings already published, we had to choose, for the same monument, between two or three sketches made at different times by the professor himself, Mrs. Ramsay, or M. Wilson, during the various visits they paid to the monuments. To select from among these sketches, accompanied by very succinct notes, was not by any means an easy task. We think that, all things considered, we did the best that could be expected under the circumstances. Professor Ramsay points out some few mistakes. His remarks appear to us to bear, for the most part, upon details of very trifling importance; and in the impossibility of comparing the two sets of pictures, it is often difficult to make out wherein the discrepancy lies. It seems to us that, could they be placed side by side, the difference complained of would very often go undetected.

Consult also, by the same, "Syro-Cappadocian Monuments in Asia Minor" (*Mittheilungen des k. d. Archæ. Athen*, tom. xiv. pp. 170–191).

It will be quite a business for future bibliographs to collect the valuable papers which Professor Ramsay has scattered up and down in more publications than can be counted on one's fingers. Great economy of labour would have been effected had he thought fit to bring them out in book form!

Page 8, note 1. In his recent work Professor Ramsay adduces fresh and convincing data in support of his conjecture as to the Ionian origin of the Phrygian alphabet (*Journal*, vol. x. pp. 186–189).

Page 32, foot-note. Whoever may have been the author of the treatise of *Isis and Osiris*, attributed to Plutarch, there is no doubt as to his having thoroughly grasped the under-current of ideas that pervaded the religious rites referred to. "The Phrygians believe," he writes (§ 69), "that the god sleeps in winter and wakes in summer. In their orgiac festivities they now celebrate his going to sleep (κατευνασμοὺς), now his awaking (ἀνεγέρσεις). The Paphlagonians declare that in winter he is held in fetters and a prisoner, but that he breaks his iron chains in spring and moves again."

Page 58, note 1. M. Humann has published a new edition of the pamphlet cited by us, with illustrations, in *Mittheilungen* of the Institute at Athens, 1888, p. 22, under the heading, "Die Tantalosburg im Sipylos."

Page 114 and following. As already observed, the restoration made by Professor Ramsay of the Broken Tomb agrees in every respect with our own. We submitted the results reached in consequence of his sketches, and we are happy to find that, at least in this instance, he acknowledges our having used them correctly (*Journal*, vol. ix. pp. 354–364, Figs. 1–9). His inner restoration coincides, so to speak, with every touch of M. Chipiez' inner perspective view.

Page 120. In *Journal*, vol. x. pp. 164, 165, Fig. 18, Professor Ramsay engraves another specimen, the Yapuldak tomb, of which a plan and two sections will be found p. 181, Fig. 18. Our Fig. 75 represents the façade alone.

Page 146 and following. For the description of Midas city and its remains, whether of roads, walls, buildings, altars, or cisterns, see RAMSAY, *Journal*, vol. ix. pp. 374–379, Figs. 11, 12. The plan (Fig. 11) was laid down with great accuracy. In it are carefully indicated the traces left by the wall that once surrounded the plateau; the stones have disappeared, but the place they formerly occupied is shown by the grooves cut in the rock to receive them.

Page 223. Professor Ramsay does not share our view with regard to the Broken Tomb and the Lions' (rampant) Tomb. He would place them, in time, before the Midas monument (*Journal*, vol. ix. pp. 364–377; x. pp. 152–154). We adhere to our expressed opinion, that those tombs grouped around the Midas monument, exhibiting geometrical and vegetable decorative forms, are, like the monument itself, older than the exemplars of the Ayazeen necropolis, whereon are sculptured animal and human figures, lions and warriors. In our estimation it is scarcely compatible with analogy to suppose that a decorative scheme wholly made up of linear elements, which everywhere else belongs to the beginnings of art, should have followed here a period during which the presentment of the living form was handled with a certain degree of freedom. Then, too, the shaft or well deliberately chosen, as means of approach to the vault in the majority of specimens forming the group of tombs embellished with meanders and lozenges, is a disposition of a more primitive character than the ornate doorway.

Page 242, note 1. Professor Sayce thinks that he has found a Lydian inscription. It consists of three lines engraved in small characters on a soft, dark-coloured stone, supposed to have been picked up among the ruins of Sardes. Such was the statement made to the Rev. Greville Chester, when, in 1887, he acquired the monument at Smyrna for the Ashmolean Museum at Oxford. The letters of the inscription seem to belong to the Carian alphabet, to which Professor Sayce has devoted so much attention. We leave the care of commenting and publishing the text to the accomplished philologist.

Page 244. Inscriptions have fully confirmed the assertion of Herodotus (i. 92), to the effect that most of the columns in the temple of Ephesus were gifts from Crœsus. Fragments of the first temple of Ephesus, exhumed by the late M. Wood, after having lain forgotten a long time in the British Museum, were pieced together by M. Murray, who succeeded in restoring one column of the ancient temple. On the fragments of a torus that forms part of a base—the profile of which is most curious—nine letters were discovered by means of which the votive inscription has been reconstituted: Βα[σιλεὺς] Κ[ροῖσος] ἀνέ-[θηκ]εν. See HICKS, *Manual of Greek Inscriptions*, No. 4, and A. S. MURRAY, "Remains of Archaic Temple of Artemis at Ephesus" (*Journal of Hellenic Studies*, vol. x. pp. 1–10).

Page 279, § 3. This was ready for the press when M. A. S. Murray, Keeper of the Greek and Roman antiquities at the British Museum, sent me photographs of the two bas-reliefs figured on this and the next page, which form part of the collection under his care (Figs. 281, 282). They came out of one of the tombs that M. Dennis explored at Bin Tepe. They are two long slabs of white marble which appear to have belonged to a frieze. The figures stand out with a slight

FIG. 281.—Lydian bas-relief. Length, 36 c. British Museum.

FIG. 282.—Lydian ... Museum.

projection from the field, enframed by a flat border. On one of these fragments (Fig. 281) are three horsemen. The animals are of stout breed; their bridles are adorned by embroidery and top-knots. The riders sit their animals well; they are clad in a short tunic reaching nearly to the knee; a mantle seems to be rolled across the shoulder. All carry a spear in their left hand, whilst on the back of one of them is some object resembling a quiver. The heads are terribly mutilated, but helmets do not seem to have been worn. We have perhaps here a representation of the famous horsemen whom Cyrus defeated. The work shows that effort was made to introduce variety. On the other hand, the deer, to the number of three, figured on the other slab are uniform (Fig. 282). They are fairly well drawn, with their heads down, grazing in a meadow. They recall those rows of animals depicted on Greek archaic vases. These two fragments may have been part of a hunting-scene which decorated the walls of one of the funereal chambers. The sculptor's hand is already very skilful, especially in the delineation of the animals. But the repetition of the same figures, which only differ from each other in trifling details, or are precisely alike, savours of archaism. It is quite possible that the sculpture is older than the fall of the Lydian empire. Should it be called Lydian work? However that may be, it was used in the decoration of a Lydian building.

Page 287. The most elegant vases seem to have been manufactured in Lydia. The specimen found by M. George Dennis in one of the tumuli of Bin Tepe belongs to this superior style of pottery (Fig. 283). The form is not wanting in elegance, but its claim to originality resides in the style of its ornamentation, which consists of wavy black lines standing out on the red ground of the clay, evidently imitated from the *chevronné* glass products of Egypt and Phœnicia (*Hist. of Art*, tom. iii. p. 732, Plate VIII. Figs. 1–3; Plate IX. Fig. 1.) The

FIG. 283.—Lydian vase. Height, 15 c. British Museum.

painter was not content with the mere tracing of the chevrons; by varying the intensity of his black pigments, he succeeded in obtaining the effect of glass. The upper edge of the vase is adorned in the same taste. This happy adoption of devices proper to glass testifies to the dexterity of the Lydian potter.

Page 328. The affirmation contained in these lines has ceased to be true. In 1887 M. Bent visited Cape Krio, near Cnidos. "At the point," he writes, "where the promontory contracts into a narrow isthmus, we saw traces of tombs recently laid bare by tropical rains, in which we found a number of small marble figures, like those I collected at Antiparos and described in this *Journal* (vol. v. p. 50). One represents a personage seated in a chair playing on a harp, the facsimile of that held by a figurine from Amorgos, now in the Museum at Athens; another is a female figure with a crescent on her head, resembling in every respect the Tenos exemplar. All these statuettes have a strong family likeness to those which come from the islands; in them we have another proof that the primitive inhabitants of the islands—as held by Thucydides—belonged to the Carian stock" ("Discoveries in Asia Minor," *Hell. Studies*, vol. ix. pp. 82–87). Should other discoveries of the like nature be made in Caria, they would not only confirm the inference to be drawn from this first "find," but forthwith solve the problem; we could then boldly assign a Carian origin to all the statuettes of the islands.

Page 390, note 4. Closer examination of the cylinder, which exhibits an offering to the dove, has led M. Ménant to withdraw the attribution of it to Persia. He now finds that the intaglio is not connected in any way with the Achæmenidæ, and that the so-called king is a woman. See *Catalogue de la collection Le Clercq*, tom. i. pp. 211, 212, and note No. 385.

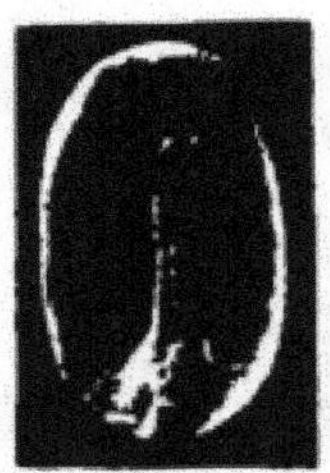

INDEX.

I.

K.

L.

M.

T.

V.

W.

X.

Y.

Z.

PRINTED BY WILLIAM CLOWES AND SONS, LIMITED, LONDON AND BECCLES.

www.ingramcontent.com/pod-product-compliance
Lightning Source LLC
Chambersburg PA
CBHW032313280326
41932CB00009B/799

* 9 7 8 3 7 4 4 6 4 6 0 8 6 *

J. E. Cairnes

Essays in Political Economy

J. E. Cairnes

Essays in Political Economy

ISBN/EAN: 9783741177613

Manufactured in Europe, USA, Canada, Australia, Japa

Cover: Foto ©Suzi / pixelio.de

Manufactured and distributed by brebook publishing software
(www.brebook.com)

J. E. Cairnes

Essays in Political Economy

ESSAYS

IN

POLITICAL ECONOMY.

THEORETICAL AND APPLIED.

BY

J. E. CAIRNES, M.A.

Emeritus Professor of Political Economy in University College, London.

London:

MACMILLAN AND CO.

1873.

PREFACE.

The following Essays have appeared in various periodicals at intervals in the course of the last fourteen years. They consist in part of attempts to apply the principles of economic science, as that science has been understood by the ablest writers in this country and in France, to the solution of actual problems, of which those presented by the Californian and Australian gold discoveries, and by the state of land tenure in Ireland, are the most important. So much of the volume may not improperly be described as Essays in Applied Political Economy. The remaining Essays deal mostly with topics of a theoretical kind; one—Political Economy and *Laissez-faire*—is expository of the character of economic science, and two—those on Comte and Bastiat—are critical and to some extent controversial. To two of the Essays relating to the Gold Question I have appended postscripts, in which the principal facts involved in the particular aspect of the movement treated in each are traced down to the present time. I have also in some instances subjoined notes, where later events have served to throw light on the questions discussed.

These remarks will sufficiently indicate the general character of the present volume. On one portion of its contents, however,—that which relates to the gold discoveries and their effects,—it has seemed to me that something further in the way of comment and elucidation would be desirable. The problem there discussed is one of which the practical solution is still in process of being worked out; and since the papers which attempt to deal with it were written, a considerable period of time has elapsed, in which the movement forming the object of the inquiry has continued to unfold itself. Such an experience offers an opportunity of bringing the views therein advanced to the test of experiment. I venture to think that, fairly judged, they will be found capable of standing this test, and that in the main the anticipations formed respecting the course of wages and prices under the action of the new gold have been sustained by the event. But in order to apply the criterion fairly, the conditions under which the experiment has proceeded ought to be taken account of. I have therefore thought it well to prefix to this portion of the volume an introductory chapter, in which the subject is discussed from the advanced standpoint we have now attained, and the reader is furnished with the data requisite for a just estimate of the speculation.

I take this opportunity of acknowledging with thanks the courtesy of the proprietors of the several periodicals in which these Essays originally appeared in consenting to their re-appearance in the present form; and, at the same time, I am anxious to express my deep obligations to my valued friend Professor Fawcett, at whose suggestion it was that they were collected, and by whose kind encouragement and effective aid I have profited largely in preparing them for the press.

J. E. C.

KIDBROOK PARK ROAD, S.E.

CONTENTS.

ESSAYS TOWARDS A SOLUTION OF THE GOLD QUESTION.

APPENDICES.

ESSAYS.

ESSAYS.

ESSAYS ON THE GOLD QUESTION.

INTRODUCTORY.

In submitting to the judgment of the public that portion of the present volume which relates to the economic aspects of the Gold Question, I am desirous at the outset to guard myself against two possible misapprehensions. In the first place I desire it to be understood that the question discussed in the Essays on that subject is, not the gold discoveries and their consequences, but the much narrower one involved in the economical effects of the increased supplies of gold. The two problems, though to some extent mutually implicated, are substantially distinct. To the one belongs the impulse given to the movement of population, which has resulted in the rapid peopling and definitive settlement of districts that without this stimulus might long have continued the slow and chequered career which up to that time had characterized their march, together with all the social and political consequences which have flowed from that movement both in Europe and in the scenes of the discoveries; to the other, the effects resulting from the increased abundance of money on the industry and trade of nations and the fortunes of individuals: and it is to the solution of this latter problem alone that the Essays on the Gold Question are addressed. And, secondly, the reader will do me the favour to remember that the views expressed on the subject of the future of trade and price are to be understood, not as predictions of the actual course which events would take, but only as an attempt to forecast the directions in which that course would be modified by the increased supplies of gold; in other words, to trace the consequences which would result from this cause, supposing all other things to remain the same. The conditions of productive industry and the needs of human beings are constantly undergoing change, and, wholly irrespective of the increased supplies of money, a variety of powerful agencies have during the period under consideration been acting upon trade and prices. The actual course which the phenomena have taken, therefore, has not been the consequence of any single influence, such as that proceeding from the increased production of gold, but the composite result of the combined action of many; so that to judge of the operations of any particular cause it becomes necessary, as far as possible, to eliminate, and, in mercantile phrase, discount what is due to the action of other contemporaneous causes. These points being premised, I proceed to consider how far the views advanced in the Essays on the Gold Question have been borne out by the test which an experience of some fourteen years since they were written has furnished.

On one point the opinion alike of economists and of the public seems now to be at one. It is now generally agreed that within twenty years a substantial advance in general prices has taken place. But beyond this general conviction there is little accord. People differ as to the extent of the advance, and as to its cause. The former point is one on which the opinion of even the best informed statistician cannot be regarded as more than conjecture. The data for anything approaching to exactness in such an estimate do not exist; and I shall certainly not attempt now, as I have not attempted in what I have formerly written, to offer any estimate pretending to exactness. I content myself with the general admission that a substantial advance has occurred, and that so far my anticipations have been borne out by events. But prices having risen, to what is the rise to be attributed? Here too, as I have said, there is a divergence of opinion. Amongst economists I think it is pretty well agreed that the advance is, at least in large measure, due to the effects of the gold discoveries. But, on the other hand, there is, on the part of commercial writers, and in general of all who view the question from the standpoint of practical business, a strong disposition to ignore, or altogether to deny, the influence of this cause in determining the results. The enhanced scale of wages and prices is not disputed, but it is referred to such causes as "the recent great development of trade," "changes in supply and demand," or "the effect of strikes;" and the facts seeming in each given instance to be traceable to one or more of such influences, the incident of an increased abundance of gold is regarded as something superfluous and irrelevant, and which need not be taken account of in seeking their explanation. Such a mode of argument, however, I do not hesitate to say, implies a fundamental misconception as to the nature of the problem to be solved. For to show that an advance of prices is connected with a development of trade,* with changes in supply and demand, or with the action of strikes, is not to prove that it is *not* due to the gold discoveries. An increased supply of money does not, and cannot, act upon prices, or upon the value of the metal composing it, in any other way than by being made the instrument of trade, by affecting demand and supply, or by furnishing employers with the means and the motives for advancing the wages of their workmen; and, consequently, however clearly the advance may be traceable in each given case to an occurrence of this nature, the problem still lies open: nothing has been done towards determining the question whether the increased monetary supplies may not have been an indispensable condition to the

* I may here remark that "a development of trade," which is so frequently assigned in explanation of a high *régime* of prices, not only is inadequate in itself to explain this result, but, so far as it operates at all upon general prices, tends to lower them, partly by cheapening the cost of commodities, and partly by increasing their quantity; for the effect of having more commodities to exchange is to create an increased need for circulating medium, which must, in the absence of an increased supply, tend to raise its value—*i.e.* to lower prices. In point of fact, the increased development of trade since 1850 has been one of the causes which has helped to neutralize to some extent the effects of the increased supplies of gold.

realization of the advance. I have said the problem still lies open; but in saying this I have conceded too much. It sometimes happens that the proximate occurrence to which the rise in price is referred is of a kind which necessarily implies an increased supply of money as the remote cause. I will illustrate my meaning by an example. In the sixth volume of the "History of Prices," * Mr. Newmarch had shown that an advance of prices on an extensive scale had taken place between 1851 and '56; and the question arose, whether this was to be referred to the action of the new supplies of gold. Mr. Newmarch decides in the negative, on the ground that the results were traceable to an increase in the demand for commodities relatively to the supply; to an increase, that is to say, in the demand for commodities in general, for nothing less than this would suffice to explain the facts. Now I maintain that, had Mr. Newmarch's object been to establish the contradictory of the conclusion he had in view, had he aimed to show that the high prices then prevailing were the result of the increased money supplies, no more effectual line of argument could have been taken for this purpose than the one he has adopted; for, putting aside the case of an increased demand resting on an undue inflation of credit (undoubtedly one of the causes in operation in 1856, though it is not referred to in Mr. Newmarch's explanation), an increase in the demand for commodities relatively to the supply can mean nothing else than an increase of *money* demand in relation to commodities; and to show that prices generally have risen from this

* Pp. 224, 225.

cause is simply to show that money has become depreciated. Mr. Newmarch's argument, so far as he made his position good, was thus a complete demonstration of the monetary depreciation which it was his purpose to disprove.

And a nearly similar criticism may be made on that explanation which refers the high scale of prices to the effects of strikes. The argument commonly takes this form. The men, it is said, having enforced their demands for increased wages, their employers are obliged to raise the prices of their commodities in order to secure their profits. But this being equivalent to a withdrawal of a portion of the advance—since the same money no longer purchases the same goods—the workmen, to make good their position, strike again, and obtain a further advance, which is followed on the employer's part by a further rise in prices, and so the cycle is repeated. Such was the explanation offered a little time since in the leading columns of an influential journal. It did not occur to the writer, that, if the principle of his argument was sound, there is no reason why the upward movement in prices should ever stop. It is, however, beyond question that an advance in price has in some instances been established in the way described, that is to say through a successful strike issuing in a higher price for the commodity; but those who have perceived this much, have failed to perceive what rendered this consummation possible. How has it happened that the capitalist producer has been enabled to maintain the advance in price urged on him by the action of his workmen? In many instances the commodities so raised in price are produced for foreign markets. How comes it that our foreign customers acquiesce in the demand? In the energetic competition which English products have now to encounter on all sides, why do they not rather turn to other markets, or become producers of the commodity themselves? There are but two possible modes of explaining the result: either prices in other markets have risen proportionally with prices in our own, in which case we have to consider whence comes the money which supports those prices; or money has become a cheaper commodity with our foreign customers, so that they find it more profitable to pay the increased price demanded by the English producer, than to divert their capital from its actual investment—an investment which enables them, directly or indirectly, to procure gold on those cheaper terms. Adopt which hypothesis you please, and the same fact will in the end confront you—an increased supply of money rendering possible an advance in general prices, which, but for this condition, could never have occurred.

I venture to lay down broadly this proposition, that, when an advance in the price of any of the great staples of industry becomes definitive (monopoly apart), there are two, and only two, adequate explanations of the fact: either the cost of producing the article (understanding by cost, not the money outlay, but the real difficulties of production) has increased; or the cost of producing or obtaining money has diminished. A change in supply and demand will indeed produce temporary effects on prices, but apart from the conditions just stated it is incapable of permanently altering them. For example, the present high price of coal is certainly due to an increased demand for the commodity as its proximate cause; * but will this high price become definitive? Only on one or other or both of the conditions I have stated being satisfied. If the increased demand can only be met by incurring increased physical difficulties of production so great as to need the present high rates to compensate them, then the present rates will become the normal rates for coal. Or again, the cost of producing coal remaining the same, if the present prices, in consequence of the increased abundance of money, do not represent a greater real cost than the lower prices of former years, in this case too the present scale of prices will be maintained. Or once more, if both these conditions are partially satisfied,—if the real cost of producing coal be raised in some degree, and the real cost of obtaining money reduced in some degree,—on this assumption also, the alterations in cost being sufficiently great, we should be justified in expecting a continuance of present rates. It thus appears that the question of an advance in price, where the advance becomes established and normal, is in all cases (monopoly apart) a question of cost of production: it is due either to an increased cost of producing the commodities, or to a diminished cost of producing or obtaining money, or to a combination of both these conditions. All explanations which fail to trace the

* The two latest returns of the quantity raised, Professor Jevons informs me, are as follows:—

1870. 110,430,000 tons.
1871. 117,439,000 "

phenomenon to one or other, or to some combination of these, are of the kind which would place the earth upon an elephant, and the elephant on a tortoise, leaving the tortoise to find his footing as best he may.

The doctrine advanced in the following Essays not merely asserts a prospective depreciation of gold as a consequence of the gold discoveries, but attempts to state the *modus operandi* of depreciation; in other words, the order of advance by which the ultimate higher level of prices would be reached. At the time the Essays were written, the opinion was nearly universal, and indeed it would seem still to be far from extinct, that a depreciation of money could only show itself in a uniform action upon all prices—not, I presume, that it was supposed that the prices of all commodities would necessarily advance *pari passu*, but that, in so far as they were affected by the increase of money, this would be the nature of their progress; and, accordingly, no such uniform movement being discoverable in the actual phenomena, it was invariably concluded that such enhancement of price as was found to exist must be due to some other cause than the increased supplies of gold. This view I ventured to combat; and, as just intimated, not content with recording a mere general denial of the current doctrine, and with asserting a definitive depreciation of gold as even then accomplished, I attempted further to state the mode and order in which the monetary movement, as it proceeded, would be developed. As regards the first portion of my thesis, I need not hesitate now to say that it has been fully verified by events. A general rise of prices has admittedly occurred; but in this general advance there are no traces of that uniformity in the march which the prevailing view anticipated. What has happened has been a great rise in the prices of some commodities, a more moderate rise in those of others, in the case of some a very slight rise or none at all. Further, up to a certain point, I am entitled to claim a substantial verification of the views I put forward as to the order of the advance of prices. For example, I had said that, resolving commodities in general into the two grand classes of crude products and manufactured goods, the rise in price would be more rapid in the former than in the latter class; while, as amongst commodities of the former class, I asserted that animal products would advance more rapidly than those of vegetable growth. Now I think I shall not need to go into details to prove that, speaking broadly, this has in fact been the course which prices have followed. The articles of which the advance in price has been most marked have been such as butcher's meat, butter, bacon, and other provisions of the animal kind. Mineral products and agricultural products of the vegetable kind have come next in order; while manufactured goods, unless where, as in the case of cotton, the raw material has been affected by causes of a very exceptional nature, have shared but slightly in the upward movement, or not at all. So far, I say, I can claim for the views advanced a substantial verification from the course of events. With regard, however, to that part of my speculation which attempted to describe the order of the movement in prices as it would be felt in different countries, only a more qualified claim to verification can be advanced. Not that I am disposed to make any retractation as regards the economic principles on which the speculation rests: so far as I am aware, the tenor of events has only tended to corroborate and fortify these; but in some instances, the action of the cause I was investigating has been overborne by influences of a violently disturbing kind, not foreseen at the time the Essays were written, and of course, therefore, not taken account of in my speculation. This has been especially the case with what I have said respecting the probable course of prices in the United States and in India. The civil war in the former country causing a sudden cessation in the supply of cotton, and leading to a large increase of taxation and to the issue of an inconvertible paper currency, operated powerfully upon the whole course of commercial and monetary affairs; nor was its influence by any means confined to the immediate scene of its occurrence. Its effect in the United States was to accelerate powerfully the upward movement of prices, already sufficiently marked,* not merely as measured in the depreciated paper currency, but as measured in gold; for the enlarged issue of paper currency had the effect of setting free a large quantity of gold formerly required for the maintenance of cash payments; and the increased taxation, so far as it fell upon commodities, acted on prices directly in proportion to its amount. The result has been that prices in the

* See Appendix G.

United States, instead of advancing, as I expected would happen, nearly *pari passu* with prices in England, have progressed with much greater rapidity.* On the other hand, the civil war in the United States caused a large diversion of the demand for cotton from that country to India. This would of course lead to an increase of specie remittances to the latter country; and other causes, more particularly a sudden development of railway enterprise, resulting in an investment of upwards of 60,000,000*l*. sterling, acted powerfully in the same direction. At the same time, while gold and silver were thus pouring into India in an exceptionally large stream, the credit system of the country was, by the establishment of numerous banks of issue and deposit, undergoing rapid extension. All these occurrences have conspired to give an impulse to the movement of prices in India, far beyond what it was possible to anticipate fourteen years ago. Accordingly, the exceptional slowness, which I was led to expect would characterize the advance of prices in Asiatic countries, has certainly, so far as India is concerned, not been realized. At the same time I am not prepared to admit, even as regards India, that the deviation from the course I had ventured to trace is by any means as great as the round assertions frequently made about Indian prices would seem to imply. These assertions may be true, so far as they go; but India, it must be remembered, is a country of vast extent; the means of communication over the greater part of it are still very imperfect; and, consequently, the

* See Mr. Wells' Reports.

widest discrepancies in the scale of prices prevail in different districts. Some interesting evidence of this will be found in Mr. Ollerenshaw's paper on "The Export Trade in Cotton to India" (Manchester Statistical Society, April 1870), in which he remarks that, "even in the same presidencies, prices have been in one place double those in another, and that this is not exceptional, but constant." And I find in Mr. Brassey's recent work the following striking differences in the rates of wages recorded as prevailing in Bombay and Bengal:*—

	In Bengal per month. Rupees.	In Bombay per month. Rupees.
Carpenters . . .	9 .	. . 25
Masons . . .	$5\frac{6}{16}$.	. . 21
Labouring Coolies .	6 .	. . $9\frac{1}{8}$
Horse-keepers . .	5 .	. . $8\frac{6}{16}$

I believe the truth to be that a great advance in wages and prices has taken place in and around particular localities; for example, the cotton districts north and east of Bombay, and in general wherever railway or public works are being carried on. The reports which come to us in this country respecting Indian prices are derived mostly, if not entirely, from observation of what is taking place in those districts; but that the state of things in those favoured centres of activity is no safe criterion of the general condition of prices throughout India, we need only refer to the prices of her leading staples in the great commercial markets to satisfy ourselves. Of these a considerable number, including Rice, Sugar, Tea, Rum, and Sago,

* "Work and Wages," p. 60.

have positively fallen since 1850; while of the rest, though a few, such as cotton and hemp, that have been subject to exceptional influences, have risen very greatly, the larger portion show but a moderate advance.* I may here add that I have been not a little fortified in my conviction of the essential soundness of the view which I took as to the bearing of the increased money supplies upon the relation of prices in Europe and in the East, by the remarkable corroboration which that view has since received from the independent investigations of my friend Professor Jevons. In a paper read before the London Statistical Society in 1865,† Professor Jevons showed, in an elaborate series of tables, not only that the course of Oriental and European prices down to that year had in the main been coincident with the course foreshadowed in my essay, but that a similar phenomenon—namely, a divergence of prices as between Europe and tropical countries—had manifested itself in the early part of the present century, when various causes—partly economical and partly political—had led to a temporary redundancy of the precious metals in Europe. In a word, it appears from Professor Jevons' investigations that, on two distinct occasion within the present century, an exceptional abundance of the precious metals was followed by the same results—those results being what theory applied to the facts had led me to anticipate.

Another incident which I was led to expect would

* I am indebted for these facts to information kindly furnished me by Professor Jevons.

† See London Statistical Society's Journal for 1865.

accompany the course of monetary depreciation was a more rapid advance of prices and rates of wages in England than on the Continent of Europe. In effect I had placed the Continent, as regards the order of advance in prices, in an intermediate position between England and the United States on the one hand, and Asiatic countries on the other. In the main I believe the results have been in accordance with my forecast; though it would seem that the general coincidence has not been without some serious exceptions. As I learn from Mr. Brassey's work, just referred to, the rates of wages in the engineering trades and other branches of industry which minister to railway construction have, within twenty years, risen much more rapidly in France and Germany than with us; and, what is a noteworthy feature of the phenomenon, while these particular industries are those in which the rise in wages has been greatest on the Continent, they are those in which it has been least in this country; indeed, it appears from Mr. Brassey's tables that in some of those trades no sensible advance at all had been established in England up to 1869,* though I apprehend the case would be different if the figures were carried on to the present year. Both facts—the exceptional rapidity of the rise in engineering and other ancillary trades on the Continent, and the exceptional slowness of their advance here—are,

* "Work and Wages," p. 157. It is pertinent to my purpose to observe that Mr. Brassey's tables commence with 1854—three years, that is to say, after the occurrence of the gold discoveries, and when that ascending movement in wages and prices which culminated in 1857 had already made considerable progress.

I have no doubt, mainly due to the cause to which Mr. Brassey assigns them. "The real explanation is to be found in the circumstance that, as the railway system was first established in this country, so we were the first in the field as locomotive engine builders" (p. 192);—that is to say, in the period between 1840 and '50 England had a practical monopoly of the engineering business of the world. "The science of building locomotives was an occult science on the Continent;" and during the period of Continental apprenticeship which followed, the rates of pay in that calling would naturally be low. But as skill and knowledge were acquired with experience, a portion of the world's demand was naturally transferred from us to them. It necessarily followed that engineering wages suffered abatement here just as they were beginning to advance abroad, and the impulse then given has not yet spent itself. I may add to Mr. Brassey's explanation, that a succession of great wars on the Continent during the period under review must have brought into special and exceptional requisition the products of engineering skill; and this, I have no doubt, has also contributed to the result we are considering. It has thus happened, comparing the Continent with England, that the movement in wages in the callings in question has been in opposite directions in relation to the general movement of prices. It has shot in advance there while here it has lagged behind. If, however, we have regard, not to particular employments, but to the general progress of industry here and abroad, I think it will be found that the evidence goes on the whole to support the view which I had advanced. I rest this opinion chiefly on the general tenor of the reports from our agents in foreign countries, published in the early part of this year. Taking these reports as a whole, they seem to me to speak in that sense. But I think the same conclusion may be deduced from facts furnished by Mr. Brassey, though it would seem that his own opinion favours the opposite view. For example, I find it stated (pp. 18, 19) that "inquiries in Spain and France, Belgium and Prussia, show that provisions in those countries are from 20 to 30 per cent. dearer than twenty years ago." Now, though I do not pretend to have gone of late minutely into the question, I will venture to assert that the advance in the prices of provisions in England during the same time has been very considerably greater than this. To take a few important items, I find that, comparing 1851 with the present year, the advance in the price of mutton has been 58 per cent.; of beef, 68 per cent.; of butter, 42 per cent.; of bacon, 60 per cent.* And I have little doubt that, omitting the article of flour (the movements in which since 1851 have been substantially uniform over Western Europe), the less important articles of provisions, such as potatoes, poultry, cheese, fresh vegetables, &c., have experienced a rise little, if at all, short of that shown by these figures. Accepting then Mr. Brassey's statement as to the advance in the prices of this class of articles in the leading Continental countries, I am justified in saying that the rise has been considerably greater here than there. But this fact, duly weighed,

* See *Economist*. Prices current for those years.

will be found to go far to decide the whole question; for, if we consider what the commodities are in which a serious deviation of local prices from the common standard is possible, we shall find that, with the exception of houses, they consist mainly of provisions. Of dry goods and articles of general manufacture—of all commodities, in a word, not quickly perishable and easily portable—the prices in different European countries, allowance being made for the effect of tariffs, will, as a rule, not differ by more than the cost of carriage between the compared localities. A more rapid advance, therefore, in the price of provisions in England than on the Continent, means a more rapid advance of local prices here than there. And it means more than this. The great consumers of provisions are the masses, whose expenditure it is that must in the main determine for this class of goods the fluctuations of price. Where, therefore, the prices of provisions have in a given period advanced more rapidly in one country than in another, the reasonable inference is that the movement in prices has been preceded by a parallel or nearly parallel movement in wages.

On no other hypothesis, so far as I can see, is the phenomenon explicable. I am inclined, therefore, notwithstanding the evidence Mr. Brassey has brought forward of a more rapid rise of wages in engineering and kindred trades abroad than with us, to abide by the view taken in the Essays. Comparing prices and wages here and on the Continent of Europe, and making allowance for disturbing causes, they appear, on the whole, to have progressed, under the influence of the increased supplies of money, much as I ventured to predict they would progress; that is to say, they have advanced more rapidly here than there. Such at least seems to me to be the tenor of the evidence down to the present time.

With these remarks I now submit these speculations to the judgment of the reader.

I.

ESSAY TOWARDS A SOLUTION OF THE GOLD QUESTION.

THE AUSTRALIAN EPISODE.[*]

In the discussions which have taken place respecting the probable consequences of the Californian and Australian gold discoveries, there is a branch of the general question which has not yet received from economists that degree of attention, to which from its scientific importance it seems to be entitled. I allude to the effects produced by those events in the countries which have been the scene of their occurrence. In the great world of commerce, the action of the new money for the most part escapes notice amid the variety and complexity of the phenomena in which it is involved. The area over which the increasing supplies have to act is immense, the extraneous incidents affecting the course of their diffusion are numerous, and the real tendency of the movement is thus in these cosmopolitan transactions not easily discoverable. But within the more limited sphere of the auriferous countries this is not the case. The gold

[*] *Fraser's Magazine*, September 1859.

discoveries have there been the predominant influence, and being less controlled by circumstances the real character of the new agencies and the results to which they are leading come distinctly and prominently into view. California and Australia, during the period of their auriferous history, furnish us with what Bacon would call "an ostensive or predominant instance" of the action of such agencies, showing their nature (to borrow his language) "naked and palpable, and even in its exaltation, or in the highest degree of its power—that is to say, emancipated or freed from impediments, or at least, by force of its native energy, dominating over these, suppressing and coercing them." * Hence, by studying the effects of the gold discoveries in these countries, we may gain a clearer and steadier view of the real nature of the causes which are at work than we are likely to obtain from the more extended and complicated transactions of general commerce. By tracing the events which are there presented, we may be guided to conclusions which (if the illustration be allowed) may serve as a sort of economic chart of the new monetary influences—a chart which, though it may be drawn upon an exaggerated scale, will all the more clearly indicate the true direction of the currents, and the ultimate goal whither they are bearing us.

With this view, I propose in the following paper to examine the effects of the gold discoveries in Australia on its trade, industry, and pecuniary relations. The course of events in California during its auriferous history has been extremely similar, and the

* "Novum Organon," Lib. ii. Aph. 24.

description of the movement in the former country will in its main features be found applicable to the latter.

Regarded in its economic aspects, the discovery of gold in Australia may be thus briefly described: It was an occurrence by which a common labourer was enabled, by means of a simple process requiring for its performance little capital or skill, to obtain about a quarter of an ounce of gold—in value about £1 sterling—on an average in the day.* This is the fundamental fact from which the remarkable series of events which we have lately been contemplating took its rise, and to which the whole movement following upon the gold discoveries is ultimately traceable. The immediate effect was a general disorganization of industry throughout the Australian colonies. The ordinary pursuits of the place were for a time entirely suspended; and the imaginations and hopes of the community outstripping even the marvellous realities of the case, the whole industrial population rushed as by a single impulse to the gold-fields. The gold fever, however, in this its first and full intensity, was not of long duration. Actual trial soon reduced the extravagant expectations raised by the first announcements to a more sober and correct appreciation of the true conditions of the discovery. Those who had overrated the gain, as well as those whose constitution and habits unfitted them for the toils and exposure of gold-digging, and who did not fall victims to their mistake, returned after a short trial to their former occupations. The extraordinary excitement subsided;

* "Correspondence relative to the late Discoveries of Gold in Australia." Presented to Parliament, February 1852. Pages 32, 51.

but in the meantime a change had taken place in the conditions of Australian industry, a new and vigorous branch of production had struck root, overshadowing all the old occupations of the country and entirely superseding many of them, and a new monetary *régime* had been inaugurated.

The immediate result of the change was a general rise of money wages throughout the country. Formerly the wages of common labour in Australia had ranged from 3*s.* to 5*s.* a day. The same labour was now, by washing the auriferous sand, capable of producing gold worth 20*s.* a day. It followed as a necessary consequence that, other things being equal, hired labourers would not work for less. Other things indeed were not equal. The toil of gold-digging was severe, its results were precarious, and the further the removal from the coast the higher was the price of provisions. All these circumstances influenced wages in different occupations and in different localities; but, making allowance for these, the standard of pecuniary remuneration in Australia was henceforth the rate of earnings on the gold-fields.

During the two years immediately following the first discoveries, this standard continued at the high point above indicated—namely, about a quarter of an ounce of gold per man each day, equal to about £1 sterling; but towards the close of 1853 a great decline in the proceeds of gold-digging took place. The cream of the richest auriferous deposits had by this time been skimmed away; and it was henceforth necessary to dig deeper for materials which, when reached, proved of inferior quality. The Commissioners appointed in the following year to report on the gold-fields accordingly describe a great falling off at this time from the richness of the early returns;* and although many new gold-fields have since been opened the high average standard of the early discoveries has not again been reached.† During the two years just passed (1857 and 1858), the rate of gold earnings per man has not exceeded on an average ten shillings a day—a decline of one-half from the early returns. On the whole, we may say that during the first and most productive period of gold-digging, the standard of money wages in Australia rose in rather more than a fourfold proportion as compared with the pre-gold times, and that during the last five years this proportion has been reduced by one-half; so that money wages in Australia are at the present time (1859) rather more than double those which formerly prevailed.‡

But this rise in the pecuniary remuneration of the labourer involved further consequences. The Australian employer could not continue to pay quadruple or double rates to his workmen while the commodities which he sold remained at their former price. In order to the maintenance of his profit, it was necessary that the price of Australian productions should rise in proportion as wages had risen; and this result accordingly followed in due course.§

* "Further Papers relative to the Discovery of Gold in Australia." Presented to Parliament, February 1856. Page 55.

† Westgarth's "Victoria" (1857), p. 171.

‡ Ibid. p. 150. [Since 1859 the rates, with occasional variations, have on the whole slightly declined, following the course of gold production (1872).]

§ As to the connection between wages and prices when money is falling in value, see *post*, pp. 58–60, and note * to latter.

The advance, however, in money wages and prices which these circumstances necessitated, though rapid, was not instantaneous.* For more than a year after the gold discoveries had occurred, it was held sensibly in check by the peculiar state of the local currencies. For there was at this time no mint in Australia; the increased requirements for coin could only be met by a transmission of bullion to London, there to be coined, and afterwards re-imported; and this process required from six to eight months at the least for its accomplishment. Pending the arrival of the new coins, prices were not indeed prevented absolutely from rising; for numerous expedients were in their absence freely resorted to for supplying the place of the ordinary currency; † but nevertheless prices were, by the straitness of the circulation, kept very considerably under their natural level, as determined by the cost of gold,—a fact which was sufficiently proved by a remarkable fall in the price of gold throughout the whole of this period.‡ The arrival, however, of sovereigns in large quantities from England, in the winter of 1852–53, quickly put an end to this exceptional state of the markets. The price of gold, and with it the prices of other things, rose to their natural level; and pecuniary rates generally throughout the country were brought permanently

* See the Table of Prices contained in Mr. Westgarth's "Address to the Melbourne Chambers of Council," given in the Appendix to his "Victoria, or Australia Felix." 1853.

† Of which expedients the passing of the Bullion Act by the Government of South Australia was the most important.

‡ A fall from £3 17*s.* 10½*d.* per ounce, the London Mint price, to 60*s.*, 50*s.*, and, it is stated, in some instances to 40*s.* per ounce. See the Appendix to Westgarth's "Victoria, or Australia Felix." 1853.

into conformity with the new conditions of producing gold.

But the advance in general prices, which was thus easily and rapidly effected within the limited area of the gold districts, could by no means be accomplished with the same facility amongst the great commercial populations of the world. The disturbance of industrial pursuits in the larger theatre, though resulting in an extensive emigration, was yet, in comparison with the general business of the world, inconsiderable, while the supply of gold required, in order to render possible a fall in its value over so large an area of transactions, was immense. The necessary conditions, therefore, to a rise in general prices not being susceptible of speedy fulfilment, money rates throughout the world at large did not, and could not, advance with the same rapidity with which they advanced in the gold countries. A divergence of local prices and rates in Australia from the general level of commercial countries has been the necessary consequence,—a divergence which has altered fundamentally her commercial position in relation to the rest of the world, and has been followed by a series of changes in her domestic industry and foreign trade which I shall now attempt to describe.

The great staple industry of Australia has, from an early period in the history of the colony, been her cattle-farming; the advantages which the country possesses for this pursuit in her extensive open plains, covered with rich natural grass, being unsurpassed in any part of the world. The fruits of this industry are the usual pastoral products, of which butcher's meat, wool, and tallow are the principal. Until the occurrence of the remarkable events we are considering, the two latter of these constituted the leading commodities of the foreign trade of the country. For the former—butcher's meat—as it was unfit for a distant traffic, she was compelled to trust for a market to the local population, which being extremely limited, the supply of meat was with difficulty disposed of, and the article was consequently often a drug in the colonial markets. The difficulty, however, thence arising to the pastoral interest, was met by the conversion of a large portion of their meat into tallow, and by the starting of an export trade in this commodity. By this means the several branches of trade connected with pastoral farming in Australia were placed upon a sound foundation, and by the beginning of 1851 they were in a highly flourishing condition. But in the summer of that year the gold discoveries occurred, and the consequences which have ensued in this leading department of her industry have been not a little remarkable.

On the first outbreak of the gold mania in 1851, the pastoral interest was subjected to the same inconvenience which was felt by all other occupations in Australia. The minds of shepherds and shearers were not proof to the attractions which had acted so powerfully on workmen in every other walk of industry, and the "squatting" stations were for a time abandoned for the more enticing pursuits of the gold-fields. As the only means of obtaining the requisite supply of labour, the squatters were obliged to submit to the same advance in wages which at this time took place in all other occupations. But, as has been pointed out, a rise in money wages requires (if profits are to be maintained) a corresponding rise in the price of the commodities which the more highly-priced labour produces. This necessary rise was effected without difficulty in articles produced in Australia for domestic consumption; but the chief product of the pastoral industry was wool, and the chief market for wool was Europe, in which a fourfold or a twofold rise in price—such a rise, that is to say, as would have indemnified the Australian farmer for the advance in his labour rates—was simply impossible, or at the least could only have been obtained by a curtailment of supply, which, as Europe had other resources for this material besides the Australian sheep farms, it was not in the power of Australia to effect. On the news, therefore, of the gold discoveries reaching this country, great alarm was felt for the stability of this trade. Mr. Lalor, in his work on "Money and Morals," strongly urged upon Government the duty of assisting the emigration of shepherds, with a view to supply the necessary labour. But supposing this were done, what security was there that the emigrating shepherds would not follow their predecessors to the gold-fields? In truth the wool trade was at this time in serious jeopardy. It has been saved from the danger that was impending through a circumstance which, in the first excitement of the movement, escaped the attention of observers—through the influence, namely, which the same event that endangered the supply of wool has exercised on other branches of the industry to which wool belongs. The immense immigration which followed the gold discoveries created a sudden demand for butcher's meat; a more than quadruple rise in the price of meat in Australia has been the consequence,—a rise which has covered the increased outlay on sheep-farming, thus providing the necessary inducement for the continuance of the supply of sheep, and therefore of wool. The wool trade of Australia has thus been preserved from extinction; but it is important to observe that it is now upon a different footing from that on which it formerly stood. Previous to the gold discoveries, while wool formed the leading product of pastoral industry, the extension of sheep-farming depended principally on the extension of the demand, chiefly in Europe, for this article. But since that event, wool has, in the calculation of the farmer's profits, become subordinate to meat, which is now the great support and mainstay of his trade. The progress of pastoral farming will therefore in future be governed, not by the requirements of Europe for wool, but by those of Australia for meat,—in other words, by the increase of the colonial population; and as this cannot be expected to keep pace with the general demand for wool, a falling off in the rate of increase at which this branch of industry was formerly progressing may accordingly be looked for; indeed, the decline has already become very apparent.*

So far as to the pastoral industry of Australia. Let us now trace the influence of the gold discoveries

* See Westgarth's "Victoria" (1857), p. 118; and "Statistical Abstract of the United Kingdom" (1858), p. 17. [Since this was written, the trade in preserved meats has sprung up, and this will of course enlarge, and already has perceptibly enlarged, the limits of the wool production (1872).]

upon the occupation which, along with pastoral pursuits, forms in general the principal resource of young communities—agriculture.

If we are to accept the very high authority of Humboldt, the discovery of the Australian gold-fields should rather assist than hinder the progress of its agriculture. In his "Political Essay upon the Kingdom of New Spain," that eminent writer thus observes:—

"It cannot be doubted that, under improved social institutions, the countries which most abound with mineral productions will be as well if not better cultivated than those in which no such productions are to be found. But the desire natural to man of simplifying the causes of everything has introduced into works on political economy a species of reasoning which is perpetuated because it flatters the mental indolence of the multitude. The depopulation of Spanish America, the state of neglect in which the most fertile lands are found, and the want of manufacturing industry, are attributed to the metallic wealth, to the abundance of gold and silver; as, according to the same logic, all the evils of Spain are attributed to the discovery of America, or the wandering race of the Merinos, or the religious intolerance of the clergy!

"We do not observe that agriculture is more neglected in Peru than in the province of Cumana or Gugana, in which, however, there are no mines worked. In Mexico the best cultivated fields, those which recall to the mind of the traveller the beautiful plains of France, are those which extend from Salamanca towards Silao, Guanaxuato, and the Villa de Leon, and which surround the richest mines of the known world. Wherever metallic seams have been discovered in the most uncultivated parts of the Cordilleras, on the isolated and desert table lands, the working of mines, far from impeding the cultivation of the soil, has been singularly favourable to it. Travelling along the ridge of the Andes, or the mountainous parts of Mexico, we everywhere see the most striking examples of the beneficial influence of the mines on agriculture. Were it not for the establishments formed for the working of the mines, how many places would have remained desert? how many districts uncultivated in the four intendancies of Guanaxuato, Zacatecas, San Luis Potosi, and Durango, between the parallels of 21° and 25°, where the most considerable metallic wealth of New Spain is to be found? If the town is placed on the arid side or the crest of the Cordilleras, the new colonists can only draw from a distance the means of their subsistence and the maintenance of the great number of cattle employed in drawing off the water, and raising and amalgamating the mineral produce. Want soon wakens industry. The soil begins to be cultivated in the various ravines and declivities of the neighbouring mountains wherever the rock is covered with earth. Farms are established in the neighbourhood of the mine. The high price of provisions, from the competition of the purchasers, indemnifies the cultivator for the privations to which he is exposed from the hard life of the mountains. Thus from the hope of gain alone, and the motives of mutual interest, which are the most powerful bonds of society, and without any interference on the part of the Government in colonization, a mine, which at first appeared insulated in the midst of wild and desert mountains, becomes in a short time connected with the lands which have long been under cultivation." *

It seems unquestionable that, in the manner described by Humboldt in the above passage, a discovery of the precious metals, by attracting people to a locality otherwise undesirable, or of which the other recommendations were previously unknown, may hasten the progress of agriculture over the earth, or may lead to the cultivation of districts which, but for such discoveries, might for ever have remained barren;

* Vol. ii. pp. 405-8

nor will anyone dispute the opinion of so competent a witness that the neglect of agriculture in some of the States of Spanish America was due in a large degree to defects in their social institutions; but, accepting thus far the opinion of Humboldt, I yet venture to question the doctrine (for to this length does the passage I have quoted seem to go) that, speaking with reference to a country *in which occupation has been effected and society established*, the possession of mineral treasures is favourable, or can be otherwise than unfavourable, to the cultivation of the soil. It is one of the best established principles of economic science—the principle on which the whole theory of foreign trade is based—that the possession by a country of any extraordinary advantage in production operates, in proportion to the extent of the advantage, as a premium against all other industrial pursuits. And the grounds of the principle are sufficiently obvious; for the possession of exceptional facilities in production makes it clearly the interest of the country which enjoys them to satisfy its wants for other things, rather through the medium of an exchange with other nations of the article to which such special facilities apply, than by the direct production of commodities in raising which the country has no special advantage. And this being the general principle which regulates foreign exchange, it is one which, from their portability and the universality of the demand for them, applies to the precious metals in an especial degree. I therefore find it impossible to believe that the mineral resources of the Spanish American States did not exercise on these countries an influence prejudicial to the progress of their agriculture, and that these were not among the causes which contributed to that backward state of cultivation which Humboldt notices and describes.

And this conclusion is entirely confirmed by the recent experience of Australia. It is not indeed contended that the discovery of mineral treasures in that country has not given an impulse to cultivation by hastening its general settlement, in the same manner as in the metalliferous districts of America. What I contend for is, that, the country being once occupied and settled, the presence of rich gold-fields must operate unfavourably upon its agriculture, or, to put the same point differently, that the area of cultivation, under the influence of this cause, will be confined within limits short of those which it would have attained, had the community reached the same stage of advance under different economic conditions; and this, I think, is sufficiently proved by the recent history of Australia,—a history which exhibits the strange, and I believe unprecedented, spectacle of a country, possessing an immense unoccupied territory, and a soil of more than average fertility, importing more than one-half its food.*

I am quite aware, indeed, that other causes besides the gold discoveries are responsible for the past history of agriculture in Australia—more particularly a land system contrived with singular ingenuity to cramp and pervert the natural development of the country. But injurious in many respects as may have been, and may still be, the operation of this system,—amongst others, in excluding from the possession of land, and in fact

* The *Times* (Melbourne Correspondent), February 3rd, 1858.

driving from the colony, a class of small proprietors whom on social grounds it would be most desirable to retain,—it can scarcely be maintained that this is at present the principal cause of the failure of Australian agriculture, when we find that of the land which has been sold only a small portion has been brought under actual cultivation.* If the quantity offered in the market is insufficient for the agricultural wants of the country, this circumstance would only give an increased value for this purpose to the land which *has* been sold; and yet the greater portion of this remains as yet untilled. It appears to me that this state of things can only be explained by reference to other causes than the restraints of the land system; and what these causes are our former reasonings sufficiently indicate. Obviously they are to be found in the new money *régime* introduced by the gold discoveries. The high rate of wages thus established, being peculiar to the gold countries, places the Australian farmer, in common with other employers of Australian labour, under an exceptional disadvantage in competing in the markets of the world, and compels him, therefore, to confine cultivation to soils in which the superior richness of the natural agent compensates the cultivator for the high pecuniary charges with which he has to contend. It is thus that the gold-fields of Australia present a barrier to the development of its agricultural resources —a barrier which, after all the restrictions of the land system are removed, must continue to operate, and

* Westgarth's "Victoria" (1857), p. 81. Further Papers, &c., February 1856, p. 33. *Australian and New Zealand Gazette*, December 11th, 1858, p. 568.

which will probably for many years to come render its richest provinces a drain upon the subsistence of over-peopled Europe, instead of what under happier conditions they might become,—liberal contributors towards our already heavily-tasked resources.

Against this reasoning it will perhaps be urged that agriculture has made considerable progress in California, which has already become an exporter of food. This is true, and is a striking proof of the fact to which every traveller in that country has borne testimony, the extraordinary fertility of the Californian soils,—a fertility which enables agriculture to hold its own even against the competition of the gold mines. The fact, however, in no degree invalidates the principle above stated; it only proves that California enjoys over other countries an advantage in raising food, up to a certain point, *as great as she enjoys in obtaining gold.*

The extension of agriculture in Australia has thus, though stimulated for the moment, suffered a real check from the gold discoveries; and the same influence has been felt throughout every branch of industry in that country, gold mining alone excepted. The premium which has operated against sheep-farming and tillage has operated against all other industrial pursuits. Many districts in the northern portion of New South Wales are represented as favourable to the growth of cotton. "In Moreton Bay," says a colonial writer, "the cotton-tree grows most luxuriantly, and appears more inclined to assume a perennial form than in even the most favoured districts of America. But," he adds, "up to the present time the cost [price] of cultivation has been found too high to make the business of cotton-growing profitable." Tin and antimony, we are told by another authority, abound in many parts of Victoria. Some of the richest tin ores in the Ovens districts have, it seems, been worked to some profit; but although antimony ore "appears to be unlimited in quantity," "the value in the home market [more properly the price of raising it in Australia] will not admit of its being touched as yet by the eager fingers of commerce." * Such has been the effect on the industry of raw produce; and in manufacturing industry the influence of the gold discoveries has been still more complete and sweeping, nothing in the nature of a manufactured product, even of the coarsest kind, being now made in the colony, which can by any possibility be imported.†

As a proof of the soundness of our economic knowledge, it is interesting to observe that all this has happened in strict conformity with the established principles of economic science. According to these principles, the exchange of commodities among different nations is regulated, not by the absolute, but by the comparative, cost of the commodities exchanged‡—not by the circumstance that the commodity imported

* Westgarth's "Victoria" (1857), pp. 112-13.

† "We all wear imported boots and shoes," says the *Times'* Correspondent, "and it is cheaper to buy new than to get the old mended."

‡ See chapter on "Foreign Trade," Ricardo's Works, pp. 76-7; also Mill's "Principles of Political Economy," Book III. chap. xvii. The reader must observe that by "cost" is meant the *real difficulty* involved in the production of a commodity, *not the amount of money* necessary to remunerate the labour by which this difficulty is overcome. The only commodity of which the *cost* was affected by the gold discoveries was gold; but the *price* of producing everything was altered.

from a foreign country may be produced with less labour in the country from which it is obtained than in the country which imports it, but by this, that it may be produced by *comparatively* less labour than some *other* commodity, which is also made the subject of exchange. Thus the essence of the gold discoveries, regarded economically, consisted, as has been said, in the reduction in the cost of raising gold which was thereby effected,—a reduction which, not being shared by other countries, involved a change in the comparative costs of Australian and foreign productions. The consequence of this change has been a corresponding change in the character of her foreign trade, brought about, as we have seen, through an action on money wages. Thus Australia, instead of raising her own corn, as under ordinary circumstances she would do, imports the greater portion of it. If we ask why is this? we shall be told that the price of labour is there so high that she cannot afford to compete with foreign countries. This is true; but why is the price of labour so high in Australia? The answer is, because the cost of gold is so low; the rate of money wages, as we have seen, always rising and falling as the facilities of producing gold increase or diminish.* The true explanation, therefore, of the importation of corn into a country possessing abundant resources for

* Which shows, by the way, the absurdity of attempting to measure the cost of gold, as some writers have done (see Tooke's "History of Prices," vol. vi. p. 226), by the *pecuniary* outlay necessary to its production. The fact is that *this* (so far as *gold* is the money employed) scarcely ever varies; the gold price of producing gold representing merely the ratio of the outlay to the return, or the rate of profit, so that if *price* be taken as the criterion of *cost*, the cost of gold would never vary unless so far as the rate of profit varies.

agriculture is, that she possesses *comparatively* still greater resources for the production of gold; so that she finds it profitable to obtain her corn rather through the medium of her cheap gold, than by its direct production. And the same explanation applies to every circumstance of her recent trade: *e.g.*, previous to the gold discoveries Australia produced her own cheese and butter; she now largely imports these articles.* To what is this change due? The pastures of New South Wales and Victoria offer unusual facilities for dairy-farming, and these facilities have not deteriorated since 1851: the cost of butter now is the same as then; † and yet, with these resources at her disposal, Australia draws her chief supplies of butter from Ireland,—an old and densely peopled country. The explanation of this singular commerce is that which has just been given. The natural facilities possessed by Australia for raising butter, superior though they are to those which we in this country possess, are yet not so much superior as her facilities of raising gold are superior to our means of commanding it. It therefore manifestly becomes her interest to turn her capital and labour to gold-mining, rather than to dairy-farming, and to satisfy her requirements for butter through the medium of that commodity in which her advantage is pre-eminent. By following this course she enjoys the same, or nearly the same, advantage over other countries, in obtaining her butter,

* The sum paid by the colony of Victoria alone to Great Britain on this account in the last year reached the large amount of £800,000.—*Australian and New Zealand Gazette.*

† The reader will bear in mind the distinction between the *cost* and the *price* of production. See *ante*, p. 36, note ‡.

which she enjoys in obtaining her gold, and, strange as it may seem, secures this commodity at less cost—at a smaller sacrifice of ease and leisure—than its production exacts from the Irish farmer who raises it.*

The importance of thus conceiving the commercial effects of the gold discoveries is, that it enables us at once to perceive the precise nature and bounds of the advantage which Australia and California reap from their gold-fields. By means of them they are enabled to obtain their gold at rather less than one-half the sacrifice formerly necessary; and, therefore, unless so far as the purchasing power of the metal has since declined, they can, through the medium of it, obtain all their other commodities on terms proportionally easier. We have seen that, as regards domestic productions, these have all risen in price in the same proportion as gold has fallen in cost, whence it follows that, so far as this portion of their consumption is concerned the gold countries derive no advantage from their cheap gold. They obtain in return for a given sacrifice, twice as much gold as formerly, but they also pay twice as much for every domestic production. With their foreign trade, however, it is otherwise. Prices throughout the world have not risen in the same degree as the cost of gold has been reduced; and consequently upon this portion of their dealings Australia and California are gainers,—gainers directly in proportion to the reduced cost of their gold, modified by the rise, so far as it has taken place, in foreign prices. A given exertion of labour enables them to command, not only

* A possibility which was foreseen and pointed out by Ricardo. See his Works, p. 77.

more gold, but more of every other thing which foreign countries can supply. It is thus exclusively in the foreign branch of their trade that the advantage of their cheap gold resides : it is only *in so far as they part with their money* that they derive from it any benefit; and yet, so completely in Political Economy is the ostensible at variance with the real, and so inveterate, consequently, are the prejudices of mere experience, that the cry of 'Protection' has been heard even in Victoria. It might, perhaps, shake the Victorian protectionist's faith in his doctrine, if he would reflect that his most effectual protection against the foreigner would be the exhaustion of his own gold-fields.

Such have been the results of the discovery of gold on the industry, trade, and general interests of Australia. Let us now observe the light which these conclusions throw on the more general questions connected with this occurrence. And, in the first place, as to the extent of the prospective depreciation. We have seen that, in the disturbance in the value of gold, or, what comes to the same thing, in the gold prices of commodities, which followed the discoveries, there was a point about which the fluctuations moved, and beyond which the advance or decline did not permanently pass. Prices were in the first instance forced upwards through an increased demand for commodities; the increase of demand led to an increase of supply, and this to a reaction in prices towards their former level. In the case of imported commodities this reaction was carried to the full extent of the previous rise, but in domestic products the decline was arrested at a higher point, the further fall being prevented by the check given to production through the high rate of money wages. The natural level of Australian prices, and therefore the value of gold in Australia, was thus determined by the rate of wages measured in gold, and this, as we have seen, was regulated by average earnings on the gold-fields. The rate of gold earnings, or, as this is in technical language expressed, "the cost of gold," is therefore the circumstance which, in the final resort, regulates the value of the metal, and sets the limit beyond which depreciation cannot permanently pass. Now we have seen that in Australia gold wages have, in consequence of the gold discoveries, risen in rather more than a twofold proportion; and since, whether gold is raised from mines or imported in exchange for commodities, gold wages, or the return to labour in gold, will always represent the cost of the metal,* it follows that the cost of gold has been reduced in Australia by the gold discoveries to the extent of about fifty per cent. Fifty per cent., therefore,—equivalent to a twofold advance in prices,—gives the maximum beyond which (on the supposition that no more productive mines are discovered) the general value of gold cannot permanently fall. Further, it has appeared that, although a reduction in the cost of gold tends to cause a corresponding fall in its value, the actual realization of this result depends upon the possibility of so enlarging the circulation as to render this fall possible. Thus we have seen that the price of gold in Australia fell, pending the enlargement of the currency, by the importation of sovereigns from England, which is, in other words, to

* See on this point Senior's Essay "On the Cost of obtaining Money."

say that the value of the currency was, during this period, maintained above its natural cost level. This severance of value from cost was indeed in Australia of brief continuance, because, the local circulation being small, it required but a short time to double, quadruple, or otherwise augment it as the occasion might render necessary. But throughout the world at large, the process of augmentation, owing to the vast dimensions of its currencies, is one necessarily of slow accomplishment, and, pending its fulfilment, the value of gold is of necessity maintained above the level prescribed by its cost. It is this which at present sustains the value of gold in the general markets of commerce, notwithstanding the cheapening of its production effected by the gold discoveries. Whether that value will ever be lowered in the same proportion, whether gold will ever fall throughout the world at large as it has fallen in Australia and California, depends upon whether the conditions which have lowered its value in them can be generally satisfied—that is to say, depends upon *whether the increased supply which such a fall would render necessary can be obtained at the present cost.* Into the further discussion of this question I do not now enter,* the object of this paper being to point out the principal issues which the general problem involves, not to attempt their solution. But from the facts which have been stated, we are justified in concluding that, so long as the present want of conformity between the cost and the value of gold continues, so long a constant premium will exist

* The reader will find some remarks on this aspect of the question in the Fourth Essay, *post*, p. 109 *et seq.*

on its production, and so long our supply of gold will continue to increase.

But, secondly, let us consider what light our conclusions respecting the gold countries throw upon a question which has been much discussed,—I mean the effect of this movement on the real wealth, the substantial well-being, of the world. That the gold discoveries have added to the real wealth of the inhabitants of Australia and California is indeed exceedingly apparent; but what has been their effect upon the interests of other nations? Has the cheapness of Australian or Californian gold added equally to the effectiveness of *their* industry, and extended *their* command over the comforts and enjoyments of life? The answer of some writers to this question has been very strongly in the affirmative; but, with the light derived from the previous discussion, we may perhaps see grounds for arriving at a different conclusion. We have seen that the gain of Australia and California from their gold-fields is confined to that portion of their trade which they carry on with foreign countries; that it is only *in so far as they part with their gold* that they derive from it any benefit. Now the world, as a whole, has no *foreign* trade; it has no means of exchanging for the productions of other planets the gold which it produces; from which it seems to follow that, regarded as a single community, the world is incapable of realizing those conditions on which the benefit to be derived from cheap money depends. The conclusion to which this consideration points is, that the operation of the new gold will be confined to causing a new distribution of real wealth in the world without affecting its aggregate amount; and that, consequently, the gain of the gold countries must be reaped at the expense of other nations.

This conclusion is no doubt much at variance with prevailing notions, and with the deep-seated prejudices of the "mercantile system;" and will not, therefore, be easily admitted. Nevertheless, if we reflect on the character of the commerce which has arisen out of these discoveries, we may see reason for accepting its truth. The trade between the gold countries and the rest of the world is one in which consumable commodities on one side are exchanged against money, or the materials of money, on the other. A large portion of the industry of the world is, through the medium of this trade, employed in ministering to the real wants—the appetites, tastes, and other human needs—of Australia and California. Let us inquire what is the want to which these countries minister in return. It will be said to the want of more gold—the want of an enlarged circulating medium. True; but what is the foundation of this want? and in what way does its satisfaction promote human happiness? Human industry is not rendered more efficient, nor human happiness more full, by the use of two coins instead of one. Why, therefore, may not the business of production and exchange be carried on upon the former terms? I apprehend that the correct answer to this question is that gold—the great medium of exchange and universal equivalent—having been cheapened in Australia and California, these countries of necessity possess an exceptional advantage in their commercial dealings with the rest of the world, until the gold prices of commodities in other countries are proportionally raised, and that to effect this object—to raise the prices of their productions in proportion to the diminished cost of gold—the quantity of their gold circulation must be increased. The nations of the world have thus by the gold discoveries been placed under the necessity of enlarging their currencies; and this can only be accomplished by parting with their productions in exchange for the required supply. Hence the character of the traffic which we are now witnessing,—a traffic in which consumable goods are exchanged for money, and real for nominal wealth. It is therefore no natural want to which this one-sided trade is subservient, no desire, the satisfaction of which adds an iota to human enjoyment: it is merely an artificial requirement, a disagreeable and unprofitable necessity, originating in the gold discoveries, and satisfied at the expense of commercial nations.

I am aware indeed that there are writers who regard gold not simply as a convenient medium for the exchange of commodities independently produced, but as in itself a source of productive energy, as "the motive power of all industry and commerce," * and who accordingly consider "an addition to the quantity of money to be the same thing as an addition to the fixed capital of a country" †—as equivalent in its effects upon industry to "improved harbours, roads, and manufactories." ‡ According to such views the influence of the gold discoveries must be universally

* Seyd's "California and its Resources," p. 5.

† Tooke's "History of Prices," vol. vi. p. 46. ‡ Ibid.

beneficial,—beneficial, not merely in relation to the countries which produce the cheap money, but in a still more eminent degree in relation to those which permanently retain it. But in spite of the plausibilities of the mercantile theory, common sense, no less than economic science, will continue to ask how the world is enriched by parting with its real wealth?—how the well-being of Europe and Asia is promoted by parting with the materials of well-being, receiving in return not materials of well-being, not augmented supplies of wool and tallow, corn and provisions, not those commodities which new countries are specially fitted to produce, and of which old countries are pressingly in need, but what?—increased supplies of the precious metals, a more cumbrous medium of exchange!

So singular and abnormal indeed has been the course of industrial affairs hitherto in the gold countries,—so strange has been the spectacle of a country abounding in resources which she dares not touch, and drawing from other countries commodities which she is specially fitted to produce,—that it has not failed to attract the attention of thoughtful observers, and to suggest the pertinent inquiry, how long is this state of things to continue? Is the development of the great and varied resources of Australia and California to be perpetually subordinated, if not indefinitely postponed, to the single pursuit of gold-mining? Are the other nations of the world destined to continue for ever labouring in the service of the gold countries, for no other than the barren reward of an addition to their circulation? These questions have been frequently put, but I am not aware that they have as yet been satisfactorily answered. The writers who have started them have indeed, correctly enough, connected the present condition of Australian industry with the high price of labour in that country, but they do not seem to perceive very clearly upon what the maintenance of this high price of labour depends. It is commonly spoken of as resulting from the scarcity of workmen, and the inference appears to be made that it will gradually disappear as population increases; but this mode of reasoning arises from confounding the temporary with the permanent causes which regulate wages. India is a less densely peopled country than Great Britain, but the rate of wages in India is many times less than the rate of wages in Great Britain. The fact is, the average rate of money wages in a country is regulated, not by the movements of population, but by the causes which determine for it the cost of its money.* In the gold countries, as we have seen, these causes are the productiveness of industry in raising gold: and, therefore, so long as the present productiveness of the gold-fields is maintained, the rate of money wages in Australia and California cannot fall permanently below its present level. How long this rate of productiveness is likely to last, is a question the discussion of which would carry me entirely beyond the necessary limits of this paper; but on the supposition of its being maintained, we can have no difficulty in discovering the condition on which the industrial development of the gold countries depends.

That condition is briefly this—that prices throughout the world should rise in proportion as the cost of gold

* See Senior's Essay "On the Cost of obtaining Money."

in the gold countries has fallen. So long as the present pecuniary rates of the gold countries are *exceptional*, so long Australian and Californian producers of other commodities than gold will labour under a disadvantage in their competition with gold miners; and so long the non-monetary exports of those countries will be limited to that small class of commodities, in which their advantage over other countries is as great as it is in their command of gold. But with the advance of gold-prices in foreign markets, this class of commodities will be extended. With the fall in the value of money, it will become less profitable to raise and export money; with the rise in the price of other things, it will become more profitable to raise and export them; and a larger share of the whole labour and capital of the country will consequently be turned to the latter purposes. We may illustrate the principle by an actual case. For several years subsequent to the gold discoveries timber was largely imported into Australia from the Baltic; and I perceive that it is still upon the list of her imports. But during all this time there have been within a few miles of the localities where this Baltic timber has been used, extensive forests of gum-trees, inviting the axe of the pioneer, capable of affording timber perfectly suited to the purposes for which timber in the mining districts is principally required. Indeed this gum-tree timber has been freely employed where it could be obtained close to the spot where it was wanted, but rather than go fifty miles to cut it, the Australian workman prefers to import it from the other side of the globe. The explanation of this conduct is the low comparative cost of Australian gold. A day's labour employed in crushing quartz or in digging auriferous clay, enables the Australian to obtain more timber than the same labour employed in felling trees. Every rise in prices, however, in foreign markets, will diminish the cost of gold to the foreigner, and thus lessen the comparative advantage of gold digging: the domestic production will gradually gain upon the foreign trade, and the area over which timber-cutting is profitable will be extended. This process has already taken place to some extent, partly through the rise in the cost of gold, with the exhaustion of some of the richer deposits, partly through the advance in the price of timber in foreign markets; and it will doubtless continue. It is obvious that the same principle will operate equally in the case of every commodity which the gold countries are capable of producing. With every rise in gold prices throughout the world, gold will become a less profitable remittance; other commodities will become more profitable; and this will continue, until either prices throughout the world rise in proportion to the reduction in the cost of gold —that is to say, to double their present amount— or until through the exhaustion of the present gold-fields, gold can no longer be produced at its present cost.*

It will not be till one or other of these contingencies happens, that the industrial development of the gold countries can be fully accomplished, or that the world can derive from their commerce that contribution to its real well-being and happiness, which their great and varied resources render them so competent to yield.

* See Postscript, p. 50.

POSTSCRIPT.

The history of the Australian trade since this essay was written furnishes so striking an illustration of the views put forward in this paragraph, that perhaps I may be pardoned for referring to it. During the whole of this time, the double process referred to—the gradual exhaustion of the richer gold-fields, and the simultaneous rise in prices throughout the world external to the gold countries—has been in operation; and every step in the movement has witnessed some new development of Australian industry. Thus, while between 1856 * and 1870 the production of gold in Victoria had fallen from 11,943,000*l.* to 6,119,000*l.*, or to a little more than one-half of its former amount, the non-monetary exports of the colony had increased from 3,546,000*l.* in 1856 to 6,351,000*l.* in 1870; the increase taking place chiefly in wool, tallow, and preserved meats. But the effect of the double process of failing gold mines and rising prices in foreign countries has been felt, up to the present, far less in increasing the number and the amount of exports than in curtailing those of imports, and in developing domestic production. The foreign trade of Victoria presents the singular and almost unique spectacle of a steady decline in its amount over a period marked by an extraordinarily rapid growth of population and general wealth. I have no returns of the population of that colony for 1856 (the date at which the commercial statistics begin).

* I commence with 1856, this being the first year of the publication of "The Statistical Abstract for the Colonies," from the last number of which (1872) the figures in the text are taken.

but it was probably between 300,000 and 400,000; in 1861, it was 541,000, and in 1870, 729,000; in other words the population must have nearly doubled itself in these sixteen years; the general prosperity of the country during the same time being almost unexampled. But the noteworthy circumstance is, that while the country was thus prospering, its external trade was undergoing constant contraction, falling from a total of 15,489,000*l.* in 1856, to 12,470,000*l.* in 1870. The fact, I may mention in passing, shows how little the foreign trade of a country, as measured by its exports and imports, furnishes a correct criterion of its industrial progress or growth in real wealth. The explanation of the phenomenon is that which I have given in the foregoing essay: with every decline in the productiveness of the mines, and with every advance in foreign prices, the gain on importation decreased and home production became relatively more profitable. The result has been that, from being a large importer of breadstuffs, butter, beer, boots and shoes, provisions, spirits, &c., Victoria has either discontinued altogether or greatly curtailed her importation of all these commodities, which she now produces from her own internal resources. Is this course of development for the advantage of Victoria? Plainly, I think, if we have regard to her general interests, social and political as well as pecuniary, we must answer in the affirmative; though, as economists, we must also recognize that, looking at the question from a purely material standpoint, this affirmation cannot be made good; since it is certainly a fact that the diminishing returns of her gold-mines have deprived her of that command of foreign markets which she formerly possessed; while the resort to her own fields of production in lieu of foreign markets, being as it is a *dernier ressort*, cannot but indicate a diminishing productiveness of her general industry. But whatever may be the interests of Victoria herself in this matter, as regards the interests of other countries the case is clear. Had her gold-mines continued as rich and productive as they were during the first few years following the discoveries, and had gold prices through the world remained at the then level, Victoria would have continued to export gold in quantities ever increasing as her population and capital increased, for which the world would have had to pay in the commodities of real wealth. In return for the products of their labour in the form of the conveniences and comforts of life, foreign countries would have gained an addition to their circulation. Instead of this, their industry is now being gradually relieved from this task of adding to their currencies, while the returns on their trade, no longer consisting of barren metal, take the form of increasing supplies of wool, tallow, and meat.

II.

ESSAY TOWARDS A SOLUTION OF THE GOLD QUESTION.*

THE COURSE OF DEPRECIATION.

No one, I think, who has attended to the discussions occasioned by the recent gold discoveries, can have failed to observe, on the part of a large number of those who engage in them, a strange unwillingness to recognize, amongst the inevitable consequences of those events, a fall in the value of money. I say, a strange unwillingness, because we do not find similar doubts to exist in any corresponding case. With respect to all other commodities, it is not denied that whatever facilitates production promotes cheapness—that less will be given for objects when they can be attained with less trouble and sacrifice: it is not denied, *e.g.*, that the steam-engine, the spinning-jenny, and the mule have lowered the value of our manufactures; that railways and steamships have lessened the expense of travelling: or that the superior agricultural resources of foreign countries, made available through free-trade, keep down the price of our agricultural

* Read before the British Association, September 1858.

products. It is only in the case of the precious metals that it is supposed that a diminution of cost has no tendency to lower value, and that, however rapidly supply may be increased, a given quantity will continue to command the same quantity of other things as before.

Amongst persons unacquainted with economic science, the prevalence of this opinion is doubtless principally due to those ambiguities of language, and consequent confusion of ideas, with which our monetary phraseology unfortunately abounds, many of which tend to encourage the notion of some peculiar and constant stability in the value of the precious metals. Thus, the expression "a fixed price of gold" has led some people to imagine that the possibility of a depreciation of this metal is precluded by our Mint regulations. The double sense, again, of the phrase, "value of money," has countenanced the same error; for people, perceiving the rate of interest (which is the measure of the value of money in one sense of the phrase) remaining high, while the supply of gold was rapidly increasing—perceiving money still scarce according to this criterion, notwithstanding the increase in its production—have asked whether this did not afford a presumption that its value would be permanently preserved from depreciation; a bank rate of discount at 6, 8, or 10 per cent., as they remarked, affording small indication of money becoming too abundant.

It appears to me, however, that misconceptions respecting the influence of an increased supply of gold upon its value and upon general prices are by no means confined to the class who could be misled by such fallacies, but that even among economists (at least among economists in this country) we may observe the same indisposition to believe in an actual and progressive depreciation of this metal. It is not indeed denied—at least, I presume it is not denied—by anyone pretending to economic knowledge, that the enlarged production of gold now taking place has a tendency to lower its value; but it seems to be very generally supposed that the same cause—the increased gold production—has the effect, through its influence on trade, of calling into operation so many tendencies of a contrary nature, that, on the whole, the depreciation must proceed with extreme slowness, the results being dispersed over a period so great as to take from them any practical importance, and that, at all events, up to the present time no sensible effect upon prices proceeding from this cause has become perceptible.

The existence of this opinion amongst economists is, I apprehend, to be attributed in some degree to the circumstance that so few have taken the pains to compare the actual prices of the present time with those of the period previous to the gold discoveries, but much more to the fact, that the character of the new agency and the mode of its operation are not in general correctly conceived. I believe the most general opinion with reference to the action of an increased supply of money upon its value is, that it is uniform—takes place, that is to say, in the same degree in relation to all commodities and services, and that therefore prices, so far as they are influenced by an increase of money, must exhibit a uniform advance;* and, no such uniformity being observed in the actual movements of prices, the inference has not unnaturally been drawn, that such enhancement as has taken place is not due to this cause; that it is not money which has fallen, but commodities which have risen in value.

Now I am quite prepared to admit that an increase of money tends ultimately, where the conditions of production remain in other respects the same, to affect the prices of all commodities and services in an equal degree; but before this result is attained a period of time, longer or shorter according to the amount of the augmentation and the general circumstances of commerce, must elapse. In the present instance the additions which are being made to the monetary systems of the world are upon an enormous scale, and the disturbance effected in the relation of prices is proportionally great. Under such circumstances it is very possible that the inequalities resulting may not find their correction throughout the whole period of progressive depreciation; a period which, even with our present facilities of production and distribution, may easily extend over some thirty or forty years. During this transitionary term the action of the new gold on prices will not be uniform, but partial. Certain classes

* "In relation to the influence of the gold discoveries on the prices of agricultural produce, it is plain that it could be only the same upon them as upon those of any other class of commodities. *If it has caused a rise of 20 per cent. in their favour, it must have caused a rise of 20 per cent. in everything else.*"—*Times*, City article, August 6, 1852. And the same assumption, either expressed or implied, runs through most of the reasoning which I have seen on this question.

of commodities and services will be affected much more powerfully than others. Prices generally will rise, but with unequal steps. Nevertheless there will be in these apparent irregularities nothing either capricious or abnormal. The movement will be governed throughout its course by economic laws; and it is the purpose of the present inquiry to ascertain the nature of these laws and the mode of their operation.

The process by which an increased production of gold operates in depreciating the value of the metal and raising general prices appears to be twofold: it acts, first, *directly* through the medium of an enlarged money demand, and, secondly, *indirectly* through a contraction of supply.*

When an increased amount of money comes into existence, there is, of course, an increased expenditure on the part of those into whose possession it comes, the immediate effect of which is to raise the prices of all commodities which fall under its influence. It is obvious, however, that the advance in price which thus occurs will be, in its full extent, temporary only; since it is immediately followed by an extension of production to meet the increased demand, and this must again lead to a fall in price. Some writers who have treated this question, observing this effect, have somewhat hastily concluded that under the operation of this

* According to Mr. Newmarch ("History of Prices," vol. vi. pp. 224-25) the depreciation of money may occur by a process which is neither of these, when money operates upon prices neither through demand nor yet through supply, but "by reason of augmented quantity." I must confess myself wholly unable to conceive the process here indicated.

principle the level of prices would never permanently be altered, since, as they have urged, each addition to the circulating medium, forming the basis of a corresponding increase of demand, gives a corresponding impetus to production; every increase of money thus calls into existence an equivalent augmentation in the quantity of things to be circulated; and the proportion between the two not being ultimately disturbed, prices, it may be presumed, will return to their original level.* The least reflection, however, will show that this doctrine has been suggested by a very superficial view of the phenomena.

For—not to press the obvious *reductio ad absurdum* to which this argument is liable—how is this extension of production to be carried out? In the last resort it is only possible through a more extended employment of labour. But, when once all the hands in a community are employed, the effect of a further competition for labour can only be to raise wages; and, wages once being generally raised, it is plain (supposing all other things to remain the same) that profits can only be maintained by a corresponding elevation of prices. When, therefore, the influence

* [It may be worth while to preserve a specimen of the sort of Political Economy that was talked and written on this subject some fifteen years ago. A leading article in the *Examiner* (December 13, 1856) contains the following:—"The additional supply of the precious metals has stimulated the industry of the world, and in fact produced an amount of wealth in representing which they have been themselves, as it were, absorbed." . . . . "But the produce of the Australian and Californian gold, as well as that of silver which has accompanied it, is likely to go on; and it may be asked if this must not in course of time produce depreciation. We think it certainly is not likely to do so; . . . . on the contrary, it will surely be absorbed by increasing wealth and population as fast as it is produced."]

of the new money has once reached wages, it is evident that there will be no motive to continue production to that point which would bring prices to their former level, and that consequently an elevation of price must, at this stage of the proceeding, be permanently established.

So far as regards articles which fall *directly* under the action of the new money. With respect to those which do not happen to come within the range of the new demand, price is, I conceive, in their case raised by an indirect action of the new money in curtailing supply.

We have seen that the effect of the efforts to extend production in the directions indicated by the new expenditure must be to raise wages; but it is plainly impossible that wages should continue to advance in any of the principal departments of industry without affecting their rates in the rest; whence it will happen that, under the operation of the new monetary influence, some departments of industry will experience a rise of wages before any advance takes place in the prices of the commodities produced by the labourers whose wages have risen. It is evident that in all departments of industry which may be thus affected—in which prices will not have shared the advance which has affected wages—profits will fall below the general average; the effect of which must be to discourage production until, by a contraction in the supply of the articles thus furnished, the price shall be raised up to that point which will place the producers on the same footing of advantage as those in other walks of industry.

An increased supply of money thus tends, by one mode of its operation, to raise prices in advance of wages, and thus to stimulate production; by another, to raise wages in advance of prices, and thus to check it; in both, however, to raise wages, and thus ultimately to render necessary, in order to the maintenance of profits, a general and permanent elevation of price.*

This being the process by which increased supplies of money operate in raising prices, in order to ascertain the laws of their advance we must attend, first, to the direction of the new expenditure; secondly, to the facilities for extending the supply of different kinds of commodities; and, thirdly, to the facilities for contracting it.

With regard to the first point—the direction of the new expenditure—this will naturally be determined by the habits and tastes of the persons into whose possession the new money comes. These persons are the inhabitants of the gold countries, and, after them, those in other countries who can best supply their wants. Speaking broadly, we may say that the persons who will chiefly benefit by the gold

* It must not be supposed that this is inconsistent with the fundamental doctrine maintained by Ricardo, that "high wages do not make high prices." That doctrine assumes the value of money to be constant. Ricardo was quite aware of the exception to the general principle, and points it out in the following passage :—

"Money, being a variable commodity, the rise of money-wages will be frequently occasioned by a fall in the value of money. A rise of wages *from this cause* will, indeed, be invariably accompanied by a rise in the price of commodities; but in such cases it will be found that labour and all commodities have not varied in regard to each other, and that the variation has been confined to money."—RICARDO'S *Works* (Second Edition), p. 31.'

discoveries belong to the middle and lower ranks of society; in a large degree to the lowest rank, the class of unskilled labourers. The direction of the new expenditure will consequently be that indicated by the habits and tastes of these classes, and the commodities which will be most affected by it will be those which fall most largely within their consumption.

With respect, secondly, to facilities for extending supply, these will be found to depend principally upon two circumstances: first, on the extent to which machinery is employed in production; and, secondly, on the degree in which the process of production is independent of natural agencies which require time for accomplishing their ends. The distinction marked by these two conditions, it will be found, corresponds pretty accurately with two other distinctions—with the distinction, namely, between raw and manufactured products; and, amongst raw products, with that between those derived from the animal and those derived from the vegetable kingdom. An article of finished manufacture, in the production of which machinery bears a principal part, and which is independent, or nearly so, of natural processes, may after a short notice be rapidly multiplied to meet any probable extension of demand. An article of raw produce, being in a less degree under the dominion of machinery, and depending more upon natural processes which require time for their accomplishment, cannot be increased with the same facility; and production will consequently, in this case, be comparatively slow in overtaking an extension of demand. But of raw products, those derived from the animal are still less under the dominion of machinery than those derived from the vegetable kingdom, and still more dependent on the slow processes of nature, and, consequently, production must in their case be still more tardy in overtaking demand. Supposing, then, the extension of demand to be in all three cases the same, the immediate rise of price will, *cæteris paribus*, be in all the same; but in the case of articles of finished manufacture, this rise will be quickly corrected by the facilities available for increased production, while in raw vegetable products the correction will take place more slowly, and in raw animal products more slowly still.*

But, thirdly, I said that the progress of prices under

* The following passage occurs in the "History of Prices," vol. vi. p. 170:—"The groups of commodities which exhibit the most important instances of a rise of price are the raw materials most extensively used in manufactures, and the production of which does not admit of rapid extension; and, second, the groups of commodities in which there is little, if any, rise of price in 1857, as compared with 1851, are articles of colonial and tropical produce, the supply of which drawn from a variety of sources does admit of being considerably and expeditiously enlarged." The *fact* of the rise of price in raw materials is here admitted, though, in ascribing that rise, as by implication the passage does, to the paucity of the sources of supply, the explanation is, as I conceive, erroneous. The sources, *e.g.*, from which tea and sugar are drawn are not more various than, nor indeed so various as, those from which beef and mutton, butter and provisions, timber, tallow, and leather are drawn; yet all these latter articles have very considerably advanced in price. Again, amongst colonial and tropical produce Mr. Newmarch includes rum and tobacco, and he might also have included cotton; yet these articles, though falling within the class which he says admits of being expeditiously enlarged, and which therefore, according to his theory, should *not* have risen in price, *have in fact risen* in a very marked manner. It appears to me that these phenomena can only be understood by reference to the principle which I have endeavoured to explain further on—namely, the efficacy of the currency of different countries in determining local prices.

the influence of the gold supplies would be governed by the facility with which supply can be contracted. Everyone who has practical experience of manufacturing operations is aware that, when capital has once been embarked in any branch of production, it cannot at once be removed to a different one the moment the needs of society may require a change; whence it happens that, on any sudden change taking place in the direction of a nation's expenditure, or when from miscalculation production has been extended beyond existing wants, producers frequently choose to continue their business at diminished profits, or even at a positive loss, rather than incur still greater damage by suffering their capital to lie idle, or by attempting to transfer it suddenly into some new branch of production. The supply of a commodity is not therefore always, or generally, at once contracted on the demand for it falling off, or on its production becoming less profitable, and, where this is so, it is evident that prices must at times continue depressed below the normal level; the duration of the depression depending on the length of time required to effect a transference of the unproductive capital to some more lucrative investment. Now the difficulty of accomplishing this will generally be in direct proportion to the amount of fixed capital employed; and the principal form in which fixed capital exists is that of machinery. It is, therefore, in articles in the production of which machinery is extensively employed—that is to say, in the more highly finished manufactures—that the contraction of supply will be most difficult; and this, it will be observed, is also the kind of commodities for extending the supply of which the facilities are greatest. While, therefore, manufactured articles can never be very long in advance of the general movement of prices, they may, of all commodities, be the longest in arrear of it.

The operation of this principle will be shown chiefly in that class of articles which feels the effect of the new gold only through its indirect action—that is to say, through its action upon wages. With respect to such articles there is no extension of demand, and the price consequently can only be raised through a contraction of supply. It is evident that of all commodities this is the class in which the rise of price must proceed most slowly.

From the foregoing considerations, then, I arrive at the following general conclusions:—

First.—That the commodities, the price of which may be expected first to rise under the influence of the new money, are those which fall most extensively within the consumption of the productive classes, but more particularly within the consumption of the labouring and artisan section of these.

Secondly.—That of such commodities, that portion which consists of finished manufactures, though their price may in the first instance be rapidly raised, cannot continue long in advance of the general movement, owing to the facilities available for rapidly extending the supply; whereas, should the production, from over-estimation of the increasing requirements, be once carried to excess, their prices, in consequence of the difficulty of contracting supply, may be kept for some considerable time below the normal level.

Thirdly.—That such raw products as fall within the consumption of the classes indicated, not being susceptible of the same rapid extension as manufactures, may continue for some time in advance of the general movement, and that, among raw products, the effects will be more marked in those derived from the animal than in those derived from the vegetable kingdom.

Fourthly.—That the commodities last to feel the effects of the new money, and which may be expected to rise most slowly under its influence, are those articles of finished manufacture which do not happen to fall within the range of the new expenditure; such articles being affected only by its indirect action, and this action being in their case obstructed by impediments to the contraction of supply.

This is one class of laws by which I conceive the ascending movement in prices will be governed; and up to this point I have the satisfaction of finding my conclusions very fully corroborated by the independent investigations of a French economist, M. Levasseur, who, in some articles lately contributed by him to the *Journal des Économistes*, has, by an entirely different line of investigation from that which I have followed—namely, by generalizing on the statistics of prices in France during the period of 1847 to 1856—arrived at conclusions in the main points identical with those which I have now advanced.*

There is, however, another principle to which I venture to call attention, which has not, so far as I know, been noticed by any of the economists who have

* See Appendix, for a summary of M. Levasseur's conclusions.

treated this question, but which, it appears to me, must exercise a powerful influence on the course of the movement. The principle to which I refer is that efficacy which resides in the currency of each country, into which any portion of the new money may be received, for determining the effect of this infusion on the range of local prices.

It is evident that the quantity of metallic money necessary to support any required advance of prices throughout a given range of business will vary with the character of the currency into which it is received; that the quantity required will be greater in proportion as the metallic element of the currency is greater; and, on the other hand, less in proportion as the credit element prevails. If the currency of a country be purely metallic, a given addition of coin will increase the aggregate medium of exchange in that country only by the same amount; if, on the other hand, the currency consist largely of credit contrivances, each addition to its coin becomes the basis of a new superstructure of credit in the form of bank-notes and credits, bills of exchange, cheques, &c., and the aggregate circulation is increased not simply by the amount of the added coin, but by the extent of the new fabric of credit of which this coin is made the foundation. Applying this principle to the different countries of the world, it follows that a given addition to the metallic stock of Great Britain or the United States, in whose monetary systems credit is very efficacious, will cause a greater expansion of the total circulation, and therefore will support a greater advance in general prices, than the same addition to the currency of countries like France, in which credit is less active; and that, again, the effect in countries like France will be greater than in countries like India or China, in which the currencies are almost purely metallic, and where credit is comparatively little used.

Now, this being so, if we consider further that the countries which receive in the first instance the largest share of the new money—namely, England and the United States—are also those in which from the character of their currencies a given amount of coin will produce the greatest effect; and, on the other hand, that Asiatic communities, in which from the weakness of the credit element the currencies are least expansible, receive but a small portion of their share of the new money direct from the gold countries;* being compelled to wait for the remainder till it has flowed through the principal markets of Europe and America, affecting prices in its transit;—if, I say, we consider these facts in connection with the principle to which I have adverted, I think we must recognize in that principle—in the influence of the currency of

* [From statistics recently furnished by the *Economist*, I learn that the facts have not been as I here assumed, at least since 1858 (the date from which full returns of specie imports have been published by the Board of Trade); and it is probable I was mistaken in my supposition with regard to what had occurred before that time. Since 1858, of 90,000,000*l.* of gold received and retained by India and the East, some 49,000,000*l.*, more than a half of the whole, appear to have gone there *directly* from Australia, the remainder only having come through Europe. This error as to matter of fact will, no doubt, affect to some extent the conclusion contended for. The causes tending to a divergence of European from Asiatic prices have not been, it seems, as powerful as I had supposed; and, in point of fact, this feature in the movement has been less marked than I sketched it; but for this, other causes besides that noticed here have been responsible (1872). See Introductory Chapter, p. 12.]

each country on the range of its local prices—an agency which must modify in no small degree the general character of the movement which is now in progress.

In speaking of the influence of the currency of a country on the range of its local prices, I should explain that I use the words "local prices" in a somewhat restricted sense—namely, with reference to the locality in which commodities are *produced*, not to that in which they are sold, their price in the latter place being always determined by their price in the former. Thus, when I speak of Australian, English, or Indian prices, I shall be understood to mean the prices of their several products in Australia, England, or India.

Understanding the words, then, in this sense, let us see how far local prices are likely to be affected by the cause to which I have adverted.

In the first place, then, let it be observed that a very remarkable divergence of local prices from the range previously obtaining in the international scale has already taken place.* The prices of all articles *produced* in Australia and California are at present on an average from two to three times higher than those which prevailed previous to the gold discoveries; these rates have now been maintained for several years, and are likely to continue: but, while this advance has taken place in the gold countries, in no part of the world external to those regions have prices advanced by so much as one-third. The possibility of a divergence of local prices is thus, as a matter of fact, established; and the explanation of the phenomenon I take to be

* See *ante*, pp. 24, 25.

this. The sudden cheapening of gold in Australia and California quickly led, through the action of competition amongst the different departments of industry, to a corresponding advance in the prices of everything produced in those countries; *this advance being in their case possible*, because, from the limited extent of the transactions, the local circulation was quickly raised to the point sufficient to sustain a double or triple elevation; but it was impossible that the currencies of all countries should be expanded in the same proportions in the same time; and, consequently, prices in other countries have not risen with the same rapidity. The cause, therefore, of this divergence of local prices—the circumstance which keeps general prices in arrear of that elevation which they have attained in Australia and California—is the difficulty of expanding the currencies of the world to those dimensions which such an advance would require. This expansion, however, is being gradually effected by the process we are now witnessing,—the increased production of the precious metals, and their diffusion throughout the world. But, as I have said, the diffusion is not uniform over the various currencies, nor are the currencies receiving the new supplies of uniform susceptibility; and the inequalities are such as to aggravate each other; the currencies which are the most sensitive to an increase of the precious metals receiving in the first instance nearly the whole of the new gold; while the least sensitive currencies are the last to receive their share. And these, it appears to me, are grounds for expecting amongst other countries further examples of that phenomenon of local divergence, of which one has already been afforded by the gold countries.

To judge, however, of the extent to which such local variations of price can be carried, we must advert to the corrective influences which the play of international dealings calls into action; and these appear to me to resolve themselves into the two following:—namely, first, the corrective which is supplied by the competition of different nations, producers of the same commodities, in neutral markets; and, secondly, that which exists in the reciprocal demand of the different commercial countries for each other's productions.

The first form of the corrective is obviously the most powerful, and must, so far as its operation extends, at once impose a check upon any serious divergence. Thus it is evident that prices in England and the United States could not proceed very much in advance of prices on the continent of Europe, since the certain effect of such an occurrence would be to send consumers from the dearer to the cheaper markets, and thus to divert the tide of gold from the currencies of England and America to the currencies of France, Germany, and other continental states,—a process which would be continued until prices were restored to nearly the same relative level as before. But it is only amongst nations which are competitors in the same description of commodities that this equalizing process comes into operation: as between countries like England and America on the one hand, and India and China on the other—in which the climate, soil, and general physical conditions differ widely, in which consequently the staple industries are different, and whose productions do not, therefore, come into competition in the markets of the world—this corrective influence would be felt slightly or not at all. The only check which could be counted on in this case would be that far weaker one which is furnished by the action of reciprocal demand in international dealings. Thus, supposing prices to rise more rapidly in England than in India, this must lead, on the one hand, to an increased expenditure in England on Indian commodities, and, on the other, to a diminished expenditure in India on English commodities, with this result—a steady efflux of the precious metals from the former to the latter country. Such an efflux, as commercial men are well aware, has long been a normal phenomenon in our Eastern trade, but it has lately assumed dimensions which constitute it a new fact needing a special explanation. I believe that explanation is to be found in the circumstances to which I am calling attention.

English and American prices, and with them money incomes in England and America, have, under the action of the new gold, been advancing more rapidly than prices and incomes in Oriental countries; and the result has been a change in the relative indebtedness of those two parts of the world, leading to a transfer to the creditor country of corresponding amounts of that material which forms the universal equivalent of commerce. It is true, indeed, that other causes have also contributed to this result, and in particular I may mention the failure of the silk crop in Europe, which has largely thrown us upon China, as a means of supplementing our deficient supplies. But the main cause of the phenomenon in its present proportions is, I conceive, to be found, not in any such mere temporary disturbances, but in the natural overflowing (consequent upon the increase of the precious metals) of the redundant currencies of Europe and America into the more absorbent and impassive systems of Asia.* This, then, I say, is the only substantial corrective afforded to the advance of prices in Europe and America beyond their former and normal level in relation to prices in the East; and the question is, will this corrective be sufficient to neutralize the tendency to a divergence? Will the flow of the precious metals from West to East suffice to keep prices in England and America within the range prescribed by the inelastic metallic systems of Asia? I do not conceive that the corrective will be adequate to this end, and I rest this conclusion upon the facts and principles which I have stated—the vast proportion of the whole gold production which finds its way in the first instance into the markets of England and America, the comparatively small portion which goes direct to the markets of Asia,† the highly elastic and expansible currencies of the former coun-

* Accordingly we find that the drain which, during the revulsion of trade following on the commercial crisis of 1857, had for a while ceased, has, with the revival of trade, recommenced. As a proof how little mere practical sagacity is to be trusted in a question of this kind, it may be worth while to mention that, only three months since, mercantile writers were confidently predicting *the turning of the tide of silver from the East to England.* The following is from a circular of Messrs. Ellisen & Co., quoted in the *Times'* City article, July 28th, 1858, apparently with the editor's approval:—"The time is rapidly approaching when silver will also be shipped from here (China) to England." So far from this being the case, the drain to the East has again set in, and gives every indication of assuming its former dimensions. Every mail to India during the present month (November 1858) has taken out large amounts of silver.

† See *ante*, p. 67, note *.

tries, and the extremely impassive and inexpansible currencies of the latter.

We find, therefore, two sets of laws by which the progress of prices, or (which comes to the same thing) the depreciation of gold under the action of an increased supply, is regulated: first, those which I explained in the earlier portion of this paper, which depend chiefly on the facility with which the supply of commodities can be adjusted to such changes in demand as the new money expenditure may occasion; and, secondly, those which result from the action of the new money on the currencies into which it is received. According to the former principle, the rise in price follows the nature of the commodity affected; thus it will in general be greater in animal than in vegetable productions—in raw produce than in finished manufactures. According to the latter principle, the advance follows the economic conditions of the locality in which the commodity is produced. Thus the rise in price has been most rapid in commodities produced in the gold countries; having in these at a single bound reached its utmost limit—the limit set by the cost of procuring gold. After commodities produced in the gold regions, the advance I conceive will proceed most rapidly in the productions of England and the United States; after these, at no great interval, in the productions of the continent of Europe, while the commodities the last to feel the effects of the new money, and which will advance most slowly under its influence, are the productions of India and China, and, I may add, of tropical countries generally, so far as these share, as regards their economic conditions, the general character of the former countries.

Such appear to be the general principles according to which a depreciation of the precious metals, under the action of an increased supply, tends to establish itself. With a view to ascertain how far, in the progress of prices up to the present time (1858), any trace of their operation can be discerned, I have drawn up some statistical tables;* and, although from the imperfect nature of the materials which I have been able to collect, I cannot claim for the result a complete verification of the theoretic conclusions which I have ventured to advance, I think they are such as to justify me in placing some confidence in the general soundness of those views. Before, however, stating the results of the tables, two or three remarks must be premised.

First, I would crave attention to this fact, that the present time [1858] is one singularly free from disturbing influences, and that such as do exist are of a kind rather to conceal than to exaggerate the effects of depreciation. Thus, we have had three harvests in succession, of, I believe, more than average productiveness (the last year of deficiency being 1855); and this cause of abundance has been assisted by free trade, which has opened our ports to the produce of all quarters of the world. Again, although in the period under review we have passed through a European war, yet we have now enjoyed two years and a half of peace, during which, I think, the economic influences of the war may be taken to have exhausted themselves.

* See Appendix.

It is true, indeed, that we have an Indian revolt still on hands, besides having but just concluded some hostile operations in China. But these disturbances have not been of a kind to interfere seriously with the general course of trade, except in some few Oriental commodities in which their effects are slightly apparent.

But what renders the present time peculiarly important as a point of comparison with former periods, is its being in immediate sequence to a severe commercial crisis. The effect of the crisis of last winter has been effectually to eliminate one great disturbing element from those causes to which a rise of price might be attributed—the element of credit. Trade is now suffering depression in almost all its branches; and prices, after a period of undue inflation, have, through an ordeal of bankruptcy, been brought to the test of real value. In the fluctuations of commerce we have reached the lowest point of the wave; whatever, therefore, be the range of prices at the present time, we may at least be sure that no commercial convulsion is likely to lower it.

We have further to remember that in an age like the present, in which science and its applications to the arts are in all civilized countries making rapid strides, there exists in most articles of general consumption (but more particularly in the more finished manufactures) a constant tendency to a decline of price, through the employment of more efficient machinery and improved processes of production. Now, taking all these circumstances together,—the propitiousness of the seasons, the action of free-trade, the absence of war, the contraction of credit, and the general tendency to a reduction of cost proceeding from the progress of knowledge,—it appears to me that, were there no other cause in operation, we should have reason to look for a very considerable fall of prices at the present time, as compared with (say) eight or ten years ago. Prices, however, as the following tables will show, have not fallen; they have on the contrary very decidedly risen, and the advance has moreover, as the same tables will also show, on the whole proceeded in conformity with the principles which I have in this paper endeavoured to establish. And this is my ground for asserting that the depreciation of our standard money is already, under the action of the new gold, an accomplished fact.

III.

ESSAY TOWARDS A SOLUTION OF THE GOLD QUESTION.

*INTERNATIONAL RESULTS.**

In a former essay† it was attempted, from a review of the industrial history of Australia since the late discovery of gold, to make some general deductions respecting the character of that event, and of its influence upon national interests. Among other conclusions it was maintained that the tendency of the gold discoveries, or, to speak with more precision, the tendency of the increased production of gold, was rather to alter the distribution of real wealth in the world than to increase its amount; the benefit derived by some countries and classes from the event being for the most part obtained at the expense of others. It was shown, for example, that the gain to Australia and California from their gold-fields accrued to them exclusively through their foreign trade—their cheap gold enabling them to command on easier terms than formerly all foreign productions; while, on the other hand, the only result to foreign nations of the traffic

* *Fraser's Magazine*, January 1860.
† Essay I. of this Series.

thence arising was an increase in their stock of money —a result rendered necessary indeed by the new conditions of raising gold introduced by the gold discoveries, but in itself destitute of any real utility. It was shown, in short, that, as regards commercial nations, the effect of the gold discoveries was to place them under the necessity of enlarging their currencies, compelling them to pay for the requisite increase by an increased export of their productions.

To this conclusion I was led by direct inference from the facts presented in the gold countries. In the present paper it is proposed to follow up the inquiry, with a view to a more particular ascertainment of the consequences formerly described; the object being to discover in what manner the loss arising from the gold movement is likely to be distributed among commercial nations, and how far this loss may in particular cases be neutralized or compensated by other influences which the same movement may develop.

In the discussions which have hitherto taken place upon this question, the inquiry into the consequences of the gold discoveries has been confined almost exclusively to that aspect of the event in which it is regarded as affecting fixed contracts through a depreciation of the monetary standard.* As soon as the probability of depreciation is settled, and the effects of

* See Stirling's "Gold Discoveries and their probable Consequences;" Chevalier "On the probable Fall in the Value of Gold;" Levasseur's contributions to the *Journal des Économistes*, 1858; M'Culloch's article 'Precious Metals,' in the "Encyclopædia Britannica." In all these, and in many other minor productions on the same subject, almost the only consequences of the gold discoveries which are taken account of are those which occur in fixed contracts through a depreciation of the standard.

this upon the different classes of society, according as they happen to be debtors or creditors under fixed contracts, explained, the subject for the most part is considered as exhausted. I venture, however, to think that this mode of treatment is very far from exhausting the question. It seems to me that, independently altogether of the existence of fixed contracts, independently even of gold being a standard of value, the increased production of this metal which is now taking place will be attended—indeed has already been attended—with very important results. Let us observe for a moment the movement which is now in progress. Australia and California have during the last eight or ten years sent into general circulation some two hundred millions sterling of gold. Of this vast sum portions have penetrated to the most remote quarters of the world; but the bulk of it has been received into the currencies of Europe and the United States, from which it has largely displaced the silver formerly circulating; the latter metal, as it has become free, flowing off into Asia, where it is permanently absorbed. Viewing the effect as it occurs in the mass of the two metals combined, it may be said that the stream which rises in the gold regions of Australia and California flows through the currencies of the United States and Europe, and, after saturating the trade of these countries, finally loses itself in the hoards of China and Hindostan. The tide which comes to light in the sands and rocks of the auriferous regions, disappears in the accumulations of the East. In conjunction, however, with this movement there has been a counter one. With every advance in the metallic tide, a stream of commodities has set in in the opposite direction along the same course,—a stream which, issuing from the ports of Europe, America, and Asia, and depositing as it proceeds a portion of the wealth with which it is charged, finds its termination in the markets of the gold countries. Here, then, we find a vast disturbance in the conditions of national wealth,—a disturbance originating in the gold discoveries, and resulting in a transfer, on an enormous scale, of consumable goods—the means of well-being—from one side of the globe to the other. This disturbance, it is evident, is entirely independent of the accident that gold happens to be in some countries a standard of value, as well as of the existence of fixed money-contracts; for it includes within the range of its influence countries in which gold is not, no less than those in which it is, the monetary standard; and it affects alike persons whose bargains are made from day to day, and those who engage in contracts extending over centuries. The fact is, the movement in question is the result, not of gold's being a standard of value, but of its being a source of purchasing power; and the influence of the gold discoveries having been hitherto regarded almost exclusively with reference to the former function, the vast effects which they are producing through the action of the latter—that is to say, by altering the distribution of purchasing power in the world—have been almost wholly overlooked. It has indeed been perceived that a great influx of the precious metals is taking place, accompanied with certain consequences on the trade of the world; but so far as I know, beyond some general phrases respecting the stimulus given to production by an increase of money, and the great development of commerce which it is causing, no attempt has yet been made to state the principles by which the movement is governed, or the effects which may flow from it. It is to these questions, then, that I would now solicit the reader's attention, and towards their solution the following remarks are offered as a contribution.

Those who have followed the course of this controversy are aware that, by most persons who have taken part in it, it has been assumed, almost as an axiom, that no depreciation of gold in consequence of the gold discoveries has, up to the present time, taken place.* As a matter of fact, however, we know that the gold prices of all commodities produced in Australia and California have risen in at least a twofold proportion; † while we have seen that (so long as the conditions of producing gold remain as at present) this rise must be permanent. To express the same thing differently:—in the purchase of every commodity raised in the gold countries two sovereigns are now required, and (the above conditions being fulfilled) will continue to be required, where one was formerly sufficient; and if this does not amount to a fall in the

* The principal exceptions to this statement are M. Levasseur (who, in an article in the *Journal des Économistes*, March 1858, estimates the rise of prices in France since 1847 at 20 per cent. on all commodities), and Dr. Soetbeer of Hamburg, who, in his table of prices given in his "Contributions to the Statistics of Prices in Hamburg," arrives at a similar result (see Appendix). Many other writers, indeed, acknowledge that prices have risen, but the rise is always attributed to causes distinct from the increased production of gold.

† See *ante*, p. 24.

value of gold, I must confess myself unable to understand the meaning of that expression. It is not to be supposed that so remarkable a fact as this should have escaped the attention of those who have written on this question: it seems to me rather that the ignoring of it in the discussion is to be attributed to a want of definite ideas respecting value in the precious metals, as well as respecting the mode in which changes in their value are accomplished. The language which is commonly used on the subject would seem to imply that gold and silver possess throughout the world a uniform value, and that all changes therein proceed in a uniform manner, showing themselves at the same time in all countries, and in respect to all commodities. But nothing can be further from the truth than such a notion. Gold and silver, like all other things which are the subjects of international exchange, possess local values;* and it is by a succession of operations on the local values of gold of an unequal and fluctuating character, that its depreciation is being effected, and that (the conditions of production remaining as at present) its value will continue to decline. The two-fold rise of prices in the gold countries forms the first step in this progress; and it will be through a series of similar partial advances in other countries, and not by any general movement, that the depreciation of the metal throughout the world will be accomplished, if that consummation is indeed to take place. With the question of depreciation, however, I am at present no

* See on the subject of the local values of the precious metals, Ricardo's "Works," pp. 77—86, and Mill's "Principles of Political Economy," Book iii., chaps. xix. and xxi.

further concerned than may be necessary to show the bearing of these changes in the local values of gold upon the movements of trade, and, through these, upon national interests.

There is no need here to resort to argument to prove that a general rise or a general fall of prices, provided it be simultaneous and uniform, can be attended—always excluding the case of fixed incomes and contracts already entered into—with no important consequences either to nations or to individuals. It is evident that such a change would merely alter the terms in which transactions are carried on, not the transactions themselves. But when the rise or fall of prices is not general—in other words, when the change in the values of the precious metals is merely local—it will be seen that important consequences must result. Supposing, *e.g.*, the prices of all commodities produced in England to be doubled, while prices throughout the rest of the world remained unchanged, it is evident that half the commodities exported from England would, under these circumstances, be sufficient to discharge our foreign debts. With half the capital and labour now employed in producing goods for the foreign markets, we should attain the same result as at present—the procuring of our imports; while the remaining half would be set free to be applied to other purposes—to the further augmentation of our wealth and well-being. England would, therefore, in the case we have supposed, be benefited in all her foreign dealings to the full extent of the rise in price. On the other hand, foreign countries would, in exchange for the commodities which they send us, receive in return of our commodities but half their present supply. Their labour and capital would go but half as far as at present in commanding our productions, and they would be losers in proportion. It is evident, therefore, that while nations have not, any more than individuals, any interest in the positive height which prices may attain, every nation, as well as every individual trader, is interested in raising, *in relation to others,* the price of its own productions. The lower the local value, therefore, of the precious metals in any country, the greater will be the advantage to that country in foreign markets.

This being the manner in which nations are interested in changes in the value of gold, let us now observe the effect which the gold discoveries are producing in this respect. As has been already stated, the local value of gold in Australia and California has fallen to one-half,—the prices of their productions having risen in a twofold proportion;* and prices in other parts of the world having undergone no corresponding change, these countries realize the position which we have just been considering in our hypothetical case. A given quantity of their capital and labour goes twice as far as formerly in commanding foreign productions, while a given quantity of foreign labour and capital goes only one-half as far in com-

* This statement is not given as strictly accurate. On the whole, the advance of local prices in the gold countries is at present (1859) considerably more than this, some leading articles, as house-rent, meat, &c., having risen in a fourfold proportion and upwards. I adopt the proportion of two to one, because money wages have risen in about this ratio, and money wages, under a depreciation of the precious metals, ultimately govern money prices.

manding theirs. The world has thus, through the gold discoveries, been placed in its dealings with California and Australia at a commercial disadvantage; and from this disadvantage it can only escape (always supposing the present conditions of producing gold to continue) by raising the prices of its productions in a corresponding degree. Every country, therefore, is interested in raising as rapidly as possible the prices of its productions,—in other words, in the most rapid possible depreciation in the local value of its gold.* The sooner this is effected, the sooner will the country be restored to its natural commercial footing in relation to Australia and California; while in relation to countries where prices do not rise with the same rapidity, it will possess the same kind of advantage which is now enjoyed by the gold countries.

This conclusion, I find, is directly at variance with the opinion of some economists of eminence. Mr. M'Culloch, for example, in his recent contribution to the "Encyclopædia Britannica," † maintains "that the mischievous influence resulting from a fall in the value of the precious metals depends in a great measure on the rapidity with which it is brought about." But I apprehend the difference between Mr. M'Culloch and myself arises from his attending exclusively to a single class of consequences,—those, namely, which result, in the case of fixed contracts, from a depreciation of the standard. With respect to this

* For the general ground of this assertion the reader is referred to Mr. Mill's chapters on 'International Values,' and on 'Money as an imported Commodity,' in his "Principles of Political Economy;" also to Mr. Senior's Essay "On the Cost of obtaining Money."

† Article 'Precious Metals.'

class of effects, it is quite true that the evils which they involve will be increased by the rapidity of the depreciation; but as I have shown, the new gold is producing effects quite independently of its operation upon fixed contracts; and it is to those other effects that the statement I have just made is intended to apply. The distinction which I have in view will be best exemplified by recurring to the experience of the gold countries. In these the value of gold fell by more than 50 per cent. in a single year, the depreciation involving a proportional loss to creditors with a corresponding gain to debtors, and entailing in addition those numerous incidental evils which always result from a sudden disturbance of social relations. No one, however, on this account, will say that the sudden depreciation of gold in Australia and California was not for these countries a great gain. The nature and extent of that gain I endeavoured on a former occasion to estimate.* It consisted, as I showed, in the increased command conferred by the cheapness of their gold over markets in which gold prices had not proportionally risen. With every rise in the price of Australian and Californian products, or, what comes to the same thing, with every fall in the local value of their gold, their power of purchase in foreign markets increased,—an increase of purchasing power which, as we know, was immediately followed by a sudden and extraordinary influx of foreign goods. Now, precisely the same principle applies in the case of other countries. A fall in the value of gold will, where gold is the standard, lead to a disturbance in fixed contracts, with the concomitant

* See *ante*, p. 39.

evils; but it will at the same time, as in the case just considered, place the countries in which it occurs in a better position commercially in the markets of the world. Supposing, *e.g.*, a rise in prices to take place in all commercial countries equivalent to that which has occurred in California and Australia, the consequence would be what I endeavoured to explain in the paper just referred to: the export of gold from California and Australia, at least on its present scale, would at once cease, and the world would receive instead an increased supply of agricultural and pastoral products, and of other commodities which those countries are fitted to produce,—a result which, I venture to think, would be a gain for the world. On the other hand, supposing the rise in price to be confined to a single country—say to England—then England would at once be placed on a footing of commercial equality with California and Australia, while as regards other countries she would occupy the same vantage-ground which California and Australia now possess. She would, in short, obtain her gold at half its present cost (for she would receive twice as much as at present in return for the same expenditure of labour and capital), while the gold thus obtained would be expended on foreign commodities of which, according to the hypothesis, the prices had not risen. Notwithstanding, therefore, the evils which undoubtedly attend variations in the standard of value, more especially in an old and highly artificial community like ours, it is nevertheless, I maintain, for the interest of every country, that, a fall in the cost of gold having been effected, the progress of depreciation should *in it* be as rapid as possible. Until, by a depreciation of gold corresponding to that which has occurred in California and Australia, the value of that metal is brought into harmony with its cost, we must continue to receive from those countries little more than a barren addition to our stock of money. But with each successive step in the progress of depreciation, there will be for the nation in which it occurs a nearer approach to the footing of commercial equality with the gold countries from which it has been temporarily displaced; while in its dealings with other places where the decline has been less rapid, the nation so circumstanced will, during the period of transition, enjoy a commercial superiority. As a general conclusion, therefore, we may say, that in proportion as in any country the local depreciation of gold is more or less rapid than the average rate elsewhere, the effect of the monetary disturbance will be for that country beneficial or injurious.

This conclusion, I may in passing remark, throws light upon a practical question of some interest at the present time,—I mean the question of introducing a gold currency into India. The measure has been advocated by Mr. M'Culloch, on the ground that, by providing a new market for the increased supplies of gold, its effect would be to "counteract that fall in its value which is so generally apprehended." * There can be no doubt that the effect of the measure would be what Mr. M'Culloch describes; but, if the above reasoning be sound, this circumstance, instead of being a reason for introducing gold into the currency of India, affords (*so far as the interests of India are con-*

* "Encyclopædia Britannica:" article 'Precious Metals.' p. 473.

cerned) a strong reason against the adoption of this course. Mr. M'Culloch does not state whether the effect which he anticipates upon the value of gold would be general or local; whether extending over the whole commercial world, or confined to the markets of India,—a point of vital importance in determining the character of the result. If the effect were general—if, while counteracting depreciation in India, it influenced the value of gold *proportionately* in other parts of the world—then it must be conceded that the result would be entirely beneficial. The evils incident to a disturbance of fixed contracts would be avoided, and no others would be incurred. But this is just the point which I venture to deny. The adoption of gold as the monetary standard of India would certainly not affect the local value of gold in Australia and California; for, as I proved on a former occasion, the value of gold in these countries is determined by its cost, and its cost depends on the productiveness of the gold-fields. Nor, for reasons which will be hereafter stated, would it influence more than in a slight degree the range of gold-prices in England and the United States. The operation, therefore, of the measure would be to depress gold-prices in India, or at least to prevent them from rising in that quarter as rapidly as they otherwise would; while in California and Australia, in England and the United States, it left their course substantially unaffected. Now this result would tend undoubtedly to the advantage of California and Australia, of England and the United States, but, as it seems to me, would as clearly be injurious to India. The purchasing power of the former countries over the markets of India would, through the relative superiority of their prices, be increased, but the purchasing power of India over *their* markets would, for the opposite reason, be diminished. An English or American merchant, instead of discharging his debts as at present through the medium of silver which he has to purchase with gold at 62*d.* per ounce (and may soon have to purchase at a higher rate), might discharge the same debts with gold directly; and gold being by hypothesis more valuable in India than before, the same amount would of course go further. But an Indian purchaser of English or American commodities would have the same sum in gold to pay as if no change had taken place in the currency of India; while the gold prices of his native productions being lower, his ability to pay would of course be less. It seems to me, therefore (and the considerations here adduced are entirely independent of the reasons which exist on the score of good faith—the Indian debt having been contracted in a silver currency), that, viewing the matter from the side of Indian interests, the introduction of a gold currency into India must be regarded as a measure decidedly detrimental.*

* Referring to the adoption of a silver standard by Holland in 1851, Mr. M'Culloch characterizes it as a measure "in opposition to all sound principles." I confess I am at a loss to conjecture what sound principle was violated in preferring as the standard of value that metal, the value of which there was every reason to believe would be the steadier of the two. [I may say now (1872) that I am disposed to assign much less importance to this question of a change in the monetary standard of India than I did when the above passage was written. The reasoning assumes the possibility of a serious divergence in the relative values of gold and silver; but I now believe that such a divergence is practically out of the question.

Returning once more to the general question, we may consider the following conclusions as established:—1st, that the effect of the cheapening of gold upon commercial countries being to compel them to enlarge their metallic currencies, for which enlargement they must pay by an export of their productions, each country will endure a loss upon this head to the extent of the additional sum which may be requisite for each; and 2ndly, that while there will be a general loss from this cause, yet the progress of depreciation over the world not being uniform or simultaneous, the primary loss may, through the disturbance in international values thence arising, in particular cases, be compensated, or even converted into a positive gain; the loss or gain upon the disturbance being determined according as the rise of prices in any country is in advance or in arrear of the general average. To ascertain, therefore, the effect of the movement upon any particular nation, we must consider the manner in which, in its case, these two principles will operate.

With respect to the first, I am aware that, in speaking of the loss imposed on a country by the necessity of enlarging its currency—by the necessity of receiving and keeping increased supplies of gold

the grounds for which opinion will be found further on (*post*, p. 141). This circumstance, however, does not affect the theoretic point argued with Mr. M'Culloch. *If* the exchange of the existing silver for a gold standard in India were calculated to produce the effects Mr. M'Culloch expected from it, the measure, it still seems to me, would be open to the objections I have urged against it. But I do not believe that the effects in question would result; and I can well conceive that, having regard to the general convenience of commerce, the change might on the whole be advantageous.]

and silver—I am using language which, notwithstanding what was said on a former occasion in its justification, and notwithstanding that it is merely in strict conformity with the most elementary principles of economic science, will still appear paradoxical to many. I would therefore, before proceeding further with this branch of the argument, ask the reader to consider the case of a private merchant who is compelled to increase the stock of cash with which he carries on his business. The metallic circulation of a country performs in relation to the community functions precisely analogous to those which are discharged for a merchant by his cash reserve. If a merchant can safely dispense with a portion of his ready cash, he is enabled, with the money thus liberated, either to add to his productive capital, or to increase his private expenditure. On the other hand, if he finds it necessary to increase his reserve of cash, his productive capital must be proportionally encroached upon, or his private expenditure proportionally curtailed. And precisely the same may be said of the currency of a nation. Where a country does not itself yield gold or silver,* every increase of its metallic circulation must be obtained—can only be obtained—by parting with certain elements of real wealth—elements which, but for this necessity, might be made conducive to its well-being. It is in enabling a nation

* Even where it does yield these metals, the necessity of augmenting the currency is not the less an evil, since the operation will occupy, with no result but that of avoiding an inconvenience, a portion of the labour and capital of the country, which, but for this, might have contributed to its positive welfare.

to reduce within the narrowest limits this unproductive portion of its stock, that the chief advantage of a good banking system consists; and if the augmentation of the metallic currency of a country be not an evil, then it is difficult to see in what way the institution of banks is a good. In regarding, therefore, the necessity imposed upon commercial countries of enlarging their metallic currencies as injurious to their interests, I make no assumption which is not in perfect keeping with the best known and most generally recognized facts of commercial experience.

An increase in the metallic currency of a country, then, being an evil, let us consider what the circumstances are by which the augmentation rendered necessary by the gold discoveries will be determined. This, it is evident, will principally depend—the amount of business to be carried on being given—on the extent to which substitutes for metallic money are in use; in other words, on the degree of perfection which the banking system of each country has attained. To illustrate this, let us suppose a given sum of metallic money—say a million sterling—to be introduced into two countries in which the currencies are differently constituted, *e.g.*, into England and India. In India coin is the principal medium of circulation* — in many

* [The reader will bear in mind that this was written in 1859. The state of the Indian currency at that time may be gathered from the following extracts from a paper on "The Trade and Commerce of India," read before the British Association in 1859.] "Intimately connected with Indian trade and commerce is a sound system of banking. At present there are only three banks of importance in India—the banks of Bengal, Bombay, and Madras. These have no branches, the absence of which constitutes one of the main defects of the system. The few other banks in India do not issue notes, and employ their capital in making advances

parts the only one, and consequently a million sterling introduced into the currency of India would represent only an equal, or little more than an equal, addition to its total medium of circulation—to the whole monetary machinery by which the exchange of commodities is effected and prices maintained. But in England, where the currency is differently constituted, the result would be different. The great bulk of the circulating medium of this country consists of certain forms of credit; and the amount of these credit media standing in a certain large proportion to the coin in the country,

on bills of lading, in exchange operations, and in some instances in loans to members of the Service, at high rates of interest; but afford no banking facilities for conducting the internal trade of the country." The writer then refers to a table, showing the state of the three leading banks (Bengal, Bombay, and Madras) in the preceding June, from which it appears that the bullion at that time in the coffers of the banks was *in excess* of the notes in circulation, the amount of these latter being, for the whole of India, 2,241,471*l.*, or about one-tenth of the amount issued by the Bank of England alone; while the total amount of "accounts current" was only 1,855,000*l.*—about one-sixth of those held by some of the private banks of London, and not one-fifteenth of those of the Bank of England. The total amount of commercial bills discounted in these three leading banks of India is set down at 278,900*l.*! "And this," it is observed, "in a country where the gross annual revenue is 34,000,000*l.*; the export trade, on an average of the last five years, 24,000,000*l.*; the import trade, on the same average, 23,000,000*l.*, with an internal trade to an extent almost impossible to estimate." ("The Trade and Commerce of India," by J. T. Mackenzie, read before the British Association, 1859, pp. 15, 16.) In the evidence taken before the late Committee "On Colonization and Settlement in India," Mr. Alexander Forbes, when questioned with reference to the large absorption of silver in India, expressed his opinion that the silver was all required for current coin. "It has often been said that the natives hoard silver: now my experience is that they do not hoard silver; they hoard gold; and that the silver is actually required for the commerce of the country." And this he traces (Answers 2,222, 2,223, 2,372–80) to the want of banking accommodation and the imperfect means of communication generally in the country. See also the evidence of Mr. Mangles (Answers 1,625–1,631).

the effect of introducing a million sterling into our currency would be to increase the medium of circulation by an amount very much greater than that of the added coin. Let us consider for a moment what becomes of a sum of coin or bullion received into England. I do not now speak of that moving mass of metal which passes (so to speak) *through* the currency of the country—which, received to-day into the vaults of the Bank of England, is withdrawn to-morrow for foreign remittance—but of gold which is permanently retained to meet our genuine monetary requirements. Of such gold a portion—greater or less, according to circumstances—will always find its way into the channels of retail trade; and so far as it follows this course, its effect in augmenting the circulation will be, as in India, only to the extent of its actual amount. But a portion will also be received into the banks of the country, where, either in the form of coin, or of notes issued against coin, it will constitute an addition to their cash reserves. The disposable cash of the banks being thus increased, an increase of credit operations throughout the country would in due time follow. The new coin would become the foundation of new credit advances, against which new cheques would be drawn, and new bills of exchange put in circulation, and the result would be an expansion of the whole circulating medium greatly in excess of the sum of coin by which the new media were supported. Now credit, whatever be the form which it assumes, so long as it is *credit*, will operate in purchases, and affect prices in precisely the same way as if it were actually the coin which it represents. So far forth, therefore, as the new money enables the country to support an increase of such credit media—to support them, I mean, by cash payments—so far it extends the means of sustaining gold-prices in the country; and this extension of the circulating medium being much greater than in proportion to the amount of added coin, the means of sustaining gold-prices will be in the same degree increased. Thus, supposing the ratio of the credit to the coin circulation of the country to be as four to one (and the proportion is greatly in excess of this), the addition of one million sterling of coin would be equivalent to an increase in the aggregate circulation of four millions sterling,* and one million sterling of gold would consequently, in England, for a given extent of business, support the same advance in gold-prices as four times that amount in India. It follows from these considerations, that, in order to raise prices throughout a given range of transactions to any required level, the quantity of metallic money which will be necessary will vary in different countries, according to the constitution of their currencies; the requirements of each increasing generally in an inverse ratio with the efficiency of its banking institutions.

* Strictly speaking, this conclusion would not follow on the above supposition, the efficiency of different forms of credit in performing the work of circulation being (as pointed out by Mr. Mill, "Principles of Political Economy," vol. ii., pp. 58—61) different, and only some of them being in this respect equal to coin. But such distinctions do not affect the general truth of the principle contended for in the text, that the necessity for coin varies inversely with the use of credit. Besides, as I intimated, the proportion of credit to coin in our circulation is much greater than I have assumed; and a million of coin taken into our currency would really be equivalent to more than four millions added to a purely metallic one.

We may thus see how very unequal will be the operation of the gold discoveries with respect to commercial communities. The reduction in the cost of gold to which they have led has, as we have seen, produced in the gold countries a twofold rise of gold-prices; and supposing the present conditions of raising gold to continue, the same cause must ultimately lead to the same result throughout the world; imposing upon each country the necessity of so enlarging its currency as to admit of this advance. But we have seen that the quantity requisite for this purpose varies according to the monetary status of the country for which it is required; and inasmuch as the new money must be paid for by commodities, the abstraction of commodities, and therefore the loss of the means of well-being, to which each country must submit, will vary with the same circumstance. On the supposition, therefore, on which we are arguing, the quantity of new money which England would require would be, when compared with the extent of her business, extremely small, and her loss of real wealth small proportionally. The same would be true of the United States, where credit institutions have also attained a high degree of efficiency, and whose paper consequently forms a large proportion of the whole circulation. In France, the use of credit being more restricted, the requirements for coin would be greater, and consequently also the loss of consumable commodities; while in India and China, and indeed in Asiatic communities generally, the circulating medium being almost purely metallic, the requirements for coin would, in proportion to the business in which it was employed, attain their maximum, with a corresponding maximum of loss in the elements of well-being.*

The operation of this principle is indeed, in the actual circumstances of the world, in some degree concealed by the complex conditions under which it comes into play. Thus Great Britain and the United States, instead of obtaining the smallest shares, receive in the first instance nearly the whole of the new gold. On the other hand, the quantity which goes to India and China from the gold countries is comparatively trifling;† and although a large drain of treasure has set in thither from Europe, yet this consists chiefly of silver. If, however, passing by the accidents of the movement, we attend to its essentials, we shall find that the results are entirely conformable to the principle I have endeavoured to describe. For though the bulk of the new gold comes in the first instance to England and the United States—determined thither by the course of international demand—yet England

* It is curious to observe the contradictions in which persons are involved who, still under the influence of the mercantile theory of wealth (and there are few even among professed economists who are free from its influence), are nevertheless sensible from experience of the advantages of a system with which it is incompatible. Thus several witnesses before the late Committee on Indian Colonization refer to the large influx of silver into India in recent years as a sure indication of the increasing prosperity of that country; yet, almost in the same breath, they speak of the deficiency of banking accommodation as among its most pressing wants. Now it is certain that, just in proportion as banking accommodation is extended, the absorption of silver by India will decline; whence it would follow, if the reasoning of the witnesses be sound, that the effect of the extension of banks would be to check the growing prosperity of the country. See "Minutes of Evidence," Questions 1,625–1,633, 2,221–2,273.

† This order in the diffusion of the new gold has not been sustained. See *ante*, p. 67, note.

and the United States do not form its ultimate destination. The monetary requirements of these countries being easily satisfied, the mass of the metal, on reaching these markets, becomes immediately disposable for foreign purchases; by which means the United States and England are enabled to transfer to other countries this unprofitable stock, the commodities with which in the first instance they parted being replaced by others which they more require. So also, although the metallic drain to the East is composed principally of silver, the efflux—at least in its present proportions—is not the less certainly the consequence of the increased production of gold; for the silver of which it consists has been displaced from the currencies of Europe and America by the gold of Australia and California; and the drain to the East is only not a golden one, because silver alone is in that region the recognized standard. As the final result of the whole movement, we find that, while the metallic systems of England and the United States are receiving but small permanent accessions, those of India and China are absorbing enormous supplies. The former countries, though the first recipients of the treasure, yet, not requiring it for domestic purposes, are enabled to shift the burden to others, whose real wealth they command in exchange; while the latter, requiring what they receive, are compelled to retain it. Having parted with their commodities for the new money, they are unable afterwards to replace them. As their stock of coin increases, their means of well-being decline, and they become the permanent victims of the monetary disturbance.

But, secondly, we concluded that the loss of real wealth resulting from the augmentation of their currencies would in particular countries be compensated, and might in some be even converted into positive gain, by the disturbance which, during the period of transition, would take place in international values. As has been already remarked, a general rise of prices in all countries, if simultaneous and uniform—since it leaves the proportions in which commodities are exchanged undisturbed—leads to no change in international values, and produces no effect upon national interests. But where prices rise unequally, international values, and through these, national interests, are affected. We have therefore to consider how far, in the actual circumstances of the world, a rise of prices in particular countries, unaccompanied by a corresponding advance in others, is possible, and, in so far as it is possible, in what order the several changes may be expected to occur.

As regards the question of possibility, this is placed beyond controversy by the example of California and Australia. It is a matter of fact that prices in those regions have advanced in a twofold proportion, while no corresponding rise of prices has occurred throughout the world. The circumstances, however, of the gold countries will probably be thought of too exceptional a character to form the basis of any general conclusion; and it will therefore be desirable to advert for a moment to the causes which produced in California and Australia that local elevation of price, with a view to consider how far the same conditions are capable of being realized elsewhere.

These causes, as was formerly shown,* were the special facilities for producing gold enjoyed by California and Australia, combined with the limited range of their domestic transactions. The sudden cheapening of gold, involving a corresponding increase in money earnings, placed an extraordinary premium on the production of the metal, while the limited range of their domestic trade rendered the necessary enlargement of their monetary systems an easy task. On the other hand, the immense extent of the aggregate commerce of the world required, in order to secure a similar advance, a proportional increase in its aggregate stock of money, an augmentation which could only be accomplished after the lapse of a considerable time. Prices therefore rose rapidly in the gold countries, while over the area of general commerce the rise has been but slow.

Such being the circumstances which produced the local divergence of prices to which I have called attention, it will at once be seen that of the two conditions which I have stated, the latter—the necessary enlargement of the local currency—may in most countries, though not in all at the same time, be fulfilled, if not with the same rapidity as in Australia and California, still after no very long delay. It has been computed,† for example, that the total quantity of gold coin circulating in Great Britain amounts to 75,000,000*l*. sterling. Assuming this to be correct, it would follow (all other conditions being supposed

* See *ante*, pp. 25, 26.

† "History of Prices," vol. vi. app. xxii. This also is Mr. M'Culloch's estimate: "Encyclopædia Britannica," article 'Precious Metals,' p. 465. [It will be borne in mind that these estimates apply to the period immediately preceding the first publication of these Essays (1859-60).]

identical) that an addition of 75,000,000*l.* would be sufficient to effect an elevation of our local prices equivalent to that which has occurred in Australia. Now at the present rate of production, the quantity of gold which arrives annually in Great Britain cannot fall much short of 30,000,000*l.* sterling;* so that were we merely to retain all that we receive, we should at the end of two years and a half be in a position, so far as the augmentation of our currency is concerned, to maintain the same advance in price as has occurred in the gold countries. If, then, prices in Great Britain have not risen in the same degree, the result, it is evident, cannot be due to the difficulty of procuring the supply of gold necessary for the enlargement of our currency. It remains, therefore, to be considered how far those special facilities for procuring gold which have operated in the gold countries may come into play in other parts of the world.

The extraordinary facilities for procuring gold enjoyed by Australia and California depend, of course, on the possession of their gold mines; and this being so, it might seem as if all countries, not being like them auriferous, were by the nature of the case precluded from fulfilling this condition of the problem; but this by no means necessarily follows, as will be evident if we reflect that there are other modes of obtaining gold than by direct production, of which modes the efficiency enjoyed by different countries differs almost as much as the degrees of fertility in

* [20,000,000*l.* would have been nearer the mark, but, at the time this paper was written, no trustworthy statistics of gold imports existed. Either amount, however, answers equally well the purpose of the argument (1872).]

different gold mines. Where countries do not themselves produce gold, the mode by which they obtain it is through their foreign trade. Now it is a fact well known to economists * that, with reference to the cost of commodities, the terms on which foreign trade is carried on differ greatly in different countries, the labour of some going much further in commanding foreign productions than that of others. According, however, to the conditions on which foreign productions generally are obtainable, will be those on which gold may be obtained. If a country possess special facilities for supplying markets where gold can be given in exchange, it will obtain its gold more cheaply—at a less sacrifice of labour and capital—than countries which do not share these facilities, and amongst such countries it will therefore occupy precisely the same position as an auriferous country whose mines are of more than the usual richness among the countries which yield gold. It is thus possible for a non-auriferous, no less than for an auriferous, country to possess exceptional facilities in the means of procuring gold, and therefore to fulfil the second of the conditions by which a divergence of local prices from the ordinary level of the world may be effected.

Now, it appears to me there are two countries which possess in an eminent degree the qualifications requisite for attaining this result—I mean Great Britain and the United States: the former, as being *par excellence* the great manufacturer among civilized

* See Ricardo's "Works"—chap. vii., on Foreign Trade. Mill's "Principles of Political Economy," chaps. xvii., xix. Also Senior's Essay, "On the Cost of obtaining Money."

nations—the manufacturer more particularly of descriptions of goods—as cotton, woollen, linen, and iron—which enter largely into the consumption of the classes by whom chiefly the gold countries are peopled; and the latter, as the principal producer of raw material, as well as of certain commodities—as grain, tobacco, sugar, and rice—which are also largely consumed by the same classes. In these circumstances, Great Britain and the United States enjoy peculiar advantages in the markets of the gold-countries, and these advantages are extended and confirmed by other important incidents of their position. Thus they possess the greatest mercantile marine in the world, by which they are enabled to give the fullest scope to their manufacturing and agricultural superiority, while by race, language, and religion they are intimately connected with the producers of the new gold,—a connection from which spring ties, moral, social, and political, to strengthen and secure those which commerce creates. Great Britain and the United States thus possess in their foreign trade a rich mine,* worked by their manufacturers, planters, and farmers, tended by their mercantile marine, and protected by their naval power,—a mine by means of which they are enabled to obtain their gold on terms more favourable than other nations. The effect of this, in ordinary times, is shown by a scale of money rates, wages, salaries, and incomes, permanently higher than that which

* "The mine worked by England is the general market of the world: the miners are those who produce those commodities by the exportation of which the precious metals are obtained."—SENIOR'S *Essay* "*On the Cost of obtaining Money*," p. 15.

elsewhere prevails; but, in times of monetary disturbance like the present, when the cost of gold having been reduced its value is falling, these advantages, it seems to me, must tell, as analogous advantages have told in the gold countries, in a more rapid realization of the results which are in store—in a quicker ascent towards that higher level of prices and incomes, which the cheapened cost of gold is destined ultimately to produce.

There is reason, therefore, on considerations of theory, to expect a repetition in England and America of that phenomenon which has been already exhibited in Australia and California,—a divergence of local money-rates from the average level of surrounding countries. On a future occasion I shall endeavour to ascertain how far, in the case of Great Britain, these *à priori* conclusions are supported by facts—how far prices and incomes have here, under the influence of the gold discoveries, outstripped the corresponding movement in other countries.* Having settled this point, we shall be in a position to form a general estimate of the benefit which may thence accrue to us. Meanwhile, however, I may, in conclusion, point out the mode in which the advantages incident to the monetary position we shall occupy are likely to be realized.

And here it may be well to call the reader's attention

* [Some evidence on the point will be found in the Appendix; but the inquiry here contemplated was never carried into effect. A very interesting and carefully prepared paper on the subject, however, was read some years later by my friend Professor Jevons before the London Statistical Society, when I had the satisfaction to find that the results of his entirely independent investigations to a very large extent corroborated the conclusions at which I had arrived, mainly by way of deduction from the general principles of the science.]

to the distinction, sometimes overlooked, between a fall in the value of gold and a rise in the price of commodities. A rise in the price of commodities, if general, implies commonly a fall in the value of money; but, according to the ordinary use of language, alike by economists and in common speech, money would, I apprehend, in certain circumstances be said to have fallen in value, even though the prices of large classes of commodities remained unaffected. For example, supposing improvements to have been effected in some branch of production resulting in a diminished cost of the commodity, the value of money remaining the same, prices would fall: if under such circumstances prices did not fall, that could only be because money had not remained the same, but had fallen in value. The continuance of prices unaltered would, therefore, under such circumstances amount to proof of a fall in the value of gold. Now when, in connection with this consideration, we take account of the fact that over the greater portion of the field of British industry improvement is constantly taking place, it is obvious that the mere movements of prices here, taken without reference to the conditions of production, are no sure criterion of changes in the value of gold.

The truth is, in a large class of commodities—in all those to which mechanical or chemical inventions are extensively applicable—even on the supposition of a very great depreciation of gold, no considerable advance in price is probable. Gold, for example, might have fallen since the beginning of the present century to the extent of 75 per cent.—that is to say, four sovereigns now might be equal to no more than one sovereign at the commencement of the period—and yet in a large class of manufactured goods no advance in price would be apparent, the reduction in the cost of production being in more than an equal proportion. In ordinary times, agricultural operations escape in a great degree the influence of industrial progress; but within the last ten years—that is to say, since the repeal of the Corn Laws, which nearly synchronized with the gold discoveries—the spirit of improvement has been as busy in agriculture as in any other department of industry, and, in conjunction with importations from foreign countries, has acted, and must for some time at least continue to act, powerfully upon the price of raw products in this country.

The depreciation of gold, therefore, may be realized either in a corresponding advance of prices, or in the neutralization of a fall which in the absence of depreciation would have occurred; but in whatever form it may come to us, our gain or loss as a nation will be the same, and will depend upon the condition I have stated—the more or less rapid depreciation of our currency as compared with the currencies (convertible, like ours, into gold) of other countries. Whether, the conditions of production remaining unaltered, the depreciation be indicated by a corresponding advance of prices, or, those conditions undergoing improvement, the fall in the value of gold merely operates in neutralizing, as regards price, the effects of the cheapened cost of commodities—in either case *the gold price of the products of English labour and abstinence will rise.* A given exertion of English industry will reap a larger *gold* reward than before; and foreign commodities not rising in price in the same degree, the larger gold reward will indicate, *over so much of our expenditure as is directed to foreign productions*, a real augmentation of well-being. As regards that portion of our expenditure which falls upon the products of our own industry, individuals and classes will, according to circumstances,* be benefited or injured by the change; but as a nation, we shall neither gain nor lose, since here the increased cheapness of gold will be exactly neutralized either by a corresponding advance in price, or by the prevention in the same degree of a fall which would otherwise have taken place. It is in this way—by the increased command which she obtains over foreign markets by her cheap gold—and not, as is commonly supposed, by finding an outlet for her wares in California and Australia, that England will benefit by the gold discoveries. That outlet for her productions—were the movement to stop here—however it might benefit individuals, would for the country at large be an injury and not a boon; it would deprive her of that which might conduce to her comfort and happiness, and would give her "a breed of barren metal" in exchange. But the movement does not stop here. The money which she obtains from the gold countries, instead of absorbing, like India or China, she employs in purchasing the goods of other nations. It is in the enlarged command which she acquires over such goods that her gain consists, and it is thus that she indemnifies herself, though at the expense of the nations who ultimately retain the new gold, for the loss—the indubitable loss—which she is called on in the first instance to sustain.

* On this point see *post*, p. 147 *et seq.*

IV.

ESSAY TOWARDS A SOLUTION OF THE GOLD QUESTION.

*SUMMARY OF THE MOVEMENT. M. CHEVALIER'S VIEWS.**

It is now rather more than three centuries since the conquest of Mexico and Peru by the Spaniards, and the discovery of rich mines of the precious metals in those regions, excited the cupidity of Europe and opened a new epoch in human affairs. Of the numerous occurrences which conspired about that time to break the spell of old ideas, and to carry the world rapidly over the border line of mediævalism into the full movement of modern civilization, this was certainly not the least powerful. The subsequent depreciation of gold and silver, and the revolutions in private property, though the most conspicuous, were by no means the sole, nor even the most important, consequences of that event. The rage for gain — the *auri sacra fames*—awakened by the golden visions of the new Eldorado, hurried across the Atlantic those numerous and daring adventurers who laid the foundation of the Transatlantic states. The vast sums of gold and silver liberated

* *The Edinburgh Review*, July 1860.

by their exertions supplied, and rendered possible, the remarkable expansion of Oriental trade which forms the most striking commercial fact of the age that followed. Less directly, but still intimately, connected with the same event, were the sudden growth and temporary splendour of the Spanish monarchy, as well as its rapid decline; the establishment of the Poor Laws in England; the financial embarrassments of Charles I., which resulted in the Long Parliament and the Revolution; and the rise and progress of British maritime power.

Once more after the lapse of three centuries, the world has witnessed another great discovery of the precious metals. The auriferous sands and rocks of California and Australia are as much superior, in richness and abundance, to those which rewarded the industry of the Spanish adventurers, as these latter were superior to all which had been previously known; and gold has now for eight years been pouring into Europe in an exuberant tide of wealth beyond all former experience. What, then, will be the result of these Californian and Australian discoveries? and how far will they resemble in their scope and influence their prototypes of the sixteenth century? These are questions which, in the presence of such facts, cannot but force themselves upon every thoughtful mind.

But since the epoch of which we have spoken—since the day when the sparkling veins on the sides of Potosi attracted the eye of the Indian shepherd—a mighty change has come upon the world. Society in all its constituents has been profoundly modified. Commerce has grown to dimensions of which the merchants of the sixteenth century could have formed no conception. The entire foreign trade of the greatest commercial nation then in existence probably did not much exceed that which is now carried on in a single English or American port. The total tonnage of the united galleons which constituted the Spanish mercantile marine only amounted a century later, as we are informed by Robertson, to 27,500 tons—little more than the tonnage of the *Great Eastern* steam-ship. Some of the most populous and wealthy communities of the present day had not yet begun to exist; and the whole quantity of the precious metals then in use was probably less than that which now circulates in some second-rate European kingdoms. The conditions under which the experiment of the sixteenth century was tried are no longer those with which we have now to deal, and the precedents of that period may therefore be thought to have little application to the present time.

But, on the other hand, if we examine the details of this change, we shall find that the facts of which it consists are of a nature, in relation to the influence of the gold discoveries, in a great degree to counteract and neutralize each other; some of them tending not less powerfully to enhance, and give increased efficacy to that influence, than others tend to impair it. The stability of trade has increased with the increase of its mass; but, on the other hand, the agencies at our disposal for acting upon trade have increased in a still greater proportion. The quantity of the precious metals now in existence may be twenty or thirty times greater than when Columbus made his memorable voyage, and the difficulty of affecting their value may be proportionably greater; but against this we have to consider, that for one Spaniard who in the sixteenth century engaged in mining, twenty or thirty English or Americans are now thus employed, and that these latter are equipped with means and appliances of production far superior to any which their predecessors could command. The area of commercial intercourse has been greatly enlarged, and commercial relations indefinitely multiplied: but not more so than the means of locomotion and the facilities of postal communication; while we have further to note, that commerce possesses now, in the agency of credit, an auxiliary to metallic money of wondrous potency, which in the earlier period was entirely unknown. Notwithstanding, therefore, the changes which have taken place in the trade and wealth of the world, the circumstances of the present time are not such as to preclude the possibility of a recurrence of events similar or analogous to those which the first American discoveries drew after them. Those events were, as we have said, of the greatest moment to mankind: they included the rapid colonization of America by European races; great and lasting changes in the channels of trade; striking vicissitudes in the fortunes of nations; and a monetary revolution the effects of which have been felt in every quarter of the globe.

The precedents of history, then, no less than the character of the facts, give to the Californian and Australian gold discoveries an interest of no ordinary kind, and we have therefore to tender our thanks to M. Michel Chevalier and his translator, for having brought to the notice of the public the momentous questions which those discoveries involve. The subject indeed has not been entirely overlooked in this country, but it has not yet been treated, either here or elsewhere, by any writer whose opinions command the same respect as those of M. Chevalier; and we therefore welcome the appearance of his volume as undoubtedly the most important contribution which has yet been made to this discussion.

But, while we gladly bear testimony to the ability and learning with which M. Chevalier has treated this subject, and to the logical acuteness with which he has dissected and expounded many of its problems, it certainly seems to us that he has failed to seize fully the nature and the extent of the principles which the increased production of gold has brought into play. In the work before us, the discussion is confined to a single aspect of the gold question—"the probable fall in the value of gold," and the effects of this on our pecuniary relations: to another, and not less important view of the movement—the changes which the new gold, by altering the distribution of purchasing power in the world, may produce in the movements of trade and the fortunes of nations, changes of which some striking illustrations have already been afforded,—to this aspect of the case M. Chevalier scarcely alludes.

And yet the distinction on which it rests is real.* If, to borrow the illustration of Hume, the world should awake some morning, every one finding in his pocket an additional sovereign, or (modifying slightly

* As has been shown in the preceding essays.

the supposition) every one finding his money income increased in some certain proportion,—such an occurrence would tend to lower the value of money, but (unless so far as it affected fixed contracts) would not alter the relative purchasing power of individuals, nor therefore the distribution of commodities, nor the interests of mankind. But if, instead of being dispensed with this impartiality, the entire addition of new sovereigns should fall to the lot of a few persons, the money incomes of the rest remaining as before, this —supposing the amount of the addition to be in each case the same—would tend, equally as in the former case, to lower the value of money; but its effects would not end here: while increasing the total quantity of money, it would at the same time alter the relative purchasing power of individuals—a result which would be followed by a corresponding change in the distribution of real wealth amongst them, and consequently of general well-being. This view of the case M. Chevalier has neglected to expound. He has discussed with considerable fulness the effects of a depreciation of money; but he has altogether overlooked the results which may follow from a redistribution of purchasing power over the world. We have in the outset called attention to this incompleteness (as we deem it) in his mode of treating the gold question, because we think he has thus been led, not only to omit from his consideration an interesting range of topics, but to attribute to a depreciation of money results which are due to a different cause. The justification and pertinence of this criticism will appear in the course of the following observations.

The facts which form the ground for expecting a fall in the value of gold are thus stated by M. Chevalier. At the beginning of the present century the quantity of gold which arrived every year to augment the metallic wealth of Christendom amounted, in round numbers, to about 2,500,000*l.* sterling. By the year 1848 this supply had increased to upwards of 8,000,000*l.*; the field of production having been in the meantime extended by the opening of new mines in the Ural Mountains, and the discovery of auriferous sands in Siberia. In 1848 the Californian discoveries occurred, which were followed in 1851 by those in Australia. The result of the whole has been to raise the rate of production from 2,500,000*l.*, the annual yield at the commencement of the century, to 38,000,000*l.* sterling, the present annual yield; being an increase, as compared with that time, in the proportion of 15 to 1, or, as compared with the period immediately preceding 1848, of 5 to 1.

Or the facts of the case may be thus represented. The region which, until the discovery of the mines of Siberia, was the chief seat of gold production for European nations, was America. Now the total quantity of gold raised throughout the whole continent of America during the interval from the first voyage of Columbus to the discovery of the mines of California—that is to say, during a period of 356 years—amounted in round numbers to about 400,000,000*l.* sterling. At the present time (as has been stated above) the *annual* supply has reached 38,000,000*l.* sterling. It thus appears that the civilized world receives now in a single year nearly one-tenth of all the gold obtained in the principal field of supply throughout the whole period from the discovery of America down to the year 1848.

Or, once more, the altered conditions of producing gold may be presented through the medium of the average produce of a day's work. M. Chevalier has not furnished us with any standard with which to compare the present rate of gold earnings, except the returns of the gold-washers of the Rhine, which scarcely afford a fair basis of comparison. We learn, however, from Humboldt that, at the commencement of the century, when he visited New Spain, the Mexican miner, "who was the best paid of all miners," "gained at least from twenty-five to thirty francs per week of six days." * This would be equivalent to from 3*s.* 6*d.* to 4*s.* 2*d.* a day of our money, which amount, since the rate of wages in mining always follows the average returns to mining labour,† we may take as representing the average earnings of miners at the commencement of the century. Now, according to some authorities quoted by M. Chevalier, and which are fully confirmed by statements which we have seen, as well as by the current rate of wages in the country, the average earnings of gold miners in California at present are at the rate of nineteen francs per man daily, equal to about 15*s.* 2*d.* The earnings in Australia he sets down at the same amount; but we are convinced that this is an over-estimate. From official accounts, confirmed by private information, we have no hesitation in saying

* "Political Essay on New Spain," vol. iii. pp. 237—240.

† See *ante*, p. 23.

that gold earnings in Australia at present do not exceed on an average 10*s.* a day per man. Even, however, reducing to this amount M. Chevalier's estimate, we have still an average produce for the two countries of 13*s.* per man daily, a rate of return nearly four times greater than that which was obtained from the best mines of Mexico half a century since. When, in connection with this fact, we consider the greater accessibility — arising partly from political causes, partly from the progress of the art of navigation—of the present gold countries, the superior enterprise and skill of the miners, and the larger capital at their disposal, we may form some conception of the immense increase which has taken place in the world's means of obtaining gold.

Such is the present state of gold production. But before these facts can be made the data for conclusions respecting the future, it is important to ascertain the extent of our existing resources. What are the auriferous capabilities of California and Australia, and of those other regions from which gold is now derived? Will the golden tide now pouring in continue with perennial flow? or will it, after inundating us for a while, suddenly disappear, like the Australian streams whence it is extracted? These are questions on which geology should be able to enlighten us, and some eminent authorities in that science are of opinion that the present extraordinary production cannot long continue. We are reminded, that auriferous formations are for the most part superficial; that the richest deposits are those which lie nearest the surface; that the countries which were once the chief seats of supply, as Spain and Lusitania, are auriferous no longer; and that, consequently, in proportion to the energy and skill with which the new gold fields are worked, will be the rapidity of their exhaustion.

"Judging from experience," says Sir Roderick Murchison, "all gold veins in the solid crust of the earth diminish and deteriorate downwards, and can rarely be followed to any great depth except at a loss in working them. Again, as the richest portions of the gold ore have been aggregated near the upper part of the original veinstones, so the heaps of gravel or detritus resulting either from former powerful abrasion, or from the diurnal wear and tear of ages, and derived from the *surface* of such gold-bearing rocks, are, with rare exceptions, the only materials from which gold has been, or can be, extracted to *great* profit. These postulates, on which I have long insisted, in spite of the opposition of theorists and schemers, have every year received further confirmation, and seem on the whole to be so well sustained as matters of fact, that the real problem we have now to solve is, how much time will elapse before the gold of Australia is finally riddled out of these heaps or basins, or extracted from a few superficial veinstones?" *

And with respect to the prospects of quartz mining, Sir Roderick adds:—

"So long as the miner is near the surface, these veinstones will unquestionably repay the cost of working them. When,

* "Address to the Geographical Society, 1857," pp. 453—455. In referring to Sir Roderick Murchison's opinion, it is proper to add that his views respecting the practical results of gold mining have reference to the state of mechanical science, as applied to mining operations, *at the time when he wrote*. In a note to the first edition of his "Siluria" (p. 436), he expressly guards himself on this point: "I would further guard any inferences I have drawn from our previous state of knowledge, by saying that my opinions were formed irrespective of the new discoveries in mechanical science, crushing machines, &c. The improved application of mercury may indeed liberate a notable quantity of ore from a matrix of apparently slight value, and thus set at nought the experience of ages." And see also the recent edition of the same work, pp. 489 *et seq.*

however, they are followed downwards into the body of the rock, they have usually been found impoverished, either thinning out into slender filaments, or graduating into silver or other ores; so that these insulated thin courses of auriferous quartz—mere threads in the mountain masses—will soon be exhausted for all profitable purposes, when the upper portions shall have been quarried out." *

To this view of the case M. Chevalier opposes the consideration of the vast extent of California and Australia, and the great richness of the alluvium which has been hitherto worked.

"The conditions in which deposits are found in California and Australia are such, that it is not a very sanguine view to suppose that in each of these countries alluvial ground will be found equal to 60,000 hectares of deposits of a metre in thickness, and of the richness of 1 to 100,000" (P. 65):

conditions which, he says, would give an annual yield for each country of 16,000,000*l.* sterling for a hundred years. We think it, however, more to the purpose to quote the following passage from the report of Mr. Selwyn, who lately conducted the geological survey of Victoria, and who is referred to by Sir Roderick Murchison as a competent witness. "The trap-plains," says Mr. Selwyn, "to the westward are very extensive; and there is every probability of gold deposits existing underneath the trap over the greater portion of them. The limit, therefore, to the period during which these tertiary gold deposits of Victoria may be profitably worked, may be regarded as indefinitely remote."* We may add, that the accounts received from practical

* "Address to the Geographical Society, 1857."

† "Quarterly Journal of the Geological Society," p. 534.

persons in the gold countries are far from supporting the opinion that the gold formations are extremely superficial. On the contrary, we hear on all hands of digging being carried on with profit at a very considerable depth, ranging frequently from 100 to 300 feet below the surface, and of quartz veins improving as they descend.* But, besides such statements, which may not be free from exaggeration, there are undisputed facts which it seems difficult to reconcile with the theory of speedy exhaustion. For example, the most extensive gold fields in Victoria are those of Ballarat and Mount Alexander; they were amongst the earliest discovered; they have been worked without intermission for eight years; and it is from them that the principal portion of the Australian supply is still derived.† Nor ought we, in estimating the prospects of the future, to overlook the probability of improvements in the means of production. The modes of extraction at present in use are generally of a very crude description. Frequent interruptions of work occur from want of water; and, though this obstacle has been overcome in California by the erection of extensive water-works, this obvious remedy has still to be applied in Australia. There is thus great room for improvement in the business of producing gold, and, with Anglo-Saxon enterprise and

* See "Further Papers relative to the Gold Discoveries," presented to Parliament, February 1856, pp. 47, 48, 56. See also Westgarth's Victoria," pp. 178, 185; Seyd's "California," pp. 30—44; and *Times*, February 16, 1858, San Francisco Correspondence.

† The Brazils also furnish instances of gold fields which have maintained their productiveness for a long period, as well as (as Sir Roderick Murchison admits) of "successful subterraneous mining."

intelligence directed to the task, we cannot doubt that improvement will be effected. On the whole, if we might venture an opinion respecting a matter on which we make no pretension to practical knowledge, we should say that, in speculating upon the auriferous resources of the new gold countries, too implicit a reliance has been placed on mere experience. It is admitted that the detritus of California and Australia greatly exceeds in richness any auriferous material hitherto known: why then may it not exceed any former material in extent as well as in quality? The history of gold digging in those countries up to the present time, and the accounts we continue to receive from a succession of travellers of the great auriferous tracts which are still untouched, certainly afford ground for this presumption; and we are therefore disposed to concur with M. Chevalier in the opinion, that the present extraordinary supply of gold is likely to be continued for, at least, some considerable period.

We assume, then, that the present production of gold will continue; and what we have now to consider is the probable effect of this upon the value of the metal. The tendency of an increased production of any commodity is to lower its value, and this tendency will be realized in fact, unless the demand for the commodity at the original value increase in a corresponding degree. On the supposition, therefore, that the production of gold continues at its present rate, the maintenance or decline of its value will depend upon the extension which may contemporaneously take place in the means of employing it. This is the position of M. Chevalier, and it is one which will, we believe, be accepted by all competent reasoners as the true ground on which the question should be argued.

By those who deny the probability of an impending fall in the value of gold we are reminded of the numerous circumstances which are likely to occur to occasion an increased demand for it. We are told of the extraordinary rapidity with which cosmopolitan commerce is now expanding; of the increased requirements for money incident to an increase of population; of enlarged consumption of gold in plate, jewelry, and decoration; of countries now circulating inconvertible paper which will soon adopt a metallic standard; of the loss from hoarding and shipwrecks; of the loss from "wear and tear;" and of other possible purposes and occasions which may create a need for an increased supply of gold. These various requirements, it is maintained, will generate a demand for the new metal as fast as it is sent forth from the mines, and will thus prevent any fall in its value. This argument M. Chevalier has met by a comprehensive review of the various incidents here enumerated, in which he endeavours, by a careful analysis of the facts of each, to estimate the probable amount which it may be able to absorb. The result of this investigation is the conclusion, that the utmost quantity which can be disposed of in the modes suggested, after allowing in the most liberal manner for every contingency that may arise, will not at the end of ten years exceed 1,275,000 kilogrammes of gold, or about 178,000,000*l.* sterling. On the other hand, on the supposition of the present rate of production continuing, the increase of supply at the end of ten years will not be less than 2,500,000 kilogrammes, or 350,000,000*l.* sterling. The result of the comparison carried over a period of ten years is thus to show an increase in the supply of gold greatly in excess of the probable requirements of the world at its present value; the inevitable consequence of which, as M. Chevalier contends, must be a general fall in the value of the metal. Such is the conclusion of this eminent economist—a conclusion full of warning to this and every other civilized community, and which has been adopted certainly on no slight or unconsidered grounds. For the extensive and interesting array of facts and reasonings by which this opinion is supported, we must refer our readers to M. Chevalier's volume. We shall confine ourselves here to some remarks on those branches of the argument which appear to us of most importance.

And here, before engaging in the discussion, it may be well to enter a *caveat* against an ambiguity of language which has introduced much confusion into popular reasonings upon this subject. We allude to the expression so frequently used in the controversy—"a demand for gold." With reference to this phrase, it must always be understood that the demand spoken of is a demand *at some given value of the metal;* since, without this qualification, an inquiry into the probable extension of the demand for gold would be an inquiry without an object, and indeed destitute of all significance. There can be no doubt that the increased supplies, however great, will find a market somehow, and be absorbed in the commerce and consumption of the world; but the question is, *upon what conditions?* upon the condition of retaining its value as at present, or of submitting to a reduction? 1600 millions sterling of gold and silver have been supplied to the world by America since the time of Columbus, and this vast amount has been absorbed; but observe upon what terms. On the terms of a fall in the value of silver in the proportion of 6 to 1, and in that of gold of 4 to 1.* "The present essay," therefore, says M. Chevalier, "is not written to prove that this extraordinary production of the precious metals cannot be employed on any terms, which would be absurd," but to prove that it cannot be absorbed consistently with maintaining its present value in relation to other commodities. "Mankind is not rich enough, nor will it soon be, to pay at so dear a rate for so large a mass." Such is the question to be solved; let us now consider some of the facts on which the solution depends.

Of the numerous causes which have been suggested as likely to afford a vent for the new gold, none seems at first sight to present so large a field for absorption as the expanding dimensions of commerce; and yet there is none on which so little expectation in this respect can be legitimately founded. The expansion of general commerce in the last half-century has indeed been enormous. In the United Kingdom, in the United States, throughout the continent of Europe, in California and Australia, even in India and China, the progress has been rapid beyond all precedent.

* These are M. Chevalier's estimates. We are inclined to think they are excessive, but they are used here merely in illustration of the principle in question.

This rapid expansion, moreover, has been more especially remarkable during the last ten years, and the causes of it (among which the adoption of a free-trade policy by this country must be considered the principal), so far from having exhausted themselves, are not considered as having yet yielded more than their first-fruits. Instead, therefore, of any slackening of commercial progress, we have rather to look for an acceleration of its pace. The wealth of the world is thus rapidly increasing, and the augmented wealth, it is urged, will require for its circulation a medium of exchange proportionately large. Here, then, is a field for the new gold of almost boundless extent. Here is an outlet into which the rising tide may flow off without any danger of surcharging those channels of circulation which are already full.

To this argument we might object, that the increase of international transactions (by which it is customary to estimate the progress of trade), although it always indicates an increase in the elements of real wealth, by no means indicates a corresponding increase, still less a corresponding increase in the *value* of such elements, or therefore in the need for a circulating medium. But, without entering into the somewhat complicated considerations connected with this point, and admitting, as we do, the probability of a considerable increase in the requirements of the world for a circulating medium, the question remains, Is gold the material by which such requirements will be met? M. Chevalier contends, and we think with good reason, that it is not. The proportion of the trade of the world which is carried on with metallic money is daily diminishing, and constantly tends to diminish; and the probability is, that the future expansions of trade will be chiefly supported, not with coin, but with those contrivances of credit and of paper currency, the immense advantages of which over metallic money we have already learned to appreciate.

Few persons, who are not practically engaged in business on a large scale, have an adequate conception of the extent to which credit expedients of one kind or another are now employed in the conduct of commercial affairs. In the principal commercial countries it may with little exaggeration be said, that the great wholesale transactions of trade are effected exclusively through this medium. Perhaps the most striking example of what can be accomplished by this means is afforded by the London Clearing House—the institution in which the accounts of the London bankers are daily settled.

"In 1839 this establishment had already attained such efficiency that for the annual liquidation of 950,000,000*l*. sterling, or 3,000,000*l*. daily, it only required, on an average each day, 200,000*l*. in sovereigns, or rather in bank-notes. At present, with a mass of transactions amounting to 1,500,000,000*l*. or 2,000,000,000*l*. sterling annually, instead of a proportionate addition to the 200,000*l*. required for the daily balance being necessary, not a shilling is wanted; the Clearing House now dispenses completely with the use of bank-notes; all is settled by the transfer of sums from one account to another in the books of the Bank of England." (P. 84.)

To such perfection has the system of credit been brought in this country. But, to appreciate the full force of the argument founded on the resources of credit, we should consider that, besides the field opened for its employment in the future expansions of trade, a large one exists in much of that which is now carried on. In Great Britain and the United States, the use of credit may indeed be thought to have reached its maximum; but this cannot be supposed of other portions of Europe and America, and still less of the vast communities of Asia. In India, though more than a century under British rule, the advantages of credit, as a medium of exchange, are only beginning to be understood. The circulation of bank-notes is exceedingly limited, and is still confined to some of the Presidency towns; cheques, by which so large a portion of the business of this country is carried on, are but slightly used; and the great mass of transactions is effected by a transfer of rupees bodily in every sale. The magnitude of the transactions conducted in this manner may be estimated by the fact stated by Sir Charles Napier, that the escort of treasure constituted one of the severest duties of the late Bengal army; from 20,000 to 30,000 men being constantly occupied in this manner. The quantity of the precious metals employed in thus carrying on the internal traffic of India has been variously estimated between 150,000,000*l.* and 300,000,000*l.* sterling. But this state of things is evidently not destined to be of long continuance. Mr. Wilson's recent minute gives grounds for believing that the Indian Government are alive to this subject, and that India will soon enjoy the advantages of an effective paper system. Such an event cannot fail to be attended with important consequences on the trade and industry of that country; and among these consequences we may expect this, that, instead of requiring, as now, continuous large additions to her present enormous stock of metallic money, she will not only be enabled to dispense with these, but will find it for her interest to part with a large portion of what she now employs: the coin thus liberated will form a new tributary to swell the increasing supplies, and the influences tending to depress the value of gold will be increased.

These observations apply to the wholesale transactions of commerce: they are not, in the same degree, applicable to the retail dealings of individuals. We say, not in the same degree, because they are applicable to a certain extent even to them. Amongst the upper and middle classes, at least in this country, the practice is becoming every day more general of paying private accounts through the medium of bankers' cheques, in which way retail transactions, in the aggregate of very large amount, are settled without the employment either of bank-notes or of metallic money. This practice, however, is confined to that comparatively limited portion of society whose private dealings assume dimensions sufficiently large to render the employment of credit convenient. For the mass of the population, who live mostly from hand to mouth, and whose dealings are on a very small scale, credit accounts are obviously unsuitable, and their purchases are accordingly effected almost wholly with coin. In this department of business, therefore, we find a field for the employment of gold which credit cannot well occupy, and which will increase with the increase of population. It becomes, therefore, important to ascertain the extent of the outlet which may be afforded in this direction for the increasing supplies.

With a view to this, M. Chevalier has instituted a comparison between the rate at which population is now advancing and that at which gold is increasing; the result of which is to show that, while population in civilized countries is advancing at the rate of one and a half per cent. per annum, gold—at least that portion which goes into general circulation—is increasing by more than 10 per cent. per annum.* Or, to put the same point differently, that while to satisfy the requirements of population an annual production of 3,000,000*l.* would be sufficient, the amount actually applicable to this purpose will, supposing the present scale of production to continue, not fall short of 20,000,000*l.* annually. It would seem, therefore, that the mere growth of population promises but an inadequate market for the new gold. And this conclusion is further confirmed by the fact, of which M. Chevalier reminds us, that in the dealings of the masses the metal which is principally employed is not gold, but silver or copper. The lowest gold piece in this country is worth ten shillings, the lowest in France is worth four shillings, and the inconvenience which would result from a smaller coin sets a limit to further reduction. It is, therefore, among a portion only of the working classes—those whose purchases are sufficiently large to make the use of such coin possible—that gold circulates at all, or can be expected to circulate; and this circumstance, he argues, must reduce within very

* This proportion is not given by M. Chevalier, but may be deduced from his statements.

narrow limits the field for its employment in this direction.

These considerations would seem to settle the question, so far as the requirements of the masses are concerned. Nevertheless there is an element of the case, not included in M. Chevalier's reasonings, which leads us to assign greater importance to this application of the new gold than the facts which he has stated would seem to warrant. The industrial history of Great Britain since the gold discoveries supplies us with a fact but little in accordance with the above calculations; the fact, namely, that since the year 1851 the population of this country, which at the utmost has not increased in the interval by more than 10 per cent., has absorbed into its retail circulation (according to the best estimate which we have been able to form) an addition to its gold currency of not less than 40 per cent.*—an addition which, though not wholly unaccompanied by an advance of prices, has not been productive of any effect in this respect commensurate with its amount. Now to what are we to attribute this anomalous circumstance? How are we to explain the fact that the gold currency of this kingdom has increased in a degree entirely out of proportion to the apparent requirements of its population, *without undergoing any corresponding depreciation in its value?* It appears to us that the explanation is to be found in the operation of a principle to which we adverted in the opening of this article, and to which we shall

* See on this point the facts and estimates given in Appendix xxii. to the sixth volume of the "History of Prices;" also the statistics of gold coinage given in the same volume, p. 154.

have occasion again to advert,—the tendency of the increased production of gold to alter the distribution of wealth throughout society. This principle, operating through our trade with the gold countries, has for the last eight years been acting upon the pecuniary relations of different classes in this country; and the result has been a change in the distribution of our national wealth sensibly in favour of the industrial portion of the social body. We do not here enter into the grounds of this opinion, which would involve us in economic discussions of an inconvenient length. But, in illustration of the general tendency of the gold discoveries to favour the industrial classes, we may refer to the triple and quadruple wages now enjoyed by those amongst them who have emigrated to California and Australia, and to the remarkable advance which during the last eight years has taken place in the wages of almost every class of labourers at home,*—an advance which has been accompanied by no corresponding movement in the incomes of other classes. A large increase has thus taken place in that portion of the general wealth which circulates among the industrial population; and this is just the portion in which the circulation of coin is most extensive. It is evident therefore (assuming, as we do, this fact to represent a general tendency) that, under the influences engendered by the new discovery, the demand of the population for gold coin may augment much more rapidly than a mere regard to the increase of its numbers would lead us to suppose. As the produc-

* See Dr. Strang's "Papers on Wages," published in the London Statistical Journal.

tion of gold continues, the proportion of the aggregate wealth of the world which goes to the industrial classes will increase; and, the field for credit contracting as we descend in the scale of society, the necessity for coin will increase also. In this way, it seems to us, a market may be opened for the new gold greatly more extensive than the considerations adduced by M. Chevalier would lead us to suppose; and a large amount of the new supplies may be thus disposed of, without involving the necessity of a fall, or at least of a corresponding fall, in their value. At the same time we are far from thinking that the demand thence arising will be sufficient to prevent the ultimate depreciation of the metal; though, as the example of this country proves, it may sensibly retard this result. At all events, the principle is one which should not be overlooked in an examination of the causes which may neutralize the direct tendencies of the gold movement.

So far as to the demand afforded to the gold supplies by the progress of trade and population. Let us now consider briefly another mode of disposing of the new gold, on which some writers have laid much stress: we mean the employment of it in the arts, in plate, and for decorative purposes. And here, as in the case we have just been considering, an examination of the facts shows upon what slight grounds they proceed who anticipate a large absorption of gold by these uses. The desire for display, at least in that gross form of the propensity which finds satisfaction in the possession of gold plate or in the wearing of massive ornaments, is an attribute of semi-barbarous life, which, instead of increasing, declines with the advance of society.

"The display of gold in utensils more or less massive is the luxury of the less refined part of the community, whose eye is instinctively attracted by the glare of a dazzling metal, and whose desire is excited for an object to which there is vulgarly attached the idea of great riches. It is a species of magnificence which was reserved for the sovereigns of primitive nations; it constituted the splendour of the Incas, and that of Attila and of Genseric; it was the pride of the savage races whom the Europeans discovered in America." (P. 98.)

The same passion for ornaments is a powerful instinct amongst the native races of Hindostan, with whom they serve at once as a mode of investment and a means of decoration. But, as civilization makes progress, tastes of a different order are developed. Vanity perhaps loses nothing of its power, but it exhibits itself under a different guise, and is directed to different objects. Luxury, in its modes of display, as in other respects, undergoes refinement, and mankind seek enjoyment, less in the gratification of external sense, and more in the cultivation of the higher faculties. The superfluous expenditure of a nation advancing in civilization is accordingly devoted less and less to objects which absorb mere masses of gold and silver, and more and more to purposes of a higher order—to the beautifying of its domains, the embellishing of its houses, the general cultivation of its tastes; and parks and mansions, pictures, sculpture, and books, take the place of accumulations of plate and collections of jewelry.

This tendency of civilization to check the consumption of the precious metals is very strikingly shown by some figures quoted by M. Chevalier. From returns given in Porter's "Progress of the Nation," it appears that the consumption of gold plate in England during the first half of the present century has not kept pace even with the progress of population. Notwithstanding the great increase which has taken place in the means of all classes during the interval, the average Englishman of the present day consumes less gold than the Englishman of fifty years back.

"From the first quinquennial period of the century to that which closed in 1850, the increase in the quantity of gold which paid duty was 50 per cent.; during the same time the increase of population was much greater: it doubled. Then if we take into account the quantity of gold required for this manufacture, we are amazed at its smallness. It is an atom in comparison with the total production. During the last quinquennial period of the half-century, the annual average has only been 7,636 ounces." (Pp. 92, 93.)

For the two years 1855 and 1856 the average consumption in this form was ten thousand ounces. For the same years the total production was nearly ten millions—that is to say, nearly a thousand times greater! In France a similar state of things is exhibited. There also the consumption of the precious metals proceeds more slowly than the increase of population.

But it will be said, if the fashion of using gold in plate and ornaments is declining, other forms of this kind of expenditure have amazingly increased.

"Paris gilds itself not a little, and is surprisingly addicted to gold lace. Is there not in these two employments a consumption large enough to enable the producers of gold to dispose of their precious commodity, almost indefinitely, without any reduction in its value? To reply to this question, let us calculate the quantity of metal which is required to gild a given surface. Gold, as is known, is the most malleable of metals; it is so to a degree of which it would be difficult, without ocular illustration, to form an idea. The goldbeater makes it into leaves which, thanks to the progress of his art, are now so thin that 14,000 form only the thickness of a millimetre, and, consequently, 14,000,000 of leaves laid one upon another would make a thickness of only a metre (about 39 inches). A cubic metre of solid gold, which would not weigh less than 680,440 ounces, would suffice to gild a surface of 3,450 acres, and 35,300 ounces would cover with gold 179 acres. It is a result which quite confounds the imagination. And yet the metal used in the manufacture of gold lace is spread over a much larger surface. The substance of the threads of which this lace is made consists of silver, the surface alone being gold, and one gramme of gold, worth 2*s.* 10*d.*, suffices to gild a thread 120 miles in length. In a piece of 20 francs (16*s.*), there is gold enough to cover a thread which would extend from Calais to Marseilles. . . . . . Let us now suppose that a room, suitably gilded, consumes five square metres of gold leaf, which is, I believe, sufficient. At this rate 35,300 ounces would gild 144,000 saloons or apartments; that is to say, at least twenty times the number which are thus embellished in one year in all those cities where the houses are of a character to require their interiors to be gilded. With the remainder, what a multitude of picture-frames, books, kettle-drums, cloths, epaulettes, and all kinds of objects, might be clothed in a dazzling covering of gold! Let the number of gold leaves required for each apartment be multiplied, let the number of books and picture-frames be augmented, and still we shall arrive at no result which deserves a moment's consideration. At Paris, where nearly all the gold leaf is beaten which is consumed in France and a part of Europe, the quantity of gold operated upon does not exceed 40,650 to 42,400 ounces." (Pp 95—97.)

It would therefore seem that not much is to be expected from the extending use of gold in manufactures as a means of disposing of the new supplies. No doubt, as depreciation sets in, the fall in the value of the metal will, as in the case of other commodities, have some effect in inducing a larger consumption; but, with the facts before us which have just been cited, this can scarcely be expected to occur to an extent which would materially retard the fall.

And here we may mention an incident of the decline in the value of gold, which is strangely at variance with popular anticipations, and will probably be cited as a proof that no depreciation has taken place. People generally imagine that as gold declines in value gold manufactures of all kinds will become cheaper. In one sense they will; they will be obtainable at a less outlay of labour; but they will not become cheaper in the sense in which the word is commonly understood—that is to say, they will not be obtainable *at a lower price*. On the contrary, in all countries where, as in this, gold is the standard metal, as its value declines *the price of gold manufactures will rise*. A little reflection will make this plain. Suppose the exchange-value of gold to fall, let us consider what will be the effect of this upon the price of a gold snuff-box. So far as the *material* of the article is concerned, it is evident that the fall in the value of gold will have no effect, will be simply nugatory, since the same cause which will reduce the value of the material will reduce also the value of the coin (or notes convertible into coin) with which it is procured; the relation between money and raw gold will continue the same as before, and the price of the material of the box will therefore continue unaltered. But the material is only one element of the cost; there is, besides this, the labour expended in the making, and this also must be included in the price of the snuff-box. Now the effect of a fall in the exchange-value of gold will be to raise the money-price of labour in common with other things; whence it is plain that, with the progress of this fall, the price of the snuff-box, which must cover the cost of labour as well as that of raw material, must constantly rise. The effect may not be very perceptible in gold articles of much solidity; but in such manufactures as gold lace, in which the value of the workmanship greatly exceeds the value of the material, the rise in price will be nearly as remarkable as if gold did not enter into their composition.

Such are the two principal outlets which have been suggested as likely to create a market for the new gold; and, considerable as they at first sight appear, this examination of them has shown how entirely inadequate they must prove to sustain its value, supposing the production of the metal to continue at its present rate. The facts of the case thus distinctly point to a general depreciation of gold as the inevitable result of the causes now in action.

Against this conclusion, however, will be urged our experience of the movement up to the present time. Already, it will be said, for eight years the golden stream has been flowing: not less than 200,000,000*l.* sterling of metal have already been added to the common stock; and yet we look in vain for those signs of depreciation which, if there be any foundation for the apprehensions which have been expressed, should surely by this time have displayed themselves. No perceptible change, it is asserted, has yet taken place in the general level of prices, no disturbance has been experienced in our pecuniary relations. If, then, under the weight of this large augmentation, the value of the metal has been sustained, there is clearly some fact or principle at work which has been overlooked in the reasonings on the subject; and if this fact or principle (whatever it may be) has been hitherto efficacious in preventing a fall, may we not expect that it will continue to be so? If no sensible effect has up to the present been produced, why, with only the same influences to contend against, need we be apprehensive for the future?

This argument is to be met by a twofold answer: first, by a denial of the fact which is assumed, that no change has taken place in the value of gold; and secondly, by pointing to a circumstance which has hitherto retarded its decline, but the influence of which must soon diminish.

With respect to the first point it should be observed, that it must always be a matter of considerable difficulty to ascertain whether, in point of fact, gold has during a given time fallen in value or not, unless the fall happens to be of a very marked and unequivocal kind. This must be so from the absence of any independent standard of value by which its variations can be measured, as well as from the variety of causes which, besides the value of money, affect the prices of commodities, and thus complicate the problem. There is, moreover, a principle in constant operation which, in a large class of cases, tends to conceal any fall which may occur in the value of the precious metals—we mean, the progress of the industrial arts. Every improvement in productive industry tends to promote cheapness and to lower price; and, as such improvements are constantly occurring, a fall in the value of gold will be as often shown in preventing a fall in the price of other things as in causing a rise. To ascertain, therefore, whether a change in the value of gold has really occurred must always be a difficult problem, requiring for its solution not only an extensive collection and accurate analysis of prices, but also a careful examination of the various causes affecting production on the one hand and consumption on the other: and it is a problem which, applied to the last ten years, presents, owing to the numerous causes of powerful disturbance which have been in action during that time, even more than the usual difficulty. We do not, therefore, propose to enter into this question here, but shall content ourselves with referring in a note * to some publications, in which it has been discussed with considerable fulness. By reference to these the reader will find that the facts of the case, far from being favourable to the assumption that the value of gold has been unaffected by the increased supply, lead rather to the conclusion, that there are grounds for believing that a definitive depreciation of the metal has already taken place.

* See tables of prices from 1851 to 1857 ("History of Prices," vol. vi. pp. 160—167); also an article by M. Levasseur in the *Journal des Économistes*, March 1858; also tables published by Dr. Soetbeer of Hamburg, giving returns of prices from 1831 to 1857; also the Appendix to this volume.

But, secondly, the above reasoning is to be answered by pointing to a circumstance which has undoubtedly acted up to the present time in counteraction of the causes tending to depress the value of gold, but the efficacy of which is diminishing, and may soon be entirely exhausted. This circumstance is the displacement of silver by gold in some currencies, and more particularly in that of France—a circumstance to which M. Chevalier very forcibly directs our attention, and which ranks unquestionably as of primary importance amongst the causes which have modified the gold movement up to the present time.

In the controversies which have taken place on this question, it has been almost uniformly assumed on the one side and conceded on the other, that, for the purpose of detecting variations in the value of gold, no better test can be selected than the price—that is, the gold-price—of silver;* and the price of silver not having risen more than 3 or 4 per cent. in the last ten years, it is argued that this ratio represents the utmost extent of the depreciation which can have taken place in gold. Indeed some writers have pressed this argument so far, as to maintain that gold has not fallen even to this extent; the rise in the price of silver, as they allege, being due rather to the increase in the demand for it than to the fall in the value of gold.

* Strange to say, even M. Chevalier makes this concession, although the facts which he adduces effectually expose its fallaciousness. "The only good measure of the rise or fall occurring in the value of gold, is that which takes place in its price in silver money." He adds: "Then it must be premised that no disturbance shall have arisen to cause a sudden change in the value of silver." But such a disturbance is produced *ipso facto* by a change in the value of gold.

But surely nothing can be more fallacious than the test of value which is thus set up. If anything unfits one commodity for measuring the value of another, it is the circumstance that they may both be applied to common purposes. No one would think of measuring the fluctuations in wheat by comparing it with oats, because, both grains being employed for the same or similar purposes, any change in the value of one is sure to extend to the other. When, *e.g.*, the wheat crop is in excess while the oat crop is an average one, it always happens that a portion of the consumption, which in ordinary years falls upon oats, is thrown upon wheat; the effect of which is at once to check the fall in the price of the more abundant grain, while, by diminishing the need for the other, it causes it to participate in the decline. The influence of the increased abundance of one commodity is thus distributed over both; the fall in price being less intense in degree in proportion as it is wider in extent. Now this is precisely what is happening in the relations of gold and silver. The crop of gold has been unusually large; the increase in the supply has caused a fall in its value; the fall in its value has led to its being substituted for silver; a mass of silver has thus been disengaged from purposes which it was formerly employed to serve, and the result has been that both metals have fallen in value together; the depth of the fall being diminished as the surface over which it has taken place has been enlarged. The scene on which this interchange of gold and silver has hitherto been exhibited on the largest scale is the currency of France, in which, owing to the existence of a double standard,—or (if M. Chevalier prefers the phrase) a double legal tender,—one or the other metal is employed according as its worth in the markets of the world happens to vary in relation to its valuation at the French Mint. Until a recent period, the metal which formed the staple of the French currency was silver, but, owing to the fall in the value of gold consequent upon the discoveries, gold is now rapidly taking its place, and becoming the principal medium of circulation. Up to the year 1852 the importation of silver into France was always largely in excess of its exportation; but in that year the tide turned, and has since continued flowing outward with increasing volume. M. Chevalier states that by the end of 1857 France had parted with 45,000,000*l.* sterling of silver. On the other hand, during this time she had coined more than 100,000,000*l.* sterling of gold. The currency of France has thus, to borrow the curious but not unapt figure of our author, played towards gold the part of a parachute to moderate its descent. But in proportion as gold has thus found a market, silver has been deprived of one; and the 45,000,000*l.* of silver liberated from the currency of France is as much an addition to the disposable supply in the world, and tends as effectually to lower its value, as if it had been raised immediately from the mines. The fall in the value of gold has thus, up to the present time, been at once checked and concealed,—checked by being substituted for silver, and concealed by being compared with it.*

* We are aware it has been maintained that the value of silver, so far from having fallen, has really risen during the last few years; in proof of

This substitution, however, of gold for silver in French circulation is not a process which can be carried on indefinitely, and M. Chevalier shows that it has already nearly reached its natural termination. When this has happened, the new gold will be deprived of that which has hitherto constituted its best market, the parachute which has moderated its descent will no longer be available; and what will be the consequence?

"From that moment," says M. Chevalier, "the fall in gold will be rapid. In a word, if, down to the present time, the immense production, of which Australia and California have been the theatre, has not produced a greater fall in gold, it is France which is the cause." (P. 62.)

which we are referred to the increased demand for it for Oriental remittance. That silver has risen in its *gold*-price owing to this circumstance, we admit, but we deny that this is a proof of a rise in its *value*, any more than a rise in the gold-price of any other commodity would prove a rise in its value at a time when the supply of gold was rapidly increasing. During the last two years (1858 and 1859) the demand for silver for the East has been affected a good deal by requirements connected with the Indian Mutiny; but if we investigate the causes of the extraordinary demand which has characterized the last four or five years, we shall find that they are in a principal degree traceable to the increased production of gold, operating through the expenditure of enlarged money incomes in England and the United States on Oriental productions; and that thus the increased demand for silver, which is alleged as a proof that silver has risen in value, *is in reality a consequence of the large amount of gold available for its purchase.* Now if a disturbance in the relative values of the precious metals, arising from *this* cause, is to be taken as a proof, not that gold has fallen, but that silver has risen in value, then it would be quite impossible ever to prove a depreciation of gold. The same argument might be applied to all other commodities; in each case it could be shown that the rise in price was the result of an increased demand for the article, and every advance in general prices would be attributed, not to the depreciation of money, but to the enhancement of commodities. In short, since money can only fall in value by being made the instrument of demand, the value of money could, according to this mode of reasoning, never fall.

We are disposed to qualify in some degree our assent to this opinion. We think that, on the occurrence of the contingency in question—the exhaustion of silver from the French currency—the depreciation of gold will be more rapid, but we question if the acceleration of the decline will be as great as the words we have quoted seem to imply. M. Chevalier appears to assume that, when the process now going on in France is completed, all further substitution of one metal for the other will be at an end, and that the action of future supplies, concentrated on gold alone, will tell in the depreciation of this metal with proportionate effect. But we question the correctness of this assumption. We are inclined to think that the substitution of gold for silver in France is only a very striking example of a process which has been in unobserved operation over a much wider area, and which will continue after the French movement has ceased. In India, where there is an immense silver currency, the process has already begun, and signs are not wanting that it will soon assume more important dimensions. The Indian Government, for reasons set forth in Mr. Wilson's Minute on the introduction of a gold currency, have indeed refused to establish a double standard in that country; and we cannot, therefore, count upon a contingency of this kind as likely to carry on in the East the process which must ere long be complete in France: still, considering the great suitability of gold for the purposes of ornamental manufacture, and of hoarding—purposes which prevail so extensively in India, and for which gold is much better adapted than silver—we cannot doubt but that, as, in the course of depreciation, the metal becomes obtainable on more favourable terms, it will gradually find its way, if not into the circulation, at least into the ornaments and hoards, and eventually displace silver to a considerable extent. These considerations do not apply to India alone: they are applicable more or less extensively to other countries where silver is the currency, and more particularly to China, where there is a large silver circulation, and where the habits of the people are in many respects similar to those of the people of Hindostan. For these reasons, we cannot concur in the assumption, that, when the movement in the French currency is concluded, the future action of the new gold must be concentrated upon the gold currencies of the world. We think that its effect will still continue to be shared, though probably in a less degree than heretofore, by the other precious metal; and that consequently the fall in gold, though accelerated, will not proceed with that rapidity which M. Chevalier seems to anticipate.*

* [The writer can now (1872) claim the verdict of events in favour of the view which he here ventured to maintain against that taken by M. Chevalier. Indeed, the course of depreciation has been even less affected by the completion of the process of substituting gold for silver in the currency of France than he anticipated. That process would seem to have been completed about the year 1861, when the coinage of gold in France fell from 27,000,000*l.* and 18,000,000*l.*—the amounts which it had reached in the years 1859 and 1860—to less than 4,000,000*l.* (See *Economist*, 29th June, 1872, article "On the Coinage of Gold.") But he is not aware that any sensible change in the rapidity of the depreciation of gold can be traced to that period. It would be difficult indeed to determine this question by reference to general prices; but if any effect, such as M. Chevalier anticipated, occurred, it would have shown itself in a rise in the price of silver. In point of fact, the price of silver has undergone little change over the whole of this period, and is now rather lower than when M. Chevalier wrote. This may be partly due to the increased production of silver in recent years, which would more or less counteract any tendency to an advance in its price; but I have no doubt the principal cause is that

But, although for these reasons we do not anticipate that rapid and sudden fall in the value of gold which M. Chevalier regards as the sure result of the exhaustion of silver from France (or more correctly, of the repletion of the French currency with gold), we nevertheless fully admit, supposing the present production to continue, that the contingencies to which we have adverted can at the utmost delay, they cannot prevent, this catastrophe. Regarding therefore, with him, an extensive depreciation of gold as probable, we shall conclude this article by adverting to some of the consequences which this result is likely to entail.

These consequences are at once so numerous and so complicated, they will be felt in such large and in such minute transactions in life, that to develop them fully would require a volume instead of a few pages. As we have already intimated, there is a wide department of this question on which M. Chevalier does not enter at all *—of the existence of which indeed he scarcely seems to be aware; but even within the range to which he has confined himself, the questions which arise are both numerous and important.

One of the most important aspects of every social change is its effect on the working classes—those who

assigned in the text—the extensive substitution of gold for silver, not only in various currencies in different countries, but in all those uses in which the two metals may be indifferently employed. In truth, so completely are gold and silver identified as economic agencies by this capacity for mutual substitution, that in judging of the probable effect of increased supplies of either metal, the safest course would probably be to consider them as one commodity, and to compare, not gold with gold and silver with silver, but the aggregate additions made to both metals with the aggregate quantities of both previously existing.]

* That discussed in Essay III. of this volume.

live by the sweat of their brow, and who in every country form the bulk of the population. Let us then inquire, What will be the effect of the gold discoveries on the interests of this large section of mankind? Will the event tend on the whole to improve or to deteriorate, to raise or to depress, their condition? The opinion of M. Chevalier is that, during the period while depreciation is in progress—a period which may extend over ten or twenty, or possibly over thirty or forty years—the effect may be prejudicial. As soon indeed as the movement shall have reached its lowest point, and gold shall have found its natural level, then he conceives the wages of the workman will rise in the same proportion as the price of his food, so that, while paying and receiving larger sums of money, he will be placed substantially in the same position as at present; but, pending the attainment of this result, the ordeal of depreciation will, as he thinks, be for the working classes a disastrous one.

"Experience shows that, when provisions rise, wages are not necessarily raised in the same proportion. Not that an upward movement of wages does not follow a continued dearness of provisions, but in the majority of employments it follows far behind. The working population are of all classes of society the most dependent, because they are the most necessitous. Being the least able to wait, owing to the pressure of want, they are the more apt to resign themselves to the terms offered them. Hence it is that the benefits which they expect to derive from a rise of wages are only yielded to them after many delays. It were easy to cite examples in proof of this assertion. It has been the subject of remark by Mr. Tooke in his important work on the 'History of Prices.' In his historical inquiry respecting the precious metals, Mr. Jacob has several remarks in the same sense, and among others he states his opinion that the institution of the Poor Law, which it is known dates from the reign of Elizabeth, was in England the effect of the changes caused by the fall in the precious metals." (Pp. 117, 118.)

From this opinion of M. Chevalier (which is endorsed by Mr. Cobden in his preface) we venture to dissent. We do not believe that the working classes, *as a body*—whatever may be the case with particular sections of them or in particular countries—will be injured by the depreciation of gold. We hold, on the contrary, that the general effect of the gold discoveries will be to alter the distribution of wealth in their favour, and on the whole to benefit them.

According to M. Chevalier, the industrial classes will suffer during the progress of the depreciation of gold, because the prices of the commodities they consume will constantly rise in advance of the rise in their wages. Now this we conceive to be, as a general proposition, essentially impossible. If the prices of the labourer's provisions and clothing rise, this result can only happen (assuming that the rise proceeds from an abundance of money) because more money is spent on those commodities; and, inasmuch as the labouring classes themselves immensely outnumber all classes who consume the same commodities, it is plain that it is *their* expenditure, and consequently *their* wages, which must substantially regulate the rise. The rise in wages, in short, is (where it proceeds from an abundance of money) the cause of the rise in the price of commodities, and consequently cannot be preceded by its own effect.

The circumstance which misled M. Chevalier appears from his reference to the remark of Mr. Tooke; for the case which Mr. Tooke had in view was the rise in the prices of corn and provisions which occurred during the last French wars—a rise due indeed in some slight degree to the depreciation then existing in the English currency, but, according to the opinion of Mr. Tooke, and we believe of all persons who have examined the facts of that time, due principally to the unusual number of deficient harvests which then occurred, aggravated as this circumstance was by the interruption of supplies from abroad during the war. The rise in prices at that time proceeded, in short, from a dearth of commodities, not from an abundance of money; and the rise in wages which followed, as a matter of necessity, fell short of the advance in provisions, since it was only thus that consumption could be kept within the limits of supply. It is by confounding the effects of these two very different cases that M. Chevalier has fallen into the error of supposing that the labouring classes, as a body, must suffer from the depreciation of gold.

But the view thus suggested has probably been confirmed by another circumstance. It would seem, as a matter of fact, that prices *in France* have up to the present time advanced more rapidly than wages.*

* See the articles by M. Levasseur, published in the *Journal des Économistes*, February and March 1858. [Since 1858 the relative advance in wages and prices, at least in some important trades, would seem to be in an opposite sense. The following I quote from Mr. Brassey's recent work (pp. 158, 159):—"Mr. Fane says, in his report to Lord Stanley, that 'the general rate of money wages in France has increased about 40 per cent. in the last fifteen years, in those industries which

This, however, is not a necessary or general consequence of the depreciation of gold, but, like the case of England in the sixteenth century to which Jacob refers, is to be attributed to that other operation of the gold movement, of which we have more than once spoken—the change it is causing in the distribution of national wealth. In the sixteenth century this disturbance was in favour of the Spanish, the Portuguese, and the Dutch; while the English, further removed from the spring-head of the new metal, received their supplies more slowly and in scantier streams. Money incomes in England therefore rose less rapidly than prices in common markets, and the population of England suffered accordingly. We have no doubt that this was a leading cause of the industrial distress which prevailed throughout a portion of the reign of Queen Elizabeth,* and which led to the introduction of the Poor Law. In the present gold movement, however, the tables have been turned, and the monetary disturbance is now in favour of the Anglo-Saxon. It is now England and the United States that have their hands in the till, and the money which they extract is employed in raising prices against the nations

compete with foreigners in the neutral markets. This rise in the money wages has been accompanied by a considerable rise in the price of food and clothing; still, the relative proportions in which money wages and the prices of commodities have risen, leave a margin in favour of the former.' "]

* See on this point a curious work, entitled "A Briefe Conceipte touching the Common Weale of this Realme of England," published in 1581 and attributed to William Stafford. Of this work Anderson, in his "Annals," conjectures that it was written by direction of the Queen's ministers, "since scarcely any ordinary person in those early days could be furnished with so copious a fund of excellent matter."

which in the sixteenth century were gainers at their expense. It is to this cause—the disturbance created by the gold discoveries in the distribution of purchasing power in the world—that the movement of prices in France in advance of incomes (so far as this is a fact) is to be attributed, and not to any tendency in prices during a depreciation of money to rise more rapidly than the incomes by the expenditure of which alone they can be raised.

And here we may remark, as bearing on the practical purpose which M. Chevalier had in view in this discussion—the change of the monetary standard in France from gold to silver—that the consideration here urged goes directly to the root of his argument. If the sufferings of the French workmen during the period of transition be the result of a depreciation of the standard, then of course the disaster may be avoided by substituting for gold, as our author recommends, a metal such as silver, of which the value is steady; but if, as we contend, the evil in question be the result of the increased purchasing power of other nations, it is plain that the proposed remedy must be futile. No change in the Mint regulations of France will prevent the nations which are in possession of the new gold from appropriating an increased proportion of the aggregate wealth of the world. To effect this, it would be necessary not merely to deprive gold of its character as a standard, but to annihilate its purchasing power altogether, to dethrone it from its position as the universal equivalent of commerce.

As we have already intimated, we conceive that the gold movement, whatever may be its effect in particular cases, will, on the whole, operate favourably for the industrial classes of society, by throwing into their hands an increased share of the purchasing power of the world. It is this which we regard as the great redeeming incident of the gold discoveries. In almost every other aspect in which we contemplate the occurrence, it is fraught with inconvenience, hardship, and injustice, introducing uncertainty into mercantile dealings, disturbing contracts which were designed to be fixed, stimulating the spirit of commercial speculation, already too strong, and bringing unmerited loss upon classes who have the strongest claims on our sympathy, and whom upon social grounds it is most desirable to sustain.

If we inquire who the people are who will suffer by the impending monetary changes, the answer is, in the first place and principally, those whose incomes consist in fixed sums of money, or whose property depends on fixed contracts expressed in the current gold coin of the realm. Adopting the assumption of M. Chevalier (which with him we make for the sake of distinctness, and not as expressing a matured opinion), that the fall in the value of gold will be 50 per cent., then the loss to the holders of all such incomes will be to the extent of one-half of their means. They will receive the same nominal amount as at present, the same number of bank-notes, which will be exchangeable for the same number of sovereigns of the same weight and fineness; but these bank-notes or sovereigns will only procure one-half as much of the necessaries, comforts, and luxuries of life as they would do in the absence of a depreciation of money. This is surely a serious matter, and its gravity is not diminished when we consider who the persons are that by the course of events (always supposing the production of gold to continue) will be placed in this position. They are, in the first place, fundholders and mortgagees, a class who, whatever may be the popular idea upon the subject, really deserve as much consideration and sympathy as any other in the community. For of what is a large portion of funded property, and of property lent on mortgage, composed? To a very large extent, as is well known, of trust money, constituting as such, the provision made for widows and orphans, for younger children and minors, and others who from their age, sex, or circumstances are incapacitated for taking part in the active pursuits of life. The persons thus provided for are also very frequently persons whose social rank is rather in advance of their pecuniary means of supporting it, with whom, therefore, a reduction of income will frequently necessitate, not merely a curtailment of physical enjoyment, but a descent in the social scale, a loss of caste and position, with the many distressing mortifications which such a loss involves. Again, trust money includes the property of endowed bodies, of charitable and benevolent institutions, schools, hospitals, and churches, all which, with the fall in the value of gold, will be deprived of a corresponding proportion of their income, and thus find abridged their means of public usefulness. Further, the depreciation of money will fall heavily on those, not confined to any class, but in general the most deserving of all classes, who seek to provide against the precariousness of uncertain incomes, by adopting the practice of life assurance. All contracts of this kind are purely monetary contracts, and as such based ultimately upon gold; and with the fall in the value of gold, every person in whose favour a life is insured will be damnified to the full extent of the depreciation. He will receive indeed the same nominal sum for which he bargained; but this sum will be worth less to him for all the practical purposes of life. Instead of representing, as is commonly imagined, secure affluence, and pensioned idleness—interests which may well bear some additional pressure—the interests at stake in funded or mortgage property, as well as those at stake in life assurance, are among the most helpless as well as the most important which society comprises. It would be nearer the truth to say that they represent the classes on whom a pecuniary loss will inflict the maximum of harm.

But the loss from the depreciation of money will not be confined to the recipients of fixed money incomes. Those also will be sufferers by the change, though in a less degree and for a temporary period, whose remuneration is determined more by custom than by competition; and this description includes a much larger number of persons than is commonly supposed. It includes, *e.g.*, two of the three learned professions, the medical and the legal, and a not unimportant portion of the third. It includes also the large number of officials, whether civil or military, whether in public or private employment, who are hired on yearly salaries. With respect to this large class, although their remuneration will probably in the end be brought into harmony with the altered state of pecuniary affairs, yet during the period of transition the adjustment will always be in arrear of events; and those who are comprised in it will suffer accordingly. The rise in prices will be very palpable before a doctor's or barrister's fee will be increased, or salaries in the Civil Service raised.

On the other hand, it must be remembered (and although M. Chevalier has not overlooked this side of the question, he has scarcely, we think, given it its due weight) that for every loss of this kind there is, from the nature of the case, a corresponding gain. If the national creditor be mulcted to the extent of one-half of his property, the tax-payer pockets an equal sum; if the mortgagee loses, the mortgagor gains; if the professional classes are curtailed in their earnings, the public who employ them obtain their services so much the more cheaply. There is thus in all cases a set-off; and this being so, it might seem as if, whatever were the case with individuals, with the community as a whole there would be neither loss nor gain, neither benefit nor injury. But we must not lightly acquiesce in so indiscriminate a conclusion; for, putting aside entirely the substantial injustice involved in the discharge of obligations in a sense different from that in which they were incurred; putting aside all the dangers of a change affecting deeply an extensive mass of interests, and opening to society an ordeal which M. Chevalier thinks sufficiently formidable to deserve the epithet 'revolutionary;' putting these considerations aside, and considering solely the effect of the pecuniary transfer, the question still remains, whether the changes of condition thus produced are, on the whole, salutary or the reverse; whether they conduce to the gain or loss—social and moral as well as purely economical—of the nation in which they occur. We have already stated our opinion that the effect of the gold discoveries will be to improve the physical status of the great body of the people; and this we regard as a gain on the whole sufficient to outweigh all the concomitant evils. Yet we are far from thinking those evils either trifling or few. It affords slight matter for congratulation that a large number of respectable people in narrow circumstances, many of them old and helpless, should be deprived of one-half of their livelihood in order that tax-payers may be discharged from a portion of their fair liabilities; or that the recipients of charitable endowments, widows and orphans, the sick and infirm, the needy in mind and in body, should be stinted in their supplies for the purpose of relieving landlords of their encumbrances: and as little do we think it a matter for rejoicing that the mercantile and manufacturing classes should be aggrandized at the expense of physicians, barristers, and members of the Civil Service. It may be said, indeed, that such a transfer of property tends to strengthen the motives to enterprise and accumulation, and thus to promote the growth of national wealth. But, before conceding much weight to this argument, we may ask if the strengthening of such motives be at present such a social desideratum, either in Great Britain or in the United States (the countries which will reap the largest profit from the movement), as to be worth procuring at such a cost.

It seems to us that the instincts of commercial

enterprise are already sufficiently strong in the Anglo-Saxon race, and that it is not so much more wealth that we want, as a higher sense of the responsibilities of wealth, and that more judicious expenditure of it which would accompany more just perceptions. If this be so, we may well doubt if the pecuniary disturbances with which we are threatened, are likely to prove as purely beneficial as those whose faith in progress is more robust than our own are accustomed to describe them. The mode in which wealth is distributed is always of more importance than its aggregate amount; and a process which increases the aggregate amount of wealth only by operating on its distribution, is therefore, at best, a questionable specific. We have seen what the nature of the impending changes is. They will in many instances increase, instead of mitigating, existing inequalities of condition. They will enrich the cosmopolitan merchant at the expense of the petty trader. They will enrich the commercial classes, as a whole, at the expense of possessors of fixed incomes, of the professional classes, and of salaried *employés*. Landlords will probably, on the whole, be gainers; they will lose temporarily where the outstanding leases are long, but they will gain permanently through the lightening of their fixed encumbrances; the balance of gain being obtained by encroaching on the incomes of their mortgagees. The tendency of the movement, as amongst the middle and higher portions of society, will thus be to aggrandize the wealthy at the expense of the indigent; to tax the more liberal and enlightened for the benefit of the more narrow-minded and selfish; to enrich those whose command of wealth is perhaps already somewhat in advance of their sense of its responsibilities, from the means of classes at once more necessitous and more cultivated. These are the evils of the change, and against these we have to set the benefit to the working classes, and the ultimate gain to the world from the opening of new and fertile regions to man's industry, and the extension of his dominion over the earth.

That good will on the whole predominate, we believe; but let us not, on this account, close our eyes to the serious cost at which this preponderance of good will be obtained. To a very great extent the cost is inevitable and must be met, but something may be done towards lessening the evils of the crisis by giving timely warning of its approach. Means may be found in the framing of settlements and leases, and in the selection of investments, to mitigate its severity; the grand rule being, to avoid as much as possible purely monetary securities, such as the funds, mortgages, preference shares, and, in general, investments the returns on which do not rise with the advance in prices and salaries. The foresight of Lord Burleigh, warned by the changes which he saw around him, effected in the sixteenth century the partial substitution of corn for money rents, and in this way the incomes of colleges and other institutions have been preserved, which but for this precaution would have long since dwindled into insignificance.* The plan adopted under the Tithe

* [The example of Lord Burleigh may be commended to the wise people who are now, in the full flow of depreciation, recommending the compul-

Commutation Act, for regulating rent-charge by the price of agricultural produce, suggests another means by which the crisis may be moderated. A permissive law, facilitating arrangements of this kind, would be free from all objection on the score of justice, and might be attended with public advantage. But, after all is said, I fear it must be confessed that the great evils of the transition are not of a kind that can be largely alleviated. In the main they must be borne, and the sufferers must endeavour to console themselves with the reflection, that while "the individual withers," "the world is more and more."

POSTSCRIPT.

The reader will probably be interested to learn the course of the gold movement since the foregoing essays were written. To enable him to appreciate this in connection with what had gone before, it will be well to state here the leading facts of the production and distribution of the new gold from the outset down to the present time. These I am enabled to set forth in a form at once brief and authentic, thanks to a series of carefully prepared

sory sale of corporate property in land and the investment of the proceeds in the funds, and this *in the interest of the corporations!* Lord Burleigh was no political economist, but he was an extremely shrewd man, and knew what he was about. The supporters of the above proposal no doubt consider themselves strong in political economy, and would gladly make the science responsible for their projects. Whatever may be thought of their economic pretensions, one can at least have no difficulty in admitting that they too may know what they are about. Some very large fortunes have been made within the last few years; and it would, no doubt, be extremely convenient for some people that land in large quantities should suddenly be thrown upon the market.

articles which have been recently published on this subject in the *Economist.*[*]

The first facts to be noted are (1) the total stock of gold in the world at the date of the Californian and Australian discoveries, and (2) the rate at which the production of gold was taking place in the period immediately preceding. These were as follows:—

The total (estimated) stock of gold in the world in 1848, was 560,000,000*l.*

As for the annual production, it had varied considerably since the beginning of the century. In 1800 it was, according to the best estimates, rather over 3,000,000*l.* But at a later period important discoveries of gold were made in Asiatic Russia, and for the five or six years ending 1848 the annual produce would seem to have varied from 5*l.* to about 8,000,000*l.*

Such was the state of things immediately preceding 1848. In that year the Californian discoveries took place, and these were followed by the discoveries in Australia in 1851. For these three years the annual average production is set down by the *Economist* at 9,000,000*l.*, but from this date the production suddenly rose to, for 1852, 27,000,000*l.*, and continued to rise till 1856, when it attained its maximum of 32,250,000*l.* At this stage a decline in the returns occurred, the lowest point reached being in 1860, when they fell to 18,683,000*l.*, but from this they rose again, and for the last ten years have maintained an average of about 20,500,000*l.*; the returns for the year 1871 being 20,811,000*l.*

The total amount of gold added to the world's

* See the *Economist*, June 29th, August 3rd and 31st, 1872.

stock by this twenty years' production has been about 500,000,000*l.*, an amount nearly equal to that existing in the world at the date of the discoveries in other words, the stock of gold in the world has been nearly doubled since that time.

As regards the distribution of this enormous sum, those who desire details will find them very fully and carefully tabulated in the articles of the *Economist* to which reference has just been made. For my present purpose it will suffice to indicate the main currents of the movement; and these can only be given for the period since 1858, that being the year when specie imports began to be regularly published by the Board of Trade. Since that year the production of gold has been about 300,000,000*l.*, and this has been distributed through three principal channels. The first and largest is that of which the tributaries, flowing from Australia and California, and in the latter case passing through the United States, converge on England, whence the body of the stream passes on to the Continent of Europe, and in large part finally to the East. About 190,000,000*l*, out of the 300,000,000*l.* produced since 1858, have been thus disposed of. The stream of next importance is that which passes from the new gold countries direct to the East, and chiefly to India, by which way some 50,000,000*l.* have been carried off. This disposes of the whole of the Californian and Australian production, with the exception of 26,000,000*l.*, retained by Australia for her own purposes. Lastly, there is the Russian supply, which appears to have passed in large part to France, whence, in greater or less amount, it has been transferred to other Continental countries.

These have been the principal channels of distribution; but an important consideration remains—in what proportions have the various countries permanently absorbed the gold thus flowing through the channels of commerce? The following are the results arrived at by the *Economist*, still, the reader will recollect, for the period between 1858 and the present:—

Retained in England	£68,000,000
„ in Continental Europe (chiefly in France)	105,000,000
„ in Portugal and some other countries not included in the last entry . .	12,000,000
„ in South America	8,000,000
„ in India and the East	90,000,000
„ in Australia	26,000,000
* Total production since 1858	£309,000,000

The only other point connected with the movement which it will be needful here to refer to is the net addition which, as the result of the whole, has accrued to our own currency. As has been seen, it follows from the figures given by the *Economist*, that of the whole amount of gold passing through England since 1858 (about 190,000,000*l.*) 68,000,000*l.* have been retained in the country. The question arises, how has this sum been disposed of? The *Economist* answers that 28,000,000*l.* have been absorbed by our currency;

* So the figures are set down by the *Economist;* yet no place is given in the table to the United States; which, including California, must surely (notwithstanding the existence of an inconvertible currency) have retained some portion of the supplies.

60,000,000*l.* having been coined from the new gold, and 32,000,000*l.* of this having gone abroad. The 28,000,000*l.* thus added to our gold circulation would, as the *Economist* remarks, of course be a maximum sum. Taking it at 25,000,000*l.*, and accepting Mr. Newmarch's estimate of the coin in circulation in 1857 as 75,000,000*l.*, this would bring our gold currency at the present time up to 100,000,000*l.*—rather more than double the amount estimated by Mr. Newmarch as in circulation a few years previous to 1848. Assuming the facts to stand thus, our gold circulation would have been about doubled since the gold discoveries. This, however, only accounts for, at most, 28,000,000*l.* out of the 68,000,000*l.* retained in one form or another in the country since 1858; and here a question arises as to what has become of the remaining 40,000,000*l.* retained at home, but not entering into the circulation? The answer given to this question by the *Economist* appears to me, I confess, the least satisfactory part of its statement. It in effect amounts to this, that, allowing for 12,000,000*l.* as probably existing in the form of foreign coin, partly in the reserves of the Bank of England, and partly in the hands of exchange dealers, the remainder—28,000,000*l.*—has been used up for purposes of art and manufacture; in other words, that the United Kingdom has, in this way, consumed about 2,000,000*l.* of gold annually since 1858. As far as appears, there are no grounds for supposing such a consumption except the difficulty of otherwise accounting for the gold. For my part, in presence of M. Chevalier's facts and arguments on this subject, I find it quite impossible to accept this explanation, and should even prefer to believe, were there no other alternative, that a considerable portion of the missing sum had somehow escaped from the country without getting into the Government returns.

The foregoing statements give an outline of the movement during the period under review, so far as *gold* is concerned; but the real character of its effects on the monetary systems of the world cannot be understood without taking into account the simultaneous operations in silver. For example, one of the most important considerations connected with the subject is the proportions in which the additions made to the monetary stock have been absorbed by the different commercial countries. From the table given above it would seem as if the Continent of Europe was the largest absorbent—larger even than India and the East; but in point of fact the greater portion of the 105,000,000*l.* of new gold retained by Continental Europe has been employed in substitution for silver formerly existing in her currencies, the silver thus parted with having in the main been passed on to the East. The addition therefore made to the metallic currencies of the Continent, as the result of the gold movement, is greatly less than the mere gold statistics would indicate; while the addition made to Oriental currencies is very much greater. I have no data from which to estimate the precise amount thus transferred, nor is there any need here to go into details. A single fact will suffice to give an idea of the scale on which this silver movement has been proceeding. I find that the amount of silver which passed to the

East by way of Egypt alone during the last fifteen years has amounted to no less than 95,000,000*l.*; of this the greater portion was taken from the currencies of Europe, and principally from that of France, and the whole has been added, over and above the 90,000,000*l.* of gold stated above, to the currencies of India and the East. The largest absorbents, therefore, of the vast additions now being made to the monetary stock of the world have not been the countries of Continental Europe, but Oriental countries, mainly India and China. We thus find, in conformity with the mode of distribution described in the third of the foregoing essays, that, although England and the United States receive the chief portion of the new supplies in the first instance, yet of these only a small part is retained permanently in their currencies. The rest is passed on to the Continent of Europe and to Asia; while, again, of the portion sent to the Continent probably the largest part finds its way ultimately to the East, not indeed always in the form in which it entered the Continent,—not, that is to say, as gold,—but in that of silver, into which it has been transmuted on the way.

V.

CO-OPERATION IN THE SLATE QUARRIES OF NORTH WALES.*

THE public must now be tolerably familiar with the story of the Rochdale Equitable Pioneers, and of the numerous societies, founded upon the same principles, which in various parts of the country have already accomplished such great things for the working people, and given earnest for the future of still greater achievements in their behalf. It has heard something also of other and more genuine examples of "co-operation,"—where associates not only trade but "work" together, where the labourers are also the capitalists, and wages and profits return to the same hands; experiments which, small as have been the actual fruits they have hitherto yielded, form yet, in the opinion of those who have most deeply pondered the problem of industrial reform, the most solid grounds of hope for the future permanent elevation of the labouring class.† But there is, besides

* *Macmillan's Magazine*, January 1865.

† See an article of great interest in the *Westminster Review* for April 1864, entitled "Strikes and Industrial Co-operation," in which the whole subject is handled with remarkable ability and knowledge.

these, a third species of "co-operation," prevailing throughout some large industries in Great Britain, which has not, so far as I am aware, received any consideration in the numerous and instructive discussions which have within the last few years taken place upon this subject, but which is nevertheless well worthy of attention. I refer to the method of employing labour which prevails extensively in mining and other analogous occupations, and is known as the "bargain" or "contract" system. Having lately had an opportunity of witnessing this system in the slate quarries of North Wales, I propose to describe briefly the method and its results. It will, I think, be seen that it is a genuine instance of "co-operation"—one, moreover, which exhibits the beneficial tendencies of that plan in some respects in even a more striking light than other and better known examples.

The mountains of North Wales, as is well known, constitute the principal source of the wealth of that region. They are extremely metalliferous, containing lead and copper ore, besides sulphur; but their most important constituent is the slate formation. Veins of this rock, varying in thickness from four and five to four and five hundred yards, and traceable, in some instances, for a length of many miles, traverse the country, but more especially the mountain ranges of Caernarvon and Merioneth. The importance of the industry to which they give occasion may be judged from the fact, that three slate quarries—those of Penrhyn, Llanberis, and Festinog—give employment to not fewer than 7,000 men, representing a population of perhaps 20,000 persons. These are, indeed, by much the most extensive of the slate quarries in that region, but they form but a small fraction of the whole number. It is impossible to wander in any direction over the mountains of those two counties without finding abundant evidence how widely the popular enterprise is engaged in this branch of production. No mountain side is so inaccessible that the slate prospector has not reached it, and the most secluded glens and passes are heard to echo the thunder of the quarrier's blast.

The great majority of the slate quarries are worked by companies — either private co-partneries or joint stock companies; but a few, and notably the two largest—the quarries of Penrhyn and Llanberis—are in the hands of individuals, the proprietors of the mountains where the slate-formation occurs. In the former case the capitalist or capitalists working the quarry pay a royalty, which is generally one-twelfth of the produce. It must be observed that the slate does not, as is frequently supposed, and as might be inferred from a cursory glance at a slate quarry, constitute the mass of the mountain in which the quarry is cut. It runs in distinct veins which, on rising towards the surface, deteriorate,—a circumstance to which is due the risk which this mode of employing capital so largely involves; for it is always difficult to say from the appearance of the vein at the surface what may be its quality at a lower depth. Before this can be known, a mass of from two or three to sometimes twenty or even thirty yards in vertical depth must be removed—a tedious and costly operation, which must be completed before slate-quarrying, properly so called, begins, and which is often performed to no purpose; the quality of the rock, when thus ascertained, not proving such as to justify the further prosecution of the work. Cases have been mentioned to the writer of quarries having been abandoned after 20,000*l.*, of others having been given up after 80,000*l.*, had been expended on preliminary operations. This incident of slate-quarrying serves to explain what will be presently referred to—the unwillingness of the working quarriers to embark their savings in this kind of speculation.

The business of making slates is an exceedingly simple operation—one, however, which not the less demands from the workman no small amount of intelligence, exactness, and dexterity, besides a good deal of practical acquaintance with the nature of the materials with which he has to deal. It consists in detaching the slate formation in blocks from the mountain side; in sawing the blocks when thus detached into suitable sizes; lastly, in splitting and dressing, so as to bring them into proper shape—a process which is performed sometimes by machinery, but more generally by hand labour. It is to the industrial arrangements by which this operation is carried out that it is desired now to invite the reader's attention. They are as follows:—The portion of the slate which it is proposed to work is divided into sections carefully marked out, which are let out as "bargains" to as many small co-partneries, consisting generally of three or four working men. These co-partneries "contract" to produce slates—each from the section of the rock assigned to it—according to sizes and shapes at so much per thousand.

The men who take part directly in these contracts form, perhaps, a third of the whole quarrying population; they are, as might be expected, the older, more experienced, and better-off portion; the remainder are employed by them as labourers at fixed wages under the name of "germyns," apparently the Welsh equivalent for "navvies." The capital employed in the undertaking is furnished principally by the proprietors or lessees, as the case may be, of the quarry; but a portion is also provided by the "contractors." Thus the former supply the larger and more expensive machinery, such as the tramways, waggons, steam-engine, if there be one, pumps, slate-saws and planes, &c., while the latter furnish the smaller tools, as well as the gunpowder used in blasting. The practice, moreover, being to pay wages monthly, this supposes, on the part of the workmen—unless so far as they may have recourse to the pernicious aid of the tally-shop—an amount of saving sufficient, at least, to support them during this interval of delay. The relations of the actual workers having been established on this footing, and the contracts entered into, the functions of the principal capitalist or capitalists are thenceforward of an extremely limited kind; they consist chiefly in keeping the machinery in proper order, and seeing to the number and quality of the slates turned out. As for the rest—the plan of operations adopted, the distribution of the labour, its superintendence and reward—of all this the "contractors" undertake the sole and entire charge. It should be added that the "contracts" are supplemented by an understanding, doubtless originating in the felt necessity of mitigating for the working men the inevitable risks of such undertakings, to the effect that, where from the inferior quality of the rock, as ascertained on trial, the returns fall below a certain standard, the reduced earnings of the "contractors" shall be aided by a "poundage," or additional allowance, varying inversely with the amount of their gains. This poundage, so far as I could make out, though for the most part regulated by custom, is also in some degree discretionary on the part of the owner of the quarry, and is not the same for all districts. It applies, however, only to the less fortunate class of "bargains;" the better "bargains" are amply remunerated within the terms of the contract.

Such, in brief, are the arrangements under which industry in the Welsh slate quarries is carried on. I think it will be seen at once that this "contract system" constitutes a true case of "co-operation." It is at least certain that it fulfils what I venture to think are the most important conditions of that method of industry: there is associated effort; there is common interest in the results of the work; and these results depend, subject to the natural conditions of the case, and the customary qualification of the strict contract just indicated, directly on the energy, skill, and mutual good faith with which the workers perform their part. It has also been said that the "contractors" advance a portion of the capital; but I should not be disposed to attach much importance to this as a distinctive feature of the "contract system;" for, though as a matter of fact the men who take part in contracts have generally accumulated some little capital, and though this circumstance no doubt facilitates in some degree their proceedings in carrying out the undertaking, still the possession of capital does not by any means constitute an indispensable condition to becoming a contractor, it being always easy for a man of good character to obtain the requisite tools and materials on credit from small shopkeepers established in the quarrying districts, and established chiefly with a view to supplying such needs. The only item of capital which in practice the contractor is in the habit of advancing is the money expended on his own support during the monthly interval that elapses before the returns to his industry come in; and, so far as this is concerned, the "germyn" whom he employs—a labourer at fixed wages—has an equally valid title to take rank as a capitalist; the earnings of the "germyn" being also postponed for the same period of time. The value of the experiment, therefore, and that which entitles it to be regarded as an example of "co-operative" industry, lies, in my opinion, in the other conditions to which I have referred—in the fact that the system enlists working men in a joint undertaking, of which the results for them depend in large part on the skill, energy, and conscientious zeal with which it is carried through.

And now let us endeavour to appreciate the bearing of these conditions on the well-being of the quarrying community. We shall consider in the first place the position of the contractor, who, as I have already said, represents about a third of the whole quarrying population. He will not, of course, for a moment be confounded with the important and generally wealthy personage by whom our railways and great public works are carried on. The latter, a capitalist pure and simple, has no other relations with the actual workers than that of paymaster. But the contractor of the slate quarries is himself a manual worker—generally, indeed, a skilled worker, taking to himself the more difficult processes of the undertaking, but still in the strictest sense a working man—working in the same place, and often at the same operation, as the labourer whom he employs, and socially in no respect his superior. But, though a manual labourer, our contractor is also something very different from the ordinary labourer for hire. His remuneration is no fixed sum, but depends upon the success of his exertions, which he has therefore the strongest interest to increase to the utmost. Nor, again, is he to be confounded with the labourer at task-work. In the first place, the undertaking in which he embarks is of an altogether more important character than any that falls to the lot of the ordinary task-work labourer. Before he commits himself to his engagements, a calculation, not altogether free from complication—requiring, besides an acquaintance with arithmetic, and a tincture of mathematics, some practical knowledge of the different qualities of certain rocks—must be performed. Then the undertaking itself comprises several distinct operations—quarrying, cleaving, dressing—the carrying out of which, effectively and economically, calls for deliberation, forethought, and organizing skill. Again, the contractor, while a labourer himself, is also a purchaser of the labours of others, holding towards his "germyn" the position of a capitalist proper, and is thus led to look at the business of production in some degree from the point of view of an employer,—a circumstance which may go some way in accounting for the noteworthy fact, that in the districts of the slate quarries strikes are unknown. Lastly, and to this I attach the greatest importance of all, the contractor is a member of a partnership, acquiring rights and incurring responsibilities in relation to his fellow-contractors, taking part in their labours on equal terms, sharing their anxieties, and interested in common with them in the ultimate result of their common efforts.

But the influence of the arrangements I have described is not limited to the class which comes immediately under their operation. A circumstance which gives especial importance to the status of the contractor in the slate quarry is that, placed as nearly as possible midway between the position of the ordinary labourer and that of the capitalist pure and simple, it forms an easy stepping-stone for the elevation of the masses from the precarious position of dependence upon the general labour-market,—a position which, if there be value in experience, is absolutely incompatible with any substantial and permanent improvement of their state.

The mode in which the ascent is made will be illustrated by a remark made to the writer by the lessee of the Dolwydellan slate quarry—a gentleman to whose kindness he is indebted for most of the information contained in this paper. In reply to a question with reference to a difference in the rates of wages prevailing in different localities, he observed that the men before us would be very slow to leave their present occupation even for the prospect of a considerable advance in their wages—"because," he explained, pointing to a large quarry hole filled with water, "so soon as this is pumped dry, there is not a man amongst them who does not know that he will have a chance of a share in the new contracts which will then be opened." Thus the labourers who have not yet attained to the rank of contractors are ever working in full view of an early promotion to this position, their attainment of which, however, depends entirely on their success in recommending themselves to the favourable consideration of the owner of the quarry, as well as to that—an equally important condition—of their own fellow-workmen, without whose approval and co-operation they would hope in vain to take advantage of the opportunities which are daily opening. Even the less important class of workmen, who are employed in clearing away refuse, also pass occasionally into the ranks of the quarriers proper, and ultimately into those of the contractors, and thus feel in some degree the stimulus which such prospects supply. The whole society is thus kept constantly under the incentive of the public opinion of the *élite* among its own members —a state of things which serves to diffuse throughout the entire organization an influence of the healthiest kind.

Nor has the beneficent tendency of these arrangements failed to become effectual in the actual condition of the population of the slate quarries. Their ordinary earnings, according to information supplied to me from various sources, may be set down as follows:—

For carters of refuse, from 12*s.* to 17*s.* per week.
For "germyns" (quarriers at fixed wages, many of whom are mere boys), 12*s.* to 20*s.* per week.

In the case of the contractors the variations are much more considerable; the results ranging from 3*l.* to 8*l.*, and occasionally to 10*l.* per month. In a small quarry near Dolwydellan which I visited, three contractors had just concluded a "bargain," in which they had netted for the month of July the sum of 9*l.* each. On the whole, so far as I could make out, the earnings of the contractors average something like 5*l.* monthly.

These rates are, I should suppose, about equal to those prevailing in corresponding occupations—I mean occupations in which the toil, risk, and skill are about the same—in the most favoured industrial districts in England; and such a result is surely very creditable to the industrial system of Wales. For it must be remembered that capital is very far from increasing with the same rapidity in Caernarvonshire and Merionethshire as in (say) Lancashire and Staffordshire; while, on the other hand, owing to the general ignorance of the English language which prevails in the former counties,—a circumstance which cannot but operate in some degree as an impediment to emigration,—the relief afforded by this safety-valve to the labour market there is likely to be considerably less than in other portions of the United Kingdom. The external conditions affecting wages in the Welsh counties are therefore decidedly less favourable than they are in the more progressive districts of England; and yet the labouring classes in the former localities are, it seems, comparing analogous modes of labour equally well off. The explanation, as will be anticipated, is to be found in the slower movements of population in the Welsh districts. In Caernarvonshire population advanced in the decade 1851 to 1861 at the rate of 9 per cent.; in Merionethshire at the rate of 3 per cent.; in both counties at an average rate of 6 per cent.; while over the whole of England and Wales population during the same period went forward at the average rate of 12 per cent., and in the more prosperous parts of the country—for example in Lancashire and Staffordshire—at the rates respectively of 20 per cent. and 23 per cent.*

The comparatively slow growth of capital in those counties of North Wales is thus, as regards its effect on the condition of the people, neutralized by a growth of population proportionately slow; and the practical result is a rate of remuneration fully up to the English level. The defect in respect to material conditions is compensated by greater vigour in the moral. Now, I think it is impossible not to connect this satisfactory

* I do not give these figures as accurate exponents of the relative growth (by way of natural increase) of population in the several districts. No doubt the results in all instances have been much modified both by emigration and by migration within the limits of Great Britain. So far as the former cause is concerned, the probability is, for the reason stated, that, could its effect be ascertained (unfortunately the Emigration Reports do not distinguish the natives of Wales), the result would considerably strengthen my case. And as regards the latter, though there is no doubt a considerable Welsh movement towards the manufacturing centres of England, this proceeds in the main from the agricultural districts; while, to be set against this, there is an Irish immigration into Wales. On the whole, I think the figures I have given may be accepted for the purpose for which they are adduced, as corroborative illustrations of tendencies which there are independent grounds for believing to exist.

state of things with the *régime* of industry under which it has come to pass. Indeed, to what else can it be ascribed? Religious influences, no doubt, are powerful in North Wales. Nothing apparently can exceed the activity and zeal of the Dissenting bodies; and the good effect on the morals and general demeanour of the people is very observable. But, however compatible a strong sense of religion may be with worldly prudence in those matters on which the growth of population depends, the mundane virtue can yet scarcely be regarded as a specific religious result: certainly it is not one which it is usual to hear inculcated from the pulpit. Nor can the fact be attributed to education in the ordinary sense of the word; for, notwithstanding the strongly pronounced literary instincts of the Welsh people, literary education in North Wales seems to be in a decidedly backward state. Improvements, it is said, of an important kind have in recent years been effected in the primary schools; but this has occurred since the mass of the present generation of Welshmen have entered upon active life. It is rare, out of the principal towns, to find working people over the age of thirty who can exchange more than a few words of English: hundreds of thousands cannot accomplish even this little: and even in the towns it is not uncommon to meet substantial shopkeepers who are unable to sign their names to their own bills. In one quarry I was told that some considerable number of the workmen were unable to read and write. It is therefore not to the superiority of their school instruction that the industrial population of these Welsh counties are indebted for the remarkable circumspection and self-control which they display in their most important social relations. I can only regard this phenomenon, therefore, as the fruit of that practical training in habits of thrift and wise foresight which is provided for them in the industrial system under which they live.

It thus appears that, in point of pecuniary returns, the position of the Welsh quarriers does not suffer by comparison with that of workmen in analogous occupations even in the most prosperous districts of England—districts far more favourably circumstanced, as regards the physical conditions affecting the remuneration of the labourer, than those of the slate quarries. But mere pecuniary return affords after all but an inadequate criterion of the labourer's condition. Fully as important as the amount which he earns is the mode in which his earnings are spent; and it is here that the peculiar strength of the co-operative principle comes into play. Those who have watched the working of "co-operative stores" have been struck with their effect in awakening and stimulating the saving spirit among the working classes—a result which has been attributed to the strong temptations to frugality presented by those establishments, in the opportunities they afford for investing small sums at a fair rate of profit. In the particular form of co-operation, however, to which I have in this paper called attention, this incident of the co-operative plan as it is conducted elsewhere—the provision, that is to say, for small investments—does not exist. As I have already intimated, to qualify a man for taking part in a "bargain," no capital is needed beyond the moral capital of a good character. Even should he be in a position to decline the credit which is readily extended to him, the amount required for the purchase of such implements and tools as it falls to his share of the bargain to provide would be exceedingly small. Nor does he find in the other branches of industry flourishing around him those special opportunities which are wanting in his own. Co-operative stores have indeed, as I have been informed, been established in one or two localities in North Wales, and with excellent results; but they do not yet exist on such a scale that they can be supposed to have sensibly affected the habits of the people. As regards the larger operations of slate quarrying, they are, as it happens, peculiarly ineligible as a field for small investments. This will at once be understood if regard be had to what has been already stated—that the amount of capital required to start a slate quarry is very large, while the risk of the speculation is very great. The former obstacle might indeed be overcome by recourse to the joint-stock expedient, were the joint-stock plan capable of being applied with advantage to this branch of production; but this seems not to be the case; at least, so think the working quarriers, and their opinion would seem to be borne out by facts.* In the case of

* Numerous joint-stock companies are at present (1864) working quarries in North Wales; but, as a rule, I understand they are not flourishing concerns; all the most prosperous undertakings being in the hands of individuals or private co-partneries. The reasons for the superiority of the latter are apparent enough. There is no need that the business organizations of such an undertaking should be other than extremely simple. In Penrhyn Quarry, for example, where the operations are on an immense scale, the entire business of keeping the accounts, &c. is performed by two clerks. This cannot but give a great advantage to

the population of the slate quarries, therefore, there seems to be an entire absence of those special incentives to frugality and providence which have been incidents of the co-operative plan in its better-known forms. Nevertheless frugality and providence are found to characterize this population in a remarkable degree. The mere fact that, according to the prevailing custom, wages are paid at so long an interval as once a month, implies of itself a considerable fund of accumulated savings existing among the body of the people. But this would give but an inadequate idea of their saving disposition. It is, I am assured, quite common to find in the ranks of the contractors men who have laid by from one to three and four hundred pounds. In one quarry which I visited, a man was pointed out to me—a manual labourer—who was known to be in receipt of between 80*l.* and 100*l.* a year, independently altogether of his current earnings—the return on capital saved and invested. This, no doubt, was an extraordinary case, but not, I was assured, by any means without a parallel. Well, where is the field for the investment of these considerable accumulations? A portion goes into agricul-

individuals and small co-partneries over the necessarily more cumbrous organisation of a joint-stock company. Again, the special knowledge and singleness of design which are so essential in this branch of industry are much more likely to be realised by individuals, or associations consisting of a few partners, than by a more numerous body. In addition to the reasons mentioned in the text, it is probable that some distrust of the Saxon enters into the Welsh workman's reluctance to commit his savings to undertakings which are carried on largely by Saxon capital: this seems to be expressed in his proverb: "Os bydd y gweli sais ac engine yn dyfod ir gwaith pacia dy bethan." [When you see an Englishman with his engine coming to the work, pack and be off.]

ture; prosperous quarrymen turning farmers in their latter days, or sometimes combining with farming pursuits occasional adventures in their old line. Retail trade again absorbs some. But probably the largest part of the funds finds its way into the associations known as "building societies." These "building societies" might with more propriety be called loan societies; their functions consisting in advancing money to be invested in building speculations, which, though for the most part undertaken by the members, are yet carried on on individual account, resembling in this respect the "Vorschussvereine" described by Professor Huber in his interesting paper on "Co-operation."* These societies are extremely popular with the workmen; and as to their range of operations, the reader will be able to form some notion when I state that several considerable towns in North Wales have been almost entirely built by the capital supplied through this agency. Thus the pretty town of Bethesda, within five miles of Bangor, is almost entirely the creation of the enterprise of working men deriving their funds from this source. Llandudno, Rhyll, and Upper Bangor owe their existence in large part to the same cause. As to the substantial comfort in which the people of the quarry districts live, no one who has visited these districts will, I think, feel any doubt. Nor is it comfort merely. The style and finish of the workmen's houses are very remarkable, more particularly in Bethesda and the neighbourhood of the Penrhyn quarries, where the elegant model furnished by Colonel Pennant in his own village has been turned to

* Published in the "Social Science Transactions" for 1862.

excellent account. A feature in the architecture is the variety of modes in which the staple material is brought into requisition. Roofing is but a small part of the purposes to which the slate is applied: there are slate door-posts, slate window-settings; the ground story is generally flagged with slate, which makes its appearance besides in many places where one would little expect to find it. I know not whether the extreme cleanliness of the Welsh is to be attributed in any degree to the advantages of this material; but they are certainly pre-eminent in this virtue. The exquisite neatness of some of the cottages in Bethesda and Trefriw is such as I imagine would not easily be matched out of Holland. The kitchen-parlour is quite a marvel of cleanliness, tidiness, and order—with its slate floor swept till it shines, its "varnished clock" clicking "behind the door," and its furniture, though mostly made of common wood, polished to such brightness that it does not pale even before the constellations of brass knobs which glitter all around. In the village where I was staying I have watched an old woman who lived on the opposite side of the street come out in showery weather to scrub her door-slab clean as fast as it was soiled by the footsteps of each careless passer-by: the apparition would follow on the clearing away of a shower almost with the regularity of the lady in the toy barometer. Nor should we omit to say that some attempt at a library is rarely absent from these quarriers' cottages. The selection may not contain the newest publications, and is not perhaps very choice; but at least it shows literary aspirations—a soul for something above the quarry.

The Bible, generally in Welsh, I observed, held a constant and honoured place in the literary store.

The simplicity of character and kindness of heart among the poorer classes of Welsh people are very striking and attractive. In illustration of these qualities I may mention an admirable trait, which may, I think, be fairly connected with their co-operative system.

The occupations of the slate quarry involve, as may readily be believed, no small amount of risk to the limbs and lives of those who engage in them; the accidents from blasting, falling in of rocks, &c. being unfortunately very numerous, and frequently fatal; and, as might be expected, there is no lack of provision against such disastrous contingencies. Besides the ordinary friendly societies which flourish in immense numbers all over the country, no quarry of any importance is without its sick club. Numerous associations exist framed with a special view to compensate for the losses incident to mutilation and death. But such machinery does not satisfy the cravings of the fraternal feeling that subsists among the workmen. The assistance from this source is almost invariably supplemented, where the accidents are of a serious nature involving calamitous consequences to the family of the injured man, by voluntary contributions raised among his fellow-workmen. "As a class," writes a correspondent, himself extensively engaged in this business, to whom I have already expressed my obligations,—" As a class, quarriers are very liberal. If by accident a father of a family is killed, the wife will go through the quarry and frequently gets (if her husband has been a man of good character) from 10*l.* to 20*l.* At other times collections are made in the chapels, and almost in every instance they show great liberality." He adds that these occurrences are unfortunately very frequent; several such calls on the workman's pocket having quite recently been made in a single quarry in the short space of a few months.

Such, then, is the "contract system" of the slate quarries, and such are its fruits. Divested as it is of certain extraneous advantages which accompany other forms of "co-operation," it sets, as it seems to me, in all the stronger light the inherent virtue of the principle itself—the principle of combining the exertions of labourers towards a common result in which they have a joint interest—an interest varying with the success of their common efforts. The results here obtained are obtained not so much through the increased force of the external inducements to prudent or righteous conduct, as by strengthening the character of the workman, calling into action qualities of mind which in the ordinary condition of the labourer's life lie dormant, enlarging his mental horizon, stimulating his reflective powers, widening his sympathies—in a word, developing those principles and habits which furnish the only solid basis for any permanent improvement of his state.

How far the particular arrangement which I have described admits of being extended to other departments of production is what actual experiment can alone determine. *Primâ facie*, it would seem that one condition only was indispensable to its adoption—the possibility of splitting up the work to be done into a number of small and independent tasks. It is at all events certain that the success of the plan in the instances in which it has been tried has been remarkably great; and this, considered with reference to commercial, no less than to social results. As an expedient for the practical solution of the labour-problem, the weakness of the "contract system" seems to me to lie in the fact that under it the labourer and the capitalist are still distinct persons; the two capacities do not coalesce in the same man. The difficulty which, under the ordinary relations of labour and capital, occurs in settling the rate of wages might equally occur under the "contract system" in settling the terms of the contract. That it does not in practice arise is to be ascribed, I imagine, chiefly to the circumstance to which I have already adverted—the double capacity in which the contractor acts, as at once employer and employed; and, for the rest, to the general intelligence which the system engenders

VI.

POLITICAL ECONOMY AND LAND.*

Various as have been the schemes recently offered to public notice for the settlement of the Irish land question, one feature is noticeable as more or less prominently characterizing them all—a profound distrust of Political Economy. Just in proportion as a plan gives promise of being effective, does the author feel it necessary to assume an attitude, if not of hostility, then of apology, towards this science. It is either sneered at as unpractical and perverse, or its authority is respectfully put aside as of no account "in a country so exceptionally situated as Ireland." This state of opinion is perfectly intelligible. In its earlier applications to practical affairs Political Economy found itself inevitably in collision with numerous regulative codes, partly the remnants of feudalism, partly the products of the commercial doctrines of a later age, but all founded on the principle of substituting for individual discretion the control of those in power. It thus came naturally to be

* *Fortnightly Review*, January 1870.

identified with the opposite principle; and was known to the general public mainly as a scientific development of the doctrine of *laissez-faire*. The Free-trade controversy of course gave great prominence to this side of the system, and of late the idea that all Political Economy is summed up in *laissez-faire* has been much fostered by the utterances of some public men and writers, who have acquired a certain reputation as political economists, chiefly, it would seem, through the pertinacity with which they have enforced this formula, insisting on its sufficiency, not merely in the domain of material interest, but over the whole range of human life. If *laissez-faire* is to be taken as the sum and substance of economic teaching, it follows evidently enough that intervention by the State to determine the relative status of those holding interests in the soil involves an economic heresy of the deepest dye; and it is not strange, therefore, that those who accept or defer to this idea of the science should, in attempting to deal with the Irish problem, evince some susceptibility in reference to Political Economy. In effect, it is very evident that two courses only are open to economists of this hue. Either they must hold by their maxims, and, doing so, remit the solution of the Irish difficulty to civil war and the arbitrament of armed force; or, accepting the plea of Ireland's exceptional condition, they must be content to put aside their science for the nonce, and legislate as if it were not. The latter is the course that fortunately has for the most part been taken. Economic laws—so it seems now to be agreed upon by thinkers of this school—do not act except where circumstances are favourable, and have no business in a country so unfortunately situated as Ireland. This is one view of the relation of Political Economy to such questions as that presented by the present state of Ireland. In my opinion, it is a radically false, and practically a most mischievous view; one, therefore, against which, alike in the interest of the peace of Ireland and for the credit of economic science, I am anxious with all my energy to protest. I deny that economic doctrine is summed up in *laissez-faire;* I contend that it has positive resources, and is efficacious to build up as well as to pull down. Sustained by some of the greatest names—I will say by every name of the first rank in Political Economy, from Turgot and Adam Smith to Mill—I hold that the land of a country presents conditions which separate it economically from the great mass of the other objects of wealth,—conditions which, if they do not absolutely and under all circumstances impose upon the State the obligation of controlling private enterprise in dealing with land, at least explain why this control is in certain stages of social progress indispensable, and why in fact it has been constantly put in force, wherever public opinion or custom has not been strong enough to do without it. And not merely does economic science, as expounded by its ablest teachers, dispose of *à priori* objections to a policy of intervention with regard to land, it even furnishes principles fitted to inform and guide such a policy in a positive sense. Far from being the irreconcilable foe, it is the natural ally of those who engage in this course, at once justifying the principle of their undertaking, and lending itself as a minister to the elaboration of the constructive design.

As regards the main ground on which the distinction between land and other forms of wealth depends, little more needs be done than unfold the argument contained in a few weighty sentences in which Mr. Mill has summed up the case:—"Moveable property can be produced in indefinite quantity, and he who disposes as he likes of anything which, it can be fairly argued, would not have existed but for him, does no wrong to anyone. It is otherwise with regard to land, a thing which no man made, which exists in limited quantity, which was the original inheritance of all mankind, and which whoever appropriates keeps others out of its possession. Such appropriation, when there is not enough left for all, is, at the first aspect, an usurpation on the rights of other people." Where wealth is provided by human industry, its having value is the indispensable condition to its existence—to its existence at least in greater quantity than suffices for the producer's own requirements; and the most obvious means of rendering this condition efficacious as a stimulus to industry is to recognize in the producer a right of property in the thing he has produced. This, I take it, is, economically speaking, the foundation on which private property rests, and is, if I mistake not, the most solid and important of all the reasons for the institution. It is one which applies to all the products of human industry—a category comprising (with some unimportant exceptions) moveable wealth in every form, as well as some forms of immoveable wealth, but which obviously can have no application to a commodity which "no man has made."* It has been urged, indeed, that this reasoning is not rigorous, and that strict logic would require us to extend the description given of land to every form of wealth, moveable as well as immoveable, elaborated by the hand of industry or still lying crude in the earth, since, in the last resort, all is traceable alike to materials furnished by nature—which "no man has made." But this is to fall into the error of the Physiocrates, and to confound wealth with matter. The street and palace, the corn and cotton, the goods that fill our warehouses, whatever be the form imparted to them by industry, all, no doubt, derive their material existence in the last resort from things which no man has made: no man has made the matter of which they are composed; but, as *wealth*, as things possessing exchange value, they exist, not through the liberality of nature, but through the labour and enterprise of man. According to the economic formula, their value (omitting the, in most

* [To guard against misapprehension, it may be as well to state that I do not recognize in this argument any proof of a "natural right" to property in anything, even in that which our hands have just made. If it is right it should belong to us, it is not (if we go to the root of things) because we have made it, but because it is expedient that property so acquired should belong to him who so acquires it. The distinction is all-important. If the product belonged to us in virtue of the fact of our having produced it, that fact being past and unalterable, there could be no limitation to our right in the absence of voluntary cession upon our part, and we should in strict justice be entitled to prescribe its destination to all future ages. On the other hand, belonging to us only in virtue of considerations of expediency, our right to the product will be limited by the expediency from which our right springs. The distinction, then, between landed property and property in the products of industry is not that in the latter case there is a "natural right" to property which does not exist in the former, but that there are grounds of expediency for recognizing the right in the one case which have no place in the other.]

instances, infinitesimal portion of it which covers rent) corresponds to their cost of production. It is not so with land, which possesses value, and often high value, even in its crudest form; with respect to which, therefore, whatever other reasons may be urged in favour of giving it up to private ownership, that reason cannot be urged which applies to the mass of the other objects of wealth—namely, that this mode of proceeding forms the natural and most effective means of encouraging industry useful to man.

It will be said, however, that the fact in question is after all pertinent to the controversy only while land remains in a state of nature, and that my argument ceases to have practical force as soon as the soil of a country has been brought under cultivation and is improved by industry. This exception, I admit, is to a certain extent well founded—only let us carefully note to what extent. Of the labour employed on land, all that is directed to the raising of the immediate produce, and of which the results are realized in this produce—that is to say, the great bulk of all the labour applied to the land of a country—finds its natural remuneration in these results, in this immediate produce. Such labour, recompensed as it is by the immediate returns, and leaving the soil substantially as it found it, cannot form a ground for rights of property in the soil itself. No more can labour employed, not upon the cultivated soil at all, but in extrinsic operations—in making roads, bridges, harbours, in building towns, and in general in doing things which, directly or indirectly, facilitate the disposal of agricultural produce. It is very true indeed that labour thus employed affects the value of land; and there are writers who have relied upon this fact, as identifying in principle landed with other property, showing as it does a connection between the value of land and labour expended.* Unfortunately for the analogy they seek to establish, the labour that is expended is expended, not upon the land whose value it affects, but upon other things; and the property which results accrues, not to those who exert or employ the labour, but to other persons. The fact, instead of making good the analogy, brings into sharp contrast the things compared. A bale of cloth, a machine, a house, owes its value to the labour expended upon it, and belongs to the person who expends or employs the labour: a piece of land owes its value, so far as its value is affected by the causes I am now considering, *not* to the labour expended upon it, but to that expended upon something else—to the labour expended in making a railroad, or building houses in an adjoining town; and the value thus added to the land belongs, not to the persons who have made the railway or built the houses, but to some one who may not even have been aware that these operations were being carried on—nay, who perhaps has exerted all his efforts to prevent their being carried on. How many landlords have had their rent-rolls doubled by railways made in their despite?† In considering the above exception, therefore, we must

* [In particular Mr Carey, the American economist, and M. Bastiat, who has borrowed his doctrine of rent from Mr. Carey. That doctrine owes such plausibility as it possesses entirely to overlooking the distinction here pointed out.]

† [" Pourrait-on sérieusement considérer cette rente, qui est exclusivement attribuée aux propriétaires, comme la rémunération d'avances et de travaux auxquels les propriétaires n'ont contribué que pour une part, et

put aside as irrelevant to the question all the industry expended upon land of which the effects are limited to the immediate crop, as well as all that employed in the general material development of the country, apart from the cultivation of the soil; and we thus narrow the argument to the effects of the labour directed to the permanent improvement of the cultivated soil itself—to rendering this a more efficient instrument for productive purposes than nature gave it to us. So far as this has been done—so far as the productive qualities of the soil have been permanently improved—so far, undoubtedly, the value added to the soil by such operations, and property in this value, when it vests in the producer, rests economically upon the same foundation as property in corn, or wine, or houses. The transformation of the Lincolnshire fens and the lagoons of Holland into tracts of golden wheat land has been referred to by Lord Dufferin: the reclamation of bog and hill-side by Irish peasant occupiers equally illustrates the principle; and the mention of this last instance will at once indicate what a very short way the analogy in question will carry those who have urged it towards the goal they seek. On the assumption that property in land were measured by the value added to land by human labour—to land as distinct from its products—and that this property vested in the person who created the value, landed property would, thus conditioned, be assimilated in principle to property in other things. As

qui avait un but tout autre que celui d'accroître la valeur des propriétés foncières."—*Précis de la Science Économique et de ses principales Applications*, par A. E. Cherbuliez: 1862. An admirable treatise, too little known in this country.]

matters actually stand, I need scarcely say none of these conditions is fulfilled. Property in land is not measured by the value which industry has added to the land, but is co-extensive with the whole value of the commodity, from whatever causes arising; while the property in such results as human labour has fixed in the soil does not pass to him whose exertions have produced them, but to him who happens at the moment to be legal owner of the improved ground. The fact, in short, does not advance us a step towards the required assimilation: it merely shows us this, that there is a portion of landed property which man has made, which is strictly the product of human industry; which, therefore, would rest on the same footing as property in other industrial products, were only the laws of landed property something wholly different from what they are.

It follows, then, that the distinction drawn between property in land and property in other things, founded on the fact that "no man made the land," by no means terminates (as might at first be supposed) with land in a state of nature: unless so far as the existing value of land is due altogether to the industry expended upon it—unless in such rare instances as the lagoons of Holland or the fens of Lincolnshire, or reclamations of waste land previously valueless—the distinction applies equally to all lands, cultivated or wild. Property in cultivated, no less than in wild land, consists largely in value which no human industry employed upon the land has created. The ordinary economic considerations, therefore, which apply to and justify property in other forms of wealth, do not apply here. There may be good reasons for the institution of property in land—on that I am not for the moment concerned to express an opinion—but they are not the reasons which support the institution in its other forms; in particular, landed property is wanting in that foundation—in the judgment of most people, I apprehend, the strongest of all those on which property rests—the expediency of securing the labourer in the fruit of his toil.

The argument, as thus far conducted, carries me, I admit, no further than to this negative conclusion. It rebuts an *à priori* objection to legislative action in such cases as Ireland presents, founded upon an assumed analogy between land and other kinds of wealth. To exhibit the positive reasons which explain and vindicate a policy in the direction contemplated we must go a step further, and bring into view the causes which determine the existence and growth of agricultural rent, and, in relation to these causes, the position occupied by the owners of land on the one hand, and by the general community on the other.

The phenomenon of agricultural rent, let me briefly explain, is, economically considered, of this nature:—it consists of the existence in the returns to agricultural industry of a value over and above what is sufficient to replace the capital employed in agriculture with the profit customary in the country. This surplus value arises in this way. The qualities of different soils being different, and the capital applied even to an area of uniform fertility not being all equally productive—farms differing besides in respect of their situation, proximity to market, and other circumstances—it happens that agricultural produce is raised at varying costs; but it is evident that when brought to common markets it will, quality for quality, command the same price. Hence arises, or rather hence would arise in the absence of rent, a vast difference in the profits upon agricultural industry. The produce raised on the best soils, or under other circumstances of exceptional advantage, will bear a much larger proportion to the outlay than that raised under less favourable circumstances; but as it is clear that, in a community where people engage in agriculture with a view to profit, even this latter portion would need to carry such a price as would give the producer the same profits which he might obtain in other occupations (for otherwise he would not engage in its production), it follows that all the produce except this, sold as it is, quality for quality, at the same price, must yield a profit over and above the customary profit of the country. This surplus profit is known to political economists as "rent," and we may henceforth conveniently distinguish it from the rent actually paid by cultivators as "economic rent." Arising in the manner described, "economic rent" cannot properly be said to owe its existence to either labourer, capitalist, or landlord. It is rather a factitious value incident to the progress of society under external physical conditions which necessitate the raising of raw produce at different costs.* This being its essential nature, it is plain that, so long as the rent paid by the cultivator of a farm does not exceed what the amount of "economic rent" would be, so long those engaged in agricultural industry will

* See Note at the end of this Essay.

be on neither a better nor a worse footing than those engaged in other occupations. The labourer will have the ordinary wages, the capitalist the ordinary profit of the country.* On the other hand, it is evident that if the cultivator be required to pay more than this—if the rent exacted from him encroach upon the domain of wages and profits—he is so far placed at a disadvantage as compared with other producers, and is deprived of the ordinary inducements to industry. It thus becomes a question of capital importance, what provision exists in the conditions of an industrial community to prevent this result; what security we have that—the land of a country being once given up to private speculation—the limits set by "economic rent" shall, in the main, be observed in the actual rent which landlords obtain. Does the principle of *laissez-faire*—that play of interests developed by competition which in manufacturing and trading operations maintains the harmony of individual with general interests—does this suffice to secure, under ordinary circumstances, the same harmony in the transactions of which land is the subject? If it shall appear that it does not, then, I think, a case will have been made out, for the interposition of some other agency—public opinion, custom, or, failing these, direct State action—to supply that which the principle of unrestricted competition has failed to supply—to secure an end which cannot but be regarded as among the legitimate ends of government—the coincidence in an important field of human activity of the individual with the general well-being.

* This position, to be accurate, needs a qualification which it will receive further on. As it stands it is correct for the purposes of the argument.

The influence which is ordinarily supposed to suffice for this purpose is the competition with agriculture of other modes of investing capital. The farmer, we are told, before taking a farm, will consider what rent he can pay consistently with obtaining the usual returns upon his industry; if the landlord demands more than is consistent with this, he will decline the bargain, and embark his means in some other occupation. Rent, it is said, can thus never rise for any length of time, or, as a general rule, above the level prescribed by the economic conditions of the case. But, as has often been pointed out, and as is obvious at the first blush, this argument supposes a state of things which exists in but few countries in the world, if indeed it exists, or ever can exist, in any. It supposes all farmers to be capitalists—capitalists on a scale implying the possession of disposable wealth in substantial amount; and it supposes a variety of occupations other than agriculture, soliciting investment, into any of which—a landlord proving unreasonable—farmers can turn their capital. The countries in which these conditions are realized in the highest degree—rather, I should say, in which the nearest approximation to their realization has been attained—are England and Scotland; and yet it is very evident that in England and Scotland the uncontrolled play of the principle of competition in dealing with land is not found sufficient for keeping the relations of landlord and tenant in a satisfactory state. If it be, then what is the meaning of the current language upon this subject? of "good" and "bad" applied to landlords in a sense in which the same epithets are never applied to traders in other commodities than land; of such phrases as "what a good landlord would do"—this being assumed to be something quite different from what his pecuniary interest would lead him to do; of the constant appeal to the moralities of the landlord and tenant relation?* What is the meaning of landlords, of English landlords, boasting that they do not let their lands at a competition rent?† What, again, is the meaning of courts of law deferring to local customs, and overriding and modifying the strict terms of a contract? The whole state of feeling and all the current language in reference to this subject imply a deeply-felt conviction that the exigencies of this relation are not, even in England and Scotland, satisfactorily met by mere commercial motives, but that public opinion and custom, custom in some instances enforced by law, are needed to supplement and qualify the mere commercial rule.

In England and Scotland the interposition of these agencies to qualify the action of competition in transactions of which land is the subject is more or less masked; in almost all other fully-peopled countries it is open and undisguised. In Asia the land has never, as a general rule, been given up to private speculation: it has remained in the hands of the

* It will be said, perhaps, that the phrase "good and bad employers" is used with a similar connotation. In general, I think the words mean no more than persons employing largely or scantily at the market rates. If they mean more than this, it is when used by those who regard labour as an exceptional commodity, the remuneration of which should not be left to the play of competition. The exception thus proves the rule.

† ["Farms in England," says Lord Derby in a recent speech, "are habitually let at a lower rent than they would fetch if competed for in open market."]

State; and the condition of the agricultural population has accordingly varied with the greater or less degree of enlightenment or of sound moral feeling existing in the rulers. Over Europe, wherever the land is not owned by the cultivators, custom or law very generally regulates or largely modifies the relations of landlord and tenant. The position of the cultivators is one not determined by contract, but, to a large extent, resting on status. In fact it would be intolerable were it otherwise; for nowhere in Europe, England and Scotland excepted, has an approximation ever been made towards a state of society in which are fulfilled the conditions that alone render tolerable the commercial treatment of land—in which the cultivators are capitalists, and a practical alternative to rural occupation exists for large masses of the people. The soil is over the greater portion of the inhabited globe cultivated by very humble men, with very little disposable wealth, and whose career is practically marked out for them by irresistible circumstances as tillers of the ground. In a contest between vast bodies of people so circumstanced and the owners of the soil—between the purchasers without reserve, constantly increasing in numbers, of an indispensable commodity, and the monopolist dealers in that commodity—the negotiation could have but one issue, that of transferring to the owners of the soil the whole produce, *minus* what was sufficient to maintain in the lowest state of existence the race of cultivators. This is what has happened wherever the owners of the soil, discarding all considerations but those dictated by self-interest, have really availed themselves of the full strength of their position. It is what has happened under rapacious governments in Asia; it is what has happened under rapacious landlords in Ireland; it is what now happens under the bourgeois proprietors of Flanders;* it is, in short, the inevitable result which cannot but happen in the great majority of all societies now existing on earth where land is given up to be dealt with on commercial principles unqualified by public opinion, custom, or law.

It seems to me that I have made out my case, and shown that the incidents attaching to land not only separate it economically from wealth in other forms, not only therefore rebut *à priori* objections to special land legislation founded on assumed economic analogies, but—regard being had to the conditions of industrial society actually prevailing in the world—furnish positive reasons for this course,—for setting limits, where public opinion and custom are not efficacious for the purpose,—for setting limits by law to the free action of competition in dealing with this commodity. So far as to the general principle. I turn now to consider its application to Ireland.

The discussions on the Irish question, whatever differences of opinion they may have disclosed, have at least made one point clear: no settlement of Irish land can be effectual which still leaves with landlords the power of indefinitely raising rent. I think it may be said that amongst those who know the country, and have seriously grappled with the problem, there is a very general agreement upon this point. The end

* See M. Laveleye's Essay, "Cobden Club Essays," vol. i. pp. 255, 256.

may be approached by different paths and realized in different forms. Compulsory leases, recognition and extension of tenant-right, simple fixity of tenure, are amongst the modes; arbitration courts, the opinion of official experts, the prices of produce, have been suggested as the methods of procedure; but in whatever manner, through whatever machinery, the plans that really promise to be effectual involve at bottom the principle of depriving landlords of the power of raising rent—the principle, therefore, of imposing on the State the obligation of saying what a "fair rent" is. It is very evident that this must be so—that the landlord, with the power still left him of raising his rent at will, could easily defeat the most stringent provisions of the most apparently drastic land code. Of what avail to the cultivator would be a right of occupancy if the landlord can attach to that right impossible conditions? Of what advantage the right of selling the good-will of his farm, if the rent can be raised at the landlord's discretion against the incoming tenant? Where would be the gain from leases if the limits of the rent are not known? The regulation of rent is thus of the very essence of the case; it is felt to be so by all who have really grasped the problem; and yet it will be found that this topic has in general been kept rather carefully in the background. The reason for this hesitancy it is not difficult to guess. Few Englishmen can hear without something of a cold tremor a proposal to fix rent by law. And yet the consequences are perhaps unfortunate. For all the reserve, it is felt that the efficacy of the several competing schemes really depends in the last resort upon this condition. *Omne ignotum pro mirifico.* Imagination magnifies the difficulty which is kept so carefully out of sight. Conscious that it lies behind, people hesitate to venture into what they expect will prove an economic *cul-de-sac;* or, if they must choose, the danger is they will choose the scheme, not which is most efficacious, nor even which is least revolutionary, but which best contrives to veil this terrible bugbear. Now, if the fixing of rent by State authority be really indispensable to an effective settlement of this question, it is surely well that the fact be frankly accepted. I have already shown that Political Economy furnishes no presumption against the propriety of this course. Let us now see if it cannot practically help the solution.*

According to some who pass for authorities, Political Economy has very little to say upon this subject. The worth of land is so much money as it will bring; and to seek a criterion for rent—nay, to attempt to conceive rent at all—otherwise than as it is determined by the market, is in the opinion of these wise persons a hopeless, if not an absurd undertaking. Had they reflected that what they pronounce to be an impossibility is, in point of fact, performed by not a few landlords in Ireland—by every landlord there who does not let his lands on the admittedly ruinous principle of competition—they might have seen reason to distrust

* [Throughout the discussions on the Irish Land Act the Government again and again denied their intention to interfere with the landlord's power of raising his rent; but nothing is more certain than that the Act does interfere, though in a circuitous and indirect way, with this power; and further, that it owes whatever success it has achieved to the knowledge shared alike by tenants and landlords that this power resides in the new law.]

the accuracy of scientific knowledge which led to conclusions so flagrantly at variance with fact. Unless, however, in what I have said above on the doctrine of rent I have very grossly misrepresented economic teaching, Political Economy is involved in no such conflict with fact as the view in question would imply. On the contrary, it recognizes in the returns from land the existence of an element—that which I have designated "economic rent"—which is no other than the "fair valuation rent" of good landlords.* It not only recognizes this element, but can state the conditions determining its amount and the laws of its growth. The "fair valuation rent" of the popular platform admits, in short, of being reduced to strictly scientific expression. The only point really debatable is as to the means of practically determining the entity in question in given cases. But, as I have just said, the thing is in fact done every day, with sufficient accuracy for practical purposes, by those who manage Irish estates; and that can scarcely be an insoluble problem which scores of landlords and land-agents solve every year.

In approaching the practical problem, there are two parts that will need to be kept distinct—the first starting of the new system, and the keeping it going after it has been started. Over and above the determination of a fair rent, the former will involve the much more serious practical difficulty of appraising tenants' past improvements. Some able writers have

* The "fair valuation rent" *plus* the returns on permanent improvements of the soil, as will presently be more particularly explained *post*, pp. 211, 212.

expressed themselves as if this latter difficulty might be evaded by permitting to occupiers the sale of their good-will. This would no doubt be so, were the question of rent once settled; but with this still open, the value of the occupation right would be uncertain, while the settlement of the rent plainly cannot take place till the abatement in consideration of tenants' improvements is known. Thus the necessity of an independent valuation of tenants' improvements, wherever landlord and tenant cannot themselves come to an agreement, is inherent in the case. Questions of this kind, involving, as they often will, disputes about minute details, can obviously only be satisfactorily dealt with by authorities adjudicating in the localities, and taking evidence in disputed cases from competent persons who have inspected the farms. Complicated and delicate questions no doubt they will be, demanding from those to whom the settlement is entrusted no small amount of patience, sagacity, and firmness; but questions not less complicated and delicate have already been unravelled by Englishmen in India; and it is hard to see why the same qualities of mind which have threaded their way through the mazes of Hindu customary law to results of order and substantial justice should not be equal to dealing with the problem, analogous, but less complicated, and less remote from English modes of thought, presented by Irish land.

These will be the initiatory difficulties; but these once surmounted, past improvements once ascertained, existing rents once adjusted to existing circumstances, there is no reason that the future working of the status principle should not be brought under general rules, and reduced to a system. Confining our attention to rent, with which alone I am at present concerned, the problem, as I conceive it, will then lie in such an adjustment of this element from time to time as shall satisfy and reconcile the two following conditions:—(1) to secure to the cultivators, so long as they fulfil the conditions of their tenure, the due reward of their industry; and (2) to do substantial justice to the reasonable expectations of those who, on the faith of Acts of Parliament and the past policy of the country, have embarked their fortunes in Irish land.

And here we must endeavour to attain to some definite conception of what constitutes the due reward of the industry of the cultivator. I have already stated what I conceive to be the economic basis of property—the right of the producer to the thing he has produced. Accepting this as our principle, the point to be determined will be the amount of the produce which is properly referable to the industry of the cultivator. To bring the question to a clear issue, I will take an extreme, but not absolutely impossible, case: I will suppose a farm which owes nothing of any kind to the landlord's outlay, on which the whole capital, fixed and circulating, in buildings, fences, manure, and wages, has been advanced by the cultivator; and I will suppose, further, that the soil of this farm is of the worst quality compatible with profitable cultivation. These conditions being supposed, how much of the wealth produced from the farm represents the due reward of the cultivator's exertions? I answer, the whole; and for this reason, that less than the whole would, according to the terms of the hypothesis, leave the cultivator without that ordinary remuneration which the conditions of industrial production in the country warrant — without, therefore, such an adequate motive for his industry, as cultivator of the soil, as in a healthy condition of society would exist. In short, my imaginary farm represents the possible case in which, in conformity with Ricardo's theory, land under a *régime* of capitalist farmers would yield no rent. Passing from this peculiar case, I will vary the hypothesis by supposing the farm to be no longer entirely composed of the worst cultivable land, but to be, we will say, of average natural fertility, while the other conditions remain as before; the entire capital and labour being supplied by the farmer. Under such circumstances,—and still recognizing the principle that the producer is entitled to what he produces,—how far will the tenants' claim to the produce extend? Many people would say, on my principle, to the whole, and would regard the result as a *reductio ad absurdum* of the principle. But I hold this conclusion to be unwarrantable.

In a society constituted according to the principles of modern industrial civilization, in which each member enjoys the general advantages arising from separation of employment and exchange, we are bound, I think, in estimating the effect of a man's labour, to distinguish the value from the commodity. In a state of patriarchal isolation the goods which the labour of a family produces are wholly unaffected by anything which other people do, and therefore rightly belong in absolute property to the family. But when the producer is a member of an industrial society, the commodity he makes may acquire a value—a power of commanding the labour and goods of other people—not by reason of what he has done, but through an importance given to his industrial function by the circumstances of society. Social circumstances may cause what he produces to bear a higher value than his labour would naturally give it, were others free to take advantage of the situation which society has permitted him to occupy. He may, in short, be the monopolist of a favoured situation, in the advantages arising from which, as they are no part of the fruit of his toil, he can, on the principle on which we proceed, have no right to property. Such advantages, so far as they are peculiar to the situation, are not properly the result of his labours, but of the social circumstances which have made the situation specially advantageous, and, on the principle we have recognized, would belong not to him, but to society at large. Now the case I have put will be found to fall within this reasoning. The corn and roots and grass which constitute the agricultural return, no doubt result, nature assisting, from the labours of the cultivator; but the value of these things—the power they confer of commanding the resources of society—is not measured by those labours, but depends on causes extrinsic to the cultivator's operations. The produce bears the price it does, not in virtue of what the farmer has done, but because society needs food—needs food in quantities which can only be obtained by bringing lands under cultivation inferior to the best on his farm. That portion of the value of his produce which is due to this circumstance is, so far as he is concerned, an accident;

something to which he has no more right than anyone else. As it does not result from his exertions, so it offers no encouragement to his industry; his claim to it is therefore wanting in that basis which constitutes the justification of property from the economic point of view. My conclusion, then, is that the due reward of the cultivator's industry, even where he supplies the entire labour and capital employed in production, is not necessarily co-extensive with the whole produce of his farm. It is only so on the supposition that he enjoys in raising it no exceptional advantages arising out of his relations with other people. But where he enjoys such exceptional advantages,—that is to say, where he farms land better than the worst that yields the current profit of the country,—the principle of property, economically considered, is satisfied by his retaining so much of the produce as shall give him the average remuneration, leaving to society the remainder to be disposed of as it shall think fit.

The other element of the problem is to do substantial justice to the reasonable expectations of the landlord. I say "reasonable" expectations, because if the State is to be bound, not by what landlords might reasonably expect when investing their money in land, but by what they actually expected, or do now expect, there is an end to the question; nothing remains but to recognize their right of property in its most absolute sense, and lend the power of the empire to its maintenance. *Risu solvuntur tabulæ.* But if this extreme ground is not to be maintained, then the claims of the landlord and tenant are reconciled, become in fact the correlatives of each other; for "reasonable" expectations must be bounded by the considerations set by public policy; and public policy manifestly requires that agriculture should enjoy the advantages common to other industries in the country,—a result which is only attained when the ordinary rewards of industry are left with the cultivators of the soil. So much as to the nature of the problem.

Let me here recall to the reader the nature of "economic rent," and the causes to which it owes its existence. It is that portion of the value of the returns from land which remains after the outlay of production has been replaced with customary profit; and its existence results from a permanent discrepancy between the price of agricultural produce and the cost of production of a large portion, the price being regulated by the highest standard of cost and being consequently more than sufficient to remunerate the outlay on all produce raised at a cost less than this. These being the causes which determine "economic rent," the amount will evidently be measured by the extent of the discrepancy; and consequently will vary, the price of produce being given, with the productiveness of the soil, or, the productiveness of the soil being given, with the price of produce. Now these phenomena—the prices of agricultural produce and the productiveness of the soil as indicated by its average yield—are already made the subject of record in our official statistical returns. Here then we have two available criteria which measure the growth of "economic rent." Let us see how far they will help us in the solution we are in search of.

The definition of "economic rent" as being so much of the value of the produce as exceeds the due remuneration of the cultivator's industry, might seem to identify this element with that which is properly, on the principle of distribution just laid down, the landlord's share; and the inference would be just, if we were to include in the cultivator's industry, not merely the capital and labour employed in raising the annual crops, but also that employed in adding to the productive qualities of the soil. But, as economists are aware, when the results of labour and capital are once made a part of the land itself, the returns upon them are governed, not by the laws of profit, but by those of rent, and become in practice inextricably blended with the rent due to natural fertility; while for the same reason they are distinguished from the returns which accrue on the ordinary annual outlay. In describing, therefore, "economic rent" as the value which remains in excess of what is needful for the due remuneration of the cultivator's industry, it must be understood that that industry only is spoken of which is employed in the direct production of the annual returns. Bearing this in mind, and having regard to what the tenant may do in the way of permanent improvement of the soil, it will be seen that the future growth of the landlord's share will not be commensurate with the future growth of "economic rent," and will not consequently follow the same indications. "Economic rent" gives us the maximum which the landlord's share can possibly attain; but in determining the amount which in the actual circumstances is properly his, we must discriminate the causes on which the productiveness of agriculture depends. What we want, in short, is some test which shall enable us to detach from the general value of the raw produce of the country that portion of it which is the result of causes external to the cultivator's operations. It is this portion only which society, in sanctioning private property in land, has consented to give up to the landlord.

Of the two criteria just mentioned—prices of produce and the productiveness of the soil—the former, agricultural prices,[*] plainly cannot be affected (at least in a way to raise rent) by any conduct on the tenant's part. An advance of price of a durable kind can only arise from one or both of two conditions—either from a fall in the value of money, or from such an augmented demand for food as should necessitate for its satisfaction the bringing under cultivation, without contemporaneous improvement in the art of agriculture, less fertile soils than any now cultivated. The latter contingency is one exceedingly unlikely to occur; but the former is at the present moment in process of realization, and amongst the causes immediately affecting the pecuniary interests of landlords is perhaps the most important. Changes in the price of produce can thus only occur as the result of causes operating through society at large; it follows that all such changes would indicate grounds for a corresponding change in the pecuniary amount of the landlord's share. This

[*] [Which should of course include the price of all that is raised from the soil—butcher's meat for example. M. Laveleye mentions (Cobden Club Essays, p. 245) that in Belgium, where rents have doubled in thirty years, the price of corn has hardly increased. The advance is due to other products, and in a large degree to the advance in live stock.]

has been generally recognized by the advocates of fixity of tenure in Ireland, and may be taken as a settled point in the controversy. It remains to consider whether this criterion alone adequately satisfies the justice of the case.

The only other cause which can affect economic rent being the productiveness of the soil, it might seem as if—unless where the landlord undertakes or concurs with the tenant in undertaking improvements of a permanent kind (cases which might easily be provided for by special arrangements between the parties)—I say it might seem, excluding such cases, as if all future increase of productiveness in the soil must necessarily be the result of the action of the tenant, and that consequently all future augmentation of economic rent, not referable to an advance in prices, should properly be assigned to him. But plausible as this inference is, I think it may be shown to be unwarrantable.

Let us consider the following case. Suppose some country village, at present of small account, to grow into a town of some importance. It would naturally soon be connected by railways with the chief industrial centres of the country, and, as an inevitable consequence, agricultural rent in the neighbourhood would greatly rise: it would rise for two reasons. First, because the local demand would raise the local prices, and, thus far, the criterion of prices would assign the increase to the landlord; but it would rise, secondly, because the proximity of a town and the facilities offered by railway communication would greatly cheapen production. The farmer would now be able to procure his ploughs and harrows, his threshing and reaping machines, his artificial manures, his tiles for draining, on greatly cheaper terms than before. Farming at greater advantage, he would be able (and that irrespective of any advance of price) to cultivate soils which formerly it would not have paid to cultivate, and in general to employ with profit a larger capital on his farm.* The soil, without supposing any change in its physical properties, would now yield a larger return, and in effect become more productive. The larger capital employed upon it would yield a larger return, while of this increase a portion would be obtained at a lower cost than the current prices (without supposing any advance beyond what had previously prevailed) would suffice to remunerate. These are conditions which imply an advance in "economic rent"—an advance not due to prices, and not indicated by prices; and the question is, to what cause is this result to be attributed—to the industry of the tenant, or to the progress of society in the locality? The tenant is very evidently a co-operator in the result. Without his capital and industry the increased produce could not be obtained; but that capital and industry would find their due reward in a corresponding augmentation of wages and profits; and the fact we have to deal with is the existence of a new increment over and above this due remuneration. It is with this part of the phenomenon only that we are concerned; and the point to be determined is its proper cause. Now it seems to me, for

* I have to thank my friend Professor Waley for having called my attention to the importance of this aspect of the case.

the same reasons which apply to the phenomenon of rent in other cases, that it is properly referable, not to the action of the cultivator, but to the progress of society.

The principle involved in this illustration is of very great importance, since it represents an influence that is constantly operating in all progressive countries, and which cannot but operate in Ireland if it is not to remain for ever in the slough of despond. Every fresh invention in the arts of productive industry applicable to agriculture, every extension of railway communication, every new development of internal trade, of external commerce, would be attended with consequences analogous in character to those which happened in the rural environs of our imaginary town. If Englishmen desire an illustration on a grand scale, they have only to look around them. The immense growth of rent in England and Scotland within a century is wholly unexplained by any corresponding rise in the price of produce, and is far from being adequately explained by the improvements effected in the permanent qualities of the soil, considerable as these have been. The phenomenon only becomes intelligible when we take account of the influence of industrial and commercial progress generally in cheapening agricultural production. Here, then, we find a source of growth for "economic rent," born of circumstances extrinsic to the tenant's sphere, and which should, therefore, on the principle of discrimination we have adopted, properly accrue to swell the landlord's share. But augmentations of rent thus arising would not be accompanied with any corresponding advance, nor, necessarily, with any advance at all in agricultural prices.

I am, therefore, brought to the conclusion that the criterion of prices, taken simply, and without reference to other circumstances, would fail to furnish an adequate basis for the periodical adjustment of rent. Its adoption would, in effect, transfer to the tenant that for which the State has permitted and encouraged the landlord to pay. I own the considerations just adduced, not to mention others that might be urged in the same sense, go strongly—at least so it seems to me—to show the fundamental impolicy of giving up land to private speculation. But that is not the question here. Land in Ireland has been given up to be thus dealt with; and, this being the policy of the country, those who have embarked their fortunes in this venture are entitled to be protected in its legitimate fruits.

There is, therefore, need of some criterion to supplement that of prices, some criterion which shall mark the growth of rent proceeding from causes not embraced by price, nor yet identical with the operations of the tenant in improving the soil. In a word, we want a test which shall discriminate so much of the increased productiveness of the soil as arises from enhanced efficacy of the productive instrument itself, from that increased productiveness which is, so to speak, the agricultural expression of the progress of the age. After some consideration I am inclined to think that such a test may be found in the average yield per acre of the staple produce of the soil over the whole country—information supplied already by

Irish agricultural statistics. This average productiveness would not, I think, in the main, be very seriously affected by the permanent outlay of tenants, for it must be remembered that a large portion of their improvements are in the nature of reclamations of waste land; and such land will, from the nature of the case, be the least productive in the country. Thus the effect of tenants' improvements would largely be to bring down the average level of productiveness throughout Ireland. On the other hand, there would be improvements, such as thorough draining, effected in the better lands, which would tend to raise the level. As between the two modes of influence I strongly incline to think that the tendency to depress the level would prevail; though I do not believe the preponderance in this direction would be so great as seriously to affect the correctness of the test.* This, however, might be matter for investigation. But proceeding on the assumption that, so far as tenants' improvements are concerned, an equilibrium would result, any positive advance in the average yield per acre over the country could only be referred to causes of that general kind which

* Applied to *land under tillage* in Ireland since 1847—the period from which the present system of statistics dates—the criterion shows a very great decline in the productiveness of the soil; but the explanation of this is to be found in the fact of its being partially applied. The newly-reclaimed land is always, at least in the first instance, brought under tillage; and since 1847 a large portion of the soil of Ireland, as is well known, has been converted from tillage to pasture; the portion so converted being, as a general rule, land of superior quality. Thus the test, confined to tillage land, would necessarily show a decline of productiveness. Were the returns from the grass lands, as measured by the increase of stock, taken into account, I have no doubt the balance would be more than redressed.

are incident to the progress of society.* I would, therefore, be disposed to combine this index with that of prices in seeking a rule for periodical readjustments of rent. Not that I would propose to fix those who might be charged with the duty of re-valuation absolutely to the results obtained from these data. It would obviously be necessary, particularly at first, to apply any general rule with discrimination and regard to local circumstances. But, I believe, the data in question constitute the main elements of a sound rule, the perfecting of which could only be the work of time and experience.

If these conclusions possess any value, they are applicable to all plans for the settlement of Ireland, which partially or generally, directly or indirectly, involve control by the State of the landlord's power over rent. But the plan which I have had mainly

* Those who have not firmly seized the doctrine of rent will probably see in the proposal to deprive the cultivator of any portion of the results accruing from the increased efficiency of his labours, a violation of equality as between him and those engaged in other industrial occupations. I will ask those who think so to consider what would be the effect of increased efficiency of industry, say in some manufacturing operation. Would it not be a proportional fall in the price of the commodity affected by the improvement? Now if a similar fall took place under similar circumstances in agriculture, the cultivator of the soil and the manufacturer would be on a footing of equality. But, in point of fact, this does not happen; and why? Simply because, owing to the limited extent of the better soils, competition cannot be brought to bear in the one case as in the other. Notwithstanding the immense progress made in the art of agriculture, assisted as this has been by the action of free trade, no serious impression has been made on agricultural prices, while the prices of manufactured articles steadily fall as new improvements come into operation. The deduction, therefore, made from the cultivator's profits of what is due to the exceptional position he occupies, so far from disturbing equality as between him and those engaged in other industries, is the necessary condition towards establishing equality.

in view in this speculation is that which has been propounded by Mr. George Campbell in his work on Irish land.* In this work Mr. Campbell has unfolded a scheme for the solution of the Irish problem incomparably (in the writer's judgment) the best deserving of attention of any that have solicited public notice—a scheme of which the characteristic and peculiar merits are that, at the cost of a minimum of disturbance to the actual machinery of Irish society, it would accomplish what would be a real and effective security of tenure for the Irish Tenant—would accomplish this in a manner suited to the ideas and habits of the country, while combining with this end the further considerable advantage of reserving for landlords under the new system a place and function in the national economy. Mr. Campbell's proposal proceeds upon the plan of distinguishing those parts of the country, or more properly those farms, where tenants now hold their land under definite contracts—where, in effect, the English system of managing property prevails—from those on which what may be called the Irish practice is followed: that of letting land from year to year, the task of providing for the permanent requirements of the farm being left to the occupier. With the state of things

* "The Irish Land," by George Campbell, Chief Commissioner of the Central Provinces of India. (Trübner & Co.) 1869. [I have allowed my remarks on Mr. Campbell's proposal to remain, partly because the principle of his scheme, though not its form or modes of procedure, has been embodied in the Irish Land Act, and therefore the comments which I have made on it are to a large extent applicable to that measure; and partly also because the objections urged against Mr. Campbell's plan continue still to be urged against all legislation with similar aim, and their refutation consequently cannot yet be considered as out of date or superfluous.]

existing on farms in the former category Mr. Campbell does not propose to interfere. But the tenants occupying under the latter conditions—a description which it is scarcely necessary to say covers the mass of the cultivators of Ireland—he would place upon a new footing, constituting them tenants under status, in contradistinction to those in the other category who would be regarded as tenants under contract. Once upon the footing of status, no tenant would be evicted except for defined reasons, of which the non-payment of rent, subdivision or sub-letting without the landlord's permission, are the chief; nor could his rent be raised against him except with the sanction of an authority representing the State. With a view to the working of the system, Mr. Campbell proposes the creation of a court or commission with large discretionary powers under an Act of Parliament prescribing its duties and mode of procedure. It would be the business of this court, in the first place, to settle the present position of tenants under status, to consider their claims on the score of past outlay on their farms, and, due allowance made for these, to settle the rent; and it would fall to the same commission to readjust the rent from time to time in conformity with the changing circumstances of the country, either at periodical re-valuations or on the requirement of either landlord or tenant. By such provisions security of tenure at fair rents would be realized for the cultivators of Ireland. But it is very far from Mr. Campbell's aim that his plan should work as a cast-iron system, stereotyping Irish society in its existing form. He would permit, where circumstances rendered this advisable, the re-appropriation by landlords of land in possession of tenants, but only on the terms of compensating the dispossessed tenant for his improvements, and indemnifying him for the inconvenience he sustained by dispossession; while, subject to the sanction of the landlord, the transference of farms from tenant to tenant would take place with perfect freedom. In providing for transactions of this kind, Mr. Campbell takes custom and Irish ideas as his guide; indeed, the recognition of custom as at once the outcome of history and the surest starting-point of reform may be said to be the *idée mère* of his whole scheme. He, therefore, naturally has recourse to the tenant-right of Ulster, in the legalization and extension of which he finds the practical solution of the thorny question of compensation for tenant's improvements. By a most ingenious argument Mr. Campbell shows that, on any view of the case which does not amount to practical confiscation of the tenant's interests, this is what compensation in the case of small farmers, as those under status would almost universally be, must come to. In this opinion those who look closely into the matter will be apt to agree with Mr. Campbell. When we have to deal with improvements on a substantial scale, carried on upon farms of considerable extent, there would be little practical difficulty in arriving at a tolerably correct estimate of their value; but when the problem is to ascertain the worth of a thatched shed, or a gateway, or of a rood of reclaimed bog in a farm of ten acres, there is really no other criterion possible than this—how much will another tenant give for them?

I venture to offer two suggestions in the way of corollary to Mr. Campbell's plan. It would only be in keeping with the whole principle of his scheme, that, where the State has once charged itself with determining the tenants' rent, no higher rent than that named by the State should be recoverable in a court of law. A provision to this effect would effectually prevent sub-letting, at least in the usual form of that practice. The occupier, it is true, could sell his right of occupancy; and it will no doubt be urged against Mr. Campbell's plan that the sum paid for this by the incoming tenant would, in effect, amount to an increased rent—the objector will doubtless add, on the authority of Adam Smith and Lord Dufferin—of the worst kind. The value of this objection I shall presently consider; but, before doing so, let me state my second suggestion, which is that the occupancy right should only be disposable to an incoming tenant. I believe that this restriction would be attended with very beneficial consequences. It would, in the first place, render impossible the mortgaging of the good-will; and secondly, it would indirectly, but I believe very effectually, restrain competition for land within healthy limits. The intending purchaser of the occupancy of a farm might, of course, still raise the money for the purchase of the tenant-right on his personal credit. This is a use of his position and circumstances with which it would be neither possible nor proper to interfere; but, in order to obtain the farm, one of two things he must have—either cash to pay for the good-will, or credit to induce some capitalist to lend him the money necessary for that purpose; either, that is to say, he must already be the master of realized property, or his character must be such as to make those who know him believe that he is likely to be a prosperous man. The restriction of competition for land to persons satisfying these conditions would render absolutely impossible, under the system of status-tenancy, anything at all resembling, or in any respect analogous to, the impossible rents promised by pauper peasants when the whole population enter the list of competition.

It appears then that, even conceding the argument that the purchase of the occupancy right would for the incoming tenant be equivalent to an increase of rent, still this increase—supposing the practice limited by the restriction I have indicated—would fall greatly short of what rents may attain under the present *régime*. But then we are told that the vice of the practice lies in the form, that the sale of the good-will is in effect a fine paid on entry, and that this has been condemned by Adam Smith. The use so constantly made of Adam Smith's authority in this connection, I must plainly say, does him flagrant injustice—injustice which it is difficult to conceive how anyone should commit who had really studied his excellent remarks on the tenure of land. The ruling thought of all that he has said on this subject is the supreme importance of security of tenure for the tenant, as the essential foundation and mainspring of all agricultural progress. He eulogizes leases, and, failing leases, customs, or whatever conduces to realizing this indispensable condition. "It is those laws and customs," he tells us, "which have perhaps contributed more to the present grandeur of England than all their boasted regulations of commerce taken together." What he says upon the subject of fines is wholly irrelevant to the issue in the present case. He is comparing leases at full rent with leases in which a portion of the rent is fined down—that is to say, alternatives either of which offers equal security to the tenant—and his decision is in favour of that one in which no fine is paid. What relevancy has a judgment on such a point to the question involved in the tenant-right controversy, where the alternative lies, not between different modes of attaining equal security, but between absolute security obtained through a fine accompanied by a moderate rent, and no security accompanied by a high rent without a fine? Had the issue in the Irish controversy really come under Adam Smith's review, no one, who knows anything of the spirit pervading the "Wealth of Nations," can doubt what his decision would have been. At all events, his authority would need to be greater even than it is to outweigh the overwhelming force of the argument from Irish experience. The universal testimony borne to the prosperity of the tenant farmers in Ireland, wherever the custom of Ulster prevails—a prosperity all the more conspicuous from its contrast with the general wretchedness of the same classes in other parts of the country,—and the almost equally universal recognition of the connection between the system and the results, are facts which no statesman can overlook. Mr. Caird, with all his strong and undisguised prepossessions in favour of Scotch farming, was unable to resist the evidence; and the *Times* Commissioner, in his singularly impartial descriptions written from direct observation, has recently confirmed the most favourable accounts of the system. In presence of such facts it is idle to talk of Adam Smith, or any other authority. All that has been said, or that can be said, against the practice of tenant-right really amounts to this—that the incoming tenant would be better off if he could get the farm with the advantages of the custom while keeping the money which is the price of those advantages. No doubt he would; and so, and in a still greater degree, would be the purchaser of a peasant property if he had not to pay the purchase-money; and yet peasant proprietors, working at this disadvantage, have contrived notwithstanding to cultivate their farms to some purpose. In neither case can a man spend his capital and have his capital; but he may in either case have that which is worth to him more than capital—the peace of mind that is born of security, the enterprise inspired by the prospect of reaping where he has sown.

[There is a mode of reasoning on this question which, if it is not positively fallacious, at least suggests a fallacy against which it may be well to insert a warning here. It is said * that a farmer at a full rent will, with a given capital, be able to work a larger farm than he would were he to employ a portion of his capital in purchasing his farm or in fining down the rent; and that, having regard to the existing price of land, he will, by adopting the former course, derive a larger income from his whole capital. The fact may

* See Judge Longfield's Essay on 'The Tenure of Land in Ireland,' "Cobden Club Essays," vol. i.

be so; but, inasmuch as there are farmers, nevertheless, who prefer a smaller farm which is their own property to a larger one at a full rent, this only shows that the position of proprietor is regarded by some as sufficiently advantageous to compensate for a certain loss on annual revenue. Of this, affecting as it does the person concerned only, farmers may be allowed to be themselves the best judges; and true policy will lie in removing all obstacles to their making the freest possible choice. But the line of reasoning to which I have referred implies that there is more than this in the matter; that, looking at the question from the point of view of public interest, an economic gain results from the farmer's remaining a tenant at a full rent, an economic loss from his becoming a proprietor. What is suggested is that the capital of the community available for agriculture is diminished by the adoption of the latter course, and here it is that the fallacy intrudes itself. The farmer who purchases his farm no doubt reduces thereby the amount of his own capital available for cultivation, but he does not curtail in any degree the capital of the community applicable for this purpose; for the purchase-money of his farm, in passing from his hands, at once becomes in the hands of the vendor a fund disposable for productive purposes. He will seek to derive an interest from it, and he can do this in no other way than by investing it. One, and not an improbable mode of investment, would be to lend it on mortgage, in which way, it is conceivable, the same capital might come back to the hands of the very farmer who had parted with it. It will perhaps be said that the farmer proprietor would be thus brought under a rent in another form; but there would be this distinction between his position now and formerly; that, whereas he was formerly a tenant paying rent and subject to all the insecurity of that position, he is now an owner subject to a fixed rent-charge. I have supposed the capital rendered disposable by the farmer's purchase to be invested on mortgage; but it is of no consequence what supposition we make with regard to the mode of investment. Suppose it were invested in the Funds, it would still be disposable in the hands of the vendor of stock, and, however it might for a time pass from hand to hand, must ultimately, if it is to yield a revenue, find its way to the sustenance of some branch of production—doubtless to the sustenance of whatever branch had most need of it. If agriculture were that branch, then, in the absence of artificial obstacles, to the support of agriculture it would go. If it did not go back to agriculture this would only be because the interests of the community were better served by a different disposition of the fund.]

Perhaps the greatest danger of the present moment is that on which so much English legislation has made shipwreck—the danger that our statesmen, meaning well but embarrassed by their position, will be drawn into the middle course of a weak compromise—a compromise which will solve nothing, but embroil everything. The plan recommended by Mr. Caird, a high authority in practical agriculture, fulfils in a remarkable manner the conditions of such a settlement. The inducements which he holds out to landlords to grant leases would be simply inappreciable, when weighed against the reasons which would still remain, from their point of view, for refusing them; and what would be the value of leases without some guarantee against an indefinite rise of rent? But while this plan would wholly fail to give a sense of security to the tenant, it would be very effectual in hampering the action of the landlord. What landlord would care to take an active part in working his estate when he could only do so by passing his transactions with his tenants through the ordeal of public advertisement in leading newspapers, and waiting for the expiration of a five years' notice to quit before getting possession of his land? Of two things, one. The material development of the country may, on plausible grounds, be entrusted to the initiative either of landlord or of tenant. There is something to be said for both plans. The landlord has naturally the advantage of the tenant-farmer—at least of the Irish tenant-farmer as he now exists—in enterprise and command of capital. On the other hand, enterprise and capital may, as others think, be developed in a far higher degree by giving real security to the tenant. But a system for which there is absolutely nothing to be said is that which would fail to evoke either of these motive powers; which would shackle the landlord without freeing the tenant, and under a net of inducements and counter-inducements, of checks and counter-checks, would stifle all vigorous life. Such, I venture to think, would be the effect of the solution of the Irish problem recommended by Mr. Caird. But such a result could scarcely prove definitive. Things have gone too far for that. The attempt to accomplish it would, however, immensely aggravate all the dangerous elements of the situation, and probably in the end involve us in extreme courses, which might now be avoided.

NOTE TO P. 197.

[This is what Mr. Mill has since, in the programme of the Land Tenure Reform Association, designated "the unearned increase" from land, all future additions to which he proposes on certain conditions to appropriate to the State. The discussions which have arisen on this proposal of Mr. Mill's have, by the flagrant weakness of the arguments employed against it, brought into strong light the essential soundness of Mr. Mill's position. Thus, one of the principal of those arguments is derived from a supposed analogy between Land and Stocks—*e.g.* the public funds. It is urged that the public funds, like land, rise in value with the progress of society; that the advance in their price which has occurred since they were first created has been "unearned" by the fundholder; and that therefore the same principle which applies to the "unearned increase" from land would require us to mulct the fundholder of this portion of his property. The argument is founded upon a gross confusion, which perhaps it may be well to clear up. A rise in the price of stocks, where it is due to the progress of society, represents a larger *capitalized* value *of the same annual sum*: it merely indicates a change in the relation of capital to interest. But land rises in value, not merely from this cause, but also because rent, the annual return, rises. A rise in the price of stocks, so far as it is due to the progress of society, would be shared by all stocks in an equal degree. The stockholder, consequently, unless so far as the advance gives him greater confidence in the stability of his property, derives no advantage from the change. His income remains as before. He may indeed sell it for a higher price; but, on reinvesting the price, he would have to pay proportionally higher for whatever productive fund he chose to buy. To deprive stockholders of the increase in the capitalized value of their stock would not be to keep their means of living at the same point at which it stood before the advance in price took place, but to reduce it below that point just in proportion to the amount abstracted. In other words, the recognition of their right to all increase in the capitalized value of their income is the condition of leaving that income unimpaired. The case of land is totally different. The capitalized value of a given rent rises with the progress of society precisely as the price of stocks rises. So far the landlord stands on the same footing with the fundholder. *But then his rent rises also;* and this makes all the difference. While the fundholder's income remains the same as society progresses, the landlord's steadily rises: his means of living steadily increase. The capitalized value of his estate consequently increases not simply *pari passu* with the increase in the price of stock, that is to say with the increase in the capitalized value of a given yearly sum, but in this proportion compounded with the increase in his annual rents. Now, it is to the increased value of land incident to the increase of annual rent, and to this alone, that Mr. Mill's proposal applies.

Another argument relied upon by Mr. Mill's opponents is the analogy to the case of land supposed to be furnished by the advance in the price of works of art and objects of *vertu* which also occurs with the progress of society. But surely the case must be felt to be desperate when such an argument is seriously put forward. Conceding the analogy to be perfect, is it not sufficient to reply *de minimis non curat lex?* Special legislation on such a subject as the land of a country may surely be permissible where it would not be worth the legislator's while to regulate by special enactment the irregular gains of a few picture-dealers. But in truth the cases are not analogous. In the first place picture collectors perform a useful social function by cultivating the public taste in the direction of art; the increase in the value of their property is therefore not altogether "unearned." And, secondly, pictures differ from land in this, that they do not *as a rule* rise in value with the progress of society. A few rise in value, and a great many more fall. The picture-dealer takes his chance: and it would be gross injustice, while compelling him to bear his losses, to compel him also to relinquish the occasional gains which form their natural compensation.]

VII.

POLITICAL ECONOMY AND LAISSEZ-FAIRE.*

Great Britain, if not the birthplace of Political Economy, has at least been its early home, as well as the scene of the most signal triumphs of its manhood. Every great step in the progress of economic science (I do not think an important exception can be named) has been won by English thinkers; and while we have led the van in economic speculation, we have also been the first to apply with boldness our theories to practice. Our foreign trade, our colonial policy, our poor-laws, our fiscal system, each has in turn been reconstructed from the foundation upwards under the inspiration of economic ideas; and the population and the commerce of the country, responding to the impulse given by the new principles operating through those changes, have within a century multiplied themselves manifold. This London, in the midst of which we find ourselves, what is it but a mighty monument of economic achievement?—the greatest practical illus-

* An Introductory Lecture delivered in University College, November 1870.

tration which the world has seen of the potent influence of those principles which it is the business of the political economist to expound? In view of such facts, one might expect that, if there was on the globe a spot where a keen interest would be felt in the study of Political Economy—where the science which unfolds the laws of industry and commerce would be held in honour—it would be London. Now I wish to call your attention to a singular fact, for singular it surely is. In this vast London, so energetic, so enterprising, so enlightened; in this great centre of the world's commerce; in this metropolis of the country which has produced Adam Smith, Ricardo, Malthus, Mill; which has produced, again, Pitt and Huskisson, Peel, Cobden and Gladstone; in this focus of economic activity and power; the systematic study of economic science is almost without practical recognition. I wish to be accurate, and I therefore say "almost," and I use the qualification "practical"; for in London there are, I believe, three chairs from which Political Economy, or matter connected with Political Economy, is taught—two in King's College and one here. But what is the number of students attracted from this great population to study Political Economy under those chairs? I have no exact statistics upon the point, and the subject is perhaps of too delicate a nature to warrant me in going into details. But I am certainly not overstating the case when I say, that the aggregate number of students attending all the public economic schools in London falls very much short of a hundred individuals—one hundred individuals, that is to say, out of a population of three millions! I wish I could say that we in this college could claim one-half, or even a quarter, of this not very overwhelming grand total.

I do not know whether it is necessary to go into comparisons in order to point the significance of these figures; but I will venture to mention one other case, as it has come under my own personal observation. In the not very flourishing town of Galway, with which I have had till lately an official connection, there is a chair of Political Economy. The number of students who during my time attended the lectures from that chair varied ordinarily from six to ten persons. Now, if we compare the proportion which these numbers bear to the population from which they were drawn with the proportion which, let us say, the sixty or one hundred students attending London chairs bear to the population of this metropolis, and if we take this proportion as an indication of the interest felt in economic studies in the two places, we arrive at this rather surprising result—that in that remote, and I regret to say decaying, Irish town, the degree of interest taken in economic science is many times, perhaps five or six times, greater than here—greater, that is to say, in the "*ultima Thule*" of Connaught than in this metropolis of modern industrial civilization.

Now it seems to me that this is a very remarkable fact, and one that deserves the attention of those who, in this country, have charged themselves with this branch of speculation. I have called attention to it, partly in the hope that those who have better opportunities of acquainting themselves with the opinions of the London public than I have may take it into consideration, and partly with a view to bring under your notice such a partial explanation of the phenomenon as occurs to myself. Let me say here, in passing, that there is one explanation of the fact, which to many people will seem the sufficient and obvious one, which, nevertheless, I cannot allow to be either a satisfactory or a complete account of the matter. I shall possibly be told that the reason the people of London are not attracted to the lectures delivered from its economic chairs is simply that those lectures are not attractive; that, in short, the fault lies, not with the people of London, but with those who fail to set Political Economy before them in an interesting light. The facts may be as this explanation suggests, at least I have no desire to deny them, so far as my own particular share in the transaction is concerned: but I submit that the allegation fails to meet the point. The professors of Political Economy in London are not the creators, but the creatures, not the cause, but the effect, of the requirements of the people of London with respect to this subject. I do not deny that there is a connection between the mode in which a subject is taught and the interest taken in it, that the public taste may be sensibly influenced by the quality of those who occupy the seats of learning in a country. But, conceding this, I still hold that the public cannot escape from its responsibilities towards science and learning by sheltering itself under an alleged incompetency on the part of those to whom it has intrusted their interests. If the teachers of Political Economy in London are not up to the mark, why does not

London supply itself with better? Why is London content to have Political Economy inadequately taught? And thus I am brought back to the fact which I have proposed for consideration: that, in this great centre of English commercial and political life, Political Economy, the one science which is pre-eminently an English product, which has been built up by English thinkers, and applied, with most striking effect, by English statesmen, is, as a branch of liberal education, all but practically ignored.

There are those who would probably explain this singular state of things by reference to a supposed distaste or inaptitude for abstract speculation characteristic of the average English mind. I will not undertake to say that there may not be some slender basis of truth in this view. Englishmen are apt to value themselves on being a practical people; and, as every excellence is said to have its compensating defect, it is conceivable that this English virtue may have a tendency to run to excess, and that it may have issued in a mental habit unfavourable to the cultivation of economic science, which, it must be admitted, shares the attributes common to all scientific knowledge. Certainly, the very slender attention bestowed in London on some other branches of philosophical speculation—I may instance mental philosophy and jurisprudence—affords some countenance to this view. Still, I cannot admit this to be a complete account of the matter. English distaste for abstract speculation, assuming it to exist, is, at all events, not so strong that it may not be overcome by the prospect of practical advantage. What do we see in the Universities?

Branches of learning of the most abstract character, others, if not abstract, at all events as far removed as learning can conceivably be from utilitarian ends, but nevertheless pursued with extraordinary eagerness. And why? For no other reason, that I know of, than because certain large pecuniary prizes are attached to success in them. But this is perhaps a somewhat coarse illustration of the facility with which the practical English mind may be drawn contrary to its natural bent. More creditable evidence may be found in the large and increasing attention now given to the physical sciences; for physical science, though deriving its data from particular facts, nevertheless, as science, consists, not in statements regarding particular facts, but in abstract doctrines. What is a law of nature but a relation between phenomena considered apart from all particular exemplifications of the relation?—that is to say, an abstract doctrine. Yet this has not prevented the keenest possible pursuit of physical knowledge. In short, let it once be made clear that abstract speculation is not barren speculation, that scientific doctrines have a real bearing on the practical concerns of life—and by practical concerns of life I do not mean simply making money, but all that concerns human beings in shaping their conduct in the world—let this only be made clear, and I think we have no reason to suppose that a fair proportion of the community will not be drawn to their cultivation. And this brings me to what, it seems to me is the true explanation, or at least one principal cause, of that indifference towards economic studies of which the limited attention given to them in the seats of learning in London affords so remarkable an indication. I seem to observe in the literature and social discussions of the day signs of a belief that Political Economy has ceased to be a fruitful speculation. Nay, I fear I must go further, and admit that it is even regarded by some energetic minds in this country as even worse than unfruitful—as obstructive, a positive hindrance in the path of useful reform. I am anxious to state, as accurately as I can, what I understand to be the precise nature of those injurious prepossessions. Before attempting to prescribe remedies, it will be well to make a careful diagnosis of the disease.

Few persons of decent education will now deny that vast benefits have accrued to the world, and in an especial degree to this country, from the study of economic science. I have already referred to the great practical reforms that have been accomplished in obedience to its teaching in the principal departments of our public life. And over and above such tangible achievements, candid people will acknowledge that its influence has been felt throughout the whole range of our legislative and administrative systems, and with largely beneficial effect. We are all now very familiar with such commonplaces as that individuals are the best judges of their own interests; that monopolies should not be permitted in trade; that contracts should be free; that taxation should be equal, and should be directed to the maintenance of the revenue, not to the guidance of commerce; and the like. These seem now to be very trite maxims, but a century ago they were paradoxes; and, in truth, they represent nothing less than a revolution in the modes of governing and administering the country, the result of the new modes of thought introduced by economic study. Well, the benefits conferred by economic science being thus evident and palpable, it may seem surprising that opinions such as I have just hinted at should obtain, and obtain not merely amongst the ignorant, but among well-informed and instructed people. How are we to reconcile the recognition which must be accorded to the past achievements of this science with the beliefs in its present unfruitfulness, still more with the opinion held by some of our more advanced social thinkers, that it has become an obstacle in the forward path of reform?

I put the question thus broadly, because it is only when these impressions are brought into juxtaposition with the admitted facts of the case that the attitude of a large portion of the educated classes towards this study can be understood. It is too easily assumed by economists that, the past services of their science once established, its importance as a branch of modern education must be forthwith acknowledged. But this by no means follows. Not a few schemes of doctrine may be named which have been useful in their time, but which, having served their purpose, have ceased to possess interest for those who desire to take part in the working life of the world; nay, the burthen of which on the memory might even be felt by such as an encumbrance and a drag. The rules of chivalry once served a very useful purpose. The doctrines of the scholastic logic for many centuries greatly aided the progress of the speculative intellect. Numerous systems of dogmatic theology, now extinct or becoming so, have for a time served as scaffolding for moral ideas more or less valuable. The theory of the social contract, fanciful and barren as it may now seem to us, was potent among the active forces which produced the great intellectual ferment of the last century in France. Yet a knowledge of all or of any of these phases of thought would scarcely be considered as an indispensable part of the mental equipment of an educated man in the present day. Now this consideration may help us to understand the attitude taken towards Political Economy by a large number of instructed and active-minded people. It is not denied that the science has done some good; only it is thought that its task is pretty well fulfilled. The process of abolishing monopolies and removing impediments to industry is thought to have well-nigh reached its natural termination; or, if there is work to be done, then it is held to be work of a different order from most of that which has been hitherto accomplished—work, in the carrying out of which the maxims of economic science not only cannot help us, but may even prove an obstruction. These opinions, it is evident, must connect themselves with the idea entertained of economic science by those who hold them; and this brings me to what I regard as the root of the matter—the notion prevailing among the great majority of educated people respecting the nature and functions of Political Economy.

That notion, I imagine, takes somewhat this shape. Political Economy has of course to do with wealth; so far there is no question in dispute. But what is the problem concerning wealth which it undertakes to solve? I think the prevailing notion is that it undertakes to show that wealth may be most rapidly accumulated and most fairly distributed—that is to say, that human well-being may be most effectually promoted—by the simple process of leaving people to themselves; leaving individuals, that is to say, to follow the promptings of self-interest unrestrained either by the State or by public opinion, so long as they abstain from force and fraud. This is the doctrine commonly known as *laissez-faire;* and, accordingly, Political Economy is, I think, very generally regarded as a sort of scientific rendering of this maxim,—a vindication of freedom of industrial enterprise and of contract, as the one and sufficient solution of all industrial problems. Such, I apprehend, is the current notion; and it must be owned that it falls in very well with most of what is known respecting the practical applications of the science. How far this view is well founded I shall presently examine; but I wish first to show how it has produced that indifference towards the study amongst a large proportion of educated people, and that hostility on the part of a few, to which I have in the preceding remarks called your attention.

You will observe, then, that, taking the foregoing as a correct description of the scope and functions of economic science, its utility, with a view to the practical requirements of a country, will entirely depend upon what those requirements happen to be. If the industrial system of a country be of that character which was universal in Europe eighty or a hundred years ago, if trade and industry be hampered in all directions by artificial rules and restrictions, obviously there will be great scope for a scheme of doctrine embodying and expounding the principle of *laissez-faire*. But if this is not the case, if all, or nearly all, the reforms covered by this maxim have been already carried, then Political Economy, as its scientific expression, can, it is evident, have little relevancy to the practical work of the country. How, then, stands the case with regard to ourselves? Do we find State action here in the sphere of industry greatly overdone? Are the legal restraints on individual enterprise, still unremoved, of a serious kind? Is our trade still in shackles? Is our freedom of contract injuriously restricted? I think most candid people will acknowledge that, while something may still be needed in some or all of these directions, it is not of a very formidable character, and that this little may safely be trusted for its accomplishment to the impetus which still remains from the movement which carried the greater economic reforms. Looking around us on the social needs of the time, we are bound, I think, to confess that we do not find much work of a merely negative sort to do; and we must therefore acknowledge that, if Political Economy be merely what a widely prevalent opinion supposes it to be, if the sum and outcome of its teaching be *laissez-faire*, the field for its activity, in this country at least, must henceforth be a narrow one. Under these circumstances, it is not strange if the interest felt in the study is of a languid sort. Where the opinion prevails that *laissez-faire* marks the limit of industrial reform, that when we have set individual enterprise free we have done all that in such matters can be done,

Political Economy will naturally be regarded with a good-natured tolerance in consideration of its past services, combined with a profound indifference, based on the conviction that it has become in the course of events a practically obsolete scheme of thought. Such, it seems to me, is in point of fact the state of feeling on this subject amongst a large number of educated people in this country at the present time.

Amongst a large number, but not universally; for there are those whose faith in *laissez-faire* is not quite so absolute as that of the majority; who hold that there are ends to be compassed in social and industrial life which can only be reached through the action of society as an organized whole; and that, while the mere negative and destructive part of industrial reform has been well-nigh completed, a work of positive and reconstructive reform still lies before us. What will be the attitude of this section of thinkers towards a speculation putting itself forward as a scientific vindication of the principle of "letting things alone"? Inevitably one of hostility. When people think they see before them a field for useful action, in which good may be done by measures of a positive kind, they naturally feel impatient of a system propounding *laissez-faire* as the last word of human wisdom. Thus, if I have correctly seized the current impression respecting this branch of speculation, we have found at least a partial explanation of the phenomenon which I have proposed for consideration. People neglect Political Economy because they regard it as practically obsolete, as out of relation to the actual work of the time; or they oppose it because they think it has begun to be obstructive; and the view taken by depreciators and opponents is in each case the natural result of the conception they have formed of the study. And here it is that I join issue with both classes. I altogether deny the correctness of their view of the science; and, as the most effectual means of exploding it, I shall now endeavour to show that the maxim of *laissez-faire* has no scientific basis whatever, but is at best a mere handy rule of practice, useful, perhaps, as a reminder to statesmen on which side the presumption lies in questions of industrial legislation, but totally destitute of all scientific authority.

In proceeding to argue this point, I must ask you, in the first place, to note what this doctrine of *laissez-faire*, if it is to be taken as a scientific principle, really means. The implied assertion, as I understand it, is this: that, taking human beings as they are, in the actual state of moral and intellectual development they have reached; taking account, further, of the physical conditions with which they are surrounded in the world; lastly, accepting the institution of private property as understood and maintained in most modern states,—the promptings of self-interest will lead individuals, in all that range of their conduct which has to do with their material well-being, spontaneously to follow that course which is most for their own good and for the good of all. Such is the assertion with which we have now to deal; and you will at once see that it involves the two following assumptions: first, that the interests of human beings are fundamentally the same—that what is most for my interest is also most for the interest of other people; and, secondly, that individuals know their interests in the sense in which they are coincident with the interests of others, and that, in the absence of coercion, they will, in this sense, follow them. If these two propositions be made out, the policy of *laissez-faire*—the policy, that is to say, of absolute abstention on the part of the State in all that concerns material well-being—follows with scientific rigour. But can they be made out? For my part I am disposed to accept the first one; I am disposed to believe that human interests, well understood, are fundamentally at one: only let me in passing suggest a caution. Let us not confound the statement that *human* interests are at one with the statement that *class* interests are at one. The latter I believe to be as false as the former is true, and, moreover, to be one of those plausible optimist falsities against which it especially behoves us in the present day to be on our guard. But accepting the major premiss of the syllogism, that the interests of human beings are fundamentally the same, how as to the minor?—how as to the assumption that people know their interests in the sense in which they are identical with the interests of others, and that they spontaneously follow them *in this sense?* It is a remarkable thing that Bastiat, the great apostle of *laissez-faire*, in the work he has devoted to the glorification of this principle, absolutely overlooks this indispensable step of the argument--wholly fails to prove his minor premiss. He thus states the case:—"Human interests," he says, are either "naturally harmonious," or "naturally antagonistic."* If antagonistic, then the solution of the social problem must lie in some form of constraint. But if human interests be harmonious, then, he argues, the solution must lie in leaving people free to follow them—in the unqualified adoption, that is to say, of the principle of *laissez-faire*. Now I beg you to mark the strange assumptions that underlie this reasoning. Human interests are naturally harmonious: *therefore* we have only to leave people free, and social harmony must result; as if it were an obvious thing that people knew their interests in the sense in which they coincide with the interests of others, and that, knowing them, they must follow them; as if there were no such things in the world as passion, prejudice, custom, *esprit de corps*, class interest, to draw people aside from the pursuit of their interests in the largest and highest sense! Here is a fatal flaw on the very threshold of Bastiat's argument; and it is a flaw which no follower of Bastiat has repaired—which, for my part, I believe to be irreparable. Nothing is easier than to show that people follow their interest, in the sense in which they understand their interest. But between this and following their interest in the sense in which it is coincident with that of other people, a chasm yawns. This chasm in the argument of the *laissez-faire* school has never been bridged. The advocates of the doctrine shut their eyes and leap over it.

For, to examine the question more nearly, and to come at once to the important point—granting that

* As if even this were necessarily true; as if it might not be that some human interests were in harmony and some opposed.

people may, in a certain sense, be trusted to see most clearly their own interest, and to pursue with avidity what they so regard, what is it that people understand to be their interest? What did landlords, as a class, understand to be their interest down to 1846, when they maintained the Corn Laws as indispensable to their rents, and the prop of their political power? What do the same class now understand as their interest, when they avail themselves of the power given them by the law to put their estates in settlement, create life-interests, entails, collateral charges, interposing endless artificial obstacles between the land of the country and the living people who inhabit it, to the practical exclusion from the possession of land of the enormous majority of Englishmen? What do Irish landlords understand to be their interest when they are only withheld by fear of assassination, or by law, from evicting their tenants in order to consolidate their estates? What did employers in former days understand to be their interest when they enacted statutes of labourers? or, in more recent times, when a ten hours' Act has become necessary to protect women and children against the consequences of an unscrupulous pursuit of gain? What is the notion those farmers form of their interest who employ the gang system as described in recent parliamentary reports? or, again, those members of trades-unions, who pass rules against task-work and in favour of uniform wages for the skilful and the inept, the idle and the industrious, rules against machinery and in favour of inefficient methods of manual-labour, rules against the admission of their fellows to sharing with themselves the opportunities of a livelihood offered by the market, rules, in a word, against the most efficacious use of man's power over nature, and the fair distribution of the proceeds of toil—what, in the idea of these trades-unionists, is their interest? To give one instance more, what was the notion of their interest entertained by the slaveholding aristocracy in the Southern States of the American Union, who, seeing with their own eyes the exhausting and ruinous effects of the system they upheld; seeing its influence in preventing the rise of a skilled industrial class, and in thus almost wholly excluding manufacturing industry from the States where it prevailed; seeing its effects in consigning to lawless barbarism more than a half of the entire rural population,—nevertheless rose in arms to maintain it, and not merely to maintain, but to extend it far and wide over the continent of America? Or, turning from particular examples to broad results, can any one seriously consider the present condition of the inhabitants of these islands—these islands where industrial freedom has for nearly half a century had greater scope than in any previous age or in any other country, but where also the extremes of wealth and poverty are found in harsher contrast than they have been ever found elsewhere; where one man consumes more value in a single meal than goes to feed and clothe the family of another for a month; where the entire land of the country is owned by less than a hundred thousand persons out of a population of thirty millions; where one in every twenty persons is a pauper; where the great bulk of the agricultural population look forward with calm resignation to spending their old age in a workhouse; while the artisan population of the towns find themselves about once in ten years in the midst of a frightful commercial catastrophe, which consigns hundreds of thousands to ruin—I ask if any one can seriously consider this state of things, and yet repose in absolute satisfaction and confidence on his maxim of *laissez-faire?* Nor is it merely the co-existence of this state of things with an unparalleled freedom in all directions of industrial and commercial enterprise that we have to consider. The truly significant circumstance is that the policy in question, the policy expressed by *laissez-faire*, has been steadily progressive for nearly half a century, and yet we have no sign of mitigation in the harshest features of our social state. I beg of you to consider the lesson taught by the repeal of the Corn Laws. That was one of the most important steps ever taken in carrying out the policy of *laissez-faire*—as all economists believe a thoroughly sound and wise step. Well, now, observe what the repeal of the Corn Laws has done for us, and also what it has not done for us. It has given an immense impulse to our general trade; our exports and imports have, since the passing of the measure, enormously increased; our wealth and population have advanced with unexampled rapidity. But the able men who led the agitation for the repeal of the Corn Laws promised much more than this. They told us that the Poor Laws were to follow the Corn Laws; that pauperism would disappear with the restrictions upon trade, and the workhouses ere long become obsolete institutions. I fear this part of the programme has scarcely been fulfilled. Those ugly social features, those violent contrasts of poverty and wealth, that strike so unpleasantly the eye of every foreign observer in this country, are still painfully prominent. The signs of the extinction of pauperism are not yet very apparent. In a word, "the grand final result" promised by Bastiat as the double goal towards which *laissez-faire* conducts mankind—"the indefinite approximation of all classes towards a level which is always rising; the equalization of individuals in the general amelioration"—seems as yet, with all our freedom of trade, scarce perceptibly nearer—nay, one might be tempted to say, seems further off than ever. I say this is a significant fact, and one fitted, it seems to me, to abate our confidence in mere *laissez-faire* as the panacea for industrial ills.

There is then no evidence, either in what we know of the conduct of men in the present stage of their development, or yet in the large experience we have had of the working of *laissez-faire*, to warrant the assumption that lies at the root of this doctrine. Human beings know and follow their interests according to their lights and dispositions; but not necessarily, nor in practice always, in that sense in which the interest of the individual is coincident with that of others and of the whole. It follows that there is no security that the economic phenomena of society, as at present constituted, will always arrange themselves spontaneously in the way which is most for the common good. In other words, *laissez-faire* falls to the ground as a scientific doctrine. I say as a scientific doctrine; for let us be careful not to overstep the limits of our argument. It is one thing to repudiate the scientific authority of *laissez-faire*, freedom of contract, and so forth; it is a totally different thing to set up the opposite principle of State control, the doctrine of paternal government. For my part I accept neither one doctrine nor the other; and, as a practical rule, I hold *laissez-faire* to be incomparably the safer guide. Only let us remember that it is a *practical rule*, and not a doctrine of science; a rule in the main sound, but like most other sound practical rules, liable to numerous exceptions; above all, a rule which must never for a moment be allowed to stand in the way of the candid consideration of any promising proposal of social or industrial reform. It is from this point of view that the argument I have been urging assumes a practical aspect. *Laissez-faire*, freedom of contract, and phrases of like import, have of late become somewhat of bugbears with a large number of people. It is enough to mention them, to discredit by anticipation the most useful practical scheme. What did we hear during the discussions on the Irish Land Bill? Political Economy again and again appealed to as having pronounced against that measure. Now, what did this mean? Simply that the Bill interfered with freedom of contract, violated the rule of *laissez-faire*—charges perfectly true, and which would have been decisive against the Bill had these phrases really possessed the scientific authority which members of Parliament supposed them to possess. Now, it is against this understanding of the doctrine that my argument is directed. So understood, I hold it to be a pretentious sophism, destitute of foundation in nature and fact, and rapidly becoming an obstruction and nuisance in public affairs.

Well, if Political Economy is something else than the doctrine of *laissez-faire*, what is it? If it possesses capabilities in relation to positive and reconstructive, no less than in relation to negative and destructive, reform, I may fairly be required to point them out. And this is what, in the further remarks I have now to offer you, I shall attempt to do. If then I am asked what is Political Economy, I say it is the Science of Wealth; and for those who clearly apprehend what science, in the modern sense of the term, means, this ought sufficiently to indicate at once its province, and what it undertakes to do. Unfortunately, many who perfectly understand what science means when the word is employed with reference to physical nature, allow themselves to slide into a totally different sense of it, or rather into acquiescence in an absence of all distinct meaning in its use, when they employ it with reference to social existence. In the minds of a large number of people everything is Social Science which proposes to deal with social facts, either in the way of remedying a grievance, or in promoting order and progress in society. Now I am anxious here to insist upon this fundamental point: whatever takes the form of a plan aiming at definite practical ends—it may be a measure for the diminution of pauperism, for the reform of land-tenure, for the extension of co-operative industry, for the improvement of the coinage; or it may assume a more ambitious shape, and aim at reorganising society under spiritual and temporal powers, represented by a high priest of humanity and three bankers—it matters not what the proposal be, whether wide or narrow in its scope, severely judicious or wildly imprudent—if its object be to accomplish definite practical ends, then I say it has none of the characteristics of a science, and has no just claim to the name. Consider the case of any recognized physical science—Astronomy, Dynamics, Chemistry, Physiology—does any of these aim at definite practical ends? at modifying in a definite manner, it matters not how, the arrangement of things in the physical universe? Clearly not. In each case the object is, not to attain tangible results, not to prove any definite thesis, not to advocate any practical plan, but simply to give light, to reveal laws of nature, to tell us what phenomena are found together, what effects follow from what causes. Does it result from this that the physical sciences are without bearing on the practical concerns of mankind? I think I need not trouble myself to answer that question. Well, then, Political Economy is a science in the same sense in which Astronomy, Dynamics, Chemistry, Physiology, are sciences. Its subject-matter is different; it deals with the phenomena of wealth, while they deal with the phenomena of the physical universe; but its methods, its aims, the character of its conclusions, are the same as theirs. What Astronomy does for the phenomena of the heavenly bodies; what Dynamics does for the phenomena of motion; what Chemistry does for the phenomena of chemical combination; what Physiology does for the phenomena of the functions of organic life; that Political Economy does for the phenomena of wealth: it expounds the laws according to which those phenomena co-exist with or succeed each other; that is to say, it expounds the laws of the phenomena of wealth.

Let me here briefly explain what I mean by this expression. It is one in very frequent use; but, like many other expressions in frequent use, it does not always perhaps carry to the mind of the hearer a very definite idea. Of course I do not mean by the laws of the phenomena of wealth, Acts of Parliament. I mean the *natural* laws of those phenomena. Now what are the phenomena of wealth? Simply the facts of wealth; such facts as production, exchange, price; or again, the various forms which wealth assumes in the process of distribution, such as wages, profits, rent, interest, and so forth. These are the phenomena of wealth; and the natural laws of these phenomena are certain constant relations in which they stand towards each other and towards their causes. For example, capital grows from year to year in this country at a certain rate of progress; in the United States the rate is considerably more rapid; in China considerably slower. Now these facts are not fortuitous, but the natural result of causes; of such causes as the external physical circumstances of the countries in question, the intelligence and moral character of the people inhabiting them, and their political and social institutions; and so long as the causes remain the same, the results will remain the same. Similarly, the prices of commodities, the rent of land, the rates of wages, profits, and interest, differ in different countries; but here again, not at random. The particular forms which these phenomena assume are no more matters of chance than the temperature or the mineral productions of the countries in which they occur are matters of chance; or than the fauna and flora which flourish on the surface of those countries are matters of chance. Alike in the case of the physical and of the economic world, the facts we find existing are the results of causes, between which and them the connection is constant and invariable. It is, then, the constant relations exhibited in economic phenomena that we have in view, when we speak of the laws of the phenomena of wealth; and in the exposition of these laws consists the science of Political Economy. If you ask me wherein lies the utility of such an exposition of economic laws, I answer, in precisely the same circumstance which constitutes the utility of all scientific knowledge. It teaches us the conditions of our power in relation to the facts of economic existence, the means by which, in the domain of material well-being, to attain our ends. It is by such knowledge that man becomes the minister and interpreter of Nature, and learns to control Nature by obeying her.

And now I beg you to observe what follows from this mode of conceiving our study. In the first place, then, you will remark that, as thus conceived, Political Economy stands apart from all particular systems of social or industrial existence. It has nothing to do with *laissez-faire* any more than with communism; with freedom of contract any more than with paternal government, or with systems of *status*. It stands apart from all particular systems, and is moreover absolutely neutral as between all. Not, of course, that the knowledge which it gives may not be employed to recommend some and to discredit others. This is inevitable, and is only the proper and legitimate use of economic knowledge. But this notwithstanding, the science is neutral, as between social schemes, in this important sense. It pronounces no judgment on the worthiness or desirableness of the ends aimed at in such systems. It tells us what their effects will be as regards a specific class of facts, thus contributing data towards the formation of a sound opinion respecting them. But here its function ends. The data thus furnished may indeed go far to determine our judgment, but they do not necessarily, and should not in practice always, do so. For there are few practical problems which do not present other aspects than the purely economical—political, moral, educational, artistic aspects—and these may involve consequences so weighty as to turn the scale against purely economic solutions. On the relative importance of such conflicting considerations Political Economy offers no opinion, pronounces no judgment, thus, as I said, standing neutral between competing social schemes; neutral, as the science of Mechanics stands neutral between competing plans of railway construction, in which expense, for instance, as well as mechanical efficiency, is to be considered; neutral, as Chemistry stands neutral between competing plans of sanitary improvement; as Physiology stands neutral between opposing systems of medicine. It supplies the means, or, more correctly, a portion of the means, for estimating all; it refuses to identify itself with any.

Now I desire to call particular attention to this characteristic of economic science, because I do not think it is at all generally appreciated, and because some serious and indeed lamentable consequences have arisen from overlooking it. For example, it is sometimes supposed that, because Political Economy comprises in its expositions theories of wages, profits, and rent, the science is *therefore* committed to the approval of our present mode of industrial life, under which three distinct classes, labourers, capitalists, and landlords, receive remuneration in those forms. Under this impression, some social reformers, whose ideal of industrial life involves a modification of our existing system, have thought themselves called upon to denounce and deride economic science, as forsooth seeking to stereotype the existing forms of industrial life, and of course therefore opposed to their views. But this is a complete mistake. Economic science has no more connection with our present industrial system than the science of mechanics has with our present system of railways. Our existing railway lines have been laid down according to the best extant mechanical knowledge; but we do not think it necessary on this account, as a preliminary to improving our railways, to denounce mechanical science. If wages, profits, and rent find a place in economic theories, this is simply because these *are* the forms which the distribution of wealth assumes as society is now constituted. But it comes equally within the province of the economist to exhibit the working of any proposed modification of this system, and to set forth the operation of the laws of production and distribution under such new conditions. And, in connection with this point, I may make this remark, that, so far from its being true that economic science has done its work, and thus become obsolete for practical purposes, an object of mere historical curiosity, it belongs, on the contrary, to a class of sciences whose work can never be completed, never at least so long as human beings continue to progress; for the most important portion of the data from which it reasons is human character and human institutions, and everything consequently which affects that character or those institutions must create new problems for economic science. Unlike the physicist, who deals with phenomena incapable of development, always essentially the same, the main facts of the economist's study—man as an industrial being, man as organized in society—are ever undergoing change. The economic conditions of patriarchal life, of Greek or Roman life, of feudal life, are not the economic conditions of modern commercial life; and had Political Economy been cultivated in those primitive, ancient, or mediæval times, while it would doubtless have contained some expositions which we do not now find in it, it must also have wanted many which it now contains. One has only to turn to the discussions on currency and credit which have accompanied the great development of our commerce during the last half-century, to see how the changing needs of an advancing society evolve new problems for the economist, and call forth new growths of economic doctrine. At this moment one may see that such an occasion is imminent. Since the economic doctrines now holding their place in our text-books were thought out, a new mode of industrial organization has established itself in this and other countries. Co-operation is now a reality, and, if the signs are not all deceptive, bids fair to transform much of our industry. Now the characteristic feature of co-operation, looked at from the economic point of view, is, that it combines in the same person the two capacities of labourer and capitalist; whereas our present theories of industrial remuneration presuppose a division of those capacities between distinct persons. Obviously, our existing theories must fail to elucidate a state of things different from that contemplated in their elaboration. We have thus need of a new exposition of the law of industrial remuneration —an exposition suited to a state of things in which the gains of producers, instead of taking the form of wages, profits, and rent, are realized in a single composite sum. I give this as an example of the new developments of economic theory which the progress of society will constantly call for. Of course it is an open question whether this *is* the direction in which industrial society is moving; and there are those, I know, who hold that it is not towards co-operation, but rather towards "captains of industry" and organization of workmen on the military plan, that the current is setting. It may be so; and in this case the economic problem of the future will not be that which I have suggested above; nevertheless, *an* economic problem there still will be. If society were organized to-morrow on the principles of M. Comte, so long as physical and human nature remain what they are, the phenomena of wealth would exhibit constant relations, would still be governed by natural laws; and those relations, those laws, it would still be important to know. The function of the economist would be as needful as ever.

A far more serious consequence, however, of ignoring the neutral attitude of this study in relation to questions of practical reform is the effect it has had in alienating from it the minds of the working classes. Instead of appearing in the simple guise of an expositor of truths, the contributor of certain data towards the solution of social problems—data which of themselves commit no man to any course, and of which the practical cogency can only be determined after all the other data implicated in the problem are known—instead of presenting itself as Chemistry, Physiology, mechanical science present themselves, Political Economy too often makes its appearance, especially in its approaches to the working classes, in the guise of a dogmatic code of cut-and-dried rules, a system promulgating decrees, "sanctioning" one social arrangement, "condemning" another, requiring from men, not consideration, but obedience. Now when we take into account the sort of decrees which are ordinarily given to the world in the name of Political Economy—decrees which I think I may say in the main amount to a handsome ratification of the existing form of society as approximately perfect—I think we shall be able to understand the repugnance, and even violent opposition, manifested towards it by people who have their own reasons for not cherishing that unbounded admiration for our present industrial arrangements which is felt by some popular expounders of so-called economic laws. When a working man is told that Political Economy "condemns" strikes, hesitates about co-operation, looks askance at proposals for limiting the hours of labour, but "approves" the accumulation of capital, and "sanctions" the market rate of wages, it seems not an unnatural response that "since Political Economy is against the working man, it behoves the working man to be against Political Economy." It seems not unnatural that this new code should come to be regarded with suspicion, as a system possibly contrived in the interest of employers, which it is the workmen's wisdom simply to repudiate and disown. Economic science is thus placed in an essentially false position, and the section of the community, which is most vitally interested in taking to heart its truths, is effectually prevented from even giving them a hearing. I think it, therefore, a matter not merely of theoretic, but of the utmost practical importance, that the strictly scientific character of this study should be insisted on. It is only when so presented that its true position in relation to practical reforms, and its really benevolent bearing towards all sorts and conditions of men, will be understood, and that we can hope to overcome those deep-seated but perfectly natural prejudices with which the most numerous class in the community unfortunately regard it.

And now I trust I have made it clear that the branch of knowledge, with whose interests I am charged in this college, possesses other claims upon our attention than those which rest upon its past services; that it has a real and vital connection with all existing problems which involve the material interests of human beings, as well as a field for development in new directions, which can never fail so long as society continues to progress. Above all, I trust I have placed it beyond doubt that, rightly conceived, economic science can never be an obstacle to the fair consideration and discussion of any plan of human improvement. Those schemes only need fear Political Economy which are conceived in ignorance of human nature, or of the laws of the physical universe. And surely it is a singular position which those social reformers take up who deliberately slight or neglect this study. They desire, they tell us, to improve the condition of their fellow-creatures. They have perhaps drawn up elaborate and highly complex plans for achieving this end; but they object to have their proposals tested by scientific methods. Better they think to take a leap in the dark, than to examine beforehand by the lamp of science the ground to which they invite us to commit ourselves. In a striking passage of an admirable address, Professor Huxley has pointed out how all true education, so far as education is an art, is but a mode of acquiring knowledge which Nature herself, where we omit this means of acquiring it, is pretty sure to bring home to us after her own rude fashion. The teaching of Nature, says Professor Huxley—

"Is harsh and wasteful in its operation. Ignorance is visited as sharply as wilful disobedience—incapacity meets with the same punishment as crime. Nature's discipline is not even a word and a blow, and the blow first; but the blow without the word. It is left to you to find out why your ears are boxed.

"The object of what we commonly call education—that education in which man intervenes, and which I shall distinguish as artificial education—is to make good these defects in Nature's methods; to prepare the child to receive Nature's education, neither incapably, nor ignorantly, nor with wilful disobedience; and to understand the preliminary symptoms of her displeasure without waiting for the box on the ear. In short, all artificial education ought to be an anticipation of natural education. And a liberal education is an artificial education which has not only prepared a man to escape the great evils of disobedience to natural laws, but has trained him to appreciate and to seize upon the rewards, which Nature scatters with as free a hand as her penalties."

What is it then that those persons ask us to do who would dispense with the study of Political Economy? Simply to deprive ourselves of the aids of artificial education in the most complicated, most difficult, and most momentous concerns of life. Rather than take the trouble to understand "the preliminary symptoms of Nature's displeasure" in the government of her economic kingdom, they think it better we should rush into action and learn—by having our ears boxed. I do not know whether you will feel inclined to hearken to their advice. But I pray you to understand that the *soufflets* administered by Nature in punishment of economic ignorance are by no means trifling penalties. They are known by the names of bankruptcies, commercial crises, conflicts of capital and labour, Sheffield outrages, excess of population, pauperism, internal insurrections, international jealousies often issuing in foreign wars. This metropolis in its eastern quarter could just now supply some striking illustrations. Ireland, with its wretched peasantry, demoralized by centuries of industrial insecurity, could furnish a few more. What is it that led France to surrender her liberties into the hands of a saviour of society? What but the spectre of socialism—that rank growth of economic ignorance? Thus economic ignorance, when it has conceived, brings forth socialism, and socialism breeds despotism, and despotism, when it is finished, issues in war, misery, and ruin. Other causes, no doubt, have contributed to the terrible catastrophe which we now witness and deplore; but most assuredly economic ignorance is deeply responsible in the matter. These horrors, then, are some of the chastisements which Nature administers to those who choose to remain in ignorance of the signs of her displeasure in economic affairs. Would it not be as well to avoid them? Nay, would it not be even worth while to seize on some of the rewards which here, no less than in her physical realm, Nature scatters with as free a hand as her penalties?

VIII.*

M. COMTE AND POLITICAL ECONOMY.

Of the writers who during the last half century have contributed to place Social Philosophy on the footing which it now holds, none deserve more deference on questions of classification and method than Auguste Comte. Opinions will differ as to the value of his views on the regeneration and reorganization of society, but M. Comte has rendered services to the cause of social and historical speculation which are quite independent of the system of doctrines distinctively connected with his name. Even those who reject what are known as Positivist doctrines, and who feel themselves in imperfect sympathy with the spirit of Positivism, may gratefully acknowledge that social studies have taken a new place in the domain of speculative thought since M. Comte devoted to them his mind and life, and may recognize in his work an achievement not without analogy to that accomplished by Bacon in a different though neighbouring field. In neither case, they will probably

* *Fortnightly Review*, May 1870.

think, did the value of the performance consist in the positive contributions made to our knowledge, whether of physical nature by Bacon, or of the principles of social union by M. Comte,—though it will be allowed that our obligations to M. Comte on this score are vastly greater than any which can be credited to the author of the "Novum Organum,"—but in the distinctness and vividness of the conception which each alike had formed of the path of investigation to be followed in the pursuit of that knowledge which each had taken for his special goal, and in what was the consequence of this: the strength of conviction and the unfaltering faith with which each delivered his message. Bacon's dreams of a New Atlantis to be reached by experiment and induction were not more in advance of the current speculation of his time than were the analogous dreams of M. Comte of a society regenerated by Positive Philosophy. While the poet was singing that—

"Through the ages one increasing purpose runs,"

the French philosopher believed that he had divined that purpose, and could lay bare its scope. And he not only conceived the design, but, in the opinion of eminent judges, took important steps towards its realization.

The high authority, then, of M. Comte in the domain of Social Philosophy will scarcely be disputed—certainly will not be disputed by the present writer; and it must therefore be allowed that the absolute proscription by him of a branch of social inquiry carries with it a certain presumption—some will think a weighty presumption—against the legitimacy of the speculation falling under this bar. Now this presumption, whatever may be its weight, lies, it must be frankly admitted, against the branch of study which it is the purpose of the following pages to promote.* It was M. Comte's opinion that Political Economy, as cultivated by the school of Adam Smith's successors in this country and in France, failed to fulfil the conditions required of a sound theory by Positive Philosophy, and was not properly a science. He pronounces it to be defective in its conception, "profoundly irrational" in its method, and "radically sterile" as regards results. Such an opinion, proceeding from a philosopher of M. Comte's eminence, is a fact which ought not to be lightly passed by. M. Comte, moreover, has supported this unfavourable judgment by a train of elaborate argumentation; but, so far as I know, his arguments have not yet been seriously grappled with. I am very sensible to what an extent I shall leave myself open to the imputation of presumption in venturing on a task which has been avoided by so many incomparably better fitted than I am for its effective discharge. Nevertheless, the task is one which I feel bound to undertake; for it seems to me that I should be guilty of even greater presumption were I to enter upon an investigation such as I propose to make the subject of the present volume, without, at all events, attempting to do justice, so far as my abilities permit, to M. Comte's views. As a preliminary step, therefore, to an examination of the

* [It should be stated that the present Essay was intended as the preliminary chapter of a work on "The Logical Method of Political Economy."]

character and method of Political Economy, I have to ask the reader to follow me in an examination of the grounds of M. Comte's judgment against the scientific pretensions of this study.

And, in the first place, let me endeavour to state the precise question on which M. Comte is at issue with the student of economic science. M. Comte does not deny that the phenomena of wealth are important elements in determining the condition and progress of society; still less does he deny—on the contrary, it is his emphatic assertion—that these phenomena, like all others which in the aggregate constitute the social state, are subject to invariable law. On the other hand, political economists—those political economists, at least, whose views the present writer shares—make no pretension to constitute Political Economy as the science of society. It is fully admitted that the subject-matter of their science is but one among many elements which go to form the aggregate social condition; and they are consequently bound to acknowledge, as they do acknowledge, that the most complete acquaintance with economic facts and laws furnishes of itself no adequate basis for general social speculation. But agreeing thus far, M. Comte and the political economists differ here:—while admitting that economic phenomena are subject to law, M. Comte denies that the law can be ascertained by study of the phenomena. His position is, that the facts of wealth are, in the form in which they actually present themselves to our observation, so inextricably interwoven with facts of a different order—with facts, for example, of the intellectual, moral, and political order—that the determination of the laws which govern them is only possible when they are considered in connection with such associated facts; that consequently a science of Political Economy is impossible; just as for the same reason a science of Psychology, or of Jurisprudence, or of any distinct and separate order of social relations is impossible. It was accordingly with him a fundamental canon of philosophical method, that all investigations into the structure and laws of society should proceed on the principle of dealing with social facts, to use M. Comte's language, in the *ensemble*. Society, he said, should be contemplated in the totality of its elements; and no investigation should be undertaken into any portion of those elements except in constant connection with parallel investigations carried on contemporaneously into all co-existing portions of the complex whole. All isolated study of a single aspect of social life, of a particular order of its relations apart from the rest, he regarded as essentially vicious and doomed to failure in advance.* Such a view is, of course, altogether inconsistent with the existence of a science of wealth; and here, accordingly, the student of Political Economy comes into collision with the teaching of M. Comte. Instead of proceeding by the method of the *ensemble*, and studying society in all its elements at once, the political economist proceeds by an opposite rule: he breaks up the aggregate social phenomenon into the elementary groups of which it is composed, and, select-

* "Philosophie Positive," Leçons 47 and 48. See also the "Politique," vol. iii. p. 585 (1853), from which it will be seen that M. Comte's views on this point underwent no change in his later years.

ing one of these, studies it apart from all the others. He does not indeed, as has been already intimated, confound the laws at which he thus arrives, the laws of this detached group, with the laws of society; but the laws of society itself, he holds, are only to be ascertained by working on the plan which he has adopted,—by making, that is to say, each distinct order of relations involved in the composite phenomenon of society the subject of a distinct and separate investigation, leaving it to the social philosopher properly so called—the speculator on society as a whole,—to combine the results of the labours of students of special branches in elucidation of the general problem.*

Such is the question at issue between the student of Political Economy and M. Comte. Now, adverting to the history of inductive research, it will at once be seen that the view taken by the political economist has this weighty presumption in its favour: it is in strict analogy with the course followed by all fruitful investigation from the dawn of scientific discovery to the present time.

* "Notwithstanding the universal *consensus* of the social phenomena, whereby nothing which takes place in any part of the operations of society is without its share of influence on every other part; and notwithstanding the paramount ascendancy which the general state of civilization and social progress in any given society must hence exercise over all the partial and subordinate phenomena; it is not the less true that different species of social facts are in the main dependent, immediately and in the first resort, on different kinds of causes; and therefore not only may with advantage, but must, be studied apart: just as in the natural body we study separately the physiology and pathology of each of the principal organs and tissues, though every one is acted upon by the state of all the others; and though the peculiar constitution and general state of health of the organism co-operates with, and often preponderates over, the local causes, in determining the state of any particular organ."—MILL'S *System of Logic*, vol. ii. p. 480. 3rd Ed.

When men first began to speculate on the facts of the universe, the line of investigation they fell into was precisely that which M. Comte holds to be the proper one in sociological inquiry. They contemplated nature in the *ensemble*, and propounded the question, What is the origin of all things? But so long as the problem remained in this form, nothing valuable issued from the efforts to solve it beyond the discipline afforded to the minds thus employed—nothing but a series of vague guesses more or less ingenious, yielding, it may be, some satisfaction to the speculative intellect, but incapable of throwing any light on the real relations of objective existence. In time, however, and by slow degrees, the spirit of the *ensemble* gave way to another spirit—that of specialization and detail. Influenced mainly by the practical necessities of life, in some degree also by the exceptional conspicuousness of certain phenomena, people turned from speculation on the universe as a whole to observation and reasoning upon certain limited orders of facts. Thus geometry arose out of the practical requirement of measuring the earth; and, beginning as an art, grew into a science, taking as its subject-matter the particular class of relations brought into view in that practical operation. The order followed in the genesis of the science of geometry is typical of the whole course of scientific development. In each case practical exigencies, or exceptional conspicuousness, have called attention to phenomena of a special kind—to the movements of the heavenly bodies, to the play of mechanical forces, to the composition of material substances, to the structure or functions of the human body—from the investigation of which have arisen the sciences of Astronomy, of Mechanics, of Chemistry, of Anatomy, of Physiology. Each science, called into existence by the anxiety to explain striking experiences, or to provide and justify practical expedients, has taken in charge some special and limited order of relations, has detached these from the mixed and heterogeneous body of physical phenomena, and has made them the subject of isolated and special study. The laws of the various orders of physical relations have thus been determined; and the rays of scientific light emanating from the separate investigations of perfectly independent workers have been made to converge in elucidation of the actual composite facts of the outer world.

This has been the course of development in physical science, the method by which the secrets of external nature have been unlocked. It has been a method, not of study in the *ensemble*, but of study through the elements—of analysis followed by synthesis. In perfect analogy with this mode of proceeding is the political economist's conception of the path of inquiry to be followed in dealing with the facts of social life. He proposes to break them up into their elementary groups, and he takes one of these groups—the phenomena of wealth—as the subject of his special investigation. It may be remarked, moreover, that, in selecting this particular group of phenomena, he has been influenced by considerations in all respects analogous to those which have determined the separate treatment of the various classes of physical phenomena. Political Economy, like Geometry, Astronomy, Mechanics, Chemistry, had its origin in practical exigencies, and made its *début* as an art. It aimed at the practical object of enriching particular nations by means of trade. For this purpose highly complicated machinery—encouragements for particular industries, prohibitions of others, bounties, drawbacks, in a word the whole body of commercial regulations known as the Colonial and Mercantile systems—was brought into play. These expedients, if they favoured some interests, damaged others: the conflict of interests brought on discussion; and the argument rapidly passed from attack and defence of practical plans to examination of the natural laws governing the order of relations which it was the purpose of these plans to control. The limits of the debate were not at first, perhaps, very distinctly defined, but by degrees they grew clear. The facts of wealth became detached for the purposes of discussion from the other classes of facts with which in actual existence they were blended; and Political Economy, as the science of those facts, emerged. As regards origin and mode of development, therefore, the parallel between Political Economy and the physical sciences is complete; nor have I any reason to suppose that M. Comte would dispute the general correctness of the description I have given: indeed, he frankly admits that the precedents of physical science are against him.* What, then, is his line of argument? It is this: he contends that the cases are not similar; that the problems presented, on the one hand by physical nature, on the

* "Philosophie Positive," vol. iv. pp. 353-54. Edit. 1839.

other by social life, are so radically discrepant that the method applicable to the one must be, not only modified, but reversed, in dealing with the other. To follow in social inquiry the precedents of physical research is, according to M. Comte, in oblivion of essential distinctions, to practise a "blind imitation." This is the position which we are now called upon to consider.

Most people who take an interest in questions of the kind we are now discussing are familiar with M. Comte's classification of the sciences. As is known, it proceeds upon the plan of arranging the various branches of scientific knowledge in the order indicated by the relative complexity of their subject-matter. Thus it places first in the scale the sciences which deal with the most simple order of relations—number and extension. After these comes Mechanics, as involving relations one degree more complex; next to Mechanics, Astronomy, which is followed by Physics, and so on through the whole circle of scientific knowledge; each science, according to its place in the scale, representing a degree of complexity greater than those preceding and less than those following it. It results from the principle of the arrangement that the organic sciences, having for their subject matter the complex phenomena of the vegetable and animal world, should occupy the later portion of the scale, and that Sociology, or the science of human society, as concerned with the most complex of all phenomena, should conclude and crown the whole. As regards the merits or demerits of this classification—a question on which the highest authorities are not agreed—it would be unbecoming in me to pretend to express an opinion. I only refer to it in order to render M. Comte's argument against Political Economy intelligible. As has been said, then, the sciences are arranged in the order indicated by the degree of complexity in their subject-matter; those occupying the first or lower portion of the scale embracing phenomena but little complex, while the phenomena embraced by the sciences in the later portion are complex in a high degree. It is on this distinction that M. Comte grounds his argument for disregarding in sociological speculation the precedents furnished by physical research. According to him, the method of investigation that has been followed in the study of physical nature—the method, that is to say, which proceeds by breaking up composite phenomena into the elementary groups composing them, studying apart the elementary groups, determining their laws, and afterwards combining these laws in explanation of the original aggregates,—this method, according to M. Comte, owes its efficacy to the uncomplex character of the phenomena submitted to the process. As phenomena become more complex, the method, he contends, becomes less suitable, less efficacious, till at length a point is reached at which it fails altogether, and it becomes necessary to adopt a contrary mode of procedure, the mode of procedure, namely, which he describes as investigation through the *ensemble*. This point in the scale of the sciences coincides, he tells us, with that at which the transition is made from inorganic to organic nature. The method of investigation by disintegration and separate study should thenceforth give way to that which proceeds by treatment in the *ensemble*. Accordingly, he holds that the organic sciences generally should be cultivated in conformity with this principle; but in the study of social phenomena, the most complex and intricate of all, the rule becomes absolute and imperative.*

And here one is led to ask why the method of specialization should lose its efficacy as problems become more complex? The very opposite is what one would naturally expect. If a problem involving no more than two or three distinct elements can only be resolved by the process of analysis and separate consideration of the parts, the necessity for this would seem to be still more urgent as the elements engaged became more numerous. M. Comte's reason for reversing this inference is very peculiar.† He says that as phenomena become more complex, the elements composing them become more *solidaires*. In the physical universe, the complexity of the phenomena is not great, and consequently their "solidarity" is but "slightly pronounced:" "the elements are here better known to us than the *ensemble*." But the reverse is the case with the organic world, and more especially

* As to the nature of the complexity of social phenomena see Mill's "Logic," vol. ii. p. 475 *et seq.* 3rd Edit.

† This argument has appeared to me so weak—indeed, M. Comte's whole case against Political Economy is, as it seems to me, so weak—that I have felt it difficult at times to repress the suspicion that his reasons for rejecting it were not purely and simply of a philosophical kind. "Il s'agit malheureusement," he says in one passage, "et sans que rien puisse m'en dispenser, de tenter une création philosophique qui n'a jamais été jusqu'ici ébauchée ni convenablement conçue par aucun de mes prédécesseurs." "Sociology" could not be constructed in its entirety by M. Comte if Political Economy were a legitimate speculation. But M. Comte felt it to be his mission to construct Sociology in its entirety. The conclusion seems evident.

with that portion of the organic world which constitutes the social organism. The phenomena are here characterized by a very high degree of complexity, and therefore, says M. Comte, by a very high degree of solidarity: "the *ensemble* of the subject is better known to us and more accessible than the parts." On the fundamental principle, then, of inductive logic, which requires us to proceed from the known to the unknown, from the better to the less known, we are bound, in dealing with the phenomena of organic nature, but more especially with the phenomena of society, to begin our investigations with the study of aggregates, and only after we have determined *their* laws to address ourselves to those of the less known elements. M. Comte admits that this mode of proceeding must "gravely augment" the fundamental difficulties already incident to the extreme complication of the subject-matter; but this, he conceives, is only a reason for reserving the study of society for "the highest scientific intelligences."

In attempting to criticise this argument, it becomes necessary to assign a distinct meaning to its several propositions. We encounter, in the first place, the expression, "the *ensemble* of society," and the statement that this is better known to us than the "elements." In the most obvious meaning of the word the statement is manifestly not true. By the *ensemble* of society most people would, I think, understand the aggregate of the human beings composing society—of those human beings considered in their social relations; and by the "elements," the individual social men and women. In this sense I say it is manifestly untrue that we know society better in its *ensemble* than in its "elements,"—so manifestly so, that it cannot for a moment be supposed that this was M. Comte's meaning. When, for example, an Englishman travels in France, it is not with the *ensemble* of French society that he comes into contact, but with certain railway officials and hotel proprietors, exemplifying a very limited range of French social existence. As he prolongs his residence he may extend his knowledge; but the course which his acquisitions take will, I need scarcely say, be in the opposite direction to that which M. Comte's maxim affirms. Nor can a French philosopher attain a knowledge of French social existence by any different path; he, too, must proceed from individuals to classes, and from classes to the social whole. But there is another sense in which M. Comte's language may be understood. Social phenomena, like all other phenomena, meet us not simple, but composite. We do not encounter purely religious, or purely industrial, or purely political men and women. Social acts, social situations, can rarely be referred to any single influence. Human beings, as they exist, are not abstract, but historical, human beings, in a greater or less degree under the influence of all the causes that have been affecting the race from its origin down to the present time. Thus regarded, society, or more properly social phenomena, may be said to present themselves to us in the *ensemble;* and thus understood, the statement that we know society through its *ensemble*, not through its elements, is undoubtedly true. If this be M. Comte's meaning, the proposition cannot be disputed; but then it must be remarked that the assertion is equally true as applied to the phenomena of the physical universe. Physical forces also act in constant conjunction. Unless we effect the separation by artificial means we encounter no purely chemical, or purely optical, or purely mechanical phenomena, but phenomena in the production of which a variety, greater or less, of physical forces concur—that is to say, we know physical nature also through its *ensemble*. We are thus brought back to the point from which we started: why are we—the phenomena of social life and those of physical nature being made known to us under similar conditions—to reverse in our study of society the method of investigation which has been found efficacious in dealing with the physical world?

M. Comte's reply at this stage of the argument resolves itself into the doctrine I have already stated, that the solidarity of phenomena varies directly with their complexity. It is true, he seems to admit, that we know physical nature equally with social through its *ensemble*; but the *ensemble*, in the former case, is composed of fewer elements, and these, in proportion as they are fewer, are less *solidaires*—are therefore more easily broken up and submitted to separate examination. Hence arises an increased facility of applying the method of disintegration and separate study in their case. But, in the first place, this does not meet the difficulty, since the answer admits that physical nature *is* known to us through its *ensemble*—an admission which, on M. Comte's principles, seems to draw with it the obligation of studying physical nature through this, its most familiar manifestation. Waiving, however, this point, I wish to examine M. Comte's position, which is really the root of his whole argument against Political Economy, that phenomena in proportion as they are more complex are more *solidaires*. If this assumption be not well founded, there is absolutely nothing for his reasoning to rest upon.

To test the doctrine, let us consider it in a concrete case. I take the instance of water, a composite physical phenomenon exemplifying a variety of physical laws. Considered chemically, its complexity is of the lowest degree, containing as it does but two elements, oxygen and hydrogen. According to M. Comte's doctrine, water, being chemically of the lowest degree of complexity, ought to exhibit, in the relation of its chemical elements, the lowest degree also of solidarity. The fact, I need scarcely say, is exactly the reverse. As everyone knows, the solidarity—by which I understand intimacy of relationship, closeness of interdependence—existing between the elements composing water is of an extremely intense kind, so much so that the analysis of water constituted an epoch in chemical history. On the other hand, if we take a phenomenon of greater complexity, say water in combination with lime, we find the solidarity diminish as the number of the elements is increased; the water or the lime being much more easily detached from the hydrate of lime than the elements composing the water, or than those composing the lime, are from each other. Nor is this a solitary example: rather it represents a rule holding extensively throughout chemical combination. In inorganic chemistry the salts are in general easily decomposed, while the less complex elements composing them—the oxides of the metals and the acids—are mostly of very difficult analysis. And in organic compounds a similar rule prevails. So far, therefore, the relation between complexity and solidarity appears to be the reverse of that for which M. Comte contends. The case just considered illustrates the incidents of complexity within the range of a single order of relations. How stands the fact when the orders of relation exemplified in the phenomena are different? For example, water possesses—besides chemical—mechanical, optical, electrical, and other physical properties. Is it true that, as between these several orders of physical phenomena, the solidarity is, as M. Comte asserts, "little pronounced"—that the chemical, mechanical, optical, and electrical attributes of water are but slightly interdependent—less interdependent than, for example, physiological and moral qualities in a human being, or political and industrial conditions in a body politic? No one denies that here also there is solidarity; but the question is, not as to the existence of solidarity, but as to the degree. What M. Comte had to show was that the solidarity of co-operating agencies was greater in the case of the phenomena of society than in that of the phenomena of the physical world—so much greater as to necessitate in their case an inversion of the method of investigation practised in the study of physical nature; but to establish this he has not advanced a particle of proof. For my part, I can imagine no more eminent example of the solidarity of forces than that presented by the most ordinary phenomena of the physical world—the ebb and flow of the tides, the succession of the seasons, the freezing and thawing of water, a shower of rain, a drop of dew. Yet this has been no bar in the study of these phenomena to the employment of methods which M. Comte would nevertheless exclude from the domain of social science on the ground that its phenomena are *solidaires*.

So much for the grounds of general philosophy on which M. Comte relies in refusing to recognize Political Economy as a science; and he finds, as he conceives, corroboration of the soundness of the view he has taken in the history and actual condition of economic speculation. M. Comte opens his criticisms on the history and existing state of Political Economy with the remark, that its scientific pretensions could not well have been otherwise than inane, considering the sort of persons by whom it has been cultivated. These have, he tells us, nearly all proceeded "from the ranks of advocates and *littérateurs*:"*—"Strangers by their education, even with regard to the least important phenomena, to every idea of scientific observation, to every notion of natural law, to every sentiment of true demonstration, it was impossible for them, whatever might have been the intrinsic force of their intelligence, to apply duly to the complicated problems of society a method of reasoning the simplest applications of which they were wholly ignorant of,—destitute, as they were, of any other philosophical preparation than certain vague and inadequate precepts of general logic." From this sweeping characterization he excepts Adam Smith, and Adam Smith alone,

* "Philosophie Positive," vol. iv. p. 266.

whose judgment is commended in having avoided the "vain pretension" of founding a special science, and in confining the aim of his work to the elucidation of some detached points of social philosophy. But with the single exception of the "Wealth of Nations," the whole dogmatic portion of the pretended science presents, according to M. Comte, the simple metaphysical character—a phrase which, as M. Comte's readers are aware, supplies the strongest form of reprobation known to the Comtian vocabulary. Of the truth of this conclusion, if further evidence were needed, ample is found in "the avowal, spontaneous and decisive, of the respectable Tracy," implied "in the insertion of his treatise on Political Economy between Logics and Ethics, as a fourth part of his general treatise on Ideology."

The impression which these comments will leave on readers acquainted with the leading economical writers of France and England, will scarcely, I should think, be favourable to M. Comte's candour and sagacity. It is, in fact, quite evident that M. Comte had no effective knowledge of the branch of science which he denounced; and it is scarcely credible that he could even have remembered, as he wrote the passage from which I have made the above extracts, who its cultivators had been; for the list includes, to mention no others, the names of Turgot, Hume, Bentham, Ricardo, and the two Mills. There need be no hesitation in saying—and the remark implies no disrespect to M. Comte—that any one of these writers had quite as accurate a conception of what constitutes a law of nature, and of the sort of proof by which a law of nature is established, as M. Comte himself. It would seem, indeed, as if M. Comte's mind lost its proper balance and edge on coming into contact with Political Economy. Not only does he forget what is due to the able thinkers who preceded him, and who—could he have believed it—were his fellow-labourers in building up that science of society of which he wished to constitute himself the sole and exclusive founder, but his sense of logical cogency seems to fail him: I know not how else to account for his reference to the collocation of topics adopted by M. Destutt de Tracy in his treatise on Ideology, as "decisive" evidence of the unpositive character of Political Economy. What M. Comte's reasons were for excepting Adam Smith from the general condemnation passed upon the cultivators of economic science, it is not easy to surmise. One is almost tempted to believe that his acquaintance with the eminent masters in the science was confined to the author of the "Wealth of Nations." Had he known, for example, and to mention no other instances, Turgot's brief but pregnant "Essai sur la Formation et la Distribution des Richesses"—a work for which his biographer Condorcet, not unreasonably, prefers the claim of being "the germ of the 'Wealth of Nations'"—or Ricardo's "Principles of Political Economy and Taxation," it is not easy to believe that he could have committed himself to a distinction not less unjust than invidious. Two works more thoroughly saturated with the severest spirit of the Positive Philosophy would not easily be found in the literature of scientific speculation.

But, passing from the personal question, M. Comte

proposes to try the Positive character of economical speculation by two tests, "continuity" and "fecundity." These qualities, he remarks, are the least equivocal symptoms of really scientific conceptions. "When the work of the present time, instead of presenting itself as the spontaneous sequel and gradual consummation of former work, takes, in the case of each new author, a character essentially personal, and the most fundamental notions are incessantly brought into question; when the dogmatic constitution of a science, far from engendering any sustained progress, results habitually in the sterile reproduction of illusory controversies, ever renewed, never advancing; when these indications are found, there we may be certain we have to do, not with positive science, but with theological or metaphysical dissertation. Now is not this the spectacle which Political Economy has presented for half a century? If our economists are in reality the scientific successors of Adam Smith, let them show us in what particulars they have effectively improved and completed the doctrine of that immortal master, what discoveries really new they have added to his original felicitous *aperçus*?"

The tests proposed are indubitably sound. The challenge is a fair one. If Political Economy cannot make good its pretensions by the criteria of continuity and fecundity, it deserves to be relegated to the limbo to which M. Comte consigns it.

But in proceeding to the ordeal it is necessary to distinguish. There would, it must at once be admitted, be no difficulty in showing that a great deal of writing on economical subjects, now no less than when M. Comte published his criticisms, is of the sort which he describes as "metaphysical,"—that is to say, vague, "personal," full of "sterile and illusory controversies;" it must further be acknowledged that this style of writing prevails to a far larger extent in the discussions of Political Economy than in those of any physical science. The least reflection, however, will show, what has often been pointed out, that this incident of economic speculation is quite inevitable. It results from two circumstances: first, the intimate relation in which social questions, economic included, stand to personal and class concerns, and through them to general politics, and the keen interest consequently felt in such questions by the general public; and, secondly, the absence of a technical nomenclature, and the necessity which hence arises for employing popular language in the exposition of the doctrines of social and economic science. The inevitable consequence of this state of things has been to attract to the discussion of such topics a crowd of unqualified persons. The incident, however, is not peculiar to Political Economy; and, if a science is to be made responsible for all the unscientific and superficial argumentation to which it gives occasion, Sociology would have quite as much, perhaps rather more, to answer for than economic science. The question, therefore, cannot be decided by extracts drawn at random from the miscellaneous literature of economic discussion: it is not by extracts from such sources, but by the doctrines of the science as expounded in the works of acknowledged masters, that the issue must be determined. From the writings of M. Comte's *avocats* and *littérateurs* I must appeal to those of Malthus, of Say, of Ricardo, of Tooke, of Senior, of Mill. These I take to be the veritable scientific successors of Adam Smith—after him and Turgot, the true founders and accredited expositors of economic doctrine. Limiting the controversy to this arena, I venture to assert that a more remarkable example of continuity of doctrine, of development of seminal ideas, of original *aperçus* extended, corrected, occasionally re-cast, of new discoveries supplementing, sometimes modifying, the old—in short, of all the indications of progressive science—will not easily be found even in the history of physical speculation.*

The portion of economic science which Adam Smith carried furthest, and in which he left least for his successors to correct or supplement, is probably the theory of production. With true instinct, he fixed on labour and land as the great original sources of wealth. Of these agencies, that furnished by nature being a constant force, he saw that the progress of wealth must depend on the progressive efficiency of that other which man contributed. The problem of production thus resolved itself into ascertaining the conditions determining the efficiency of human industry. These conditions he grouped under three leading categories—division of labour, machinery, and

* "L'économie politique," says M. Courcelle-Seneuil, "bien que jeune encore, présente une suite de travaux dont l'objet, le but et la méthode, sont les mêmes, qui forment un corps, établissent une tradition et des croyances communes, une science enfin dans laquelle les conceptions, même fautives et imparfaites, servent à élever des théories moins fautives et moins imparfaites; dans laquelle chaque vérité découverte est recueillie et conservée et chaque erreur signalée comme un écueil à éviter."

the accumulation of capital. Such, stated in a few words, is the theory of production propounded in the "Wealth of Nations." It has been submitted by his successors to a searching criticism; but it has emerged from the ordeal, in the main, unaffected as regards the essence of the doctrines, though more or less modified in detail. Land—though, without doing much violence to language, we may extend the term to cover all that the land contains, all the material objects, therefore, which form the subject-matter of wealth, and even those productive powers resident in the earth—can yet scarcely be understood as comprising the forces in general of physical nature. Adam Smith, at all events, did not so employ the term; and, accordingly, his generalization of the sources of wealth into land and labour is defective in not paying sufficient regard to the part performed in production by these latter agencies. As he overlooked their co-operation, so he necessarily failed to perceive the conditions on which it was rendered, and the consequences involved in the varying efficacy of those conditions—an omission which has been supplied by his successors, with important consequences in the general theory of economic development. Again, his conception of capital has been carefully sifted by more than one later writer, and has been cleared in the process of discussion of some extraneous elements which obscured the true nature of the functions performed by that agent of production. Division of labour, again, which he regarded mainly in its more obvious applications, has been shown to be a particular case of a larger principle, co-operation, which embraces not merely the class of phenomena adverted to by Adam Smith, but the great transactions of international commerce, and industrial organization in its most extended sense. Subject to modifications of this minor kind, however, the doctrines of Adam Smith, in the theory of production, have been retained, and remain an integral portion of the existing body of economic science.

Passing to another field, and turning to his speculations on the phenomena of exchange value, one may with great truth apply to them what M. Say has said of his entire work: "The more we extend our knowledge of Political Economy, the more highly we shall appreciate both what he has done and what he has left for others to do." There are passages in the "Wealth of Nations" which touch the very core of the true theory of value. When, for example, he says: "The real price of everything, what everything really costs to the man who wants to acquire it, is the toil and trouble of acquiring it. What everything is really worth to the man who has acquired it, and who wants to dispose of it, is the toil and trouble which it can save to himself, and which it can impose upon other people:"—when, again, he says: "Labour was the first price—the original purchase-money that was paid for all things,"* he expressed truths which had only need to be firmly grasped to unravel for him the complications of this

* Turgot also saw in industrial production the original act of exchange: "L'homme est encore seul; la nature seule fournit à ses besoins, et déjà il fait avec elle un premier *commerce* où elle ne fournit rien qu'il ne paie par son travail, par l'emploi de ses facultés et de son temps."—*Valeurs et Monnaies*, quoted by M. Courcelle-Seneuil, vol. i. p. 304, note.

most intricate order of phenomena. But he has hardly laid hold on the clue when he lets it go, and proceeds to exclude from the operation of the principle he had enunciated all stages of social existence except the earliest—that "rude state of society which precedes the accumulation of stock and the appropriation of land." The doctrine of value, as he finally developed it, though vitiated by a defective analysis of the elements of cost, nevertheless had the great merit of connecting the phenomena with cost as its governing principle, and the further still higher merit—in which I think he was entirely original—of bringing into view the conception of "natural," as distinguished from "market" values—that "central price towards which the prices of all commodities are continually gravitating." These were considerable achievements, as those will acknowledge who are acquainted with the failure of even the most able of his predecessors to get beyond superficial generalizations—one might say the commonplaces of the subject—in this fundamental branch of Political Economy,* or who observe the futile efforts to excogi-

* Turgot's exposition of the doctrine of value (*Formation et Distribution des Richesses*, §§ 33—35) does not go beyond proximate causes, namely, the reciprocal wants and means of buyers and sellers in a given market; in modern phrase, demand and supply. But incidentally in another part of his work (§ 61), he falls into a groove of thought which all but leads him up to the principle of "natural price" and "cost of production." "C'est lui" [the capitalist], he writes, "qui attendra que la vente des cuirs lui rende, non seulement toutes ses avances, mais encore un profit suffisant pour le dédommager de ce que lui aurait valu son argent s'il l'avait employé en acquisition de fonds; et de plus du salaire dû à ses travaux, à ses soins, à ses risques, à son habileté même; car sans doute, à profit égal, il aurait préféré vivre sans aucune peine d'un revenu d'une terre qu'il aurait pu acquérir avec le même capital." But having thus touched on the true solution, he afterwards (§ 67) recurs to his former position:

tate a theory of the numerous modern writers who rush into economic speculations with no better guidance than the light of nature. In this form the theory was accepted by Say * without substantial change, but in the hands of Ricardo it underwent important modifications, and in effect was recast. Starting from Adam Smith's conception of "natural price," and of cost as the regulator of this, he did much to elucidate the position by simply excluding from his exposition of the subject all that was inconsistent with these primary assumptions. But he did more than this. His clearer view of the nature of exchange value, and the firmer grasp he had attained of the bearing of that "first price," that "original purchase-money" on all the secondary results in the play of industrial exchange flowing from the necessity of its payment, enabled him to show that the same principle which governed exchanges in primitive societies, and which Adam Smith imagined was peculiar to such societies, obtained equally, though masked by the more complicated machinery of advanced civilization, in all stages of industrial development; and finally enabled him to bring within the scope of his general theory a class of phenomena of which the theory, as left by Adam

"Ce sont toujours les besoins et les facultés qui mettent le prix à la vente," &c.

* M. Say's doctrine of value—so far as a distinct doctrine can be elicited from his very contradictory statements—differed in some respects from Adam Smith's; but Ricardo has shown (Works, p. 172) that where he differed, it was to go wrong. The essentials of Adam Smith's doctrine, that value was governed by cost of production, and that cost of production consisted of wages, profits, and rent, in such sense that a rise or fall of any of these elements necessitated a corresponding rise or fall of value—all this M. Say fully held.

Smith, failed to give any intelligible account—the phenomena of agricultural prices;—a generalization from which he was immediately led to his celebrated doctrine of rent. From the facts of value, as presented within the limits of a single industrial community, Ricardo advanced to the more complicated phenomena presented by international exchange; and here, again, with unfailing instinct, he laid his hand on the salient elements of the problem; though it was reserved for Mr. Mill, by his theory of the "equation of international exchange," first propounded in his "Essays on Unsettled Questions in Political Economy,"* to complete this portion of the docrine. In the more important and fundamental speculation, however, on the governing principle of "natural value" in domestic transactions, Ricardo left little for his successors to supply. Mr. Senior improved the exposition by giving a name—Abstinence—to an element of cost, not unrecognized by Ricardo, and implied in his exposition, but not brought into sufficient prominence by him; and Mr. Mill, in his chapter on the "ultimate elements of cost of production," has effected some modifications in detail, and given greater precision to some of the conceptions involved; but in essentials the doctrine remains as it came from the master's hand.

In the field of foreign trade, Adam Smith achieved important results, though mainly of a negative kind. His onslaught on the mercantile theory of wealth, and his advance from the destruction of that fetish to the

* "Un travail," says M. Cherbuliez of Geneva, "le plus important et le plus original dont la science économique se soit enrichie depuis une vingtaine d'années."

establishment of the doctrine of Free Trade, are among his best-known exploits. Yet it is nevertheless true that Adam Smith wholly failed to give a rational account of the principle which occasions and governs the interchange of commodities between nations, and by consequence to explain in what consists, or what measures, the gain of foreign trade. His language on this subject, in not a few passages, exhibits all the vacillation and contradiction of the mercantile school. While alive to the important and fundamental truth that "consumption is the sole end and purpose of production," and drawing the sound inference that "the interests of producers ought to be attended to only so far as they promote the interests of consumers," the main tenor of his exposition of the nature and effects of foreign trade is nevertheless conceived distinctly from the producer's stand-point. Foreign markets are regarded as beneficial, because affording a "vent for surplus productions," and the gain of commerce is supposed to lie mainly in its conducing to maintain a high range of mercantile profit. On the whole, it must be said, in spite of some admirable maxims and pregnant hints which occur throughout the discussion, that the theory of foreign trade, as developed in the "Wealth of Nations," constitutes a mass of confused thought and misapprehended fact. The whole of this portion of the science was still essentially chaotic, and, notwithstanding the partial elucidations effected by M. Say in his exposition of the doctrine that "products are the markets for products," remained in this condition until here again the genius of Ricardo, by a few masterly generalizations, introduced order and light into the jarring elements. One of these, known to economists as the doctrine of "comparative cost," set forth, for the first time, the fundamental conditions which determine the profitableness of international exchange. Adam Smith's negative conclusions were not only corroborated but supplied with a basis in the general theory of the subject, while the small element of truth contained in the doctrine of the Mercantile school was ascertained and discriminated. Phenomena, moreover, which Adam Smith had wholly overlooked, and which his doctrine would have been powerless to explain—for example, the continued importation of a commodity produced under less favourable conditions than those available for its production in the importing country—were brought into view, and shown to be the necessary consequences of the fundamental law which governed this province of exchange. The theory of foreign trade, thus for the first time placed upon a rational foundation, has since been taken up by Mr. Mill, at whose hands it has received important additions and modifications, but additions and modifications, as Mr. Mill himself is careful to point out, which are all in the nature of developments of the original doctrine—all, therefore, of that kind which are the natural incidents and best evidence of progressive science.

Let me briefly trace the history of one important economic doctrine more. The true nature and functions of money, as employed within the limits of a single country, were apprehended with great clearness by Adam Smith. When he distinguished the coin of a country—"the great wheel of circulation"—from the goods which it circulates; when he likened the use of paper money to the substitution for this wheel of another, less costly and more convenient; and, by a still more apt image, to a road through the air which should enable the people of the country to turn to the purposes of cultivation the space previously occupied by the ordinary highway; when, following out this illustration, he showed how the conversion was effected through the substitution, by means of interchange with foreign countries, of productive capital for the barren gold; when he set the subject of a mixed currency in this light,—he supplied or suggested principles adequate to explain the most important phenomena of domestic circulation. These principles have all been accepted by his successors, and are to be found in all good text-books of Political Economy: some of their consequences, too, have been embodied in legislative measures. But the same weakness of his general doctrine on the side of international exchange which excluded him from clear insight into the movements of cosmopolitan commerce, disabled him also in his attempt to deal with the phenomena of international money. On the causes regulating the distribution of gold and silver throughout the world, and the relative range of prices amongst commercial nations, Adam Smith has thrown little or no light; but, as the reader will anticipate, his shortcomings were here again supplemented by the same able thinker who had solved the general problem of international trade – a problem of which the question of international money was but a part. In other directions, also, monetary doctrines have progressed since the time of Adam Smith. It would be strange indeed were it otherwise. The disturbance of monetary relations caused by the great wars following on the French Revolution, the suspension of cash payments for twenty years by the Bank of England, the immense development of credit which has signalized the last half-century, have brought to light monetary phenomena of a range and complexity unknown in the earlier period. The investigations of the Bullion Committee of 1810, and the admirable labours of Mr. Tooke, preserved in his "History of Prices," have turned these opportunities to excellent account, and shed new light over the whole of this extended and intricate field; which has been still further elucidated by the discussion arising out of the controverted question of the policy of the Bank Act of 1844.

Such, then, in four capital departments of Political Economy, has been the course of speculation since the publication of the "Wealth of Nations;"* and there would be no difficulty in extending the illustration to other doctrines of the science. But I think I may stop here, and ask if there is nothing in all this but "the reproduction of sterile controversies, ever renewed, never advancing?" Is this a spectacle of purely theological and metaphysical dissertation? Is it

* In the foregoing argument I have drawn my illustrations mainly from the works of English economists; not that I have any wish to ignore what has been done by other schools, but because the capital discoveries in the science have, so far as I know, been made by Englishmen. This, I observe, is freely admitted by one of the most eminent of recent contributors to economic speculation on the Continent. M. Cherbuliez, of Geneva, writes:—"On peut considérer Adam Smith comme le fondateur d'une école, de cette école Anglaise, à laquelle la science est redevable de presque tous les théorèmes importants dont elle s'est enrichie depuis le commencement de ce siècle."—*Précis de la Science Économique*, vol. i. p. 30.

true that the successors of Adam Smith have nothing to show of effective contribution to the doctrines of their master, no really new discoveries to add to his "felicitous *aperçus*"? Are we not, on the contrary, justified in affirming that Political Economy presents, and that in a very eminent degree, one at least of those symptoms which M. Comte has declared to be among the least equivocal evidences of really scientific conceptions—continuity of doctrine?

The other criterion by which M. Comte proposes to try Political Economy is fecundity, or the test of fruit. And here it is probable many people would meet his challenge by adducing the general results of modern industrial and commercial legislation—such results, for example, as the extinction of trade corporations, the abolition of usury laws, the more or less extensive adoption by the leading nations of Europe of the principle of free trade, English colonial policy, English financial, monetary, and poor-law reforms—achievements which, it will scarcely be denied, may be fairly credited to Political Economy. They are unquestionably in general conformity with its principles; and they were carried into effect by men more or less under the influence of, some of them deeply imbued with, the spirit of its teaching. Nevertheless I must demur to the test of fecundity as thus understood. More than one even of the physical sciences might find themselves in straits if required to make good their pretensions by a criterion of this sort. Geology is counted a science, yet amongst practical miners, whether in Wales and Cornwall or in California and Australia, empirical experience, coupled with native sagacity, stands, if I have not been misinformed, for much more than the most profound geological knowledge. Zoology, Botany, perhaps also Biology, if brought to the same test, might find themselves in similar difficulties; and I rather think Professor Max Müller would find it no easy matter to establish the scientific character of those philological studies of which he is the learned advocate, by the criterion of fruit in this sense of the word. Are we then to say that these several branches of scientific knowledge have borne no fruit—that they have no results to show in evidence of their scientific pretensions? Rather, I think, it behoves us to consider whether such results as those of which examples have been given above—applications, that is to say, of scientific principles to the practical arts of life—constitute the proper fruit of a science. It is in this sense that M. Comte applies the test to Political Economy, and even in this sense, as has been seen, Political Economy emerges triumphant from the ordeal; but the criterion, as thus understood, is vicious, and ought not to be accepted. Practical applications of scientific principles are, I submit, not the proper fruit, but the accidental consequences of scientific knowledge; or if fruit, then fruit of the kind typified by the apple of Atalanta, against the attractions of which Bacon warns the aspirant in the scientific race as apt to draw him aside from the nobler pursuit. It is not in such tangible results that we shall find the genuine fruit of science; these may, and in the end generally will, come in abundant supply, but they are not of the essence of the plant; it is not in these, but in that power which is the end and aim of scientific knowledge—the power of interpreting nature, of explaining phenomena. This is a test from which no true science will shrink, and by the result the scientific claims of Political Economy, as of all other subjects of speculation, must stand or fall. Now the question is, has Political Economy given evidence of fecundity as thus understood? Has it increased our power of interpreting the facts of industrial and commercial life? To deny this would, it seems to me, be as futile as to make a similar denial respecting any of the physical sciences. M. Comte, indeed, does not go this length. On the contrary, he admits, if not in terms, at least by implication, that Political Economy is equal to the interpretation of economic phenomena. But his objection is, that it has not succeeded in preventing the injurious consequences which are incident to some of the laws it expounds. To state, for example, the effects of the extended use of machinery in the production and distribution of wealth, if the exposition be unaccompanied by the suggestion of practical remedies for the industrial evils incident to the process, is, according to M. Comte, a proceeding "vraiment dérisoire," equivalent to proclaiming "the proper social impotency" of economic science—a complaint which, it seems to me, is about as philosophical as if we were to condemn the science of electricity, because, in spite of lightning-conductors, houses are sometimes struck by lightning, or to reproach mechanical science because railway-trains come into collision, or to denounce astronomy because it is powerless to prevent eclipses. Political Economy, it must be owned, has no panacea to offer for the cure of social evils, but it has that to offer which it is in the nature of science to furnish—light as to the causes on which those evils, so far as they proceed from economic agencies, depend. It reveals the laws according to which wealth is produced, accumulated, and distributed; according to which capital increases, and profit declines, and rent grows, and wages, prices, and interest fluctuate; according to which, in a word, economic phenomena are governed; it thus extends our power of interpreting nature, and, "by obeying, of conquering her;" and, in doing so, it has given evidence of fecundity in the only sense in which fecundity can be properly required of a science.

A great deal has been made by M. Comte of the divergence of view on fundamental points revealed by the discussions of economic science. The fact, whether to be regretted or not, cannot be denied; but it may be asked what there is in the controversies of economists that has not been paralleled again and again in the history of every physical science? What, for example, has been the history of chemical progress but a succession of controversies upon points of the most fundamental character; controversies which have not yet been closed? There is, indeed, no little analogy between the course of Chemistry in this respect and that of Political Economy. While Adam Smith and the French Physiocrats were discussing the fundamental problem as to the nature and ultimate sources of wealth, a parallel controversy was raging between the followers of Stahl in England, and those of Lavoisier in France, on the most fundamental of chemical problems—the nature of combustion. Both controversies, after periods of about equal duration, were closed by the definitive triumph of English views in Political Economy, of French views in Chemistry; but closed only to be opened again on new, but still fundamental issues. There are French economists who refuse to accept the doctrines of population and rent propounded by Malthus and Ricardo. And there are chemists, English and French, who, holding by the theory of Lavoisier as to the primary character of chemical combinations, reject the subtle speculations of a more modern school. At the present moment, as I learn from a recent article in the *Revue des deux Mondes*, there are no less than three distinct positions taken by chemists on the question of the molecular constitution of bodies :—

> "Can it be said," asks the writer, "that the theory of atomicity reigns now without challenge in chemical science? No, we have not reached that point. There are still amongst *savans* of the highest authority some declared partisans of the theory of Lavoisier. There are chemists who, while abandoning the ancient doctrines, refuse to accept the new, and for the moment acknowledge no general idea of a kind to guide investigators. One may foresee, however, that the principle of atomicity will, at no distant day, rise superior to opposition and doubt." *

With such facts before us it will scarcely be maintained that divergence of view amongst the cultivators of a science on even fundamental points is inconsistent with its positive character; and we can, therefore,

* See an article in the *Revue des deux Mondes*, 15th July, 1869, by M. Edgar Savenez: 'L'Évolution des Doctrines chimiques depuis Lavoisier.'

afford to admit the existence of English and French schools of Political Economy, without being forced to take rank as outcasts from the Positive pale, among metaphysical and theological dissertators. We may even go further than this, and contemplate the possibility of economic generalizations which shall supersede some now holding their place in our text-books. Whatever may ultimately become of our existing doctrines of value, of rent, of profits, of international trade, they can scarcely meet a harder fate than befell the phlogistic theory of combustion, or than seems likely to befall the binary theory of chemical combination. Those doctrines, as they stand, do in fact explain a vast number and variety of the phenomena of wealth presented by modern industrial societies. This alone, on Positive principles, constitutes a valid title, at all events, to the claim of provisional acceptance. Subsequent examination will show whether they do not also satisfy the second condition required for their definite recognition as natural laws.

The above considerations will probably be deemed a sufficient answer to M. Comte on the criterion of fecundity as applied to Political Economy; but in connection with this topic, that philosopher has some remarks on the subject of scientific prevision as practicable in the social sciences, the bearing of which on Political Economy it may be well here briefly to examine.

M. Comte has laid it down as the attribute of a true social science, that it be able to establish a "rational filiation in the succession of events, so as to permit, as for every other order of phenomena, and within the general limits imposed by a superior complication, a certain systematic prevision of their ulterior succession." The point to which I wish to call attention is the extent to which Political Economy satisfies the condition here required of a social science.

That in a certain sense "prevision" is attainable in the phenomena treated by Political Economy will be at once seen if we consider that its principles have been frequently taken as a guide in practical legislation. It is true the rules by which a practical art is conducted may be empirical; but this character cannot be attributed to the conclusions of Political Economy: the common objections to it lie, indeed, all in the opposite direction. It cannot be denied, for example, that the doctrine of Free Trade is a product of systematic reasoning: true or false, it is at least no rule of thumb. We had no experience of Free Trade when Adam Smith and Turgot preached it. The announcement, then, that free trade would enrich a country, like the announcement that water would ascend in the exhausted tube of a pump, formed a distinct prediction—a prediction that certain effects would follow from certain causes; and a prediction which, wherever the experiment has been tried,* has been verified by the event. It is clear, therefore, that to this extent Political Economy lays claim, and not without valid grounds, to the power of prediction.†

* Using the term 'experiment' in the loose sense in which alone experiments in social science are possible. See Mill's "Logic," ii. p. 456, &c.

† "Elle peut prévoir les conséquences de tel ou tel acte, et c'est dans cette faculté de prévoir les fruits à venir qu'elle trouve, comme la physique, la contre-épreuve de la théorie, le signe de leur certitude."—*Traité d'Économie Politique*, par J. G. Courcelle-Seneuil, vol. i. p. 10.

But the faculty contemplated by M. Comte, in the passage I have quoted, would seem to comprehend something more than this. It was to be a power of foreseeing, not merely a single consequence, however general and wide-reaching, but a train of consequences depending by "rational filiation" on an original cause. Can it be said that Political Economy satisfies this requirement? Before answering this question, let us observe what the requirement involves.

We have seen that Political Economy has predicted certain results as flowing from the policy of Free Trade; but it is not more certain that freedom of trade favours the best distribution of industrial forces, and thus conduces to the augmentation of wealth, than it is that an accelerated growth of capital promotes an accelerated increase of population; while it is equally certain that, where other things are equal, density of population is attended with certain economic advantages—advantages which in their turn converge to the same result, intensifying the original impulse towards augmented wealth and population. Further it might be shown, remembering that the material well-being of a people depends in the last resort upon their habits as affecting their disposition and power to keep their numbers within the limits of the means of support;—remembering again that the habits of a people are liable to be modified by changes in its condition if these be sufficiently long continued; —I say it might be shown, having regard to these considerations, that a Free-trade policy would have a tendency, not merely to enrich a country and augment the number of its people, but also, through an action upon their habits, to raise permanently the standard of well-being among the population whose numbers it had contributed to increase. This, perhaps, will suffice for the purpose of illustration; but if the reader desires to see examples of this mode of reasoning on social affairs applied to actual questions of momentous interest, he has only to turn to Mr. Mill's celebrated chapters in the second volume of his "Political Economy" on the "Influence of the Progress of Society on Production and Distribution." In such instances, then, we find a "rational filiation" established in the succession of economic influences.

But does it amount to prevision of the actual order of economic events, and would it justify a distinct prediction of a remote economic result? At this point I think the answer must be in the negative; and for this reason: the realization of the results described is contingent in each case on the action of contemporaneous agencies influencing the course of events, but not included in the economic premisses. In short, the economic prevision is a prevision, not of events, but of tendencies—tendencies which would be liable, in a greater or less degree, or even completely, to be counteracted by others of which it takes no account.*

* "It is evident, in the first place, that Sociology, considered as a system of deductions *à priori*, cannot be a science of positive predictions, but only of tendencies. We may be able to conclude, from the laws of human nature applied to the circumstances of a given state of society, that a particular cause will operate in a certain manner unless counteracted; but we can never be assured to what extent or amount it will so operate, or affirm with certainty that it will not be counteracted, because we can seldom know, even approximatively, all the agencies which may co-exist with it, and still less calculate the collective result of so many combined elements. The remark, however, must here be once more repeated, that

This incapacity, however, of forecasting events, let it be noted, argues no imperfection in economic science; the imperfection is not here, but in those other cognate sciences to which belongs the determination of the non-economic agencies which are the unknown quantities in the problem. When these cognate social sciences shall have been brought up to the same stage of advancement which has been attained by Political Economy, something approaching to that systematic prevision of events contemplated by M. Comte will be possible. Meanwhile it is no slight gain, in speculating on the future of society, to have it in our power to determine the direction of an order of tendencies exercising so wide, constant, and potent an influence on the course of human development as the conditions of wealth. It is to hold in our hand one, and that not the weakest, of the threads of destiny.

So much for that highest form of scientific fruit—"forecast of the future." The principle, however, of establishing a filiation in events may take the more modest form of explaining the past; and here, it seems to me, we have a field in which if abundant fruit has not been reaped, it is only because the ground

knowledge insufficient for prediction may be most valuable for guidance. It is not necessary for the wise conduct of the affairs of society, no more than of anyone's private concerns, that we should be able to foresee infallibly the results of what we do. We must seek our objects by means which may perhaps be defeated, and take precautions against dangers which possibly may never be realized. The aim of practical politics is to surround any given society with the greatest possible number of circumstances of which the tendencies are beneficial, and to remove or counteract, as far as practicable, those of which the tendencies are injurious. A knowledge of the tendencies only, though without the power of accurately predicting their conjunct result, gives us to a certain extent this power."—MILL's *System of Logic*, vol. ii. p. 477. Third edition.

has not been adequately cultivated. That Political Economy—assuming that it fulfils its limited purpose of unfolding the natural laws of wealth—is capable of throwing light on the evolutions of history, will scarcely be denied, if only it be considered how large a proportion of all human existence is absorbed in the mere pursuit of physical well-being, how extensively the material interests of men prevail in determining their political opinions and conduct, and in how many subtle ways worldly considerations gain an entrance into the heart and conscience, and help to give the cue to moral and religious ideas. It is scarcely possible, I say, to reflect on this, and not perceive that to the right interpretation and correct exposition of the conduct of men in past times—that conduct which makes history—a knowledge of the laws of wealth, a knowledge of the direction in which, in a given epoch, material interests draw the men who live in it, forms an indispensable qualification. Obvious, however, as this reflection is, the truth (except in a few eminent instances) has been all but wholly ignored. Speaking generally, it is not yet supposed—notwithstanding Mr. Buckle's admirable efforts to raise the standard of requirement on this point—that a knowledge of Political Economy is any necessary part of the equipment of an historian. It is impossible to doubt that the consequences of this view of things to historic study have been very serious; that many precious indications, which to a student furnished with the economic key would have opened light through not a few of the dark but important crises of history, have been wholly lost to us—thrown away upon investigators who, however rich in erudition, perhaps embarrassed with their riches, were unprovided with this potent instrument. Our historians have but rarely been economists, and I fear it must be acknowledged that our economists have quite as rarely been profound students of history; and it has thus come to pass that this important field of economic research has as yet produced but scanty fruit.

NOTE ON AN ESSAY BY FREDERIC HARRISON, WRITTEN IN REPLY TO THE FOREGOING, WHICH APPEARED IN THE "FORTNIGHTLY REVIEW" FOR JULY 1870.

I quite agree with Mr. Harrison that the comparing of opinions by the disciples of two parallel schools of thought, "where there is mutual respect, no spirit of rivalry, and an active sense of a common purpose," may be as useful in eliciting truth, as controversy, in the theological sense of the term, is generally efficacious in hiding it; and I trust I shall not be thought oblivious of this, or unappreciative of the gracious and highly flattering terms in which he has recognized my attempts to deal with a difficult problem, if I desire to append some observations in vindication of my own accuracy on some points on which he has impugned it. I am quite content that the arguments I have used in defence of the scientific pretensions of Political Economy against the attacks of Comte should be taken subject to whatever modification of their force or scope Mr. Harrison's strictures may be thought to have shown that they require; but on one or two points his criticisms amount to a challenge of my accuracy in stating Comte's doctrine. On a question of this kind those only are qualified to judge who are students of Comte's writings, and even they may not find it convenient to verify at once the passages on which the issue turns. I am anxious, therefore, to lay before the readers of Mr. Harrison's Essay and mine the means of judging between us upon this part of the case.

At p. 40 Mr. Harrison corrects me in these terms:—

"Comte *does not* 'contend that the problems presented, on the one hand, by physical nature, and, on the other, by social life, are so radically discordant that the method applicable to the one must be, not only modified, but reversed, in dealing with the other.' He is speaking of the *inorganic*, not of the *physical* world. Comte insists that the organic phenomena of all sorts—zoological, physiological, moral, and social—cannot be pursued by a method which is very useful in the inorganic," &c. (The italics are Mr. Harrison's.)

It seems to me that most readers would by "physical," in the passage quoted from my Essay, understand "inorganic." Those sciences which deal with the physical phenomena of the organic world, as zoology, botany, &c., are, I think, more commonly called "natural sciences;" the term "physical" being rather reserved for the sciences dealing with inorganic nature, such as astronomy, dynamics, chemistry, &c. But however this may be, it was, I submit, scarcely open to Mr. Harrison to fix upon this passage and proceed to comment upon it in language which implied that I was ignorant of the true character of Comte's distinction, when the page from which he quoted contained the following:—

"As has been said, then, the sciences are arranged in the order indicated by the degree of complexity in their subject-matter. . . . As phenomena become more complex, the method [of disintegration and separate study], he contends, becomes less suitable, less efficacious, till at length a point is reached at which it fails altogether, and it becomes necessary to adopt a contrary mode of procedure, the mode of procedure, namely, which he describes as investigation through the *ensemble*. *This point in the scale of the sciences coincides, he tells us, with that at which the transition is made from inorganic to organic nature.* The method of investigation by disintegration and separate study should thenceforth give way to that which proceeds by treatment in the *ensemble*. Accordingly he holds that the organic sciences generally should be cultivated in conformity with this principle."

Again, at p. 45, Mr. Harrison writes:—

"I turn to the reasoning of Professor Cairnes against what he says is M. Comte's position—'that phenomena, in proportion as they are more complex, are more *solidaires*.' For my own part, I cannot find in Comte any such doctrine, at least so stated."

Now I beg to call Mr. Harrison's attention to the following passage:*—

"Mais on doit, à ce sujet, reconnaître, en principe, que *le consensus devient toujours d'autant plus intime et plus prononcé qu'il s'applique à des phénomènes graduellement plus complexes* et moins généraux; en sorte que, suivant ma hiérarchie scientifique élémentaire, l'étude des phénomènes chimiques forme, par sa nature, à ce titre, comme à tout autre, une sorte d'intermédiaire fondamental entre la philosophie inorganique et la philosophie organique, ainsi que chacun peut aisément s'en convaincre. D'après ce principe, il reste néanmoins incontestable que, conformément aux habitudes philosophiques prépondérantes, *c'est surtout aux systèmes organiques, en vertu de leur plus grande complication, que conviendra toujours essentiellement la notion scientifique de solidarité et de consensus,* malgré son universalité nécessaire."

If M. Comte does not here state that "phenomena, in proportion as they are more complex, are more *solidaires*," I must confess myself incompetent to interpret him. I may add that the same doctrine is implied (as I read his words) in the whole tenor of his exposition of sociological method.

The passage just quoted supplies an answer to another of Mr. Harrison's criticisms. At p. 41 he writes:—

"'But why,' says Professor Cairnes, 'the method of *ensemble* in studying the organic world?' Why? Because the organic world is an *ensemble*. Every organism is an *ensemble*. Every organic system and order is an *ensemble*. The organic means something which has a complex function over and above that of any of its elements. The study of the organic is simply the study of this complex function (*i.e.* of an *ensemble*)."

Now, whatever be the merit of this answer, what I am concerned here to show is that it is not Comte's: not only is it not Comte's answer, it is inconsistent with Comte's answer. Mr. Harrison says the organic world must be studied in the *ensemble*, "because it is an *ensemble*. Every organism is an *ensemble*;" but according to M. Comte (as will be seen by reference to the passage just quoted), the reason for this is that the phenomena comprised in the organic world are "more complex," and, "in virtue of their greater complication," more "*solidaires*," than those of the inorganic world—a reason which, a little reflection will show, by no means runs

* "Philosophie Positive," vol. iv. p. 350. Edit. 1839.

on all fours with the former. For example, as M. Comte states the case, one can see why the study of chemical phenomena should occupy an intermediate position between organic and inorganic philosophy. It is intermediate, because —the whole distinction turning on a question of degree—the phenomena it deals with are more complex than other inorganic phenomena, less complex than organic. But how does this accord with Mr. Harrison's rendering of the argument? Where is the room for a middle term between organic and inorganic if the distinction turns upon the consideration of the presence or absence of organic character, of "complex function"? Are chemical phenomena semi-organic? Do they exhibit "complex function" in a rudimentary form? If not, how is Mr. Harrison's statement of the argument consistent with assigning chemical studies an intermediate place?

Further, if the fact of "organic character," of "complex function," be the ground of the distinction, the reasons for the method of the *ensemble* will be strong or weak according as the phenomena to be dealt with partake of this character, manifest this "complex function." Now does Mr Harrison contend that a society is an organism in a stricter sense than an individual man; that the adaptation of structure to function is *more* complete in the case of a nation than in that of a human being? I hardly think he will say so; nay, I am sure he will admit that the reverse is the fact; but, if so, his reason for the method of the *ensemble* has less force in relation to social investigations than in relation to the study of individual life—is less applicable to sociology than to biology—a conclusion which exactly reverses one of Comte's most frequently reiterated opinions. Comte held that the reasons for studying social facts in the *ensemble* are incomparably stronger than those which apply to biological investigations. This is entirely in harmony with his doctrine as I have stated it; social phenomena being "more complex" than biological; but, as it seems to me, absolutely irreconcilable with Mr. Harrison's exposition.

IX.

BASTIAT.*

SCIENCE belongs to no country; yet the method of cultivating a science cannot but be affected by the habits of philosophic thought which prevail among its cultivators; and this influence will obviously be stronger in proportion as the subject-matter of science comes more directly into contact with human intelligence and will. I have lately pointed out in this Review† that, even in a speculation so eminently positive as Chemistry, there is room for difference of opinion on problems of a fundamental kind, and that in England and France opposing schools have ranged themselves round conflicting theories from the infancy of chemical science down to the present hour. It is not, then, strange that similar phenomena should manifest themselves in Political Economy, so much more closely connected than Chemistry with human conduct and pursuits; and we need not be surprised if we find in France modes of thinking on this subject more or less out of relation with those

* *Fortnightly Review*, October 1870. † *Ante*, p. 301.

which prevail among ourselves. The fact unquestionably is so; but it is important that we should not overrate its extent or significance. Indeed, I think, it must be considered as no slight testimony to the influence of the scientific point of view in keeping speculation straight, that, in spite of the divergent tendencies of national philosophies, the most characteristic doctrines of the English school of Political Economy should have found some of their most powerful champions and most skilful expositors on the other side of the Channel; and that such men as Say, Duchâtel, Garnier, Courcelle-Seneuil, and Cherbuliez, while contributing not a few original and important developments to economic doctrine, should have been the interpreters to their countrymen of Adam Smith and Malthus, Ricardo and Mill. In effect, the main stream of economic thought has in both countries flowed in the same channels; while the idiosyncrasies of the national mind have, on each side, made themselves felt in producing certain eddies of speculation apart from the main current. No one can be at any loss in finding examples of aberrations due to this cause among ourselves. Among French political thinkers one of the most noteworthy is presented by the writings of Bastiat.

The name of Bastiat is, perhaps, the most familiar in this country of all French economists; a result to which several circumstances have contributed besides the merit of his writings. At a critical period of our reforming career he threw himself with extraordinary ardour into our contests, and lent effective assistance to the side that has triumphed. He is known on more than one occasion to have made himself the generous defender of English policy and character against the unreasoning prejudices of his countrymen. He was, moreover, the friend of Cobden—in itself, in the judgment of most, a sufficient voucher for economic acquirement; and he has been fortunate enough to find excellent translators for his principal works. This last circumstance cannot, indeed, be fairly separated from the merits of the writings themselves; and it must be owned that these were in some respects of a high and rare order. As examples of dialectical skill in reducing an opponent to absurdity, of simple and felicitous illustration, of delicate and polished raillery, attaining occasionally the pitch of a refined irony, the "Sophismes Economiques" might almost claim a place beside the "Provincial Letters." The petition of the candle-makers and other manufacturers of light to the Legislative Body, praying the exclusion by legislative enactment of the light of the sun, is alone almost enough to make a reputation in this line; and Swift himself has hardly shown greater art in the logical conduct of an absurd proposition than that with which the reader, in this modest proposal, is led, step by step, from the avowed premisses of Protection, through a series of the most natural and irrefragable deductions, straight to the preposterous conclusion advocated by the petitioners.

"What we pray for is, that it may please you to pass a law ordering the shutting up of all windows, skylights, dormer-windows, outside and inside shutters, curtains, blinds, bull's-eyes—in a word, of all openings, holes, chinks, clefts, and fissures, by or through which the light of the sun has been allowed to enter houses, to the prejudice of the meritorious manufactures with which we flatter ourselves we have accommodated our country—a country which, in gratitude, ought not to abandon us now to a strife so unequal. . . . . .

"And, first, if you shut up as much as possible all access to natural light, and create a demand for artificial light, which of our French manufactures will not be encouraged by it?

"If more tallow is consumed, then there must be more oxen and sheep; and, consequently, we shall behold the increase of artificial meadows, meat, wool, hides, and, above all, manure, which is the basis and foundation of all agricultural wealth.

"If more oil is consumed, then we shall have an extended cultivation of the poppy, of the olive, and of colewort. These rich and exhausting plants will come at the right time to enable us to avail ourselves of the increased fertility which the rearing of additional cattle will impart to our lands.

"Our heaths will be covered with resinous trees. Numerous swarms of bees will, on the mountains, gather perfumed treasures, now wasting their fragrance on the desert air, like the flowers from which they are derived. No branch of agriculture but will then exhibit a cheering development. . . . .

"If you urge that the light of the sun is a gratuitous gift of nature, and that to reject such gifts is to reject wealth itself under pretence of encouraging the means of acquiring it, we would caution you against giving a death-blow to your own policy. Remember that hitherto you have always repelled foreign products, *because* they approximate more nearly than home products to the character of gratuitous gifts. To comply with the exactions of other monopolists, you have only *half a motive;* and to repulse us simply because we stand on a stronger vantage-ground than others, would be to adopt the equation $+ \times + = -$; in other words, it would be to heap *absurdity* upon *absurdity*. . . . . .

• • • • • • •

. . . . ."Make your choice, but be logical; for as long as you exclude, as you do, coal, iron, corn, foreign fabrics, *in proportion* as their price approximates to *zero*, what inconsistency would it be to admit the light of the sun, the price of which is already at *zero* during the entire day!"

But it was not on the "Sophismes Économiques" that Bastiat would have been content to take the verdict of posterity as to his pretensions as an economist. Indeed, whatever might be the controversial and literary merits of these admirable tracts, they added nothing to already familiar economic truths. The theory of Free Trade had been fully thought out by a succession of able writers before Bastiat took it in hand, and all that he here could do was what, in fact, he did—furnish new and apt illustrations of a familiar doctrine, or, by well-selected instances, reduce opponents to glaring absurdity. But in 1848 the advent of the democratic republic brought other questions to the front, and stirred controversies more fitted to try the metal of a philosophic thinker. Socialism had raised its grim visage, and was propounding those solutions of the social problem, the mere recollection of which has since so often sufficed to frighten France from her propriety. Louis Blanc, Considérant, Leroux, Proudhon, were thundering against the existing industrial order; and for those who cared to maintain that order the need of the hour was a philosophy adapted to the popular apprehension, which should be capable of furnishing a plausible reply to their attacks. At this time Bastiat was at the height of his reputation in Paris. He had frankly and sincerely accepted the Revolution, though sensible of the unpreparedness of the country for the new *régime*, and alive to the inevitable dangers incident to this state of things. His views, however, did not extend beyond political changes, and while recognizing the generous aims of the Socialists, he shrank with horror from their subversive proposals. He accordingly came forward eagerly to defend the menaced social structure. In a series of clever brochures—"Propriété et la Loi," "Propriété et Spoliation," "Justice et Fraternité," "Capital et Rente," "Maudit Argent,"—he propounded his reply to the "despotic organizers"—"ces pétrisseurs de l'argile humaine." As he wrote, his ideas took firmer hold of his mind, and gradually shaped themselves into a system. The needed philosophy was, he thought, to be found in a recast of Political Economy, and the "new exposition" he undertook to furnish in his "Harmonies Économiques." Unfortunately, Bastiat did not live to complete this work; but enough was accomplished to render perfectly clear the essential character of the conception and the general scope of his design. The English reader has now an opportunity of studying it in Mr. Stirling's excellent Translation.

Political Economy, as treated by the predecessors of Bastiat—by Adam Smith and his successors in this country, by Say and his successors in France—aimed at unfolding the natural principles—natural in the sense of having their foundation in the nature of man and of his environments—which govern the facts of material well-being. Those economists did not, indeed, hold themselves precluded from pointing out, when occasion offered, the moral and social bearing of their doctrines; but, in general, they recognized the distinction between such practical lessons as they believed deducible from their expositions and the doctrines of the science which they taught. In effect, Political Economy, in their hands, was a positive science, in the modern sense of that expression; its methods were combined induction and deduction; its conclusions embodied hypothetical truths of precisely the same character as those of any of the deductive physical sciences; and its purpose was to explain phenomena. As thus constituted, however, Political Economy did not meet the need which it was the object of Bastiat to satisfy. What he aimed at supplying was, not a positive science, not a body of doctrines which should simply *explain* the facts of wealth, but one which, while explaining, should also *justify* those facts,—should justify them, that is to say, as manifested in the results of those fundamental institutions of modern society, private property, freedom of industry, of contract, and of exchange. As his biographer, M. de Fontenay, puts it, his aim was—

"To combine together and fuse into one the two distinct aspects of Fact and of Right; to recur to the formula of the Physiocrats—'La science des faits au point de vue du droit naturel;' to prove that *that which is*, in its actual *ensemble*, and still more in its progressive tendency, is conformable to *that which ought to be*, according to the aspirations of the universal conscience."

In Bastiat's own words, he sought—

"To demonstrate the Harmony of those laws of Providence which govern human society," by showing "that all principles, all motives, all springs of action, all interests, co-operate towards a grand final result, ... the indefinite approximation of all classes towards a level which is always rising; in other words, the *equalization* of individuals in the general *amelioration*."* "The conclusion of the Economists," he says in another place, "is for liberty. But, in order that this conclusion should take hold of men's minds and hearts, it must be solidly based on this fundamental principle:—Interests, left to themselves, tend to harmonious combinations, and to the progressive preponderance of the general good."†

Such was the scheme of renovated economic science propounded by Bastiat; and the question which I desire here to consider is, how far this conception of the inquiry represents a legitimate philosophical speculation, and, more particularly, how far the actual treatment of economic questions from this point of view by Bastiat has resulted in what all will allow to be among the primary and main ends of economical investigation—the elucidation of the facts of wealth.

And here the first remark that occurs is, that, as set forth in the above extracts, the problem of Political Economy is not properly the problem of a science at all. Not only is it not *the* problem of a science, it is not even a scientific problem; for I apprehend it is of the essence of all scientific investigation that the conclusion be left free to shape itself according to the results of the inquiry. Science has no foregone conclusions; but to prove a foregone conclusion is *the* problem of Political Economy, as propounded by Bastiat. What Bastiat proposes to do is, not to ascertain what the consequences of a given set of social arrangements are—that would have been a scientific investigation—but *to prove that they are of a certain kind;* to prove that "left to themselves, human

* Stirling's "Translation," p. 105. † Ibid. p. 7.

interests are harmonious." By the very form in which he states his case, he constitutes himself the advocate of a system, instead of the expositor of a science.

But his conception of the problem involves a still graver error: as we have seen, it was of the essence of his scheme to "fuse together the two distinct aspects of Fact and Right." The "harmony" of human interests which he undertook to establish was not a mere coincidence of certain manifestations of material well-being with certain others, but extended to the moral consequences involved—an extension of view which, according to his biographer, constituted the great merit of his speculation. In effect, Bastiat, however widely separated from his opponents on the question of practical policy, was thoroughly at one with them on the most fundamental article of his philosophic creed: he and they alike accepted the doctrine of "natural rights." They differed, indeed, in their interpretation of the code of nature, but they were quite agreed as to its existence, and as to the obligation of bringing their doctrines to the test of its maxims. A new order of ideas thus found entrance among the premisses of economic science; and the appeal, which had formerly been to facts,—to facts exclusively, mental or physical,—as the ground and evidence of doctrine, was henceforth extended to "rights," "*les plus simples éléments de la justice,*" "*bonne équité,*" and phrases of similar import.* It was

* His Essay on Free Trade opens with this announcement:—"Exchange is a natural right, like Property. Every citizen who has created or acquired a product, *ought* to have the option either of applying it immediately to his own use, or of ceding it to whosoever, on the surface of the globe, consents to give him in exchange the object of his desires.

thus that Fact and Right were fused. The principle of value, as understood by Bastiat, was not simply the law to which the facts of value conform, but such a presentation of that law as should reconcile the facts with what the expositor held to be the dictates of natural justice. The problem involved in the payment of interest on capital was not simply the determination of the physical and mental conditions which render possible the permanent payment of interest, and which govern its amount and fluctuations, but such a mode of presenting the practice as should amount to its moral vindication,—to show that it is "natural, just, legitimate, as useful to him who pays as to him who receives it."* And so of the other problems of the science. Political Economy, in short, became in Bastiat's hands one more example of that style of reasoning on political and social affairs which flourished so luxuriantly in France during the latter half of the last century, and is not yet quite extinct, of which the "Social Contract" may be taken as the type, and the "Declaration of the Rights of Man" as the best known practical outcome—a species of hybrid philosophy, consisting, to borrow the language of Mr. Mill, "of attempts to treat an art like a science, and to have a deductive art." "I speak," says Mr. Mill, "of those who deduce political conclusions, not from laws of nature, not from sequences of phenomena, real or imaginary, but from unbending practical maxims.

To deprive him of this faculty, while he makes no use of it contrary to public order or good morals, and solely to satisfy the convenience of another citizen, is to legalize spoliation, is to do violence to the law of justice."

* "Œuvres Complètes," vol. v. p. 26.

Such are all who found their theory of politics on what is called abstract right." *

Now is such a mode of speculation philosophically legitimate? It seems to me not, and for this reason —that, from the very form in which the problem is stated, the argument is involved from its outset in a *petitio principii*. The question, What is? and the question, What ought to be? are distinct questions. It may be that the answers to them coincide; that *that which is*, is also *that which ought to be;* but, then, this is a thing to be proved, not to be taken for granted; and it can only be proved by working out each problem independently of the other. Instead of this, Bastiat formally identifies them—"fuses" them into one. But fusion of the questions implies fusion of the answers;—that is to say, it is assumed that the same form of words which tells us what is, will tell us also what ought to be. Such a scheme of speculation, it is obvious, could only be worked out in one way—namely, through the instrumentality of terms capable of lending themselves at need to either point of view—capable either of simply expressing a matter of fact, or of connoting with the fact expressed a moral judgment. And such, in truth, is Bastiat's method of proceeding. Availing himself of the double meaning of such "passionate" terms as "principle," "value," "worth," "service," and the like, he has produced a theory which affects to cover both solutions—at once to explain and to justify the facts to which it applies. The economic vocabulary unfortunately lends itself only too readily to this sort of theorizing, and few

* "System of Logic," vol. ii. p. 466. Third ed.

writers have entirely escaped illusion from this cause. Bastiat's distinction is that he has contrived so to propound the problem of Political Economy that it can only be answered by an *équivoque*.

It may be added, that even though the questions of Fact and Right, of Science and Morality, were conceived and argued as distinct, there would still be strong, and, I venture to think, decisive reasons against combining them in the same scheme of speculation. To mention one reason only: such a mode of investigation would present the constant temptation to sacrifice one solution to the other, the scientific to the moral, or the moral to the scientific. The student would be constantly solicited to overlook or ignore, or, on the other hand, to strain or overrate, data, according asthey might seem to involve conclusions in one branch of the speculation in conflict with, or corroborative of, conclusions deemed to be of more importance in the other. Investigation, thus pursued, would no longer be disinterested; science would lose its singleness of purpose. This objection would lie against the combined treatment of the two problems even if they were conceived and discussed as distinct. But the objection to Bastiat's method goes far deeper than this: that method not merely combines science and morality, it confounds them.

Passing from the question of the logical legitimacy of Bastiat's conception of Economic Science let us consider now the results which have accrued from this mode of conceiving and dealing with the problems of wealth. What, in a word, have been the scientific fruits of Bastiat's method? What new light have his speculations shed on the facts which form the subject-matter of his inquiry?

The doctrine on which Bastiat founded his pretensions as an original thinker in Political Economy was his Theory of Value. According to him this theory comprised potentially the whole of Economic Science; and, in point of fact, all that is peculiar to his views flows directly from this source: his conception of value is the *idée mère* of his entire scheme. It is, then, in this doctrine that we shall find the fairest evidence of his work as an economist, and I shall make no apology for examining it at some length.

The following passages from Mr. Stirling's Translation of the "Harmonies" set forth with sufficient fulness the salient features of the doctrine.

"Let us analyse the co-operation of nature of which I have spoken. Nature places two things at our disposal—*materials* and *forces*.

"Most of the material objects which contribute to the satisfaction of our wants and desires, are brought into the state of *utility* which renders them fit for our use only by the intervention of labour, by the application of the human faculties. But the elements, the atoms, if you will, of which these objects are composed, are the gifts—I will add, the *gratuitous* gifts—of nature. This observation is of the very highest importance, and will, I believe, throw a new light upon the theory of wealth.

* * * * * *

"It is very evident, that, if man in an isolated state must, so to speak, *purchase* the greater part of his satisfactions by an exertion, by an effort, it is rigorously exact to say that, prior to the intervention of any such exertion, any such effort, the materials which he finds at his disposal are the *gratuitous* gifts of nature. After the first effort on his part, however slight it may be, they cease to be *gratuitous*; and if the language of Political Economy had been always exact, it would have been to material objects in this state, and before human labour had been bestowed upon them, that the term *raw materials* (*matières premières*) would have been exclusively applied.

"I repeat that this *gratuitous* quality of the gifts of nature, anterior to the intervention of labour, is of the very highest importance. I said in my second chapter that Political Economy was the *theory of value;* I add now, and by anticipation, that things begin to possess *value* only when it is given to them by labour. I intend to demonstrate afterwards that everything which is *gratuitous* for man in an isolated state is gratuitous for man in his social condition, and that the gratuitous gifts of nature, *whatever be their* UTILITY, have no value. I say that a man who receives a benefit from nature, directly and without any effort on his part, cannot be considered as rendering himself an *onerous service*, and, consequently, that he cannot render to another any service with reference to things which are common to all. Now, where there are no services rendered and received, there is no *value*.

"All that I have said of *materials* is equally applicable to the *forces* which Nature places at our disposal. Gravitation, the elasticity of the air, the power of the winds, the laws of equilibrium, vegetable life, animal life, are so many forces which we learn to turn to account. The pains and intelligence which we bestow in this way always admit of remuneration, for we are not bound to devote our efforts to the advantage of others gratuitously. But these natural forces, in themselves, and apart from all intellectual or bodily exertion, are *gratuitous* gifts of Providence, and in this respect they remain destitute of *value* through all the complications of human transactions. This is the leading idea of the present work.

"This observation would be of little importance, I allow, if the co-operation of Nature were constantly uniform; if each man, at all times, in all places, in all circumstances, received from Nature equal and invariable assistance. In that case, science would be justified in not taking into account an element which, remaining always and everywhere the same, would affect the services exchanged in equal proportions on both sides. As in geometry we eliminate portions of lines common to two figures which we compare with each other, we might neglect a co-operation which is invariably present, and content ourselves with saying, as we have done hitherto, 'There is such a thing as natural wealth; Political Economy acknowledges it, and has no more concern with it.'

"But this is not the true state of the matter. The irresistible tendency of the human mind, stimulated by self-interest, and assisted by a series of discoveries, is to substitute natural and gratuitous co-operation for human and onerous concurrence; so that a given utility, although remaining the same as far as the result and the satisfactions which it procures us are concerned, represents a smaller and smaller amount of labour. In fact, it is impossible not to perceive the immense influence of this marvellous phenomenon on our notion of value. For what is the result of it? This, that in every product the *gratuitous* element tends to take the place of the *onerous;* that *utility*, being the result of two *collaborations*, of which one is remunerated and the other is not, value, which has relation only to the first of these united forces, is diminished, and makes room for a *utility* which is identically the same, and this in proportion as we succeed in constraining nature to a more efficacious co-operation. So that we may say that mankind have as many more *satisfactions*, as much more *wealth*, as they have less *value*. Now the majority of authors having employed these three terms, *utility*, *wealth*, *value*, as synonyms, the result has been a theory which is not only not true, but the reverse of true. I believe sincerely that a more exact description of this combination of natural forces and human forces in the business of production—in other words, a juster definition of value—would put an end to inextricable theoretical confusion, and would reconcile schools which are now divergent."

* * * * * *

"Thus, the definition of the word value, in order to be exact, must have reference not only to human efforts, but likewise to those efforts which are exchanged or exchangeable. Exchange does more than exhibit and measure values—it gives them existence. I do not mean to say that it gives existence to the acts and the things which are exchanged, but it imparts to their existence the notion of *value*.

"Now, when two men transfer to each other their present efforts, or make over mutually the results of their anterior efforts, they *serve* each other; they render each other reciprocal *service*.

"I say, then, VALUE IS THE RELATION OF TWO SERVICES EXCHANGED."* [The italics and capitals are the author's.]

To appreciate this, Bastiat's principal contribution to economic science, we must endeavour to separate in the above exposition the doctrines which he held in common with the most eminent economists who preceded him from the element or elements which he has himself added to the theory. It may be at once stated that in the main positions taken by Bastiat there is nothing at issue between him and the leading economists of England and France. He appears, indeed, not to have been of this opinion himself, and to have thought that, in asserting the "gratuitousness of the gifts of nature," he was announcing a truth which had hitherto escaped universal observation; and, strange to say, this claim seems to be admitted by some who have commented on his works in this country. But it is certain that on this point he deceived himself. Adam Smith has indeed expressed himself in some passages as if it were in agriculture only that nature gave anything to man except on the terms of what Bastiat would call "onerous services"—an error which Smith shared with the Physiocrats; but Ricardo has called particular attention to this erroneous limitation of an important principle, and

* Stirling's "Translation," pp. 61-63.

has shown that, so far from this being true, it is, on the contrary, in agriculture only, or at all events mainly, that nature in her co-operation with man has set any limit to her munificence.

"Does nature," Ricardo asks, "nothing for man in manufacture? Are the powers of wind and water, which move our machinery, and assist navigation, nothing? The pressure of the atmosphere and the elasticity of steam, which enable us to work the most stupendous engines—are they not the gifts of nature? To say nothing of the matter of heat in softening and melting metals, of the decomposition of the atmosphere in the process of dyeing and fermentation, there is not a manufacture which can be mentioned, in which nature does not give her assistance to man, *and give it, too, generously and gratuitously.*" *

Say, again, though differing from Ricardo in many points, is at one with him here. In language quite as emphatic as any that Bastiat has used, he insists on the point:—

"It is thus that nature is almost always in partnership of labour with man and his instruments; and in this partnership, we gain so much the more in proportion as we succeed in saving our labour and that of our capital, which is necessarily costly, and get performed, *through the gratuitous services of nature*, a larger portion of what is to be done." And again he observes, "Of those wants, some are satisfied by the use which we make of certain things with which *nature has furnished us gratuitously*, such as the air, water, the light of the sun. We may name these things *natural wealth*, since nature alone is at the cost of them. So far as she gives them indifferently to all, no one is obliged to obtain them at the cost of any sacrifice whatever. They have, therefore, no exchangeable value."†

* Works, p. 40, *note*. † Traité d'Économie Politique, vol. i. p. 36.

It would be idle to multiply quotations from later writers, who have, so far as I know without an exception, followed on this point the teaching of Ricardo and Say. Nor can it be alleged that, while recognizing the fact, there was any failure to appreciate its due significance. So far from this, it has been taken as the basis of no less fundamental a doctrine than that of cost of production—a doctrine which merely asserts in other words that exchange-value in commodities, susceptible of indefinite production at a uniform cost, finds its determining principle in the efforts of man; the utility derived from nature going for nothing in the result.

It is not, therefore, in the recognition of the gratuitous character of nature's services in her co-operation with the industry of man, that what is peculiar to Bastiat's views on value is to be found. It is not in this, but in an assumption with which he accompanies his recognition of this circumstance. Ricardo, Say, and the great majority of succeeding economists have held that, however gratuitous may be the gifts of nature, such gifts are not necessarily on that account incapable of acquiring value. In order to this, they must be not only gratuitous, but also in such abundance, and so accessible to all, that none who desire them need be without them. Water, they would say, when not produced by artificial process, is a gratuitous gift of nature; but water—spring water for example—may or may not have value according to circumstances. If in sufficient abundance for the wants of a neighbourhood, and also accessible to all who live there, it can have no value—none at least beyond what would represent the labour employed in drawing it from the spring; but water in insufficient supply, though a gift of nature, may have value, and this value will have no necessary relation to the human exertion employed in obtaining it. And what is true of water is true, they would say, of all natural objects: in particular it is true of the natural productive forces residing in the materials of the earth. These, though to the persons who are at liberty to take advantage of them "gratuitous gifts of nature," yet not being bestowed on man in unlimited quantity, not being after the appropriation of the soil of a country accessible to all, may and do acquire value, and enter as elements into the causes which give value to land. Now it is this position which Bastiat denies; and of which his denial, together with the consequences which he draws from it, forms the ground of his claim to having reconstituted economic science. According to him, a gift once obtained gratuitously from nature—a spring of water, a field of natural fertility, a pearl picked up on the sea-shore—can never afterwards acquire value except in virtue of human effort bestowed upon it. "The materials and forces given by God to man gratuitously at the beginning have continued gratuitous, and are and must continue to be so through all our transactions; for* in the estimates and appreciations to which exchange gives rise, the *equivalents* are *human services*, and not the *gifts of God*." † This was the capital assumption of Bastiat's economic philosophy, that alone in which his theory of value differed from that generally

* The reader will note the begging of the question in this "for," &c.

† Stirling's "Translation," p. 221.

accepted. On it all that is peculiar to his scheme of speculation rests; and, this failing, the entire fabric inevitably collapses.*

Perhaps the most singular circumstance about the speculation is that Bastiat should have thought the principle just stated self-evident. He was wholly unable to conceive that a gift of nature should be at once "gratuitous" and not "common to all." A gratuitous gift limited in supply, and capable of acquiring value, was for him an impossible thought. Again and again throughout his writings he rings the changes on the grotesqueness of such a supposition. "Who," he asks, "can have the audacity to exact payment for this portion of *superhuman* value?" "The purchaser of corn must pay for it, though it has cost nothing to anybody, not even labour! Who then dares to come forward to demand this pretended *value?*" Accordingly, in speaking of gratuitous gifts of nature, Bastiat always assumes that such gifts are "common to all."

"It is that portion only of utility," he says, "which is due to human labour that becomes the object of exchange, and, by consequence, of remuneration. This latter varies doubtless much in proportion to the intensity of the labour, of its skill, promptitude, and suitability to the circumstances of the case (*son à-propos*), of the need which is felt for it, of the momentary absence of competition, &c. But it is not the less true that the concurrence of natural laws, *belonging to all*, enters for nothing into the price of the product." †

Where natural laws, or forces, or objects "belong to all," the conclusion is irrefragable. No one will pay

* It should be stated that Bastiat's originality in this, the capital element of his theory, has been challenged by Mr. Carey in his work on Social Philosophy—it seems to me on good grounds.

† "Œuvres Complètes," vol. iv. p. 41. The italics are mine.

for what he can get from nature without payment; but the question is, do natural laws, forces, and objects *in all cases* "belong to all"? Those natural laws and forces of the soil in particular, which constitute its fertility, are they incapable of appropriation by some to the exclusion of others? Are they incapable, in virtue of such appropriation, of acquiring value in exchange? This is the gist of the whole argument; and it is, I repeat, in assuming this point in the sense I have described, that Bastiat's special contribution to the economic theory of value consists.

Bastiat's doctrine, then—keeping in view the facts which it expressed, the form apart—resolved itself into the statement that exchange-value under all circumstances is due to human effort as its sole and exclusive cause—to human effort as distinguished from natural gift and endowment, material or mental. What was given to man by nature was not only, he conceived, gratuitous in its origin, but must, in all cases, and (so long as exchange is free) under all circumstances, be incapable of acquiring value. Stated thus nakedly, however, the doctrine is not easily reconcilable with some very obvious facts. For example, the value of a pearl picked up accidentally on the sea-shore; the high remuneration obtained by persons endowed with natural gifts of an exceptional kind—painters, singers, and *artistes* generally; above all, the value of land possessing natural fertility or peculiar advantages of situation;—value in these and other similar instances does not seem to lend itself very easily to the doctrine that all value consists in and represents human effort. To give the theory plausibility, it needed to be clothed in other words. A term, in short, was wanting, which, while designating "effort," should be capable also of suggesting other considerations fitted to meet cases of the above kind. More than this, it was necessary (bearing in mind the moral side of the problem as conceived by Bastiat) that the term, while satisfying the conditions indicated, should also be capable of conveying a moral judgment on the facts to which it was applicable. Such a term Bastiat found in the word "service;" and it is in the uses to which he turns this word—as at once universal solvent of economic difficulties, and what Bentham would call a "sacramental" term in the warfare with Socialism—that the peculiar character of his speculation reveals itself.

In propriety of speech the term "service" should, I apprehend, be limited to personal exertions made in another's behalf. It is in this sense that it is commonly used in economic writings, and, so understood, it is a convenient economic term. But it is obviously possible, without doing any great violence to language, to give it a wider signification. Thus, for example, if a friend were to warn me that I was about to drink poison, he might be said to render me a service, though the effort involved in the announcement would be quite inappreciable. Similarly, a musician might be said to render a service to an audience whom he gratified by the performance of a piece of music, however slight the effort incident to the performance might happen to be. And so, again, might the owner of an island just risen from the sea, on which no human being had ever set foot, be said to render a "service" to the person to whom he should consent to transfer his property so circumstanced. Service, in short, may be understood to mean, not exclusively personal effort in another's behalf, but any act whereby another is served, *i.e.* benefited, wholly irrespective of whether the act consist in onerous exertion, in the passive surrender of property to another's use, or in a mere utterance of words from which some useful or pleasant consequence may flow. "Service" thus fulfilled the first of the conditions required; and it is accordingly substituted by Bastiat for "human effort" in the exposition of his theory. "Value" is said to depend upon "service," and to vary with the magnitude of the "service;" and all exchange is described as an "exchange of services." In a word, what Bastiat did was this: having been at infinite pains to exclude gratuitous gifts of nature from the possible elements of value, and pointedly identified the phenomenon with "human effort" as its exclusive source, he designates human effort by the term "service," and then employs this term to admit as sources of value those very gratuitous natural gifts the exclusion of which in this capacity constituted the essence of his doctrine. I acknowledge it seems scarcely credible that a writer of Bastiat's distinguished reputation should put forward an elaborate speculation, purporting to be "a new exposition of economic science," in which principles established or accepted by a succession of eminent predecessors are challenged, and which should after all resolve itself into so gross a fallacy as this; but a few quotations will show whether I have overstated the case.

"To make an effort in order to satisfy another's want is to render him a service. If a service is stipulated in return, there is an exchange of services . . . . If the exchange is free, the two services exchanged are worth each other . . . . Less effort implies less service, and less service implies less value." *

So far he is propounding (doubtless in vague and somewhat equivocal terms, and without the due limitations) the doctrine of cost of production, and to this he for some time adheres; but, further on, we find this passage :—

"I take a walk along the sea-beach, and I find by chance a magnificent diamond. I am thus put in possession of a great value. Why? Am I about to confer a great benefit on the human race? Have I devoted myself to a long and laborious work? Neither the one nor the other. Why then does this diamond possess so much value? Undoubtedly because the person to whom I transfer it considers that I have rendered him a great *service*—all the greater that many rich people desire it, and that I alone can render it."

Here, it will be observed, he wholly abandons the idea of "effort" as the fundamental consideration. It is no longer "effort in satisfying another's want" that creates and measures the "service," but the capacity of the *natural object* in this respect in connection with the limitation set by *nature* to objects possessing this capacity. Further on, having to deal with the case of the high remuneration obtained by eminent *artistes*, he has these remarks :—

"Among the amusements which the people of Paris relish most is the pleasure of hearing the music of Rossini sung by Malibran or the admirable poetry of Racine interpreted by Rachel. There are in the world only two women who can

* Stirling's "Translation," pp. 44, 45.

furnish these noble and delicate kinds of entertainments, and unless we subject them to the torture, which would probably not succeed, we have no other way of procuring their services but by addressing ourselves to their good-will. Thus the services which we expect from Malibran and Rachel are possessed of great value." *

The reason assigned, it will be observed, being the same as in the case of the diamond—the power of satisfying a widely felt desire, coupled with the limitation of the number of persons possessing the natural endowments which give the power.

These, however, are rather "fancy" cases: the real hitch lies in the application of the theory to value in the case of land. I beg the reader's attention to Bastiat's mode of dealing with this point:—

"Land," he says, "has value, because it can no longer be acquired without giving in exchange the equivalent of this labour [the labour expended upon it]. But what I contend for is that this land, on which its natural productive powers had not originally conferred any value, has still no value in this respect. This natural power which was gratuitous then is gratuitous now, and will be always gratuitous. We may say that the land has *value*, but when we go to the root of the matter we find that what possesses value is the human labour which has improved the land, and the capital which has been expended on it." †

But then comes the question, which he puts into the mouth of an objector, how is this doctrine reconcilable with the fact of the value attaching to natural fertility?

"Everyone," says the objector, "who purchases a land estate examines its quality, and pays for it accordingly. If of two properties which lie alongside each other, the one consists

* Stirling's "Translation," p. 121. † Pp. 249, 250.

of rich alluvium, and the other of barren sand, the first is surely of more value than the second, although both may have absorbed the same capital, and, to say truth, the purchaser gives himself no trouble on that score." *

The objection is fairly stated; and now mark the answer:—

"The answer to the objection now under consideration is to be found in the theory of value explained in the fifth chapter of this work. I there said that value does not essentially imply labour; still less is it necessarily proportionate to labour. I have shown that the foundation of value is not so much the *pains taken* by the person who transfers it as the *pains saved* to the person who receives it; and it is for that reason that I have made it to reside in something which embraces these two elements—in *service*. I have said that a person may render a great service with very little effort, or that with a great effort one may render a very trifling service. The sole result is that labour does not obtain necessarily a remuneration which is in proportion to its intensity, in the case either of man in an isolated condition, or of man in the social state." †

In other words, the difficulty is surmounted through the equivocal meaning of "service," which, with curious *naïveté*, we are informed in this passage was selected by the philosopher expressly because its meaning was equivocal.

Now what is the significance and what the worth of a theory, of which the efficacy, as a means of elucidating phenomena, lies entirely in the shifting uses of an ambiguous term? After the concessions made in these passages, it is evident that there is no longer any question of fact between Bastiat and the

* Stirling's "Translation," p. 255. † P. 256.

economists whose views he controverts. In entire disregard of what he had contended for as a fundamental principle, he here admits that value depends upon other conditions than human effort—upon such condition as the degree of satisfaction which the valuable object or act is capable of conferring; upon such condition, again, as the degree of limitation set to the supply of natural objects or of acts depending upon natural endowment; lastly, upon such condition as the natural superiority of some agents furnished by nature over others—for this is what the explanation in the passage last quoted obviously comes to. After these concessions, I say, there is no longer between Bastiat and those whom he so vehemently controverts anything that can be called a question of fact; and yet the issue is very far from being verbal merely. The real difference is not as to the facts, nor yet as to the names by which the facts are to be called, but as to the method of dealing with them—a difference again which resolves itself into the different aims with which Bastiat and those whom he opposes have gone into the inquiry. Thus Ricardo, seeking to ascertain the laws to which exchange-value in its various manifestations conforms, analyses the various conditions under which the phenomenon is found to present itself, classifies them according to their essential distinctions, marking these distinctions by distinct names, and is thus enabled to show in what way and under what circumstances each class contributes to the ultimate result—the phenomenon of value. Bastiat, aiming, not at the interpretation of facts, but at the defence of a system, proceeds by a wholly different course—repudiates analysis, classification, distinctive nomenclature; nay, avowedly selects as the central term of his doctrine a word which designates combinations of facts of the most diverse character. The difference of aim leads to difference of method, and issues in a different result; for whereas Ricardo's doctrine *does* succeed in explaining a vast variety of the most important and most complicated facts of exchange-value, Bastiat's, I have no hesitation in asserting, fails to solve even the simplest case. Let us test it by an example:—I desire to know if the recent gold discoveries will lower the value of gold. How am I helped to this by being told that value represents "service," and is in proportion to "service"? "Service" may import half-a-dozen things—effort exerted, effort saved, satisfaction conferred by the possession of natural objects, limitation of supply, and various combinations of these—and its import in the case in hand I have no means of determining. Gold, it is true, is now obtained by less "effort" than formerly. With Ricardo's doctrine before me I know what interpretation to place upon that circumstance. Enlightened by Bastiat's, I am precluded from drawing any inference whatever; for though the effort of production has been diminished, it may not be on effort that "service" in this case depends: "On peut rendre un grand service avec un très-leger effort, comme avec un grand effort on peut ne rendre qu'un très-médiocre service." Take a simpler case still. A machine is invented which cheapens the production of cloth:—will this lower the value of cloth? It would be quite consistent with Bastiat's theory that it should not do so, because it would be open to him to say, as he does say in the case of the diamond and of Madame Malibran's singing, that though the effort of production was diminished, the satisfaction which the commodity was capable of conferring remained unaffected. To tell me then that value represents "service" and varies with "service" is to tell me nothing, unless I am told further the elements of "service" which are operative in the given case. This is what Ricardo's theory in effect does: this is what Bastiat's theory fails to do; and in this difference lies the entire difference between the two doctrines. It is much as if a chemist were to propound as a solution of the problem of the composition of bodies, that matter is composed of elementary atoms, omitting to classify the various forms of matter according to their elementary constitution, or to say in what proportion in each class the elements combine. Such a generalization is no generalization in the scientific sense of the term: it is a mere confounding of a crowd of unanalysed phenomena under an ambiguous word.

So utterly, so glaringly inadequate is Bastiat's Theory of Value as a means of explaining phenomena, that its enunciation by a reasoner of Bastiat's remarkable acuteness would be altogether inexplicable had economic explanation been his principal object. But this, as we have seen, if an object with Bastiat at all, was quite secondary in his scheme. His paramount aim was, in truth, not economic, but moral; he sought, not simply to explain, but also, and mainly, to justify the social facts which he undertook to expound. And this brings me to the second and more important *rôle* played by the term "service" in his theory. For service not merely designates a fact, but connotes a moral judgment. No one will deny that a man's services are properly his own—that he has a right to be remunerated for his services by him who requires to have them rendered to him; if, therefore, property is resolvable into the right to certain values, and values in all cases represent, and vary with, services, we have the moral sentiment at once enlisted in the support of property. To maintain property—property, let us say, in the ground-rent of houses in the centre of London—is to maintain the right of a man to the product of "services"—of "services" rendered to society by himself or by those from whom he has derived. To maintain freedom of contract is to maintain the right of one who has rendered "services" to exchange those "services" on such terms as he pleases against the "services" of others who are equally free. Thus all industrial and commercial operations under a *régime* of freedom were resolved by Bastiat into instances of the reciprocity of services—"*services pour services;*" than which, he asks, what can be more just? "*Services pour services*"—the phrase has the unmistakeable ring of an axiom of "natural justice." Like the "droit du travail," "a fair day's wages for a fair day's work," and other kindred expressions, it, so to speak, sounds in equity. Whatever can be brought under the formula of "*services pour services*" has already received its moral ratification. We see, then, what Bastiat really accomplished. By dint of such explanations as I have given examples of, he succeeded in bringing the principal phenomena of value within the comprehension of a single term; this term being one which, from its etymological associations, connoted a moral judgment on the facts to which it was applied. Armed with the shibboleth of *services pour services*, Bastiat felt himself strong to encounter Communists on their own ground, and was able to return in kind the bolts launched at him from the arsenal of the Rights of Man.

So much for the "new exposition of Political Economy," by which Bastiat proposed to defend social order menaced by socialistic attacks. The degree of faith which he placed in his specific is certainly surprising; for, however he may have failed to convince others, it is beyond question that he succeeded in fully convincing himself. He entirely believed that the Theory of Value set forth above contained the key to the social problem—furnished the sufficient foundation for a policy of the most rigid *laissez-faire*. Considered with reference to the practical purpose for which it was designed—as a corrective to the intoxicating appeals of socialistic writers—the antidote must, I think, be pronounced to be extraordinarily weak, a veritable pill to cure an earthquake. Nor would it seem that Bastiat's writings have produced any sensible impression upon the general course of economic thought in France. He has left no school, and even those who yield a general assent to his system for the most part qualify their adhesion by reservations on essential points. The most important of recent French treatises on Political Economy—those, *e.g.*, of M. Cherbuliez and of M. Courcelle-Seneuil—scarcely refer to him, and, when they do, it is for the purpose of refutation. It will, perhaps, occur to the reader that there was little need, under these circumstances, for the somewhat elaborate examination of his system of economic philosophy attempted in the foregoing pages. It may be said of Bastiat, however, as of some other eminent French thinkers, that Englishmen seem disposed to attach greater weight to his authority than it finds amongst his own countrymen; and it happens that his capital doctrine is in immediate contact with one of the most urgent of our own social questions—that of land-tenure reform. Since the free-trade controversy was settled, no question has come up for political discussion on which economic theory has a more direct and decisive bearing than on this. It is evident that the nature and extent of the prospective reform will mainly be determined by the economic standpoint from which the question is regarded—according, that is to say, as it is regarded from the standpoint of absolute property and commercial contract, or from that which recognizes a fundamental distinction between land and the ordinary products of industry. The latter view flows as an immediate corollary from the theory of rent propounded by Ricardo—one of those "pretty problems," by the way, which some eminent authorities would rank, as regards its social importance, with "the resolution of double stars," and "theories of irregular verbs." The former—the absolute property and commercial contract view of the case—can, on the other hand, only find its justification in some theory tantamount to Bastiat's, of which the capital feature is the identification of value, and, therefore, of property, in all its forms, as a phenomenon depending on the same causes, a product of the same essential conditions. Accept Bastiat's theory of value, and for any reform in land beyond the assimilation of real and personal property (for thus far it does carry us) we are without scientific warrant. The principle which governs contracts in the case of moveable wealth must be allowed to govern them in the case of land. The Irish Land Act, and all legislation in the same direction, are, of course, in this view, an injustice and a blunder. Such is one of the practical bearings of Bastiat's doctrine; and Bastiat's reputation in this country being what it is, it has seemed to me not out of place—more especially in the presence of fresh translations of his principal work—to attempt some estimate of the scientific value of his speculation.

APPENDICES.

A.

PRODUCTS OF VICTORIA—*Prices in Melbourne.**

	Sheep, wethers, each.	Cows and Heifers, each.	Bullocks, working, per pair.	Hay, per ton.	Bread, retail, per 4 lb. loaf.	Beef, retail, per lb.	Mutton, retail, per lb.	Butter, fresh, per lb.	Eggs, per dozen.	Turkeys, each.	Ducks, per couple.	Fowl, per couple.	Potatoes, wholesale, per cwt.	Potatoes, retail, per lb.	Carrots, per bunch.	Turnips, per bunch.	Cabbages, each.
	s. s.	£ £	£ £	£ £	d. d.	d. d.	d. d.	d. d.	s. d.	s. s.	s. s.	s. s.	s. d. s. d.	d.	d.	d.	d.
Pre-gold period	4 to 5	1 to 3	8 to 14	2 to 5	5 to 8	1 to 2	1 to 2	12 to 18	0 9	7 to 9	2 to 5	2 to 4	6 6 to 8 0	1	6	2	2
Single Average	4s. 6d.	£2 10s.	£11 0s.	£3 10s.	6½	1½	1½	15	0 9	8s. 0d.	3s. 6d.	3s. 0d.	7s. 3d.	1	6	2	2
1851	—	—	—	8 10	12	—	—	—	1 3	6 9	3 0	4 0	8 0	2½	6	1½	4½
1852	5 6	5 10	19 0	10 0	16	4	4½	24	2 0	8 3	10 0	9 0	13 0	10	3½	2½	8
1853	14 3	11 10	31 0	29 0	21	6½	6½	43½	3 0	17 0	14 0	14 6	23 6	15	6½	6	19
1854	13 3	8 13	30 0	33 0	10½	8	8	43½	2 6	23 4	22 8	20 0	23 4	5½	9½	7½	3½
1855	16 8	8 7	—	15 0	10½	6	5½	44	3 0	27 6	18 0	22 6	17 4	4	6	3½	6
1856	18 4	7 0	29 3	8 0	17	5	5	39	4 11	17 6	16 6	10 0	10 0	3½	3½	7½	4
August, 1858	23 0	7 5	23 10	7 10	—	6½	7½	39	4 0	22 6	9 0	9 0	13 6	—	3	6	17
October, 1858	23 0	6 0	18 0	6 0	10½	9½	7	33	2 0	20 0	14 0	9 0	—	6	3½	2½	10
	s. d.	£ s. d.	£ s.	£ s.	d.	d.	d.	d.	s. d.	s. d.	s. d.	d.	s. d.	d.	d.	d.	d.
Average of 1858	24 0	6 11 6	20 3	6 15	10½	8	6½	36	3 0	21 3	10 0	9	13 6	6	3½	4½	1[illegible]

The first line, showing prices in the pre-gold period, is taken from the tables in the "History of Prices," vol. vi. pp. 830-41, slightly altered in some instances in conformity with returns given by Mr. Westgarth. The remaining figures to 1856 are averages taken from the same tables. The two last quotations are taken from the local papers.

* Wool and Tallow have been omitted from this table by an oversight; but it may be stated that their prices have not differed very materially from those of home wool and tallow; the explanation of which is, that these articles are merely parts of a larger production, namely cattle, which, it will be seen, have advanced in a threefold proportion; the rise in beef and mutton compensating the comparatively stationary condition of the other elements of the products.

B. PRODUCTS OF THE UNITED KINGDOM.—*Forty Commodities.*

	PROVISIONS.			Butcher's Meat at Leadenhall and Newgate Markets, by the carcase.		RAW MATERIALS.				METALS.			
	Butter, Waterford, per cwt.	Bacon, Waterford, per cwt.	Pork, small, by the carcase, per 8 lbs.	Beef, per lb.	Mutton, per lb.	Leather, English Butts, 16-24, per lb.	Tallow, Home, per cwt.	Wool, Fleeces, South Down, per pack of 240 lbs.	Soda Ash, per cwt.	Copper, Tough cake, per ton.	Iron, British Bars, per ton.	Lead, English Pig, per ton.	Tin, English Bars, per ton.
	s. s.	s. s.	s. d.	d.	d.	s. d. s. d.	s. d.	£ s. £ s.	s. d.	£ s.	£ s. £ s.	£ s.	£
1849—January	70 to 78	54 to 57	4 3	4½	3½	0 9 to 1 4	44 0	10 0 to 11 0	9 11	79 10	6 0	15 15	80
" April	56 – 60	58 – 59	3 9	4½	3½	0 9 – 1 4	—	11 10 – 12 10	—	88 10	6 15 to 6 17	15 17	90
" June	68 – 70	60 – 64	3 10	4	5	0 9 – 1 4	40 6	11 12	9 9	79 10	5 10 – 6 10	15 8	74
" October	66 – 70	48 – 56	4 1	4½	5	0 9 – 1 4	30 8	11 10	9 11	84 0	6 0	15 17	74
1850—January	66 – 70	40 – 47	3 9	4½	4½	0 9 – 1 4	38 1	12 10 to 13 10	10 3	84 0	6 0	15 17	85
" April	66 – 70	44 – 48	3 9	3½	4½	0 9 – 1 4	—	12 10 – 13 10	—	88 0	5 17 – 5 18	18 0	81
" July	62 – 66	40 – 60	3 9	4½	4½	0 9 – 1 4	38 4	12 0 – 13 10	10 3	84 0	5 17 – 5 18	16 0	78
" October	72 – 76	46 – 52	4 1	4	4½	0 9 – 1 4	39 6	13 10 – 14 10	9 9	79 0	5 7 – 5 10	17 1	81
1851—January	78 – 80	43 – 45	3 10	4	4½	0 10½ – 1 4	39 7	13 10 – 14 10	9 7	84 0	5 15 – 5 16	17 10	84
" April	76 – 78	48 – 54	3 9	4	4½	0 11 – 1 4	—	14 0 – 14 10	—	84 0	5 15 – 5 16	17 11	83
" July	72 – 74	52 – 56	3 7	4	4½	0 10½ – 1 4½	40 3	14 0 – 14 10	9 6	84 0	5 7	17 0	83
" October	74 – 76	50 – 53	3 8	4	4½	0 10½ – 1 4½	39 0	13 0 – 13 10	9 6	84 0	5 7	17 0	83
	s. d.	s. d.	s. d.	d.	d.	s. d.	s. d.	£ s. d.	s. d.	£ s. d.	£ s.	£ s. d.	£ s.
Average of three years, 1849, '50, '51	70 8	54 3	3 10	4½	4½	1 0½	39 10	12 17 1	9 10	83 11 6	5 17	16 16 7	81 5
1852—January	72 to 76	41 to 45	3 9	4½	4½	0 10 to 1 4	38 3	13 0 to 14 10	8 6	88 0	5 0	16 17	90
" July	64 – 68	56 – 58	3 6	4½	5	0 10½ – 1 4½	44 4	14 10 – 15 10	8 5	102 10	5 10	17 10	98
1853—January	80 – 86	51 – 59	3 7	4½	5½	0 10½ – 1 4	41 6	17 10 – 18 10	8 8	107 10	10 0	24 0	107
" July	84	64	5 0	5½	6	1 3 – 1 7	37 8	17 0 – 18 0	9 3	107 10	9 0	23 0	124
1854—January	104	60 to 63	4 8	5½	5½	1 3 – 1 6	64 6	15 10 – 16 0	9 6	126 0	9 5 to 9 10	23 10	130
" July	100 to 104	58 – 61	4 8	5½	6½	1 3 – 1 6	64 0	12 0 – 13 10	8 6	126 0	10 10	24 15	130
1855—January	104	—	—	5½	5½	—	56 0	12 10 – 13 10	8 6	126 0	8 10	23 0	119
" July	100	—	—	5½	6	—	66 6	14 0 – 15 0	8 11	126 0	8 15	22 10	111
1856—January	104 to 108	—	—	5½	5½	—	54 9	14 10 – 15 0	9 3	126 0	8 17 to 9 0	25 15	130
" July	104	—	—	5½	6	—	51 6	17 10 – 18 0	9 3	107 10	8 15 – 9 0	25 15	130
1857—January	110 to [illegible]	64 to 67	4 11	5½	6½	[illegible]	68 6	[illegible]	9 6	133 0	8 17 – [illegible]	23 0	[illegible]
" April	100	73 – 74	4 10	5½	5½	1 0 – 1 7	—	21 10 – 22 0	—	135 0	8 10 – 8 15	24 15	147
" July	98 to 100	74 – 78	4 5	5½	5½	1 1 – 1 6	60 6	19 0	10 6	117 0	8 5	25 5	131
" October	106 – 110	78 – 80	4 11	5½	5½	1 0 – 1 3	59 0	20 0 – 21 0	11 6	121 10	8 5 to 8 10	24 7	141
1858—January	106 – 112	54 – 58	4 0	5½	5½	1 6 – 1 8	58 0	13 0	9 6	107 0	7 0 – 7 10	21 0	119
" April	112 – 114	56 – 60	3 8	4½	5½	1 0 – 1 10	—	13 0 to 14 0	—	107 0	7 0 – 7 10	22 10	113
" July	108 – 112	68 – 70	3 6	5½	5½	1 0 – 1 10	52 0	14 10 – 15 0	10 3	107 10	7 0 – 7 5	21 15	119
" September	104 – 106	63 – 64	3 10	5½	5½	1 0 – 1 9	52 0	15 0 – 16 0	10 3	102 10	7 0 – 8 0	21 10	119
	s. d.	s. d.	s. d.	d.	d.	s. d.	s. d.	£ s. d.	s.	£ s.	£ s. d.	£ s. d.	£
Average price, 1858	109 3	61 6	3 10½	5½	5½	1 6½	53 4	16 3 9	10	108 10	7 5 7½	21 3 9	119

B (*continued*). PRODUCTS OF THE UNITED KINGDOM.

	P — * MANCHESTER MANUFACTURES.								P — LINEN MANUFACTURES.					
	No. 40 Mule Yarn, fair and quality, per lb.	No. 30 Water Twist, fair and quality, per lb.	⅞ Printer's 66 reed, 29 yards.	⅞ Shirting, 66 reed, 37½ yards.	32-in T cloths, 24 yards.	39 in. Domestics, 60 yards.	Good Seconds, Water Twist, 60 yards.	Good Seconds, Mule Twist, 60 yards.	Frontings.	Hucks.	Drills.	¾ Linens.	Sheeting.	Bed Ticks.
									per yard.					
	d.	d.	s. d. s. d.	s. d. s. d.	s. d. s. d.	d. d.	d. d.	d. d.	d.	d.	d.	d.	s. d.	d.
1849—January	[illegible]	7	.. ..	.. ..	.. ..	..	..	..	4½	5½	5½	5½	[illegible]	9½
" April	[illegible]	7	.. ..	.. ..	.. ..	..	..	..	4	5	5½	4½	[illegible]	9½
" July	[illegible]	7	.. ..	.. ..	.. ..	..	..	..	3½	4½	5	6	[illegible]	9
" October	9	8	.. ..	.. ..	.. ..	..	..	..	3½	4	5	6½	[illegible]	8½
1850—January	10	9	.. ..	.. ..	.. ..	..	..	..	3½	4½	5½	5	[illegible]	9
" April	10½	9	4 9 to 5 3	8 0 to 8 9	3 9 to 4 0	1½ to 3½	8½ to 8½	10½ to 10½	3½	4½	5	5½	[illegible]	9
" July	11½	11	.. ..	.. ..	.. ..	..	..	..	..	..	..	..	..	..
" October	11	11	.. ..	.. ..	.. ..	..	..	..	..	5½	5½	5½	[illegible]	9½
1851—January	11	11	.. ..	.. ..	.. ..	..	..	..	3½	5½	5½	5½	[illegible]	9½
" April	11	10	4 8 to 5 0	8 3 to 9 0	4 1½ to 4 4½	[illegible] to 4	9½ to 10	11½ to 11½	..	..	..	..	..	..
" July	9½	9	.. ..	.. ..	.. ..	..	..	..	3½	5	5½	5½	[illegible]	9
" October	9	9	.. ..	.. ..	.. ..	..	..	..	3½	5½	5½	5½	[illegible]	9½
Average price of three years, 1849, '50, '51	d. 10	d. 9½	s. d. 4 10½	s. d. 9 0	s. d. 4 0½	d. [illegible]	d. 9	d. 10½	d. 3½	d. 5	d. 5½	d. 5½	s. d. 1 1½	d. 5½
1852—January	9	9	4 4½ to 5 0	7 3 to 8 6	3 4 to 3 9	1½ to 4	7½ to 8	8½ to 8½	3½	5½	5½	5½	[illegible]	9
" July	9½	9	.. ..	.. ..	.. ..	..	..	..	3½	4½	4½	5	[illegible]	8½
1853—January	9½	9	4 10½ to 5 3	7 6 to 8 9	3 4½ to 3 10½	[illegible] to 3	8½ to 8½	9½ to 9½	..	..	..	..	..	..
" July	10	9	.. ..	.. ..	.. ..	..	..	..	..	..	..	..	..	..
1854—January	9	9	4 3 to 5 0	7 3 to 8 6	3 6 to 3 10½	[illegible] to 3	7½ to 8½	9 to 9½	3½	..	5½	5½	[illegible]	9
" July	9	9	.. ..	.. ..	.. ..	..	..	..	4	5½	5½	5½	[illegible]	9½
1855—January	[illegible]	..	3 9 to 4 6	7 0 to 8 0	[illegible] to 3 5	1½ to [illegible]	7½ to 7½	8½ to 9	..	..	..	..	..	..
" July	9	..	.. ..	.. ..	.. ..	..	..	..	..	..	..	..	..	..
1856—January	9	..	4 3 to 5 0	7 0 to 8 4½	3 1½ to 3 9	1½ to [illegible]	8½ to 8½	9½ to 9½	3½	5½	5½	5½	[illegible]	9½
" July	10	..	.. ..	.. ..	.. ..	..	..	..	4½	..	5½	5½	[illegible]	9½
1857—January	11	10	.. ..	.. ..	.. ..	..	..	..	..	..	..	..	[illegible]	..
" April	12	11	4 7½ to 5 7½	8 6 to 9 9	3 9 to 4 3	[illegible] to 3½	8½ to 9½	11 to 11½	..	..	..	6½	..	..
" July	12½	11	.. ..	.. ..	.. ..	..	..	..	4½	5½	5½	6½	[illegible]	9½
" October	13	11	.. ..	.. ..	.. ..	..	..	..	4½	5½	5½	6	[illegible]	9
1858—January	10	9	.. ..	.. ..	.. ..	..	..	..	..	..	..	..	..	..
" April	11	10	4 4½ to 5 3	8 3 to 9 4½	3 9 to 4 7½	[illegible] to 3½	8½ to 9½	10½ to 10½	3½	5½	5½	5½	[illegible]	8½
" July	11	11	.. ..	.. ..	.. ..	..	..	..	3½	..	..	..	..	..
" September	11	11½	.. ..	.. ..	.. ..	..	..	..	4½	5½	5½	6½	[illegible]	9½
Average price of 1858	d. 11½	d. 10½	s. d. 4 9½	s. d. 8 9½	s. d. 4 4½	d. [illegible]	d. 9	d. 11	d. 4	d. 5½	d. 5½	d. 5½	s. d. [illegible]	d. 8½

* Average prices during the early months of each year.

B (*concluded*). PRODUCTS OF THE UNITED KINGDOM.

	GRAIN.								WEST INDIES.				
	Wheat,* per imperial quarter.	Barley,* per imperial quarter.	Oats,* per imperial quarter.	Rye, per imperial quarter.	Beans, per imperial quarter.	Peas, per imperial quarter.	† Whiskey, Patent Still, per proof gallon (bond).	Turpentine, English Spirits, without casks.	Coffee, Jamaica, fine ord. to middling, per cwt. (in bond).	Rum (Jamaica) 10 to 20 O.P. per gallon (bond).	Logwood (Jamaica), per ton.	Sugar, B.P. Brown, per cwt. (bond).	Sugar, B.P. good and fine, per cwt. (bond).
	s. d.	s. d.	s. d.	s. d.	s. d.	s. d.	s. d.	s. d.	s. d. s. d.	s. d. s. d.	£ s.	s. d. s. d.	s. d. s. d.
1849—January	46 10	27 9	17 6	28 6	33 11	38 9	..	30 3	38 0 to 46 0	1 6 to 1 10	3 15	20 0 to 22 0	21 0 to 26 0
" April	..	..	..	26 5	28 1	39 6	..	33 3	35 0 " 44 0	1 6 " 1 10	4 17	21 0 " 25 6	25 6 " 27 6
" July	45 1	..	..	28 1	30 1	33 10	..	31 9	35 0 " 44 0	1 3 " 1 8	4 15	24 0 " 25 6	28 6 " 29 0
" October	..	..	..	25 9	29 1	31 8	1 5½	30 9	36 0 " 48 0	1 3 " 1 8	4 15	23 0 " 24 0	24 0 " 27 0
1850—January	41 3	23 5	16 6	24 11	26 11	28 5	1 6	31 3	50 0 " 56 0	1 3 " 1 8	6 7	21 6 " 24 0	25 0 " 27 0
" April	..	..	..	21 6	27 8	24 5	1 4½	30 0	50 0 " 56 0	1 3 " 1 8	6 7	22 0 " 24 0	24 0 " 27 0
" July	38 11	..	..	23 8	26 10	28 4	1 4½	29 6	40 0 " 46 0	1 3 " 1 8	4 7	22 0 " 23 6	24 0 " 28 0
" October	..	..	..	20 7	25 6	30 0	1 6	29 9	50 0 " 56 0	1 3 " 1 8	3 15	24 6 " 26 6	27 0 " 30 0
1851—January	41 5	24 9	18 7	22 8	27 5	28 1	1 6	30 9	53 0 " 58 0	§1 8 " 2 8	3 15	26 0 " 28 0	29 6 " 33 0
" April	..	..	..	18 5	25 7	24 6	1 4½	33 9	41 0 " 41 0	§1 6 " 2 8	3 15	23 0 " 27 6	29 0 " 32 0
" July	38 6	..	..	26 11	24 1	29 1	1 6½	33 9	43 0 " 46 0	§1 6 " 2 8	3 7	23 0 " 24 0	30 0 " 28 0
" October	..	..	..	25 0	27 8	26 7	1 6½	33 3	40 6 " 42 0	§1 4 " 1 6	3 7	20 0 " 23 6	29 0 " 30 0
	s. d.	s. d.	s. d.	s. d.	s. d.	s. d.	s. d.	s. d.	s. d.	s. d.	£ s. d.	s. d.	s. d.
Average price of three years, 1849, '50, '51	43 0	25 3½	17 6	25 9	28 7	29 0	1 5½	31 8	45 6	1 6½	4 1 10	23 10	27 –
1852—January	38 7	28 6	19 1	28 1	27 1	29 0	1 7½	31 0	44 0 to 47 6	§2 2 to 2 4	3 7	18 0 to 22 0	22 0 to 26 0
" July	40 11	..	..	31 0	38 4	38 0	1 10½	30 9	41 0 " 43 6	§2 0 " 2 7	3 7	17 6 " 22 0	20 0 " 26 6
1853—January	40 10	33 7	21 0	30 7	34 6	37 0	1 10½	48 3	48 0 " 59 0	§2 8 " 2 10	4 0	22 0 " 25 0	25 0 " 30 0
" July	45 0	..	..	36 9	43 0	41 6	1 1	60 0	50 0 " 58 0	§2 8 " 2 10	5 7	20 6 " 23 6	24 0 " 28 6
1854—January	60 11	36 0	27 11	47 5	46 0	50 3	1 3	57 0	51 0 " 60 0	4 4 " 4 6	5 10	22 6 " 25 0	25 6 " 29 0
" July	79 1	..	..	49 10	45 11	48 7	1 3	54 3	50 0 " 58 0	2 9 " 3 0	7 6	25 6 " 25 0	25 6 " 29 0
1855—January	65 8	34 9	27 5	..	..	..	1 5	..	49 0 " 58 0	4 0 " 4 6	6 10	..	..
" July	71 7	..	..	..	..	..	1 8	..	51 0 " 60 0	3 6 " 3 9	4 11	..	..
1856—January	77 7	41 1	25 7	..	..	..	1 4½	..	54 0 " 63 0	§3 8 " 4 0	6 5	..	..
" July	72 8	..	..	..	..	..	1 4½	..	54 0 " 61 0	§3 0 " 3 3	6 15	..	..
1857—January	67 9	41 1	25 0	39 7	41 1	40 9	1 8	43 8	58 0 " 67 0	§3 8 " 3 10	5 0	36 6 " 37 6	37 6 " 41 0
" April	..	..	..	37 8	39 4	39 1	1 6	39 9	66 0 " 73 0	§4 3 " 4 9	5 0	34 0 " 37 6	37 6 " 40 0
" July	56 9	..	..	41 11	45 11	44 5	1 7	43 0	68 0 " 80 0	§4 6 " 4 9	5 5	39 0 " 43 0	41 0 " 47 0
" October	..	..	..	35 6	41 6	43 4	1 11½	39 6	66 0 " 75 0	§3 10 " 4 4	5 0	30 6 " 34 0	34 0 " 42 0
1858—January	47 7	31 10	23 8	30 1	39 1	32 4	1 11½	31 0	50 0 " 60 0	§3 8 " 4 0	5 5	21 6 " 26 0	27 6 " 33 0
" April	44 5	30 10	23 5	31 1	40 4	41 9	1 8½	40 0	58 0 " 69 0	§3 8 " 4 0	5 5	21 6 " 26 0	29 0 " 33 0
" July	43 0	30 1	25 10	33 10	41 3	40 3	1 8	43 0	58 0 " 70 0	§3 4 " 3 8	5 5	19 0 " 24 0	26 6 " 30 6
" September	45 3	34 0	27 3	34 6	46 7	45 1	1 0	30 9	55 0 " 70 0	§3 2 " 3 6	5 5	22 0 " 26 6	26 6 " 32 0
	s. d.	s. d.	s. d.	s. d.	s. d.	s. d.	s. d.	s. d.	s. d.	s. d.	£ s.	s. d.	s.
Average price of 1858	45 4½	34 3¼	24 11¼	32 11	41 7½	40 10½	1 9¼	38 1¾	60 9	3 7½	5 5	23 6	30

* The figures in these columns represent averages. † The dates for Whiskey are January, March, October, and December for each year.
‡ After January 1856, twopence added to compensate change in law. § 15 to 25 O.P.

C. PRODUCTS OF NORTH AMERICA.—*Ten Commodities.*

	Cotton Wool. Middling Orleans, per lb.	Cotton Wool. Fair Orleans, per lb.	Ashes, First Sort Pearl, U.S. per cwt.	Duty 1s. per load. Timber, Canadian red pine, per load	Resin, American, per cwt.	Tobacco, Maryland, per lb. bond.	Tobacco, Virginia, per lb. bond.	Beef, American and Canadian, per tierce.	Pork, American and Canadian, per barrel.	Indian Corn, Yellow American, per quarter.	Rice, Carolina (American dressed), per cwt.
	d.	d.	s. d.	s. s.	s. d.	d. d.	d. d.	s. d.	s. s.	s. s.	s. d. s. d.
1849—January	4½	4½	35 9	60 to 70	6 8	4 to 5	3½ to 6	91 0	40 to 65	31 to 36	18 6 to 20 6
" April	4	4	36 [illegible]	58 " 65	..	4 " 5	3½ " 6	80 6	60 " 70	28 " 30	18 6 " 19 0
" July	4½	5½	35 6	58 " 65	5 6	4 " 6½	4 " 5½	80 6	60 " 70	28 " 31	20 0
" October	6½	6½	37 [illegible]	60 " 65	5 0	4 " 6½	4 " 7½	80 6	60 " 70	25 " 26	21 6 to 23 6
1850—January	6½	7½	36 6	60 " 78	6 0	4 " 6½	4½ " 8	85 6	60 " 70	27 " 28	22 6 " 25 0
" April	6½	7	32 6	55 " 70	..	5½ " 6½	4½ " 6½	80 6	62	27 " 27	19 6 " 25 6
" July	7½	7½	27 6	57 " 65	5 11	5½ " 6½	4½ " 6½	80 6	54 to 60	27 " 28	21 6 " 27 6
" October	7½	8	31 3	55 " 65	5 6	5½ " 6½	7 " 10	85 6	..	27 " 28	21 6 " 27 6
1851—January	7½	7½	30 9	57 " 70	6 3	5 " 11	4½ " 18	80 6	..	28 " 30	17 6 " 28 0
" April	6	7	28 9	57 " 70	..	6 " 9	4½ " 18	80 6	..	28 " 30	16 0 " 26 6
" July	4½	5½	30 6	55 " 65	6 8	6 " 9	4½ " 18	82 6	..	29 " 30	26 6
" October	4½	5½	29 9	57 " 80	5 0	5½ " 9	4 " 11	80 6	..	27 " 28	20 6 to 26 6
Average price of three years, 1849, '50, 51	d. 6	d. 6½	s. d. 31 8½	s. d. 62 1	s. d. 6 4	d. 6	d. 6½	s. d. 83 6	s. d. 62 1	s. d. 28 7	s. d. 20 10
1852—January	4½	4½	28 3	45 to 57	6 6	3½ to 9	2½ to 9	80 6	..	25 to 28	..
" July	5½	6½	27 9	53 " 57	3 4	3½ " 8	2½ " 8½	..	..	29 " 30	21 6 to 28 6
1853—January	5½	6½	27 9	60 " 80	6 7	3½ " 8	2½ " 9½	121 0	..	30 " 32	21 6 " 31 6
" July	6½	7	28 3	80 " 95	8 6	3½ " 8	2½ " 15	137 6	..	33 " 38	21 0 " 37 0
1854—January	5½	6½	30 3	90 " 105	9 0	3½ " 8	2½ " 11	137 6	63	45 " 48	21 0 " 37 0
" July	5½	6½	30 3	90 " 105	7 3	3½ " 8	2½ " 10	137 6	63	48 " 50	20 0 " 37 0
1855—January	5½	5½	33 6	..	7 6	..	4 " 11	137 6	..	..	..
" July	6½	7	34 0	..	7 0	..	4 " 10½	157 6	..	..	..
1856—January	6½	6½	43 6	..	7 6	..	4 " 10½	157 6	..	..	..
" July	6½	7	42 0	..	10 0	..	4 " 11	160 0	..	..	..
1857—January	7½	8	43 6	80 to 90	8 3	7 to 9	8 to 11	160 0	80	..	23 6 to 27 6
" April	7½	8½	42 6	80 " 90	..	7 " 9	8 " 12	130 0	80	..	23 0 " 27 0
" July	8½	8½	45 0	70 " 90	8 3	7 " 9	8 " 11	130 0	80	36 to 38	21 6 " 28 0
" October	8½	8½	44 3	70 " 90	8 6	7 " 9	8 " 11	..	..	35 " 36	21 6 " 27 6
1858—January	6½	6½	36 0	70 " 80	9 6	7 " 9	8 " 11	..	..	30 " 35	20 0 " 28 0
" April	6½	7½	37 0	70 " 80	..	6 " 9	6 " 11	..	..	32 " 34	20 0 " 23 6
" July	7	7½	36 10	70 " 80	8 0	6 " 9	6 " 11	..	72	32 " 34	20 0 " 24 0
" September	7½	7½	36 10	70 " 80	11 6	6 " 9	6 " 11	120 0	..	34 " 36	20 6 " 25 0
Average price of 1858	d. 6½	d. 7½	s. d. 37 6	s. d. 73 9	s. d. 9 8	d. 7½	d. 8½	s. 120	s. 72	s. 34	s. d. 20 7

D. PRODUCTS OF CONTINENTAL EUROPE.—*Fifteen Commodities.*

	P. T. B. Flax, Riga, per ton.	Hemp, St. Petersburg, clean, per ton.	Hides, Riga, Russia, dry, per lb.	Leather, Foreign Butts, 16-56, per lb.	Oils, Gallipoli, per 252 gallons.	Oil, Seal pale, per 252 gallons.	Oil, Palm, per 252 gallons.	P. Tallow, Russian, per cwt.
	£ £	£ s. £ s.	s. d. s. d.	s. d. s. d.	£ s.	£ s.	£ s.	s. d.
1849—January	34 to 40	31 10	0 9 to 0 9½	0 9 to 1 1	40 10	36 10	30 10	44 0
„ April	34 to 40	30 0 to 30 5	9	0 9 to 1 1	42 5	32 5	34 5	..
„ July	34 to 40	31 0	9	0 9 to 1 1	41 5	32 15	30 10	39 6
„ October	34 to 38	28 10 to 28 15	0 8 to 0 10	0 9 to 1 1	44 15	30 5	30 15	38 6
1850—January	34 to 42	30 10 to 31 0	0 9 to 0 10	0 9 to 1 1	48 5	30 5	32 5	38 6
„ April	38 to 46	31 0 to 31 10	0 9 to 0 10	0 9 to 1 1	47 8	37 5	32 17	..
„ July	38 to 46	30 5	0 9 to 0 9½	0 9 to 1 1	41 15	32 [illegible]	30 5	38 0
„ October	38 to 46	30 0 to 31 0	0 9 to 0 9½	0 9 to 1 1	43 15	32 5	30 [illegible]	37 6
1851—January	38 to 46	30 0 to 30 10	0 9 to 0 9½	0 10 to 1 1	43 5	37 5	28 15	40 4
„ April	39 to 48	30 0 to 30 10	0 9 to 0 9½	0 10½ to 1 1	42 5	32 17	28 15	..
„ July	42 to 48	30 0 to 30 10	0 9 to 0 9½	0 10½ to 1 1	38 15	31 5	28 8	39 5
„ October	42 to 48	31 0	0 9 to 0 9½	0 10½ to 1 1	40 5	32 10	27 15	39 4
Average price of three years, 1849, '50, '51	£ s. d. 40 10 10	£ s. d. 30 1 3	d. 9½	d. 11½	£ s. d. 42 18 9	£ s. d. 33 4 5	£ s. d. 30 6 7	s. d. 39 9
1852—January	47 to 48	31 10 to 31 0	0 8 to 0 9½	0 10½ to 1 1	44 5	30 5	36 17	37 10
„ July	42 to 53	30 0 to 30 10	0 8 to 0 8½	0 10 to 1 0	46 17	35 15	38 12	44 4
1853—January	42 to 53	34 15 to 39 0	0 8 to 0 8½	0 10 to 1 0	50 10	35 15	34 5	47 0
„ July	.. ..	35 0 to 36 5	0 10½ to 0 10½	1 3 to 1 5	67 10	32 17	40 5	56 6
1854—January	55 to 52	41 10 to 40 0	0 10½ to 0 10½	1 0 to 1 5	63 5	41 0	42 15	64 0
„ July	55 to 58	62 0 to 63 10	0 10½ to 0 11	1 0 to 1 5	58 10	40 0	46 5	65 0
1855—January	57 to 58	55 0 to 58 0	.. ..	.. ..	57 15	47 5	48 0	57 0
„ July	57 to 56	46 0 to 47 0	.. ..	.. ..	56 5	53 5	42 0	72 0
1856—January	51 to 54	43 0 to 42 12	.. ..	.. ..	53 15	56 5	48 10	51 0
„ July	53 to 54	33 0 to 35 0	.. ..	.. ..	57 5	48 15	46 0	56 6
1857—January	50 to 53	36 0 to 37 0	1 9½ to 1 3½	1 11 to 0 4	60 5	49 15	42 15	63 [illegible]
„ April	52 to 53	35 0 to 36 0	1 9½ to 1 9½	1 11 to 2 4	58 5	48 15	45 5	..
„ July	55 to 56	32 0 to 34 10	1 9 to 1 3	1 11 to 2 3	57 5	45 0	46 5	60 0
„ October	56 to 56	32 0 to 32 0	1 0 to 1 9	1 8 to 1 10	62 10	43 15	40 5	59 6
1858—January	53	29 10	0 11 to 1 0	1 0 to 1 0	50 10	39 0	39 10	58 0
„ April	50	30 0	0 8 to 0 9½	1 0 to 1 9	47 10	33 15	31 15	..
„ July	58	29 0	0 8 to 0 9½	1 0 to 1 9	45 0	37 15	38 15	53 6
„ September	55 to 61	30 0	0 8 to 0 9½	1 2 to 1 9	45 5	38 10	33 5	51 9
Average price of 1858	£ 55	£ s. d. 29 12 6	d. 9½	s. d. 1 0½	£ s. d. 47 6 3	£ s. 38 10	£ s. d. 33 6 3	£ s. 53 0

D (*concluded*). PRODUCTS OF CONTINENTAL EUROPE.

	Tallow, St. Petersburg, New Y. C., per cwt.	Timber, Dantzic and Memel fir, per load (hewn).	WOOL. German, 1st and 2nd elect, per lb.	WOOL. (Sheep's) Northern Germany, Inferior, per lb.	Tar, Stockholm, per barrel.	Iron, Swedish, per ton.	Steel, Swedish, in Kegs, per ton.
	s. d. s. d.	*s. d. s. d.*	*s. d. s. d.*	*s. d.*	*s. d. s. d.*	*£ s. £ s.*	*£ s.*
1849—January	41 6 to 43 0	60 0 to 70 0	2 9 to 4 3	1 9	17 0 to 17 3	10 15 to 11 5	15 10
" April	38 6 " 38 9	60 0 " 75 0	2 10 " 4 4	1 10	17 6 " 18 0	11 0 " 11 10	14 0
" July	38 3 " 38 6	60 0 " 75 0	2 10 " 3 6	1 7½	16 6 " 17 0	11 0	14 0
" October	37 6 " 38 0	60 0 " 70 0	2 10 " 3 6	1 7½	16 0 " 16 3	11 0 to 11 10	14 0
1850—January	38 9 " 39 0	60 0 " 70 0	3 6 " 4 6	1 5	16 9 " 17 0	11 0 " 11 10	14 5
" April	36 9 " 37 0	55 0 " 70 0	3 3 " 4 6	[illegible]	16 9 " 17 0	11 10	14 5
" July	36 9 " 37 0	55 0 " 65 0	3 3 " 4 6	[illegible]	17 0 " 17 3	11 5	14 10
" October	38 3 " 38 6	55 0 " 65 0	3 3 " 4 6	[illegible]	19 0 " 19 6	11 10 to 11 15	14 0
1851—January	37 3 " 37 6	60 0 " 70 0	3 3 " 4 6	[illegible]	20 6 " 21 0	11 15	14 17
" April	40 0 " 40 3	60 0 " 75 0	3 3 " 4 6	[illegible]	19 0 " 19 6	11 15	14 17
" July	37 6 " 37 9	50 0 " 65 0	3 3 " 4 6	[illegible]	17 6 " 18 0	11 15	14 17
" October	37 3 " 37 6	50 0 " 65 0	3 3 " 4 6	[illegible]	16 9 " 17 0	11 15	14 17
Average price of three years, 1849, '50, '51	*£ s.* 38 8	*s. d.* 63 4	*s. d.* 3 8¾	*s. d.* [illegible]	*s. d.* 17 9	*£ s. d.* 11 18 11	*£ s. d.* 14 9 9
1852—January	36 6 to 36 9	45 0 to 60 0	3 3 to 4 6	[illegible]	16 3 to 16 6	11 10 to 11 15	14 17
" July	38 0	50 0 " 65 0	3 3 " 4 6	[illegible]	14 6 " 14 9	11 0 " 11 5	15 0
1853—January	46 0 to 46 3	67 0 " 77 0	3 3 " 4 6	[illegible]	15 6 " 16 0	11 10	20 0
" July	53 6	75 0 " 80 0	3 3 " 4 6	[illegible]	15 6 " 16 0	11 10 to 12 0	19 10
1854—January	60 6 to 62 0	70 0 " 95 0	3 1 " 4 4	[illegible]	17 6 " 17 9	11 10	16 10
" July	63 9 " 65 0	65 0 " 90 0	3 4 " 4 4	[illegible]	24 0	11 10	16 10
1855—January	69 6	80 0 " 95 0	.. ..	[illegible]	28 6 to 31 0	11 10	18 10
" July	52 9 to 53 0	65 0 " 91 0	.. ..	[illegible]	17 6 " 18 0	13 10 to 14 10	18 0
1856—January	68 0 " 68 3	60 0 " 82 0	.. ..	[illegible]	15 0 " 15 6	15 0 " 16 0	20 10
" July	50 6	60 0 " 80 0	.. ..	[illegible]	16 0 " 16 6	14 0 " 18 0	20 10
1857—January	58 0	58 6 " 77 6	3 4 " 4 6	[illegible]	18 0	14 0 " 17 0	21 0
" April	54 3	57 6 " 77 6	3 4 " 4 6	[illegible]	17 6	14 10 " 17 5	21 0
" July	59 6	49 6 " 70 6	3 4 " 4 6	[illegible]	15 9 to 16 0	14 10 " 17 0	21 10
" October	57 6	53 6 " 77 6	3 4 " 4 6	[illegible]	15 0 " 15 3	14 10 " 17 0	22 5
1858—January	51 9	49 6 " 77 6	3 4 " 4 6	[illegible]	13 0 " 14 0	14 0 " 16 0	22 5
" April	55 9 to 56 0	50 6 " 67 6	3 4 " 4 6	[illegible]	14 6 " 15 0	14 0 " 15 0	21 10
" July	50 9 " 51 0	47 6 " 67 6	3 4 " 4 6	[illegible]	16 0 " 16 3	13 0 " 14 0	21 0
" September	50 6	48 6 " 63 6	3 4 " 4 6	[illegible]	14 6 " 15 0	13 0 " 14 0	19 0
Average price of 1858	*£ s.* 50 3	*s. d.* 58 2¾	*s. d.* 3 11	*s. d.* [illegible]	*s. d.* 14 9¼	*£ s. d.* 14 2 6	*£ s. d.* 20 18 9

E.

PRODUCTS OF ASIA.—*Seventeen Commodities.*

	Cotton, Bengal, Madras, and Surat, per lb.	Hemp, Jute, per ton.	Silk (raw) China Tsatlee, per lb.	Rape, per last of 10 qrs.	Coffee, Native, Ceylon ordinary to good, per cwt. (bond).	Tea, Congou, per lb. (bond).	Tea, Hyson, per lb. (bond).	Sugar, Bengal: Brown, per cwt. (bond).	Sugar, Bengal: Yellow and White, per cwt. (bond).
	d. d.	£ s. £ s.	s. d. s. d.	£ £	s. d. s. d.	s. d. s. d.	s. d. s. d.	s. d. s. d.	s. d. s. d.
1849—January	2¾ to 3¼	11 0 to 18 0	11 6 to 17 6	24 to 27	31 6 to 32 6	0 8 to 1 9	1 0 to 3 7	14 0 to 19 0	17 0 to 30 0
" April	3 " 4½	13 0 " 18 0	11 0 " 17 0	26 " 30	30 6 " 34 0	0 8 " 1 9	1 0 " 3 7	16 0 " 21 0	20 6 " 28 0
" July	3½ " 4½	13 0 " 17 0	11 0 " 17 6	31 " 34	30 6 " 33 0	0 8 " 1 9	1 0 " 3 7	18 0 " 26 6	21 0 " 33 0
" October	3¾ " 4¾	13 0 " 17 0	13 6 " 20 0	28 " 30	30 6 " 40 0	0 8 " 1 9	1 0 " 3 7	18 0 " 26 6	21 0 " 34 0
1850—January	3¾ " 5	13 0 " 17 0	14 6 " 19 6	30 " 33	33 6 " 37 0	0 10 " 1 9	1 3 " 3 7	17 0 " 27 0	21 6 " 34 0
" April	4 " 5	13 0 " 19 0	16 0 " 20 0	31 " 36	31 0 " 31 6	0 9 " 1 9	1 4 " 3 7	21 6 " 29 6	23 0 " 33 0
" July	4¼ " 6¼	13 0 " 19 0	15 0 " 21 0	32 " 37	43 0 " 43 6	0 [illegible] " 1 7	1 [illegible] " 3 6	16 0 " 26 0	23 0 " 33 0
" October	4¾ " 7	13 0 " 19 0	17 6 " 22 0	24 " 28	33 0 " 35 0	1 0 " 1 7	1 3 " 3 6	17 6 " 29 6	25 6 " 34 6
1851—January	4¾ " 7	13 0 " 19 0	18 6 " 22 0	25 " 26	35 0 " 38 6	1 0 " 1 10	1 3 " 3 6	19 0 " 28 0	27 0 " 37 0
" April	4¾ " 5¾	10 0 " 16 0	18 6 " 20 0	28 " 30	41 0 " 43 0	0 10 " 1 10	1 3 " 3 6	18 0 " 22 0	25 6 " 33 0
" July	3¾ " 4¼	10 0 " 16 0	18 6 " 21 0	28 " 31	37 0 " 38 0	0 8 " 1 8	1 0 " 3 6	16 0 " 29 0	24 6 " 34 0
" October	3¼ " 4	10 0 " 16 0	14 6 " 20 0	19 " 22	40 6 " 42 0	0 8 " 1 6	1 0 " 3 6	13 0 " 17 0	22 0 " 28 0
Average price of three years, 1849, '50, '51	d. 4¼	£ s. d. 16 16 8	s. d. 17 7½	£ s. d. 28 14 0	s. d. 43 3	s. d. 1 3½	s. d. 2 4½	s. d. 19 7	s. d. 27 9
1852—January	2¾ to 4	10 0 to 16 0	14 6 to 17 6	19 to 22	38 6 to 40 0	0 7½ to 1 6	1 1 to 3 6	13 0 to 25 6	20 0 to 33 6
" July	3½ " 4¼	10 0 " 16 0	16 6 " 20 6	20 " 23	42 0 " 44 6	0 6½ " 1 6	1 1 " 3 6	15 0 " 25 0	21 0 " 34 0
1853—January	3 " 4½	13 0 " 18 17	16 6 " 20 6	20 " 23	40 0 " 47 0	0 10 " 2 0	1 0 " 3 0	26 0 " 29 0	25 6 " 30 0
" July	3 " 4½	20 0 " 24 0	16 0 " 19 0	26 " 28	45 0 " 46 6	0 11½ " 2 0	1 4 " 3 0	27 0 " 31 0	23 0 " 31 0
1854—January	2¾ " 4½	20 0 " 24 0	10 6 " 20 0	30 " 36	40 6 " 50 0	1 2 " 1 10	1 4 " 3 0	26 0 " 22 0	23 6 " 30 6
" July	3¾ " 4½	20 0 " 25 0	7 0 " 18 0	30 " 36	.. ..	0 11 " 1 10	1 4 " 3 0	27 0 " 30 0	20 6 " 30 6
1855—January	3¾ " 4½	.. ..	8 0 " 18 6	..	.. ..	0 9½ " 1 10	1 4 " 3 0	.. ..	.. ..
" July	3 " 4½	.. ..	8 0 " 18 6	..	.. ..	0 [illegible] " 2 4	1 3 " 3 6	.. ..	.. ..
1856—January	3½ " 4½	.. ..	9 0 " 19 6	..	.. ..	0 9 " 2 4	1 6 " 3 6	.. ..	.. ..
" July	4 " 5½	.. ..	9 6 " 21 6	..	.. ..	0 [illegible] " 2 4	1 6 " 4 0	.. ..	.. ..
1857—January	4¾ " 5¾	24 0 " 33 0	28 6 " 37 6	42 " 44	46 0 " 57 0	1 1 " 2 3	1 6 " 4 0	26 0 " 33 0	36 0 " 40 0
" April	4¼ " 6	27 0 " 36 10	32 6 " 38 6	42 " 44	61 0 " 62 6	1 0¾ " 2 3	1 6 " 4 0	26 0 " 34 0	37 0 " 40 0
" July	4¾ " 6	28 0 " 36 0	24 0 " 37 0	41 " 44	64 0 " 65 0	1 1 " 2 3	1 6 " 4 0	31 6 " 36 0	45 0 " 49 0
" October	3 " 7¼	20 0 " 27 0	21 6 " 32 0	37 " 39	60 6 " 62 0	1 2 " 2 6	1 6 " 4 0	25 0 " 30 0	35 0 " 45 6
1858—January	3¼ " 5¼	14 0 " 21 0	15 0 " 20 0	37 " 39	51 0 " 50 6	0 11 " 2 4	1 4 " 3 6	20 0 " 22 6	30 0 " 37 6
" April	4 " 5¾	15 10 " 19 0	17 6 " 19 6	37 " 39	50 0 " 54 0	0 9 " 2 6	1 2 " 3 6	21 0 " 28 0	29 0 " 33 0
" July	4¼ " 6	13 10 " 19 0	15 0 " 20 0	34 " 35	43 6 " 47 6	0 9½ " 2 3	1 4 " 3 0	18 6 " 20 6	29 0 " 34 0
" September	4¼ " 6	13 10 " 19 0	15 0 " 20 0	34 " 33	44 0 " 50 0	0 9 " 1 4	1 3 " 3 0	16 0 " 22 6	31 0 " 35 0
Average price of 1858	d. 5	£ s. d. 18 13 3	s. d. 17 9	£ s. d. 33 13 4	s. d. 49 9	s. d. 1 1½	s. d. 2 3½	s. d. 18 3	s. d. 32 6

E (*concluded*).

PRODUCTS OF ASIA.

	SUGAR, MAURITIUS.		Rice, Bengal Yellow, and White, per cwt.	SPICES.				Sago, Pearl, per cwt.
	Brown, per cwt. (bond).	Good and Fine Yellow, per cwt. (bond).		Black Pepper (heavy and light), per lb. (bond).	Cinnamon, 1st, 2nd, and 3rd qualities, per lb. (bond).	Cloves, Amboyna and Bencoolen, per lb. (bond).	Cassia Lignea, ordinary to good, per cwt. (bond).	
	s. d. s. d.	s. d. s. d.	s. d. s. d.	d. d.	s. d. s. d.	s. d. s. d.	s. s.	s. d. s. d.
1849—January	[illegible]	[illegible]	[illegible]	[illegible]	[illegible]	[illegible]	[illegible]	[illegible]
" April	[illegible]	[illegible]	[illegible]	[illegible]	[illegible]	[illegible]	[illegible]	[illegible]
" July	[illegible]	[illegible]	[illegible]	[illegible]	[illegible]	[illegible]	[illegible]	[illegible]
" October	[illegible]	[illegible]	[illegible]	[illegible]	[illegible]	[illegible]	[illegible]	[illegible]
1850—January	[illegible]	[illegible]	[illegible]	[illegible]	[illegible]	[illegible]	[illegible]	[illegible]
" April	[illegible]	[illegible]	[illegible]	[illegible]	[illegible]	[illegible]	[illegible]	[illegible]
" July	[illegible]	[illegible]	[illegible]	[illegible]	[illegible]	[illegible]	[illegible]	[illegible]
" October	[illegible]	[illegible]	[illegible]	[illegible]	[illegible]	[illegible]	[illegible]	[illegible]
1851—January	[illegible]	[illegible]	[illegible]	[illegible]	[illegible]	[illegible]	[illegible]	[illegible]
" April	[illegible]	[illegible]	[illegible]	[illegible]	[illegible]	[illegible]	[illegible]	[illegible]
" July	[illegible]	[illegible]	[illegible]	[illegible]	[illegible]	[illegible]	[illegible]	[illegible]
" October	[illegible]	[illegible]	[illegible]	[illegible]	[illegible]	[illegible]	[illegible]	[illegible]
Average of three years, 1849, '50, '51	s. 21	s. d. 26 6	s. d. 9 8½	d. 3½	s. d. 2 6	s. d. 1 4½	s. d. 91 9	s. d. 21 1
1852—January	[illegible]	[illegible]	[illegible]	[illegible]	[illegible]	[illegible]	[illegible]	[illegible]
" July	[illegible]	[illegible]	[illegible]	[illegible]	[illegible]	[illegible]	[illegible]	[illegible]
1853—January	[illegible]	[illegible]	[illegible]	[illegible]	[illegible]	[illegible]	[illegible]	[illegible]
" July	[illegible]	[illegible]	[illegible]	[illegible]	[illegible]	[illegible]	[illegible]	[illegible]
1854—January	[illegible]	[illegible]	[illegible]	[illegible]	[illegible]	[illegible]	[illegible]	[illegible]
" July	[illegible]	[illegible]	[illegible]	[illegible]	[illegible]	[illegible]	[illegible]	[illegible]
1855—January	.. ..	.. ..	.. ..	.. ..	.. ..	.. ..	.. ..	.. ..
" July	.. ..	.. ..	.. ..	.. ..	.. ..	.. ..	.. ..	.. ..
1856—January	.. ..	.. ..	.. ..	.. ..	.. ..	.. ..	.. ..	.. ..
" July	.. ..	.. ..	.. ..	.. ..	.. ..	.. ..	.. ..	.. ..
1857—January	[illegible]	[illegible]	[illegible]	[illegible]	[illegible]	[illegible]	[illegible]	[illegible]
" April	[illegible]	[illegible]	[illegible]	[illegible]	[illegible]	[illegible]	[illegible]	[illegible]
" July	[illegible]	[illegible]	[illegible]	[illegible]	[illegible]	[illegible]	[illegible]	[illegible]
" October	[illegible]	[illegible]	[illegible]	[illegible]	[illegible]	[illegible]	[illegible]	[illegible]
1858—January	[illegible]	[illegible]	[illegible]	[illegible]	[illegible]	[illegible]	[illegible]	[illegible]
" April	[illegible]	[illegible]	[illegible]	[illegible]	[illegible]	[illegible]	[illegible]	[illegible]
" July	[illegible]	[illegible]	[illegible]	[illegible]	[illegible]	[illegible]	[illegible]	[illegible]
" September	[illegible]	[illegible]	[illegible]	[illegible]	[illegible]	[illegible]	[illegible]	[illegible]
Average price, 1858	s. d. 20 9	s. d. 29 1	s. d. 8 6½	d. 3½	s. d. 1 4	d. 10½	s. d. 110 6	s. d. 19 9½

* Duty, 6d. per cwt. † Duty, 2½d. per cwt.

F. ARTICLES SUBJECT TO EXCEPTIONAL INFLUENCES.—*Six Commodities.*

	Potatoes (York Regents) at Waterside Market, Southwark, per ton.	Saltpetre, Bengal, per cwt.	Silk, Italian (Raw), and descriptions, per lb.	Indigo, Bengal, Oude and Madras, per lb.	WINE. Port (duty 5s. 6d. per gallon) per pipe.	WINE. Sherry (duty 5s. 6d. per gallon) per butt.
	s. d.	s. d. s. d.	s. d. s. d.	s. d. s. d.	£ £ s.	£ £
1849—January	155 0	[illegible] 6 to 27 6	13 0 to [illegible] 6	1 3 to 5 3	17 to 51 0	[illegible] to 76
" April	140 0	[illegible] 6 .. [illegible] 6	[illegible] 6 .. [illegible] 0	1 3 .. 5 6	17 .. 51 0	12 .. 76
" July	190 0	[illegible] 0 .. 28 6	17 6 .. [illegible] 0	1 6 .. 5 6	17 .. 51 0	19 .. 76
" October	75 0	[illegible] 0 .. 26 0	[illegible] 0 .. [illegible] 0	1 6 .. 5 5	17 .. 51 0	[illegible] .. 76
1850—January	[illegible] 0	25 0 .. 26 0	[illegible] 0 .. [illegible] 0	1 6 .. 5 5	17 .. 50 0	[illegible] .. 76
" April	[illegible] 0	25 0 .. [illegible] 0	16 0 .. [illegible] 0	1 10 .. 5 5	17 .. 51 0	[illegible] .. 76
" July	[illegible] 0	25 0 .. 27 6	18 0 .. [illegible] 0	1 10 .. 5 7	19 .. 51 0	[illegible] .. 76
" October	[illegible] 0	26 6 .. [illegible] 0	19 0 .. [illegible] 0	3 0 .. 6 10	[illegible] .. 51 0	[illegible] .. 76
1851—January	97 6	27 0 .. 29 6	19 0 .. [illegible] 0	3 0 .. 6 10	[illegible] .. 51 0	[illegible] .. 76
" April	[illegible] 0	[illegible] 0 .. [illegible] 6	17 0 .. [illegible] 6	2 8 .. 6 6	[illegible] .. 51 0	12 .. 76
" July	[illegible] 0	[illegible] 0 .. [illegible] 6	19 0 .. [illegible] 6	1 10 .. 6 1	[illegible] .. 51 0	[illegible] .. 76
" October	70 0	[illegible] 0 .. 19 0	[illegible] 0 .. [illegible] 6	1 9 .. 6 3	[illegible] .. 51 0	[illegible] .. 76
Average price of three years, 1849, '50, '51	s. d. 103 6	s. d. 27 [illegible]	s. d. 21 6½	s. d. 3 11	£ s. d. 36 0 10	£ 44
1852—January	70 0	24 6 to 28 6	17 0 to [illegible] 0	1 9 to 6 3	[illegible] to 51 0	18 to 76
" July	97 0	[illegible] 0 .. 29 0	19 0 .. 27 0	1 9 .. 6 3	[illegible] .. 51 0	19 .. 76
1853—January	117 6	24 0 .. 29 6	19 0 .. [illegible] 0	[illegible] .. 7 [illegible]	[illegible] .. 51 6	18 .. 76
" July	117 6	25 6 .. 30 0	[illegible] 0 .. 30 0	1 9 .. 7 [illegible]	[illegible] .. 50 0	10 .. 70
1854—January	[illegible] 0	27 0 .. 31 0	[illegible] 0 .. 25 0	1 6 .. 8 0	[illegible] .. 50 0	10 .. 70
" July	[illegible] 0	31 0 .. 36 [illegible]	19 0 .. 25 0	1 6 .. 7 [illegible]	[illegible] .. 50 0	18 .. 80
1855—January	112 6	[illegible] 6 .. [illegible] 6	18 0 .. 30 0	1 9 .. 7 6	..	.. ..
" July	[illegible] 0	[illegible] 6 .. 30 0	[illegible] 0 .. [illegible] 0	1 3 .. 7 0	..	.. ..
1856—January	[illegible] 0	29 0 .. 37 6	[illegible] 0 .. [illegible] 0	1 0 .. 7 6	..	.. ..
" July	[illegible] 0	[illegible] 0 .. 34 0	[illegible] 0 .. [illegible] 0	1 0 .. 7 7	..	.. ..
1857—January	100 0	[illegible] 0 .. [illegible] 0	[illegible] 0 .. [illegible] 0	[illegible] .. [illegible]	[illegible] .. 60 0	[illegible] .. [illegible]
" April	117 6	[illegible] 0 .. 40 6	33 0 .. 45 0	1 3 .. [illegible] 0	[illegible] .. 65 0	[illegible] .. [illegible]
" July	105 0	[illegible] 0 .. 41 6	[illegible] 0 .. 45 0	1 0 .. 7 8	42 .. 75 0	28 .. 85
" October	100 0	35 0 .. 65 0	[illegible] 0 .. 50 0	[illegible] 0 .. 6 0	40 .. 75 0	30 .. 85
1858—January	142 6	31 0 .. 41 0	24 0 .. 37 0	[illegible] 6 .. 10 0	47 .. 75 0	30 .. 85
" April	165 0	[illegible] 0 .. 37 0	23 0 .. [illegible] 0	0 11 .. 9 0	48 .. 65 0	27 .. 80
" July	150 0	[illegible] 0 .. [illegible] 0	24 0 .. 37 0	0 11 .. [illegible] 0	42 .. 75 0	28 .. 85
" September	65 0	36 0 .. [illegible] 0	23 0 .. 31 0	0 11 .. [illegible] 6	30 .. 65 0	[illegible] .. 80
Average price of 1858	s. d. 133 1	s. d. 36 9	s. d. 29 10½	s. d. 5 1½	£ s. 54 10	£ 55

G.

RATIO OF PRESENT PRICES TO THE AVERAGE PRICES OF 1849, 1850, AND 1851.

(The latter being taken as 100) deduced from the foregoing Tables.

PRODUCTS OF VICTORIA.	1849, '50, and '51.	1858.
Cattle—Sheep, Cows, Bullocks	100	327·1
Hay	100	192·8
Bread	100	161·5
Butcher's Meat—Beef, Mutton	100	474·9
Butter	100	240·0
Farm-yard Produce—Eggs, Turkeys, Ducks, Fowl	100	312·8
Potatoes	100	186·3
Potatoes, retail	100	600·0
Garden Vegetables—Carrots, Turnips, Cabbages	100	349·1
PRODUCTS OF THE UNITED KINGDOM.		
Provisions—Butter, Bacon, Pork	100	123·1
Butcher's Meat—Beef, Mutton	100	122·2
Leather	100	148·0
Tallow	100	133·6
Wool	100	110·2
Soda Ash	100	102·0
Copper	100	129·1
Iron	100	124·4
Lead	100	131·8
Tin	100	141·5
Wheat	100	104·7
Barley	100	135·1
Oats	100	141·5
Rye	100	127·8
Beans	100	145·4
Peas	100	143·4
Cotton Manufactures (8 articles)	100	103·3
Linen Manufactures (6 articles)	100	105·8
Whiskey	100	123·3
Turpentine	100	120·5
Coffee	100	133·5
Rum	100	147·0
Logwood	100	128·3
Sugar (2 qualities)	100	104·7

PRODUCTS OF NORTH AMERICA.	1849, '50, and '51.	1858.
Cotton Wool—Middling Orleans, Fair Orleans ...	100	115·5
Ashes	100	114·8
Timber	100	120·1
Resin	100	152·6
Tobacco—Maryland, Virginian	100	127·8
Provisions—Beef, Pork	100	130·0
Indian Corn	100	118·0
Rice	100	108·9
PRODUCTS OF CONTINENTAL EUROPE.		
Flax	100	135·6
Hemp	100	101·5
Hides	100	100·6
Leather	100	159·7
Tallow (2 qualities)	100	136·4
Timber	100	92·8
Wool (2 qualities)	100	103·8
Tar	100	83·2
Oils—Gallipoli, Palm, Seal	100	117·8
Iron	100	118·2
Steel	100	144·5
Wheat	100	104·7
Barley	100	135·1
Oats	100	141·5
Rape	100	124·2
PRODUCTS OF ASIA.		
Cotton	100	114·1
Hemp	100	88·0
Silk	100	100·1
Rape	100	124·2
Coffee	100	115·0
Tea—Congou, Hyson	100	106·4
Sugar—Bengal (2 qualities), Mauritius (2 qualities)	100	104·8
Rice	100	88·6
Spices—Black Pepper, Cinnamon, Cloves, Cassia Lignea	100	97·2
Sago	100	94·7
COMMODITIES SUBJECT TO EXCEPTIONAL INFLUENCES.		
Potatoes	100	122·2
Saltpetre	100	135·1
Silk	100	136·6
Indigo	100	130·0
Wine—Port, Sherry	100	138·1

H ABSTRACT OF DR. SOETBEER'S TABLES.

Given in his Contributions to the Statistics of Prices in Hamburg.

1831—40	Percentage rates compared with the average of the years 1831—40.								
	1831/40	1841/50	1851	1852	1853	1854	1855	1856	1857
Coffee	100·0	68·5	75·6	74·4	81·8	88·5	81·7	86·2	95·4
„ Domingo	100·0	71·3	77·3	72·7	83·1	98·4	86·5	65·5	105·8
„ Java	..	..	..	..	..	..	..	..	..
Cocoa	..	100·0	82·4	104·0	105·0	98·3	105·1	140·9	165·0
Tea	100·0	110·7	86·5	73·8	85·8	81·7	84·8	81·4	94·0
Unrefined Sugar	100·0	83·3	75·8	71·4	82·3	85·5	96·8	112·6	117·8
Refined do.	100·0	80·4	74·7	78·0	77·2	89·7	80·8	112·6	116·5
Tobacco	100·0	90·0	111·0	94·4	85·7	84·6	84·6	98·7	100·7
Rice	100·0	85·5	67·2	80·9	77·0	93·0	103·3	86·0	96·7
Pepper	100·0	80·3	84·8	87·6	98·6	100·5	109·5	100·4	111·2
Almonds	100·0	95·0	90·8	89·2	94·1	99·7	110·1	111·6	120·8
Raisins	100·0	99·5	89·7	84·7	137·9	163·5	127·6	183·3	154·7
Currants	100·0	71·9	59·7	67·1	164·5	173·5	184·2	200·3	135·0
Wine	100·0	77·5	98·4	101·6	120·3	148·3	171·0	169·7	197·8
Rum	100·0	80·0	96·8	57·5	78·8	96·7	106·2	120·0	107·2
Geneva	100·0	92·8	134·0	137·5	167·0	170·0	189·0	186·8	161·0
Wheat	100·0	120·0	108·3	116·7	150·0	193·8	215·3	206·9	144·4
Rye	100·0	110·9	118·2	140·0	161·8	175·4	209·2	203·6	150·0
Barley	100·0	113·1	111·8	136·0	157·4	178·7	200·0	210·8	160·9
Oats	100·0	111·7	117·4	110·9	143·5	167·4	187·0	191·3	169·6
Wheat (meal)	..	100·0	90·0	94·9	170·7	154·3	185·7	160·7	109·3
Herrings	100·0	79·8	67·5	107·9	103·5	98·4	106·8	118·3	132·5
Ham	100·0	110·0	93·7	127·3	141·0	167·6	160·0	158·5	159·4
Beef	100·0	119·3	113·4	124·7	142·9	167·8	172·5	172·9	175·3
Butter	100·0	108·4	105·0	105·8	131·4	140·4	146·3	154·0	155·3
Cheese	100·0	101·1	103·6	103·6	113·9	127·8	144·0	151·7	..
Indigo	100·0	83·9	91·5	89·0	91·5	86·6	87·8	97·6	103·7
Logwood	100·0	85·1	68·8	66·7	89·0	97·8	91·5	100·0	96·8
Saltpetre	100·0	97·9	89·1	89·4	98·3	140·8	152·3	164·0	145·8
Soda	..	..	..	..	..	..	..	..	..
Clover Seed	100·0	95·1	106·7	113·4	128·1	139·0	146·2	176·6	139·3
Rapeseed	100·0	..	..	..	..	..	..	..	..
Rapeseed Oil	100·0	105·0	98·9	94·3	103·1	114·1	139·0	148·7	140·8
Tar	100·0	108·2	111·5	103·1	100·0	164·1	171·9	118·7	104·7
Tallow	100·0	96·8	84·6	84·9	113·8	134·3	109·0	118·9	130·0
Wool	100·0	83·8	85·6	90·9	99·2	91·7	99·7	109·9	109·9
Cotton	100·0	70·6	81·3	71·1	81·8	77·8	77·0	84·1	105·6
Hemp	..	100·0	88·1	56·7	105·6	138·9	113·6	98·7	98·7
Linen	100·0	65·4	70·4	65·5	61·6	60·0	59·3	56·1	64·9
Rags	100·0	105·0	175·9	140·1	175·9	172·4	158·6	148·3	137·9
Skins	100·0	76·3	79·2	80·0	68·0	110·0	118·4	143·3	185·7
Calf Skin	100·0	98·0	83·8	78·4	87·6	95·8	100·1	109·2	135·1
Iron	100·0	91·8	77·0	74·0	109·7	120·6	110·8	124·0	118·9
Zinc	100·0	139·4	93·3	104·7	140·7	148·7	156·3	163·1	191·3
Lead	100·0	107·7	98·3	98·0	129·3	137·0	153·0	137·6	138·0
Copper	100·0	96·8	94·3	106·6	121·9	123·6	108·9	116·0	135·0
Tin	100·0	101·3	103·0	108·7	152·0	155·1	151·4	171·5	186·4
Pit Coal	100·0	100·0	85·7	85·7	106·3	118·6	128·6	128·6	100·0

The above table is framed on a basis of the average prices of 1831–40. This is represented by 100 in the first column; the second column represents the average of prices with reference to this basis, during 1841–50, and the remaining columns the averages, with reference to the same basis, of each year from 1851 to 1857, inclusive. By comparing the first and second columns it will be seen that, on the whole, the prices of 1841–50 had fallen as compared with those of 1831–40, while by carrying the eye forward, the reader will find that after 1850 there is in the great majority of cases a rise, which in 1857 reaches a very high point, not only in relation to 1841–50, but in relation to 1831–40. The rise in prices thus shown is very much greater than that indicated by my tables, which is accounted for by the circumstance, that mine have been carried on to 1858, when the full effect of the reaction from the crisis of 1857 had been felt.

I.

STATEMENT OF THE CONCLUSIONS ARRIVED AT BY M. LAVASSEUR.

("JOURNAL DES ÉCONOMISTES," MARCH 1858.)

[*From the official statistics of French Prices, including all commodities produced or consumed in France from 1847 to 1856, inclusive.*]

NATURAL PRODUCTS.

	Per cent.	Per cent.
Actual increase in prices during the above period . . .		67·19
Proportion of increase due to war and scarcity	20	
Ditto to speculation	5	25·00
Increase in price of natural products		42·19

MANUFACTURED PRODUCTS.

	Per cent.	Per cent.
Actual increase in prices during the above period . . .		14·94
Proportion of increase due to war and scarcity	2	
Ditto due to speculation	5	7·00
Increase in price of manufactured products		7·94

By adding these results together and dividing by two, the average increase in price of all commodities is made out to be 25 per cent., from which 5 per cent. is deducted as an allowance "for the development of industry and the increase of consumers," thus bringing the advance in price, due to the depreciation of gold, to 20 per cent.

Exception might, I think, be taken to some of the principles by which M. Lavasseur arrives at this result; *e.g.* the plan of averages is very apt to be deceptive, unless the commodities from which the averages are taken, are of equal or nearly equal importance; and the principle of the last deduction of 5 per cent. as an allowance for "the development of industry and the increase of consumers," appears to me to be fallacious; the development of industry and the increase of consumers having, except in the case of agricultural produce, a tendency to lower, instead of raising, price. But, passing by these considerations, the important fact remains, that French prices, comprehending those of all articles produced or consumed in France, have, after making liberal allowance for the effects of war, scarcity, and undue speculation, undergone since 1847 a marked rise, and that this rise has taken place (so far as the classification has been carried) in the manner according to which, supposing it to have proceeded from an increase of money, it might be expected to take place; a fact which, I submit, affords a strong corroboration of the general truth of the views which I have advanced.

K.

EXTRACTS FROM DR. STRANG'S PAPER ON WAGES IN GLASGOW AND THE WEST OF SCOTLAND.

[*Read at the Meeting of the British Association in* 1858.]

AVERAGE RATE OF WAGES OF WORKERS IN FACTORIES (numbers not less than 30,000 in 1851, 1856, and 1858).

	1851.		1856.		1858.	
	s.	d.	s.	d.	s.	d.
Power-loom Weavers	8	9	10	9	9	9
Spinners	25	0	30	0	27	0
Winders	8	0	9	0	9	0
Warpers	12	0	17	0	16	6
Dressers	32	0	40	0	35	0
Tenters	30	0	40	0	38	0
Twisters	9	0	12	0	12	0
Mechanics	24	0	27	0	26	0
Labourers	12	0	17	0	15	0

WORKMEN IN MINES AND IRON WORKS (in number 31,900, total wages paid in 1854–5 1,976,000*l.*, ten hours a day).

	1852.		1854.		1856.		1858.	
	s.	d.	s.	d.	s.	d.	s.	d.
Miners	2	6	5	0	5	0	3	0
Blast furnace keepers ...	5	0	6	8	7	9	5	0
Do. assistants...	3	2	4	2	4	2	3	3
Do. fillers ...	2	8	3	10	4	2	3	9
Puddlers, including under hands	7	6	10	6	10	0	9	0
Rollers (chief rollers) ...	10	0	14	6	13	6	12	0
Labourers	1	6	2	1	2	0	2	0

ENGINEERS AND MECHANICS (per day).

Year.	Shillings.	Year.	Shillings.
1851	3·43	1855	3·99
1852	3·52	1856	4·00
1853	3·82	1857	3·97
1854	3·97	1858	3·92

WORKMEN ENGAGED IN THE BUILDING TRADE (ten hours a day).

QUARRIERS.		QUARRIERS.	
Year.	Shillings.	Year.	Shillings.
1851	16 per week.	1855	20 per week.
1852	16 "	1856	22 "
1853	17 "	1857	22 "
1854	19 "	1858	19–20 "

MASONS.

	s.	d.	
Summer of 1850 and '51	21	0	per week of 60 hours.
Winter do. do.	18	0	ditto.
Summer of 1852	21	0 & 18s.	ditto.
Do. 1853	23	9	ditto.
Do. 1854	25	0	ditto.
Do. 1855	25	0	ditto.
Do. 1856	25	0	ditto.

In September 1856, a change was made, and the rate fixed per hour, as follows:—

	d.		s.	d.	
September 19th, 1856 ...	5⅔	per hour or	26	11¼	per week of 57 hours.
December 12th, "	5¼	"	24	11	ditto.
May 15th, 1857	5	"	23	9	ditto.
July 24th, "	5¼	"	24	11	ditto.
Aug. 7th, "	5½	"	26	1½	ditto.
Nov. 6th "	5	"	23	9	ditto.
March 1st, 1858	4¾	"	22	6¾	ditto.
August 1st, "	4¾	"	*22	6¾	ditto.

CARPENTERS AND JOINERS.

	s.			s.	
1851	21	per week of 60 hours.	1855.........	24	per week of 57 hours.
1852	24	ditto.	1856.........	24	ditto.
1853	23	ditto.	1857 to Nov.	26	ditto.
1854	24	ditto of 57 hours.	1858.........	†24	ditto.

COMMON LABOURERS (connected with all matters of house construction).

	s.	d.	
1850, '51, and '52	12	0	per week of 57 hours.
1853	14	0	ditto.
1854-5-6	17	0	ditto.
1857	16	0	ditto.
1858	15	9	ditto.

* Equal to 23s. 8¾d. per week of 60 hours. † Equal to 25s. 3d. per week of 60 hours.

HAND-LOOM WEAVERS (per week, for men, boys, and girls).

	s.	d.		s.	d.
1851	5	8	1856	7	1
1852	6	9	1857	6	4
1853	7	0	1858	5	9

HAND-LOOM WEAVERS (fancy work).

	s.	d.		s.	d.	
1856	9	3	to	14	0	per week.
1858	7	0	to	5	9	„

Dr. Strang remarks that there has been a gradual diminution of hand-loom weavers during the last few years.

It will be desirable to add a few words in the way of explanation and comment on the tables now presented. And first, as to the standard of comparison which has been adopted. It appeared to me that, in selecting this, three leading considerations should be kept in view: first, that it should be taken from a period sufficiently long to allow, by the use of averages, of the elimination, as far as possible, of what is casual and exceptional; secondly, that this period should exclude occasions of violent commercial agitation; thirdly, that it should be continued to a point of time coinciding as nearly as possible with that at which the action of the new supplies of gold began to be felt. The period extending over 1849, 1850, and 1851, though not free from objection, appears to me, on the whole, to fulfil these conditions with tolerable fairness. It is in respect to the first that it principally errs, but the necessity of complying with the second and third (which I thought the more important conditions) left me no choice on this point; for, had I extended the period from which the average is taken further back than 1849, it would have been brought under the influence of the powerfully disturbing occurrences of the years 1845, 1846, and 1847, including the Railway speculation of 1845 and 1846, the Irish famine of 1846 and 1847, and the commercial crisis of the last year; while, on the other hand, to have carried it to a date later than 1851 would have been to bring it under the influence of the gold discoveries—that is to say, subjected that which was to be our standard of comparison to the action of the agency, the character of which it was our object to investigate. Indeed, with a view to American prices, the year 1851 is too late; the demand springing up in California consequent on the gold discoveries, having previous to the close of that year produced a very decided effect on the American markets; a circumstance which prevents the rise in American prices, as shown in the tables, from being as marked as it otherwise would be. If it be said that these objections might be obviated by taking a *longer* period *anterior* to 1845, this is true; but, by doing so, we should have incurred others of a more serious kind. In the first place, there was to this course the practical objection arising from the difficulty of obtaining extensive returns of prices from so distant a period—a difficulty of which no one who has attempted to construct a table of prices on a large scale will think lightly; while it would have been further objectionable as not fulfilling the third of the three conditions which I have stated above—that of taking the standard of comparison from a period as close as possible to the epoch of the gold discoveries. To disregard this condition would be in no small degree to conceal the operation of the agency in question; there being a constant tendency in the progress of the mechanical arts and applied sciences to cheapen production, and thus, when any considerable period of time is allowed to elapse, to neutralize the effect of any cause, which, like the new gold, tends to raise prices. But, though not free from objection, I conceive the years 1849, 1850, and 1851 to form on the whole a fair basis of comparison; and this I think will appear from the following extracts from the Trade Reports of that time, which have been taken partly from the *Economist*, and partly from the 5th volume of the "History of Prices."

During the whole of 1848 the country was suffering from the depression consequent upon the reaction from the crisis of 1847, but by the close of that year and the opening of 1849 its prospects became more cheering. This is shown by the following extracts from the *Economist*, January 6th, 1849. *Lime Street, London.*—"At the close of this year, which has been so sadly eminent for dulness in the produce market, I have the pleasure to announce a decided improvement, which is more important for being so very unusual just at this period. The reports from our manufacturing districts are more favourable." *Manchester.*—"We have the satisfaction, at the termination of another remarkable and eventful year, of communicating to you the continuance of a decided improvement in the trade of this district." *Liverpool.*—"The wool-market continued in a state of great depression till the end of October. . . . During the past two months, however, we are glad to notice a considerable change for the better; a large business has been done both for the home trade and for export, and prices both of foreign and domestic wools have an upward tendency." On the other hand, the corn market is reported as at this time in a very depressed condition, "all classes holding back for the period of free trade becoming a great act; anticipating a still further reduction in value under its dreaded influence;" as were also the markets for colonial produce.

The anticipations, however, expressed in the passages I have extracted, of a general revival of commercial activity, were not realized during the first half of 1849, which must be regarded as a time of more than ordinary depression. About the middle of 1849, however, a decided improvement took place, as appears from the following report, dated October 31st, 1849:—"With the single exception of some branches of the cotton trade, I have the satisfaction of reporting a continued improvement up to a late period, and with every appearance of continued activity, at least for some months to come, to the extent to which it has now reached. The worsted stuff trade has been the one most active; this trade has never before reached anything like the extent to which it has now attained. Plain and fancy woollens have varied, ... but on the whole they have been very satisfactory. The silk trade has been brisk and prosperous." At the close of October (1849), the historian of prices informs us ("History of Prices," vol. v. p. 244)—that "there sprung up in the colonial markets a marked disposition to a speculative rise of prices. The tendency first manifested itself in coffee. . . . . From coffee the speculation gradually spread to several other articles." This buoyant state of the market, it appears, continued till the end of January 1850, at which time the reports announce that "the speculations in colonial produce appear to have in some measure subsided." The commercial character of 1849 appears thus to have been one of depression during the first half of the year, followed by a general revival of trade in the latter half, accompanied by a speculative rise of prices of certain markets: on the whole, we may consider the range of prices during this year as somewhat under the normal level.

At the opening of 1850 we are told, "the trade of the country was moderately active" ("History of Prices," vol. vi. p. 249): and this representation is fully supported by quotations from the Trade Reports. Thus from Yorkshire the accounts say:—"I continue to receive very satisfactory reports as to the state of trade in all branches of manufactures throughout my district, except that portion engaged in spinning low numbers of cotton yarns, or manufacturing heavy cotton goods. The general condition of the factory workers, as regards employment and their ability, by good wages and low prices, to obtain food and clothing, is also satisfactory." (Ibid. p. 250.) The principal complaints at this time appear to have been in the cotton trade respecting the high price of raw cotton, which we are told "were general throughout 1850." In April 1850, the account from Lancashire was as follows:—"All the accounts I receive represent the woollen, worsted, flax, and silk mills to be in an active and prosperous state, and I have received similar good accounts of the larger portion of the different branches of trade in print works." (Ibid. pp. 250–1.) On July 6, 1850, the following reports appear in the *Economist*:—"Nothing has occurred during the past month to disturb the even and satisfactory course in which the commerce of the country appears to be now steadily proceeding. . . . The low prices of many foreign articles might have been expected to offer a sufficient inducement to speculative investment; but such has not been the case, business having been in most instances restricted to the supply of the actual consumptive and export demand; so great, however, is this demand at present for many of our silk, cotton, and woollen fabrics, that higher rates are obtainable than have been current for some years past; and so far from the stocks of manufactured goods increasing, there is difficulty in getting orders executed except for forward delivery. From Liverpool the account at the same time was as follows:—"Throughout the manufacturing districts there is full employment, and trade is in the highest degree flourishing. At this season of the year there is generally a large business doing in domestic wools, but the transactions have been to a greater extent than usual." From Manchester, owing to the cause already adverted to, the scarcity and dearness of raw cotton which continued throughout this year, the accounts were less favourable. In the review of this year's cotton trade (December 1850) given in the "History of Prices," vol. v. pp. 255, 256, the following statements appear :—"On the 1st of January, 1850, this quality (Middling Orleans) was worth 6½*d.* per pound, being 50 per cent. *higher* than at the commencement of 1849, and also of 1848. Speculators came freely into the market early in 1850, basing their operations on the promising appearance of trade in the manufacturing districts, and the unfavourable prospects of the crop of American cotton. . . . . There was a trifling reaction in August; in September and October a recovery; but in November a considerable fall, arising in apprehension of a war on the Continent. In December, more activity; and the year 1850 closed with a price of 7¾*d.* per pound, or nearly 20 per cent. higher than at the opening." "In coffee," we are told, "there were considerable fluctuations during the year; the price in January 1850 having risen very considerably, under the influence of bad crops from Brazil, and speculative purchases," falling in June and rising again in September, from which time it rose steadily till the end of the year. "In indigo and silk there were also some fluctuations arising out of reports of deficient crops." "In the sugar market the year 1850 has been marked, on the whole, by a very steady maintenance of prices." Of the ship-building trade we are told that "new British ships have fully maintained our last quotations; indeed, we have felt the want of a larger supply of good vessels, which would have met with a ready sale at fair prices if at hand." The review of this year is thus summed up :—"As a general rule there was a disposition in the latter half of 1850, in all the great markets of produce, to look forward to considerably higher prices, on the twofold ground of increasing consumption, and of the probable failure of the usual supplies." (Ibid. p. 258.)

The opening of the year 1851 is thus chronicled :—"The year 1851 opened with fair prospects. . . . . Prices of colonial produce were firm and rising; and already the export trade to the United States began to exhibit the influence of the large consumption in California." (Ibid. p. 258.) A reaction, however, from this favourable condition of things occurred in the spring, and on April 3, 1851, there was the following report from Yorkshire :—"In various branches there has been a considerable quantity of machinery either unemployed or working for a shorter period than for many previous months. This has not been extended to all branches of trade at the same time or in the same degree. . . . . In the neighbourhood of Huddersfield nearly all branches of the woollen trade are represented to be at this moment very flat and depressed." (Ibid.) At Liverpool the price of cotton had fallen at the end of May to a point as much as 60 or 70 per cent. below the prices current in the previous January. "Throughout July, August, and September there was great depression in the produce markets of London and Liverpool. Prices had failed to correspond with expectations formed, and had fallen considerably instead of having risen. . . . About the end of September, however, the markets began to revive. The reports from Manchester represent the home trade as decidedly better." (Ibid. p. 261.) "When the period arrived for taking a review of the twelve months, the retrospect was of a mixed character. . . . But, as a general rule, the close of 1851 was distinguished by a range of prices in almost every branch of trade and manufacture *lower* than had prevailed for a very long period."

On a survey of the three years we may say that they embraced a period of chequered character, not free from commercial vicissitudes, but undisturbed by commercial convulsion. The range of prices in 1849 was perhaps rather under the usual level, but on the other hand "in 1850 prices had in most cases risen considerably above their ordinary level." ("Hist. of Prices," vol. v. p. 265.) This high range of prices appears to have culminated in January 1851, from which point there was a decline, which appears to have touched its lowest range about August of this year, after which a revival set in; prices, however, at the end of the year remaining still greatly depressed when compared with the high level they had attained at its opening. There is one important class of articles, indeed, which throughout the whole of this period continued at a low range, namely agricultural produce: this was owing principally to two causes, viz. favourable seasons and free trade which had at this time just come into force: but, on the other hand, there were others scarcely less important, which ruled throughout at prices much above what had been their usual level for many years previously, *e.g.* raw cotton and wool; the former of these articles being maintained throughout the greater portion of the whole period at from 50 to 80 per cent. above what had for many years been the prevailing price; and the latter also at what were considered very high rates.

Such being the grounds on which the years 1849, 1850, and 1851 have been taken as a standard of comparison, it remains that I should explain the principles on which the tables have been constructed, and the significance of the results which they embody.

And first as to the sources from which the foregoing returns have been taken: these are as follows, viz.—for agricultural produce, the Gazette returns, as given either in the Statistical Abstract published by Government, or in the *Economist;* for butcher's meat and potatoes, the Registrar-General's quarterly returns; for cotton (American), a series of tables published lately by Mr. Spence of Manchester, entitled, "The Course of Corn, Cotton, and Money;" the figures in the columns marked P in the tables have been furnished to me by private merchants extensively engaged in transactions with the articles to which they relate; a few columns have been taken from the tables in the sixth volume of the "History of Prices," and the remainder from the Prices Current published weekly in the *Economist.* The prices are, as a general rule, the prices of the London markets, though in some instances they refer to others, but the locality of the market is evidently unimportant, provided the quotations for any given article refer throughout the whole period to the *same* market, and this rule has been always observed. The same principle obviously applies to foreign as well as to home commodities. The prices, *e.g.* of cotton wool, of tobacco, of tea, or of sugar, will always be higher (I speak of bond prices) in London than in the countries of their production, by the cost of transmission *plus* the profit on the capital invested in the trade, and these elements, it is true, will vary for short intervals, but taken over long periods they will on an average be the same. The variations of prices therefore in the London markets will on an average show the variations of prices in the markets of the producing countries.

Of articles subject to import duties, the prices quoted are, with one or two unimportant exceptions which are duly notified in a footnote, the *bond* prices.

From the commodities comprised in the tables silver has been designedly excluded, because, contrary to what is sometimes supposed, silver, of all articles, forms the most fallacious criterion of changes in the value of gold, owing to the circumstance that silver and gold, wherever a double standard of value exists, and to some extent even where it does not, are made to perform the same functions, and can be reciprocally substituted one for the other; the effect of which is that a fall in the value of gold is always attended with a fall in the value of silver, though not necessarily to the same extent.

The tables have been constructed with a view to exhibit the operation of the principles which in the preceding paper I have endeavoured to establish; the classification being made according to the countries in which the commodities are produced, and the mode of their production. To the complete carrying out of this principle several practical difficulties occur. Thus there is an important group of commodities which are not produced in any of the leading commercial countries of the world, and which do not therefore properly fall under any of the above heads—West Indian commodities. These are obviously too important to be omitted from any table purporting to represent the progress of prices, but, on the other hand, they do not conveniently fit into any of the departments laid down. As on the whole the least objectionable plan, I have added them as a distinct group to the productions of the United Kingdom; for, although tropical commodities, they are the produce for the most part of British capital, and are more under the influence of our monetary system than that of any other country. Again, it will be found that there are many commodities which are common to several classes. Of these grain is by far the most important; the others being cotton, rice, tallow, oils, rape, and a few more. It is, as I have pointed out (*ante*, pp. 70, 71), through the medium of such commodities that the most powerful corrective is supplied to that local divergence of prices which it is the object of these tables to illustrate. In proportion therefore as such commodities are found in the several tables, will the operation of the principles to which I call attention be neutralized, and the phenomenon in question be less striking.

The tables, though containing altogether about one hundred commodities, I must admit to be in a very incomplete state. It will be remembered, however, that *I do not base any theory upon them.* The theory which I have advanced stands on entirely independent grounds, namely, the conditions of production affecting different classes of commodities, the peculiar character of the monetary systems existing in different countries, the commercial channels by which the new gold is diffused, and lastly the principles of monetary science. In their present form I cannot even claim for these tables a verification of that theory: all that I assume for them is that they afford so extensive an illustration of the principles which I have advanced as to warrant me in feeling considerable confidence in their general soundness. Thus, if the reader will glance over Table G, which shows at one view the result of the comparison instituted in the previous returns, he will find that out of the whole number of commodities included in it, which amounts to nearly one hundred, only six have fallen since the epoch of 1849–51: the remainder have all risen, and the greater number in a very marked manner; and he will find further, that in this progress of prices the advance has on the whole taken place in the order in which, as I have endeavoured to show, prices may be expected to advance under an increase of the precious metals. Thus he will find Victorian prices to have advanced in the proportion of about 200 per cent., or rather more. He will find the movement in English and American prices on the whole greater than in the prices of Continental Europe, while these latter show a greater advance than prices in Asia. This local divergence of prices will be very remarkable if we take some leading commodities of British and American produce, and contrast them with some of the leading products of Asia. Thus, if we take provisions and butcher's meat, the metals, agricultural produce, raw cotton, and tobacco, and compare these with some principal Asiatic products, as cotton, silk, coffee, tea, sugar, rice, and spices, we shall find that while the prices of the former articles have risen from 15 to 45 per cent. as compared with their prices in 1849–51, the prices of the latter have in no case risen more than 15 per cent., and have in several cases positively fallen—in one important article, rice, by so much as 11 per cent. The only important Asiatic products in which a marked rise in price has taken place are saltpetre and indigo, and in both these cases the rise is owing to causes of an exceptional nature—in saltpetre to a greatly increased consumption during the last four years, consequent upon causes too numerous here to mention, combined with the obstacles presented to a rapid extension of the supply by the scarcity of the peculiar clays from which this article is principally obtained; and in indigo owing to the interruption given to the operations of the indigo planters by the Mutiny, and to the speculative transactions to which this event gave occasion. It will be seen, too, that, on the whole, the other doctrines of the paper are pretty well borne out. Thus the advance in raw materials is much greater than in manufactured articles, while amongst raw materials the advance is most marked in animal than in vegetable products; such articles, *e.g.*, as leather, tallow, provisions, and butcher's meat showing a very remarkable rise.

I have appended to my own tables an abstract of the results arrived at by Dr. Soetbeer of Hamburg, in his "Beiträge zur Statistik der Preise," for which I am indebted to the kindness of the Archbishop of Dublin, as well as a statement of M. Levasseur's conclusions as to the progress of prices in France during the period of 1847 to 1856. It will be seen that the conclusions of both these writers, derived from independent data, and reached by modes of investigation entirely different from mine, concur in supporting not only the general position of a rise in prices, but also, *so far as they go*, the particular doctrines which I have ventured to advance respecting the mode in which this rise must take place. On the other hand Mr. Newmarch (the author, in conjunction with the late Mr. Tooke, of the fifth and sixth volumes of the "History of Prices"), in a communication made to the British Association at its meeting in Leeds in *September*, 1858, maintained that prices were then *rather lower than previous to the gold discoveries*, and that no depreciation in the value of money had up to that time taken place; resting his conclusions on certain tables which he then produced. To account, however, for the discordance of Mr. Newmarch's conclusions as well with mine as with those of others who have investigated the same problem, it is only necessary to state, first, that the tables on which he based his conclusions contained *not more than twenty commodities*, and excluded almost all those in which the advance has been most marked; and secondly, that the standard of comparison which he adopted was *a single quotation in January*, 1851; that being, as I have shown above, as well from Mr. Newmarch's own writings as from other authorities, *the culminating point of an ascending movement* in prices which had commenced in the beginning of the preceding year. Under these circumstances, the standard of comparison being exceptionally high, the object of comparison—that is to say, the prices in *September*, 1858—being (owing to the reaction consequent on the commercial crisis of the previous autumn) exceptionally low, and the comparison being limited to a select number of commodities, it is not strange that the conclusion should have been different from that of other writers who proceeded upon different principles.

For the returns of wages in Glasgow and the West of Scotland, given in Table K, I am indebted to Dr. Strang, who kindly allowed me to copy them from the valuable paper on that subject which he read before the British Association in September last. I had hoped to have extended this portion of the subject by adding to these some returns of wages in Ireland, but the materials which I have yet obtained for this purpose are not sufficiently extensive to be worth publication. It will be seen, however, that Dr. Strang's tables, so far as they go, fully support the general views advanced.

I cannot conclude without gratefully acknowledging the assistance I have received, while compiling these tables, from several gentlemen, both in this country (Ireland) and in England, to whom I have had occasion to apply for information, and who, as well by procuring me returns as by the observations with which in some instances they have accompanied them, have afforded me very material aid. I shall only further add that, as I cannot but fear that many inaccuracies may have found their way into the foregoing tables notwithstanding my anxiety to avoid them, I shall feel obliged to anyone who will do me the favour of pointing out any error he may detect, whether in the way of omission or of commission, and still more so if he will afford me the means of correcting it. Such criticism will be the more acceptable, as I purpose carrying on these tables with a view to exhibit the future progress of depreciation, and hope on some future occasion to be able to publish them in a form less incomplete and fragmentary than that in which, owing to unavoidable circumstances, they at present appear. [This intention the writer has been prevented from carrying into effect.]

THE END.

LONDON:
R. CLAY, SONS, AND TAYLOR, PRINTERS
BREAD STREET HILL.

BEDFORD STREET, COVENT GARDEN, LONDON.
July, 1871.

MACMILLAN & CO.'S CATALOGUE of Works in BELLES LETTRES, including Poetry, Fiction, Works on Art, Critical and Literary Essays, etc.

Allingham.—LAURENCE BLOOMFIELD IN IRELAND; or, the New Landlord. By WILLIAM ALLINGHAM. New and Cheaper Issue, with a Preface. Fcap. 8vo. cloth. 4*s.* 6*d.*

The aim of this little book is to do something, however small, towards making Ireland, yet so little known to the general British public, better understood. Several of the most important problems of life, Irish life and human life, are dealt with in their principles, according to the author's best lights. In the new Preface, the state of Ireland, with special reference to the Church measure, is discussed. "It is vital with the national character. . . . . It has something of Pope's point and Goldsmith's simplicity, touched to a more modern issue."—ATHENÆUM.

Arnold.—Works by MATTHEW ARNOLD:—

THE COMPLETE POETICAL WORKS. Vol. I. NARRATIVE AND ELEGIAC POEMS. Vol. II. DRAMATIC AND LYRIC POEMS. Extra fcap. 8vo. Price 6*s.* each.

The two volumes comprehend the First and Second Series of the Poems, and the New Poems. "Thyrsis is a poem of perfect delight, exquisite in grave tenderness of reminiscence, rich in breadth of western light, breathing full the spirit of gray and ancient Oxford."—SATURDAY REVIEW. *"The noblest in it is clothed in clearest words. There is no obscurity, no useless ornament: everything is simple, finished, and perfect."*—SCOTSMAN.

Arnold—*continued.*

ESSAYS IN CRITICISM. New Edition, with Additions. Extra fcap. 8vo. 6s.

The Essays in this Volume are—"The Function of Criticism at the Present Time;" "The Literary Influence of Academies;" "Maurice de Guerin;" "Eugenie de Guerin;" "Heinrich Heine;" "Pagan and Mediæval;" "Religious Sentiment;" "Joubert;" "Spinoza and the Bible;" "Marcus Aurelius." Both from the subjects dealt with and mode of treatment, few books are more calculated to delight, inform, and stimulate than these charming Essays.

Bacon's Essays.—See GOLDEN TREASURY SERIES.

Baker.—(For other Works by the same Author, see CATALOGUE OF TRAVELS.)

CAST UP BY THE SEA; OR, THE ADVENTURES OF NED GREY. By SIR SAMUEL BAKER, M.A., F.R.G.S., With Illustrations by HUARD. Fourth Edition. Crown 8vo. cloth gilt. 7s. 6d.

"*An admirable tale of adventure, of marvellous incidents, wild exploits, and terrible dénouements.*"—DAILY NEWS. "*A story of adventure by sea and land in the good old style.*"—PALL MALL GAZETTE.

Ballad Book.—See GOLDEN TREASURY SERIES.

Baring-Gould.—Works by S. BARING-GOULD, M.A.:—

IN EXITU ISRAEL. An Historical Novel. Two Vols. 8vo. 21s.

"*[illegible] powerful [illegible]—and [illegible] of [illegible]*"—LITERARY CHURCHMAN. "*[illegible] in [illegible] and [illegible]*"—WESTMINSTER REVIEW.

Baring-Gould—*continued.*

LEGENDS OF OLD TESTAMENT CHARACTERS, from the Talmud and other sources. Two vols. Crown 8vo. 16s. Vol. I. Adam to Abraham. Vol. II. Melchizedek to Zachariah.

Mr. Baring-Gould has here collected from the Talmud and other sources, Jewish and Mohammedan, a large number of curious and interesting legends concerning the principal characters of the Old Testament, comparing these frequently with similar legends current among many of the nations, savage and civilized, all over the world. "These volumes contain much that is very strange, and, to the ordinary English reader, very novel."—DAILY NEWS.

Barker.—Works by LADY BARKER:—

"Lady Barker is an unrivalled story-teller."—GUARDIAN.

STATION LIFE IN NEW ZEALAND. New and Cheaper Edition. Crown 8vo. 3s. 6d.

These letters are the exact account of a lady's experience of the brighter and less practical side of colonization. They record the expeditions, adventures, and emergencies diversifying the daily life of the wife of a New Zealand sheep-farmer; and, as each was written while the novelty and excitement of the scenes it describes were fresh upon her, they may succeed in giving here in England an adequate impression of the delight and freedom of an existence so far removed from our own highly-wrought civilization. "We have never read a more truthful or a pleasanter little book."—ATHENÆUM.

SPRING COMEDIES. STORIES.

CONTENTS:—A Wedding Story—A Stupid Story—A Scotch Story—A Man's Story. Crown 8vo. 7s. 6d.

"Lady Barker is endowed with a rare and delicate gift for narrating stories,—she has the faculty of throwing even into her printed narratives a soft and pleasant tone, which goes far to make the reader think the subject or the matter immaterial, so long as the author will go on telling stories for his benefit."—ATHENÆUM.

STORIES ABOUT:—With Six Illustrations. Second Edition. Extra fcap. 8vo. 4s. 6d.

Barker—*continued.*

This volume contains several entertaining stories about Monkeys, Jamaica, Camp Life, Dogs, Boys, &c. "There is not a tale in the book which can fail to please children as well as their elders." —PALL MALL GAZETTE.

A CHRISTMAS CAKE IN FOUR QUARTERS. With Illustrations by JELLICOE. Second Edition. Extra fcap. 8vo. cloth gilt. 4*s.* 6*d.*

In this little volume, Lady Barker, whose reputation as a delightful story-teller is established, narrates four pleasant stories showing how the "Great Birth-day" is kept in the "Four Quarters" of the globe,—in England, Jamaica, India, and New Zealand. The volume is illustrated by a number of well-executed cuts. "Contains just the stories that children should be told. 'Christmas Cake' is a delightful Christmas book."—GLOBE.

Bell.—ROMANCES AND MINOR POEMS. By HENRY GLASSFORD BELL. Fcap. 8vo. 6*s.*

"Full of life and genius."—COURT CIRCULAR.

Besant.—STUDIES IN EARLY FRENCH POETRY. By WALTER BESANT, M.A. Crown 8vo. 8*s.* 6*d.*

A sort of impression rests on most minds that French literature begins with the "siècle de Louis Quatorze;" any previous literature being for the most part unknown or ignored. Few know anything of the enormous literary activity that began in the thirteenth century, was carried on by Rutebeuf, Marie de France, Gaston de Foix, Thibault de Champagne, and Lorris; was fostered by Charles of Orleans, by Margaret of Valois, by Francis the First; that gave a crowd of versifiers to France, enriched, strengthened, developed, and fixed the French language, and prepared the way for Corneille and for Racine. The present work aims to afford information and direction touching the early efforts of France in poetical literature. "In one moderately sized volume he has contrived to introduce us to the very best, if not to all of the early French poets."—ATHENÆUM.

Book of Golden Deeds.—See GOLDEN TREASURY SERIES.

Book of Golden Thoughts.—See GOLDEN TREASURY SERIES.

Book of Praise.—See GOLDEN TREASURY SERIES.

Brimley.—ESSAYS BY THE LATE GEORGE BRIMLEY, M.A. Edited by the Rev. W. G. CLARK, M.A. With Portrait. Cheaper Edition. Fcap. 8vo. 2s. 6d.

George Brimley was regarded by those who knew him as "one of the finest critics of the day." The Essays contained in this volume are all more or less critical, and were contributed by the author to some of the leading periodicals of the day. The subjects are, "Tennyson's Poems," "Wordsworth's Poems," "Poetry and Criticism," "The Angel in the House," Carlyle's "Life of Sterling," "Esmond," "My Novel," "Bleak House," "Westward Ho!" Wilson's "Noctes Ambrosianæ," Comte's "Positive Philosophy." "It will," JOHN BULL *says, "be a satisfaction to the admirers of sound criticism and unassuming common sense to find that the Essays of the late George Brimley have reappeared in a new and popular form. They will give a healthy stimulus to that spirit of inquiry into the real value of our literary men whose names we too often revere without sufficient investigation."*

Broome.—THE STRANGER OF SERIPHOS. A Dramatic Poem. By FREDERICK NAPIER BROOME. Fcap. 8vo. 5s.

Founded on the Greek legend of Danaë and Perseus. "Grace and beauty of expression are Mr. Broome's characteristics; and these qualities are displayed in many passages."—ATHENÆUM. *"The story is rendered with consummate beauty."*—LITERARY CHURCHMAN.

Bunyan's Pilgrim's Progress.—See GOLDEN TREASURY SERIES.

Burke.—EDMUND BURKE, a Historical Study. By JOHN MORLEY, B.A., Oxon. Crown 8vo. 7s. 6d.

"The style is terse and incisive, and brilliant with epigram and point. Its sustained power of reasoning, its wide sweep of observation and reflection, its elevated ethical and social tone, stamp it as

a work of high excellence."—SATURDAY REVIEW. "*A model of compact condensation. We have seldom met with a book in which so much matter was compressed into so limited a space.*"—PALL MALL GAZETTE. "*An essay of unusual effort.*"—WESTMINSTER REVIEW.

Burns' Works.—See GOLDEN TREASURY SERIES and GLOBE LIBRARY.

Carroll.—Works by "LEWIS CARROLL:"—

ALICE'S ADVENTURES IN WONDERLAND. With Forty-two Illustrations by TENNIEL. 33rd Thousand. Crown 8vo. cloth. 6*s*.

A GERMAN TRANSLATION OF THE SAME. With TENNIEL'S Illustrations. Crown 8vo. gilt. 6*s*.

A FRENCH TRANSLATION OF THE SAME. With TENNIEL'S Illustrations. Crown 8vo. gilt. 6*s*.

AN ITALIAN TRANSLATION OF THE SAME. By T. P. ROSSETTI. With TENNIEL'S Illustrations. Crown 8vo. 6*s*.

"*Beyond question supreme among modern books for children.*"—SPECTATOR. "*One of the choicest and most charming books ever composed for a child's reading.*"—PALL MALL GAZETTE. "*A very pretty and highly original book, sure to delight the little world of wondering minds, and which may well please those who have unfortunately passed the years of wondering.*"—TIMES.

THROUGH THE LOOKING-GLASS, AND WHAT ALICE FOUND THERE. With Fifty Illustrations by TENNIEL. Crown 8vo. 6*s*. 23rd Thousand.

In the present volume is described, with inimitably clever and laughter-moving nonsense, the further Adventures of the fairy-favoured Alice, in the grotesque world which she found to exist on the other side of her mother's drawing-room looking-glass, through which she managed to make her way. The work is profusely embellished with illustrations by Tenniel, exhibiting as great an amount of humour as those to which "Alice's Adventures in Wonderland" owed so much of its popularity.

Carroll—*continued.*

PHANTASMAGORIA, AND OTHER POEMS. Fcap. 8vo. gilt edges. 6s.

"Those who have not made acquaintance with these poems already have a pleasure to come. The comical is so comical, and the grave so really beautiful."—LITERARY CHURCHMAN.

Chatterton: A BIOGRAPHICAL STUDY. By DANIEL WILSON, LL.D., Professor of History and English Literature in University College, Toronto. Crown 8vo. 6s. 6d.

The author here regards Chatterton as a Poet, not as a "mere resetter and defacer of stolen literary treasures." Reviewed in this light, he has found much in the old materials capable of being turned to new account: and to these materials research in various directions has enabled him to make some additions. He believes that the boy-poet has been misjudged, and that the biographies hitherto written of him are not only imperfect but untrue. While dealing tenderly, the author has sought to deal truthfully with the failings as well as the virtues of the boy: bearing always in remembrance, what has been too frequently lost sight of, that he was but a boy;—a boy, and yet a poet of rare power. The EXAMINER *thinks this "the most complete and the purest biography of the poet which has yet appeared."*

Children's Garland from the Best Poets.—See GOLDEN TREASURY SERIES.

Church (A. J.)—HORÆ TENNYSONIANÆ, Sive Eclogæ e Tennysono Latine redditæ. Cura A. J. CHURCH, A.M. Extra fcap. 8vo. 6s.

Latin versions of Selections from Tennyson. Among the authors are the Editor, the late Professor Conington, Professor Seeley, Dr. Hessey, Mr. Kebbel, and other gentlemen. "Of Mr. Church's ode we may speak in almost unqualified praise, and the same may be said of the contributions generally."—PALL MALL GAZETTE.

Clough (Arthur Hugh).—THE POEMS AND PROSE REMAINS OF ARTHUR HUGH CLOUGH. With a

Clough (Arthur Hugh)—*continued.*

Selection from his Letters and a Memoir. Edited by his Wife. With Portrait. Two Vols. Crown 8vo. 21*s.* Or Poems separately, as below.

The late Professor Clough is well known as a graceful, tender poet, and as the scholarly translator of Plutarch. The letters possess high interest, not biographical only, but literary—discussing, as they do, the most important questions of the time, always in a genial spirit. The "Remains" include papers on "Retrenchment at Oxford;" on Professor F. W. Newman's book, "The Soul;" on Wordsworth; on the Formation of Classical English; on some Modern Poems (Matthew Arnold and the late Alexander Smith), &c. &c. "Taken as a whole," the SPECTATOR *says, "these volumes cannot fail to be a lasting monument of one of the most original men of our age." "Full of charming letters from Rome," says the* MORNING STAR, *"from Greece, from America, from Oxford, and from Rugby."*

THE POEMS OF ARTHUR HUGH CLOUGH, sometime Fellow of Oriel College, Oxford. Third Edition. Fcap. 8vo. 6*s.*

"From the higher mind of cultivated, all-questioning, but still conservative England, in this our puzzled generation, we do not know of any utterance in literature so characteristic as the poems of Arthur Hugh Clough."—FRASER'S MAGAZINE.

Clunes.—THE STORY OF PAULINE: an Autobiography. By G. C. CLUNES. Crown 8vo. 6*s.*

"Both for vivid delineation of character and fluent lucidity of style, 'The Story of Pauline' is in the first rank of modern fiction."—GLOBE. *"Told with delightful vivacity, thorough appreciation of life, and a complete knowledge of character."*—MANCHESTER EXAMINER.

Collects of the Church of England. With a beautifully Coloured Floral Design to each Collect, and Illuminated Cover. Crown 8vo. 12*s.* Also kept in various styles of morocco.

In this richly embellished edition of the Church Collects, the paper is thick and handsome and the type large and beautiful, each Collect, with a few exceptions, being printed on a separate page. The dis-

tinctive characteristic of this edition is the floral design which accompanies each Collect, and which is generally emblematical of the character of the day or saint to which it is assigned; the flowers which have been selected are such as are likely to be in bloom on the day to which the Collect belongs. Each flower is richly but tastefully and naturally printed in colours, and from the variety of plants selected and the faithfulness of the illustrations to nature, the volume should form an instructive and interesting companion to all devout Christians, who are likely to find their devotions assisted and guided by having thus brought before them the flowers in their seasons, God's beautiful and never-failing gifts to men. The Preface explains the allusion in the case of all those illustrations which are intended to be emblematical of the days to which they belong, and the Table of Contents forms a complete botanical index, giving both the popular and scientific name of each plant. There are at least one hundred separate plants figured. "This is beyond question," the ART JOURNAL *says, "the most beautiful book of the season." "Carefully, indeed livingly drawn and daintily coloured," says the* PALL MALL GAZETTE. *The* GUARDIAN *thinks it "a successful attempt to associate in a natural and unforced manner the flowers of our fields and gardens with the course of the Christian year."*

Cowper's Poetical Works.—See GLOBE LIBRARY.

Cox.—RECOLLECTIONS OF OXFORD. By G. V. COX, M.A., late Esquire Bedel and Coroner in the University of Oxford. Second and cheaper Edition. Crown 8vo. 6*s.*

Mr. Cox's Recollections date from the end of last century to quite recent times. They are full of old stories and traditions, epigrams and personal traits of the distinguished men who have been at Oxford during that period. The TIMES *says that it "will pleasantly recall in many a country parsonage the memory of youthful days."*

Dante.—DANTE'S COMEDY, THE HELL. Translated by W. M. ROSSETTI. Fcap. 8vo. cloth. 5*s.*

"The aim of this translation of Dante may be summed up in one word—Literality. To follow Dante sentence for sentence, line for line, word for word—neither more nor less, has been my strenuous endeavour."—AUTHOR'S PREFACE.

Days of Old; STORIES FROM OLD ENGLISH HISTORY. By the Author of "Ruth and her Friends." New Edition. 18mo. cloth, gilt leaves. 3*s.* 6*d.*

The Contents of this interesting and instructive volume are, "Caradoc and Deva," a story of British life in the first century; "Wolfgan and the Earl; or, Power," a story of Saxon England: and "Roland," a story of the Crusaders. "Full of truthful and charming historic pictures, is everywhere vital with moral and religious principles, and is written with a brightness of description, and with a dramatic force in the representation of character, that have made, and will always make, it one of the greatest favourites with reading boys."—NONCONFORMIST.

De Vere.—THE INFANT BRIDAL, and other Poems. By AUBREY DE VERE. Fcap. 8vo. 7*s.* 6*d.*

"Mr. De Vere has taken his place among the poets of the day. Pure and tender feeling, and that polished restraint of style which is called classical, are the charms of the volume."—SPECTATOR.

Doyle (Sir F. H.)—Works by SIR FRANCIS HASTINGS DOYLE, Professor of Poetry in the University of Oxford:—

THE RETURN OF THE GUARDS, AND OTHER POEMS. Fcap. 8vo. 7*s.*

"Good wine needs no bush, nor good verse a preface; and Sir Francis Doyle's verses run bright and clear, and smack of a classic vintage. . . . His chief characteristic, as it is his greatest charm, is the simple manliness which gives force to all he writes. It is a characteristic in these days rare enough."—EXAMINER.

LECTURES ON POETRY, delivered before the University of Oxford in 1868. Crown 8vo. 3*s.* 6*d.*

THREE LECTURES:—(1) *Inaugural, in which the nature of Poetry is discussed;* (2) *Provincial Poetry;* (3) *Dr. Newman's "Dream of Gerontius." "Full of thoughtful discrimination and fine insight: the lecture on 'Provincial Poetry' seems to us singularly true, eloquent, and instructive."*—SPECTATOR. *"All these dissertations are marked by a scholarly spirit, delicate taste, and the discriminating powers of a trained judgment."*—DAILY NEWS.

Dryden's Poetical Works.—See GLOBE LIBRARY.

Dürer, Albrecht.—HISTORY OF THE LIFE OF ALBRECHT DÜRER, of Nurnberg. With a Translation of his Letters and Journal, and some account of his Works. By Mrs. CHARLES HEATON. Royal 8vo. bevelled boards, extra gilt. 31*s.* 6*d.*

This work contains about Thirty Illustrations, ten of which are productions by the autotype (carbon) process, and are printed in permanent tints by Messrs. Cundall and Fleming, under licence from the Autotype Company, Limited; the rest are Photographs and Woodcuts.

Estelle Russell.—By the Author of "The Private Life of Galileo." Crown 8vo. 6*s.*

Full of bright pictures of French life. The English family, whose fortunes form the main drift of the story, reside mostly in France, but there are also many English characters and scenes of great interest. It is certainly the work of a fresh, vigorous, and most interesting writer, with a dash of sarcastic humour which is refreshing and not too bitter. "We can send our readers to it with confidence."—SPECTATOR.

Evans.—BROTHER FABIAN'S MANUSCRIPT, AND OTHER POEMS. By SEBASTIAN EVANS. Fcap. 8vo. cloth. 6*s.*

"In this volume we have full assurance that he has 'the vision and the faculty divine.' . . . Clever and full of kindly humour."—GLOBE.

Fairy Book.—The Best Popular Fairy Stories. Selected and Rendered anew by the Author of "John Halifax, Gentleman." With Coloured Illustrations and Ornamental Borders by J. E. ROGERS, Author of "Ridicula Rediviva." Crown 8vo. cloth, extra gilt. 6*s.* (Golden Treasury Edition. 18mo. 4*s.* 6*d.*)

"A delightful selection, in a delightful external form."—SPECTATOR.
Here are reproduced in a new and charming dress many old favourites, as "Hop-o'-my-Thumb," "Cinderella," "Beauty and the Beast," "Jack the Giant-Killer," "Tom Thumb," "Rumpelstiltzchen," "Jack and the Bean-stalk," "Red Riding-Hood," "The Six Swans," and a great many others. "A book which will prove delightful to children all the year round."—PALL MALL GAZETTE.

Fletcher.—THOUGHTS FROM A GIRL'S LIFE. By LUCY FLETCHER. Second Edition. Fcap. 8vo. 4s. 6d.

"Sweet and earnest verses, especially addressed to girls, by one who can sympathise with them, and who has endeavoured to give articulate utterance to the vague aspirations after a better life of pious endeavour, which accompany the unfolding consciousness of the inner life in girlhood. The poems are all graceful; they are marked throughout by an accent of reality; the thoughts and emotions are genuine."—ATHENÆUM.

Freeman (E. A., Hon. D.C.L.)—HISTORICAL ESSAYS. By EDWARD FREEMAN, M.A., Hon. D.C.L., late Fellow of Trinity College, Oxford. Second Edition. 8vo. 10s. 6d.

This volume contains twelve Essays selected from the author's contributions to various Reviews. The principle on which they were chosen was that of selecting papers which referred to comparatively modern times, or, at least, to the existing states and nations of Europe. By a sort of accident a number of the pieces chosen have thrown themselves into something like a continuous series bearing on the historical causes of the great events of 1870—71. Notes have been added whenever they seemed to be called for; and whenever he could gain in accuracy of statement or in force or clearness of expression, the author has freely changed, added to, or left out, what he originally wrote. To many of the Essays has been added a short note of the circumstances under which they were written. It is needless to say that any product of Mr. Freeman's pen is worthy of attentive perusal; and it is believed that the contents of this volume will throw light on several subjects of great historical importance and the widest interest. The following is a list of the subjects:—I. "The Mythical and Romantic Elements in Early English History;" II. "The Continuity of English History;" III. "The Relations between the Crowns of England and Scotland;" IV. "St. Thomas of Canterbury and his Biographers;" V. "The Reign of Edward the Third;" VI. "The Holy Roman Empire;" VII. "The Franks and the Gauls;" VIII. "The Early Sieges of Paris;" IX. "Frederick the First, King of Italy;" X. "The Emperor Frederick the Second;" XI. "Charles the Bold;" XII. "Presidential Government."—"All of them are well worth reading, and very agreeable to read. He never touches a question without adding to our comprehension of it, without leaving the impression of an ample knowledge, a righteous purpose, a clear and powerful understanding."—SATURDAY REVIEW.

Garnett.—IDYLLS AND EPIGRAMS. Chiefly from the Greek Anthology. By RICHARD GARNETT. Fcap. 8vo. 2s. 6d.

"*A charming little book. For English readers, Mr. Garnett's translations will open a new world of thought.*"—WESTMINSTER REVIEW.

Geikie.—SCENERY OF SCOTLAND, viewed in Connexion with its Physical Geology. By ARCHIBALD GEIKIE, F.R.S., Director of the Geological Survey of Scotland. With Illustrations and a New Geological Map. Crown 8vo. 10s. 6d.

"*Before long, we doubt not, it will be one of the travelling companions of every cultivated tourist in Scotland.*"—EDINBURGH COURANT. "*Amusing, picturesque, and instructive.*"—TIMES. "*There is probably no one who has so thoroughly mastered the geology of Scotland as Mr. Geikie.*"—PALL MALL GAZETTE.

Gladstone.—JUVENTUS MUNDI. The Gods and Men of the Heroic Age. By the Right Hon. W. E. GLADSTONE, M.P. Crown 8vo. cloth extra. With Map. 10s. 6d. Second Edition.

"*This new work of Mr. Gladstone deals especially with the historic element in Homer, expounding that element and furnishing by its aid a full account of the Homeric men and the Homeric religion. It starts, after the introductory chapter, with a discussion of the several races then existing in Hellas, including the influence of the Phœnicians and Egyptians. It contains chapters "On the Olympian System, with its several Deities;" "On the Ethics and the Polity of the Heroic Age;" "On the Geography of Homer;" "On the Characters of the Poems;" presenting, in fine, a view of primitive life and primitive society as found in the poems of Homer. To this New Edition various additions have been made. "To read these brilliant details," says the* ATHENÆUM, "*is like standing on the Olympian threshold and gazing at the ineffable brightness within.*" *According to the* WESTMINSTER REVIEW, "*it would be difficult to point out a book that contains so much fulness of knowledge along with so much freshness of perception and clearness of presentation.*"

Globe Library.—See end of this CATALOGUE.

Golden Treasury of the best Songs and Lyrical POEMS IN THE ENGLISH LANGUAGE.—See GOLDEN TREASURY SERIES.

Golden Treasury Series.—See end of this CATALOGUE.

Goldsmith's Works.—See GLOBE LIBRARY.

Guesses at Truth.—By TWO BROTHERS. With Vignette Title, and Frontispiece. New Edition, with Memoir. Fcap. 8vo. 6s. Also see Golden Treasury Series.

These "Guesses at Truth" are not intended to tell the reader what to think. They are rather meant to serve the purpose of a quarry in which, if one is building up his opinions for himself, and only wants to be provided with materials, he may meet with many things to suit him. To very many, since its publication, has this work proved a stimulus to earnest thought and noble action; and thus, to no small extent, it is believed, has it influenced the general current of thinking during the last forty years. It is now no secret that the authors were AUGUSTUS *and* JULIUS CHARLES HARE. *"They—living as they did in constant and free interchange of thought on questions of philosophy and literature and art; delighting, each of them, in the epigrammatic terseness which is the charm of the 'Pensées' of Pascal, and the 'Caractères' of La Bruyère—agreed to utter themselves in this form, and the book appeared, anonymously, in two volumes, in 1827.*

Hamerton.—Works by PHILIP GILBERT HAMERTON:—

A PAINTER'S CAMP. Second Edition, revised. Extra fcap. 8vo. 6s.

BOOK I. *In England*; BOOK II. *In Scotland*; BOOK III. *In France.*

T[illegible] Hamerton's encampments [illegible]. The [illegible] chapters may serve to [illegible] notion of the [illegible] A Walk on the [illegible] Moors; the [illegible] for the

Hamerton—*continued.*

Highlands; The Author encamps on an uninhabited Island; A Lake Voyage; A Gipsy Journey to Glencoe; Concerning Moonlight and Old Castles; A little French City; A Farm in the Autumn, &c. &c. "These pages, written with infinite spirit and humour, bring into close rooms, back upon tired heads, the breezy airs of Lancashire moors and Highland lochs, with a freshness which no recent novelist has succeeded in preserving."—NONCONFORMIST. *"His pages sparkle with many turns of expression, not a few well-told anecdotes, and many observations which are the fruit of attentive study and wise reflection on the complicated phenomena of human life, as well as of unconscious nature."*—WESTMINSTER REVIEW.

ETCHING AND ETCHERS. A Treatise Critical and Practical. With Original Plates by REMBRANDT, CALLOT, DUJARDIN, PAUL POTTER, &c. Royal 8vo. Half morocco. 31*s.* 6*d.*

"The work is one which deserves to be consulted by every intelligent admirer of the fine arts, whether he is an etcher or not."—GUARDIAN.

"It is not often we get anything like the combined intellectual and artistic treat which is supplied us by Mr. Hamerton's ably written and handsome volume. It is a work of which author, printer, and publisher may alike feel proud. It is a work, too, of which none but a genuine artist could by possibility have been the author."—SATURDAY REVIEW.

Hervey.—Works by ROSAMOND HERVEY:—

THE AARBERGS. Two vols. Crown 8vo. cloth. 21*s.*

"All [illegible] with the more delicate flavour of [illegible] and [illegible] enriching the quiet tone of common life [illegible] [illegible] refined and [illegible]."—GUARDIAN. *"A [illegible]."*—DAILY NEWS.

DUKE ERNEST, a Tragedy; and other Poems. Fcap. 8vo. [illegible]

"[illegible] and true [illegible] [illegible] These [illegible]."—BRITISH [illegible]

Higginson.—MALBONE: An Oldport Romance. By T. W. HIGGINSON. Fcap. 8vo. 2*s.* 6*d.*

This is a story of American life, so told as to be interesting and instructive to all English readers. The DAILY NEWS *says: "Who likes a quiet story, full of mature thought, of clear humorous surprises, of artistic studious design? 'Malbone' is a rare work, possessing these characteristics, and replete, too, with honest literary effort."*

Home.—BLANCHE LISLE, and other Poems. By CECIL HOME. Fcap. 8vo. 4*s.* 6*d.*

Hood (Tom).—THE PLEASANT TALE OF PUSS AND ROBIN AND THEIR FRIENDS, KITTY AND BOB. Told in Pictures by L. FRÖLICH, and in Rhymes by TOM HOOD. Crown 8vo. gilt. 3*s.* 6*d.*

This is a pleasant little tale of wee Bob and his Sister and their attempts to rescue poor Robin from the cruel claws of Pussy. It will be intelligible and interesting to the meanest capacity, and is illustrated by thirteen graphic cuts drawn by Frölich. "The volume is prettily got up, and is sure to be a favourite in the nursery."—SCOTSMAN. *"Herr Frölich has outdone himself in his pictures of this dramatic chase."*—MORNING POST.

Jebb.—THE CHARACTERS OF THEOPHRASTUS. An English Translation from a Revised Text. With Introduction and Notes. By R. C. JEBB, M.A., Fellow and Assistant Tutor of Trinity College, Cambridge, and Public Orator of the University. Extra fcap. 8vo. 6*s.* 6*d.*

The first object of this book is to make these lively pictures of old Greek manners better known to English readers. But as the Editor and Translator has been at considerable pains to procure a reliable text, and has recorded the results of his critical labours in a lengthy Introduction, in Notes and Appendices, it is hoped that the work will prove of value even to the scholar. "We must not omit to give due honour to Mr. Jebb's translation, which is as good as translation can be. . . . Not less commendable are the execution of the Notes and the critical handling of the text."—SPECTATOR. *"Mr. Jebb's little volume is more easily taken up than laid down."*—GUARDIAN.

Jest Book.—By MARK LEMON.—See GOLDEN TREASURY SERIES.

Keary (A.)—Works by Miss A. KEARY:—

JANET'S HOME. Cheap Edition. Globe 8vo. 2s. 6d.

"*Never did a more charming family appear upon the canvas; and most skilfully and felicitously have their characters been portrayed. Each individual of the fireside is a finished portrait, distinct and lifelike. . . . The future before her as a novelist is that of becoming the Miss Austin of her generation.*"—SUN.

CLEMENCY FRANKLYN. Globe 8vo. 2s. 6d.

"*Full of wisdom and goodness, simple, truthful, and artistic. . . It is capital as a story; better still in its pure tone and wholesome influence.*"—GLOBE.

OLDBURY. Three vols. Crown 8vo. 31s. 6d.

"*This is a very powerfully written story.*"—GLOBE. "*This is a really excellent novel.*"—ILLUSTRATED LONDON NEWS. "*The sketches of society in Oldbury are excellent. The pictures of child life are full of truth.*"—WESTMINSTER REVIEW.

Keary (A. and E.)—Works by A. and E. KEARY:—

THE LITTLE WANDERLIN, and other Fairy Tales. 18mo. 3s. 6d.

"*The tales are fanciful and well written, and they are sure to win favour amongst little readers.*"—ATHENÆUM.

THE HEROES OF ASGARD. Tales from Scandinavian Mythology. New and Revised Edition, Illustrated by HUARD. Extra fcap. 8vo. 4s. 6d.

"*Told in a light and amusing style, which, in its drollery and quaintness, reminds us of our old favourite Grimm.*"—TIMES.

Kingsley.—Works by the Rev. CHARLES KINGSLEY, M.A., Rector of Eversley, and Canon of Chester:—

Mr. Canon Kingsley's novels, most will admit, have not only commanded for themselves a foremost place in literature, as artistic

Kingsley (C.)—*continued.*

productions of a high class, but have exercised upon the age an incalculable influence in the direction of the highest Christian manliness. Mr. Kingsley has done more perhaps than almost any other writer of fiction to fashion the generation into whose hands the destinies of the world are now being committed. His works will therefore be read by all who wish to have their hearts cheered and their souls stirred to noble endeavour; they must be read by all who wish to know the influences which moulded the men of this century.

"WESTWARD HO!", or, The Voyages and Adventures of Sir Amyas Leigh. Sixth Edition. Crown 8vo. 6*s*.

No other work conveys a more vivid idea of the surging, adventurous, nobly inquisitive spirit of the generations which immediately followed the Reformation in England. The daring deeds of the Elizabethan heroes are told with a freshness, an enthusiasm, and a truthfulness that can belong only to one who wishes he had been their leader. His descriptions of the luxuriant scenery of the then new-found Western land are acknowledged to be unmatched. FRASER'S MAGAZINE *calls it "almost the best historical novel of the day."*

TWO YEARS AGO. Fourth Edition. Crown 8vo. 6*s*.

"*Mr. Kingsley has provided us all along with such pleasant diversions—such rich and brightly tinted glimpses of natural history, such suggestive remarks on mankind, society, and all sorts of topics, that amidst the pleasure of the way, the circuit to be made will be by most forgotten.*"—GUARDIAN.

HYPATIA; or, New Foes with an Old Face. Fifth Edition. Crown 8vo. 6*s*.

The work is from beginning to end a series of fascinating pictures of strange phases of that strange primitive society; and no finer portrait has yet been given of the noble-minded lady who was faithful to martyrdom in her attachment to the classical creeds. No work affords a clearer notion of the many interesting problems which agitated the minds of men in those days, and which, in various phases, are again coming up for discussion at the present time.

Kingsley (C.)—*continued.*

HEREWARD THE WAKE—LAST OF THE ENGLISH. Crown 8vo. 6*s*.

Mr. Kingsley here tells the story of the final conflict of the two races, Saxons and Normans, as if he himself had borne a part in it. While as a work of fiction "Hereward" cannot fail to delight all readers, no better supplement to the dry history of the time could be put into the hands of the young, containing as it does so vivid a picture of the social and political life of the period.

YEAST: A Problem. Fifth Edition. Crown 8vo. 5*s*.

In this production the author shows, in an interesting dramatic form, the state of fermentation in which the minds of many earnest men are with regard to some of the most important religious and social problems of the day.

ALTON LOCKE. New Edition. With a New Preface. Crown 8vo. 4*s*. 6*d*.

This novel, which shows forth the evils arising from modern "caste," has done much to remove the unnatural barriers which existed between the various classes of society, and to establish a sympathy to some extent between the higher and lower grades of the social scale. Though written with a purpose, it is full of character and interest; the author shows, to quote the SPECTATOR, *"what it is that constitutes the true Christian, God-fearing, man-living gentleman."*

AT LAST: A CHRISTMAS IN THE WEST INDIES. With numerous Illustrations. Second and Cheaper Edition. Crown 8vo. 10*s*. 6*d*.

Mr. Kingsley's dream of forty years was at last *fulfilled, when he started on a Christmas expedition to the West Indies, for the purpose of becoming personally acquainted with the scenes which he has so vividly described in "Westward ho!" "In this book Mr. Kingsley revels in the gorgeous wealth of West Indian vegetation, bringing before us one marvel after another, alternately sating and piquing our curiosity. Whether we climb the cliffs with him, or peer over into narrow bays which are being hollowed out by the trade-surf, or wander through impenetrable forests, where the tops of the trees form a green cloud overhead, or gaze down glens which*

Kingsley (C.)—*continued.*

are watered by the clearest brooks, running through masses of palm and banana and all the rich variety of foliage, we are equally delighted and amazed."—ATHENÆUM.

THE WATER BABIES. A Fairy Tale for a Land Baby. New Edition, with additional Illustrations by Sir NOEL PATON, R.S.A., and P. SKELTON. Crown 8vo. cloth extra gilt. 5*s.*

"*In fun, in humour, and in innocent imagination, as a child's book we do not know its equal.*"—LONDON REVIEW. "*Mr. Kingsley must have the credit of revealing to us a new order of life. . . . There is in the 'Water Babies' an abundance of wit, fun, good humour, geniality,* élan, *go.*"—TIMES.

THE HEROES; or, Greek Fairy Tales for my Children. With Coloured Illustrations. New Edition. 18mo. 4*s.* 6*d.*

"*We do not think these heroic stories have ever been more attractively told. . . . There is a deep under-current of religious feeling traceable throughout its pages which is sure to influence young readers powerfully.*"—LONDON REVIEW. "*One of the children's books that will surely become a classic.*"—NONCONFORMIST.

PHAETHON; or, Loose Thoughts for Loose Thinkers. Third Edition. Crown 8vo. 2*s.*

"*The dialogue of 'Phaethon' has striking beauties, and its suggestions may meet half-way many a latent doubt, and, like a light breeze, lift from the soul clouds that are gathering heavily, and threatening to settle down in misty gloom on the summer of many a fair and promising young life.*"—SPECTATOR.

POEMS; including The Saint's Tragedy, Andromeda, Songs, Ballads, etc. Complete Collected Edition. Extra fcap. 8vo. 6*s.*

Canon Kingsley's poetical works have gained for their author, independently of his other works, a high and enduring place in literature, and are much sought after. The publishers have here collected the whole of them in a moderately-priced and handy volume. The SPECTATOR *calls "Andromeda" "the finest piece of English hexameter verse that has ever been written. It is a volume which many readers will be glad to possess."*

Kingsley (H.)—Works by HENRY KINGSLEY :—

TALES OF OLD TRAVEL. Re-narrated. With Eight full-page Illustrations by HUARD. Fourth Edition. Crown 8vo. cloth, extra gilt. 5*s*.

In this volume Mr. Henry Kingsley re-narrates, at the same time preserving much of the quaintness of the original, some of the most fascinating tales of travel contained in the collections of Hakluyt and others. The CONTENTS *are:—Marco Polo; The Shipwreck of Pelsart; The Wonderful Adventures of Andrew Battel; The Wanderings of a Capuchin; Peter Carder; The Preservation of the "Terra Nova;" Spitzbergen; D'Ermenonville's Acclimatization Adventure; The Old Slave Trade; Miles Philips; The Sufferings of Robert Everard; John Fox; Alvaro Nunez; The Foundation of an Empire. "We know no better book for those who want knowledge or seek to refresh it. As for the 'sensational,' most novels are tame compared with these narratives."*—ATHENÆUM. *"Exactly the book to interest and to do good to intelligent and high-spirited boys."*—LITERARY CHURCHMAN.

THE LOST CHILD. With Eight Illustrations by FROLICH. Crown 4to. cloth gilt. 3*s*. 6*d*.

This is an interesting story of a little boy, the son of an Australian shepherd and his wife, who lost himself in the bush, and who was, after much searching, found dead far up a mountain-side. It contains many illustrations from the well-known pencil of Frolich. "A pathetic story, and told so as to give children an interest in Australian ways and scenery."— GLOBE. *"Very charmingly and very touchingly told."*—SATURDAY REVIEW.

Knatchbull-Hugessen.—Works by E. H. KNATCHBULL-HUGESSEN, M.P. :—

Mr. Knatchbull-Hugessen has won for himself a reputation as an inimitable teller of fairy-tales. "His powers," says the TIMES, *"are of a very high order; light and brilliant narrative flows from his pen, and is fed by an invention as graceful as it is inexhaustible." "Children reading his stories," the* SCOTSMAN *says, "or hearing them read, will have their minds refreshed and invigorated as much as their bodies would be by abundance of fresh air and exercise."*

Knatchbull-Hugessen—*continued.*

STORIES FOR MY CHILDREN. With Illustrations. Third Edition. Extra fcap. 8vo. 5*s.*

"*The stories are charming, and full of life and fun.*"—STANDARD. "*The author has an imagination as fanciful as Grimm himself, while some of his stories are superior to anything that Hans Christian Andersen has written.*"—NONCONFORMIST.

CRACKERS FOR CHRISTMAS. More Stories. With Illustrations by JELLICOE and ELWES. Fourth Edition. Crown 8vo. 5*s.*

"*A fascinating little volume, which will make him friends in every household in which there are children.*"—DAILY NEWS.

MOONSHINE: Fairy Tales. With Illustrations by W. BRUNTON. Fourth Edition. Crown 8vo. cloth gilt. 5*s.*

Here will be found "an Ogre, a Dwarf, a Wizard, quantities of Elves and Fairies, and several animals who speak like mortal men and women." There are twelve stories and nine irresistible illustrations. "*A volume of fairy tales, written not only for ungrown children, but for bigger, and if you are nearly worn out, or sick, or sorry, you will find it good reading.*"—GRAPHIC. "*The most charming volume of fairy tales which we have ever read. . . . We cannot quit this very pleasant book without a word of praise to its illustrator. Mr. Brunton from first to last has done admirably.*"—TIMES.

La Lyre Française.—See GOLDEN TREASURY SERIES.

Latham.—SERTUM SHAKSPERIANUM, Subnexis aliquot aliunde excerptis floribus. Latine reddidit Rev. H. LATHAM, M.A. Extra fcap. 8vo. 5*s.*

Besides versions of Shakespeare, this volume contains, among other pieces, Gray's "Elegy," Campbell's "Hohenlinden," Wolfe's "Burial of Sir John Moore," and selections from Cowper and George Herbert.

Lemon.—THE LEGENDS OF NUMBER NIP. By MARK LEMON. With Illustrations by C. KEENE. New Edition. Extra fcap. 8vo. 2*s.* 6*d.*

Life and Times of Conrad the Squirrel. A Story for Children. By the Author of "Wandering Willie," "Effie's Friends," &c. With a Frontispiece by R. FARREN. Crown 8vo. 3*s.* 6*d.*

It is sufficient to commend this story of a Squirrel to the attention of readers, that it is by the author of the beautiful stories of "Wandering Willie" and "Effie's Friends." It is well calculated to make children take an intelligent and tender interest in the lower animals.

Little Estella, and other Fairy Tales for the Young. Royal 16mo. 3*s.* 6*d.*

"*This is a fine story, and we thank heaven for not being too wise to enjoy it.*"—DAILY NEWS.

Little Lucy's Wonderful Globe.—See YONGE, C. M.

Lowell.—AMONG MY BOOKS. Six Essays. Dryden—Witchcraft—Shakespeare once More—New England Two Centuries Ago—Lessing—Rousseau and the Sentimentalists. Crown 8vo. 7*s.* 6*d.*

"*We may safely say the volume is one of which our chief complaint must be that there is not more of it. There are good sense and lively feeling forcibly and tersely expressed in every page of his writing.*" —PALL MALL GAZETTE.

Lyttelton.—Works by LORD LYTTELTON :—

THE "COMUS" OF MILTON, rendered into Greek Verse. Extra fcap. 8vo. 5*s.*

THE "SAMSON AGONISTES" OF MILTON, rendered into Verse. Extra fcap. 8vo. 6*s.* 6*d.*

"*Classical in spirit, full of force, and true to the original.*" —GUARDIAN.

Macmillan's Magazine.—Published Monthly. Price 1*s.* Volumes I. to XXV. are now ready. 7*s.* 6*d.* each.

Macquoid.—PATTY. By KATHERINE S. MACQUOID. Two vols. Crown 8vo. 21*s.*

The ATHENÆUM "*congratulates Mrs. Macquoid on having made a great step since the publication of her last novel,*" *and says this* "*is a graceful and eminently readable story.*" *The* GLOBE *considers it* "*well-written, amusing, and interesting, and has the merit of being out of the ordinary run of novels.*"

Malbone.—See HIGGINSON.

Marlitt (E.)—THE COUNTESS GISELA. Translated from the German of E. MARLITT. Crown 8vo. 7*s.* 6*d.*

"*A very beautiful story of German country life.*"—LITERARY CHURCHMAN.

Masson (Professor).—Works by DAVID MASSON, M.A., Professor of Rhetoric and English Literature in the University of Edinburgh. (See also BIOGRAPHICAL and PHILOSOPHICAL CATALOGUES.)

ESSAYS, BIOGRAPHICAL AND CRITICAL. Chiefly on the British Poets. 8vo. 12*s.* 6*d.*

"*Distinguished by a remarkable power of analysis, a clear statement of the actual facts on which speculation is based, and an appropriate beauty of language. These Essays should be popular with serious men.*"—ATHENÆUM.

BRITISH NOVELISTS AND THEIR STYLES. Being a Critical Sketch of the History of British Prose Fiction. Crown 8vo. 7*s.* 6*d.*

"*Valuable for its lucid analysis of fundamental principles, its breadth of view, and sustained animation of style.*"—SPECTATOR. "*Mr. Masson sets before us with a bewitching ease and clearness which nothing but a perfect mastery of his subject could have rendered possible, a large body of both deep and sound discriminative criticism on all the most memorable of our British novelists. . . . . His brilliant and instructive book.*"—JOHN BULL.

Merivale.—KEATS' HYPERION, rendered into Latin Verse. By C. MERIVALE, B.D. Second Edition. Extra fcap. 8vo. 3*s.* 6*d.*

Milner.—THE LILY OF LUMLEY. By EDITH MILNER. Crown 8vo. 7*s.* 6*d.*

"*The novel is a good one and decidedly worth the reading.*"—Examiner. "*A pretty, brightly-written story.*"—Literary Churchman. "*A tale possessing the deepest interest.*"—Court Journal.

Mistral (F.)—MIRELLE, a Pastoral Epic of Provence. Translated by H. Crichton. Extra fcap. 8vo. 6*s*.

"*It would be hard to overpraise the sweetness and pleasing freshness of this charming epic.*"—Athenæum. "*A good translation of a poem that deserves to be known by all students of literature and friends of old-world simplicity in story-telling.*"—Nonconformist.

Brown, M.P.—MR. PISISTRATUS BROWN, M.P., IN THE HIGHLANDS. Reprinted from the *Daily News*, with Additions. Crown 8vo. 5*s*.

These papers appeared at intervals in the Daily News *during the summer of 1871. They narrate in light and jocular style the adventures "by flood and field" of Mr. Brown, M.P. and his friend in their tour through the West Highlands, and will be found well adapted to while away a pleasant hour either by the winter fireside or during a summer holiday.*

Mrs. Jerningham's Journal. A Poem purporting to be the Journal of a newly-married Lady. Second Edition. Fcap. 8vo. 3*s*. 6*d*.

"*It is nearly a perfect gem. We have had nothing so good for a long time, and those who neglect to read it are neglecting one of the jewels of contemporary history.*"—Edinburgh Daily Review. "*One quality in the piece, sufficient of itself to claim a moment's attention, is that it is unique—original, indeed, is not too strong a word—in the manner of its conception and execution.*"—Pall Mall Gazette.

Mitford (A. B.)—TALES OF OLD JAPAN. By A. B. Mitford, Second Secretary to the British Legation in Japan. With Illustrations drawn and cut on Wood by Japanese Artists. Two Vols. Crown 8vo. 21*s*.

The old Japanese civilization is fast disappearing, and will, in a few years, be completely extinct. It was important, therefore, to preserve as far as possible trustworthy records of a state of society which, although venerable from its antiquity, has for Europeans the charm of novelty; hence the series of narratives and legends translated by Mr. Mitford, and in which the Japanese are very judiciously left to tell their own tale. The two volumes comprise not only stories and episodes illustrative of Asiatic superstitions, but also three sermons. The Preface, Appendices, and Notes explain a number of local peculiarities; the thirty-one woodcuts are the genuine work of a native artist, who, unconsciously of course, has adopted the process first introduced by the early German masters. "They will always be interesting as memorials of a most exceptional society; while, regarded simply as tales, they are sparkling, sensational, and dramatic, and the originality of their ideas and the quaintness of their language give them a most captivating piquancy. The illustrations are extremely interesting, and for the curious in such matters have a special and particular value."—PALL MALL GAZETTE.

Morte d'Arthur.—See GLOBE LIBRARY.

Myers (Ernest).—THE PURITANS. By ERNEST MYERS. Extra fcap. 8vo. cloth. 2*s.* 6*d.*

"*It is not too much to call it a really grand poem, stately and dignified, and showing not only a high poetic mind, but also great power over poetic expression.*"—LITERARY CHURCHMAN.

Myers (F. W. H.)—POEMS. By F. W. H. MYERS. Containing "St. Paul," "St. John," and others. Extra fcap. 8vo. 4*s.* 6*d.*

"*It is rare to find a writer who combines to such an extent the faculty of communicating feelings with the faculty of euphonious expression.*"—SPECTATOR. "*'St. Paul' stands without a rival as the noblest religious poem which has been written in an age which beyond any other has been prolific in this class of poetry. The sublimest conceptions are expressed in language which, for richness, taste, and purity, we have never seen excelled.*"—JOHN BULL.

Nine Years Old.—By the Author of "St. Olave's," "When I was a Little Girl," &c. Illustrated by FRÖLICH. Second Edition. Extra fcap. 8vo. cloth gilt. 4*s.* 6*d.*

It is believed that this story, by the favourably known author of "St. Olave's," will be found both highly interesting and instructive to the young. The volume contains eight graphic illustrations by Mr. L. Frolich. The EXAMINER *says: "Whether the readers are nine years old, or twice, or seven times as old, they must enjoy this pretty volume."*

Noel.—BEATRICE, AND OTHER POEMS. By the Hon. RODEN NOEL. Fcap. 8vo. 6*s.*

"*It is impossible to read the poem through without being powerfully moved. There are passages in it which for intensity and tenderness, clear and vivid vision, spontaneous and delicate sympathy, may be compared with the best efforts of our best living writers.*" —SPECTATOR. "*It is long since we have seen a volume of poems which has seemed to us so full of the real stuff of which we are made, and uttering so freely the deepest wants of this complicated age.*"—BRITISH QUARTERLY.

Norton.—Works by the Hon. Mrs. NORTON:—

THE LADY OF LA GARAYE. With Vignette and Frontispiece. New Edition. Fcap. 8vo. 4*s.* 6*d.*

"*A poem entirely unaffected, perfectly original, so true and yet so fanciful, so strong and yet so womanly, with painting so exquisite, a pure portraiture of the highest affections and the deepest sorrows, and instilling a lesson true, simple, and sublime.*" — DUBLIN UNIVERSITY MAGAZINE. "*Full of thought well expressed, and may be classed among her best efforts.*"—TIMES.

OLD SIR DOUGLAS. Cheap Edition. Globe 8vo. 2*s.* 6*d.*

"*This varied and lively novel—this clever novel so full of character, and of fine incidental remark.*"—SCOTSMAN. "*One of the pleasantest and healthiest stories of modern fiction.*"—GLOBE.

Oliphant.—Works by Mrs. OLIPHANT:—

AGNES HOPETOUN'S SCHOOLS AND HOLIDAYS. New Edition with Illustrations. Royal 16mo. gilt leaves. 4*s.* 6*d.*

"*There are few books of late years more fitted to touch the heart, purify the feeling, and quicken and sustain right principles.*"—NONCONFORMIST. "*A more gracefully written story it is impossible to desire.*"—DAILY NEWS.

Oliphant—*continued.*

A SON OF THE SOIL. New Edition. Globe 8vo. 2s. 6d.

"*It is a very different work from the ordinary run of novels. The whole life of a man is portrayed in it, worked out with subtlety and insight.*"—ATHENÆUM. "*With entire freedom from any sensational plot, there is enough of incident to give keen interest to the narrative, and make us feel as we read it that we have been spending a few hours with friends who will make our own lives better by their own noble purposes and holy living.*"—BRITISH QUARTERLY REVIEW.

Our Year. A Child's Book, in Prose and Verse. By the Author of "John Halifax, Gentleman." Illustrated by CLARENCE DOBELL. Royal 16mo. 3s. 6d.

"*It is just the book we could wish to see in the hands of every child.*" —ENGLISH CHURCHMAN.

Olrig Grange. Edited by HERMANN KUNST, Philol. Professor. Extra fcap. 8vo. 6s. 6d.

This is a poem in six parts, each the utterance of a distinct person. It is the story of a young Scotchman of noble aims designed for the ministry, but who "rent the Creed trying to fit it on," who goes to London to seek fame and fortune in literature, and who returns defeated to his old home in the north to die. The NORTH BRITISH DAILY MAIL, *in reviewing the work, speaks of it as affording "abounding evidence of genial and generative faculty working in self-decreed modes. A masterly and original power of impression, pouring itself forth in clear, sweet, strong rhythm. . . . Easy to cull, remarkable instances of thrilling fervour, of glowing delicacy, of scathing and trenchant scorn, to point out the fine and firm discrimination of character which prevails throughout, to dwell upon the ethical power and psychological truth which are exhibited, to note the skill with which the diverse parts of the poem are set in organic relation. . . . It is a fine poem, full of life, of music, and of clear vision.*"

Oxford Spectator, the.—Reprinted. Extra fcap. 8vo. 3s. 6d.

These papers, after the manner of Addison's "Spectator," appeared in Oxford from November 1867 to December 1868, at intervals varying from two days to a week. They attempt to sketch several features of Oxford life from an undergraduate's point of view, and to give modern readings of books which undergraduates study. "There is," the SATURDAY REVIEW *says, "all the old fun, the old sense of social ease and brightness and freedom, the old medley of work and indolence, of jest and earnest, that made Oxford life so picturesque."*

Palgrave.—Works by FRANCIS TURNER PALGRAVE, M.A., late Fellow of Exeter College, Oxford :—

ESSAYS ON ART. Extra fcap. 8vo. 6*s.*

Mulready—Dyce—Holman Hunt—Herbert—Poetry, Prose, and Sensationalism in Art—Sculpture in England—The Albert Cross, &c. Most of these Essays have appeared in the SATURDAY REVIEW *and elsewhere: but they have been minutely revised, and in some cases almost rewritten, with the aim mainly of excluding matters of temporary interest, and softening down all asperities of censure. The main object of the book is, by examples taken chiefly from the works of contemporaries, to illustrate the truths, that art has fixed principles, of which any one may attain the knowledge who is not wanting in natural taste. Art, like poetry, is addressed to the world at large, not to a special jury of professional masters. "In many respects the truest critic we have."*—LITERARY CHURCHMAN.

THE FIVE DAYS' ENTERTAINMENTS AT WENTWORTH GRANGE. A Book for Children. With Illustrations by ARTHUR HUGHES and Engraved Title-page by JEENS. Small 4to. cloth extra. 6*s.*

"If you want a really good book for both sexes and all ages, buy this, as handsome a volume of tales as you'll find in all the market."—ATHENÆUM. *"Exquisite both in form and substance."* —GUARDIAN.

LYRICAL POEMS. Extra fcap. 8vo. 6*s.*

"A volume of pure quiet verse, sparkling with tender melodies, and alive with thoughts of genuine poetry. . . . Turn where we will throughout the volume, we find traces of beauty, tenderness, and truth; true poet's work, touched and refined by the master-hand of a real artist, who shows his genius even in trifles."—STANDARD.

Palgrave—*continued.*

ORIGINAL HYMNS. Third Edition, enlarged, 16mo. 1*s.* 6*d.*

"*So choice, so perfect, and so refined, so tender in feeling, and so scholarly in expression, that we look with special interest to everything that he gives us.*"—LITERARY CHURCHMAN.

GOLDEN TREASURY OF THE BEST SONGS AND LYRICS. Edited by F. T. PALGRAVE. See GOLDEN TREASURY SERIES.

SHAKESPEARE'S SONNETS AND SONGS. Edited by F. T. PALGRAVE. Gem Edition. With Vignette Title by JEENS. 3*s.* 6*d.*

"*For minute elegance no volume could possibly excel the 'Gem Edition.'*"—SCOTSMAN.

Palmer's Book of Praise.—See GOLDEN TREASURY SERIES.

Parables.—TWELVE PARABLES OF OUR LORD. Illustrated in Colours from Sketches taken in the East by MCENIRY, with Frontispiece from a Picture by JOHN JELLICOE, and Illuminated Texts and Borders. Royal 4to. in Ornamental Binding. 16*s.*

The SCOTSMAN *calls this "one of the most superb books of the season." The richly and tastefully illuminated borders are from the* Brevario Grimani, *in St. Mark's Library, Venice. The* TIMES *calls it "one of the most beautiful of modern pictorial works;" while the* GRAPHIC *says "nothing in this style, so good, has ever before been published."*

Patmore.—THE ANGEL IN THE HOUSE. By COVENTRY PATMORE.

BOOK I. *The Betrothal;* BOOK II. *The Espousals;* BOOK III. *Faithful for Ever. The Victories of Love. Tamerton Church Tower.* Two Vols. Fcap. 8vo. 12*s.*

"*A style combining much of the homeliness of Crabbe, with sweeter music and a far higher range of thought.*"—TIMES. "*Its merit is more than sufficient to account for its success. . . . In its manly and healthy cheer, the 'Angel in the House' is an effectual protest against the morbid poetry of the age.*"—EDINBURGH REVIEW.

"*We think his 'Angel in the House' would be a good wedding-gift to a bridegroom from his friends; though, whenever it is read with a right view of its aim, we believe it will be found itself, more or less, of an angel in the house.*"—FRASER'S MAGAZINE.

*** *A New and Cheap Edition in One Vol. 18mo., beautifully printed on toned paper, price 2s. 6d.*

Pember.—THE TRAGEDY OF LESBOS. A Dramatic Poem. By E. H. PEMBER. Fcap. 8vo. 4s. 6d.

Founded upon the story of Sappho. "He tells his story with dramatic force, and in language that often rises almost to grandeur."—ATHENÆUM.

Poole.—PICTURES OF COTTAGE LIFE IN THE WEST OF ENGLAND. By MARGARET E. POOLE. New and Cheaper Edition. With Frontispiece by R. Farren. Crown 8vo. 3s. 6d.

"*Charming stories of peasant life, written in something of George Eliot's style. . . . Her stories could not be other than they are, as literal as truth, as romantic as fiction, full of pathetic touches and strokes of genuine humour. . . . All the stories are studies of actual life, executed with no mean art.*"—TIMES.

Pope's Poetical Works.—See GLOBE LIBRARY.

Population of an Old Pear Tree. From the French of E. VAN BRUYSSEL. Edited by the Author of "The Heir of Redclyffe." With Illustrations by BECKER. Second Edition. Crown 8vo. gilt edges. 6s.

"*This is not a regular book of natural history, but a description of all the living creatures that came and went in a summer's day beneath an old pear tree, observed by eyes that had for the nonce become microscopic, recorded by a pen that finds dramas in everything, and illustrated by a dainty pencil. . . . We can hardly fancy anyone with a moderate turn for the curiosities of insect life, or for delicate French esprit, not being taken by these clever sketches.*"—GUARDIAN. "*A whimsical and charming little book.*"—ATHENÆUM.

Portfolio of Cabinet Pictures.—Oblong folio, price 42s.

This is a handsome portfolio containing faithfully executed and beautifully coloured reproductions of five well-known pictures:—"Childe Harold's Pilgrimage" and "The Fighting Temeraire," by J. M. W. Turner; "Crossing the Bridge," by Sir W. A. Callcott; "The Cornfield," by John Constable; and "A Landscape," by Birket Foster. The DAILY NEWS *says of them, "They are very beautifully executed, and might be framed and hung up on the wall, as creditable substitutes for the originals."*

Raphael of Urbino and his Father Giovanni SANTI.—By J. D. PASSAVANT, formerly Director of the Museum at Frankfort. Illustrated. Royal 8vo. cloth gilt, gilt edges. 31s. 6d.

To the enlarged French edition of Herr Passavant's Life of Raphael, that painter's admirers have turned whenever they have sought for information; and it will doubtless remain for many years the best book of reference on all questions pertaining to the great painter. The present work consists of a translation of those parts of Passavant's volumes which are most likely to interest the general reader. Besides a complete life of Raphael it contains the valuable descriptions of all his known paintings, and the Chronological Index, which is of so much service to amateurs who wish to study the progressive character of his works. The illustrations, twenty in number, by Woodbury's new permanent process of photography, are from the finest engravings that could be procured, and have been chosen with the intention of giving examples of Raphael's various styles of painting. "There will be found in the volume almost all that the ordinary student or critic would require to learn."—ART JOURNAL. *"It is most beautifully and profusely illustrated."*—SATURDAY REVIEW.

Realmah.—By the Author of "Friends in Council." Crown 8vo. 6s.

Rhoades.—POEMS. By JAMES RHOADES. Fcap. 8vo. 4s. 6d.

CONTENTS:—*Ode to Harmony; To the Spirit of Unrest; Ode to Winter; The Tunnel; To the Spirit of Beauty; Song of a Leaf;*

By the Rother; An Old Orchard; Love and Rest; The Flowers Surprised; On the Death of Artemus Ward; The Two Paths; The Ballad of Little Maisie; Sonnets.

Richardson.—THE ILIAD OF THE EAST. A Selection of Legends drawn from Valmiki's Sanskrit Poem, "The Ramayana." By FREDERIKA RICHARDSON. Crown 8vo. 7*s*. 6*d*.

"*It is impossible to read it without recognising the value and interest of the Eastern epic. It is as fascinating as a fairy tale, this romantic poem of India.*"—GLOBE. "*A charming volume which at once enmeshes the reader in its snares.*"—ATHENÆUM.

Robinson Crusoe.—See GLOBE LIBRARY and GOLDEN TREASURY SERIES.

Roby.—STORY OF A HOUSEHOLD, AND OTHER POEMS. By MARY K. ROBY. Fcap. 8vo. 5*s*.

Rogers.—Works by J. E. ROGERS:—

RIDICULA REDIVIVA. Old Nursery Rhymes. Illustrated in Colours, with Ornamental Cover. Crown 4to. 6*s*.

"*The most splendid, and at the same time the most really meritorious of the books specially intended for children, that we have seen.*"—SPECTATOR. "*These large bright pictures will attract children to really good and honest artistic work, and that ought not to be an indifferent consideration with parents who propose to educate their children.*"—PALL MALL GAZETTE.

MORES RIDICULI. Old Nursery Rhymes. Illustrated in Colours, with Ornamental Cover. Crown 4to. 6*s*.

"*These world-old rhymes have never had and need never wish for a better pictorial setting than Mr. Rogers has given them.*"—TIMES. "*Nothing could be quainter or more absurdly comical than most of the pictures, which are all carefully executed and beautifully coloured.*"—GLOBE.

Rossetti.—Works by CHRISTINA ROSSETTI:—

GOBLIN MARKET, AND OTHER POEMS. With two Designs by D. G. ROSSETTI. Second Edition. Fcap. 8vo. 5*s*.

Rossetti—*continued.*

"*She handles her little marvel with that rare poetic discrimination which neither exhausts it of its simple wonders by pushing symbolism too far, nor keeps those wonders in the merely fabulous and capricious stage. In fact, she has produced a true children's poem, which is far more delightful to the mature than to children, though it would be delightful to all.*"—SPECTATOR.

THE PRINCE'S PROGRESS, AND OTHER POEMS. With two Designs by D. G. ROSSETTI. Fcap. 8vo. 6*s.*

"*Miss Rossetti's poems are of the kind which recalls Shelley's definition of Poetry as the record of the best and happiest moments of the best and happiest minds. . . . They are like the piping of a bird on the spray in the sunshine, or the quaint singing with which a child amuses itself when it forgets that anybody is listening.*"—SATURDAY REVIEW.

Rossetti (W. M.)—DANTE'S HELL. See "DANTE."

Ruth and her Friends. A Story for Girls. With a Frontispiece. Fourth Edition. Royal 16mo. 3*s.* 6*d.*

"*We wish all the school girls and home-taught girls in the land had the opportunity of reading it.*"—NONCONFORMIST.

Scott's Poetical Works.—See GLOBE LIBRARY.

Scouring of the White Horse; or, the Long VACATION RAMBLE OF A LONDON CLERK. Illustrated by DOYLE. Imp. 16mo. Cheaper Issue. 3*s.* 6*d.*

"*A glorious tale of summer joy.*"—FREEMAN. "*There is a genial hearty life about the book.*"—JOHN BULL. "*The execution is excellent. . . . Like 'Tom Brown's School Days,' the 'White Horse' gives the reader a feeling of gratitude and personal esteem towards the author.*"—SATURDAY REVIEW.

Seeley (Professor).—LECTURES AND ESSAYS. By J. R. SEELEY, M.A. Professor of Modern History in the University of Cambridge. 8vo. 10*s.* 6*d.*

CONTENTS :—*Roman Imperialism: 1. The Great Roman Revolution; 2. The Proximate Cause of the Fall of the Roman Empire; 3. The Later Empire.—Milton's Political Opinions — Milton's Poetry—Elementary Principles in Art—Liberal Education in Universities—English in Schools—The Church as a Teacher of Morality—The Teaching of Politics: an Inaugural Lecture delivered at Cambridge.* "*He is the master of a clear and pleasant style, great facility of expression, and a considerable range of illustration. . . . The criticism is always acute, the description always graphic and continuous, and the matter of each essay is carefully arranged with a view to unity of effect.*"—SPECTATOR. "*His book will be full of interest to all thoughtful readers.*"—PALL MALL GAZETTE.

Shairp (Principal).—KILMAHOE, a Highland Pastoral, with other Poems. By JOHN CAMPBELL SHAIRP, Principal of the United College, St. Andrews. Fcap. 8vo. 5*s.*

"*Kilmahoe is a Highland Pastoral, redolent of the warm soft air of the western lochs and moors, sketched out with remarkable grace and picturesqueness.*"—SATURDAY REVIEW.

Shakespeare.—The Works of WILLIAM SHAKESPEARE. Cambridge Edition. Edited by W. GEORGE CLARK, M.A. and W. ALDIS WRIGHT, M.A. Nine vols. 8vo. Cloth. 4*l.* 14*s.* 6*d.*

This, now acknowledged to be the standard edition of Shakespeare, is the result of many years' study and research on the part of the accomplished Editors, assisted by the suggestions and contributions of Shakespearian students in all parts of the country. The following are the distinctive characteristics of this edition:—1. The text is based on a thorough collation of the four Folios, and of all the Quarto editions of the separate plays, and of subsequent editions and commentaries. 2. All the results of this collation are given in notes at the foot of the page, together with the conjectural emendations collected and suggested by the Editors, or furnished by their correspondents, so as to give the reader a complete view of the existing materials out of which the text has been constructed, or may be amended. 3. Where a quarto edition differs materially from the received text, the text of the quarto is printed literatim *in a smaller type after the received text. 4. The lines in each scene are numbered separately, so as to facilitate reference. 5. At the end of each play a few notes, critical, explanatory, and illustrative, are added. 6. The Poems, edited on a similar plan, are printed at the end of the Dramatic Works. The Preface contains some notes on Shakespearian Grammar, Spelling, Metre, and Punctuation, and a history of all the chief editions from the Poet's time to the present. The* GUARDIAN *calls it an "excellent, and, to the student, almost indispensable edition;" and the* EXAMINER *calls it "an unrivalled edition."*

Shakespeare, Globe.—See GLOBE LIBRARY.

Shakespeare's Tempest. Edited with Glossarial and Explanatory Notes, by the Rev. J. M. JEPHSON. Second Edition. 18mo. 1s.

This is an edition for use in schools. The introduction treats briefly of the value of language, the fable of the play and other points. The notes are intended to teach the student to analyse every obscure sentence and trace out the logical sequence of the poet's thoughts; to point out the rules of Shakespeare's versification; to explain obsolete words and meanings; and to guide the student's taste by directing his attention to such passages as seem especially worthy of note for their poetical beauty or truth to nature. The text is in the main founded upon that of the first collected edition of Shakespeare's plays.

Smith.—POEMS. By CATHERINE BARNARD SMITH. Fcap. 8vo. 5s.

"Wealthy in feeling, meaning, finish, and grace; not without passion, which is suppressed, but the keener for that."—ATHENÆUM.

Smith (Rev. Walter).—HYMNS OF CHRIST AND THE CHRISTIAN LIFE. By the Rev. WALTER C. SMITH, M.A. Fcap. 8vo. 6s.

"These are among the sweetest sacred poems we have read for a long time. With no profuse imagery, expressing a range of feeling and expression by no means uncommon, they are true and devoted, and their pathos is profound and simple."—NONCONFORMIST.

Song Book, the.—See GOLDEN TREASURY SERIES.

Spenser's Works.—See GLOBE LIBRARY.

Spring Songs. By a WEST HIGHLANDER. With a Vignette Illustration by GOURLAY STEELE. Fcap. 8vo. 1s. 6d.

"*Without a trace of affectation or sentimentalism, these utterances are perfectly simple and natural, profoundly human and profoundly true.*"—DAILY NEWS.

Stephen (C. E.)—THE SERVICE OF THE POOR; being an Inquiry into the Reasons for and against the Establishment of Religious Sisterhoods for Charitable Purposes. By CAROLINE EMILIA STEPHEN. Crown 8vo. 6s. 6d.

Miss Stephen defines religious Sisterhoods as "associations, the organization of which is based upon the assumption that works of charity are either acts of worship in themselves, or means to an end, that end being the spiritual welfare of the objects or the performers of those works." Arguing from that point of view, she devotes the first part of her volume to a brief history of religious associations, taking as specimens—I. The Deaconesses of the Primitive Church; II. the Béguines; III. the Third Order of S. Francis; IV. the Sisters of Charity of S. Vincent de Paul; V. the Deaconesses of Modern Germany. In the second part, Miss Stephen attempts to show what are the real wants met by Sisterhoods, to what extent the same wants may be effectually met by the organization of corresponding institutions on a secular basis, and what are the reasons for endeavouring to do so. "It touches incidentally and with much wisdom and tenderness on so many of the relations of women, particularly of single women, with society, that it may be read with advantage by many who have never thought of entering a Sisterhood."—SPECTATOR.

Stephens (J. B.)—CONVICT ONCE. A Poem. By J. BRUNTON STEPHENS. Extra fcap. 8vo. 3s. 6d.

A tale of sin and sorrow, purporting to be the confession of Magdalen Power, a convict first, and then a teacher in one of the Australian Settlements; the narrative is supposed to be written by Hyacinth, a pupil of Magdalen Power, and the victim of her jealousy. The metre of the poem is the same as that of Longfellow's "Evangeline." "It is as far more interesting than ninety-nine novels out of a hundred, as it is superior to them in power, worth, and beauty. We should most strongly advise everybody to read 'Convict Once.'"—WESTMINSTER REVIEW.

Storehouse of Stories.—See YONGE, C. M.

Streets and Lanes of a City: Being the Reminiscences of AMY DUTTON. With a Preface by the BISHOP OF SALISBURY. Second and Cheaper Edition. Globe 8vo. 2*s.* 6*d.*

This little volume records, to use the words of the Bishop of Salisbury, "a portion of the experience, selected out of overflowing materials, of two ladies, during several years of devoted work as district parochial visitors in a large population in the north of England." Every incident narrated is absolutely true, and only the names of the persons introduced have been (necessarily) changed. The "Reminiscences of Amy Dutton" serve to illustrate the line of argument adopted by Miss Stephen in her work on "the Service of the Poor," because they show that as in one aspect the lady visitor may be said to be a link between rich and poor, in another she helps to blend the "religious" life with the "secular," and in both does service of extreme value to the Church and Nation. "One of the most really striking books that has ever come before us."—LITERARY CHURCHMAN.

Sunday Book of Poetry.—See GOLDEN TREASURY SERIES.

Symonds (J. A., M.D.)—MISCELLANIES. By JOHN ADDINGTON SYMONDS, M.D. Selected and Edited, with an Introductory Memoir, by his Son. 8vo. 7*s.* 6*d.*

The late Dr. Symonds, of Bristol, was a man of singularly versatile and elegant as well as powerful and scientific intellect. In order to make this selection from his many works generally interesting, the editor has confined himself to works of pure literature, and to such scientific studies as had a general philosophical or social interest. Among the general subjects are articles on the Principles of Beauty, on Knowledge, and a Life of Dr. Pritchard; among the Scientific Studies are papers on Sleep and Dreams, Apparitions, the Relations between Mind and Muscle, Habit, etc.; there are several papers on the Social and Political Aspects of Medicine; and a few Poems and Translations, selected from a great number of equal merit, have been inserted at the end, as specimens of the lighter literary recreations which occupied the intervals of leisure in a long and laborious life. "Mr. Symonds has certainly done right in gathering together what his father left behind him."—SATURDAY REVIEW.

Theophrastus, Characters of.—See JEBB.

Thring.—SCHOOL SONGS. A Collection of Songs for Schools. With the Music arranged for four Voices. Edited by the Rev. E. THRING and H. RICCIUS. Folio. 7*s.* 6*d.*

There is a tendency in schools to stereotype the forms of life. Any mind solvent is valuable. Games do much; but games do not penetrate to domestic life, and are much limited by age. Music supplies the want. The collection includes the "Agnus Dei," Tennyson's "Light Brigade," Macaulay's "Ivry," etc. among other pieces.

Tom Brown's School Days.—By AN OLD BOY.

Golden Treasury Edition, 4*s.* 6*d.* People's Edition, 2*s.*

With Sixty Illustrations, by A. HUGHES and SYDNEY HALL, Square, cloth extra, gilt edges. 10*s.* 6*d.*

With Seven Illustrations by the same Artists, Crown 8vo. 6*s.*

"We have read and re-read this book with unmingled pleasure. . . . We have carefully guarded ourselves against any tampering with our critical sagacity, and yet have been compelled again and again to exclaim, Bene! Optime!"—LONDON QUARTERLY REVIEW. *"An exact picture of the bright side of a Rugby boy's experience, told with a life, a spirit, and a fond minuteness of detail and recollection which is infinitely honourable to the author."*—EDINBURGH REVIEW. *"The most famous boy's book in the language."*—DAILY NEWS.

Tom Brown at Oxford.—New Edition. With Illustrations. Crown 8vo. 6*s.*

"In no other work that we can call to mind are the finer qualities of the English gentleman more happily portrayed."—DAILY NEWS. *"A book of great power and truth."*—NATIONAL REVIEW.

Trench.—Works by R. CHENEVIX TRENCH, D.D., Archbishop of Dublin. (For other Works by this Author, see THEOLOGICAL, HISTORICAL, and PHILOSOPHICAL CATALOGUES.)

POEMS. Collected and arranged anew. Fcap. 8vo. 7*s.* 6*d.*

ELEGIAC POEMS. Third Edition. Fcap. 8vo. 2*s.* 6*d.*

CALDERON'S LIFE'S A DREAM: The Great Theatre of the World. With an Essay on his Life and Genius. Fcap. 8vo. 4*s.* 6*d.*

HOUSEHOLD BOOK OF ENGLISH POETRY. Selected and arranged, with Notes, by Archbishop TRENCH. Second Edition. Extra fcap. 8vo. 5*s.* 6*d.*

This volume is called a "Household Book," by this name implying that it is a book for all—that there is nothing in it to prevent it from being confidently placed in the hands of every member of the household. Specimens of all classes of poetry are given, including selections from living authors. The editor has aimed to produce a book "which the emigrant, finding room for little not absolutely necessary, might yet find room for in his trunk, and the traveller in his knapsack, and that on some narrow shelves where there are few books this might be one." "The Archbishop has conferred in this delightful volume an important gift on the whole English-speaking population of the world."—PALL MALL GAZETTE.

SACRED LATIN POETRY, Chiefly Lyrical. Selected and arranged for Use. By Archbishop TRENCH. Second Edition, Corrected and Improved. Fcap. 8vo. 7*s.*

"The aim of the present volume is to offer to members of our English Church a collection of the best sacred Latin poetry, such as they shall be able entirely and heartily to accept and approve—a collection, that is, in which they shall not be evermore liable to be offended, and to have the current of their sympathies checked, by coming upon that which, however beautiful as poetry, out of higher respects they must reject and condemn—in which, too, they shall not fear that snares are being laid for them, to entangle them unawares in admiration for aught which is inconsistent with their faith and fealty to their own spiritual mother."—PREFACE.

JUSTIN MARTYR, AND OTHER POEMS. Fifth Edition. Fcap. 8vo. 6*s.*

Trollope (Anthony).—SIR HARRY HOTSPUR OF HUMBLETHWAITE. By ANTHONY TROLLOPE, Author of "Framley Parsonage," etc. Cheap Edition. Globe 8vo. 2*s.* 6*d.*

The TIMES *says: "In this novel we are glad to recognize a return to what we must call Mr. Trollope's old form. The characters are drawn with vigour and boldness, and the book may do good to many readers of both sexes." The* ATHENÆUM *remarks: "No reader who begins to read this book is likely to lay it down until the last page is turned. This brilliant novel appears to us decidedly more successful than any other of Mr. Trollope's shorter stories."*

Turner.—Works by the Rev. CHARLES TENNYSON TURNER:—

SONNETS. Dedicated to his Brother, the Poet Laureate. Fcap. 8vo. 4*s.* 6*d.*

"The Sonnets are dedicated to Mr. Tennyson by his brother, and have, independently of their merits, an interest of association. They both love to write in simple expressive Saxon; both love to touch their imagery in epithets rather than in formal similes; both have a delicate perception of rhythmical movement, and thus Mr. Turner has occasional lines which, for phrase and music, might be ascribed to his brother. . . . He knows the haunts of the wild rose, the shady nooks where light quivers through the leaves, the ruralities, in short, of the land of imagination."—ATHENÆUM.

SMALL TABLEAUX. Fcap. 8vo. 4*s.* 6*d.*

"These brief poems have not only a peculiar kind of interest for the student of English poetry, but are intrinsically delightful, and will reward a careful and frequent perusal. Full of naïveté, piety, love, and knowledge of natural objects, and each expressing a single and generally a simple subject by means of minute and original pictorial touches, these Sonnets have a place of their own."—PALL MALL GAZETTE.

Virgil's Works.—See GLOBE LIBRARY.

Vittoria Colonna.—LIFE AND POEMS. By MRS. HENRY ROSCOE. Crown 8vo. 9*s.*

The life of Vittoria Colonna, the celebrated Marchesa di Pescara, has received but cursory notice from any English writer, though in every history of Italy her name is mentioned with great honour among the poets of the sixteenth century. "In three hundred and fifty years," says her biographer, Visconti, "there has been no other Italian lady who can be compared to her." "*It is written with good taste, with quick and intelligent sympathy, occasionally with a real freshness and charm of style.*"—PALL MALL GAZETTE.

Volunteer's Scrap Book. By the Author of "The Cambridge Scrap Book." Crown 4to. 7*s.* 6*d.*

"*A genial and clever caricaturist in whom we may often perceive through small details that he has as proper a sense of the graceful as of the ludicrous. The author might be and probably is a Volunteer himself, so kindly is the mirth he makes of all the incidents and phrases of the drill-ground.*"—EXAMINER.

Wandering Willie. By the Author of "Effie's Friends," and "John Hatherton." Third Edition. Crown 8vo. 6*s.*

"*This is an idyll of rare truth and beauty. . . . The story is simple and touching, the style of extraordinary delicacy, precision, and picturesqueness. . . . A charming gift-book for young ladies not yet promoted to novels, and will amply repay those of their elders who may give an hour to its perusal.*"—DAILY NEWS.

Webster.—Works by AUGUSTA WEBSTER:—

"*If Mrs. Webster only remains true to herself, she will assuredly take a higher rank as a poet than any woman has yet done.*"—WESTMINSTER REVIEW.

DRAMATIC STUDIES. Extra fcap. 8vo. 5*s.*

"*A volume as strongly marked by perfect taste as by poetic power.*"—NONCONFORMIST.

A WOMAN SOLD, AND OTHER POEMS. Crown 8vo. 7*s.* 6*d.*

"*Mrs. Webster has shown us that she is able to draw admirably from the life; that she can observe with subtlety, and render her observations with delicacy; that she can impersonate complex conceptions and venture into which few living writers can follow her.*"—GUARDIAN.

Webster—*continued.*

PORTRAITS. Second Edition. Extra fcap. 8vo. 3*s.* 6*d.*

"*Mrs. Webster's poems exhibit simplicity and tenderness . . . her taste is perfect . . . This simplicity is combined with a subtlety of thought, feeling, and observation which demand that attention which only real lovers of poetry are apt to bestow.*"—WESTMINSTER REVIEW.

PROMETHEUS BOUND OF ÆSCHYLUS. Literally translated into English Verse. Extra fcap. 8vo. 3*s.* 6*d.*

"*Closeness and simplicity combined with literary skill.*"—ATHENÆUM. "*Mrs. Webster's 'Dramatic Studies' and 'Translation of Prometheus' have won for her an honourable place among our female poets. She writes with remarkable vigour and dramatic realization, and bids fair to be the most successful claimant of Mrs. Browning's mantle.*"—BRITISH QUARTERLY REVIEW.

MEDEA OF EURIPIDES. Literally translated into English Verse. Extra fcap. 8vo. 3*s.* 6*d.*

"*Mrs. Webster's translation surpasses our utmost expectations. It is a photograph of the original without any of that harshness which so often accompanies a photograph.*"—WESTMINSTER REVIEW.

THE AUSPICIOUS DAY. A Dramatic Poem. Extra fcap. 8vo. 5*s.*

Westminster Plays. Lusus Alteri Westmonasterienses, Sive Prologi et Epilogi ad Fabulas in S^{ti} Petri Collegio: actas qui Exstabant collecti et justa quoad licuit annorum serie ordinati, quibus accedit Declamationum quæ vocantur et Epigrammatum Delectus. Curantibus J. MURE, A.M., H. BULL, A.M., C. B. SCOTT, B.D. 8vo. 12*s.* 6*d.*

IDEM.—Pars Secunda, 1820—1864. Quibus accedit Epigrammatum Delectus. 8vo. 15*s.*

When I was a Little Girl. STORIES FOR CHILDREN. By the Author of "St. Olave's." Third Edition. Extra fcap. 8vo. 4*s.* 6*d.* With Eight Illustrations by L. FRÖLICH.

"*At the head, and a long way ahead, of all books for girls, we place 'When I was a Little Girl'"*—TIMES. *"It is one of the choicest morsels of child-biography which we have met with."*—NONCONFORMIST.

Wollaston.—LYRA DEVONIENSIS. By T. V. WOLLASTON, M.A. Fcap. 8vo. 3*s*. 6*d*.

"It is the work of a man of refined taste, of deep religious sentiment, a true artist, and a good Christian."—CHURCH TIMES.

Woolner.—MY BEAUTIFUL LADY. By THOMAS WOOLNER. With a Vignette by ARTHUR HUGHES. Third Edition. Fcap. 8vo. 5*s*.

"It is clearly the product of no idle hour, but a highly-conceived and faithfully-executed task, self-imposed, and prompted by that inward yearning to utter great thoughts, and a wealth of passionate feeling, which is poetic genius. No man can read this poem without being struck by the fitness and finish of the workmanship, so to speak, as well as by the chastened and unpretending loftiness of thought which pervades the whole."—GLOBE.

Words from the Poets. Selected by the Editor of "Rays of Sunlight." With a Vignette and Frontispiece. 18mo. limp., 1*s*.

"The selection aims at popularity, and deserves it."—GUARDIAN.

Wyatt (Sir M. Digby).—FINE ART: a Sketch of its History, Theory, Practice, and application to Industry. A Course of Lectures delivered before the University of Cambridge. By Sir M. DIGBY WYATT, M.A. Slade Professor of Fine Art. 8vo. 10*s*. 6*d*.

"An excellent handbook for the student of art."—GRAPHIC. *"The book abounds in valuable matter, and will therefore be read with pleasure and profit by lovers of art."*—DAILY NEWS.

Yonge (C. M.)—Works by CHARLOTTE M. YONGE. (See also CATALOGUE OF WORKS IN HISTORY, and EDUCATIONAL CATALOGUE.)

THE HEIR OF REDCLYFFE. Eighteenth Edition. With Illustrations. Crown 8vo. 6*s*.

Yonge (C. M.)—*continued.*

HEARTSEASE. Eleventh Edition. With Illustrations. Crown 8vo. 6*s.*

THE DAISY CHAIN. Tenth Edition. With Illustrations. Crown 8vo. 6*s.*

THE TRIAL: MORE LINKS OF THE DAISY CHAIN. Fifth Edition. With Illustrations. Crown 8vo. 6*s.*

DYNEVOR TERRACE. Fourth Edition. Crown 8vo. 6*s.*

HOPES AND FEARS. Third Edition. Crown 8vo. 6*s.*

THE YOUNG STEPMOTHER. Third Edition. Crown 8vo. 6*s.*

CLEVER WOMAN OF THE FAMILY. Second Edition. Crown 8vo. 6*s.*

THE DOVE IN THE EAGLE'S NEST. Second Edition. Crown 8vo. 6*s.*

"*We think the authoress of 'The Heir of Redclyffe' has surpassed her previous efforts in this illuminated chronicle of the olden time.*" —BRITISH QUARTERLY.

THE CAGED LION. Illustrated. Crown 8vo. 6*s.*

"*Prettily and tenderly written, and will with young people especially be a great favourite.*"—DAILY NEWS. "*Everybody should read this.*"—LITERARY CHURCHMAN.

THE CHAPLET OF PEARLS; OR, THE WHITE AND BLACK RIBAUMONT. Crown 8vo. 6*s.*

"*Miss Yonge has brought a lofty aim as well as high art to the construction of a story which may claim a place among the best efforts in historical romance.*"—MORNING POST. "*The plot, in truth, is of the very first order of merit.*"—SPECTATOR. "*We have seldom read a more charming story.*"—GUARDIAN.

THE PRINCE AND THE PAGE. A Tale of the Last Crusade. Illustrated. 18mo. 3*s.* 6*d.*

Yonge (C. M.)—*continued.*

"*A tale which, we are sure, will give pleasure to many others besides the young people for whom it is specially intended. . . . This extremely prettily-told story does not require the guarantee afforded by the name of the author of 'The Heir of Redclyffe' on the title-page to ensure its becoming a universal favourite.*"—DUBLIN EVENING MAIL.

THE LANCES OF LYNWOOD. New Edition, with Coloured Illustrations. 18mo. 4*s.* 6*d.*

"*The illustrations are very spirited and rich in colour, and the story can hardly fail to charm the youthful reader.*"—MANCHESTER EXAMINER.

THE LITTLE DUKE: RICHARD THE FEARLESS. New Edition. Illustrated. 18mo. 3*s.* 6*d.*

A STOREHOUSE OF STORIES. First and Second Series. Globe 8vo. 3*s.* 6*d.* each.

CONTENTS OF FIRST SERIES:—History of Philip Quarll—Goody Twoshoes—The Governess—Jemima Placid—The Perambulations of a Mouse—The Village School—The Little Queen—History of Little Jack.

"*Miss Yonge has done great service to the infantry of this generation by putting these eleven stories of sage simplicity within their reach.*" —BRITISH QUARTERLY REVIEW.

CONTENTS OF SECOND SERIES:—Family Stories—Elements of Morality—A Puzzle for a Curious Girl—Blossoms of Morality.

A BOOK OF GOLDEN DEEDS OF ALL TIMES AND ALL COUNTRIES. Gathered and Narrated Anew. New Edition, with Twenty Illustrations by FRÖLICH. Crown 8vo. cloth gilt. 6*s.* (See also GOLDEN TREASURY SERIES). Cheap Edition. 1*s.*

"*We have seen no prettier gift-book for a long time, and none which, both for its cheapness and the spirit in which it has been compiled, is more deserving of praise.*"—ATHENÆUM.

A BOOK OF WORTHIES.—See GOLDEN TREASURY SERIES.

Yonge (C. M.)—*continued.*

LITTLE LUCY'S WONDERFUL GLOBE. Pictured by FRÖLICH, and narrated by CHARLOTTE M. YONGE. Second Edition. Crown 4to. cloth gilt. 6*s.*

Miss Yonge's wonderful "knack" of instructive story-telling to children is well known. In this volume, in a manner which cannot but prove interesting to all boys and girls, she manages to convey a wonderful amount of information concerning most of the countries of the world; in this she is considerably aided by the twenty-four telling pictures of Mr. Frölich. "'Lucy's Wonderful Globe' is capital, and will give its youthful readers more idea of foreign countries and customs than any number of books of geography or travel."—GRAPHIC.

CAMEOS FROM ENGLISH HISTORY. From ROLLO to EDWARD II. Extra fcap. 8vo. 5*s.* Second Edition, enlarged. 5*s.*

A SECOND SERIES. THE WARS IN FRANCE. Extra fcap. 8vo. 5*s.*

The endeavour has not been to chronicle facts, but to put together a series of pictures of persons and events, so as to arrest the attention, and give some individuality and distinctness to the recollection, by gathering together details at the most memorable moments. The "Cameos" are intended as a book for young people just beyond the elementary histories of England, and able to enter in some degree into the real spirit of events, and to be struck with characters and scenes presented in some relief. "Instead of dry details," says the NONCONFORMIST, *"we have living pictures, faithful, vivid, and striking."*

Young.—MEMOIR OF CHARLES MAYNE YOUNG, Tragedian. With Extracts from his Son's Journal. By JULIAN CHARLES YOUNG, M.A., Rector of Ilmington. New and Cheaper Edition. Crown 8vo. 7*s.* 6*d.* With Portraits and Sketches.

"There is hardly a page of it which was not worth printing. There is hardly a line which has not some kind of interest attaching

to it."—GUARDIAN. "*In this budget of anecdotes, fables, and gossip, old and new, relative to Scott, Moore, Chalmers, Coleridge, Wordsworth, Croker, Mathews, the Third and Fourth Georges, Bowles, Beckford, Lockhart, Wellington, Peel, Louis Napoleon, D'Orsay, Dickens, Thackeray, Louis Blanc, Gibson, Constable, and Stanfield (the list might be much extended), the reader must be hard indeed to please who cannot find entertainment.*"—PALL MALL GAZETTE.

MACMILLAN'S

GOLDEN TREASURY SERIES.

UNIFORMLY printed in 18mo., with Vignette Titles by Sir NOEL PATON, T. WOOLNER, W. HOLMAN HUNT, J. E. MILLAIS, ARTHUR HUGHES, &c. Engraved on Steel by JEENS. Bound in extra cloth, 4s. 6d. each volume. Also kept in morocco and calf bindings.

"*Messrs. Macmillan have, in their Golden Treasury Series, especially provided editions of standard works, volumes of selected poetry, and original compositions, which entitle this series to be called classical. Nothing can be better than the literary execution, nothing more elegant than the material workmanship.*"—BRITISH QUARTERLY REVIEW.

The Golden Treasury of the Best Songs and LYRICAL POEMS IN THE ENGLISH LANGUAGE. Selected and arranged, with Notes, by FRANCIS TURNER PALGRAVE.

"*This delightful little volume, the Golden Treasury, which contains many of the best original lyrical pieces and songs in our language, grouped with care and skill, so as to illustrate each other like the pictures in a well-arranged gallery.*"—QUARTERLY REVIEW.

The Children's Garland from the best Poets. Selected and arranged by COVENTRY PATMORE.

"*It includes specimens of all the great masters in the art of poetry, selected with the matured judgment of a man concentrated on obtaining insight into the feelings and tastes of childhood, and*

D

desirous to awaken its finest impulses, to cultivate its keenest sensibilities."—MORNING POST.

The Book of Praise. From the Best English Hymn Writers. Selected and arranged by Sir ROUNDELL PALMER. *A New and Enlarged Edition.*

"All previous compilations of this kind must undeniably for the present give place to the Book of Praise. . . . The selection has been made throughout with sound judgment and critical taste. The pains involved in this compilation must have been immense, embracing, as it does, every writer of note in this special province of English literature, and ranging over the most widely divergent tracks of religious thought."—SATURDAY REVIEW.

The Fairy Book; the Best Popular Fairy Stories. Selected and rendered anew by the Author of "JOHN HALIFAX, GENTLEMAN."

"A delightful selection, in a delightful external form; full of the physical splendour and vast opulence of proper fairy tales."—SPECTATOR.

The Ballad Book. A Selection of the Choicest British Ballads. Edited by WILLIAM ALLINGHAM.

"His taste as a judge of old poetry will be found, by all acquainted with the various readings of old English ballads, true enough to justify his undertaking so critical a task."—SATURDAY REVIEW.

The Jest Book. The Choicest Anecdotes and Sayings. Selected and arranged by MARK LEMON.

"The fullest and best jest book that has yet appeared."—SATURDAY REVIEW.

Bacon's Essays and Colours of Good and Evil. With Notes and Glossarial Index. By W. ALDIS WRIGHT, M.A.

"The beautiful little edition of Bacon's Essays, now before us, does credit to the taste and scholarship of Mr. Aldis Wright. . . . It puts the reader in possession of all the essential literary facts and chronology necessary for reading the Essays in connection with Bacon's life and times."—SPECTATOR. *"By far the most complete as well as the most elegant edition we possess."*—WESTMINSTER REVIEW.

The Pilgrim's Progress from this World to that which is to come. By JOHN BUNYAN.

"*A beautiful and scholarly reprint.*"—SPECTATOR.

The Sunday Book of Poetry for the Young. Selected and arranged by C. F. ALEXANDER.

"*A well-selected volume of Sacred Poetry.*"—SPECTATOR.

A Book of Golden Deeds of All Times and All Countries. Gathered and narrated anew. By the Author of "THE HEIR OF REDCLYFFE."

". . . *To the young, for whom it is especially intended, as a most interesting collection of thrilling tales well told; and to their elders, as a useful handbook of reference, and a pleasant one to take up when their wish is to while away a weary half-hour. We have seen no prettier gift-book for a long time.*"—ATHENÆUM.

The Poetical Works of Robert Burns. Edited, with Biographical Memoir, Notes, and Glossary, by ALEXANDER SMITH. Two Vols.

"*Beyond all question this is the most beautiful edition of Burns yet out.*"—EDINBURGH DAILY REVIEW.

The Adventures of Robinson Crusoe. Edited from the Original Edition by J. W. CLARK, M.A., Fellow of Trinity College, Cambridge.

"*Mutilated and modified editions of this English classic are so much the rule, that a cheap and pretty copy of it, rigidly exact to the original, will be a prize to many book-buyers.*"—EXAMINER.

The Republic of Plato. TRANSLATED into ENGLISH, with Notes by J. Ll. DAVIES, M.A. and D. J. VAUGHAN, M.A.

"*A dainty and cheap little edition.*"—EXAMINER.

The Song Book. Words and Tunes from the best Poets and Musicians. Selected and arranged by JOHN HULLAH, Professor of Vocal Music in King's College, London.

"A choice collection of the sterling songs of England, Scotland, and Ireland, with the music of each prefixed to the words. How much true wholesome pleasure such a book can diffuse, and will diffuse, we trust, through many thousand families."—EXAMINER.

La Lyre Française. Selected and arranged, with Notes, by GUSTAVE MASSON, French Master in Harrow School.

A selection of the best French songs and lyrical pieces.

Tom Brown's School Days. By AN OLD BOY.

"A perfect gem of a book. The best and most healthy book about boys for boys that ever was written."—ILLUSTRATED TIMES.

A Book of Worthies. Gathered from the Old Histories and written anew by the Author of "THE HEIR OF REDCLYFFE." With Vignette.

"An admirable addition to an admirable series."—WESTMINSTER REVIEW.

A Book of Golden Thoughts. By HENRY ATTWELL, Knight of the Order of the Oak Crown.

"Mr. Attwell has produced a book of rare value . . . . Happily it is small enough to be carried about in the pocket, and of such a companion it would be difficult to weary."—PALL MALL GAZETTE.

Guesses at Truth. By TWO BROTHERS. New Edition.

The publishers hope, therefore, that these Globe Editions may prove worthy of acceptance by all classes wherever the English Language is spoken, and by their universal circulation justify their distinctive epithet; while at the same time they spread and nourish a common sympathy with nature's most "finely touched" spirits, and thus help a little to "make the whole world kin."

The SATURDAY REVIEW *says*: "*The Globe Editions are admirable for their scholarly editing, their typographical excellence, their compendious form, and their cheapness.*" *The* BRITISH QUARTERLY REVIEW *says*: "*In compendiousness, elegance, and scholarliness, the Globe Editions of Messrs. Macmillan surpass any popular series of our classics hitherto given to the public. As near an approach to miniature perfection as has ever been made.*"

Shakespeare's Complete Works. Edited by W. G. CLARK, M.A., and W. ALDIS WRIGHT, M.A., of Trinity College, Cambridge, Editors of the "Cambridge Shakespeare." With Glossary. pp. 1,075. Price 3*s*. 6*d*.

This edition aims at presenting a perfectly reliable text of the complete works of "the foremost man in all literature." The text is essentially the same as that of the "Cambridge Shakespeare." Appended is a Glossary containing the meaning of every word in the text which is either obsolete or is used in an antiquated or unusual sense. This, combined with the method uses to indicate corrupted readings, serves to a great extent the purpose of notes. The ATHENÆUM *says this edition is "a marvel of beauty, cheapness, and compactness. . . . For the busy man, above all for the working student, this is the best of all existing Shakespeares." And the* PALL MALL GAZETTE *observes*: "*To have produced the complete works of the world's greatest poet in such a form, and at a price within the reach of every one, is of itself almost sufficient to give the publishers a claim to be considered public benefactors.*"

Spenser's Complete Works. Edited from the Original Editions and Manuscripts, by R. MORRIS, with a Memoir by J. W. HALES, M.A. With Glossary. pp. lv., 736. Price 3*s*. 6*d*.

The text of the poems has been reprinted from the earliest known editions, carefully collated with subsequent ones, most of which were published in the poet's lifetime. Spenser's only prose work, his sagacious and interesting "View of the State of Ireland," has been re-edited from three manuscripts belonging to the British Museum. A complete Glossary and a list of all the most important various readings serve to a large extent the purpose of notes explanatory and critical. An exhaustive general Index and a useful "Index of first lines" precede the poems; and in an Appendix are given Spenser's Letters to Gabriel Harvey. "Worthy—and higher praise it needs not—of the beautiful 'Globe Series.' The work is edited with all the care so noble a poet deserves."—DAILY NEWS.

Sir Walter Scott's Poetical Works. Edited with a Biographical and Critical Memoir by FRANCIS TURNER PALGRAVE, and copious Notes. pp. xliii., 559. Price 3*s*. 6*d*.

"Scott," says Heine, "in his every book, gladdens, tranquillizes, and strengthens my heart." This edition contains the whole of Scott's poetical works, with the exception of one or two short poems. While most of Scott's own notes have been retained, others have been added explaining many historical and topographical allusions; and original introductions from the pen of a gentleman familiar with Scotch literature and scenery, containing much interesting information, antiquarian, historical, and biographical, are prefixed to the principal poems. "We can almost sympathise with a middle-aged grumbler, who, after reading Mr. Palgrave's memoir and introduction, should exclaim—'Why was there not such an edition of Scott when I was a schoolboy?'"—GUARDIAN.

Complete Works of Robert Burns.—THE POEMS, SONGS, AND LETTERS, edited from the best Printed and Manuscript Authorities, with Glossarial Index, Notes, and a Biographical Memoir by ALEXANDER SMITH. pp. lxii., 636. Price 3*s*. 6*d*.

Burns's poems and songs need not circulate exclusively among Scotchmen, but should be read by all who wish to know the multitudinous capabilities of the Scotch language, and who have the capacity of appreciating the exquisite expression of all kinds of human feeling—rich parody humour, keen wit, withering satire, genuine pathos, pure passionate love. The exhaustive glossarial index and the copious notes will make all the purely Scotch poems intelligible even to an Englishman. Burns's letters must be read by all who desire fully to appreciate the poet's character, to see it on all its many sides. Explanatory notes are prefixed to most of these letters, and Burns's Journals kept during his Border and Highland Tours, are appended. Following the prefixed biography by the editor, is a Chronological Table of Burns's Life and Works. "Admirable in all respects."—SPECTATOR. *"The cheapest, the most perfect, and the most interesting edition which has ever been published."*—BELL'S MESSENGER.

Robinson Crusoe. Edited after the Original Editions, with a Biographical Introduction by HENRY KINGSLEY. pp. xxxi., 607. Price 3s. 6d.

Of this matchless truth-like story, it is scarcely possible to find an unabridged edition. This edition may be relied upon as containing the whole of "Robinson Crusoe" as it came from the pen of its author, without mutilation, and with all peculiarities religiously preserved. These points, combined with its handsome paper, large clear type, and moderate price, ought to render this par excellence *the "Globe," the Universal edition of Defoe's fascinating narrative. "A most excellent and in every way desirable edition."*—COURT CIRCULAR. *"Macmillan's 'Globe' Robinson Crusoe is a book to have and to keep."*—MORNING STAR.

Goldsmith's Miscellaneous Works. Edited, with Biographical Introduction, by Professor MASSON. pp. lx., 695. Globe 8vo. 3s. 6d.

This volume comprehends the whole of the prose and poetical works of this most genial of English authors, those only being excluded which are mere compilations. They are all accurately reprinted from the most reliable editions. The faithfulness, fulness, and literary merit of the biography are sufficiently attested by the name of its author, Professor Masson. It contains many interesting anecdotes which will give the reader an insight into Goldsmith's character, and many graphic pictures of the literary life of London during the middle of last century. "Such an admirable compendium of the facts of Goldsmith's life, and so careful and minute a delineation of the mixed traits of his peculiar character as to be a very model of a literary biography in little."—SCOTSMAN.

Pope's Poetical Works. Edited, with Notes and Introductory Memoir, by ADOLPHUS WILLIAM WARD, M.A., Fellow of St. Peter's College, Cambridge, and Professor of History in Owens College, Manchester. pp. lii., 508. Globe 8vo. 3s. 6d.

This edition contains all Pope's poems, translations, and adaptations,—his now superseded Homeric translations alone being omitted. The text, carefully revised, is taken from the best editions; Pope's own use of capital letters and apostrophised syllables, frequently necessary to an understanding of his meaning, has been preserved; while his uncertain spelling and his frequently perplexing interpunctuation have been judiciously amended. Abundant notes are added, including Pope's own, the best of those of previous editors, and many which are the result of the study and research of the present editor. The introductory Memoir will be found to shed considerable light on the political, social, and literary life of the period in which Pope filled so large a space. The LITERARY CHURCHMAN *remarks: "The editor's own notes and introductory memoir are excellent, the memoir alone would be cheap and well worth buying at the price of the whole volume."*

Dryden's Poetical Works. Edited, with a Memoir, Revised Text, and Notes, by W. D. CHRISTIE, M.A., of Trinity College, Cambridge. pp. lxxxvii., 662. Globe 8vo. 3s. 6d.

A study of Dryden's works is absolutely necessary to anyone who wishes to understand thoroughly, not only the literature, but also the political and religious history of the eventful period when he lived and reigned as literary dictator. In this edition of his works, which comprises several specimens of his vigorous prose, the text has been thoroughly corrected and purified from many misprints and small changes often materially affecting the sense, which had been allowed to slip in by previous editors. The old spelling has been retained where it is not altogether strange or repulsive. Besides an exhaustive Glossary, there are copious Notes, critical, historical, biographical, and explanatory; and the biography contains the results of considerable original research, which has served to shed light on several hitherto obscure circumstances connected with the life and parentage of the poet. "An admirable edition, the result of great research and of a careful revision of the text. The memoir prefixed contains, within less than ninety pages, as much sound criticism and as comprehensive a biography as the student of Dryden need desire."—PALL MALL GAZETTE.

Cowper's Poetical Works. Edited, with Notes and Biographical Introduction, by WILLIAM BENHAM, Vicar of Addington and Professor of Modern History in Queen's College, London. pp. lxxiii., 536. Globe 8vo. 3s. 6d.

This volume contains, arranged under seven heads, the whole of Cowper's own poems, including several never before published, and all his translations except that of Homer's "Iliad." The text is taken from the original editions, and Cowper's own notes are given at the foot of the page, while many explanatory notes by the editor himself are appended to the volume. In the very full Memoir it will be found that much new light has been thrown on some of the most difficult passages of Cowper's spiritually chequered life. "Mr. Benham's edition of Cowper is one of permanent value. The biographical introduction is excellent, full of information, singularly neat and readable and modest—indeed too modest in its comments. The notes are concise and accurate, and the editor has been able to discover and introduce some hitherto unprinted matter. Altogether the book is a very excellent one."—SATURDAY REVIEW.

Morte d'Arthur.—SIR THOMAS MALORY'S BOOK OF KING ARTHUR AND OF HIS NOBLE KNIGHTS OF THE ROUND TABLE. The original Edition of CAXTON, revised for Modern Use. With an Introduction by Sir EDWARD STRACHEY, Bart. pp. xxxvii., 509. Globe 8vo. 3s. 6d.

This volume contains the cream of the legends of chivalry which have gathered round the shadowy King Arthur and his Knights of the Round Table. Tennyson has drawn largely on them in his cycle of Arthurian Idylls. The language is simple and quaint as that of the Bible, and the many stories of knightly adventure of which the book is made up, are fascinating as those of the "Arabian Nights." The great moral of the book is to "do after the good, and leave the evil." There was a want of an edition of the work at a moderate price, suitable for ordinary readers, and especially for boys: such an edition the present professes to be. The Introduction contains an account of the Origin and Matter of the book, the Text and its several Editions, and an Essay on Chivalry, tracing its history from its origin to its decay. Notes are appended, and a

Glossary of such words as require explanation. "It is with perfect confidence that we recommend this edition of the old romance to every class of readers."—PALL MALL GAZETTE.

The Works of Virgil. Rendered into English Prose, with Introductions, Notes, Running Analysis, and an Index. By JAMES LONSDALE, M.A., late Fellow and Tutor of Balliol College, Oxford, and Classical Professor in King's College, London; and SAMUEL LEE, M.A., Latin Lecturer at University College, London. pp. 288. Price 3s. 6d.

The publishers believe that an accurate and readable translation of all the works of Virgil is perfectly in accordance with the object of the "Globe Library." A new prose-translation has therefore been made by two competent scholars, who have rendered the original faithfully into simple Bible-English, without paraphrase; and at the same time endeavoured to maintain as far as possible the rhythm and majestic flow of the original. On this latter point the DAILY TELEGRAPH *says, "The endeavour to preserve in some degree a rhythm in the prose rendering is almost invariably successful and pleasing in its effect;" and the* EDUCATIONAL TIMES, *that it "may be readily recommended as a model for young students for rendering the poet into English." The General Introduction will be found full of interesting information as to the life of Virgil, the history of opinion concerning his writings, the notions entertained of him during the Middle Ages, editions of his works, his influence on modern poets and on education. To each of his works is prefixed a critical and explanatory introduction, and important aid is afforded to the thorough comprehension of each production by the running Analysis. Appended is an Index of all the proper names and the most important subjects occurring throughout the poems and introductions. "A more complete edition of Virgil in English it is scarcely possible to conceive than the scholarly work before us."*—GLOBE.

R. CLAY, SONS, AND TAYLOR, PRINTERS, BREAD STREET HILL.

www.ingramcontent.com/pod-product-compliance
Lightning Source LLC
Chambersburg PA
CBHW032301280326
41932CB00009B/656

* 9 7 8 3 7 4 1 1 7 7 6 1 3 *